OXFORD STUDIES IN ANCIENT DOCUMENTS

General Editors

Alan Bowman   Alison Cooley

OXFORD STUDIES IN ANCIENT DOCUMENTS

This innovative new series offers unique perspectives on the political, cultural, social, and economic history of the ancient world. Exploiting the latest technological advances in imaging, decipherment, and interpretation, the volumes cover a wide range of documentary sources, including inscriptions, papyri, and wooden tablets.

Scribal Repertoires in Egypt from the New Kingdom to the Early Islamic Period

Edited by
JENNIFER CROMWELL
EITAN GROSSMAN

OXFORD
UNIVERSITY PRESS

OXFORD
UNIVERSITY PRESS

Great Clarendon Street, Oxford, OX2 6DP,
United Kingdom

Oxford University Press is a department of the University of Oxford.
It furthers the University's objective of excellence in research, scholarship,
and education by publishing worldwide. Oxford is a registered trade mark of
Oxford University Press in the UK and in certain other countries

First Edition published in 2018
Impression: 1

Published in the United States of America by Oxford University Press
198 Madison Avenue, New York, NY 10016, United States of America

British Library Cataloguing in Publication Data
Data available

Library of Congress Control Number: 2017939059

ISBN 978–0–19–876810–4

Printed and bound by
CPI Group (UK) Ltd, Croydon, CR0 4YY

Preface

This volume was born out of a workshop held in 2009 at the University of Oxford. The conference, *Beyond Free-Variation: Scribal Repertoires in Egypt from the Old Kingdom to the Early Islamic Period*, originated from our conviction that variation in scribal texts, whether linguistic, palaeographic, or orthographic, was far from 'free' or 'random'. Rather, variation is governed by a potentially wide, but also potentially identifiable, range of factors. Preliminary research pointed to the insight that scribal variation provides a rich source for better understanding the social and cultural histories of documents, texts, and the scribes that produced them. The workshop aimed to raise questions and identify problems related to variation across boundaries of time and period, including Ancient Egyptian, up to and including demotic and Coptic, Greek, Latin, Hebrew, and Arabic. By adopting such a comparative and diachronic approach, our overarching goal was to address the stability, or instability, of scribal conventions over time, across languages, and amidst political or cultural changes. Egypt provides the perfect laboratory for testing our conviction.

A selection of the papers that were presented at the workshop are here revised and expanded, showcasing a number of studies that focus on different aspects of scribal variation. Alexander Bergs and Merja Stenroos, two historical sociolinguists of English, provide a conceptual framework or toolbox for the authors of the other studies, and act as midwife to the reconceptualization of 'free' scribal variation as symptoms of the sociocultural agency of pre-modern scribes in Egypt. Our scribes wrote texts of highly diverse types, from legal protocols to private letters to alchemical texts to literary works, and what we know about them is also diverse: the names of some scribes, as well as significant bodies of documents, have come down to us, while the names of others remain lost to history. What is shared by these studies, however, is a concern for understanding a surviving scribal document or body of documents as the one-time production of a human being in a particular time, place, and sociocultural environment.

As the fifteen chapters in this volume were shaped by the discussions that took place in Oxford in 2009, we would like to acknowledge and thank the other participants (speakers and session chairs): Mark Collier, Jacco Dieleman, Roland Enmarch, Todd Gillen, Glenn Godenho, Eva Grob, Nikolaos Gonis, Robert Hoyland, Matthias Müller, Richard Parkinson, Gesa Schenke, Petra Sijpesteijn, Mark Smith, Andreas Stauder, and John Tait. It was not possible to publish all the papers here, for a variety of reasons. In our Introduction to this volume, we have acknowledged some of the key work that was presented and has been published elsewhere. To Alan Bowman we owe special thanks, for suggesting that we submit this resulting volume to the series Oxford Studies in Ancient Documents, and for his support throughout the process. Additionally, the feedback provided by the three anonymous reviewers proved invaluable in shaping the final version of this book.

The principal difficulty in producing such a volume as this is marrying the different systems used to refer to ancient textual material, whether literary or non-literary, not only between Middle English and Ancient Egyptian, but across the different languages and language-phases used within Egypt alone. For this reason, we have chosen not to italicize any papyrological reference (sigla), name of ancient texts, or museum inventory numbers, if for no other reason than to create uniformity across the individual chapters. Greek, Latin, and Coptic papyri are referred to according to their sigla entered in the Checklist of Editions of Greek, Latin, Demotic, and Coptic Papyri, Ostraca, and Tablets (updated at: http://www.papyri.info/docs/checklist). Some readers may not be aware of the editorial conventions used to indicate the condition of an epigraphic or papyrological text in modern editions. The Leiden Conventions are used by several of our authors, as follows:

[...]	A lacuna or gap in the original text, not restored by the editor (extent known).
[– – –]	A lacuna or gap in the original text, not restored by the editor (extent unknown).
[abc]	Letters missing from the original text due to lacuna, restored by the editor.
a(bc)	Abbreviation in the text, expanded by the editor.
<ab>	Characters erroneously omitted by the ancient scribe, restored or corrected by the editor.
{ab}	Letters in the text considered erroneous and superfluous by the editor.
...	Traces of letters on the surface, insufficient for restoration by the editor.
⟦abc⟧	Characters deleted by the ancient scribe.
vac.	Space left empty (*vacat*) on the page.

The workshop itself could not have taken place without the financial support of the John Fell Fund, the Oriental Institute, the Griffith Institute, and University College (all at the University of Oxford). The Hebrew University of Jerusalem provided funds for the preparation of the manuscript, and we thank Alexandra Kellner for her invaluable assistance in proofreading the volume. Permission to reproduce images of original manuscripts has been provided by: Ägyptisches Museum und Papyrussammlung, Berlin; Mission archéologique dans la nécropole thébaine (Mant), Brussels; Institut français d'archéologie orientale (IFAO), Cairo; Syndics of the University of Cambridge; Carlsberg Papyrus Collection, Copenhagen; Instituto Papirologico G. Vitelli, Florence; Institut de papyrologie et d'Égyptologie, Lille; British Library Board, London; Bodleian Library, University of Oxford; Le Louvre, Paris; Bibliothèque Nationale et Universitaire, Strasbourg; and Österreichische Nationalbibliothek, Papyrus Erzherzog Rainer, Vienna.

We thank the various institutions with which we have been affiliated for their support of our work. In particular, Eitan Grossman would like to thank Roni Henkin-Roitfarb of Ben Gurion University of the Negev and Jean Winand of the University of Liège. Jennifer Cromwell would like to thank the Department of Ancient Egypt and Near Eastern Studies, University of Oxford, and the Department of Ancient History, Macquarie University, Sydney.

Our greatest thanks go to the fellows and staff at University College, Oxford, and Luigi Prada, for their assistance throughout the organization of the initial meeting. Our sincere thanks go to all the staff at OUP, who have provided their unwavering support. Above all, thank you to the contributors, who have been patient throughout the entire publication process. We are proud and happy to present their work and hope that this will stimulate much future work in the socio-historic study of ancient texts, from Egypt and beyond.

Jennifer Cromwell (Copenhagen)
Eitan Grossman (Jerusalem)

Contents

List of Figures

The publisher and the author apologize for any errors or omissions in the above list. If contacted they will be pleased to rectify these at the earliest opportunity.

List of Tables

List of Contributors

Alexander Bergs joined the Institute for English and American Studies at Osnabrück University in 2006 when he became Full Professor and Chair of English Language and Linguistics. His research interests include language variation and change, constructional approaches to language, the role of context in language, and cognitive poetics. His works include several authored and edited books (*Social Networks and Historical Sociolinguistics*, 2005; *Modern Scots*, 2nd edition, 2005; *Constructions and Language Change*, 2008), textbooks on English and historical linguistics, as well as the two-volume *Handbook of English Historical Linguistics* (edited with Laurel Brinton). Apart from several terms as Director of the Institute of English and American Studies, as Dean of the Faculty of Linguistics and Literatures, and as member of the University Senate, he is one of the founding directors of the Research Cluster for Cognition and Poetics at Osnabrück University.

Anne Boud'hors has been affiliated with the Centre national de la recherche scientifique (CNRS), Paris, since 1990 and is the Directrice de recherche at the Institut de recherche et d'histoire des textes (IRHT). Her research interests are in the Coptic language and its texts and manuscripts, both literary and non-literary. Her principal publications include *Le Canan 8 de Chénouté: Introduction, édition critique* (2013) and, with Chantal Heurtel, *Les ostraca coptes de la TT 29. Autour du moine Frangé* (2010) and *Ostraca et papyrus coptes du topos de Saint-Marc à thèbes* (2015).

Willy Clarysse is Professor Emeritus at the Katholieke Universiteit Leuven. He is both a papyrologist and a demotist, with special interest in the bilingual society of Graeco-Roman Egypt, in onomastics, and in prosopography. He has published extensively in each of these areas. Among his principal monographs are *The Eponymous Priests of Ptolemaic Egypt* (with G. van der Veken and S. Vleeming, 1983) and *The Petrie Papyri, Second Edition Volume 1, The Wills (P.Petr.2)* (1991). Together with Dorothy Thompson, he is the author of *Counting the People in Hellenistic Egypt* (2006), which illuminates many aspects of the relations between immigrant Greeks and the existing majority Egyptian population.

Jennifer Cromwell is a Marie Curie Research Fellow at the University of Copenhagen. She previously held postdoctoral positions at the University of Oxford and Macquarie University, Sydney. Her two primary research projects are on the role of Egyptian (Coptic) scribes in the administration of early Islamic Egypt (the subject of her 2017 monograph with University of Michigan Press, *Recording Village Life: A Coptic Scribe in Early Islamic Egypt*) and in the administration and economy of Egyptian monasteries in Late Antiquity. In addition, she is editing a corpus of Coptic writing exercises from western Thebes in the collection of Columbia University, together with Professor Raffaella Cribiore (NYU).

Eitan Grossman is Assistant Professor in the Department of Linguistics at the Hebrew University of Jerusalem, where he is also a member of the Language, Logic and Cognition Center. His research interests include language variation and change, language typology, and the description of Ancient Egyptian–Coptic and other languages, such as Nuer, a Nilotic language of South Sudan. Recent publications include *Egyptian–Coptic Linguistics in Typological Perspective* (co-edited with Martin Haspelmath and Tonio Sebastian Richter, 2014), *On Forms and Functions: Studies in Ancient Egyptian Grammar* (co-edited with Stéphane Polis, Andréas Stauder, and Jean Winand, 2014) and *Greek Influence on Egyptian-Coptic: Contact-Induced Change in an Ancient African Language* (co-edited with Peter Dils, Tonio Sebastian Richter, and Wolfgang Schenkel, 2017). Since 2016, he has headed the Dynamics of Language Lab at the Hebrew University of Jerusalem.

Hilla Halla-aho attained her PhD in 2008 from the University of Helsinki, where she has since worked as a researcher. Her publications include the monograph *The Non-Literary Latin Letters: A Study of their Syntax and Pragmatics* (2009). Her research interests focus on Latin syntax, variation and change in Latin non-literary sources and Latin papyri, bilingualism, and the influence of scribes on language use.

Rachel Mairs is Lecturer in Classics at the University of Reading. She works on multilingualism and ethnicity in the Hellenistic world, in particular Egypt and Central Asia. Her recent publications include *The Hellenistic Far East: Archaeology, Language, and Identity in Greek Central Asia* (2014), *Archaeologists, Tourists, Interpreters* (with Maya Muratov, 2015), and *From Khartoum to Jerusalem: The Dragoman Solomon Negima and his Clients, 1885–1933* (2016).

Ben Outhwaite has been Head of the Genizah Research Unit in Cambridge University Library since 2006. His Cambridge PhD thesis was on the grammatical description of Medieval Hebrew letters in the Genizah. Dr Outhwaite's research interests revolve around Hebrew and its use and transmission in the Middle Ages: the vocalization traditions of biblical (and post-biblical) Hebrew, the Medieval Hebrew language (particularly its use as a medium of communication throughout the early Middle Ages), and the documentary history of the communities who deposited manuscripts into the Cairo Genizah. His research projects have been funded by the AHRC, the Wellcome Foundation, and the Andrew W. Mellon Foundation, among others, and he is a series editor for Brill's *Cambridge Genizah Studies* series.

Stéphane Polis is Research Associate at the National Fund for Scientific Research (Belgium). With Masters degrees in classical studies (2002) and oriental studies (2004) at the University of Liège, he was awarded a Master of Advanced Studies in general linguistics in 2005. He combined the philological and linguistic dimensions in his doctoral dissertation *Modality in Late Egyptian* (2009). His fields of research are Ancient Egyptian linguistics and Late Egyptian philology and grammar. His work focuses mainly on language variation and language change in Ancient Egyptian, with a special interest on the functional domain of modality and grammaticalization processes. He supervises the development of the Ramses Project at the University of Liège (with Jean Winand).

Joachim Friedrich Quack studied Egyptology, Semitic languages, Biblical Archaeology, Assyriology, and Prehistory at the Universities of Tübingen and Paris. He received his PhD at Tübingen in 1993 and was assistant at the Egyptological seminar of the Free University Berlin from 1997 to 2002. Since 2005, he has been Professor of Egyptology at Heidelberg University. His focus of research is on Egyptian language, literature, and religion, especially of the Late and Graeco-Roman periods. His most important books are *Studien zur Lehre für Merikare* (1992), *Die Lehren des Ani. Ein neuägyptischer Weisheitstext in seinem kulturellen Umfeld* (1994), *Einführung in die altägyptische Literaturgeschichte III. Die demotische und gräko-ägyptische Literatur, Einführungen und Quellentexte zur Ägyptologie 3. Zweite, veränderte Auflage* (2009), and, together with Friedhelm Hoffmann, *Anthologie der demotischen Literatur, Einführungen und Quellentexte zur Ägyptologie 4* (2007).

Tonio Sebastian Richter is Professor at the Berlin-Brandenburg Academy of Sciences and Humanities and holds a chair for Coptology at the Egyptological Seminar of the Free University. He finished his PhD thesis on the language of Coptic legal documents in 1999 (printed as *Rechtssemantik und forensische Rhetorik*, 2nd edition, 2008) and his habilitation on Coptic land leases in 2005. His research interests include Coptic linguistics, papyrology, and epigraphy, and the history of law, economy, religion, magic, and sciences in Byzantine and early Islamic Egypt. He is co-editor of the journals *Archiv für Papyrusforschung* and *Zeitschrift für Ägyptische Sprache und Altertumskunde*, editorial board member of *Lingua Aegyptia*, and is director of the long-term projects *Database and Dictionary of Greek Loanwords in Coptic* and *Structure and Transformation of the Vocabulary of the Egyptian Language*.

Kim Ryholt is Professor of Egyptology at the University of Copenhagen and specializes in ancient Egyptian history and literature. He was director of the Centre for Canon and Identity Formation under the University of Copenhagen Programme of Excellence 2008–13 and has been responsible for the Papyrus Carlsberg Collection and its publication project since 1999. He has published extensively on Egyptian literature and the Tebtunis temple library in particular. His most recent monographs include *The Petese Stories II* (2006), *Narrative Literature from the Tebtunis Temple Library* (2010), *Catalogue of Egyptian Funerary Papyri in Danish Collections* (2016, co-authored with T. Christiansen), and *The Antiquities Trade in Egypt, 1880–1930* (2016, co-authored with F. Hagen).

Merja Stenroos is Professor of English Linguistics at the University of Stavanger in Norway. She leads the Middle English Scribal Texts Programme at Stavanger and is the main compiler of two corpora of Middle English: *The Middle English Grammar Corpus* (MEG-C) and *A Corpus of Middle English Local Documents* (MELD). Her main research interests are within historical sociolinguistics and pragmatics, as well as historical literacy studies, with particular focus on the late and post-medieval periods. She has published articles on different aspects of Middle English, including orthography, dialectal variation, and pragmatics. Together with Inge Særheim and Martti Mäkinen, she edited the volume *Language Contact and Variation around the North Sea* (2012).

Esther-Miriam Wagner is a Senior Research Fellow at the Woolf Institute and an affiliated lecturer and associated researcher at the University of Cambridge. Her research interests include Genizah Studies, Arabic linguistics and language history, sociolinguistics, and Muslim–Jewish relations. She is the author of *Linguistic Variety of Judaeo-Arabic Letters from the Cairo Genizah* (2010), and the co-editor of the themed volumes *Scribes as Agents of Language Change* (2013) and *Merchants of Innovation: The Languages of Traders* (2017).

Jean Winand has been working with the Fonds National de la Recherche Scientifique (FNRS) of Belgium for more than fifteen years, reaching the level of Maître de recherches before joining the academic staff of the University of Liège in 2003. Professor ordinarius in 2005, he was awarded the Anneliese Maier Forschung Prize of the von Humboldt Stiftung in 2015. His main research areas are the languages and literature of ancient Egypt, particularly during the period covering the Old Kingdom down to the Third Intermediate Period, as well as the writing system of ancient Egypt and in the royal ideology. He is the initiator of the Ramses Project, which he runs together with Stéphane Polis. His main publications are *Études de néo-égyptien, I La morphologie verbale* (1992), *Grammaire raisonnée de l'égyptien classique* (1999, with Michel Malaise), *Temps et aspect en ancien égyptien. Une approche sémantique* (2006), and *Les hiéroglyphes* (2013).

1

Scribes, Repertoires, and Variation

Eitan Grossman and Jennifer Cromwell

'Texts are unlikely to provide good evidence if they are used primarily to reconstruct something else' (Merja Stenroos).

§1. FREE VARIATION AND SCRIBAL REPERTOIRES

As in spoken language, variation abounds in written texts. In the case of the latter, linguistic and extralinguistic variation coexists: one finds variation in lexical and grammatical features, on the one hand, and in other textual parameters such as orthography, phraseology and formulary, palaeography, layout, and formatting, on the other. Such variation occurs both within the written output of individuals and across broader corpora that represent 'communities' of diverse types.

Scholarly reactions to such variation vary. Philologists have tended to subject variation in texts (and manuscripts) to an anachronistic aesthetic judgement, or to emend it out of existence in text editions. The assumption underlying such practices seems to be that modern scholars know better than earlier scribes; the corresponding conclusion is that modern scholars are entitled to abstract from textual variation (often viewed as 'scribal errors' or 'textual corruption') in order to reconstruct coherent, homogeneous linguistic entities. In this respect, the views of traditional philologists intersect with those of some theoretical linguists, who hold that variation and other 'extraneous' performance factors are obstacles to linguistic analysis.[1]

In contrast to such views, sociolinguists have long considered variation to be an opportunity to understand the relationships between languages and the societies in which they are embedded. However, until fairly recently, sociolinguists have

[1] See, for example, Hale (2007, 19–26). Also, on this point, see the discussion by Stenroos in the current volume.

tended to focus their attention on synchronic variation in spoken language. It is precisely in the gap left by traditional philologists, historical linguists, and synchronically-oriented sociolinguists that a broad spectrum of contemporary linguistic approaches and frameworks has emerged: from 'sociophilology' (Wright 2002) to 'historical sociolinguistics' (Bergs 2005) and 'sociohistorical linguistics' (Romaine 1982), as well as a range of critical voices emerging from diverse philological disciplines (Cerquiglini 1989 and Fleischman 2000, to name but two). These frameworks have argued that variation in texts or, more specifically, manuscripts can and should be taken as data for empirical research and as an opportunity for framing new research questions.[2]

The papers collected in this volume reflect different approaches to and perspectives on the issue of variation; some are primarily associated with linguistics, but others deal with problems that are traditionally considered to fall within the purview of philology, the critical study of manuscripts and texts. In order to encapsulate this, we use the inclusive term 'scribal repertoires', a concept that is intended to cover the entire set of linguistic and non-linguistic practices that are prone to variation within and between manuscripts. Furthermore, it is probably artificial to draw too firm a distinction between linguistic and non-linguistic features, since we are dealing with written language and the way in which linguistic forms are written. The concept 'scribal repertoires' also serves to place focus on scribes as socially and culturally embedded agents, whose choices are reflected in texts. Scribal repertoires are shaped by education and experience; while they will be shared to an extent by members of a given community, they will not be exactly the same for any two individuals.

Socio-historical approaches to texts and manuscripts have made much progress in the study of western European languages, most notably Germanic and Romance languages.[3] However, these research frameworks have barely begun to penetrate other linguistic and philological disciplines.[4] In some cases,

[2] See also Nevalainen and Raumolin-Brunberg (2003).

[3] See, for example, the references cited above.

[4] For Egypt (the focus of this volume), such studies do exist, but they are rare. Some notable examples include Eyre 1979 (see pp. 86–7 especially, on palaeography); Funk 1988 (linguistic and sociolinguistic aspects of dialects as realized in manuscripts); Goldwasser 1990, 1992, 1999 (registers and diglossia); Janssen 1987 (palaeographic variation within the writing of specific grammatical items within the texts of a single scribe and between those by several, and the possible reasons for this); Prada 2013 (use of extralinguistic marks to distinguish between grammatical features); Richter 2004a, 2004b, 2006, 2008b (language contact, genre- and register-specific repertoires, social aspects of language use in general); and Sweeney 1994, 1995, 1998 (gender, idiolects). These are demonstrative of an interest in applying historical sociolinguistic methods and concerns to the study of Egyptian, but they are still uncommon.

This is also not to say that other regions of the ancient world would not also be excellent settings for such analyses. Mesopotamia provides a wealth of written material over a long period of time. An example of variation in cuneiform tablets is found in the series of seventh-century tablets inscribed with an oath to uphold the succession of Esarhaddon, king of the Neo-Assyrian Empire, by the crown prince Assurbanipal ("Esarhaddon's Succession Treaty"). With copies and fragments found in the Assyrian cities of Nimrud and Assur, as well as a copy on the other side of the empire

this is more or less justified—relatively few of the world's past and present languages have a long and bountiful tradition of writing. But in others, the attested documentation renders the study of variation possible—and necessary—in order to better understand the premodern and modern societies with which we are concerned.

The central aim of this volume is to demonstrate some of the ways in which we can approach the fact of variation in scribal texts. In essence, the papers collected here all ask what we can learn about texts, their authors or copyists, and the social worlds in which they lived and worked if we take variation seriously. As their source material, these papers use different types of texts, from different periods, in different languages and scripts. They provide a diversity of approaches and perspectives towards the primary evidence, which can be used in the development of further studies. Furthermore, since they deal with Egypt—at once outside of Europe and yet never detached from it—they provide valuable comparative data for the field of historical sociolinguistics, which has a strong research bias towards the better-known languages of western Europe.

§2. GEOGRAPHIC AND HISTORICAL SCOPE OF THE VOLUME

The volume opens with two papers dealing with premodern English, which differ significantly from the others in time and place. While these articles might seem out of place in a collection devoted to scribal cultures of Egypt, their inclusion is crucial. Their main purpose is to sketch the scope and goals of socio-historical linguistics for the unacquainted reader. It is in the philological disciplines devoted to the study of western European languages that the most advanced theoretical and methodological frameworks have been articulated. They introduce the conceptual toolbox common to contemporary historical sociolinguistics, from notions such as 'text language', 'manuscript community', and 'social network', to innovative—even radical—perspectives about what we can ask of scribal texts. These papers frame and contextualize the papers dealing with both the indigenous and non-indigenous languages of premodern Egypt. This framework is embraced and applied to Ancient Egyptian by Polis (Chapter 4), whose paper serves as a bridge between the two worlds.

While Stenroos (Chapter 2) takes a broad approach to medieval English, Bergs (Chapter 3) focuses on two case studies in eastern England: the letters written by the Paston family, a well-known family from fifteenth-century

in Tell Tayinat, this corpus provides a wealth of textual variants—orthographic, phonetic, semantic, etc.—for analysis. Current analysis of this variation, being undertaken by Jacob Lauinger (Johns Hopkins University), focuses on scribal production and is illustrative of the potential for future work.

Norfolk, and an eleventh-century chronicle from an abbey of sixty monks in Peterborough. While removed in many ways from the Egyptian material, there are several points of contact: they deal with transitions between phases of the same language—e.g. from Old to Middle English with the Peterborough Chronicle and in a closer time frame between generations of a single family—and the potential issue of language contact and the variation that arises from writing in a non-native language, which may be the case with the Peterborough Chronicle.

As noted above, Egypt is the geographic area in focus here, but the case studies presented span thousands of years as well as a number of languages and sociocultural milieus. The scope of the papers collected ranges from the period of indigenous (Pharaonic) rulers to later times, in which Egypt was conquered and became part of the empires of foreign nations: Roman, Byzantine, and Arab. The texts were therefore written under different circumstances, from periods when traditional Egyptian religion, Christianity, and Islam were the dominant religious forces in the country. Several stages of the indigenous Egyptian language are represented (Late Egyptian: Polis, Winand; demotic: Mairs, Ryholt, Quack; Coptic: Boud'hors, Cromwell, Richter) as well as Greek and Latin (Clarysse, Halla-aho, Mairs), on the one hand, and Hebrew (Wagner and Outhwaite), on the other. These languages are written in a number of native writing systems, as well as later alphabetic scripts. The chronological range and changing political climates create the environment within which these different systems came into contact, creating bilingual (and at times trilingual) documents, as language contact becomes increasingly prevalent, or at least visible in written texts.

At present, there are significant disciplinary divides even within Egyptology. Scholars tend to focus on Coptic, demotic, or pre-demotic Egyptian, and while there are often strong links between Greek and Latin papyrology, on the one hand, and demotic or Coptic papyrology, on the other, it is only in recent years that similar links have begun to be forged between Egyptian (demotic and Coptic), Greek, and Arabic.[5] While the study of medieval Hebrew is often dealt with in connection with medieval Arabic, it is only rarely that the former is at all considered in the context of the other linguistic and textual traditions of premodern Egypt.

The nature and quantity of documentation are not equal over the four millennia covered. While some periods and places are nearly black holes for the modern observer, others provide us with almost incomparably richer materials. The Theban region in southern Egypt has produced high numbers of documents in hieratic, demotic, Greek, and Coptic, providing information, if not consistently then for much of the period, from *c.*1200 BCE to 800 CE.[6] Conversely,

[5] As an example of the working relationships being fostered between specialists in different fields, see Mairs and Martin (2008/2009) and Naether and Renberg (2010).

[6] This, and the following information, is based on statistics from Verreth (2009), concerning texts written (as opposed to found) in the sites in question, for the 1,600 years spanning the eighth century BCE to eighth century CE. For Thebes there are 349 hieratic, 3,681 demotic, 9,284 Greek,

some sites provide only a snapshot of a single time. One of the most notable of these is Pathyris (Gebelein), only 30 km south of Thebes, for which the papyrological material is mostly confined to those texts produced between 188 and 86 BCE, when the site was the location of a minor military base.[7]

Within the studies offered, four such rich situations stand out. The first is the New Kingdom village of Deir el-Medina (*c.*1500–1050 BCE) on the west bank of Thebes, the village of the workmen responsible for building and decorating the royal tombs of this period. Polis' and Winand's contributions deal with texts from this site. In the same region, but two millennia later, is the seventh-/eighth-century-CE town of Djeme, built within Medinet Habu, the mortuary complex of Ramses III. Djeme was part of a larger, connected western Theban region that included several monasteries and hermitages, which have produced a wealth of monastic and secular material. The papers by Boud'hors and Cromwell focus on texts from both domains. The west bank of Thebes is also the site of the Ptolemaic (second century BCE) priestly community dealt with in Mairs' study of bilingual legal documents. The third is the Fayum region, as represented by studies focusing on demotic (Ryholt and, in part, Quack) and Greek (Clarysse) texts, with texts coming from both the large temple estates (see the temple library from Tebtunis, examined by Ryholt) and private landowners, in the case of Greek texts.[8] Finally, there is the Cairo Genizah, a collection of over 190,000 Jewish manuscript fragments written in Hebrew, Judaeo-Arabic, and Arabic, which was found in the storeroom of the Ben Ezra synagogue in Old Cairo (Fusṭāṭ). Hebrew letters from this corpus are the focus of the study by Wagner and Outhwaite.[9]

and 3,504 Coptic texts. These statistics do not provide a chronological breakdown of when the documents were written.

[7] For Pathyris, Verreth (2009) lists 1,005 demotic and 234 Greek texts (no hieratic texts are included for the period in study and only four Coptic texts, all of which concern a fifth-century group of Blemmyes at the site). The language of these has been the focus of recent studies; see, for example, Vierros 2007, 2008, and 2012 (and the references therein). It is important to stress that the statistics in Verreth (2009) are based on the papyrological material dated after the eighth century BCE, and this is not to say that no written records survive from earlier periods. As a prime example, see the First Intermediate Period (*c.* 2125–1975 BCE) stela of Iti, which records how he supplied his town during famine (see Lichtheim 1973, 88–9 and references therein), which is vital not only for the study of the history of this period but, from a philological perspective, for the study of early Egyptian biographies. Further restrictions concerning the utility of Verreth's statistics are discussed in n. 10.

[8] As is the case with the Zenon archive, one of the studies discussed by Clarysse. This corpus is the focus of ongoing linguistic analysis, for which see especially Evans 2010a and 2012 (and see therein for background). Found at Tebtunis, but concerning a village not far to the north-west of it, is also the archive of the scribe Menches, *komogrammateus* of Kerkeosiris (see Verhoogt 1998). This archive has yet to undergo a linguistic analysis, such as that for the Zenon material (but is an excellent candidate for such a study).

[9] Research on Hebrew texts from the Genizah is far more advanced than Arabic papyrology, as noted by Grob 2010, xiii n. 1. Grob's excellent study on the form, function, content, and context of Arabic letters on papyrus from the seventh to tenth centuries starts to redress this imbalance. Here, she raises many of the same issues relevant to the issue of variation and the reasons for it,

The data available for these sites allows us to frame and pursue research questions that are difficult for other periods. In this respect, the pre-New Kingdom periods of Egypt's history (i.e. pre-1540) especially spring to mind.[10] In part, this is connected with the type of written material available for study. As will be discussed in the following sections, the majority of the case studies here take non-literary material as their primary evidence, that is, letters and other documentary genres. The exceptions are the papers by Ryholt and Quack, which primarily focus on demotic literary works, and Richter, whose study is on 'semi-literary' texts. For most of Egypt's history, especially before the New Kingdom, relatively few large corpora of non-literary documents have survived. Nevertheless, where they do survive, our knowledge of the work of individual scribes, which at times includes literary and non-literary documents, allows us to examine their repertoires, focusing on the ways in which genre/*Textsorte* or register informs their scribal choices. For example, Polis provides a detailed study of the linguistic choices of a single New Kingdom scribe, Amenakhte son of Ipuy, who wrote or copied numerous literary and non-literary texts.

To varying degrees, each period and each place was characterized by its own particular scribal culture, its own set of practices, embedded in an ever-changing socio-historical context. One of the goals of this volume is to encourage the kind of research that would make possible the search for continuities and discontinuities or transformations in scribal cultures in a single area whose texts cover a range of dates, cultures, and languages. The contributions to the current study raise several key concepts, and set up the possibilities for future research on many of these—as well as other—points.

§3. MAIN THEMES

§3.1. From Scribes to Text Communities

Bergs and Stenroos stress that the object of research in historical sociolinguistics is not the 'Holy Grail of the vernacular', but rather the constraints on variation

from language use (including whether or not a 'Documentary Standard' can be postulated on the basis of such letters as a counterpart to the Literary Standard of Classical Arabic), layout and palaeography, how speech is mapped onto the documents, how the relationships between the different parties are encoded, and so on (Grob 2010, xvii).

[10] The statistics provided by Verreth (2009) start only from the eighth century BCE, so it is not possible to produce comparable statistics that cover Egypt's entire history, and the information in question is documentary, thus excluding a wealth of other text types. For the period in question (eighth century BCE to eighth century CE), 110,174 texts are included (since the compilation of these figures on 23 August 2009, insufficient numbers of texts have been published that would significantly alter them). Of these, the overwhelming majority are Greek (76,182 = 69.1%), followed by demotic (14,136 = 12.8%) and Coptic (9,976 = 9.1%), followed by texts written in hieroglyphs (4.2%), Latin (3.6%), hieratic (1.3%), and Aramaic (1.1%), with numerous languages represented by much smaller numbers.

in written texts. Such variation often turns out to be anything but 'random, chaotic, or riddled with "free variation"'. One of the main ways of seeing past the messiness of the data—and identifying patterns of variation—is to return to the individual language user. In the context of the present volume, this often means the scribe. However, we interpret the category 'scribe' rather broadly (and conveniently) to include not only individuals who copied manuscripts, but also authors (understood broadly to include those responsible for 'everyday writing'[11]), translators, and editors. This conceptualization is necessary because modern conceptions of scribes might not be cross-culturally valid. For example, McIntosh (1963) shows that for Middle English scribes, there is a scale with *literatim* copyists at one end and translators at the other, with a wide range of interim possibilities.

In many cases dealt with in the present volume, we are lucky enough to know at least something about the scribes in question: a name, place of activity, family members or associates, the nature of his social relations with an addressee, his religious and economic practices. Even when this information is known (Clarysse and Halla-aho), the goal of the authors in this volume is not necessarily to focus on what we can deduce about the writers themselves, but about the implications of their language selection upon wider social issues. Other papers explicitly focus on certain known individuals, being close micro-studies of aspects of their work.

For example, the texts written by the scribe Amennakhte son of Ipuy from Deir el-Medina are dealt with by Polis, who analyses the parameters of linguistic variation according to the genre of his texts, allowing an identification of the written registers or selections operating within his repertoire. This detailed analysis demonstrates that the variation at the level of an individual scribe is far from being random and is almost entirely free from 'unmotivated or asystemic idiosyncracies'. Boud'hors' study contrasts the work of two monks, from seventh- and eighth-century Thebes, who lived at different times in the same cell—Mark and Frange. Palaeographic and linguistic analyses of their respective dossiers show how diverse they were as scribes. Their unequal graphic skill (Mark exhibits better penmanship) and different use of language (Frange writes in a style more influenced by regional traits and personal habits) set them apart. On one hand, this is indicative of education level and social position, but on the other hand, the time separating them (perhaps fifty years or more) must also be a factor, especially as during this period Egypt was undergoing a series of administrative changes following the Arab conquest.

It is within the same historical and geographic framework that Cromwell's study is set. In this paper, we move away from the focus on a single scribe to the work of multiple scribes producing legal documents and the degree of variation

[11] This is the term used by Bagnall (2011), which is not entirely synonymous with documentary texts and does not exclude literary and semi-literary texts, depending on their form and social usages, which are more important than content (see especially p. 3).

found between them, specifically focusing on one formulaic component. Scribes can be grouped together based on the language and formulae that they used. Here, 'used' rather than 'chose' is an important distinction, as it is argued that the decisions made by these scribes are not necessarily personal ones but are rather indicative of the type of training that they received. Again, variation is not arbitrary but influenced by factors derived from the professional networks within which the scribes worked.

These three papers collectively exhibit a spectrum, from the individual scribe to multiple scribes to scribal communities. Wagner and Outhwaite's contribution encompasses a much broader scribal community. The Judaeo-Arabic letters from Egypt are placed within the wider community of Hebrew letters from Palestine and Babylonia, as well as the native and antique Egyptian tradition and those of Arabic–Islamic correspondences. This brings us back to Stenroos' contribution and the concept of text community, a flexible term that must be defined for each study, but which refers to groups of text with something in common. In these instances, we know the region involved, the history of the period, and many of the individuals who interacted in this time. The texts were not produced in isolation, but by living and interacting language users.

This is not to say that anonymous texts, or those lacking precise provenance, have less to offer. In some scribal cultures, including within Egypt, anonymous manuscripts are the norm, but this does not mean that the study of the variation therein cannot yield new insights. Richter and Winand deal with anonymous scribes, but much can be learned about their practices as individuals and as members of scribal communities, as well as their probable sites of activity.

A recurring theme is that of scribal education and training. Many of the papers deal with this issue to a limited extent, often emphasizing how little we know about the reality of such training. However, the search for text communities is often accompanied by the assumption that the clustering of shared practices is indicative of a shared background or 'school of practices'. This matter is prominent in the paper by Cromwell, but is also discussed in the papers of Boud'hors, who mentions Frange's role as a teacher, and of Quack, who examines the local successes of particular writing styles in Roman Egypt as traces of broader sociopolitical changes with deep consequences for scribal education.

§3.2. Types of Variation

Looking at individual scribes tends to reduce the amount of variation observed in a corpus, since an individual scribal repertoire might not comprehend the totality of variation observed across a broader corpus. A focus on individual scribes intersects with another methodological issue prominent in the study of written language, namely, the conceptualization of the data used. If, in everyday parlance, one speaks of 'dead languages', there has been a trend in sociolinguistically-oriented philology and linguistics to reconfigure the data as 'text languages' (Fleischman 2000). Taking this a step further, Stenroos argues that 'text languages' are better thought of as 'manuscript languages', in order to reflect the nature of the actual data and to emphasize the kind of research questions and methods that would be appropriate for their study.

For example, contemporary scholars of variation in written texts have begun to study the relationship between individual scribes and manuscripts and the communities in which they are embedded, using a range of methods that can be described collectively as 'social network' approaches. Pioneered by Milroy (1987) for the study of spoken language, social network theory has been expanded to the study of written texts by Bergs (2005) and others. While Bergs in this volume focuses on scribal networks (e.g. in the Paston letter corpus), Stenroos develops a framework that is highly fruitful for situations in which we have anonymous manuscripts. Stenroos' flexible concept of text community, 'a group of texts that have something in common, so that it makes sense to refer to them as an entity', has yielded impressive results for the study of variation in Middle English, and it is certain that it can—and should—be applied to other 'manuscript languages'.

Both of these concepts (scribal networks and text communities) are the focus of Polis' paper on a single scribe active in Deir el-Medina. Polis deals with orthographical variation, on the one hand, and lexical, morphological, and syntactic variation, on the other, showing the significant impact of register and genre on the latter. For example, a marker of topicalization (*ỉr*) is avoided in literary registers, while abundantly attested in non-literary texts by the same author. Adjectives are shown to be rarer in non-literary texts than in literary texts. In some cases, orthography and syntax intersect: Polis shows that the graphic presence or omission of a tense-aspect marker is dependent on syntactic context. Moreover, the careful study of a single scribe's corpus over his entire career clearly demonstrates that individual scribal usage can change over time; these 'micro-diachronic' changes in the individual scribe's active repertoire are examined against the background of broader patterns of change within the scribal community at the site.

Other papers to address parameters of variation typically considered to be 'linguistic,' i.e. variation in lexical and grammatical features, include Halla-aho's. Here she shows that for dictated Greek letters from Egypt, while orthography and, to a lesser extent, morphology reflect the scribe's repertoire, syntax tends to be that of the (dictating) author. However, there is no reason that the framework of historical sociolinguistics should not be applied to other types of variation, as demonstrated by the studies here that deal with other socio-historical aspects of scribal repertoires. To take two examples, which will be dealt with in greater detail below, Clarysse discusses the ways that epistolary formulary employed by scribes encode social power asymmetries between superiors and subordinates, while Richter reconstructs the social and intellectual milieu of a group of scribes, based on their sophisticated use of different graphic codes as 'high' and 'low' varieties.

Palaeographical variation is addressed by a number of papers, although the only paper to focus almost entirely on handwriting is Quack's. Quack demonstrates that for the Ptolemaic period we can identify palaeographical regionalization—the development of distinctive local norms—in cursive (hieratic and demotic) manuscripts. It is striking that these norms can be limited to quite small areas, with considerable differences found between relatively close locales. Quack argues that this regionalization cannot be divorced from significant sociopolitical changes, especially changes in the status of political elites, the breakdown of a dominant supraregional 'centre', and the consequent decentralization of scribal training. In essence, Quack proposes that sociopolitical institutions and agents that previously held a more or less standardized norm in place were no longer able to do so, leading to the destandardization of cursive Egyptian writing. Quack concludes with several provocative proposals regarding the 'success' of certain types of hands, raising the possibility that these hands persisted due to the high prestige of the individual scribal teachers who innovated and disseminated them.

Palaeography is also emphasized, but not exclusively, in Boud'hors' study of the repertoires of two scribes from the Theban area. Boud'hors compares the respective dossiers of documents written by Mark, a seventh-century priest, and Frange, a monk active in the first half of the eighth century. Mark wrote letters and wall inscriptions, but also copied literary manuscripts, some of which have survived, while Frange's dossier mostly comprises letters, and the evidence for other forms of scribal activity, e.g. copying, is more tenuous. Boud'hors sketches the differences in their palaeographical and linguistic practices, showing how scribal repertoires changed over time in a single area. While Mark wrote a standard Sahidic dialect and shows evidence of having been trained in both Coptic and Greek, Frange's usage is heavily localized, with the linguistic features typical of the destandardized repertoire of the Theban area. Boud'hors identifies both orthographical–phonological and morpho-syntactical Theban features in Frange's repertoire, features that may have been known to Mark but were not part of his active repertoire. Some of these features, including a still poorly understood verbal construction, appear to be idiolectal marks. Moreover, while Mark's hand remained relatively stable, that of Frange—something of a palaeographic chameleon, able to imitate well the hand of others—changed throughout his career. Boud'hors attributes the differences between Mark's and Frange's repertoires to a range of factors: level of education, social position, and large-scale changes in the written representation of language after the Arab conquest of Egypt.

Cromwell takes variation in legal formulae as the basis for a preliminary study to isolate what Stenroos would call text communities in early Islamic Djeme. The religious invocation at the beginning of legal documents is used as a case study to illustrate how much information can be extracted from close analysis of language selection (here Greek or Coptic), orthography, and palaeography, and what these reveal when examined together. While orthography appears to reflect competency rather than training, palaeography is shown to be an extra dimension in language choice. Palaeographical variation reveals the intriguing phenomenon of bigraphism, the use of two different scripts in the same text by a single scribe: Djeme scribes wrote Greek either in the writing typical of Greek documents or in the same script used for writing Coptic. Some scribal repertoires included a distinction between the two, while others were limited to the Coptic system for writing both Coptic and Greek. This corpus has the great advantage that many texts are dated (a few absolutely) and bear the names of the scribes that wrote them. Dossiers of work by different individuals can be compiled as a result. Two connected observations result from this study: functional domain, i.e. the types of documents that a scribe produces, is not a unifying factor (scribes producing the same types of texts write in different styles); and scribes show greater similarities with their direct contemporaries than those writing in the previous generation or generations.

The palaeographic 'matrix system' of late Coptic alchemical manuscripts is examined by Richter, as one part of the strategies and repertoires available to scribes (see §3.3). Collectively, Boud'hors, Cromwell, and Richter provide an important contribution to the field of Coptic palaeography, which is not as developed a discipline as its Greek counterpart. Richter in particular stresses this point. Terminology that remains standard in Coptic palaeographic analyses—'uncial' is the main case in point—are no longer used by Greek scholars. A volume such as this, which brings together different languages and scripts, while showing the diversity of approaches to written material, highlights some of these discrepancies in the situation of related areas across fields. These studies do not aim to resolve this situation, but they can be used as the base from which advances can be made.

These studies show how variation in practices usually considered non-linguistic, such as orthography and palaeography, can be integrated into a more comprehensive study of scribal repertoires. Furthermore, they serve to illustrate how linguistic and extralinguistic features can be investigated together to reveal points of correlation or divergence in the type of variation exhibited.

§3.3. Repertoire

Scholars of language contact (e.g. Matras 2008) have adopted the notion of repertoire to reflect the fact that the competence of individual language users ('speakers') can comprise more than one linguistic code ('language'). In fact, it is not certain that there is a sharp division between bilinguals and monolinguals, since even the latter often have competence in different codes ('varieties', 'registers'), the choice between which is often constrained by the circumstances and contexts of use, construed broadly. The contributions illustrate the internal complexity of scribal repertoires. In some cases, we are dealing with 'multilingual' repertoires that comprise multiple codes. In other cases, the comparison of the repertoires of different scribes reveals historical change in active repertoires. Boud'hors shows that the decades separating two scribes in a single place—decades in which a radical sociopolitical change took place—were enough to allow highly local, non-standard features to become visible in texts as part of active scribal repertoires. This, of course, raises the interesting possibility that these features were part of earlier scribes' passive repertoires, but for still-unknown sociocultural reasons were barred from representation in written texts.

Cromwell, with her discussion of bigraphism, expands this conception of repertoire to the graphic—purely visual—aspect of scribal documents. Bigraphism, the use of more than one script in the same text, is parallel to situations in which language users' repertoires comprise more than one language or variety. When phrased in this way, it becomes apparent that one can ask questions very similar to those posed by sociolinguists, e.g. regarding the contexts of use in which a variant—in this case, a graphic one—is selected.

Richter also deals with the graphic 'bag of tricks' of a single scribe of whose output two late (tenth-century) Coptic alchemical manuscripts survive. While the majority of the documents are written in what Richter calls a 'matrix system', a number of alternative codes are employed by the scribe, for a variety of reasons. Richter points out that these alternative codes are a matter of pure choice, since the scribe could have relayed the content using the matrix system. Richter's discussion highlights the complexities involved in script choice in literary manuscripts. He shows that what is normally a rather specialized graphic code in most literary manuscripts, namely, the so-called 'sloping uncial' writing style (in his terminology, as applied to Coptic palaeography) has a particular functional significance when it is used outside of bigraphic situations, such as in one of the alchemical manuscripts. Its use to mark a text as of a lower 'textual level' or degree of 'literariness' reveals, in fact, contemporary sociocultural attitudes of the scribes towards the texts they themselves wrote and copied. Interestingly, this code often correlates with less standardized language. The matrix system of the other manuscript is the bimodular uncial, usually thought to be a 'high variety' used for literary manuscripts. Richter argues that this is a misconception. While the other option, the unimodular bookhand, was indeed limited to high-prestige types of text production, the bimodular uncial was often used as part of a bigraphic practice: the unimodular hand was used for writing the basic text, whereas the bimodular hand was used for paratextual units. This perspective allows Richter to analyse the choice of the 'high variety' bimodular script as a functional equivalent in one text to the clearly 'low variety' sloping uncial found in the other text.

Moving beyond the matrix system, Richter describes a range of alternative graphical codes: the use of miniscule letters, cryptographic code, Arabic letters, and alchemical symbols. He proposes several motivations for the choice of alternative codes, mainly the use of a 'group code', reflecting scribal self-consciousness and professionalism, on the one hand, and the deliberate obscuring of esoteric content, on the other. Richter traces the origins of these practices to a range of contexts: the Coptic scriptorium tradition, the Coptic documentary tradition, specific scientific traditions, and a bilingual (Arabic–Coptic) intellectual milieu.

These repertoires are connected with the writing of text, represented by different modes of scribal activity, whether *literatim* copying, translating, taking dictation, paraphrasing, or producing a partially new document on the basis of existing templates. The range of activities in which scribes were engaged is here extended. Especially interesting in this respect is Ryholt's paper, in which he focuses on a single site of manuscript production, conservation, and transmission: the library of the temple of Soknebtunis at Tebtunis in the Fayum. Ryholt provides a detailed description of the material aspects of text production at this site, from the use of fresh vs reused papyrus, the formatting of manuscripts (e.g. lines and pagination, and the choice of coloured ink), and contrasting the Tebtunis manuscripts with those found or produced at other sites. Also documented are additional scribal activities that can best be characterized as 'editorial', namely correcting and collating manuscripts, or 'conservatorial', such as repairing damaged or worn-out papyri.

Ryholt assesses what we know about the scribes active in the temple library, based on prosopography and palaeography: while very few scribes' names are known, others can be identified on the basis of handwriting. This section complements—and complicates—Quack's in-depth treatment of the regionalization of Roman demotic hands. Some manuscripts found in Tebtunis were written in hands highly similar to styles typical of other sites, which raises the possibility of some form of trade in manuscripts between temples or that scribes were mobile, that is, receiving their training in one temple and later working in another. Identifying 'manuscript communities' on the basis of palaeography also allows Ryholt to conclude that the temple library scribes were probably not specialized for particular scribal jobs or textual genres.

Also expanding the range of activities performed by scribes, Winand deals with the role of scribes in producing the New Kingdom dossier of juridical documents known as the 'Tomb Robbery Papyri', written in a particular variety of Late Egyptian. Against the reasonable expectation of a high degree of standardization, Winand identifies a considerable amount of orthographical, lexical, and grammatical variation, even within the more formulaic parts of these manuscripts. Based on this variation, Winand is able to reconstruct the production of these legal reports as a three-step process: taking notes during the questioning, composing a preliminary draft, and writing the final version. As opposed to private letters, in which the dictated content is usually largely that of the sender/author, these legal texts show a high degree of involvement on the part of the scribe, who often fills in information, rephrases what had been said during the depositions, and in general standardizes the phraseology of the final documents.

A parallel is found in a Ptolemaic bilingual dossier of legal documents in demotic and Greek, which provides Mairs with the opportunity to examine the almost invariably 'invisible' role of translators as active agents in legal proceedings. Her study of the legal formula *kata to dunaton* ('according to what is possible') leads her to identify an important, albeit often neglected, type of translation: the kind of 'functional' translation that does not require full bilingualism and whose goal is not the production of an idiomatic, native-like text in the target language. The perspective is shifted from the axiological ('bad Greek', 'translationese') to the functional, i.e. how this kind of Greek is embedded in the specific cultural activity of translating a demotic Egyptian document into an Egyptian Greek one. Mairs also points out that translation is not the only option available to scribes: transliteration, a kind of graphemic code-switching, in her view, was also a perfectly acceptable and functional choice for translators who could rely on the audience's exposure to and acquaintance with both the source and target languages.

§3.4. Genre

As noted above (§2), the papers collected here deal with both literary and non-literary textual genres. As Polis cautions, it is crucial to keep in mind that our modern genre categorizations are often anachronistic with respect to the culturally alienated premodern societies we study: in some cases, we may not identify native genres, while in others, we may argue—without necessarily reaching new insights—about the proper categorization of literary letters, pieces of literary texts preserved as scribal exercises, or a tale written according to the conventions of an administrative report. Nevertheless, a nuanced conception of genre—and its relevance for the study of variation in written language—is characteristic of most of the authors whose papers make up this volume. For example, Richter (2005) shows that even documentary texts, specifically child donation texts from the same Coptic Theban corpus examined by Cromwell, have a narrative dimension that can only be understood as intertextuality with literary texts.

In some studies genre is not the primary motivating factor, but location. This is important in Quack's study of texts, which come principally from Tebtunis, Soknopaiou Nesos, and Narmouthis in the Fayum. Sometimes, different periods produced different types of text. From Ptolemaic (third to first centuries BCE) Tebtunis the evidence is mostly documentary, but from the Roman period (first to third centuries CE) it becomes mostly literary or sub-literary. For the variation at the heart of his study, 'the dominating factor is the local one, not the text genre'. In other studies, as discussed below, a selection is made, and here non-literary texts are divided into letters and legal documents, while literary includes also semi-literary productions.

§3.4.1. *Epistolary practices*

Several papers deal with letters, letter writing, and letter writers, such as those by Boud'hors and Polis, as part of broader studies of the scribal repertoires of known individuals. In others, these receive a more focal position.

Halla-aho interrogates the process of letter composition, and the specific contribution of scribes to the process. Arguing that it is essential to know 'whose linguistic competence is presented', she points out that if the language attested in letters mainly reflects the competence of scribes, it would mean that the linguistic output of a rather circumscribed and atypical group—educated scribes—is embodied in letters. Working on Latin and Greek letters from Roman Egypt, Halla-aho poses questions that are relevant to most situations in which the sender of a letter is not necessarily the person who penned it. Taking issue with some prevalent views of the type of language production involved in dictation, Halla-aho stresses that dictated language is not 'oral language' and is not necessarily close to a putative 'spoken' language. Finally, she shows that gender is not an especially important parameter in identifying the role of the scribe in the final written output.

Clarysse deals with ways of encoding asymmetrical relations of social power between superiors and subordinates. Based on two archives of Greek letters dating between the third century BCE and the third century CE, Clarysse studies how epistolary language is used to negotiate nuanced power relations between senders and addressees. Patterns of linguistic variation correlate with differences between situations in which (a) a superior writes to a subordinate, (b) a subordinate writes to a superior, or (c) the sender and addressee are more or less of equal status. Clarysse finds that 'high-to-low' letters are characterized mainly by what is absent—namely, conventional politeness formulas—as well as the density of curt directive forms.

Wagner and Outhwaite deal with changes in the use of Hebrew and Judaeo-Arabic as written vernaculars, appropriate for use in various forms of letter writing. The authors examine the ways in which functional domain influenced language choice, focusing on the florescence of Hebrew as a written vernacular. Interestingly, Wagner and Outhwaite approach the question of language choice through the textual parameters of formulas (greetings, religious invocations, and dating), showing that in some respects, early letter writers were working with not only a bilingual linguistic repertoire but also within multiple epistolary traditions. At a later time, the differences between Hebrew and Judaeo-Arabic letters dwindled, the former coming to resemble the latter. This paper, perhaps more than the others collected here, shows how changing epistolary practices and traditions can reflect significant changes in society. For example, changing political realities in late-eleventh-century Egypt had significant consequences for the ways that Jews wrote letters, leading in the end to a discontinuity between earlier and later traditions.

§3.4.2. Legal documents

It has been noted already that the New Kingdom scribes discussed by Winand that were responsible for the 'Tomb Robbery Papyri' had more involvement in the production of these texts than scribes involved in letter writing. These texts are therefore held up as a contrast to those studied by Halla-aho. Here he deals with the evidence for processes of composing and editing legal protocols from the so-called Tomb Robberies corpus, recording the depositions of the defendants, which were written by scribes navigating constantly between the conventional and the formulaic, on the one hand, and the particular, on the other. In these texts, variation marks the unexpected, what is exceptional or remarkable, but even in these personal accounts, uniformity is encountered, showing the influence of the scribes in question.

Again, in contrast to letters, where style is accredited to the dictator, Cromwell gives the scribe full responsibility for the formulae used in the Djeme corpus. The content of the documents in question in her study and the judicial aspect of the legal activity recorded form no part of the discussion. The specific formula in question—the invocation of the Holy Trinity—is found at the beginning of sales, settlements of dispute, testaments, and other document types. Variation is not examined in order to differentiate one type of document from another, but to look at the people behind the text, the legal parties become secondary to the scribes themselves.

Mairs' study focuses on a set of translated documents drawn up for the same family some ten years apart. The two sets of papers concern the transfer of rights to perform liturgies and receive income from certain tombs in the Theban necropolis. These comprise a sale document and a cession document in each case (although only one of the cessions survives). How the translator of the demotic texts chose to translate and condense the phraseology into Greek is the key feature of this paper, but Mairs demonstrates that a comprehensive knowledge of the historical and social context of these documents is vital in understanding the choices made.

§3.4.3 Literary and 'semi-literary' texts

The term 'literary' in connection with Egyptian texts generally refers to historical and religious or mythological narrative material, as well as 'wisdom literature'. 'Semi-literary', also referred to as 'paraliterary' or 'subliterary', or '*Kleinliteratur*', primarily comprises technical literature, whether on medicine, dream interpretation, or other scientific matters. Richter's paper on alchemical texts falls into this category. These more or less elaborate compilations of alchemical recipes provide evidence for the reception and appropriation of contemporary scientific knowledge from Arabic sources in medieval Egypt. Yet, again, it is not the content of these recipes that is the focus of this study, but rather how the anonymous scribe presented them. The palaeographic component of this was discussed above, but this is just the start of the 'bag of tricks' at the scribe's disposal. This text type also allowed him to play with numbers, cryptography, and the striking use of 'scientific signs', including the sun (ϭ), the moon (☽), and the rectangle (▭) to represent gold, silver, and sheet metal respectively: a range of devices not appropriate for other genres.

Ryholt focuses on the Roman-period productions from the library belonging to the temple of Soknebtunis at Tebtunis. As noted regarding Quack's paper, the texts from this time are mostly literary in nature. This study highlights important aspects of the formal and physical elements of such texts, which are specific to this genre. One feature that is immediately clear is the very use of the demotic script for literary texts. Hieratic was still in use at the site, but it was reserved for texts directly associated with the cult, whereas the bulk of the demotic material preserve literary and semi-literary texts. This distinction in script choice is also reflected in other scribal practices, including the use of formatting lines and red ink. Both are more frequent in the hieratic manuscripts: as cultic texts, they were generally prepared more carefully.[12]

Both of these papers, by Richter and Ryholt, show that scribes had various techniques at their disposal, and were conscious in their use of them when producing works of different natures. Different genres required different considerations.

§4. MOVING ON FROM HERE: KEY ISSUES FOR FUTURE RESEARCH

As stated at the beginning, there have been studies that consider variation and scribes, but these have been relatively uncommon. This is changing, with more serious thought being given to the kinds of issues that are raised in the following

[12] Parkinson (2009, 90–112) provides a rare study of the physical features of literary manuscripts from the Middle Kingdom, specifically a scribe working *c.*1780 BCE. In some respects, this study is reminiscent of features discussed by Ryholt, including column length, margins, placement of rubrics, correction techniques including erasures with wet fingers, which in one case appears to have left a fingerprint (!) (see p. 98), mistakes, and the reasons for mistakes. Parkinson also addresses the reasons for variation between the copy made by the scribe in question and other known copies: 'Some of his orthographic idiosyncrasies may reflect something of his cultural circumstances and attitudes' (p. 115; see pp 115–19 for further detail).

contributions. In the past five years, significant works have appeared that show a general trend in this direction.[13] Impediments to this type of research, notably access to text editions and original manuscripts, remain, but these are being slowly overcome by various research tools providing online and immediate access, e.g. the online Deir el-Medina database (New Kingdom), the Datenbank demotischer Texte (demotic texts), and the Duke Databank of Documentary Papyri (initially Greek texts but now incorporating Coptic material).[14] Accurate diplomatic renderings of texts are required, so that variation can be studied rather than removed as 'corruption' by text editors.

But more broadly, we envision a change in the philological and linguistic practices of scholars working on the languages of premodern Egypt. This means taking into account the fact that the textual artefacts were written by individual human beings, who were educated or trained in particular places at particular times, and who lived and worked with social, professional, and often religious networks composed of other individuals and their interrelations. This translates into the attempt to relate scribal practices, whether found in a single manuscript or across a broad corpus of manuscripts, to the communities in which they were produced. These practices are themselves historical products, the result of processes of innovation, diffusion, and conventionalization—and they are often related to wider changes in the sociocultural and political matrices in which scribal cultures were embedded. These processes, as the papers collected here show, can be traced, given careful attention to manuscripts and scribes. The results clearly demonstrate that such perspectives enrich our knowledge of both synchronic and diachronic dimensions of written culture.

Furthermore, looking at individual scribes as social actors means investigating the ways that textual conventions of different types inform linguistic and non-linguistic scribal practices. For example, it is clear that the active repertoires visible in manuscripts depend strongly on the parameter of textual genre. Genres are also historical products that evolve over time, in ways that are often contingent on the changing reality outside the world of texts.

Finally, the historical sociolinguistic perspective—and the study of variation in particular—introduces an often-lacking dose of concrete realities (and new data) into the abstract theoretical discussions of language change. The latter often focus so strongly on gaining access to underlying linguistic systems that they forget that such systems, which are quite possibly only useful fictions, are accessible only through the concrete (and often messy) linguistic output of

[13] For example, note the papers collected in Evans and Obbink (2010) concerning Greek and Latin, Parkinson (2009) for Middle Egyptian, and Prada (2013) for the importance of orthographic variation in certain demotic texts, to name but three.

[14] See respectively, http://dem-online.gwi.uni-muenchen.de (Deir el Medine online; Nichtliterarische Ostraka aus Deir el Medine), http://www.adwmainz.de/index.php?id=44 (Datenbank demotischer Texte), and http://www.papyri.info (Duke Databank).

language users. And in the case of premodern written cultures, this usually means that one is dealing with scribes and their practices.

This paradigm—like all paradigms—is not just a set of analytical techniques or methods to be applied to data. Rather, it is first and foremost a set of questions and preoccupations, as its practitioners emphasize. In the words of Merja Stenroos, 'Rather than making the best of bad data, we should turn them into good data by designing enquiries for which they are suited.'

2

From Scribal Repertoire to Text Community

The Challenge of Variable Writing Systems

Merja Stenroos

§1. INTRODUCTION

This chapter addresses a problem in interpreting the empirical evidence for early historical languages: that of relating individual scribal usages to the linguistic variation within a community. As detailed contextual information is often absent, both the individual scribal text and the large-scale survey pose problems of representativeness: it is suggested that the study of smaller 'text communities', defined by specific parameters, may provide a better perspective. This approach, which builds upon the 'textual parameters approach' outlined by Herring, van Reenen, and Schøsler in 2000, is adopted in ongoing work within the Middle English Scribal Texts (MEST) programme at Stavanger, to which reference will be made as appropriate.[1]

The languages concerned here are those of the pre-print era, and represent what Suzanne Fleischman termed 'text languages' in a seminal paper; a logical if inelegant term for these might be manuscript languages.[2] For such languages, there are neither recordings of spoken language nor living speakers to interview; the only direct evidence consists of a body of handwritten texts which cannot be augmented at will. The evidence is generally patchy and often anonymous, and the linguistic variation is difficult to relate to known variables. On these grounds, Labov famously described historical linguistics as 'making the best use of bad data'.[3]

[1] http://www.uis.no/meg-c.

[2] Fleischman (2000, 33). Fleischman's term 'text language' refers to any historical languages for which all evidence survives in the written mode; the present paper, however, is concerned especially with manuscript languages. See also Bergs' contribution to the current volume, Chapter 3.

[3] Labov (1994, 11).

The data are not, however, necessarily bad if studied on their own terms. It has been shown by many studies in recent years that historical texts can provide good data as long as we ask them questions that they are capable of answering. This entails, first of all, an awareness of the limitations of the mode and medium of the text. The texts may represent very different writing systems, and their physical media may be various: parchment, papyrus, cloth, clay, ceramic, stone, or metal. The different systems and media pose different challenges which need to be taken into account; at the same time, all manuscript languages present certain shared problems that are very different from those faced by the students of present-day languages. Such questions have to do with the relationship between written and spoken variation, the status of scribal texts as evidence, and the problems connected with reconstruction and the messiness of real data. While the present paper uses examples from medieval English, most commonly written on sheets of parchment or paper in a Latin-based alphabet, it is hoped that the discussion is, *mutatis mutandis*, relevant for other manuscript languages as well.

Texts are unlikely to provide good evidence if they are used primarily to reconstruct something else. Traditional practice has been to disregard the variation produced by scribes in actual texts as 'corruption', and to seek instead to reconstruct the presumed 'pure' language of postulated authorial originals. In a similar way, Labovian sociolinguistics has tended to focus on the spoken 'vernacular' as the central goal of linguistic enquiry; for historical linguistics in this tradition, the task has been to identify 'texts or subtexts that have the highest probability of approximating the spoken language'.[4] However, it is clear that no written texts from early historical periods can provide good evidence for the 'vernacular'; they may, on the other hand, provide excellent evidence for written language, which is what they represent.

Taking the text on its own terms also means that the starting point of enquiry should be the individual text as we have it, uncontaminated by editorial emendation or modernization. As Roger Lass puts it: 'the only acceptable source for older materials is a diplomatic transcript, or a representation that can be made to yield one.'[5] The text should be studied in its own right, as a source of a written language produced by a scribe who knew the language (s)he was writing infinitely better than any modern editor or linguist, and whose repertoire is reflected in the actual surviving data.[6]

However, the text will make little sense if studied in isolation; any interpretation of the data, even the choice of features for study, will depend on our assumptions about their linguistic and non-linguistic context. Conversely, the history

[4] Labov (1994, 11). [5] Lass (2004, 22).

[6] In English historical studies, it was earlier customary to explain particularly variable or perplexing texts as transcribed by scribes who 'did not know English'; this so-called 'Anglo-Norman Delusion' was shown to be untenable in a classic paper by Clark (1992).

of a language will make little sense if presented as a series of individual, isolated scribal outputs: as linguists, we are interested in the dynamics of language in a community, and we wish to study the patterns of variation and change of which the individual text (and the individual scribal repertoire) forms a part.

In other words, it is necessary to relate the language of the individual scribal text to the linguistic variation within a community. This may, however, be far from straightforward. We often have little or no information about the historical context of the individual text, and scribal texts of different genres and textual histories may be problematic to compare. Corpus-based studies of historical languages often present confusing results, and it is not always possible to tell whether this reflects the natural complexity of the data or problems of sampling: samples based on historical languages often contain far too broad a geographical and/or chronological range, and it is difficult to isolate variables.

There is also a problem of description: while it is possible to study the distribution of a single feature (such as the form of the first-person singular pronoun) across a wide geographical and chronological range, we cannot study clusters of related features (such as the 'system' of personal pronouns) in such a way: there can be no 'Middle English' system of personal pronouns, as the dynamics of pronoun use and the paradigmatic relationships will vary across time and space. A useful approach might be to study variation within specific 'text communities'; this entails relating the texts to other surviving texts sharing predefined criteria, rather than trying to draw inferences about usage within the language community as a whole.

§2. TAKING TEXTS ON THEIR OWN TERMS: THE STUDY OF WRITTEN VARIATION

§2.1. Written Language as an Object of Study

The historical linguist can only rely on direct evidence of written language. This has tended to place historical linguistics into a theoretically and methodologically problematic position. For much of the twentieth century, the study of written language was marginalized or even banished from the realm of linguistics: both Saussure and Bloomfield saw writing as merely the record of language, not as language itself.[7] In the structuralist tradition, the legitimate aim of linguistics has been the study of spoken language, irrespective of the mode of the evidence, and it is still common to separate 'orthography' from 'linguistics' proper. At the same time, there has been remarkably little problematization of the written mode as evidence for spoken language.

[7] Saussure (1986, 24–25); Bloomfield (1933, 21).

The idea that written language should, in the first instance, be studied as written language, was introduced by McIntosh half a century ago and has become widely accepted within the study of Middle English;[8] however, it still remains a radical idea within many linguistic traditions. This approach, which formed the basis of *A Linguistic Atlas of Late Mediaeval English* (LALME),[9] may be summarized as follows:

1) Written language should be studied in its own right, not as a representation of speech. The patterns of variation are strictly patterns of written convention and must be analysed as such. It is only at a later stage of analysis that we may, if we wish, enquire into the relationship of written and spoken forms.
2) In the absence of a standard, written language shows orderly variation that can be studied. Many written forms show clear distribution patterns across geography that may be used for localizing texts. This is the case whether or not they might relate to 'equivalent' variation in the spoken mode.

The patterns of linguistic variation derived from written texts should thus not, in the first instance, be analysed as variation in speech, even though they may be related to such variation. Here one might refer to Labov's discussion of 'facts' and 'generalizations': only the written forms are facts and can thus form data.[10] Our inferences about their spoken meaning may be contested and thus cannot be facts or form data; rather, they are generalizations from the written data.

The study of written language in its own right also allows for the direct study of such orthographic variation that would be ignored in a study of reconstructed speech. Such information was irrelevant to the traditional scholar whose only aim was to reconstruct spoken systems; however, for an enquiry into scribal variation, it may be of crucial importance. Native varieties of English show fairly few differences between phonemic systems, something that also appears to have been the case in the Middle English period; as written texts cannot be expected to reflect the phonetic variation that must have existed, they can only provide very broad indications of dialect if interpreted as records of speech. On the other hand, they show a great deal of purely orthographic variation that may be related to specific variables. For example, the use of doubled consonant digraphs, such as <chch> or <ghgh> in *cachche* 'catch' and *neghgheþ* 'approaches', seems to be connected with a small group of West Midland manuscripts, where they tend to cluster together with other distinctive orthographic habits, such as the doubling of <w> (*powwer* 'power').[11]

[8] McIntosh (1956, 1963). [9] McIntosh, Samuels, and Benskin (1986).

[10] Labov (1994, 12). Labov does, in fact, contrast the scribal spelling (the 'fact') and our interpretation of it, although he does this on the grounds of 'the possibility of scribal error' rather than because of the difference in mode as such.

[11] This group consists of four manuscripts, all of which are connected to the north Herefordshire–south Shropshire area, but which vary considerably in date and content. They include Harley 2253, Lincoln's Inn Hale 150, Longleat, Marquess of Bath's MS 5, and Oxford, St John's College 6.

§2.2. Written Variation in Middle English

The extent of orthographic variation varies greatly in early historical languages. Some languages, such as Latin, came to be highly standardized: scribes copying these languages would in general aim at reproducing a shared conventional written variety, just as a modern typesetter would. Other languages would permit a great deal of variation in the written mode; these include Coptic, Old Norse, and, to a dramatic extent, Middle English.

Used to the fixity of Latin, earlier historical linguists tended to expect writing systems to be regular: even if there might be different written varieties, 'literate' individual writers were expected to write consistently. Variable texts were thus associated with mistakes, carelessness, ignorance, so-called 'scribal corruption'. Scholars who studied the actual surviving texts in variable historical languages were then likely to find the majority of them corrupt and unsuitable as evidence.

This used to be the case with Middle English. The extreme variability of Middle English is the result of historical circumstances. While English ('Old English' or 'Anglo-Saxon') had been a literary and administrative language before the Norman Conquest in 1066, it ceased to be used for official or national functions after the Conquest, as all positions of power were taken over by the French-speaking Normans. While Latin remained the dominant written language, gradually joined by French, English was restricted to limited functions, and few new texts in English survive from the twelfth century.

However, English continued to be the spoken language of the majority and was gradually reintroduced as a written language for a wide range of purposes. From the mid-fourteenth century onwards, a large number of English texts were produced; however, standardization did not set in until much later. There is thus a long period during which English texts appear in large numbers without any overall standard model. During this period, variation is extensive. LALME records 510 spellings of the single word 'through', including forms such as *dorwgh*, *thoroo*, *trghug*, *twrw*, *þurf*, *yoro*, *yurth*, and *yhurgh*.[12]

The number of texts that survive from the Middle English period is large, considering the relatively small area and population involved. The texts represent a wide range of genres and text types, including religious prose and verse, medical texts, herbals and alchemica, romances in rhyming and alliterative verse as well as prose, legal documents, private and official letters, cookery recipes, historical works, and treatises of various kinds.

Through much of the twentieth century, most of this material was considered more or less useless for study; as nearly all manuscripts represent scribal copies rather than authorial originals, it used to be assumed that the linguistic variation

[12] McIntosh, Samuels, and Benskin (1986.IV, 96–101). It should be noted that 'through' is exceptional even in Middle English, in that it includes two consonant clusters that show a particularly high degree of variation in their orthographic realization, and is, in addition, prone to both metathesis and epenthesis.

simply reflected scribal corruption. This was formulated by J. R. R. Tolkien in a much-quoted passage:[13]

> Very few Middle English texts represent in detail the real language . . . of any one time or place or person . . . Their 'language' is, in varying degrees, the product of their textual history, and cannot be fully explained, sometimes cannot be understood at all by reference to geography.

Tolkien's argument was largely based on the expectation that language 'proper' is regular and invariable. Like many of his contemporaries, he assumed that the scribes were remarkably incompetent: unless trained to write a standard, they would simply corrupt a text *ad infinitum*, the degree of mixture increasing with each successive copying. This made the great majority of Middle English texts of no interest for the linguist; accordingly, the study of Middle English language was based on a small minority of exceptional texts deemed to represent 'pure' dialects.

Since the 1960s, however, views on the competence of scribes have changed dramatically, as have conceptions of linguistic variability. It is now recognized that scribes were generally competent people who knew what they were doing; they did not produce random mixtures of linguistic forms, but rather the kind of complex but orderly variation that is characteristic of natural language.

§3. FROM EXEMPLAR TO OUTPUT: THE SCRIBAL REPERTOIRE

A 'scribal text' was defined in LALME as 'any consecutive written output that is a single text in the literary sense, or a part of such a text, and written by a single scribe'.[14] In this research tradition, the scribal text is the basic unit of enquiry.[15]

Each scribal text contains a specific combination of linguistic forms. In English historical dialectology, it has become common to call this an *assemblage*, borrowing a term from palaeontology and archaeology.[16] However, unlike an archaeological assemblage, the set of forms in a scribal text cannot be the product of coincidence: it cannot consist of items that just happened to be left, perhaps on different occasions, in a single place. (A bound manuscript or a group of related texts may contain this kind of assemblage; however, by definition a single scribal text cannot.) The assemblage found in a scribal text represents a specific scribal output, based on an individual scribal repertoire.

[13] Tolkien (1929, 104). [14] McIntosh, Samuels, and Benskin (1986.I, 8).

[15] In their recent work, Margaret Laing and Roger Lass (e.g. Laing and Lass 2009; Laing and Lass 2008–13 and 2013–) have used the term 'text language' to refer specifically to the language of a single scribal text; however, as this use of the term may be confused with Fleischman's (see n. 2), it is avoided here.

[16] See, e.g., Benskin (1991, *passim*).

A scribal repertoire may be defined simply as the sum of written forms available for the scribe. McIntosh et al. distinguished between 'active' and 'passive' repertoires.[17] A scribe's active repertoire consists of the range of forms used when not copying, his/her 'spontaneous usage'; the passive repertoire, on the other hand, includes all the forms that the scribe recognizes and is willing to reproduce when copying. The distinction between active and passive repertoires, while useful, should probably be thought of as fairly fluid: both are likely to be undergoing constant slight modifications, and the 'spontaneous usage' of a scribe may be heavily constrained by the context.[18] The repertoire will reflect the scribe's background, including his/her education, copying and reading experience, as well as geographical background. In England, a northern scribe accustomed to copying southern texts (and needing to sell them to southerners) would be likely to broaden his repertoire and become basically bidialectal; a northern scribe copying mainly local texts would have no incentive (nor opportunity) to do so.

The copying procedure involves two sources of input: the exemplar and the scribal repertoire (Figure 2.1). What makes this situation crucially different from any copying situation involving a standardized variety is that the scribe has to carry out a selection process: every form in the scribal text is potentially the product of a choice between different input variants. The selection, of course, will not involve conscious pondering but is likely to be automatic, at least for the most part, just like all selections made by fluent language users.[19]

There are two basic possibilities for a scribe copying from an exemplar: to copy faithfully the forms of the exemplar, or to replace them with other forms. Either choice may be carried out more or less consistently throughout a text, or some forms may be copied and others replaced. These basic possibilities were

Exemplar	+	Repertoire (scribe's background, education, experience, etc.)	→	Selection (copying strategy, status of text, audience, genre expectations)	→	ASSEMBLAGE

Fig. 2.1. The copying process leading to the assemblage present in a surviving scribal text

[17] McIntosh, Samuels, and Benskin (1986.I, 14).

[18] There is also the question of dictation: it is perfectly plausible that a scribe's orthographic habits might be affected by the spoken form in a dictation context.

[19] Written language is often considered to be characterized by 'conscious design' in a way that makes it essentially different from speech. However, it may also be pointed out that writing is highly conventional precisely because fast writing (like speech) leaves no time for active design, except as an occasional afterthought. The degree of conscious encoding will, of course, depend greatly on the skill of the writer and on the medium involved: subconscious slips are less likely on marble than on paper.

systematized by McIntosh in 1963 as three main types of scribal strategy: *literatim* copying, translation, and 'something in between'.[20] It is sometimes assumed that scribes tend to have fairly fixed habits when it comes to copying strategy: a *literatim* scribe would always copy *literatim*, and so on. The reality may, again, have been more fluid: the strategies should perhaps be seen as tendencies rather than strict categories, as many scribes would clearly be able to vary their strategy according to the situation and text.

The actual selection of forms may, then, depend on several variables: apart from the basic copying strategy, it might reflect the status of the text, the intended audience, as well as the expectations of what is appropriate for a particular type of text. The scribal strategy may be impossible to determine from a single short text copied from a single source; however, in long texts, especially ones containing portions copied by different scribes, or in multiple texts copied by the same scribe, scribal behaviour may be studied in some detail.

At the same time, the precise contribution of the scribe to a scribal text can seldom be determined. This means that, in a community where most surviving texts are the products of copying, the 'active' language of the writers is only exceptionally available for study. On the other hand, bearing in mind that any situation of language use is constrained by a multitude of variables, there is no reason why copied texts would be a priori less interesting as objects of enquiry than authorial originals. Just as with authorial originals, they reflect a specific situation of language use, and they represent a language that was produced by an individual in a specific context. Rather than a confused record of a long textual history, as held by Tolkien, a scribal text may therefore be considered a valid witness for a linguistic survey, assuming that it is possible to identify a set of useful variables for the analysis.

§4. FROM THE SCRIBAL REPERTOIRE TO A MATRIX OF TEXTS

§4.1. The LALME Typology: Fitting Texts into a Dialect Continuum

Even the most detailed study of a scribal text makes little sense in isolation. To interpret the variation present in the text, there has to be some kind of matrix of other texts to which it may be related. In order to identify patterns, the matrix has to be organized according to some suitable variable or variables. The most commonly used variables in the study of historical texts are date and geographical provenance; however, information on these is not always available, or may be

[20] Laing (2004) provides a useful discussion of these strategies, with numerous examples from actual texts.

problematic, and there are many other potential variables. Knowing the precise identity of each scribe would be ideal; however, for many manuscript languages the identity of scribes is a rare luxury.

The anonymity of texts varies greatly between manuscript languages. For medieval Norway, there is a great deal of information about scribes and writers;[21] for medieval England, on the other hand, the available information about writers and their social and historical context is very scarce indeed. In addition, Middle English texts, with the exception of legal documents, seldom provide explicit information about date and provenance.

In the absence of explicit information, manuscript texts are usually dated on palaeographic grounds; such datings are based on fitting the scripts into a typology built up on the basis of dated texts. For localization, a very similar methodology was developed by the team of LALME; this entailed the construction of a typology based on linguistic similarity. The features considered were mainly orthographic and morphological: these levels of language are assumed most likely to belong to the scribe's 'own' repertoire, while syntactic and lexical features would be more resistant to scribal change.

The LALME typology is based on the assumption that geography is the most important variable in written Middle English, just as it is in the spoken rural dialects of England. It also builds on the model of a regular unbroken continuum of written dialect across the geography: any assemblage of linguistic forms may be 'fitted' into one geographical position only, always assuming that we have enough data.

The methodology, known as the 'fit-technique', takes as a starting point those texts, mainly legal documents, for which the geographical provenance is known. Other, usually longer, texts are then placed in relation to these 'anchor texts', according to their linguistic similarity. The network of texts is then superimposed on a geographical map, which is used to produce dialect maps of linguistic features. LALME provided a localization for more than 1,000 texts from the late Middle English period (*c.*1350–1500) in this way; a daughter project, *A Linguistic Atlas of Early Middle English*, has carried out a similar localization process for the earlier period (*c.*1100–1350).[22]

The localizations are different from 'real' geographical localizations in some crucial ways. First, the dialect of a text may not always agree with its physical provenance: scribes would travel and work in different parts of the country, and a manuscript produced in London may be written in a Herefordshire dialect.[23] The LALME localizations always reflect linguistic similarity rather than external

[21] The Norwegian medieval scribes have been catalogued by Vågslid (1989).

[22] See Laing and Lass (2008–13 and 2013–). A third, recently completed, project is *A Linguistic Atlas of Older Scots* (Williamson 2008–13 and 2013–).

[23] This seems to be the case with the herbal known as 'Lelamour's herbal', contained in British Library, Sloane 5, which was localized in central Herefordshire in LALME; for a discussion of the dialect see Black (1997, 87–8).

information: if the language of a text with local associations disagrees substantially with the other evidence for that locality, and does not fit into the continuum, then it is not accepted as evidence for the dialect of that area.

Secondly, as the ordering is typological, the linguistic distance is not necessarily meant to translate into 'real' geographical distance between scriptoria or schools. In LALME, closely related copies of the same text naturally often appear close to each other on the map:[24] the linguistic similarities may here relate to textual history rather than to locally varying scribal habits.

Finally, there is the question to what extent the continuum model represents linguistic reality. Recent research into spoken dialects suggests a picture that is typically much more patchy and clustered, rather than corresponding to a regularly unfolding continuum.[25] One might also ask how far a continuum makes sense in the case of written language in an age of very restricted literacy: can we assume an unbroken continuity of writing conventions across a landscape where skilled writers were few and far between?

The difference is thus between 'historical reality' and typology, and parallels the difference between the explicit dates of legal documents and the dating of texts on palaeographic grounds. Both approaches are valid and important, and provide important knowledge about the material: it is, however, crucial that they are not confused with each other.

§4.2. Expanding the Range of Variables: Scribal Attributes and Textual Parameters

It has become common among historical dialectologists to view geographical and chronological patterns as part of a three-dimensional space: patterns of geographical variation evolve through time, and variation is the trace of change in process. Dialectologists working with modern survey materials have the advantage of knowing precisely which points of time and space each informant represents: it is thus possible to try out models of language change and test them against the actual data. For historical linguists, on the other hand, the external information is often lacking. There have been attempts to expand the 'fit-technique' to a space-time continuum, using computerized fitting;[26] while this certainly helps make 'the best use of bad data', it should be noted that the resulting three-dimensional matrix is a purely typological construct, just like the two-dimensional one.

[24] Examples are the two versions of the Prick of Conscience in British Library, Harley 2281 and Huntington, San Marino HM 130, localized on each side of the Herefordshire–Monmouthshire border, and the two versions of Robert of Gloucester's *Chronicle* in Harley 201 (scribe B) and British Library, Cotton Caligula A xi, both localized in Gloucestershire.

[25] See, e.g., Kretzschmar (2009, 125–30).

[26] See Williamson (2004).

While geography and date are unquestionably major variables, relevant for virtually any historical corpus, other variables need to be taken into account as well. The same variables will not necessarily be relevant, or available, for all manuscript languages. Most present-day surveys focus on variables associated with the speaker; in historical surveys, on the other hand, information about the scribe is usually sparse. The traditional variables of present-day sociolinguistic surveys—age, sex, and social class—are in most cases singularly unsuitable for the study of variation in manuscript languages. The age of the scribe is usually not known: while there are cases where both the date of the document and the biography of the scribe are known, these are relatively rare.[27] As regards the other two variables, it is an unfortunate fact that literacy in most early historical societies was confined to a small part of the population, usually male and by default part of a privileged educated class.

In late medieval England, this group would also be uniformly Roman Catholic and, up to the fourteenth century, almost exclusively connected to the church; on the other hand, the medieval church in England was not a homogeneous entity, and different groupings could show linguistically distinctive usages. In some highly complex societies, such as medieval Egypt, religious and ethnic background might be very important variables indeed.

In the study of manuscript languages, it is often easier to define variables associated with the text than with the scribe. In an important paper of 2000, Herring, van Reenen, and Schøsler outlined what they termed the 'textual parameters approach':

> Narrowly conceived, its subject matter is variation conditioned by properties of texts themselves – their manner of production, their notional type, their structural organization, and the like – properties which are directly reflected in the textual artefacts that come down to us through time, and hence are accessible for empirical analysis.[28]

Such properties might include poeticality (verse vs prose), text type, script, physical manuscript format, and the like. However, Herring, van Reenen, and Schøsler also admitted broader factors pertaining to the external context as 'textual parameters': these include factors such as 'writer and reader demographies, contact with other languages, the effects of language standardization'. Some of these parameters would certainly need to be based on a preliminary linguistic analysis of the texts, just like the LALME localizations do; they thus form a secondary level of labels, derived from the scribal language itself, rather than basic 'facts' such as the label 'rhyming verse'.

The rationale of the 'textual parameters', according to Herring, van Reenen, and Schøsler, is to avoid 'partial or misleading analysis' based on untypical data

[27] Letter collections may provide such material; in Middle English, they only start appearing towards the end of the period.

[28] Herring, van Reenen, and Schøsler (2000, 5).

by creating 'homogeneous subsets of data out of the heterogeneity of historical records'.[29] A good understanding of the parameters that condition linguistic variation will not, of course, solve the problem of limited data; however, it might help identify areas where meaningful generalizations may be made, and it may thus help make better use of the available data.

§4.3. An Example of Categorization: The Middle English Grammar Corpus

The research on Middle English linguistic variation begun by LALME has been continued in two further Atlas projects,[30] as well as in the ongoing MEST programme. Instead of the typological aims of the Atlases, the MEST programme aims at studying the dynamics of scribal variation in Middle English, based on a 'textual parameters' approach.

One of the main projects within the programme has been to produce an electronic corpus (the Middle English Grammar Corpus, or MEG-C) based on the *c.*1,000 texts included in LALME.[31] Rather than being placed on a map on the basis of their linguistic forms, the texts are provided with a wide range of labels representing parameters or variables associated with the text and the scribe. A list of these labels, work on which is still in progress, is provided in Figure 2.2.[32]

The categories fall into two major groups. In most categories, the values are independent of any interpretation of the language of the text. These may be historical facts such as the dating of a legal document or the association of a text with a particular religious sect, agreed categories such as register or basic script type, or inferences based on non-linguistic evidence, such as datings based on palaeography. The second group consists of categories that are based on a previous analysis and interpretation of the language and may thus lead to a circular argument if used as a priori facts: these include localizations based on the fit-technique as well as identifications of scribal behaviour. Some variables involve subcategories, which are entered into a separate field; for example, the text type 'legal document' may combine with subcategories such as 'will', 'agreement', or 'lease'.

[29] Herring, van Reenen, and Schøsler (2000, 4).

[30] Laing and Lass (2008–2013 and 2013–) and Williamson (2008–13 and 2013–).

[31] Since 2012, the main focus of the programme has been the compilation of a corpus of late medieval administrative documents, *A Corpus of Middle English Local Documents* (MELD; see www.uis.no/meld).

[32] The actual labels consist of short distinctive strings designed to be searchable; in Figure 2.2, they are expanded for intelligibility. It should be noted that the work on the Middle English Grammar Corpus is ongoing, and the categories are being continuously developed; the present list will almost certainly be augmented and refined.

Variable	Values
Language-independent	
Text	Prick of Conscience, Canterbury Tales, Liber Uricrisium subcategories (of Prick of Conscience): Main Version, Southern Recension, etc.
Register	Religious, personal, legal, medical, courtly, etc.
Text type	Letter, treatise, recipe, sermon, document, etc. subcategories (of 'document'): will, agreement, lease, etc.
Poeticality	Alliterative verse, metrical verse, prose
Localization given	Staffordshire, Lancashire, Cheshire subcategories (within each county): north, south, west, east, central
Date	14a1, 14a2, 14b1, 14b2, 15a1, etc. subcategories (when precise date is known): 1376, 1425, etc.
Date grounds	dated in text, palaeography, codicology, historical reference
Script	Anglicana, Secretary, Textura subcategories (of Anglicana): current, media, formata
Association	Wycliffite, orthodox, northern mystical
Language background	English composition, translation, adaptation subcategories (of translations and adaptations): Latin, French, other
Physical format	Codex, roll, single sheet, booklet, other
Language-based	
Localization fit-technique	Staffordshire, Lancashire, Cheshire subcategories (within each county): north, south, west, east, central
Scribal behaviour	Translation, Literatim, Constrained

Fig. 2.2. Textual parameters in the Middle English Grammar Corpus

The first parameter is the identity of the text in the literary sense: which particular romance, historical chronicle, or sermon does it represent? For literary scholars, used to the literary text as the object of study, this may be unexpected as a 'parameter' (and it is not included as one by Herring, van Reenen, and Schøsler). However, as the unit of enquiry here is the scribal text, the text identity is simply another label: for example, the Middle English poem known as the Prick of Conscience survives in some 120 copies, making up more than 120 scribal texts (as some of the versions are produced by more than one scribe). The Prick of Conscience is thus a category, which may be further subdivided into major textual groupings, such as the Main Version and the Southern Recension.[33]

[33] For textual groupings of the Prick of Conscience, see Lewis and McIntosh (1982).

The categories dealing with register and text type are perhaps the ones requiring most care; apart from the highly variable use of the terminology by different scholars, views of the categorization of a single text may vary greatly, and texts may be complex and difficult to classify. A good example of this is the long alliterative poem Piers Plowman, which might be considered to form a genre in its own right: it is an allegory, a dream vision, and a didactic work, and it contains elements of dialogue, narrative, sermonizing, and reflection. The only solution is to allow for multiple categories, and the labels should only refer to the sample included in the corpus, not to the entire work. Both the register/text type and script labels are provisional at this stage, as building up good systems of classification, suitable for the material, is a considerable project in itself.

Dates are provided in a searchable format that allows for more or less precision, reflecting the realities of manuscript dating; if the precise date is known, it is provided as well, and the source of dating is provided as an additional category.

The 'Association' category is necessarily a fuzzy one: it refers to particular communities or groupings, usually religious ones, that have either been identified as groups by contemporaries, as in the case of the Wycliffite movement, or by modern scholars, as in the case of the 'Northern mystics'. Such labels describe what might be termed historical discourse communities (cf. §5); these may be highly significant for Middle English linguistic variation and should therefore be included as labels.

A label is also provided for 'language background'. Many Middle English texts are translations from Latin or French, sometimes faithful ones and at other times only loosely based on the original (here termed 'adaptations'). This may have considerable consequences for the linguistic form, even when removed by many scribal copyings from the original English version. A good example is the early Middle English retention of Old English grammatical gender in anaphoric pronouns: while gendered pronouns could linger on for a long time in scribal versions of a text originally composed in English, they are generally more or less absent from texts that were closely translated from French.

Finally, the physical format of the text is recorded. The majority of longer Middle English texts survive on parchment or paper sheets, bound into codices or booklets or made into rolls. The format often correlates closely with the function of a text and is mostly of interest when unexpected. For other manuscript languages, on the other hand, physical format may be much more variable and could be a parameter of major significance.

The textual parameter labels allow for the sorting of linguistic data in relation to a range of extralinguistic variables, the significance of which may then be assessed. Searches may also be limited to specific groups of texts, using one or several parameters. When completed, the corpus will thus be a powerful tool for describing the linguistic variation in Middle English. There are, however, two important limitations to this kind of enquiry, which means that it has to be supplemented with other approaches. First, no matter how carefully the texts have been labelled for relevant variables, computerized searches cannot take into account the individual characteristics of a scribal text, which may be crucial for the interpretation of a pattern: in order to understand the dynamics of a single text, it should be studied in its entirety. Secondly, a corpus survey covering a wide range of texts cannot say anything about repertoires or systems. It is only capable of tracing the distribution of individual variants or the extent to which these cluster. In order to study the dynamics of variation within paradigms it is necessary to combine quantitative and qualitative analysis, and to focus on limited communities.

§5. THE CONCEPT OF TEXT COMMUNITIES

A scribal repertoire is the result of education and experience: it is shared with a community, even though no other individual repertoire may be exactly the same. The assemblage found in a scribal text should therefore be interpreted in the light of other texts in the same community; the more texts that survive, the better we can understand how any one of them works. The problem with manuscript languages is, of course, that we cannot reconstruct the entire linguistic communities within which a scribe worked and sample them at will. Indeed, the single scribal text may be the only representative for an entire linguistic period, or even a language: in such cases, not much can be done by way of linguistic contextualization.

If the language survives in numerous texts, however, it will be possible to study a scribal text in the context of other surviving texts, as part of a group. As writing is a highly social activity, the scribe demonstrably forms part of certain networks by virtue of having copied the text we have access to. For example, the scribe of a medical text may be considered to belong to a network of people dealing with medical texts. Of course, the fact that two scribes copied the same text in the same part of the country at approximately the same time does not necessarily mean that they had anything to do with each other directly. As with present-day discourse communities, we cannot assume that each member of a community is a personal acquaintance of all the others, nor even that they would recognize the existence of the community.[34]

The discourse community was defined by Barton as 'a group of people who have texts and practices in common' and 'who, by definition, have a common discourse, in the narrow sense of common ways of using language, and in

[34] This was presented as the 'Café-owner Problem' by Swales (1990, 25). He would initially not admit such groups as discourse communities; however, a more flexible view appears in Bex (1996, 64–6) and Swales (1993, 695).

the broader sense of common ways of acting in relation to knowledge'.[35] The concept of discourse communities has shown itself highly useful for the study of historical literacy and text production; for example, it was applied by Jones to the study of medical manuscripts, their scribes, and users in medieval Norfolk.[36]

The problem with discourse communities from the point of view of historical linguistics is, however, that they cannot be studied directly: discourse communities consist of language users who have disappeared long ago, together with the vast majority of linguistic utterances that they produced. It is suggested here that a useful unit for studying and describing linguistic variation in the past might, instead, consist of groups of the actual surviving texts, defined in terms of specific parameters.

Such a group may be termed a 'text group' or 'constellation'. The latter term was suggested by Williamson and relates to the concept of a 'text universe' consisting of the total network of interrelated texts.[37] A constellation is a group of texts that have something in common, so that it makes sense to refer to them as an entity: they may be associated with the same geographical area or with a particular network of writers or readers. In the case of Middle English, a constellation might consist of all the texts connected with Norfolk, or all the texts associated with the Wycliffite movement, or all the alchemical treatises, or all the copies of the Main Version of the Prick of Conscience. It is thus a flexible term like 'variety', and its scope must be defined specifically for each study.

Constellations are at the outset defined on the basis of extralinguistic parameters. No expectation of linguistic homogeneity within a text community is implied; rather, the extent to which linguistic patterns coincide with such groupings is a research question. At the same time, a constellation forms a basis for generalizations: while we cannot describe 'the Middle English system of personal pronouns', it is possible to define a constellation that forms a good framework for such a study. This approach, which is simply an application of the 'textual parameters approach', will then allow the analyst to 'make meaningful generalizations within restricted domains'.[38]

For example, studies of the loss of grammatical gender in English have often suffered from confusing and chaotic data due to a too-wide geographical and chronological range; this has led several scholars to suggest that grammatical gender in Middle English was characterized by confusion.[39] However, smaller-scale studies show that the gender loss in fact displays a very orderly development, assuming that it is studied within a limited community. A study of a group

[35] Barton (2007, 75–6). [36] Jones (2004).
[37] Williamson (2004, 110); see also Mäkinen (2006, 18).
[38] Herring, van Reenen, and Schøsler (2000, 4).
[39] Markus (1988, 248); see also Ausbüttel (1904) and Curzan (2003).

of twenty thirteenth-century religious texts associated with the south-west Midland area shows a steady variation between historically regular gendered forms and the new gender-free forms such as *the* and *it*.[40] Apart from the single, untypical text of the verse chronicle known as Laȝamon's Brut (which has been the one most studied by scholars),[41] the few 'unhistorical' forms that appear either show the result of an orthographic merger[42] or are confined to specific lexical items. As regards the progress of the change, innovative forms were clearly more common in prose than in verse, and dominated completely in close translations from French. The focus on a specific group of texts also made it possible to bring in variables that were particularly appropriate for the community: the relative frequency of French loanwords in each text also showed a clear correlation with the frequency of innovative forms.

The community associated with a particular, identified group of texts has been termed a 'text community'.[43] Unlike a spoken-language discourse community, a text community may to some extent range over time as well as space. In the medium of writing, language users interact with others at different points of time, for example through the copying of older texts. As with present-day discourse communities, some text communities may reach far across geography; however, most of them will have a restricted geographical distribution or focus.[44] Finally, both text communities and constellations may overlap, so that a single witness may belong to more than one community: a text may simultaneously represent 'texts connected with Norfolk' and 'alchemical treatises'.

It may also make sense to accept groups of texts as constellations on the basis of linguistic similarity, for example on the basis of the geographical localizations using the 'fit-technique'. Such a group of texts, consisting, for example, of all the texts that have been localized in Northamptonshire on linguistic grounds, may then be studied with the view to elucidate the non-linguistic make-up of the material: what kind of texts contain a linguistic assemblage associated with the Northamptonshire area?

Most parts of the medieval networks of texts and their users are beyond our retrieval. However, their existence may to some extent be inferred from the available texts; in terms of the space metaphor they form a 'dark matter' much larger than the visible material. While these contexts may not be studied directly, they affect the surviving material in two ways: in a real, historical sense that is lost to us, and in the sense that our conjectures about them (whether

40 Stenroos (2009). 41 London, British Library Cotton Caligula A ix.

42 This was the merger between <e> and <eo>, related to an earlier phonemic merger. It made the traditional written forms of the masculine nominative and feminine nominative/accusative definite article, *þe* and *þeo*, interchangeable as far as mapping to spoken forms was concerned; thus the masculine use of *þeo* is 'unhistorical' with regard to orthographic convention, but does not imply confusion of gender.

43 Meurman-Solin (2014).

44 Of course, no medieval text community can be freed from the constraints of geography in the way of present-day Internet-based discourse communities.

explicit or not) are often central to the interpretation of the surviving data. Conjectures about the 'dark matter' have from time to time had a tendency to shape language history; it is therefore crucial that they should be made explicit and based on the patterns found in the actual surviving constellations.

§6. POPULATING THE DARK MATTER: A 'THIRTEENTH-CENTURY STANDARD'

One of the enduring myths in the history of Middle English has been a 'thirteenth-century English literary standard',[45] which was assumed to have been used over at least a couple of generations within a small community near the Welsh border. The idea goes back to Tolkien, who in 1929 identified a remarkably regular written language that appears in more or less identical form in two manuscripts written by different scribes.[46] As Tolkien did not believe medieval scribes to be capable of either consistent dialect translation or faithful copying, unless trained to write a standard, he concluded that the texts had to represent a standardized variety of English for which all other direct evidence had been lost. He called the language 'AB'.

The two manuscripts, both of which are dated to the early thirteenth century, contain different texts that seem to relate to the same kind of audience. One of them, Cambridge, Corpus Christi College 401, contains a book of guidance for anchoresses, titled Ancrene Wisse. The second one, Bodley 34, is a collection of three female saints' lives (Katherine, Margaret, and Juliana) and two religious treatises aimed at women, together known as the Katherine Group. All of these texts survive in other contemporary copies, which show scribal usages that are clearly related but much more variable. From a linguistic perspective, they are also closely related to a further group of short devotional texts known as the Wooing Group.

Versions of these texts are combined in the same manuscripts, and there is at least one possible allusion in Ancrene Wisse to one of the Katherine Group texts: *Nabbe ȝe alswa of Ruffin þe deouel beliales broðer in ower englische boc of seinte Margarete* 'have you not also got (information) about the devil Ruffin, the brother of Belial, in your English book about Saint Margaret?'[47] Several of the manuscripts have connections with the West Midlands, in particular Herefordshire; the texts also contain Welsh loanwords, otherwise rare in Middle English. This group of texts, which has sometimes been called the 'AB group' (reflecting the assumption that all the texts were first composed in the 'AB Language') thus seems to form a constellation that belongs to a specific historical

45 The title of an article by Hulbert (1946). 46 Tolkien (1929).
47 Ancrene Wisse, fol. 66a.19, cited from Tolkien (1929, 125).

context: the reading requirements of religious ladies, at least some of whom were anchoresses, in the early-thirteenth-century West Midlands.

In accordance with contemporary thinking about linguistic variation, Tolkien assumed that the regularity and similarity of the two manuscripts could not have come about through ordinary scribal copying; as they were clearly not written by the same scribe, they could only represent an institutional model. Tolkien postulated an early Middle English standard literary language, which, unlike all the corrupt scribal usages, was based on a local spoken dialect 'connected to a soil somewhere in England'. This idea, which had obvious nationalistic appeal, was taken up and elaborated by other scholars, and presented as a fact in numerous textbooks.

The case against the theory need not be rehearsed here in detail, as it has been discussed elsewhere both by the present writer and others.[48] As was first pointed out by Smith, the other surviving texts of the 'AB group' show precisely the kind of linguistic relationship to each other that one would expect of textually related Middle English texts in the same area. It is the two texts studied by Tolkien that form the 'mystery' because of their regular and nearly identical usage.

In order to explain them in the simplest possible way, however, only one additional 'lost' text needs to be postulated. We may assume that two manuscripts, the surviving Corpus text of the Ancrene Wisse and the lost exemplar of the Bodley 34 text of the Katherine Group, were copied by a single scribe who produced an unusually regular orthography. That the Bodley 34 text was in fact copied by a *literatim* scribe, aiming to reproduce the text of the exemplar letter for letter, was established long ago on the basis of mistakes characteristic of this kind of copying.[49]

In contrast, Tolkien's explanation presupposed a centre of learning in the Welsh Marches, where a large number of scribes were producing a remarkably homogeneous standard language, surviving only in two manuscripts, even though the total number of texts must have been very large. The period around 1200 would have been a remarkably strange time for such a standard language to develop: this was when English had no official function, literacy and text production were low, and the few people writing English around the country were for the most part producing extremely variable spelling. Even after standardization set in, written English continued to be variable for a long time; the kind of regularity here suggested does not appear until the eighteenth century.

Tolkien's theory is, above all, difficult to accept because it populates the 'dark matter' with numerous postulated facts that have no precedent in the available evidence. The alternative view, on the other hand, does not postulate anything stranger than a single regular speller, one of whose scribal products was copied *literatim*. While regular spellers were not typical of the age, they are not unknown:

[48] See Black (1999) and Smith (1991).
[49] See Laing (1993) and references there cited; see also Black (1999).

a famous example is Orm, the author of the 20,000-line gospel harmony called The Ormulum. That scribes were capable of faithful *literatim* copying, even from very different dialects, is well established.

The question whether the 'AB Language' represented a standard or not makes a considerable difference to the sociolinguistic history of English; less obviously, it also makes a difference to the interpretation of many linguistic forms in this variety, as presumed 'archaic' features may in fact be explained differently. Assumptions about the 'dark matter' can thus affect our interpretation of the surviving evidence in a very real way.

This example points at a potential danger embedded in the concept of text communities: as the term 'community' suggests something real, with a historical presence, it is very tempting to try to fill the gaps in knowledge with suitable guesses. Conjectures about the 'dark matter' cannot be entirely avoided, and they are implicit in almost any discussion of scribal repertoires; however, as with any decent reconstruction, they should be based strictly on the actually existing evidence.

§7. CONCLUSION: LOOKING EVERYWHERE AT ONCE

The main perceived problems of manuscript evidence for the study of linguistic variation have to do with representativeness: the use of a few surviving written texts to describe a whole language, all the speakers of which have disappeared long ago. From this point of view, manuscript languages provide 'bad data': the description will always be partial and dependent on reconstruction.

This paper has attempted to outline an alternative approach to the evidence, building on the Middle English tradition following McIntosh and LALME, as well as on the 'textual parameters approach' advocated by Herring, van Reenen, and Schøsler. The main principle behind both these approaches is that, rather than making the best use of bad data, we should turn them into good data by designing enquiries for which they are suited.

This means that the object of study should be the actual surviving text, not a reconstruction of its original or of the spoken system 'behind' it. One of the groundbreaking points made by McIntosh was that written data should be studied and analysed as written data; this does not preclude enquiries into historical phonology, but it makes them a secondary line of enquiry, based on the interpretation of the primary, written data. This approach also focuses on the scribal text as the informant, and the linguistic choices reflected in the data are accepted as those of the scribe rather than of the original author.

As we study the written language of scribal texts, we cannot proceed directly to making generalizations about the spoken language either of the authors or of the vast majority of speakers in early historical societies that did not contribute to the written evidence. The 'textual parameters approach' focuses on the attributes of those texts that are available for us, making it possible to limit our generalizations to groups of comparable texts and to understand better the dynamics of variation within those areas of language that are represented by our evidence.

The detailed study of individual scribal texts, it is held here, should form the basis of historical linguistic enquiry. At the same time, scribal choices and repertoires need to be discussed in relation to the linguistic variation within a community. While large-scale surveys are needed to provide an overall framework, they should be combined with smaller-scale enquiries in order to ensure comparability and make possible the study of change within paradigms and repertoires. It is suggested here that such studies might focus on text communities, based on text groups or constellations defined on the basis of specific parameters.

In sum, it might be suggested that the study of linguistic variation in manuscript languages requires the kind of perspective involved in driving a car, which, for the person learning to drive, seems to ask for the impossible: looking ahead, back, and to the sides at the same time, focusing both near and far, and attempting to see where there is no visibility. Good studies should take into account all three levels (whichever of these they focus on): the large-scale framework, the constellation/text community, and the individual scribal text. Accordingly, we need both the philologist and the corpus linguist.

3

Set Them Free?!

Investigating Spelling and Scribal Variation in Language and History

Alexander Bergs

§1. INTRODUCTION

When we 'do' historical linguistics, we rarely think about sociolinguistic issues. Sociolinguistics deals with the interrelationship between language and society in the broadest sense. In order to investigate sociolinguistic problems we need both linguistic and social data. For a long time, it was assumed that the poverty of historical data—both social and linguistic—means that sociolinguistic questions cannot be discussed satisfactorily. Here is one very simple example. One of the central questions or factors in sociolinguistics is 'gender'. Before 1500, however, there is hardly any data from female authors and scribes, as females on average were illiterate. Consequently, the question of language and gender becomes very tricky if we want to go back beyond the year 1500 or so. We do have some evidence for female scribes and authors in medieval Europe and also in Greek, Latin, and Jewish antiquity and ancient Egypt,[1] but in terms of sheer numbers, it is extremely difficult to establish reliable patterns of female language use in this small database. Essentially the same can be said for many other sociolinguistic variables: age, education, social group, social network, etc. This is perhaps one of the reasons why Labov claimed that historical linguistics is actually 'the art of making the best use of bad data'.[2] In the present paper, I will try to show that this is not necessarily so. In fact, I will try to identify certain domains where current sociolinguistic questions and methods could even be more fruitful in historical linguistics than in contemporary studies. This, however, requires some rethinking and some rekeying of certain issues and problems.

[1] For ancient Egypt, note that there are no female 'authors', but there is evidence for scribes; see, for example, Bagnall and Cribiore (2006).

[2] Labov (1994, 11).

§2. WHAT IS HISTORICAL SOCIOLINGUISTICS?

§2.1. Definition and Basic Concepts

Historical sociolinguistics[3] or socio-historical linguistics[4] lies at the intersection of three different disciplines: linguistics, history, and the social sciences. It deals with linguistic variation and the social constraints on this variation in the past, including diachronic developments. Note, however, that diachrony need not be the only concern of historical sociolinguistics. Just as present-day sociolinguistics can deal with stasis, i.e. stable patterns of linguistic variation, and not just change, so can historical sociolinguistics. It is just as interesting, for example, to describe and analyse the use of infinitival patterns by different speakers in the fifteenth century as it is to discuss the prior and subsequent changes in these patterns and the developments themselves.

Working at the boundaries of three different disciplines usually means that one also has to cope with the conflicting aims, theories, models, and methods in these different areas. This is not the right place to discuss this issue in full,[5] but it needs to be stressed that there is no single unified theory, model, or method for historical sociolinguistics. On the contrary, this field thrives and survives on being decidedly eclectic in its choice of theories, models, and methods. Depending on the data and problems at hand, historical sociolinguistics may work with tools and concepts from correlational and interactional sociolinguistics. Even approaches from the sociology of language can be very illuminating, e.g. when discussing language contact, standardization, dialects, and language norms. This also means that in terms of explanations and accounts, it may look towards sociology, certain fields of linguistics, and the natural sciences when it employs deductive–nomological (Hempel–Oppenheim-style) reasoning,[6] or towards history, anthropology, and cultural studies when it provides accounts and motivations in more hermeneutical terms. Eventually, both explaining and understanding can be of value here.[7]

§2.2. Data Problems

Modern sociolinguistics has a wide array of data-gathering methods available[8] and thus also has a large amount of data types: spoken, written, electronic, from speakers of all ages and from all social groups. But its biggest advantage is that it almost always can generate more data if needed, i.e. the researcher usually can

[3] Milroy (1992a). [4] Romaine (1982).
[5] For a broader discussion, see Bergs (2005). [6] See Lass (1980 and 1997).
[7] Haussmann (1991); Manicas (2006); von Wright (1971).
[8] See Milroy and Gordon (2003).

go back to the source and unearth more data as necessary. Eventually, then, we have statistically significant, balanced, and meaningful data sets that allow us to arrive at significant patterns and conclusions.

From that point of view, historical (socio)linguistics is of course at a disadvantage. It cannot simply go back and elicit some more data: its informants are no longer alive and have only left us a limited amount of material. It has to deal with the data actually available. No more, no less. This also means that for some research questions there is simply very little or even no data available. As we have said before, we do not know what the language of female speakers in the Old English period was like. But is this a problem? Not necessarily, since there are a number of other questions that can be successfully dealt with, even with a small database. One such question concerns the language use of individuals across time and its impact on the linguistic community.

§2.3. Historical Sociolinguistics and the Linguistic Individual

For some time now, there has been a growing tendency to dehumanize linguistics, and ironically even sociolinguistics. The strive for real, natural, representative speech data led to the development of huge linguistic corpora such as the British National Corpus (100 million words of text) or the English Internet Corpus (with 90 million words). At the time of writing, even bigger corpora are being designed and developed, such as the Corpus of Contemporary American English (COCA) with more than 520 million words. These and other, similar corpora contain real, natural, representative speech samples and they allow us to develop excellent studies that investigate language variation in great detail. The keyword here is representativeness. We want the data we work with to be representative of certain groups, communities, genres, styles, etc.[9] The results are excellent correlative studies that look into language variation and its correlation with (major) social factors. For obvious reasons, this approach is very problematic for historical linguists, as we hardly ever have enough truly representative material from certain groups, genres, styles, etc. This does not mean, however, that such an approach is completely out of the question. The development of comparatively large historical corpora, such as the Helsinki Corpus of English Texts (*c.*800–1710, about 1.5 million words) or the Corpus of Early English Correspondence (1417–1681, about 2.7 million words), has been a great help in identifying major patterns and developing some statistical baselines in terms of usage for further analyses. Nevertheless, even these major projects can of course not compete with major contemporary corpora in terms of size or statistical significance and representativeness. This not only has serious consequences for language-external but also for language-internal variables. Some

[9] Cf. Biber (1995); McEnery and Wilson (1996).

structures, such as non-restrictive relative clauses introduced by *that*, were fairly rare in Middle English, and so having a very limited database means that no reliable statistics (in comparison to contemporary studies) about their use can be developed. Some of these rare structures should rather be investigated from a qualitative point of view. However, not having massive multi-million-word corpora can also mean that we now can and should concentrate on the micro level, the individual speakers, which we will now discuss.

Something contemporary studies of language variation usually do not do is look at individual speakers. The individual speaker as such has gradually disappeared from the sociolinguistic landscape, for a number of reasons. For one thing, the fetish for large corpora, statistical significance, and representativeness directs the attention away from small-scale individual variation. However, I would claim that how and why language varies at the micro level is most interesting. For the individual, we can ask how the speaker uses or even plays with certain repertoires that are available in the linguistic community, how the language of the individual changes over time, and how individual speakers as members of social networks are influenced by these networks, and how they, in turn, influence other network members. This, however, also means that we need to leave behind us the idea that individual language use—including scribal variation—is necessarily random, or chaotic, or riddled with 'free variation'. In order to look at the role of individuals in language communities, we need to approach their linguistic products—no matter whether they are spoken or written—with the basic assumption or null hypothesis that scribal variation is essentially free and random. The alternative hypothesis that we would arrive at—given that the null hypothesis can be shown to be false—is that there must be some inherent system in their own, individual language use (though maybe with some average residue of free variation).

Looking at individuals seems to be particularly promising and rewarding for historical linguistics. Virtually all of the data that we have comes from individuals, i.e. all the texts and manuscripts we work with can be traced back to a few people who composed and wrote them. Still, it is also clear that this attribution of historical texts is anything but easy. Despite the fact that some individual must have written (or at least copied) a given piece of language at one point in time, historical documents can be of several types. Therefore, one of the basic questions is whether the scribe and/or author are known. The options are represented in Table 3.1.

Table 3.1. Identifiability of authors and scribes

	Author	Scribe	Both
Known	x	–	x / –
Unknown	–	x	x / –

Table 3.1 shows that either the author or the scribe of a given text can be known, or both, or neither of them. The latter would mean that the text is completely anonymous (one example would be Beowulf), the former would mean that we know quite a few details about the development of a given text or manuscript (one example would be Chaucer as the author, and Adam Pinkhurst as the scribe, of the Consolation of Philosophy or probably even the Canterbury Tales). And there are cases where we know the author, but not the scribe (William Langland is the author of Piers Plowman, but we do not know who the scribe of Corpus Christi College, MS 201(F) was), or vice versa (we do not know the author of the Brut, but we know the scribe and translator John Shirley, who composed the copy in Harvard MS English 530 (fol 180v)). But then we also need to keep in mind that 'knowing' is a relative concept. We know quite a bit about John Shirley and his life, but only comparatively little about the person Adam Pinkhurst, and even less about the thousands of 'Hand A's and 'Hand B's who riddle our manuscripts, and so on. So, even scribal identification does not necessarily mean that we have sufficient sociological data on these people. Needless to say, the same applies to authors. While we have quite a few Chaucer biographies, there is very little to say about William Langland.

Where does that leave us? Back to square one: the art of making the best use of bad data? Not necessarily. Even if we do not know all the details of some author's or scribe's life, one can still try to locate these people in their social and cultural environment. One such example is presented by Ursula Lenker in her study on the so-called Winchester School, a network of interacting individuals and monasteries in the wake of the Benedictine Reform in late-tenth-century England.[10] We only know some of the people in this network (such as Æthelwold and Ælfric) and none of the scribes, and yet, looking at the available texts and manuscripts, Lenker is able to show that a social network analysis can shed some light on the transmission of words and word forms within this network. Eventually, we witness the growth of a particular style, the 'Winchester Vocabulary',[11] within this social and cultural environment, the Winchester network, despite the fact that we only know very little about the individual network members.

Another aspect that we need to consider is the actual influence of scribes. Say a given author dictated their texts, since he or she was illiterate. How much did the scribe interfere? How much of the language that we still see today is the scribe's, and how much of the language actually represents the author? The answer is anything but simple. There is one pilot study of the Paston Letters, i.e. documents from the fifteenth century, which might help us to get a first idea of how influential scribes actually were. These document the language of various family members between 1421 and 1503. For some family members we only have very little linguistic data, e.g. Elizabeth, who only left us three letters with about 4,000 words all in all. For others, there is ample material, e.g. John III with

[10] Lenker (2000). [11] Gneuss (1972).

seventy-eight letters and almost 45,000 words. With the Paston Letters, we have a great deal of biographical data not only about their authors, but also about their scribes. As these are mostly family letters, some of the family members occasionally acted as both authors and scribes, e.g. for female family members who could not read or write. This is a great chance to test for scribal versus authorial influence. If one author also acted as scribe for another speaker, the writings of that particular speaker either contain or do not contain features that we find with that particular scribe/author. If they contain features that do not show up in the author's own writings, but only in the dictations that he took down, we may assume that these come from the speaker who dictated. And vice versa: if the language of the author is more or less the same when he acts as scribe for somebody else, we may assume some greater influence here. Now, a careful and thorough investigation[12] shows that when speakers acted as scribes for another author and scribes for themselves or as scribes for more than one author, they show a great deal of linguistic variability. James Gloys, for example, when writing for John I, used the possessive pronoun *her(e)* nine times in 1449 (letter no. 36, 1,062 words), and modern *their* only once. When he was writing for John I's wife Margaret in 1469, he used *their* nine times and *her(e)* not at all (letter no. 200, 874 words). Similarly, John Wykes wrote for both Margaret Paston and for John Paston II, Margaret's son. He used the objective pronoun form *hem* twice, but *them* only once when writing for Margaret in 1465 (letter no. 190, 1,069 words); in 1469 when writing for John I he used *hem* only once, *them* twice (letter no. 242, 1,308 words). We see the same when we look at family members who acted as scribes. Edmond II, John II, and John III acted as scribes for their mother, Margaret. Table 3.2 shows their use of pronoun forms.

All three scribes were much more conservative when they wrote for their mother. Edmond II does not use any traditional forms in his own writings, but more than 50 per cent in letters written for his mother. Similarly, John II has a few old objective forms in his writing (less than 3 per cent), but uses 50 per cent old forms when writing for his mother. John III uses almost twice as many old

Table 3.2. The use of third person pronoun forms by scribes and authors in the Paston Letters

Scribe	Author	Hem	Them	Here	Their	Total
Edmond II	Edmond II		8		1	9
	Margaret	5	9	1		15
John II	John II	3	98		15	116
	Margaret	4	4		3	11
John III	John III	60	77	2	57	196
	Margaret	21	11	4	4	40

[12] See Bergs (2005 and 2015).

forms in the objective case as new forms when writing for Margaret, and has an equal distribution in the possessive forms. When writing for himself, he clearly prefers new forms for both functions. The same can be observed for a number of other variables and speakers.

What does this mean? As I pointed out before, the figures are nowhere near what we would expect from present-day data regarding statistical validity. Nevertheless, they suggest certain interpretations, which can be evaluated according to their plausibility. One such suggestion is that scribes had very little influence regarding the morphosyntactic and lexical shape of the letters, even when authors dictated directly. The morphosyntax and lexicon that we find can be seen as the null hypothesis, i.e. unless they can be shown to come from other sources. This must be regarded as the authors' and not the scribes' personal language use. This, in turn, opens up new ways for the cultural and sociological interpretation of those language products.

Yet another advantage that historical sociolinguistics can have with regard to individual language use is the fact that with some authors and/or scribes we have data which covers almost their entire lifespan. As long as we have not reached a high degree of standardization (i.e. before about 1500 or 1600), we can expect these writings to be highly variable and to show some linguistic developments in real time, if there are any. This in turn might help us to look into one of the currently most fascinating questions in language change theory: does change mainly happen during first language acquisition, as many generativist accounts would claim,[13] or does it also happen in later life? Should we distinguish between language change and grammar change, as Fischer et al. suggest?[14] To illustrate this, let us look once again at the Paston Letters. John III's use of the object plural pronouns between 1461 and 1503 is illustrated in Figure 3.1.

Apparently, John III did not exhibit any kind of stable use of the traditional and innovative pronoun forms. He uses only the traditional forms up until about 1473 (with two minor exceptions), and the modern forms throughout. Similarly, his brother John II is the first member of the family to begin to use the third person singular present tense inflection {(y)s}, and *yow* instead of *ye* in about 1472. Similar phenomena can also be found with other family members. What does this mean? I would suggest that discarding these changes as pure changes in language use is not very productive and does not do them any justice. After all, these are not only lexical changes but also changes in morphology, and in closed grammatical word classes. Changes like these are not very common and should not be regarded in the same way as new items in the mental lexicon. Instead, I believe that these phenomena, which can only be observed in very intensive longitudinal surveys, warrant some rethinking of the idea that language or grammar change is something that only happens in children during

[13] Going back to Halle (1962) and King (1969), but also Lightfoot (1998).
[14] Fischer, van Kemenade, and Koopman (2000, 3).

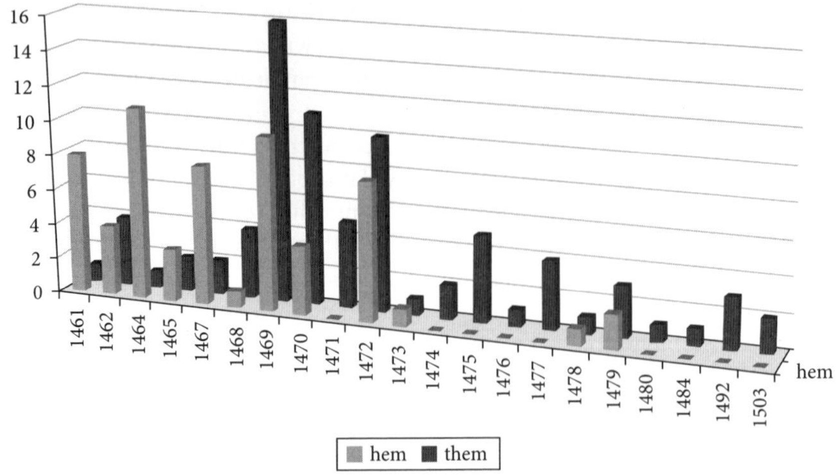

Fig. 3.1. John III's use of <them>/<hem> over time

first language acquisition. Needless to say, I also think that there is good evidence that this is the most important period for changes to happen, but apparently changes beyond simple usage can also happen at a later stage in life and we should maybe put them on our future research agenda.

§3. CASE STUDIES

In the following, I will present two case studies on earlier Englishes, which show what opportunities and perspectives a sociolinguistic approach to language variation, and in particular to scribal variation, can offer.

§3.1. The Paston Letters

In the first study, we will look at the late medieval Paston family. The Pastons are a rather well-known Norfolk family; for a number of reasons we have almost 250,000 words from documents authored by family members between 1421 and 1503. The most comprehensive and reliable edition available today is Davis (1971).[15] There is rich biographical material available,[16] so that we can reconstruct the lifestyle of many family members in great detail. As Middle English, i.e. English between 1100 and 1500, is a prestandardized period of English, we

[15] This is also available online at http://ota.oucs.ox.ac.uk/headers/1685.xml.
[16] For example, in Davis (1971), but also in Bennett (1995) and Gies and Gies (1999).

find massive linguistic variability. There is hardly any stability on any linguistic level, and morphosyntax, lexicon, spelling, etc. actually vary from speaker to speaker and even within single speakers. One of the many linguistic variables available is the form of the third person plural pronoun. Historically, the third person plural pronouns had an initial <h> in the nominative, genitive, and accusative: *heo*, *here*, *hem*. From the mid-fourteenth century onwards, we witness the gradual spread of the Norse forms with <th> (*they*, *their*, *them*) from the north, the Danelaw area, to the south.[17] It has been suspected that the actual borrowing only affected the subject form *they*, which was also the first that was borrowed, and that the objective and possessive forms developed later, maybe through analogical levelling.

The Paston Letters, written in the east of England in the mid-fifteenth century, still exhibit variability in at least the possessive and the object form. In both cases, the <h> form gradually gives way to the new, innovative <th> form, as can be seen in Figures 3.2 and 3.3.

The nature of this particular set of documents allows us to take a look at this temporal sequence from the viewpoint of familial generations. In the Paston Letter Corpus, we find data from three different generations of family members. The results of such an analysis are presented in Figures 3.4 and 3.5.

Figures 3.4 and 3.5 show that this was not a landslide-like generational shift, but rather something that must have happened in the second generation. The first generation overwhelmingly uses the older forms (*c.*75 per cent *hem*, *c.*94 per cent *here*), the third generation uses the new forms (*c.*80 per cent *them*, *c.*97 per cent *their*). The second generation is somewhere in the middle (*c.*60 per

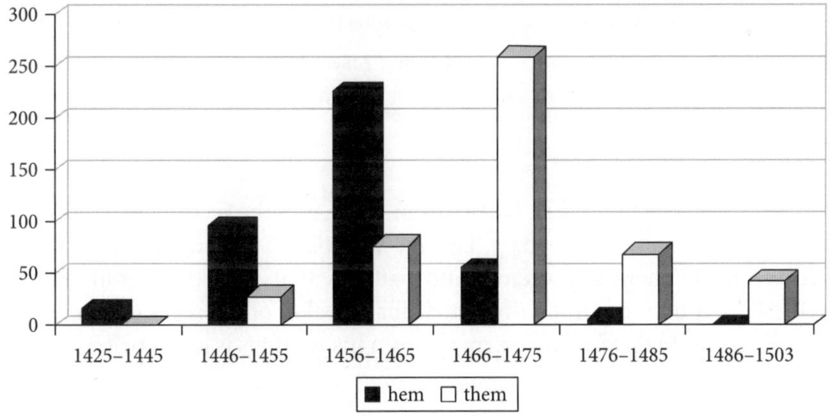

Fig. 3.2. <hem> versus <them> in the Paston Letters, 1425–1503, taken from Bergs (2005, 104)

[17] See Thomason and Kaufman (1991).

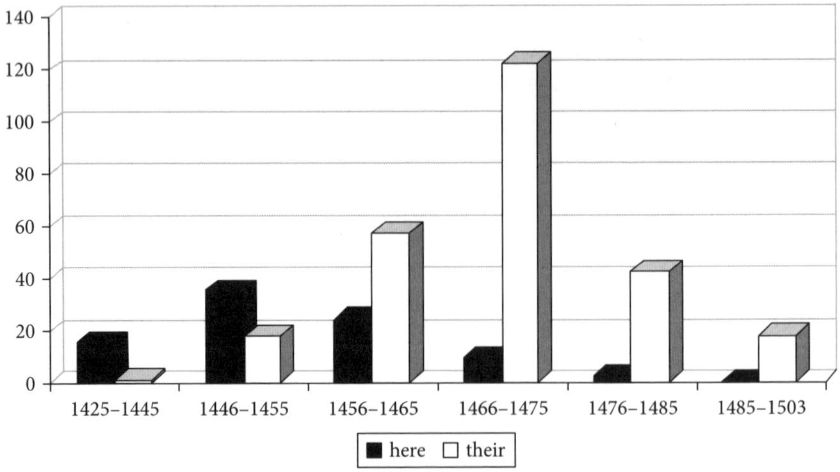

Fig. 3.3. <here> versus <their> in the Paston Letters, 1425–1503, taken from Bergs (2005, 105)

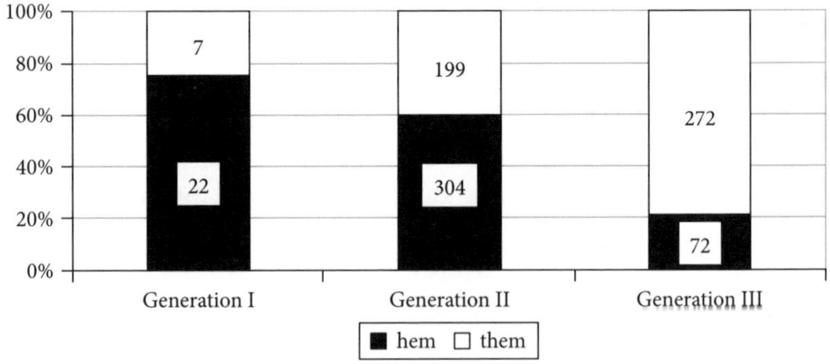

Fig. 3.4. <hem> and <them> in three generations of Pastons (total figures in columns)

cent *hem*, *c*.37 per cent *here*). Does this mean that in the second generation we find the most noise in our data, i.e. free variation between older and newer forms? Or are there any vectors and patterns that guided the authors and scribes?[18] Let us zoom in on one individual speaker of the second generation: John Paston I (1421–66). One example from his writings is given below:[19]

[18] It should be added here that not all letters were autographed. However, a detailed study of the morphosyntax of the autographed and dictated letters showed that scribal influences in the domain of morphosyntax were actually minimal and negligible; see Bergs (2005, 79–80).

[19] The square brackets in the translation signify two things: (1) both paragraphs were cancelled by a large cross; (2) the second paragraph was inserted later. See Davis (1971, 61, letter number 40).

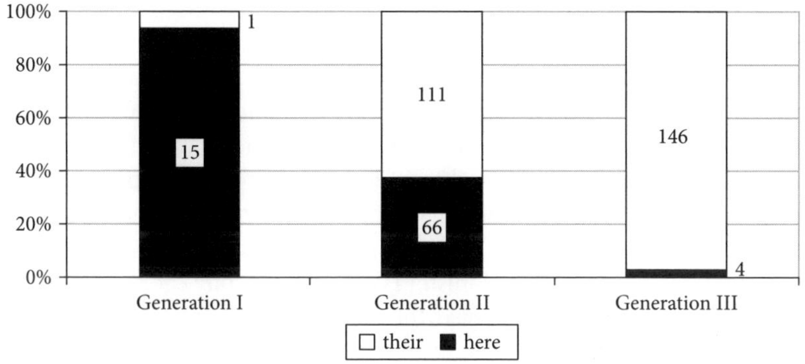

Fig. 3.5. <here> and <their> in three generations of Pastons (total figures in columns)

> *divers jentelmen and the most part of the trysty yemen and husbondis and men of good name and fame of the hundre abowte the seid Ledehams place, where the seid felechep is abydyng, and nameth* ***hem*** *wyth odyre suspecious people for risers, to the entent to hide and couer her awn gylt and to holde* ***them*** *þat be trw men and innosent [[in]] þat mater in a dawnger and feer that they shuld not gader peopell ner atempte to resiste* ***ther*** *riotows governauns of the seid reotows felechep. [Item, it is conceyved that if the seyd riotows felechep and they that drawe to* ***them*** *were dewly examyned it shuld be knowe that if there were any seche rysyng it was coniectyd, don, jmagened, and labored be the seid reotows felechep and be* ***ther*** *meanes, for aswele the seid Cherche as dyvers of the most suspeciows persones be the seid Cherche enbelled for rysers, as it is seid, be and have be of long tyme dayly in compeny wyth the seid reotows felechep.*
>
> *Item, on of the seid felechep of late tyme, as it is seide, to encresse* ***her*** *maliciows purpoce hath proferid rewardis and goode to a-nodyre persone for to take vpon hym to apele certyn persones and afferme the seying of the seid Roger Cherche.] In wytnesse of these premesses dyvers knytes and esquieris and jentelmen, whos names folwen, wheche knowe this mater be seying, heryng, or credible reporte to this wrytyng have set* ***her*** *seall, besechyng your lordcheppis to be meanes to the Kyng owre Sovereyn lord for remedy in this behalve. Wrete, &c.*

John I shows some variation both in the object and in the possessive forms. At least at first sight, there are no simple and straightforward determining factors for the different forms. Nevertheless, given the principle of no synonymy in language, i.e. a one form–one meaning and one meaning–one form correlation,[20] we might assume that the variability here is not random, but somehow systematic. The determining factors may be of a language-internal or -external nature. Let us first look at language-internal factors. An extensive study of the different forms has shown that there are no clear language-internal correlates.[21] *Them* was probably more closely associated with indirect objects, and *hem* with direct

[20] See Tobin (1988) and Bolinger (1977).

[21] Bergs (2005, Chapter 4).

objects, but this is only a tendency. One very promising additional perspective comes from psycholinguistic approaches, especially connectionism.[22] The pronouns are segmented into so-called Wickelphones, roughly something like soundbites, or phonological segments between phoneme and syllable. Each of these Wickelphones is a trigram, i.e. it has three elements (a syllable boundary (#) counts as one element). Thus, the modern English pronoun *them* [ðem] can be segmented into the Wickelphones, {ðem} and {em#}. Wickelphones (and their smaller subparts, Wickelfeatures) operate as cognitive units or associative patterns within the framework of connectionism. The more frequently a given Wickelphone or Wickelfeature is used or perceived, the more deeply it is entrenched and hence more likely to occur again.

Note that, in terms of Wickelphones, all plural pronouns share a common final part, {em#} and {er#}, respectively, but differ in the first ({#he} versus {#θ/ðe}) and middle parts ({hem/r} versus {θ/ðem/r}) between Old and Middle English. However, upon close inspection, it becomes clear that the difference lies in only one single form, or sound: [h] versus [θ/ð]. This is summarized in Table 3.3. The latter two sounds are even very closely related, as both have the Wickelfeatures [+dental] and [+fricative]. The growing frequency of the perception and production of these innovative Wickelfeatures (which can also be found in the newly established first person plural form *they*) leads to strengthening of that very link in connectionist terms and may thus facilitate learning. Moreover, the new forms have a greater sonority, and hence greater phonetic signalling value, than the old forms.

From this, it follows that the introduction of a single Wickelphone, or its respective features, and the strengthening of that connection through frequent use, may have sufficed for a change in the pronominal system. This makes a change in this particular direction, once the subject form was established, understandable and psychologically plausible. And this, in turn, explains why speakers in the second generation, despite seemingly random and free variability, may have opted for the new form.

In addition to this language-internal, psycholinguistic explanation, we can also look at language-external factors. As was mentioned above, there is plenty of biographical and socio-historical data on the family and its members available

Table 3.3. Analysis of third person plural pronoun forms in Old and Middle English in terms of Wickelphones

First Part		Middle Part		Final Part	
OE	**ME**	**OE**	**ME**		
{#he}	{#he}/ {#θ/ðe}	{hem}	{θ/ðem}	{em#}	*hem/them*
{#he}	{#he}/{#θ/ðe}	{her}	{θ/ðer}	{er#}	*here/their*

[22] Wickelgren (1969); Rumelhart et al. (1986); Pinker and Prince (2001).

to us today. In fact, we have enough data to be able to reconstruct, at least partially, the individual family members' social networks (based on factors such as gender, education, literacy, marital status, place of living, travel activities, contacts, and cluster memberships). This seems to be particularly promising and interesting for socio-historical approaches that go back beyond *c*.1500, as we do not have enough data on relevant social groups based on gender, education, social rank, etc. to be able to compare these in a traditional macro-correlational analysis. So, the focus on the individual in his or her particular social environment is both a drawback and a great advantage of historical sociolinguistics. In the Paston family, we can see that the family members with the densest, most multiplex network structures (John I, John III, Margaret) tend to be the most conservative language users, while network members with rather loose, uniplex ties (William II, John II) tend to be more innovative, i.e. they use more *th*-pronoun forms.

This result corroborates the findings of present-day sociology and sociolinguistics.[23] Milroy and others have discovered that close, dense-knit networks and clusters (such as can be found in small, traditional village communities) tend to work as norm-enforcing, conservative factors, while open, loose-knit networks more readily allow for change, e.g. through contact with other networks. John I has a rather close-knit network and shows variability in both the objective and possessive forms. His father, William I, only used the traditional forms, while his son, John II, only uses the modern forms. John I thus takes a middling role and is not completely conservative, but also did not go the whole way yet. It is very interesting to see that basically the same principles apply to historical networks and their analyses. The people who are part of loose-knit networks rather act as innovators or bridges between networks, while the core members of dense, multiplex networks on average would be more conservative in their language use. John I, as one of the core members and a variable pronoun user, probably has to be classified not so much as an innovator or bridge, but rather as a propagator of these changes.

There is one more factor, however, that we also need to take into account in historical network analysis. Many historical speech communities do not have an established linguistic standard such as present-day speech communities usually do (Standard French, High German, Standard English, Bokmål, Castilian Spanish, etc.). In other words, there may be an occasional case of something like a linguistic standard (for example, Chancery English or late West Saxon), but there is nothing like 'Received Pronunciation' or 'Standard English' before the year 1500. What does this mean for sociolinguistic approaches and, in particular, the idea that speakers could be more innovative or more conservative, and thus their networks norm-enforcing or susceptible to change? In present-day networks, virtually all network members perceive one, or probably even two

[23] For example, Milroy (1987); Mitchell (1969); Barnes (1969).

kinds of external-linguistic norms: those of the 'standard language' (this has to do with the notion of 'overt prestige' in the widest sense) and maybe even those of local norms (this may be related to the notion of 'covert prestige' in some sense). Being innovative can mean violating one or even both kinds of norms and, therefore, risking one's position in the network.[24] In prestandardized periods like Middle English and before, we do not find one single standard, but a large bandwidth of local, dialectal norms and standards. This would mean that here dense, multiplex networks must have led to the preservation of these local varieties, while loose-knit networks did not lead to standardization (note: there is no supraregional standard!), but rather to greater linguistic freedom and diversity, as members of those networks did not feel the pressure of their local groups. In other words, in Middle English and before, members of loose-knit networks show greater flexibility and may have acted as bridges and innovators.

Apart from bridges, i.e. sources that lie outside the network, innovations may also come from within the network itself—e.g. through linguistic performance or deliberate adoption of overtly prestigious forms. If the innovator is a bridge, i.e. the link between two networks, the change needs to be adopted by a core member of the network in order to spread. If the change originates with a core member, one needs to find out whether the change was noticeable or not. If it was unnoticeable, it may still be adopted (subconsciously) through prestige or frequency, or it may spread very slowly just through sheer frequency effects. Or, of course, it may simply die out. If the change was noticeable by other network members, one needs to look at their evaluation. If this was positive, there may be a rapid spread; if it was negative, again, there may be some slow spread through frequency, or the innovation may die out. This whole process can be summarized in a diagram (Figure 3.6).

Where exactly do we locate our individual speaker, John I, and his particular change in this diagram? As already discussed, John I is a rather central, core member of his networks and entertained a multiplex, dense network of relationships. The th-pronoun was already in place for the subject function, i.e. everybody already used *they*. As we have just discussed, the other new th-pronoun forms are supported by the favourable processing conditions (in connectionist terms) and their increased phonetic signalling value. In other words, their spread is at least facilitated by internal sources, such as ease of processing. However, there is no evidence available that tells us anything about the evaluation of speakers with respect to these new forms. There are no explicit discussions that tell us that speakers liked or did not like the new pronoun forms—despite the fact that it seems very likely that they would have noticed them! What we

[24] The situation may be very different for certain, mostly youth- and Internet-related, networks, where innovation is the norm. Time and space does not allow me to discuss this point in greater detail here, but see Bergs (2009) for further discussion.

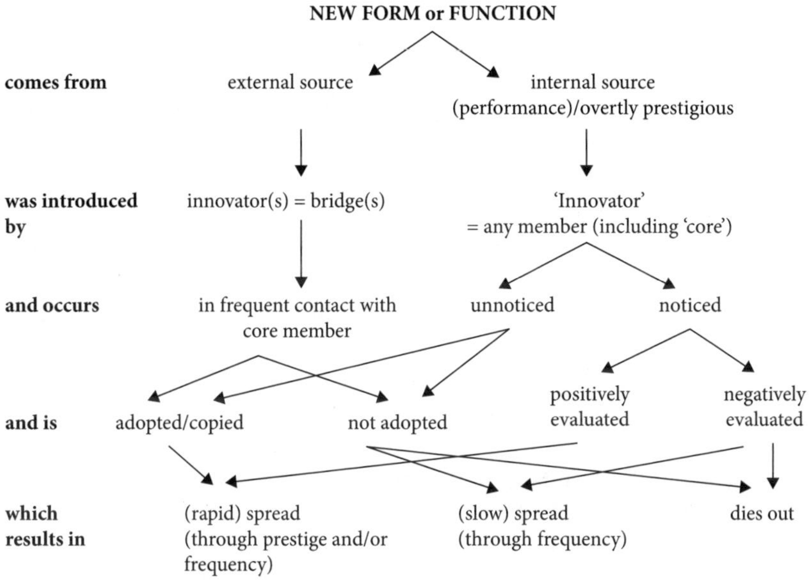

Fig. 3.6. Innovation type and change in networks (taken from Bergs 2005)

do know is that some older, more conservative speakers did not use them, while the younger, more progressive speakers did use the innovative forms. This suggests that here we see a change that was brought about by the earlier introduction of the subject pronoun *they*. This, in all likelihood, first happened through language contact in the north, i.e. the Danelaw area, and later dialect contact between speakers from the north and the south. The new objective and possessive pronoun forms *them* and *their* had greater signalling value and were easier to process than the former mixed paradigm of old and new forms. Individual speakers like John I, central and influential members of their particular networks, further supported the changes by their use of these pronouns which—metaphorically speaking—implicitly licensed their use by other, more marginal members.

§3.2. The Peterborough Chronicle

Let us now turn to the second case study. We need to go back in time, to the year 1154, to the abbey in Peterborough, a medium-sized, well-to-do monastery with about sixty monks in residence at the time. In the scriptorium, one scribe is working frantically on a manuscript which we know today as one of the earliest specimens of Middle English (ME), Bodleian MS Laud 636. It is the last part of the great Anglo-Saxon Chronicle, commissioned by Alfred the Great in about 840 and subsequently maintained and updated until 1154. The latest entries,

1132–54 of Text E of the Anglo-Saxon Chronicle, were made in one single block, by one single scribe in Peterborough (Cambridgeshire, in the east of England). It has sometimes been suggested that the irregularities that we find in this part of the manuscript are due to the fact that the scribe was actually not a native speaker of English, but of Anglo-Norman descent, and that he was not familiar with English, 'regular' orthography. This may be the cause of the apparent randomness that we find here. Bennett and Smithers, for example, in their description of the early ME Peterborough Chronicle, complain that its 'philological value is reduced by a slight admixture, not of scribal divergences from an "author's form" of ME (since they are virtually of autograph status) but of forms from the standard written language of late Old English (OE) which was WS [West Saxon, AB] and by a disordered system of spelling.'[25]

As early as 1992, Milroy[26] and Clark[27] have commented on this and have shown that such a perspective may actually rest on a rather prescriptive attitude towards spelling.[28] Eventually, this led to 'the neglect of structured variation in Middle English studies'. In the present paper, we will focus on exactly that.

The variable I am interested in is the scribal representation of the interdental fricatives [θ] and [ð]. In Old and Middle English these were allophones of /θ/. In word-medial position in native words, preceded by a stressed vowel, we find the voiced allophone [ð]. In word-initial position, finally, and in clusters we find the voiceless allophone [θ]. The two sounds were represented by the two symbols thorn <Þ> and eth <ð>. In Old and Middle English, apparently, the two symbols were used interchangeably, without any specific phonetic value attached to them. In Middle English, we also find the innovative <th> as a new way of representing these sounds. In this case, we are dealing with variation of so-called 'written-language features (W-features)', i.e. variation in features in a scribal linguistic profile (LP) 'which carry no contrasting phonic implications'.[29] Note that this does not mean that there is no system in those features. On the contrary, it is only that these are not linked to phonetics or phonology.

Why is this spelling variable so interesting in the Peterborough Chronicle? First, because the Peterborough Chronicle represents a very important document for the ME period, being one of the first examples, and a visible departure from OE. Second, in the Peterborough Chronicle we find a striking number of <th> digraphs instead of the OE forms eth and thorn (see Table 3.4).

Surprisingly, it is not until about 1400 that we see such a high percentage in a single document again.

A detailed analysis of the distribution of the three graphemes reveals that there are no major conditioning factors for their use, such as phonotactic constraints, position in the word, word class, etc. The <th> digraph was preferred

25 Bennett and Smithers (1974, 374).
26 Milroy (1992a, 193–4).
27 Clark (1992, 121–5).
28 As in Scragg (1974), for example.
29 McIntosh (1974, 46).

Table 3.4. The use of thorn, eth, and <th> in the Peterborough Chronicle. Text E. 1132–54.

Total	<þ>	<ð>	<th>
384 (100%)	266 (69%)	58 (15%)	60 (16%)

somewhat for voiced dental fricatives, while thorn occurred more often in grammatical words. However, there does seem to be some lexical motivation for the scribe: following <7> 'and' there is a very high frequency of contracted <te> 'the'. The grapheme <t> probably represents assimilated [t] from [θ], following stops. If this is so, we can assume that <t> is somehow linked to <th>, as some kind of unpacking. The same can be observed in <ph>, where the <h> adds some fricative quality. This initial motivation may have led to a gradual spread from <te> > <the> > <th> in initial position.

The grapheme <ð>, interestingly, shows the opposite tendency. On its way out of the linguistic system, it is very restricted in its use and occurs very often in only one word: <ðat>. There are only a few occurrences apart from that, and these are exclusively spellings which also appeared in the previous section of the chronicle. We may thus assume some kind of Peterborough spelling convention here, in the sense of Hockett: 'The word has a culturally prescribed spelling which the scribe has learned from others.'[30] This is not unlikely, since Peterborough scribes were usually recruited locally and the community was very small. There are only twenty-four years between the scribe of the previous section and our scribe.

Eventually, what we see here is an orderly, but not perfect idiosyncratic spelling system, and not, as has been claimed, free, random variation due to imperfect language knowledge. This again is very interesting for historical sociolinguistics. Why?

Let us return to our scribe in the scriptorium: here is a tight-knit community of sixty monks and one of the most important historical documents in English history. But, what we find is not conservative linguistic behaviour, but orderly heterogeneity, and more <th>, i.e. innovative, spellings than ever before, and the highest frequency for more than 200 years to follow. Also, as Phillips shows, there appear many innovative spellings of diphthongs and the first use of the word <scæ> 'she' in English.[31] How can this be possible? The scribe must have been under close supervision when he composed the manuscript. And why did those innovations not catch on in the linguistic community? Since Milroy,[32] we need to distinguish between innovation and change. This clearly was an act of speaker innovation. But language change only happens when the innovation spreads from the single speaker into the social group. At this point, we can observe the classical S-curve of diffusion[33] and the development of various constraints on the use of

[30] Hockett (1959), quoted in Stockwell and Barritt (1961, 77). [31] Philips (1995).
[32] Milroy (1992a). [33] See Ogura and Wang (1998) and Denison (2003).

the variable in question (stylistic, geographical, social). Eventually, we find orderly heterogeneity in a group of speakers. However, this is not what happened here. We do not have clear and solid evidence for why this change was not successful, but we need to consider the circumstances under which this scribe was working. The linguistic and social circumstances after the Norman Conquest clearly favoured Latin and French as official written languages.[34] Moreover, although there may have been adopters for the new forms, it seems plausible to assume that potential early adopters (central network members) were quickly replaced after the conquest by French and/or francophone people. This virtually eliminates the medium in which this innovation could have spread. And indeed, there is a big gap in our documentation of English between *c.*1150 and 1300. To what extent, however, the scribal innovations reflected ongoing changes in the spoken language (especially with regard to the diphthongs and the third person singular female pronoun) is impossible to tell at this point due to the lack of data.

§4. CONCLUSION

The present paper first addressed some general issues regarding the study of scribal variation and the question of free variation in general. It was pointed out that historical sociolinguistics does not necessarily suffer from a lack of data, as Labov claimed, but that it can offer some very valuable additional perspectives on the data that we have, particularly since we are dealing with only a few groups of people and individual language users. Two case studies, one on the late Middle English Paston Letters and one on the early Middle English Peterborough Chronicle, illustrated some actual possibilities here. The Paston Letters give us a very wide array of linguistic data and thus lend themselves for various investigations. Especially long-term studies of linguistic change in small groups and individuals can be carried out on this basis. The Peterborough Chronicle, on the other hand, offers some intriguing and very special linguistic data, but only very few social details on its scribe. We thus need to speculate about why certain predictable changes did not occur, while other, non-predictable innovations actually did occur. Again, using the principle of uniformity as our starting point, we can apply ideas from social network analysis to this problem and develop at least a plausible scenario that can help us to account for what we find here. There is good reason to believe that these and similar approaches can be used in the study of even older documents and in other linguistic contexts. The aim should be to gather comparable material which allows us to check

[34] See Görlach (1999).

whether some of the principles that have been developed here and in so much previous work on contemporary language variation actually hold for all languages and all language stages, or, alternatively, what sort of phenomena and principles appear to be universal (like anthropological constants) and what sort of phenomena and principles of language variation and change are language-specific.

4

Linguistic Variation in Ancient Egyptian

An Introduction to the State of the Art (with Special Attention to the Community of Deir el-Medina)

Stéphane Polis

In this chapter,[1] I explore different aspects of the variability 'inherent to human languages'[2] as it manifests itself in the corpus of pre-demotic texts[3] from ancient Egypt. More specifically, I adopt a sociolinguistic perspective and describe the types of impact that extralinguistic[4] factors have had on the written performance in this specific sociocultural setting.[5]

Four dimensions of linguistic variation[6] or, as Coseriu (1980) puts it, four dia-dimensions have long been acknowledged in linguistic studies: the temporal–historical (or diachronic) dimension, the spatial–geographical (or diatopic) dimension, the social (or diastratic) dimension, and the situational (or diaphasic) dimension. These dimensions of variation capture the fact that the intrinsic

[1] I am grateful to Todd Gillen (Liège), Ben Haring (Leiden), Joachim Friedrich Quack (Heidelberg), Baudouin Stasse (Liège), Pascal Vernus (Paris), and Jean Winand (Liège) for their comments and criticisms on first drafts of this paper. Thanks are also due to Andréas Stauder (Paris) and Daniel Werning (Berlin), who gave me access to unpublished material. I finally wish to warmly thank the editors, Jennifer Cromwell (Copenhagen) and Eitan Grossman (Jerusalem), as well as the anonymous referees, for their suggestions and improvements to the manuscript. This paper is dedicated to Eitan, in remembrance of an improbable year.

[2] Biber (1995, 1), see already Sapir (1921, 147).

[3] In this paper, the labels 'pre-demotic' and 'pre-Coptic' have a purely chronological meaning, i.e. referring to the written material of ancient Egypt that predates respectively the appearance of the demotic and of the Coptic scripts. None of the connotations sometimes linked to the 'pre-Coptic' label are implied here (on this point, see Schenkel (1983.II, 11–3) and Loprieno (1995, 371)).

[4] The question of extralinguistic motivation for language change in ancient Egypt has been recently broached by Stauder (2013a) in the introduction of his study focusing on attitudes towards the linguistic past in the Thutmoside inscriptions (i.e. inscriptions written during the first part of the Eighteenth Dynasty, *c.*1550–1350).

[5] For general considerations about the impact of non-linguistic factors, see Berruto (2010).

[6] This is why one may legitimately talk, after Labov (1994, 19), of ordered heterogeneity.

heterogeneity and complexity as well as the evolution of languages are heavily dependent on social contexts.

Traditionally, one considers the temporal dimension to be diachronic in essence whereas the three other types of variation are defined as synchronically oriented. However, this conception is misleading. On the one hand, the temporal dimension may have obvious 'synchronic' orientations, e.g. when it comes to explaining variation related to generational effects.[7] On the other hand, the dynamics of spatial, social, and situational variation often mirror language change in progress, i.e. the diachronic dimension[8] (this is called the 'Labov Principle'[9]). Therefore, for each 'synchronic' corpus,[10] one can adopt a multidimensional approach to variation that includes, at least, the four aforementioned parameters.

This chapter is structured as follows. After a general presentation of the type of linguistic data and metadata at our disposal when applying sociolinguistic methods to Ancient Egyptian (§1), I first turn to the elusive dimensions of variation related to the language users, i.e. the scribes, in the pre-demotic textual material, namely the diatopic and diastratic dimensions (§2). In a second step, the much more salient types of variation pertaining to the situation of use (the diaphasic dimension) are examined, with a discussion of the notion of genres and registers as they relate to ancient Egyptian practices (§3). Finally, I focus on a specific sociocultural environment, the community of Deir el-Medina, which was in charge of royal tomb building during the New Kingdom (§4). The goal is to describe the effects, in terms of variation, that this sociocultural environment had on the language of the written productions emanating from its community.

[7] To the best of my knowledge, an analysis of generational factors in a given 'synchronic' corpus has not been explicitly conducted in Ancient Egyptian linguistics. However, this is one of the side contributions of Sweeney's (1994) innovative approach to idiolects in the Late Ramesside Letters (a corpus of about sixty letters dating from the very end of the Twentieth Dynasty and the beginning of the Third Intermediate Period, i.e. *c.*1100) in comparing the styles of Dhutmose and Butehamon, two scribes of the Necropolis who were father and son.

[8] This idea is now becoming trivial due to the spread of grammaticalization studies. In Egyptological linguistics, see already the comments made by Loprieno (1994, 370–371) about the 'need to recognize the "trace" of history within any synchronic stage of the language'.

[9] See also Givón's (2002, 19–20) comparison with synchronic variations within a biological population. In this vein, methods of historical sociolinguistics enable us to dynamicize synchronic models of variation, just as 'diachronic typology "dynamicizes" the extant synchronic model by reinterpreting synchronic languages states as stages in a diachronic process'; Croft, Denning, and Kemmer (1990, xiii). This perspective has been adopted by Winand (1992) in his study of verbal morphology in Late Egyptian.

[10] Historical sociolinguistics is not diachronic in essence; it may deal with motivated linguistic variations in 'synchronic' corpora of the past (see, e.g., Bergs (2005, 12)). Moreover, considering the dimensions of variation synchronically—because they behave independently with respect to the speed and types of evolution depending on internal variables—appears to be a prerequisite to sound diachronic studies that focus on the evolution of the language as a whole.

§1. ANCIENT EGYPTIAN: AVAILABLE TYPES OF DATA AND METADATA

If one accepts that it is not possible to describe a whole language with the limited set of textual information at our disposal, Ancient Egyptian data are not 'bad' for variationist analyses, but they do need problematizing.[11] In this section, the methodological implications of dealing with a highly formal text language[12] are discussed first (§1.1). This is followed by a brief discussion of the quantity and type of linguistic data (and metadata) at our disposal in pre-demotic Egyptian.

§1.1. Methodological Remarks about Ancient Egyptian as a Text Language

As a text language, Ancient Egyptian is certainly not best described in relation to any kind of spoken vernacular, but should be studied as written performance in its own right.[13] The impression of having access to written-as-if-spoken Ancient Egyptian is essentially an illusion[14] that ignores the demarcation

[11] The 'unpredictable series of historical accidents' leading to uneven corpora, the 'normative' nature of written varieties (and distortion imposed on the varieties by the medium), as well as the impossibility of confirming negative evidence (gaps in the documentation are definitely unequal to statements of ungrammaticality), explain Labov's (1994, 11) pessimistic statement about historical linguistics which he considers to be 'the art of making the best use out of bad data'. Several scholars have taken this remark at face value (recently see, inter alios, Beal 2008). A refreshing counter-perspective is offered by Bergs and Stenroos (both in the current volume), arguing that the data are excellent for whoever is inclined to ask questions they can answer.

[12] The notion of text languages (also discussed in Stenroos' contribution to this volume, Chapter 2) was coined by Fleischman (2000, 34) in order 'to reflect the fact that the linguistic activity of such languages is amenable to scrutiny only insofar as it has been constituted in the form of extant *texts* [...]. [...] the data corpus of a text language is finite [...]'.

[13] See already the remarks in Baines and Eyre (1989, 103–4). This is much in agreement with Kammerzell (1998, 21–3) who argues that spoken Egyptian and written Egyptian may be considered as two distinct linguistic systems since they show marked differences on all levels of linguistic description.

[14] See, for example, Allen (1994, 1), in reference to the letters of Heqanakht that are 'generally understood to represent what Middle Egyptian must have been like as a spoken language'. Another enduring myth is the conception of Late Egyptian documentary texts as a low variety directly reflecting the spoken vernacular of the time (see below). In Egyptian linguistics, the labels 'colloquial', 'spoken', and 'vernacular' have been used as near synonyms to refer to the registers of some texts, text varieties, subcorpora, or genres, according to two usually—but not necessarily—co-occurring principles: (1) the function of the text has to be anchored in daily life (letters, administrative documents such as accounts, court reports, etc.), and (2) formal features characteristic of later stages of the language occur in the text (the functional dimension of these formal features is usually downplayed). Against this position, it is argued here that the written language is inevitably levelled in different ways—no matter how close its function to daily life and how numerous the innovative features—and is better not evaluated against a virtual spoken variety, even less so when it is seen as a coherent and monolithic variety with a linear diachronic evolution. Additionally, innovative linguistic features access the numerous written registers through complex processes of

between written and spoken realms.[15] These two independent semiotic universes deserve methodologies that are distinct, even if comparable (because of the fact that they ultimately represent the same language).[16]

This rather uncontroversial statement holds for any language, but is of paramount importance in the cultural environment of ancient Egypt. As a matter of fact, *l'espace de l'écrit* is characterized by a strong tendency towards a very high degree of formality[17] that ensues from converging cultural and sociological factors:[18] documents from ancient Egypt can be organized on a graded continuum of sacralization,[19] which is indexed by artefactual[20] parameters. This continuum of sacralization combines in complex ways with linguistic features[21] that range from greater vernacularity to greater formality.[22]

legitimization (granted by the power-holders, by the competing elite, or by the scribal intelligentsia itself). These aspects, which inevitably involve drastic selections in the spoken repertoire, are broached in Goldwasser (1999, 312–13 and 316–17). Conversely, some written varieties may be the very locus of innovation (the relation between spoken and written varieties is far from being unidirectional; see, e.g., Chafe and Tannen (1987)): some changes may originate in the written medium directly (and spread afterwards, if ever, to the spoken one; see Smith (1996, 15–17)); one can simply think of literary findings, documentary idioms (e.g. in legal texts), or even complete registers (e.g. of the *Égyptien de tradition*, see n. 21) which most certainly never occurred in the spoken medium.

[15] This does not quite mean, of course, that parts of the spoken registers may not be reflected in writing; see, e.g., the case of quoted discourses and slang idioms in the Tomb Robberies papyri mentioned by Vernus (1993) and Winand (Chapter 6 in this volume). In this respect, the linguistic differences between the registers of narratives and discourses are particularly striking, both registers showing different patterns of variation in a single text and having distinct speeds of evolution.

[16] See Goldwasser's (1999, 312) insightful comments.

[17] The notion of formality is well established in sociolinguistic theories (e.g. Bergs (2005, 18)), but it is not unproblematic; see already Halliday (1978, 224). It has been recently used in Egyptological linguistics by Stauder (2013a, especially n. 20).

[18] See below the comments about literacy, access to writing, and the status of the scribe in §2.2.

[19] See Vernus (1990, 41–3) and his distinction between documents that are 'sacralisés' and those 'qui ne le sont point'; '[l]a sacralisation est le terme marqué de cette opposition, ce qui veut dire que les documents sacralisés ont des marques positives qui les classent comme tels, alors que les documents non sacralisés n'ont pas de marques spéciales.'

[20] For example, the type of medium (from the most enduring ones, such as monuments, to the most temporary ones, such as ostraca), or the link with the iconic sphere (complementarities and interaction with pictures and, crucially, the use of the hieroglyphic script which bears the capacity to refer figuratively to the essence of things).

[21] At the linguistic level, it does not only involve the selection of formal and standardized registers at a given point in time (see Figure 4.2 below), but—given the postulated relation between language and essences in ancient Egypt—the use of a linguistic variety (called *Égyptien de tradition* after Vernus (1978, 139 n. 136; 1982, 81)) that aims at imitating and emulating, ideologically at least, the language of the First Time (*zp tpy*) and, in practical terms, parts of the Earlier Egyptian repertoire. With time, this led to a genuine diglossia between written registers (the literature is abundant; see, e.g., Jansen-Winkeln (1995a), Loprieno (1996a), and Vernus (1996)). I would, however, favour the term 'multiglossia', which is familiar to scholars of Arabic, in order to refer to the continuum of registers; see §3.2.2. We still lack a comprehensive description of the language ideologies, defined, following Silverstein (1979, 193), as 'sets of beliefs about language articulated by users as a rationalization or justification of perceived language structure or use', prevalent in ancient Egypt. The identification of evaluative attitudes held by writers is an important requisite when dealing with variation and conventionalization (see especially Ferguson (1994, 18 and 25–6)), for they play a crucial role in the diachronic spread of certain features at the expense of others.

[22] See Bergs (2005, 18).

It should be stressed that the 'vernacular' registers[23] have no characteristics that make them more interesting than other more formal registers for linguistic studies.[24] Paraphrasing Stenroos (Chapter 2, this volume), every register displays patterns of variation that are strictly patterns of written convention and deserve to be analysed as such. No register has ontological qualities that make it better suited for linguistic analysis on account of being closer to the spoken language.[25] Due to the overall cultural context of written production, we may assume that even the text varieties situated at the bottom of the formality scale (i.e. those closest to the written 'vernacular' pole) have few features and types of variations in common with spoken Ancient Egyptian. If generalizations about the relationship between written data and spoken language—or, better, varieties—have to be made, they belong to a second stage of analysis.[26]

§1.2. Linguistic Data and Metadata about Texts in Pre-Demotic Egyptian

The linguistic data at our disposal are very limited in terms of quantity when compared to modern corpora—very roughly, some 2.5 million tokens for pre-demotic Egyptian. Apart from the discovery of new written material, the set of data is closed, and we can unfortunately not elicit additional data from dead speakers. As such, whatever the type of variation under investigation may be, restrictions apply to the use of quantitative analysis, an important tool of contemporary sociolinguistics.[27] The problem is not in producing quantitative data, but in their lack of significance. Except for large-scale diachronic phenomena, mostly irrelevant in the perspective adopted here, the low token frequencies of variables and their highly unequal distribution across types often make the use of statistics meaningless (because of random distributions on which no generalization can be made). Given the low density of linguistic material and the correlatively high diversity of registers (as well as their disparity across periods), any quantitative approach to Ancient Egyptian is therefore profitably supplemented by a qualitative one, which evaluates actual number of

[23] Their description has been distinctly favoured in grammatical studies of Late Egyptian. The nature of the Earlier Egyptian corpus made this option impossible.

[24] A similar observation applies to the distinction between dialects and standard languages, which is a by-product of social, historical, and cultural factors: 'from a merely linguistic point of view there is no difference between standard and dialect' (Berruto (2010, 231)). In the same vein, see already Hudson (1996, 36) who argues that there is no distinction to be drawn except with reference to prestige, which is impossible to define based on linguistic features.

[25] Contra, e.g., Černý and Groll (1993, xlix–l).

[26] It is evidently the case when it comes to the phonological level of analysis; see Peust (1999a, 19).

[27] On methodological issues in quantitative sociolinguistics, see, for example, the conclusions of Bailey and Tillery (2004).

occurrences against an 'expected' body of evidence[28] in order to offset the vagaries of preservation. As discussed in §1.1, the data are also limited in terms of quality,[29] since the written medium mostly gives access to levelled or standardized varieties, or 'normative dialects' in Labovian terminology.[30]

Second, metadata are often lacking,[31] making it difficult to draw definitive conclusions about the dating of texts[32] and to assess the exact status of scribes and authors, when we are lucky enough to know their names. What is their place of origin?[33] What is the social structure of the community they lived in and their actual position therein for each period?[34] These issues are addressed in §2 and further illustrated in §4, when discussing the exceptional case of the Deir el-Medina community.

§2. DIMENSIONS OF VARIATION RELATED TO THE USERS (SCRIBES)

Two dimensions of linguistic variation are reflections of reasonably permanent characteristics of the 'social man', i.e. the language user, in any linguistic situation:[35] the geographical (diatopic) and social (diastratic) dimensions. These dimensions are merged in every single text, which is by definition the product of a scribe who both originates from a particular place and lives in a particular social milieu. In other words, the separation between the two dimensions is a convenient abstraction that allows the analysis to focus on specific aspects.[36] For argument's sake, the local tradition in the Coffin Text spells from Deir el-Bersha represents a clear case of diatopic variation, while the evolution

[28] This issue is discussed extensively in Stauder (2013b).

[29] Vernus (1994, 330) clearly draws the attention of the Egyptological community to this fact: '[f]aute d'informateur, nous ne disposons que d'un registre plus ou moins étendu d'énoncé qui ne reflète pas nécessairement toutes les variétés théoriquement possibles.'

[30] See, for example, Nevalainen, Klemola, and Laitinen (2006, 16–17).

[31] For this, see especially Nevalainen (1999).

[32] The question becomes especially vexing when it comes to dating literary texts. See recently Moers et al. (2013) and Stauder (2013b).

[33] Place is understood here both as location, in objective physical terms, and as meaning, an idealization of the physical resulting from a social construct; see Johnstone (2004). The second dimension is most certainly the determinant in the case studied by Uljas (2010), which shows that the region in which an individual is born is part of his social identity.

[34] This was underlined by Funk (1988, 151) concerning the Coptic dialects.

[35] I refer explicitly to Halliday's viewpoint in his chapters (1978, 8–35 and 211–35) entitled 'Language and the social man' (parts 1 and 2), where he states (p. 12) that 'language and society—or, as we prefer to think of it, language and social man—is a unified conception, and needs to be understood and investigated as a whole. Neither of these exists without the other: there can be no social man without language, and no language without social man.'

[36] Both dimensions are obviously always pregnant: every place has some social 'depth' and one may be interested in the repertoire of a social group scattered in several places.

of draughtsmen's writings during the New Kingdom can be envisioned as a diastratic one.

§2.1. The Diatopic Dimension

The diatopic dimension has attracted the attention of many scholars. Within this dimension, two main trends of research have been pursued: the identification of local varieties[37] per se and the investigation of possible correlations between macro-diachronic stages and regions of Egypt where the written 'standard' variety of a given period might originate. From this perspective, the 'standard' written language of one period is seen as predominantly reflecting a geographic dialect.[38]

Most of the local varieties that one may reasonably assume to have existed, given the considerable north–south extension of the country,[39] are elusive in pre-Coptic Ancient Egyptian. In the present state of affairs, '[i]t has been almost impossible to find clear linguistic characteristics typical for a specific geographical region.'[40] The only convincing case of diatopic variation that has been identified so far is the Napatan Egyptian dialect,[41] attested by a small set of royal inscriptions in the northern half of the Sudan (fifth to third centuries BCE). This dialect shows morphological and syntactic variations that diverge strikingly from the written norm of similar registers attested in Egypt at the same period.

None of the hypotheses correlating macro-diachronic stages of pre-Coptic Ancient Egyptian with a standard variety coming from one particular part of

[37] For the suggestions that have been put forward, see the literature quoted in Peust (1999a, 33 n. 15). Also see Vycichl (1958); Davis (1973, 168–202); Osing (1975); Meltzer (1980); Leahy (1981); Doret (1986, 14 n. 24), with previous literature; Allen (2004); Kammerzell (2005); Peust (2007); Gundacker (2010). See also the numerous features that are explained based on dialectal, i.e. diatopic, variation in Allen (2013, see indexes). The suggested patterns of variation are generally relevant, but their matching with a place is often not conclusive: the number of texts considered is small (e.g. Johnson (1977)), the argument disputable (e.g. Davis (1973, 168–202)), or the phenomenon under investigation at the fringes and inaccurately described (e.g. Groll (1987); compare Shisha-Halevy's (2007a) thorough investigation of determination-signalling environments).

[38] This position is convenient when it comes to explaining the quick emergence of a given linguistic feature; however, the argument is generally ad hoc. See, e.g., Meltzer (1990, 75).

[39] See the famous sentence of P.Anastasi I, 28,6: *st mỉ md.t n s ỉdḥ.w ḥnʿ s n ȝbw* 'they [i.e. your stories] are like the talk of a man from the Delta with a man of Elephantine,' with Loprieno's (1982, 76–7) critical comments. See also Greenberg (1990, 505), commenting on the differing local dialects in ancient Egypt.

[40] Peust (1999a, 33).

[41] See Peust (1999b) (with Quack (2002c) regarding the similarities with demotic); Breyer (2008) rejects the label 'dialect', arguing that Napatan is better characterized as 'eine Art hyperkreolisierte Schriftsprache'. For earlier material (early Third Intermediate Period), see Darnell (2006) on Queen Katimala's inscription with the critical reviews and papers by Zibelius-Chen (2007) and Collombert (2008).

Egypt has proven to be entirely persuasive.[42] This is reflected most immediately by the lack of agreement between scholars. If one puts demotic aside, Old, Middle, and Late Egyptian have all been linked in turn to Lower, Middle, and Upper Egypt, depending on the linguistic features scholars paid attention to. Definitely more promising are the approaches that identify *diaglosses* between texts coming from specific geographical areas at different stages of the language and that focus on some linguistic features without overgeneralization.[43] In-depth studies of this kind appear to be a prerequisite for further generalizations.

This apparent lack of significant geographic variation[44] points to the need for detailed analyses that envision all the possible dimensions of variation[45] and

[42] The divergent suggestions are summed up in Peust (1999a, 33 n. 15), with the previous literature on the topic. See now also Stauder (2013b, 6 n. 11). Note that Edgerton's (1951b) identification of Old and Late Egyptian with northern varieties was more recently joined by Allen (2004, 6–7), based on the analysis of the prothetic verbal forms in the Middle Kingdom versions of the Pyramid Texts: the more northern the texts, the more frequent the prothetic *yod*. On the other hand, Allen (2004, 7–10) argues for a southern origin of Middle Egyptian, given the occurrence of the negation *nn*, characteristic of Middle Egyptian, instead of *nj* in the Middle and Lower Egypt versions of Pyramid Text spells during the Middle Kingdom. Based on other features, the opposite position also has advocates; see, e.g., Schenkel (1993: 146–9), with previous literature.

[43] See, e.g., Shisha-Halevy (1981), who discusses the degree of similarity between Late Egyptian and Bohairic, exploring 'descriptive similarities of grammatical entities'; Winand (1992, 502–4), between Upper Egypt Late Egyptian and Akhmimic constructions of the Third Future with nominal subject (see now also Vernus (2013, 222–5) regarding this construction and other possible Akhmimic features in the Teaching of Amenemope); Winand (2007, 302–3 and 2011a, 547 and 550), between The Tale of Wenamun and Coptic dialects from Upper Egypt (Sahidic excluded) concerning the compatibility of the relative converter with the perfective *sḎm=f* and the past converter *wn*; Vernus suggested (pers. comm.) that, given the temporal proximity of Wenamun and the Teaching of Amenemope, 'de très maigres manifestations de variétés locales pourraient déjà être reconnues frémissantes dès le début de la Troisième Période Intermédiaire.' This observation fits well with a progressive opening of the written registers to diatopic variation, a dimension which is definitely identifiable in the demotic corpus (Quack, pers. comm.).

[44] Even if it falls outside of the scope of the present paper, it is worth mentioning that the situation in Coptic is somewhat different given that 'geographical distance is the most powerful factor behind the range of variation in Coptic as a whole' (Funk (1988, 152)). The non-defective writing system has allowed scholars to identify several 'dialects' (see, e.g., Kasser (1991)). It is not the place here to enter the debate regarding the exact nature of the variations at stake behind the graphical level, i.e. whether it actually reflects regional linguistic variation at the phonological level or merely different ways and norms of transcribing the same language according to the place where a text has been written (for the latter option, see especially Loprieno (1982)). In any event, morphological and syntactical distinctions between dialects have been fruitfully identified; see, e.g., Polotsky (1960); Shisha-Halevy (2007b) for the peculiarities of the Bohairic dialect; Grossman (2009a) about the grammaticalization of periphrastic perfects in the Coptic dialects; and Grossman and Polis (forthcoming) about the prohibitive constructions across dialects.

[45] In this respect, it seems methodologically unsound to assume that one or two linguistic features in common between 'dialects' may be sufficient to equate an entire stage of the language with another. Additionally, the grammatical consonances usually occur between specific corpora displaying similar patterns of variation and not between idealized and linguistically heterogeneous stages of Ancient Egyptian (this fact was already mentioned in Doret (1986, 14 n. 24)). Here, Shisha-Halevy's statement about Coptic (1981, 314) could be profitably extended to pre-Coptic Egyptian: 'there is really no justification, either syn- or diachronic, descriptive or comparative, for tackling Coptic *en bloc* as a monolithic phenomenon, previous to examining its

take into consideration the evanescent metadata concerning the place of origin of the authors of texts.[46] Indeed, combined sociological and cultural factors (see §2.2) lead to a high degree of standardization (or normalization[47]) of the written performance at any stage of the Egyptian language.[48] Dialectal variables therefore are evidently not numerous and mostly to be found at the fringes of the attested registers: there can be no doubt that the dialectal study of pre-Coptic Egyptian is still in its infancy.

§2.2. The Diastratic Dimension

The social (or diastratic) dimension of variation is not more self-evident than the diatopic one.[49] In both cases, this appears to follow directly from the way ancient Egyptians conceived of their national identity and from the ideology maintaining their sense of community. The Ancient Egyptian language—and more specifically the mastery of reading and writing it—was a component of paramount importance in the construction of this identity and 'must have come close to being the qualifying test for Egyptianness'.[50] In this context, the knowledge of cursive and hieroglyphic writing was integral, even if it remained chiefly the prerogative of a scribal elite dependent on various administrative and religious institutions and, ultimately, on the central state. Consequently, the social dimension of variation is limited due to at least two parameters.

The first applies also to other dimensions of variation, but is worth describing more explicitly in relation to sociological variation. Writing is an instrument of knowledge,[51] and knowledge an instrument of power.[52] As such, written performance was in the grip of a closed group of individuals at the top

components.' Here, I deliberately cast aside as a premature enterprise the further attempt to match one stage of the language with an actual geographical area.

[46] For example, of the type produced by Uljas (2010) in his study of the writings of the third person plural suffix pronoun =*sn* without the final *n* in Middle Kingdom and Second Intermediate period inscriptions.

[47] Regarding the spectrum of Coptic literary dialects, Funk (1988, 151) speaks of 'normalized texts'.

[48] On this point, see recently the pessimistic (but quite realistic) view expressed by Loprieno (2006, 167) concerning the identification of dialectal features in the Deir el-Medina documentation.

[49] Loprieno (2006, 168) uses the label 'diastratic' for referring to what is called 'diaphasic' variation in the present paper.

[50] Kemp (2006, 34).

[51] See Baines (1990, 9–10) and Vernus (1990, 37). In the framework of this paper, it is enough to quote the famous idiom *sštꜣ n mdw-nṮr* 'the secret of the hieroglyphs'.

[52] On this point, see Baines (1990, 6–10; 2007, 146–71) who problematizes the opposition between oral and written knowledge and its distribution among the literate elite. On the subversive uses of speech in the literary texts, see Coulon (1999).

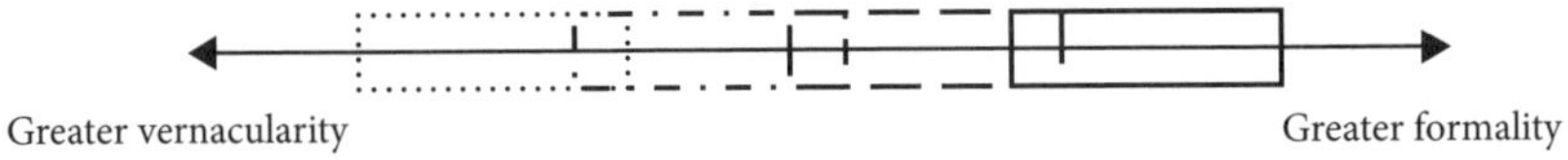

Fig. 4.1. Scale of formality of the written registers

of the social hierarchy and, undoubtedly, subject to control; it was situated within a complex system of conventions[53] imposing restrictions on the written language.[54] In linguistic terms, this led *ipso facto* to a limitation of the space for socially motivated variation: each Ancient Egyptian genre was linked to registers (see §3.1–2 below), which were conventionalized to a degree hardly reached by any other text language. As mentioned earlier, this conventionalization of registers can be conceived of as a scale[55] ranging from greater vernacularity to greater formality. Assuming four ideal registers, this may be schematized as shown in Figure 4.1.[56]

Even if the situation varied quite a bit over the course of history,[57] the proportion of literate individuals among the whole Egyptian population most certainly remained close to 1 per cent of the total adult population in pre-demotic times.[58] Literacy, understood as a social practice,[59] was the prerogative of a small group of individuals, a scribal elite occupying a position of prestige. This community of knowledge and writing[60] was always prone to self-promotion through iconic and textual representations; scribes shared values and interests, and, accordingly, acted as a highly cohesive group in the social stratification. In their writings, this is reflected by the conformity to norms acquired both

[53] The lexicon referring to the language of literature is itself tinged with axiological values (*md.wt nfr.wt* 'the good words', *ṯꜣs.w stp.w* 'the chosen maxims', etc.); see the examples quoted by Moers (2002).

[54] See Junge (2001, 18) and also Loprieno (2006, 167), who provides two examples 'in which writing conventions torpedo the recognition of dialectal, and to a certain extent even of linguistic realities altogether'.

[55] See, e.g., Bergs (2005, 18).

[56] This description of the written registers may be compared with Milroy's 'structured varieties' (1992a, 66).

[57] See Baines and Eyre (1983, 67–9).

[58] Baines and Eyre (1983, 67) suggest a rate of literacy of 1 per cent (highest estimate) for the Old Kingdom, but they think that it might have been higher for other periods. This estimation (which is disputed by Lesko (1990) without much argument) may be compared with Harris' evaluation (1989, 328) of the degree of literacy in classical Athens: 5 per cent (or possibly a bit more) of the total adult population. This percentage was to rise to 10–15 per cent in the next centuries. Quack (2006a, 95–8), based on his work on the Book of the Temple (especially the number of hands) and taking into account various degrees of literacy (people working periodically for temples, etc.), argues that, at least in urban areas, a high percentage of the male adult population must have been literate during the later periods.

[59] On this point, see Barton and Hamilton's introduction (1998, 1–22). Literacy is described as integral to its social context and may be accessed through literacy practices linked to social institutions and power relationships.

[60] See Ragazzoli (2010, 158).

through teaching and scribal practices,[61] conventions probably often best understood as an implicit or tacit agreement within the group of literates than as a proper prescriptive standard.[62] To put it otherwise, the mastering of the linguistic norm attached to each conventionalized register was indexical of their belonging to the upper class.[63] Therefore, one may refine the schema of Figure 4.1 by adding a second dimension, a continuum ranging from greater variation to greater standardization (Figure 4.2).

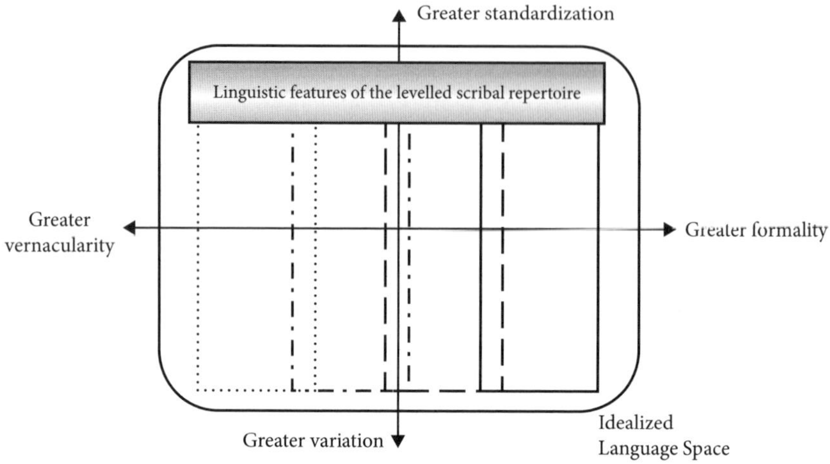

Fig. 4.2. The linguistic features of the levelled scribal repertoire

[61] This assertion does not take sides on the question of the existence of centralized teaching in ancient Egypt (see the well-known sentence in the Instruction of Kheti [P.Sallier II, 3,9–4,1] referring to 'a scribal school in the midst of the children of the officials and the foremost of the Residence' and the comments in McDowell (2000, 217–18)): the scribal practices and the assumed mobility of individual scribes are self-sufficient in explaining the emergence of levelled written registers. However, one should not downplay the influence of teaching, centralized or local, in reinforcing the convention attached to registers in the direction of greater normalization, especially during the New Kingdom when the 'Classics' of earlier times were learned and copied at school. See, e.g., Junge (2001, 21). On scribal education, see Brunner (1957), as well as 'Erzieher' and 'Erziehung' in LdÄ II, 20–2 and 22–7. On the first steps of scribal training (writing exercises (from individual signs to the copying of whole sentences), grammatical paradigms, onomastic lists, etc.), see Venturini (2007). On scribal education during the Ramesside period, see the relevant observations in Hagen (2006, about the Miscellanies, and 2007) and Goelet (2008), with previous literature.

[62] See Ferguson's definition of 'conventionalization' (1994, 15): 'Human language [...] is nevertheless largely a matter of convention, that is an implicit contract among a community of users of a language variety that certain expressions will mean certain things when used in combinations under certain social conditions. Just how this "contract" is constantly being achieved, maintained, and changed is the problem of conventionalization.' There always seems to be 'an expected norm for any single utterance, and any deviance from this expected norm is of interest to the sociolinguist and the student of language change' (Bergs (2005, 18)); see also Croft's (2000, 31) Theory of Utterance Selection.

[63] If we understand it correctly, the most famous declaration of Montuweser (St. MMA 12.184) is definitely symptomatic of this fact: *ink mdw r r-ʿ sr.w, šwy m ḏd pꜣw* 'I was someone speaking like the officials, free from saying *pꜣw*' (literature in Stauder (2013a, n. 36)). This would be a clear case of 'first order indexicality' in Silverstein's terminology, i.e. the association by a social actor of a linguistic form with some meaningful social group, the officials.

This two-dimensional graph delimits what might be labelled as an idealized 'language space', a theoretical construct encompassing all the linguistic features likely to be actualized by a scribe at any given point in time. Due to the sociological factors acknowledged above, the scribal repertoire, i.e. the sum of written forms available for the scribe, is, however, limited to tightly levelled registers,[64] which usually lack significant linguistic variation. This lack of variation, in turn, reflects the sociological context of production.

Figure 4.2 shows that a given register may be low on the formality scale, e.g. the content of a letter, but will nevertheless display a considerable degree of regularity.[65] Therefore, the Egyptian language we access through writing is, to gloss Bourdieu, an object ideologically pre-constructed by a set of socio-historical conditions: the scribal repertoire of the extant documentation is close enough to what Heinz Kloss labelled '*Dachsprache*',[66] if we understand this term as referring to the continuum of levelled registers whose prestige succeeds in obscuring those dimensions of variation that are related to the user.

So far, the identification of diastratic variation in pre-demotic Egyptian has not been a successful enterprise. The issues that we are facing in this domain may be illustrated by Sweeney's (1995) case study. She investigated whether ancient Egyptian women used language differently from men in non-literary letters from the Ramesside Period and tried to identify 'genderlectal' features. Her results are mostly negative: 'what women have in common with each other linguistically, they also have in common with men, by and large. Almost all the morphological and syntactic elements which appear in women's letters also appear in those of men.' Interestingly, from a methodological viewpoint, the author noticed some peculiarities in the phrasing of Late Ramesside Letter no. 37, sent by the chantress of Amun Henuttawy, which is less 'standardized' than other letters. However, the infrequent linguistic features that appear in this document seem to point rather to an individual style (idiolect) than to a proper genderlect, for they do not occur in other letters sent by women.

[64] The notion of 'levelling' is preferred here as a cover term to the under-theorized concept of 'standardization'. Following Milroy (2004, 162–5), 'levelling' may be described as a linguistic process 'that has the effect of reducing variability both within and across language systems and which in principle operates independently of an institutional norm', but does not exclude it. The result of this process is 'levelled registers'. 'Standardization', on the other hand, is the marked term, for it typically displays an orientation to an institutionally supported norm. Levelled registers may therefore be the result of various types of agentivity: authorization from the power-holders, cohesive norms of the scribal elite, etc.

[65] This analysis is somewhat different from, but compatible with, Goldwasser's (1999, 312–14) description of the language of the Ramesside Period. She accounted for the existence of two main 'social dialects', both comprising the Standard variety (i.e. occupying the top of the standardization scale in the present approach): the first, her 'Low variety', is the one attested in the non-literary corpus, whereas the second, the 'High variety', occurs in literary texts.

[66] The notion of koineization might be relevant to describe the evolution of language (inflectional reduction, avoidance of syntactic redundancy, etc.) attested in the documentary text of the Ramesside period (Nineteenth–Twentieth Dynasties), but this hypothesis—proposed by Goldwasser (1999, 314)—remains to be investigated.

Finally, a note by Gilula (1991) regarding the king's Egyptian in the tale of P.Westcar will serve here as a bridge between the diastratic and the diaphasic dimensions of variation. While studying two sentences with 'majestic licence' uttered by the king, Gilula argues that they may reflect 'a level of speech that is higher than that of common people and might indicate special breeding, erudition or sensitivity to the language and its eccentric usage'. This observation is certainly valid,[67] but one should not be tempted to correlate it with the actual position of the king at the top of the social hierarchy. We are dealing with a literary text and the kinds of variation observed show mostly, if not solely, that the author and scribe who wrote down this piece on papyrus was able to play in a masterly fashion with the written registers at his disposal, depending on the character.

§3. DIMENSION OF VARIATION RELATED TO THE USE OR DIAPHASIC DIMENSION

If we had to acknowledge the elusiveness of the dimensions of variation related to the user in the previous section (§2), types of variation related to the use (i.e. the diaphasic dimension of variation) are much more salient in pre-demotic Egyptian.[68] This results directly from two related parameters: the high degree of conventionalization of the registers (see §3.2) attached to each genre, and the sizeable differences in the distribution of the linguistic features between registers. In Ancient Egyptian, the overwhelming regularity of correlation between genres and registers is especially striking. Each written performance (genres are 'practices') was linked to well-defined, often prescribed, registers.[69] In other words, paraphrasing Berruto (2010), linguistic variation according to registers is an indirect reflection of the recurrent characteristics of the way the scribes used the language according to the situation of writing.[70]

[67] For 'poetic licence' induced in documentary texts by the topic dealt with, see Goldwasser (2001).

[68] See Ferguson's (1983, 154) general statement: 'register variation, in which language structure varies in accordance with the occasion of use, is all-pervasive in human language.' Biber (1995, 1–2) adds: 'Although linguistic differences among geographic and social dialect have been more extensively studied, it turns out that the linguistic differences among the registers within a language are in many ways more noteworthy.'

[69] This is immediately dependent on the sociocultural settings of the written performance (see §2.2).

[70] Berruto (2010, 228). On this point, see Goldwasser (1999, 314–15): 'the use of the different language varieties is in no way arbitrary, but prescribed; the choice of linguistic and lexical items within the literary dialect is usually conditioned by the required registers of language in every single linguistic situation.'

The investigation of this dimension of variation has been far and away the most fruitful in variationist accounts of pre-demotic Egyptian.[71] For the sake of clarity, and given the lack of agreement on the definition of these terms,[72] the relations between the notions of genre and register need first to be clarified[73] (§3.1–3).

§3.1. Genre

The notion of genre is not seen here as referring directly to language varieties associated with particular situations of use or specific communicative purposes. 'Genre' is the reflex of social practices and can be envisioned as an analytical abstraction[74] based on the structural regularities of the written production depending on the situation of use.[75] The form of the written performance within a culture (the structure of a text, including phenomena such as versification, register selection, etc.) is constrained by socially shared organizational features[76] that are characteristic of whole texts.[77] For example, a letter will typically contain an addressee, a main body with some content, and some final salutations as well as expressions of politeness, whereas poetry is expected to be written in stanzas and to conform to a specific register. The notion of genre is best defined prototypically,[78] based on the extant text varieties during one

[71] See Goldwasser (1990, 1991, and 2001), in which numerous theoretical insights are to be found; Junge (2001, 18–23), who stresses the importance of the social functions of texts as well as of grasping the linguistic register of any given text; Quack (2001, 168–9); and David (2006 and 2010). It is noticeable that such analyses have not been properly attempted for Earlier Egyptian (i.e. Old and Middle Egyptian); see, however, Junge's innovative overview in LdÄ v, 1190–3 and Junge (1985).

[72] Recently, see Biber and Conrad (2009, 21–3).

[73] See now also the discussion in Gillen (2014, 41–8). For the relationship between genres and registers in Late Egyptian, see Gohy, Martin Leon, and Polis (2013).

[74] This is much in agreement with the definition of genre in Systemic Functional Linguistics. On the epistemological issues linked with the modelling of Ancient Egyptian genres, see Baines (2003, 5).

[75] See especially Ferguson (1994, 21). The situation of use or circumstances in which the text was produced is the main criterion used by Junge (2001, 19–20) in his survey of the textual genres in Late Egyptian. The notion of genre is central in Mathieu's (1996, 129–241) description and analysis of the so-called love songs of the New Kingdom. Following G. Genette, he distinguishes between three complementary dimensions of genres: the modal one (i.e. the situation of communication), the formal one, and the thematic one. This methodological framework is endorsed by Ragazzoli (2008, 95–134).

[76] The intelligibility of any text is hugely facilitated by the genre, for writers and readers share a set of implicit conventions. However, this may become an issue for modern scholars dealing with text languages, given the elusiveness of this tacit code, which is often far from easy to reconstruct.

[77] Nowadays, there is a general recognition that genres exist 'just as much in non-literary spoken or written "texts" as in literary texts' (Ferguson (1994, 17)). On the problem of 'genres' in relation to literary pieces, especially of the Middle Kingdom, see Parkinson (2002, 32–6).

[78] See Parkinson (2002, 34): 'A genre is not a mutually exclusive class, not "all (of whose) characteristic traits need be shared by every embodiment of the type" [quoting Fowler].'

period: a text is expected to have some properties that identify it as belonging to a genre, but all the prototypical features need not occur[79] (a letter without final salutations is still a letter) and non-prototypical features may also appear (a letter might embed accounts of commodities or be written in a highly poetic register). As a practice, 'genre' is a zone of tension and negotiation between extralinguistic determinations and linguistic actualizations; as such, genres are reconfigured by every single new text[80] that will, in one way or another, play with the universe of expectations of the reader. This accounts for the 'fluid transition between individual texts' that 'may be combined into text clusters' that display permeable exterior boundaries.[81] Distinctions between genres are essentially defined in non-linguistic and emic[82] terms: differences in purpose (monumental display, archiving process, actual communication), production circumstances (*Sitz im Leben*), relation between the text producer and the intended audience, etc. When switching between genres, the scribes use the written performance to achieve different goals, and the registers selected by the genres yield language choices that are functionally motivated.

§3.2. Register

The notion of register is often considered to be an overarching concept designating 'a variety according to use'[83] (as a dialect is a 'variety according to the user') or a 'situationally defined variety':[84] it is therefore used 'as a cover term for any variety associated with a particular situational context or purpose'.[85] As a result, there is a possible confusion between genre and register, and the latter often turns out to be used in order to refer to the well-identified text types

[79] In the literary sphere, an author is therefore able to play consciously with the expected features of a genre: illustrious examples like Sinuhe or Wenamun will immediately pop up in the Egyptologist's mind, as will the literary letters of the New Kingdom (see Caminos in LdÄ I, 858 and III, 1066; Goldwasser (1991, 130–1) speaks of 'embedding' into the genre of letters), such as P.Anastasi I or the Letter to Menna.

[80] See Parkinson (2002, 34). Following, inter alios, Parkinson (2002), Bickel and Mathieu (1993), as well as Genette and Todorov in the French tradition of literary criticism, this point has been underlined by Ragazzoli (2008, 99–100).

[81] Moers (2010, 687).

[82] This point is crucial, since the types of collections of texts in single manuscripts unmistakably show that the projection of our modern understanding of the genres onto the Egyptian texts, without acknowledging the cultural settings, would lead to ineffective and inadequate categorization. Parkinson (2002, 34) labels this 'emic' approach to the genres 'historical and inductive'.

[83] See, e.g., Halliday (1978, 31), who states that register is 'a very simple and yet powerful notion: the language that we speak or write varies according to the type of situation'. Halliday's interest was in building a theory that attempts to uncover the principles which govern these variations: 'what situational factors determine what linguistic features; which kind of situational factor determines which kind of selection in the linguistic system'. On this point, see §3.3 below.

[84] In the Egyptological literature, see Junge (2001, 21): 'The conventional norm for a given situation can also be called "Register".'

[85] Biber (1995, 1).

within a culture, e.g. novels, letters, or debates. I would suggest here restricting the term 'register' to the description of the regular selections of linguistic features in the scribal repertoire in accordance with text genre. Indeed, the language of a genre will tend to display identifiable linguistic features, which are different from the language of other genres. Now three questions still hold. What kind of relation may we posit between registers and genres (§3.2.1)? How do registers differ from one another (§3.2.2)? At which level of generality do we define registers (§3.2.3)?

§3.2.1. Relationship between genres and registers

The relationship between genre and register is not seen here as a one-to-one—or biunique—relation, but rather an *n*-to-*n* relation. This modelling means that (a) several registers may be used in a single genre[86] (distinctive phrases are sometimes used as signals for the change of register, such as the so-called initiality marker *ky ḏd r-nty* in letters), and (b) a single register may occur in texts from different genres; e.g. there are few, if any, differences between discourse in Late Egyptian tales and direct (or reported) speech in actual letters of the same period. Figure 4.3 captures these two observations.

§3.2.2. Distinctions between registers

Distinctions between registers are not discrete, but are rather to be understood as a continuous space of variation.[87] Most of the time, registers differ in the characteristic distribution of pervasive linguistic features.[88] Therefore, the

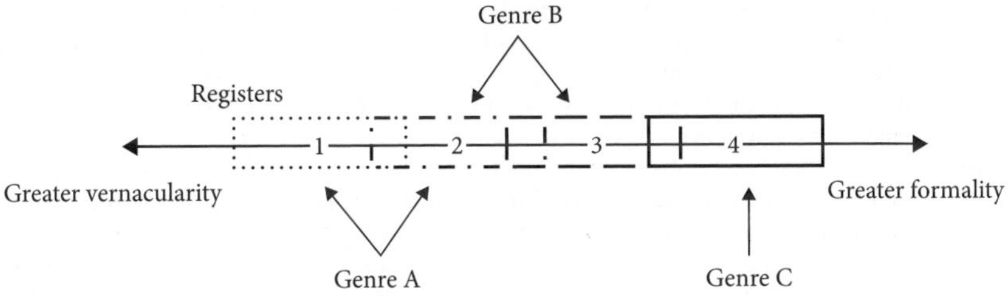

Fig. 4.3. Relationship between genres and registers

[86] See especially Baines (2003, 13): 'Any literary phase exhibits a plurality of registers. For the Middle Kingdom this is clear in teachings, which include several different styles, and more clearly in narratives, where much in the Shipwrecked Sailor and P.Westcar may travesty oral types.' In P.Anastasi I, Goldwasser (1990) showed that three distinct registers may be identified based on the criterion of grammatical forms, i.e. verbal morphology in the present case: the registers of adulation, of congratulation, and of subject discourse (the latter being itself described as a 'multi-layered register' in Goldwasser (1991)).

[87] See Biber's subtitle (1995, 7–8 and 31): 'register as a continuous construct'.

[88] For example, see Biber (1995, 28).

identification of a register generally depends not on the occurrence vs non-occurrence of an individual feature, but on the relative frequency of this feature among the various registers. As such, the use of quantitative methods is necessary.[89] Second, the distinction between registers does not reside in any single linguistic parameter, but in several parameters to be investigated at once: the co-occurrence relation among the linguistic features themselves is therefore crucial. Third, some distinctive linguistic features (that may be as strong as 'register markers') are found in some particular registers only.[90] In this case, the genre itself may be responsible for inducing or preserving specialized lexemes, idioms, or constructions in some registers.[91] In Ancient Egyptian, the phenomenon of multiglossia[92] makes the multidimensional approach to register variation especially illuminating, for a wide variety of lexical, morphological, syntactical, and constructional parameters may combine in complex ways in the conventionalization and evolution of registers.[93]

§3.2.3. Defining registers

There is no level of generality in the definition of register that is better suited for linguistic analysis than another; the aim of each study leads to the selection of an ad hoc granularity for distinguishing registers. As an illustration, in his study of verbal morphology in Late Egyptian, Winand identifies three main registers[94] across the whole corpus (using morphological features and spelling

[89] In Figure 4.3, this is what is meant by the overlapping registers 1–2–3–4: the registers 1 and 2 share some linguistic features that are susceptible to quantitative variation, and the same holds for the other theoretical registers. Needless to say, this schematization oversimplifies the relationship between registers themselves: registers not only overlap, but may also be embedded in one another or be embedded in one, but overlap with a second one. This has to do with the level of generality in the definition of registers; see below in §3.2.3.

[90] The situation of multiglossia in the New Kingdom is of special interest here. In the more formal registers, the emulation of the past textual tradition led to filtering the 'innovative' linguistic features of the scribal repertoire and to remobilizing or refunctionalizing linguistic patterns of the past (on this phenomenon, see Stauder (2013a) and Werning (2013)). This leads to observing registers with actual distinctive patterns of diaphasic variation. As a side remark, it is worth noticing that the historical knowledge of the language (see already Saussure or Labov concerning the influence on the state of the language of the individual speaker) does not seem to influence the less formal registers to a great extent: scribes seem to have had a full consciousness of the registers they were using and of the related linguistic norms; see Polis (Chapter 5, this volume).

[91] In Figure 4.3, genres A and B have one register in common (2), but genres A and C do not. This does not mean that they do not share any linguistic features (it is still the same language, after all), but that the characteristic features of their registers are always distinctive and not distributionally determined.

[92] See nn. 21 and 90. For diglossia as an extreme case of register variation, see Hudson (1994).

[93] See the case study on Amennakhte by Polis (Chaper 5, this volume).

[94] Winand (1992, 13). 'Néo-égyptien complet', a register that, in addition to the common linguistic features of classical and Late Egyptian, displays all the resources of Late Egyptian at a given time; 'néo-égyptien mixte' characterized as a Late Egyptian variant with additional features inherited from Earlier Egyptian; 'néo-égyptien partiel' that preserves some resources of Earlier

habits), while Goldwasser acknowledges the existence of three registers in a single literary text belonging to the same corpus (see n. 86): different goals lead to different levels of generality in the selection of the relevant patterns of variation. This being said, some recurrent issues in the Egyptological scholarly literature, such as the distinction between literary and non-literary texts based on linguistic criteria,[95] are probably misleading. To put it bluntly, the epistemological impossibility of such an enterprise is the result of an oversimplified conception of the notion of literature itself and of the relation between genres and registers. Texts belonging functionally to the 'literary sphere' (envisioned as an overarching genre) select a significant number of different registers in the scribal repertoire,[96] ranging from the more formal ones to the ones closer to the vernacular pole. Consequently, some literary registers are close, if not identical, to the ones used in the non-literary texts, making the identification of a language of literature as a whole dubious: the language of written registers does not determine the genre to which a text belongs.

§3.3. Relationships between Participants: Another Aspect of the Situational Parameter

Variation according to genres and registers is not the only type of variation within the diaphasic dimension. In every individual situation of written performance, the selected registers are susceptible to variation according to the role structure governing the relationships between participants (the tenor dimension in Halliday's (1978) perspective). As a result, some registers in which this kind of relationship matters (i.e. in the sphere of discourse where speaker and addressee interact in the speech situation) have an intrinsic and specific 'thickness' (see Figure 4.4). By way of illustration, Allen showed that the alternation between the negation *nj* and *nn* of an infinitive clause in the letters of Heqanakht is probably not syntactically motivated.[97] Indeed, the only occurrence of *nn* is found in a formal letter from Heqanakhte to a high-ranking official, which prompted the writer to use more formal and more levelled parts of the register typical to letters. This points to the very existence of—at least individually, but most expectedly socially—constructed language ideologies.[98] Crucially, this scribal consciousness of the possible variations in terms of formality and

Egyptian instead of the ones proper to Late Egyptian. This tripartition is similar to Junge's (2001, 23) between 'Late Egyptian', 'Medio-Late Egyptian', and 'Late Middle Egyptian'.

[95] Groll (1975) is among the first exponents of this method. Criticisms of this approach have already been put forward: see, inter alios, Quack (1994, 29–31).

[96] On the continuum between the literary and documentary registers in Ancient Egyptian, see the case study on cleft-sentences presented in Vernus (1987, 175–81).

[97] Allen (1994, 9–10).

[98] Accessible through indexical markers of various kinds; see, e.g., Silverstein (1992).

conventionalization[99] among registers according to the situation of use has had an unquestionable impact on language change in pre-demotic Egyptian, as recorded in the written documentation.

§4. DEIR EL-MEDINA: CONTEXTUALIZING A TEXT COMMUNITY

In this last section, I focus on the community of Deir el-Medina in order to describe the effects that this specific sociocultural environment had on its written productions in terms of language variation. The aim is not to suggest new insights about the social history of the village itself,[100] but—elaborating on previous studies—to evaluate the impact that the quite unique configuration of this community might have had on the shared scribal repertoire shaped by education and configured by experience.

Deir el-Medina is an isolated village[101] on the west bank of Thebes (modern Luxor) located on the border with the desert in a small valley behind the hill of Gurnet Mura'i. The texts written by the artisans who lived in this settlement—whose main task was to build the royal tombs during the New Kingdom (from the Eighteenth to the Twentieth Dynasty; *c.*1450–1050)—make it a priori a favourable site for investigating the conditions of written performance in ancient Egypt and their influences on the language preserved in the documentation for at least two reasons.

The quantity of available linguistic data is sizeable, partly thanks to the fact that the site is located in the mountains, i.e. far from the Nile floods, and was abandoned sometime during the reign of Ramses IX (*c.*1115) when the community moved away[102] from the village, mainly because work had stopped,[103] and

[99] One has to stress that the actual situation of the written performance may have an impact both on the level of formality (specific selections in the repertoire for a given register) and on the level of conventionalization (e.g. regularities at the graphemic, morphological, and constructional levels).

[100] A comprehensive synthesis of the social status of the members of this community is still lacking. Based on the evidence at our disposal, it seems, however, quite clear that, between the Thutmoside and the Late Ramesside periods, it evolves significantly in the direction of an increasing social prominence of its members, not least at the level of an individual's self-representation, who were apparently increasingly involved in official matters unrelated to the business of the Tomb itself.

[101] The classical references are Černý (2004) and Valbelle (1985). A systematic bibliography compiled by the Leiden team is available online: see http://www.leidenuniv.nl/nino/dmd/dmd.html.

[102] The *opinio communis* is that the crew moved nearby to the safer funerary temple of Medinet Habu (see, e.g., Valbelle (1985, 219)), but, except from the scribes Dhutmose and his son Butehamun, 'there is no evidence at all that the workmen ever lived within the Medinet Habu *temenos*' (Haring (2006, 111)). It has been inferred from the putative place of discovery of a great number of late Ramesside papyri (see Demarée (2008, 46)) that many inhabitants of the Theban west bank found refuge in the Medinet Habu temple that had turned into some kind of fortress.

[103] See Demarée (2008, 51).

left behind a mass of written material. According to Gasse,[104] Černý and Posener estimated that *c.*13,000 ostraca (potsherds or limestone flakes) originating from Deir el-Medina are now kept at the French Archaeological Institute in Cairo (IFAO), among which there are *c.*7,000 (copies of) so-called literary texts and *c.*6,000 'non-literary' texts. To this number, one must add a considerable number of documents coming from Deir el-Medina[105] that are scattered in Egyptological collections all over the world (Berlin, Brussels, Cairo, Chicago, Florence, London, Oxford, Paris, Turin, etc.): 15,000 non-literary ostraca might have been excavated in total.[106] If we combine this estimate with the number of papyri coming from this site (*c.*300 are published), a proper linguistic contextualization is a viable project for the registers of almost every genre: each text may be studied as representative of a group, in the context of other surviving texts.

This wealth of material also gives access to invaluable metadata of the kind that is too often lacking in historical sociolinguistics (and unparalleled in ancient Egypt, see §1.2):[107] 'The mass of documentation uncovered both in the environs of the village and from the royal work sites affords a detailed insight into the cultural, political and economic identity [...], in addition to information concerning the working techniques and bureaucratic organisation employed by the ancient craftsmen.'[108] Moreover, personal data about the official curriculum of individuals is available through the titles they bear as well as the functions they occupy in the extant documents, and it is therefore possible to reconstruct accurate prosopographies and extensive genealogical lineages.[109]

However, this rather optimistic picture concerning the quantity and quality of (meta)data at our disposal is counterbalanced by two factors. Up until now, only a small part of the texts related to Deir el-Medina has been made available through publication. Using the database of the Leiden team (see n. 101), it appears that no more than 3,344 ostraca and 308 papyri have been published so far; there is still a long way to go in this area and, even if new documents are

[104] See Gasse (1992, 51). See now the online inventory, http://www.ifao.egnet.net/bases/archives/ostraca/.

[105] This body of evidence does not only originate from the settlement of Deir el-Medina itself, but may also come from various places on the west bank of the Nile in which the crew was active at some point: the Valley of the Kings, the Valley of the Queens, the Tombs of the Nobles, and the funerary temples of Thutmosis IV, Ramses II, Ramses III, etc.

[106] The estimation of 20,000 non-literary ostraca put forward in the 'Einführung' of the Deir el-Medine Online website (http://dem-online.gwi.uni-muenchen.de/einfuehrung.php) is certainly too optimistic. Based on the number of IFAO ostraca and on the proportion of documentary ostraca in the Deir el-Medina Database that are kept in other collections, the number of usable ostraca coming from Deir el-Medina is probably closer to 13,000–15,000; I am indebted to Ben Haring's expertise on this topic. This approximate figure is in agreement with Mathieu (2003, 119), who refines Gasse's view (see n. 104): 'on recense environ 7,400 ostraca dits "littéraires", par opposition aux "documentaires", sur les 13,000 inventoriés.'

[107] As succinctly noted by Loprieno (2006, 170).

[108] Davies (1999, xviii).

[109] Among the general studies, see, for example, Černý (2004), Bierbrier (1975), and Davies (1999).

published each year,[110] decades will be needed to make the full range of documentary material accessible.

In the framework of this study, a more crucial issue is the problematic matching between the dependent linguistic variables that are found in the documents and the independent social variables when one tries to reach an optimum degree of precision, i.e. to connect a text with a scribe. Even if we do have a lot of metadata, we do not have much personalized data. Here and there, it is possible to correlate the two dimensions with some precision. The documents written by Qenhirkhopshef may be a good illustration of the methodological possibilities and limitations in terms of linguistic studies. This prominent member of the Deir el-Medina community probably occupied the office of 'scribe of the Tomb' for more than fifty years (year 40 of Ramses II to year 1 of Siptah; *c.*1240–1190[111]) and was most interested in matters 'concerning the written word, lexicography, the development of language, literature and historiography',[112] which would make his writings—easy to single out thanks to his rather unique cursive handwriting[113]—especially worth studying. However, despite such a long tenure, no more than thirty extant documents can be attributed to him with any certainty: 'this is disappointingly little'.[114] Furthermore, if all the documents are good sources for the examination of scribal practices[115] (use of drafts, etc.), only six of them can really be exploited linguistically,[116] the

[110] In this domain, Grandet's rhythm of publication for the IFAO documentary texts is admirable; see Grandet (2000, 2003, 2006, and 2010).

[111] See Černý (2004, 331), with emendations in Davies (1999, 84–6).

[112] Davies (1999, 86). Qenhirkhopshef commissioned a cryptographic inscription for a limestone funerary headrest (BM EA 63783 = KRI VII, 200; picture in Andreu (2002, 133)), wrote down onomastic lists (bureaucratic titles beginning with the grapheme *ḥry* 'superior' – O. Cairo CG 25760 [KRI III, 642–3]; a list of ten kings of the Eighteenth and Nineteenth Dynasties = O.Cairo CG 25646, see Sauneron (1951)), possessed a list of the sons of Ramses II (O. Carnarvon '300 PP', r° [KRI IV, 188,9]; for Černý (2004, 295), the hand of the recto 'does not seem to be the same as that of the verso' that is definitely written by Qenhirkhopshef), and is shown adoring the cartouches of eighteen different kings and queens on the offering table in Marseilles (n° 204, see PM I, 743; see also another offering table of our scribe PM I, 743 [KRI III, 640,11–13] mentioning the *Šms.w Ḥr* 'companion of Horus', i.e. the Pharaoh of the past; cf. Vernus (2002, 64)). See McDowell (1992, 96–7), who adds to this list the Ritual of Amenhotep of which his archive (see n. 141) contains a copy (P.Chester Beatty IX, r° 7, 5–8, 9 and r° 12, 11–13; see Gardiner (1935.I, 90 and 95, II, pls. 53 and 55). Furthermore, he made two copies of the beginning of the Battle of Kadesh based on the Ramesseum inscription (P.Chester Beatty III v° = P.BM EA 10683); see Gardiner (1935.II, pls. 9–10a) and the comments in Lesko (1994, 133–8). This papyrus also contains the notorious Dreambook that for some time was among his possessions; see Sauneron (1959b).

[113] Gardiner (1935.I, 23) asserts that: 'The writing of kenhikhopshef [*sic*] is undoubtedly the most cursive and least legible of all the scripts that have survived from the Nineteenth Dynasty'; Sauneron (1959a, XVIII and n. 7) famously spoke of an 'enfant terrible du hiératique'; see also Černý (2004, 332) and Vernus (2002, 62).

[114] Donker van Heel and Haring (2003).

[115] List and detailed discussion in Donker van Heel and Haring (2003, 41–8).

[116] A note about a special event (O.Cairo CG 25552), a list of workmen (O.Carnarvon '300 PP'), two drafts of letters to viziers (O.Cairo CG 25832 and P.Chester Beatty III v°), and the beginning of a third letter (O.Cairo CG 25807), as well as a copy of a magic spell (known by two other

rest being administrative texts dealing with things such as lamps used, labour absences and progress of work in the Tomb, deliveries of commodities, accounts, etc. Given the scarcity of material, a variationist study of the documents he wrote is not the most promising avenue of investigation.[117] Nevertheless, if one broadens the scope to the entire scribal network of his time and takes into account the written production of the other members of the community, a variationist approach becomes much more interesting.

Most of the time, though, such a matching is difficult, if not impossible, in the present state of affairs. The identification of scribes relies on convergent criteria such as (a) palaeography[118] (but we have to acknowledge the fact that scribes and authors are not always one and a single individual[119]), (b) internal evidence (usually combining prosopographical information with the context of production; e.g. a literate person figuring among the witnesses of a judicial case might be the scribe), and (c) linguistic features.[120]

Yet, these remarks do not contradict the fact that the community of Deir el-Medina is a remarkable place for socio-historical approaches to variation.

ostraca) against a demon *shḳḳ* that he filled in a letter by a fan-bearer and vizier addressed to him (P.BM EA 10731 [KRI IV, 181–2], see Černý (2004, 335–6)).

[117] Even in the case of the letters, we may expect the situational parameter (i.e. the relationship between participants) to be neutralized: all of them are drafts or model letters to (or from) high-ranking officials (regarding the socially motivated distribution of the introductory formulae in letters form the Theban Necropolis, see Haring (2009a)). Nevertheless, some questions related to Qenhirkhopshef's distinct habits as a copyist of literary texts (including the process of transposition from hieroglyphic to hieratic script) and as a scribe would be worth further investigation. In this respect, the examination of the idiosyncrasies found in the texts copied by a single scribe, like Ennene (P.d'Orbiney, P.Anastasi IV, VI, VII, and P.Sallier II), Pabasa (P.Anastasi III, P.Koller), Pentaweret (P.Sallier I), Pawehem (P.Bologna 1094), or Wentaiamun (P.Lansing; see Moers (2001)) would definitely be fruitful; on 'signed' papyri, see Quirke (1996, 382); Goelet (2008, 104); and Dorn (2009, 75).

[118] The identification of Ramesside hands is a tricky issue and a field that is still very much in its infancy. Concerning the identification of handwritings, see the pessimistic remarks in Janssen (1987), who comments on the possibility of distinguishing the handwriting of various scribes by looking at the most frequent graphemes and by observing the statistical distribution (Janssen 1994, 96, 'How difficult it is to recognize an individual hand has recently been demonstrated by Gasse [see 1992, 56–70 esp. n. 27]'). However, Baines and Eyre (1983, 87) argue that 'Few texts reveal their authorship through internal evidence, so that progress would come only from a palaeography of individual hands.' For further literature on the topic and promising avenues for future research, see Polis (Chapter 5, this volume, n. 50–3).

[119] On dictation in pre-demotic Egyptian, see, for example, Baines and Eyre (1983, 87) and Sweeney (1994, 277). Using internal evidence (requests for letters in the actual handwriting of a given scribe), Sweeney rightly points out that the scribes themselves did not always write the letters they sent. In the case of literary texts and school exercises ('miscellanies'), two good indications that the texts have been copied are: (a) the presence of a colophon, and (b) the mention of the date of copying. For colophons in school exercises, see McDowell (2000, 223), Luiselli (2003), Lenzo Marchese (2004, 365); in its fullest form, a colophon reads: 'It has come well and in peace, for A [the teacher], his assistant B.' In the case of copies, a recent typology of the kinds of variation of the written performance for which the copyists are responsible is still lacking in the Egyptological literature; see, however, Burkard (1977) and the literature quoted by Baines (2003, 26 nn. 129–30).

[120] See Sweeney's (1994) identification of idiolectal features in the Late Ramesside Letters; see n. 7.

In fact, it may be, in many respects, better suited for such analyses than many other places later in time, at least down to the Middle Ages. Take the scales of individuation of historical linguistic data established by Bergs:[121]

1. Data that are completely 'un-social' (scribes unknown; social context cannot be established).
2. Data can be ascribed to certain groups or locales (social context can only be established at some macro-level, but social data on the groups and/or locales are available).
3. Data can be ascribed to single scribes, whose social data are more or less available.

One observes that the correlation between dependent linguistic variables and independent social data oscillates generally between stages 2 and 3 for Deir el-Medina, which is exceptional for a cluster of writers dating back more than three millennia.

Furthermore, in pre-demotic Egyptian, the community of Deir el-Medina is undoubtedly the best place to study the diaphasic dimension of variation.[122] On top of the advantages cited above, it is worth noting that two factors led to a relative increase of variation—or destandardization[123]—of the scribal repertoire in this community.

First, during the New Kingdom, i.e. the period of activity of the craftsmen of Deir el-Medina, a movement of individualization, which began during the First Intermediate Period (some five hundred years before) and went top-down in ancient Egyptian society,[124] emerges clearly in the documentation through the affirmation and self-promotion of personal agentivity in numerous contexts.[125] This is found in, for example, the religious sphere (with an increase in the manifestations of personal piety[126]), the artistic domain (where several hands and actual artists' signatures are documented[127]), and the literary realm (with non-fictive authorships[128]). At a linguistic level, this personal agentivity sometimes led to the relaxation of the norms attached to written registers. As a matter

121 Bergs (2005, 51). 122 In the same vein, see Loprieno (2006, 168).

123 Following Grossman (2011), the notion of destandardization may be conceptualized as a weakening of the norm resulting in an increase in linguistic heterogeneity, in other words, as a relaxation of the selections in the scribal repertoire usually conditioned by situational constraints. This presupposes that individual scribes wish to (and may actually) exploit parts of the repertoire that are not parts of the written registers usually associated with a genre.

124 Recently, see Ragazzoli (2010, 167) with previous literature.

125 In general, see Vernus (1995). Egyptologists, perhaps influenced by the cultural context of production, generally accepted the anonymity of the works they studied.

126 See, e.g., Assmann (1997) and Vernus (2003), with previous literature, and Luiselli (2011).

127 See Keller (1984; 2003).

128 See, e.g., Assmann (1991, 307) who speaks of an 'Individualisierung der literarischen Überlieferung in „Werke" und „Autoren"' and the case study on Amennakhte in Polis (Chapter 5, this volume). Correlatively, this societal evolution is reflected in the literature itself with scribes and middle-class people becoming prominent figures; see, e.g., Ragazzoli (2010).

of fact, in this specific sociocultural setting, an increasing (and emulative) freedom of composition among the literate is anything but surprising. In this respect, the extension of belles-lettres for that time is symptomatic, for it involves the creation of new literary genres (especially linked to fictional emotional landscapes, such as literary letters, love letters and songs,[129] lyric poetry, fables, hymns to the City, etc.) and the authorization of registers previously excluded from literary and sacralized productions.[130] In spite of all this, it seems, however, that the above-mentioned relative emancipation from the conventionalized pole did not result in a similar increase of linguistic variation in all the registers[131] of the written performance in Deir el-Medina.

Second, as a result of the specialized nature of the work in digging and decorating tombs,[132] which made the workmen familiar with several types of written performance, the level of literacy in the village was undoubtedly higher[133] than the average 1 per cent of the population in the country as a whole (see above §2.2). According to a first estimate, between 5 and 7.5 per cent of the entire community (25–30 per cent of the male personnel[134]) was literate, i.e. more than five times the global rate. Janssen[135] goes as far as to state that, if one includes also semi-literates, i.e. people having passive competence sufficient to recognize hieratic signs and to understand the contents of a relatively simple text, the number comprised virtually the entire adult male population. In fact, he provides evidence showing that several ordinary workmen were definitely literate[136] (and called themselves *sš* 'scribe' when writing ostraca or graffiti, although they were definitely not professional scribes or draughtsmen[137]). These figures depend heavily on the very definition of literacy and literates in ancient societies,[138] but it appears reasonable to assume that most of the members of

[129] See Mathieu (2003, 126–7). On love songs, see, for example, Mathieu (2008). On Butehamon's famous letter to his departed wife (O.Louvre 698), see Goldwasser (1995, 191).

[130] On the relationship between language and literary genres during the New Kingdom and the artificial caesura of the Amarna Period, i.e. a caesura largely projected on the written material by the Egyptologists themselves based on historical data, see Baines (2003, 14).

[131] See Loprieno (2006, 167): 'The main problem we are facing in dealing with linguistic variety in Deir el-Medina material is the highly conventional nature of Egyptian writing altogether. This highly conventional character of Egyptian writing is less pronounced in the second portion of the linguistic history of Egyptian, i.e. in the Late Egyptian language we know from the vast majority of Deir el-Medina documents, but infinitely more invasive than the levels of intrusion of extralinguistic conventions we are used to in our own linguistic and graphic experience.'

[132] As noted by Davies (1999, xviii).

[133] 'The community is likely to have been one of the most literate of all in relation to its social status' (Baines and Eyre 1983, 86 and 90). See also Mathieu (2002, 219): 'la petite communauté de Deir el-Médineh n'est pas représentative de l'ensemble de la société égyptienne, puisque le pourcentage de lettrés, sachant lire *et* écrire, y était nettement supérieur.'

[134] Baines and Eyre (1983).

[135] Janssen (1992, 82).

[136] See, e.g., the case of *mꜣꜣ-nḫtw=f* presented in Dorn (2006).

[137] Regarding the honorary title *sš*, indicating merely that its bearer was skilled in writing, see Janssen (1982, 149).

[138] See the chart of potential literacy in Der Manuelian (1999, 286) who studied some erasures from the Amarna Period in this perspective, elaborating inter alia on the different possible

the community (including several women) had some knowledge of the written language.[139] The degree of literacy is likely to have been rather varied depending on the domain of specialization of the members of the community. It was probably rather low for the less qualified of the workmen,[140] but given the diversity of the genres attested in funerary contexts and the kinds of texts used for teaching, a good mastery of all the written registers, including the more formal ones,[141] is definitely to be assumed for the scribes and, presumably, for the chief draughtsmen as well. Moreover, the degree of literacy within the community is likely to have been subject to important diachronic change, as reflected in the documentation by the evolution of scribal activity.[142] In this respect, the label 'contingent literacy', coined by Loprieno,[143] is useful for the situation in Deir el-Medina.

The impact of these observations on the linguistic variation found in the multiglossic scribal repertoire may be sketched as follows:

(a) Few people had an active knowledge of the more formal registers,[144] which were based on a mimetic use and remobilization of the language

audiences for discrete sections of a scene or image in Egyptian art, as highlighted by Bryan (1996). One should not overestimate anachronistically the importance of written practices and should take care not to project it directly onto ancient societies in general and onto the Deir el-Medina community's daily life in particular. Between the Eighteenth and the Twentieth Dynasties, the situation underwent important changes in the direction of an increase of the use of written records; see especially Haring (2006, 107). This presumably reflects an increase in the degree of literacy in the community and, probably, an evolution of the social status of its members (cf. the presence of locally based necropolis scribes). Based on 'mistakes' in administrative documents and refusing to accept 'sheer incompetence' as a satisfactory answer, Janssen (2005, 157) argues that 'while the community of Deir el-Medîna as a whole may have had a higher level of literacy than others, it was not yet far removed from the oral tradition of recording.... [T]he whole administration rested still on a predominantly oral practice.' On this question, see already Haring (2003a and 2003b) who speaks of 'oral village culture' and describes (2006) the intensification of the use of writing in Deir el-Medina during the Ramesside period.

[139] For McDowell (1999, 4) and Haring (2006, 110), 'literacy, full or partial, reached a rate of 40% in the Twentieth Dynasty' (quote from Haring).

[140] See Davies' (1999, xix) comment concerning the innumerable graffiti throughout the Theban necropolis. Different strategies were developed in order to allow semi-literates or illiterates to take part in administrative matters. In the context of Deir el-Medina, the use of the so-called 'workmen's marks' deserves a special mention, see Haring and Kaper (2009) as well as the contributions of Haring (2009b), Killen and Weiss (2009), and Fronczak and Rzepka (2009). In a broader context, for a discussion of sealing practices as one of these strategies, see Pantalacci (1996) and Smith (2001).

[141] On this point, see Baines and Eyre (1983, 88), who state that the 'level of literate culture of the scribal elite was surprisingly high'. The Chester Beatty collection of papyri is an excellent illustration of this point; on this collection and its history, see Pestman (1982), Bickel and Mathieu (1993, 48–9, n. 103), and Demarée (2008, 47).

[142] See n. 138.

[143] Loprieno (2006, 167).

[144] Baines (2003, 17): '[those] who could exploit the stream of tradition were a small subset of the literate group, at Deir el-Medina perhaps consisting of the scribes and a couple of others.' The author subsequently argues, based on the Late Period Elephantine papyri, among others, that the knowledge of classical Egyptian was probably more widespread in proper administrative centres and temples. In any case, as has been demonstrated by, inter alios, Werning (2013), the 'profound

of the past. If we exclude copies[145] of earlier literary texts, as well as of the teaching-oriented Kemyt (which is written in columns in a distinctive style evoking early Middle Egyptian cursive; the oldest manuscript dates back to the end of the Twelfth Dynasty), most of the texts making use of these registers are monumental inscriptions (especially in tombs with the so-called Books of the Netherworld) or funerary texts on papyri (such as the Book of the Dead or the Opening of the Mouth Ritual, which use different registers, but display very few variations). The norm attached to these registers remained indisputably strong during the New Kingdom,[146] as well as in the later productions written in *Égyptien de tradition*.

(b) A slight increase of variation is documented in the literary registers of the so-called Miscellanies (Hagen 2006), as well as in the registers of some other hymns to gods and royal eulogies on papyri and ostraca. The variation within this category is, however, rather due to the fact that various genres, mobilizing several registers, belong to this category than to a significant decrease in conventionalization (basically, as far as one can see, the village seems 'to have shared an Egypt-wide idea of the educated man'[147]).

(c) The less formal registers of the texts that the community was producing for daily-life purposes, e.g. administrative texts, judicial notes, and the contents of letters, were certainly familiar to a larger part of the community. The variation found therein is consequently higher, and personal habits may be identified at different levels.

In the framework of Deir el-Medina, Figure 4.2 may therefore be refined in order to account for the different levels of conventionalization according to registers: the entire scribal repertoire is not affected in the same way by the increase of variation (Figure 4.4).

This being said, even in the less formal registers, one should not overestimate nor overemphasize the actuality of variation,[148] for the textual material shows that it actually remained quite limited. The very nature of this community can contribute to explain this fact. As a (quite isolated) social location, the community

philological and linguistic competence of certain Egyptian literates' during the New Kingdom is beyond any doubt.

[145] In strong contrast with spoken performance, written performance allows scribes to interact with each other over great temporal distance, through the copying of texts. Most of the variations that result from the copying of texts are intratextual: traces of modernizations (including reinterpretations) or misunderstandings of the model. This affects mostly the graphemic and lexical levels, but morphosyntactic variations are far from infrequent.

[146] On the 'power' of classical Egyptian, see Baines (2003, 11).

[147] McDowell (2000, 231).

[148] However, some variations in the administrative habits of the scribes (how they use drafts, etc.) appear to be quite regular and identifiable; see Donker van Heel and Haring (2003).

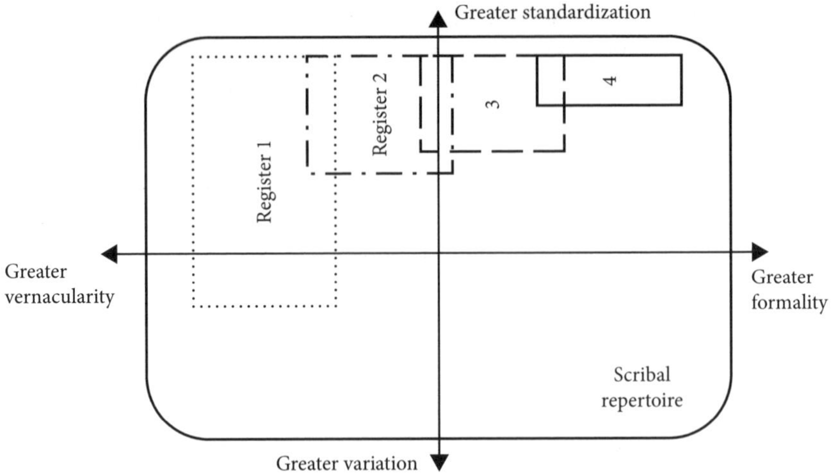

Fig. 4.4. Degree of variation in the scribal repertoire according to registers

of Deir el Medina may not be envisioned only as a microcosm of the wider Egyptian society. The inhabitants most likely reinterpreted the national idealization of the registers[149] (see §1.1) through 'locally constructed language ideologies'.[150]

In order to describe this phenomenon and to refine somewhat the description of the Deir el-Medina 'scribal network',[151] the heuristic of 'social network analysis' may be applied.[152] Thanks to the metadata at our disposal, the village of the tomb-builders may be described in terms of both structural and interactional components. These two components, i.e. the quantity and the quality of the links between individuals, play a crucial role 'in accounting for the attitudes and behaviour of a given network participant'[153] and in defining the global standpoint of the community towards linguistic conventions.

[149] It is important to note here that the education in Deir el-Medina was (at least partly) local, even though the very existence of a 'school' in the modern sense of the term may be doubted, a master-to-apprentice teaching relationship being probably more accurate. See Baines and Eyre (1983, 88): 'The large number of writing and drawing exercises found at Deir el-Medina shows that draughtsmanship and literacy were taught locally', and McDowell (2000, 230): '[…] skilled members of the gang were entitled to an assistant to whom they could then offer a proper scribal education.'

[150] Milroy (2004).

[151] To the best of my knowledge, the concept was introduced into the Egyptological literature in Reiche (2004).

[152] For a comprehensive presentation of the ideas, principles, and methods underlying and constituting social network analysis in relation to language variation and language change, see Bergs (2005, 22–58).

[153] Bergs (2005, 27).

In terms of structural components,[154] the density of the network, i.e. the number of actual links divided by the number of potential links, is high, if not maximal. We are indeed dealing with a territory-based cluster, with the number of inhabitants varying with time between *c.*100 and 400 (and probably never exceeding 630, if one includes the servants[155]), which makes it plausible that any member of the community had some interaction with all the other members of the community at some point. This is even truer if we consider only the subgroup of literates actually producing written material.

As for interactional components, they can be described as follows:

- The transactional content is massive and regular, both in professional and personal matters.
- The multiplexity of relationships, i.e. the diversity of social functions that any two participants fulfil in their relationship, is generalized. The village of Deir el-Medina was a place for working and living, which inevitably led to:
    - Hierarchical relationships in official business.
    - Ties of kinship and friendship[156] (occasionally of enmity) in the immediate neighbourhood.
    - Acquaintances and voluntary associations in the 'informal workshop', i.e. when manufacturing artefacts together for the outside world.[157]
    - Relationships with the outside world.[158]
- The types of reciprocity in relationships and related linguistic behaviours are consequently susceptible to extreme diversity.

If we use the above-mentioned criteria in order to situate Deir el-Medina on a network strength scale,[159] the community as a whole may be considered as a close-knit multiplex network. Such a close-knit network assuredly influenced the writings of the scribal network (as well as the related language ideology) in generating uniform network norms.[160] In principle, uniform network norms (that vary according to registers) are not to be mistaken for a 'standard variety': in the case of Deir el-Medina, this might have led to a proper sociolect,[161] a language constituted of levelled registers whose written conventions differ in

[154] The quick overview suggested here does not take into account external links between the administrative and religious centres of the Theban area and other parts of the country (e.g. the travels of members in places ranging from Memphis to Lower Nubia) that are attested in the documents. Note that the issues related to the centrality of given individuals and to clusters or cliques (defined as cohesive subgroups within the network) have been left almost entirely untouched and remain open to further investigation.

[155] See, e.g., Toivari-Viitala (2001, 4–5) with earlier literature.

[156] See the case study in Sweeney (1998).

[157] See especially Cooney (2006).

[158] See especially McDowell (1994).

[159] On this concept, see Milroy (1987, 142).

[160] See already Milroy and Milroy (1985).

[161] On this point, see Sweeney (1994, 317 n. 533) on the corpus of the Late Ramesside Letters.

several ways (i.e. at the graphemic, lexical, and morphosyntactic levels) from other varieties of the same language. Such a sociolect is unfortunately hardly identifiable in the documentation originating from Deir el-Medina, for at least two reasons. First, we do not have any proper *tertium comparationis*: the geographic distribution of the Late Egyptian corpus (and especially of the registers belonging to the lower part of the formality scale) is highly uneven and our knowledge of non-literary Late Egyptian is predominantly based on the documents emanating from this very community (more than 90 per cent of the extant texts). In these conditions, evaluating the differences between a possible Deir el-Medina sociolect and other varieties during the New Kingdom is a perilous task, for it usually involves an argument from silence. Second, the shared conception of language registers at the level of the country (see §1.1) makes variation between the linguistic material produced within the community and those coming from other places elusive: the local scribal network rather seems to have sustained (or reinforced) the common norm of the state than to have developed self-defined and accepted conventions for its written productions. After all, the social role and importance of the Deir el-Medina community in attending to the post-mortem destiny of the kings definitely points in the same direction.

§5. A WORD IN CONCLUSION

In this chapter, I examined the various types of extralinguistic factors that can be responsible for linguistic variation in Ancient Egyptian texts from pre-demotic times. It has been observed that, in this sociocultural environment, variations brought about by the users (geographical origin and social status of the scribes) are few, whereas the context of use has a deep impact on the linguistic registers that scribes could use and brings about significant variation across text types. Based on the more detailed discussion of the written production of the Deir el-Medina community, one can assert that, even in the framework of this highly literate scribal network of the Ramesside period, the degree of conventionalization of the various registers is significant. As such, we mostly have access to highly levelled registers for all of the genres attested. Keeping these observations in mind (and the related methodological issues), there is, however, little doubt that acknowledging the external dimensions of variation in their complexity should always go hand-in-hand with examining language-internal factors when dealing with linguistic phenomena in Ancient Egyptian. This is an epistemological requisite for any sound description of the diachronic evolution of this language.

5

The Scribal Repertoire of Amennakhte Son of Ipuy

Describing Variation Across Late Egyptian Registers

Stéphane Polis

§1. INTRODUCTION

This chapter[1] aims to investigate diaphasic variation[2] in the texts written by the Deir el-Medina scribe Amennakhte son of Ipuy in New Kingdom Egypt (*c.*1150 BCE) by analysing the graphemic and linguistic features of the registers he used when writing texts belonging to different genres. The registers are conceived here as selections operating within the scribal repertoire.[3] At an empirical level, this study is intended as a first step towards a comprehensive description of the types of linguistic variation found within the written production of the Deir el-Medina community in New Kingdom Egypt (*c.*1450–1050); at a more methodological level, it is intended as a case study testing the applicability of some historical sociolinguistic methods[4] in the field of Ancient Egyptian, which could ultimately result in refining our approach to its diachrony.

The chapter is structured as follows. After an introduction presenting the scribe and author Amennakhte (§2), I provide an overview of the corpus of texts that can be linked to this individual and justify the selection that has been made for the present study (§3). Following a discussion of graphemic regularities across

[1] I am very grateful to Andreas Dorn (Bonn), Joachim Friedrich Quack (Heidelberg), and Jean Winand (Liège) for their comments on first drafts of this paper. My thanks also go to the editors, Jennifer Cromwell (Copenhagen) and Eitan Grossman (Jerusalem), as well as to the anonymous referees, for their suggestions and improvements to the manuscript. It has not been possible to integrate fully the scholarly literature that was published after the final submission of this chapter in April 2011.

[2] On the dimensions of linguistic variation in pre-demotic Egyptian, see Polis (this volume, Chapter 4).

[3] On scribal repertoires and the need to study them in a dialectic process with the language emerging from a text community, see Stenroos' contribution in this volume (Chapter 2).

[4] On this label and the concept and methodologies behind it, see Bergs (2005, 8–21).

text types in this corpus (§4), a multidimensional description of Amennakhte's registers is proposed (§5). The results of this section are combined with a discussion of habits that can be identified in Amennakhte's writings, at the graphemo-morphological and constructional levels (§6). This allows a representation of the space occupied by each text within the continuum of registers (or language space[5]). Finally, I test the possibility of using idiolectal features to identify a scribe (or an author) in the community of Deir el-Medina, comparing the data obtained in this study with three texts closely related to Amennakhte.

§2. AMENNAKHTE: A SCRIBE AND AUTHOR

Amennakhte is an illustrious figure of the Deir el-Medina community.[6] He is known to have been a draftsman[7] before he was promoted to the office of senior scribe of the Tomb (*sš n pꜣ ḫr*) in year 16 of Ramses III, third month of the inundation season, by the vizier To.[8] He held this post for more than thirty years, until he eventually passed away in a year 6 or 7, most probably of the reign of Ramses VI.[9] He was the founder of a six-generation lineage of scribes who occupied this function within the village[10] down to the Twenty-first Dynasty. Additionally, he

[5] On the concept of language space, comprising language varieties and intrinsically heterogeneous, see especially Berruto (2010, 226 and fig. 2).

[6] See already Černý (1936) and appendix D devoted to his family in Černý (2004, 339–83); further literature in Eyre (1979, 84), Frandsen (1990, 195 n. 98), Bickel and Mathieu (1993), Vernus (1993, 172 n. 21), Nelson and Hassanein (1995), Davies (1999, 105–18), Klotz (2006, 271 n. 14), and Dorn (2006, 78). Andreas Dorn has a project that focuses on the different aspects of this individual: using all the extant records, he aims not only to account for Amennakhte's career, biography, and written production, but also at providing, through this central figure, a clearer picture of the whole sociocultural milieu of Deir el-Medina in the Twentieth Dynasty. I thank him warmly for the amount of data that he shared with me on the topic.

[7] Numerous graffiti in the Theban Mountain document this title; see Černý (2004, 240 n. 2). He probably occupied this post as early as the reign of Seti II (see graffito 621 in Spiegelberg (1921) and Davies (1999, 105)). In Year 10 of Ramses III, he is most certainly referred to as *sš-*[*qd*] in O.Michaelides 1, 5–6 (= KRI V, 452, 4–5); due to the mention of the foreman Khonsu, Černý (2004, 212) suggested emending the date to a 'Year 16', but this emendation requires further evidence. On the graffiti related to the scribe Amennakhte in general, see Peden (2001, 182–8).

[8] See Spiegelberg (1921, nos. 1111 and 1143). The beginning of the draft of one letter written by Amennakhte to the vizier To is preserved on O.Louvre N 696, r° (on this text, see below Text C). He was so grateful to the vizier that he named one of his sons after him; see, e.g., Davies (1999).

[9] See Janssen (1979 and 1994), Davies (1999, 283), and Müller (2004, 165).

[10] See especially the graffito (no. 1109) left by the scribe Dhutmose: *ḥsb.t 18 ꜣbd 1 pr.t sww 28, sš-nsw ḏḥwty-ms n ḫnw sꜣ sš-nsw ḫꜥ-m-ḥḏ.t sꜣ nsw sš ḥri-šri sꜣ sš-nsw imn-nḫt n ḫnw* 'Year 18, first month of the winter season, day 28, the king's scribe of the interior, Dhutmose, son of the king's scribe Khaemhedjet, son of the king's scribe Harshire, son of the king's scribe of the interior Amennakhte.' On this family of scribes, see already Černý (1936) and Christophe (1957). An updated list of bibliographical references and analysis of the last three generations are in Bouvier and Bouvier (2006, 23). On the evolution of the status and function of the Deir el-Medina scribes during the Twentieth Dynasty, see Demarée (2008, 51).

was a prominent intellectual figure[11] of the community during the first part of the Twentieth Dynasty (*c.*1170–1140). Indeed, not only was he in charge of the administration of the Tomb (and wrote down an impressive amount of documents regarding administrative and judicial matters), he also had a deep interest in belles-lettres and produced several literary texts,[12] such as a teaching and poems, as well as hymns to kings and gods (see below for a detailed list).

In the pre-demotic Egyptian documentation, it is quite exceptional to have access to such a variety of registers for a single scribe.[13] This is partly due to the fact that, down to the Twentieth Dynasty, the historical authors of literary pieces are almost completely elusive in the extant written records.[14] To put it briefly, in the cultural environment of ancient Egypt, the conception of authorship differs essentially from our modern understanding of the concept—partly inherited from classical philology—and one should consequently avoid projecting it back onto the Ancient Egyptian material.[15] A simplified (but quite accurate) way of describing how the Egyptians conceived of the notion of authorship before the Ramesside era is the following:[16] authors of literary texts are to be identified with the figures who are fictively presented as having the *auctoritas* on their content[17] and not with the historical scribe who actually

[11] See Bickel and Mathieu (1993, 48) who quote the famous passage of the Late Ramesside Letters (P.BM EA 10326, r° 20–2) dealing with wet papyri that were put in Amennakhte's Tomb and hypothesize, following Koenig (1981), but against Pestman (1982), that he was at some point the owner of the Chester Beatty collection of papyri. On this collection, see Polis (Chapter 4, this volume, n. 141). The title *sš n pr ꜥnḫ* 'scribe of the House of life', found after Amennakhte's name in one of the copies of his teaching (O.Cairo s.n.), could be taken as a mere indication of this prominent social and intellectual status (see Vernus (2009, 139; 2010, 56 and 369), who stresses the obvious admission of Amennakhte in 'le royaume des belles-lettres' as shown by the fact that the title of his teaching is directly followed by the Teaching of Amenemhat on O.Cairo s.n.). However, the occurrences of this title in a graffito of the Theban Mountain (no. 2173) as well as the advice *ỉry=k sš pẖr=k pr-ꜥnḫ* 'may you be a scribe and frequent the House of Life' in Amennakhte's Teaching might both be an indication that the title has to be taken at face value (see, e.g., Posener (1955, 69) and Bickel and Mathieu (1993, 36 n. 31)).

[12] This dimension of Amennakhte's life received detailed attention in Bickel and Mathieu (1993).

[13] Another case that deserves to be mentioned here is the variety of registers attested in Nebre's writings during the Nineteenth Dynasty; see KRI III, 653–9 for the texts with Goldwasser's comments (1999, 313–14 n. 11).

[14] On the play on authorship as a literary device, see, e.g., Quirke (2004, 31).

[15] On the notion of authorship in ancient Egypt, see especially Derchain (1996, 84 and 92), who stresses its importance and argues that '[l]'auteur, individu-origine du texte, dans la perspective scientifique, est une nécessité épistémologique'; the same opinion is found in Luiselli (2003, 343): '[t]he literature [...] was anonymous, and treated more as the fruit and reflections of a common "cultural memory" rather than as the work of individuals. Without the figure of the "author", however, or of a copyist [...] this "cultural memory" would never have acquired a written form.' This notion of author and its usefulness has been a matter of intense debates in literary theory; see the chapter devoted to this topic in Compagnon (1998, 51–110). In the Egyptological literature, see especially Parkinson (2002, 24–5), Quirke (2004, 29–36), and the references quoted by Moers (2009, 320 n. 8).

[16] I am grateful to Todd Gillen for discussing this topic with me.

[17] See especially Vernus (2010, 17–22). Regarding the form of the literary texts, one observes a sort of chiasm between the proclaimed respect of the original in the colophons (see Luiselli (2003, 345), with earlier literature) and the fluctuating and evolving literary tradition as documented by

composed the text. This provides a side explanation for the mention of authors only in the case of teachings and discourses[18] that offer an authoritative vision and a qualified reflection on the world. Accordingly, viziers or other famous characters of the past regularly act as guarantor for wisdom texts;[19] the 'author' may also simply be a generic figure, as in the Instruction of a Man for his Son, which emphasizes not only 'wisdom's universality',[20] but also the moral authority of the father figure. This explains why, in the didactic literature of the New Kingdom, the authorship of texts is usually attributed to the teachers themselves, who maintain metaphoric father-to-son relations with their pupils.[21] These relations are often reflected by actual acts of filial piety.[22]

It is only during the Ramesside period that external metareferences to literary texts and figures appear in the documentation.[23] In the context of this paper, it is worth mentioning that the verso of P.Chester Beatty IV, which contains the famous 'Eulogy of Dead writers'[24] (v° 2.5–3.11), has been tentatively attributed to Amennakhte himself[25] (see *infra* §4), even if this remains a hypothetical proposal. Strikingly, this coincides with the times when we are first able to match individual scribes, known by other records, with authors of literary compositions, i.e. to contextualize historically non-fictive authorships. For the present, this kind of matching has only been possible in the context of Deir el-Medina during the first part[26] of the Twentieth Dynasty,[27] i.e. when the level of literacy was substantially higher than in other places and times,[28] when textuality became

the witnesses of these texts; see Moers (2009, 321), who rightly states that we are studying productive tradition and argues against the excess and aporias of a 'Fehlerphilologie'.

[18] Coulon (1999, 132): '[l]a plupart des œuvres du Moyen Empire révèlent une affinité profonde entre l'auteur et l'orateur qu'il met en scène, au point d'ailleurs que la postérité retienne l'un pour l'autre.'

[19] See the excellent pages about 'authors and authorship' in Parkinson (2002, 75–8).

[20] As expressed by Parkinson (2002, 76).

[21] See Bierbrier (1980, 102). In the framework of this study, one has to mention in the Teaching of Amennakhte the variant *ỉr.n sš ỉmn-nḫt n sꜣ[=f]* 'made by the scribe Amennakhte for his son' in O.DeM 1248 + O.Brux. E. 6444, r° 2.

[22] In this respect, the relationship between Ramose and Qenhirkhopshef immediately springs to mind (see Černý (2004, 325–6) and Vernus (2002, 58)).

[23] See Parkinson (2002, 30–2).

[24] See Moers (2008; 2009, 319–22), Dorn (2009), and Vernus (2010, 365–7), with previous literature.

[25] See Posener (1955, 71; 1980b, 55).

[26] Except for some marginal cases, such as Butehamon's letter to his departed wife (= O.Louvre 698; beginning of the Twenty-first Dynasty), see Goldwasser (1995).

[27] On the earlier texts attributed by the Egyptian textual tradition to the scribe Khety and the question of his actual existence, see Quirke (2004, 31–3). The wisdom text attributed to Aametchu, which is inscribed in the Tomb of Useramun (see Dziobek (1998, 23–54); Eighteenth Dynasty [Thutmosis III]), might well belong to the topos of a fictive father-to-son teaching (Ptahhotep and after) rather than being an actual composition of Aametchu (this viewpoint has also been put forward by Vernus (2010, 55)).

[28] It is worth noting, after Dorn (2006), that the literary documentation from Deir el-Medina after this period (i.e. from the second half of the Twentieth Dynasty onwards) is, to say the least, limited. We certainly witness 'at first a reorganization and then a reduction of the literary activity that seems to exclude Thebes from what is going on in other regions of the country' (Loprieno 2006,

central in the community,[29] and when it was possible to embed literary production in real life,[30] with concrete functional settings, in other words, when 'thematizing life experience' became a feature of Egyptian literature.[31]

Besides Amennakhte's compositions, the three main other cases[32] in point are (1) Menna's literary letter-lament to his son Mery-Sekhmet, nicknamed Payiri,[33] (2) Hori's teaching, which was probably addressed to one of Amennakhte's sons after the death of his father,[34] and (3) Hay's hymn to Amen-Ra-Horakhty.[35] These literary pieces are not documented as having been circulated outside the community of Deir el-Medina,[36] i.e. the places where the workmen's activity was taking place.

Consequently, Amennakhte's writings are undoubtedly one of the most promising sites for investigating variation according to registers at the level of the individual scribe. Indeed, we have access to:

1. independent social data;
2. linguistic material that is rich, albeit limited in terms of token frequency, for the texts that he wrote pertain to genres that entail a great variety of registers;

166). Accordingly, it looks very much as if the times of Amennakhte constituted a kind of acme in the literary life of the community.

[29] As a working hypothesis, it could be suggested that Amennakhte was a pioneer of the practice of 'signature'. Indeed, other 'signatures' of scribes are either contemporaneous or posterior to him; see in particular his son Amenhotep (Keller (2003)), who frequently signed the figured ostraca he produced.

[30] Mathieu (2003, 136–7 and table 3) and Dorn (2009; see especially the figures on pp. 76–7 and the comments on pp. 77–82) have shown how the authors emerge in our documentation under Ramses III. It is worth noting that the selection in the written repertoire made by the scribes in these texts does not strictly emulate the Earlier Egyptian language anymore, but corresponds to high registers of Late Egyptian tinted with older constructions, lexemes, and spellings (which are indexical of their literary value) and expressly filtering some features more recently introduced in the written repertoire. This opening of the literary sphere to new registers is already documented during the Nineteenth Dynasty; see, e.g., P.Anastasi I. Strikingly, this phenomenon is reflected by the types of texts copied as school exercises, as has been demonstrated in Dorn (2009).

[31] Loprieno (2006, 167).

[32] Seven other texts might be included here, following the hypotheses put forward in Mathieu (2003, 136–7, table 3), Lenzo Marchese (2004, 365), and Dorn (2009, 77): O.Cairo CG 25225 (?Hymn?; A[men]nakhte), O.DeM 1593+O.Michaelides 82 (Hymn to Amun-Ra; Amenmes), O.DeM 1693 (Model letter; Paneferemdjed son of Amennakhte), O.Gardiner 319 (Hymn to Ra; scribe Hormin son of Hori [bare name and filiation at the end of the text]), O.Leipzig 8 (Imprecation; Amenemhat), O.Turin 57003 (Hymn to the Sun; ?Panefer?), O.Turin 57319+O. DeM 1635 (Love song; a scribe in the Place of Truth, if the 'signature' of the v° is related to the text on the r°). Possible additional candidates are mentioned in passing when analysing the formula *ỉr.n sš* PN 'made by the scribe PN', see n. 49.

[33] On the O.OIC 12074, see, for example, Fischer-Elfert (2006) and the abundant literature quoted in Vernus (2010, 469–75).

[34] This short *sbꜣy.t mtr.t* is preserved on a single ostracon, O.Gardiner 2, r°; see Bickel and Mathieu (1993, 49–51).

[35] See Dorn (2009, 77; 2011, 190–1), with two new parallels from the Valley of Kings (see pp. 457–8, nos. 745 and 746; pls. 648–56) showing that, much like Amennakhte's Teaching, this text was used as a school exercise.

[36] See Loprieno (1996b, 56–8), Baines (1996, 167), and Parkinson (2002, 76).

3. (a large amount of) other texts written within the same community, which allow us to interpret the linguistic assemblage found in each of Amennakhte's scribal productions in the light of other texts, and which serve as a *tertium comparationis*.

In the framework of this paper, the focus is on Amennakhte's writings themselves (i.e. point 2), and the analysis will be restricted to an 'internal' approach to the selections made by this individual in the scribal repertoire of his time. Thereby, I intend to describe the diaphasic variation found within the texts he produced, including issues of standardization, written formality, and idiosyncrasies, and to show that the variation—far from being 'free'—is to be conceptualized in relation to a full mastery of all the registers available to a scribe in the beginning of the Twentieth Dynasty:[37] Amennakhte was consciously using and playing with them, depending on the conditions of production and on the norms attached to each genre.

§3. THE CORPUS OF AMENNAKHTE'S WRITINGS

The corpus used for the present analysis is restricted to a body of texts whose attribution to Amennakhte son of Ipuy, as author (not necessarily as scribe, see below),[38] suffers little doubt and is agreed upon by most scholars. This option has been favoured in order to avoid uncontrolled discrepancies in the results, so as to give a description of the types of variation found in his writings that could be used later on as a 'test corpus', i.e. which (graphemic and) linguistic features may be used as criteria when one tries to corroborate or invalidate the attribution of a text to Amennakhte.

Among the literary texts, only those that bear the formula (*ỉr.n*) *sš ỉmn-nḫt* '(made by) the scribe Amennakhte' (or some variant thereof) have been included in the present corpus:

Text 1 (T1): Teaching of Amennakhte.
Ed.: Synoptic edition in Dorn (2004, 40–2)[39] with new parallels on unpublished ostraca in Ritter (2008, 83–4). **Authorship:** Consensus of the scholars, based on

[37] On this point, see already the comments made by Bickel and Mathieu (1993, 48): 'les écrivains accomplis devaient être capables de traiter tous les genres, comme le souligne l'*Enseignement*: *Il est si agréable de trouver un homme compétent dans tous les domaines*' (e.g. *nḏm zp-2 gm z ỉp m kꜣ.t nb.t*). On this sentence, see now the interpretation suggested by Vernus (2012, 420).

[38] On the identifiability of authors and scribes in ancient societies and, more specifically, concerning how much of the language that we still see today is the scribe's or represents the author, see the analysis in Bergs (Chapter 3 in this volume).

[39] Abbreviations used here: (A) O.KV 18/3.614 + 627 (Dorn (2004, 40–2 and pls. II–VII)); (B) O.BM EA 41541 (Posener (1955 , 62–3 and pl. 4); Demarée (2002, pl. 93); and Mathieu (2002, 221)); trace of a date written in red under the final line); (C) O.München ÄS 396, v° (von Beckerath (1983, 68–9)); (D) O.Cairo s.n. (Posener (1951a, 42–3; 1952, 119)); (E) O.DeM 1248 + O.Brux. E 6444 (Posener (1972, pls. 62–62a)); (F) O.DeM 1036 (Posener (1938, pls. 20–20a)); (G) O.DeM 1249

O.BM EA 41541 (rº 2: *ỉr.n sš ỉmn-nḫt—ẖry-ꜥ.f ḥr-mỉn* 'made by the scribe Amennakhte—his assistant Hormin'; see also O.KV 18/3.614 + 227, rº 1; O.Grds., rº 1–2; O.München ÄS 396, vº 3; O.DeM 1248 + Brux. E 6444, rº 1–2; O.Cairo s.n., rº 2–3), with additional prosopographical arguments by Bickel and Mathieu (1993, 37).[40]

Text 2 (T2): Lyrical poem that expresses longing for Thebes (O.Ashmolean Museum 25, rº = O.Gardiner 25, rº).
Ed.: Černý and Gardiner (1957, xxxviii, 1 rº) = KRI V, 646. **Bib.:** Černý (2004, 348); Lichtheim (1980); Bickel and Mathieu (1993, 38); Parkinson (1999, 157); Ragazzoli (2008, 31–33). **Authorship:** Consensus of the scholars, based on the formula of rº 10–11: *ø sš ỉnm-nḫt [n pꜣ ḫ]r ° pꜣ sꜣ ỉ[pwy]* 'the scribe Amennakhte of the Tomb, the son of Ipuy'.

Text 3 (T3): Satirical poem that makes fun of a pretentious person (O.Ashmolean Museum 25, vº = O.Gardiner 25, vº).
Ed.: Černý and Gardiner (1957, xxxviii, 1 vº) = KRI V, 646–7. **Bib.:** Posener (1964); Guglielmi (1985). **Authorship:** Consensus of the scholars, based on the formula of vº 8–9: *ø sš ỉnm-nḫt n pꜣ ḫr ° pꜣ sꜣ ỉpwy* 'the scribe Amennakhte of the Tomb, the son of Ipuy'.

Text 4 (T4): Encomium of Ramses IV or V[41] (O.Ermitage 1125, rº).
Ed.: Matthiew (1930). **Bib.:** Bickel and Mathieu (1993, 44–5). **Authorship:** Consensus of the scholars, based on the formula of rº 9: *ỉr.n sš ỉmn-nḫt sꜣ ỉpwy* 'made by the scribe Amennakhte, son of Ipuy'.

(Posener (1972, pls. 62–62a)); (h) O.DeM 1254 (Posener (1972, pls. 66–66a)); (i) O.DeM 1256 (Posener (1972, pls. 66–66a); with date at the end: *ꜣbd 2 ꜣḫ.t sw 23 ỉw.ỉ ḥr ḫt[?m n pꜣ ḫr?]*,  must be added to the transcription given by Dorn (2004, 41)); (j) O.DeM 1596 (Posener (1978, pls. 47–47a)); (k) O.Grdseloff (Bickel and Mathieu (1993, pls. i–vii); with date at the end: *ꜣbd 1 šmw sw 5*); (l) O.Lacau (Černý and Gardiner (1957, iii and 3)); (m) O.Turin N. 57436 (López (1982, pls. 143–143a)); (n) O.DeM 1599 (Posener (1978, pls. 49–49a)); (o) O.DeM 1255 (Posener (1972, pls. 66–66a)); (p) O.Cairo CG 25770 (Černý (1935, 96* and pl. 100)). O.Turin CG 57134 might preserve the very beginning of the text, *[sb]ꜣy.t mtr[.t]*. Based on the proposal made by Dorn (2013), the Instruction of Amennakhte could now perhaps be extended to other textual fragments: O.DeM 1606 + O.Cairo CG 25772, O.DeM 1598 II (with parallel on O.Michaelides 18), O.DeM 1218+ (with other parallels, see Fischer-Elfert 1983), O.DeM 1607, and O.DeM 1219.

[40] Bickel and Mathieu (1993, 32–3): 'Les sept ostraca [i.e. the ones known to belong to this teaching in 1993] qui contiennent cet *Enseignement* sont très proches, aussi bien pour ce qui est du texte lui-même, qui ne présente que peu de variantes, qu'au regard des écritures. Ces similitudes plaident en faveur d'une diffusion de l'oeuvre dans l'entourage immédiat de son auteur.' On this point, see Baines (1996, 167) who describes the Teaching of Amennakhte as a 'local text' (and compares it with Menna's literary letter-lament to his son (O.Chicago OI 12074, cf. n. 33)), somehow dismissing the hardly disputable literary qualities of the composition. In the same vein, see McDowell (2000, 233).

[41] If we consider, with due respect, the classifier applied to the word *sfy* ('child') in line 2, this text could hardly be anything else than a royal eulogy, although it borrows many topoi from the Love Songs corpus; see Bickel and Mathieu (1993, 44) according to whom this text might have been addressed to Ramses IV or V. Based on the 'écriture plus dense et plus rapide', Bickel and Mathieu (1993, 38) have misgivings about Amennakhte being the copyist of this text. In this respect, one can notice that it is the only literary text that contains several 'mistakes' (e.g. supererogatory *ḥr* at the end of rº 2; unexpected spellings, like *pr.w* (rº 4), *nšn* (rº 7), etc.), some apparently incomplete sentences (e.g. rº 6), and *supra lineam* additions (rº 7 and 8 (twice)). However, none of these arguments is decisive, for it could simply result from a hastier copy with self-correction, which is a well-known practice; see, e.g., Quirke (1996, 383).

Text 5 (T5): Encomium of Ramses IV (O.Turin CG 57001, r° = cat. 2161).
Ed.: López (1978, pls. 1*a*–1). **Bib.**: Assmann (1975, 498–9); Bickel and Mathieu (1993). **Authorship:** Consensus of the scholars, based on the formula of r° 9: *ỉr.n sš ỉmn-nḫt n pꜣ ḫr m ḥsb.t 4 ꜣbd 1 ꜣḫ.t sw 14* 'made by the scribe Amennakhte in year 4, first month of Akhet, fourteenth day'.

Text 6 (T6): ?Hymn to Ptah?[42] (O.Turin CG 57002 = cat. 2162 + 2164).
Ed.: López (1978, pls. 3–4*a*). **Bib.**: Bickel and Mathieu (1993, 45–7). **Authorship:** Consensus of the scholars, based on the formula of r° 9–11: *ø sš ỉnm-nḫt sꜣ ỉpwy n pꜣ ḫr, ḥsb.t 2 ꜣbd 4 pr.t sw 27 n nsw.t-bỉty* R5 'the scribe Amennakhte of the Tomb, son of Ipuy; year 2, fourth month of Peret, twenty-seventh day of the King of Upper and Lower Egypt Ramses V'.

Text 7 (T7): ?Appeal to the gods (r°; 7 lines, the lower part being slightly erased) followed by a Hymn to Osiris (v°; 8 lines)? (O.IFAO OL inv. 117).
Ed.: Dorn and Polis (2016). **Authorship:** Based on the formula of v° 8: *ỉr.n sš ỉmn-nḫt n pꜣ ḫr* 'made by the scribe Amennakhte of the Tomb'.

An eighth literary text (hymn to a king of the Twentieth Dynasty),[43] O.Berlin P 14262 r°,[44] is now to be added to Amennakhte's literary production (*sš ỉmn-nḫt* (*sꜣ*) *ỉpwỉ* [. . .] on line 6, i.e. the last line, of the ostracon), but will not be included in the corpus for it was published after the completion of the present study.[45]

[42] So far, this text has received little attention. Bickel and Mathieu (1993, 45) suggest that it could be a hymn to Ptah (two occurrences of the name *Ptḥ* (r° 3 and 5) and phraseological similarities with other hymns to this divinity (especially P.Berlin P 3048 and P.Harris I, 44.3–7)).

[43] A hymn to Amun-Re of Karnak on an uncarved stela (MMA 21.2.6) has also been attributed to Amennakhte; see Klotz (2006, 272) and the previous mentions in Černý (2004, 350 n. 8) and Davies (1999, 105 n. 289 and 109 n. 348). However, the authorship appears to rely solely on the appearance of Amennakhte (*sš-nsw.t n s.t mꜣꜥ.t Ỉmn-nht* 'Royal scribe of the Place of Truth, Amennakhte') in the lower register (followed by his son, the scribe Pentaweret and his brother, the chief craftsman Amenemope). Consequently, the attribution of this text to Amennakhte is plausible, but disputable: the two other individuals depicted on the stela could well be the artists who drew it, and we should not exclude the possibility of attributing it to other contemporary literates of the community. This question deserves special interest. If this text were to be included among Amennakhte's literary works and if he actually drew the stela himself (this question might be addressed by taking into consideration the ostracon to Ptah made by Amennakhte (Valley of the Queens, see Nelson and Hassanein (1995, 231)), as well as the ostracon to Meretseger (O.BTdK 244) recently found in the Valley of the Kings (see Dorn 2011.I, 293; II, 216–17), then a tenth text is also to be taken into consideration: the hymn addressed to the great cat (as sun god) on a stela in the Ashmolean Museum (picture and description in Winter (1963, 201–2 and fig. 18); translation in Assmann (1975, 368 and 604)). I do agree with Klotz (2006, 270; with further bibliography on the stela in n. 4) that this piece is likely to be the work of the same artisan. Unfortunately, the names of the man and woman of the lower register have never been drawn. Furthermore, Andreas Dorn has drawn my attention to two other traces of personal piety, which might have been produced by Amennakhte (Stela BM EA 374, see Parkinson (1999) and KRI V 645, 14–16 and KRI V 644, 12–14), but this remains difficult to ascertain given the lack of filiation.

[44] See Burkard (2013).

[45] A picture of the r° of this ostraca is available online on the website Deir el Medine Online (http://dem-online.gwi.uni-muenchen.de/fragment.php?id=243). Other literary texts signed by Amennakhte have been identified since then among the unpublished papyri and ostraca of the

Following other scholars, I assume that the formula (*ỉr.n*) *sš ỉmn-nḫt* '(made by) the scribe Amennakhte' that occurs at the end of the literary texts introduces, in the present case, the name of the author,[46] but not necessarily the name of the copyist or scribe; some of them could be autographs, but this remains to be demonstrated. This position, explicitly endorsed by Bickel and Mathieu,[47] is not unproblematic. Indeed, if the use of the *ỉr.n* PN formula is documented in cases when it can solely refer to the author, i.e. to the exclusion of the scribe who actually copied the text,[48] the full formula (*ỉr.n* PN) or the bare name of an individual (PN) may also occur at the end of a text in reference to the scribe who actually wrote it down. This case is especially well attested for students copying texts as a school exercise.[49] Therefore, the occurrence of the

IFAO and of the Egyptian Museum in Turin (and there are undoubtedly more to be found in other collections). They are being prepared for publication by Dorn and Polis.

[46] See especially the 'signatures' of the *sš-ḳd.w* 'draughtsmen' studied by Keller (1984; 2003, 86) who argues that 'la formule votive *ỉr(.t).n* signifie non seulement que le dessinateur en question était le dédicant de la pièce mais aussi qu'il en était le créateur' and quotes other cases in which the subject of the *ỉr(.t).n* formula cannot be the orant, but only the author. Add now the study by Dorn (2017).

[47] Bickel and Mathieu (1993, 38) state that 'la paternité unique [de ces textes] est indubitable' and consider that, maybe with the exception of T5, '[t]outes ces compositions [. . .] semblent nous être parvenues sur des documents écrits de la main même d'Amennakht.'

[48] Among the well-known *incipits* of earlier texts, see, for example, the post-Middle Kingdom versions of Ptahhotep; see Moers (2009, 323–4) who produces a penetrating analysis of the appearance of *ỉr.t.n* 'verfertigen' (vs the earlier *ḏd* 'vortragen').

[49] The same opinion is expressed in McDowell (2000, 227–8) and Lenzo Marchese (2004, 364–6) where several examples are quoted. The following list of examples can be considered: O.DeM 1022 and 1042 (copy of the Satire of the Trades with bare name of the copyist at the end, *ỉt-nfr*), and O.DeM 1560 (copy of the Satire of the Trades on the v° with the formula *ỉr.t.n sš* PN *sꜣ* PN 'made by the scribe PN son of PN' on r° 1–2); this formula is sometimes further developed with the mention of a dedicatee as in O.DeM 1027 (copy of the Hymn to the Inundation with the formula *ỉr.n sš ỉt-nfr n Ḥrỉ* at the end on v° 3–4 'made by the scribe Itnefer for Hori'). The formula *ỉr.n sš* PN is also attested in relation with exercises on specific signs (see, e.g., O.DeM 1784 with the formula *ỉr.n sš ꜣny* 'made by the scribe Ani' framed in an inked box in the middle of bull signs; exercise on a royal epithet) or on colophons (see P.Sallier IV, v° 16.2: *ỉr.n sš ỉmn-ḫꜥw* 'made by the scribe Amenkhau') after model letters (see, e.g., O.DeM 1693, r° x+6; signed by one of Amennakhte's sons, Paneferemdjed), after love songs (see, e.g., O.Turin 57319+O.DeM 1635, if the 'signature' on the v° is related to the text on the r°), after a dreambook (P.Chester Beatty III, 10.20; *ỉr.n sš ỉmn-nḫt sꜣ ḫꜥ-m-nwn* 'made by the scribe Amennakhte son of Khaemnun'), and after copies of literary texts (in this case, it follows the *ỉw=s pw nfr m ḥtp* formula: P.Sallier III, 11.9–11 [Pentaweret—Kadesh], P.d'Orbiney 19.9 [Ennene—Two Brothers], ?O.Turin 57431? [?—Teaching of Amenemhat]; bare name of the scribe without the *ỉr.n* formula, e.g. on P.Sallier II, 3.8 [Ennene—Teaching of Amenemhat], O.DeM 1014, 2.7 [Neferhotep—Satire of the Trades]). Additionally, see the famous usurpations of the scribe Nakhtsobek in P.Chester Beatty I (in the love song of r° 16.9 and in the text of Horus and Seth), and see Vernus (1992: 177 n. 37). It should also be mentioned that, after royal encomia, hymns, and prayers, besides the formula *ỉr.n* PN (see, e.g., the hymn to the sun onO.Turin CG 57003, v° 10; O.Turin CG 57396, r° 6; O.Leipzig 23, v° 7; name only in the Hymn to Ra of O.Gardiner 319, r° 5), the passive construction *ỉrw ỉn* PN is also attested for what is usually more likely to be an author (on this question, see also Mathieu (2003, 136–7, table 3) and Lenzo Marchese (2004, 365)) rather than an orant signature (much like in TA, r° 5.8; see, e.g., the Hymn to Amun-Ra of the O.Michaelides 82 + O.DeM 1593, l. 5: *ỉrw ỉn sš ỉmn-ms* 'made by the scribe Amenmes', O.Petrie 6, r° 4–5; in the *dwꜣw*-hymns, the mere agentive particle *ỉn* may be used directly after the

formula '(made by) the scribe Amennakhte' after literary texts is not sufficient if one wishes to ascertain his authorship, for it might be used to indicate a copy that he made. In order to corroborate Amennakhte's authorship for the above-mentioned texts, two additional facts can be taken into consideration:

1. He is the author of T1.
2. T4, T5, and T6 were composed quite late in Amennakhte's life (under Ramses IV and V), i.e. at a time when Amennakhte was a skilled professional in writing and had few (if any) reasons to copy such literary texts on ostraca.

Given both points 1 and 2, it is tempting to attribute T2, T3, and T7 to the same author, especially based on the fact that we have to deal with trained literary hand(s), which seems to exclude 'signed' school exercises. Hence, the probability that Amennakhte actually composed these texts is high, but this has not been definitely proven yet.

One should stress here the fact that the attribution of these literary texts to Amennakhte does not rely on the identification of his handwriting.[50] Indeed, as has been pointed out several times, the use of palaeographical arguments for dating in general,[51] and for the identification of individual handwritings in particular, still remains a risky business,[52] not least because of the similarities between hands in the Deir el-Medina community of the period.[53]

This principle also applies to the selection of documentary texts that have been included in the present corpus: their palaeography has been used very cautiously as a secondary criterion and it is only the documents for which

introduction of the prayer like in O.DeM 1197, r° 1: *dwꜣ rꜥ ḥtp=f m ꜥnḫ in sš ḳd ḥri-mnw* 'worshipping Ra when he goes down in life by the draughtsman Hormin'; see also O.DeM 1706, 1748); the status of the scribe of O.BM EA 29549 is difficult to ascertain: are we dealing with a mere copyist or with an author introduced after a long colophon by *ir(w) in ẖry-ꜥ=f* 'made by his assistant' (v° 2)? Finally, one sometimes finds the formula *sš pw* PN 'it is the scribe PN' at the end of literary texts, such as O.Leipzig 8, r° 5.

50 Such an enterprise (with a special attention to the *ductus*) is part of another project.

51 See, e.g., Eyre (1979, 86–7) and Janssen (1984, 305–6; 1987).

52 See, inter alios, Gasse (1992, n. 27); Janssen (1994, 96); Sweeney (1998, 102–3); and van den Berg and Donker van Heel (2000). For the Will of Naunakhte, see Eyre (1979, 87): 'Even within the Will of Naunakhte [calligraphic writing], the degree of deliberateness in sign formation varies quite considerably, the forms tending most to cursiveness and ligature appearing in the list of witnesses at the end of the first column.'

53 Amennakhte was a 'teacher' and Eyre (1979, 87) suggests that we could be dealing 'with a "school" of hands closely associated with his'. Further comments on the similarities between the hands that wrote the numerous ostraca of the teaching of Amennakhte are in Dorn (2004, 49). On this point, see also Parkinson (1999, 158) who states, about O.BM EA 41541 (T1b): 'This copy is well written on a carefully chosen ostraca and the scribe's handwriting seems to be modelled on Amennakhte's own.' Given r° 2 and comparing it with T1e (*n sꜣ* [lac.] 'for the son [lac.]'), one may wonder whether Hormin is actually the dedicatee (Bickel and Mathieu 1993) or rather the copyist of T1 (Dorn (2009, 77)).

strong internal evidence speaks in favour of Amennakhte's authorship that have been kept in the main corpus:[54]

Text A (TA): The testamentary deposition of Naunakhte (also known as The Last Will of Naunakhte [Doc. I] = P.Ashmolean 1945.97 = P.Gardiner 1 [cols. 1–5.8[55]]). **Ed.:** Černý (1945, VIII*a*–IX) = KRI VI, 236–40. Year 3 Ramses V or VI. **Authorship:** Amennakhte is mentioned as the scribe: *ỉrw ỉn sš ỉmn-nḫt n pꜣ ḫr ḫnỉ* (col. 5.8).

Text B (TB): The Turin Strike Papyrus[56] (= P.Turin Cat. 1880).
Ed. RAD XIV–XVII and 45–58 = n° XVIII. Year 29–30 Ramses III. **Bib.:** Pleyte and Rossi (1869–76, pls. XXXV–XLVIII [*fac simile*]); Edgerton (1951a); Frandsen (1990); Häggman (2002, 20–2); Müller (2004). **Authorship:** Based on internal evidence,[57] see, for example, Edgerton (1951a, 144–5); Frandsen (1990); Donker van Heel and Haring (2003, 40 n. 3).[58]

Text C (TC): Draft of a letter by the scribe Amennakhte (r°) and two accounts (v°); Doc. A records the amount of fresh vegetables to be delivered by the doorkeeper *ꜥn-ḫr-tr* and Doc. B records the amounts of firewood to be delivered by the same doorkeeper = O.Louvre N. 696).

[54] Usually, arguments of two kinds are invoked in arguing for the authorship of Late Egyptian documentary texts: (1) palaeographical comparison, which has been used by Eyre (1979, 86–7 and n. 57) in combination with the onomastic point of view; this results in a list of no less than twenty documents attributed to Amennakhte; see *infra*; (2) the occurrence of the name of the scribe in the document, especially when he is the only person qualified as a scribe among the people mentioned in the text and when his position in the list of witnesses is prominent or unexpected. Both arguments are used by Zonhoven (1979, 89 and 97) regarding the attribution of O.Wien Aeg 1 to Amennakhte.

[55] The end of the fifth column perhaps was written by Horisheri, son and pupil of Amennakhte; see already Černý (1945, 31). This suggestion received general approval; see, e.g., Eyre (1979, 86): 'That he is indeed correct, as also in his presumption that the later hand is that of Horisheri, is unchallengeable.' Eyre's argument is also based on the appearance of Horisheri among the witnesses to the codicil in his earliest attestation as 'Scribe of the Tomb'.

[56] This papyrus is basically a series of notes related to the strike that occurred in Deir el-Medina at this time (see, e.g., Valbelle (1985, 35), Polis (2011, 387)), even if, as it has been noted (see Eyre (1979, 90 n. 36)), the word *sḫꜣ* (lit. 'memorandum') only occurs after a later addition (*RAD* 58.14–16). One finds this term in connection with Amennakhte on O.DeM 761: [DATE] *sḫꜣ n sš ỉmn-nḫt* end (see Grandet (2000, 162)). On the notion of 'draft' in relation to this document, see Donker van Heel and Haring (2003, 1–2).

[57] The strongest argument in attributing this document to Amennakhte is maybe not so much the preponderant and positive part he plays in it, but the switch from the third to the first person pronoun that occurs in P.Turin Cat. 1880, r° 3.12–13 when the narrative resumes after direct speech: *ỉw.ỉ ḥr ỉn.t.w r-ḥry ꜥn* 'and I brought them back to the upper place'; see also the switch from the first to the third person in v° 7.3–4. This phenomenon is also attested in other documents; see, e.g., the second text on the verso of P.Turin 1879 (v° 2.7–2.22 = KRI VI, 338.3–339.5); cf. *infra* n. 59 with Janssen (1994, 92): 'the scribe suddenly introduces himself and his companions, here probably the captains of the necropolis. Structure = [DATE] *hrw pn, ỉṯꜣ sš ḥrỉ n pꜣ ḫr m-bꜣḥ pꜣ ḥm-nṯr tpy n ỉmn* [...], *ỉw.f dỉ.t sš.n nꜣ ḥmty nꜣ ḫnr n pꜣ ḫr*.'

[58] Gardiner, in his publication of the text (RAD XVI), already noticed that 'the handwriting [...] may have been due to the same scribe throughout, though the size of the writing varies in different places [...]. The scribe was a skilled professional.'

Ed.: Koenig (1991, 98–101 and 103) = KRI VII, 321. Ramses III (end of reign). **Authorship:** Amennakhte is the sender of this draft of a letter to the vizier *tꜣ* (rº 1–2: *ṯꜣy-ḫwy ḥr wnmy-nsw.t mr nỉw.t ṯꜣty tꜣ – sš ỉmn-nḫt*) and his name appears three times on the vº (see esp. Doc. B, l. 7–8: *sš ỉmn-nḫt n pꜣ ḫr r-ḫt mr-nỉw.t tꜣ*).

To the best of my knowledge, apart from these three documentary texts, the name of Amennakhte (son of Ipuy) occurs in more than 120 documents (with many variants in his title: ø, *sš*, *sš-ḳdw*, *sš n pꜣ ḫr* (*ḫny*), etc.). Among these, at least twenty ostraca and one papyrus[59] have been explicitly attributed to him by scholars (notably by Eyre,[60] who combined two types of criteria: palaeography and appearance of the name of Amennakhte in prominence):

1: O.Ashmolean Museum 4 [= O.Gardiner 4].
Ed.: HO xxvii.3 = KRI VI, 142. Year 5 Ramses IV. **Bib.**: McDowell (1999, 181–2); Helck (2002, 394).

2: O.Ashmolean Museum 68 [= O.Gardiner 68].
Ed.: HO lxvii. 3 = KRI V, 555–6. Year 31 Ramses III. **Bib.**: Allam (1973, 166–7); Helck (2002, 330).

3: O.Ashmolean Museum 104 [= O.Gardiner 104].
Ed.: HO xlvii.3 = KRI V, 555. Year 31 Ramses III. **Bib.**: Allam (1973, 171–2); Helck (2002, 329); Janssen (2005, 24).

4: O.Berlin P 10633.
Ed.: DeM-online = KRI V, 529–30. Year 29 Ramses III.

5: O.Berlin P 10645+10646.
Ed.: HOPR pl. 6–7 and DeM-online = KRI V, 527–8. Year 28 Ramses III. **Bib.**: Allam (1973, 30); Wimmer (1995.I, 29–30) [hand similar to T7].

[59] One could probably add two rather exceptional papyri to this list, even if these attributions remain problematic. [1] P.Turin Cat. 1879+1969+1899, i.e. the famous map of the mines located in Wadi Hammamat. Romer (1984, 129–30) was the first to acknowledge the fact that this map could have been drawn by a scribe from Deir el-Medina. Harrel and Brown (1989; 1992, 86) suggested that this scribe could be Amennakhte son of Ipuy (see the development on pp. 100–3). The name of Amennakhte appears several times on the (mostly unpublished) verso. The first text (vº 1.1–3 = KRI VI, 377.12–14), for instance, records an oath sworn by the scribe Amennakhte in his house, certainly in the presence of his wife (*ḥsb.t* [LAC] *ʿrḳ* [LAC *hrw*] *pn ỉn sš ỉmn-nḫt* (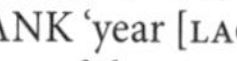) *m tꜣy=fʿ.t ḥr* [*t*]*r-n-dwꜣ.t m-bꜣḥ ʿnḫ-n-nỉw.t* [*tꜣ-wr.t-*]*m-ḥb ʿnḫ n nbʿ.w.s ḏd.n=f* BLANK 'year [LAC.] last day [LAC.] this [day] by the scribe Amennakhte in his place at sunset in front of the citizen [LAC.] oath by the lord l.p.h. that he said BLANK'). The second (vº 1.3–2.6 = KRI VI, 335.5–337.15; see Hovestreydt (1997)) and third texts (vº 2.7–2.22 = KRI VI, 338.3–339.5) are tentatively attributed to the scribe of the necropolis Hori by Janssen (1994, 92–6), but Amennakhte remains a possible candidate (see Hovestreydt 1997, 114; McDowell 1999, 94). [2] P.Turin 1885 (see Carter and Gardiner (1917), and von Beckerath (2000)), i.e. the well-known plan of the tomb of Ramses IV (name of Amennakhte on the verso).

[60] Eyre (1979, 91 n. 57), and see already Černý (2004, 342). Now, add the list provided by Burkard (2013, 67).

6: O.Berlin P 10655.
Ed.: DeM-online = KRI V, 573–4. ?Year 29 Ramses III?. **Bib.**: Allam (1973, 30–2); Helck (2002, 302).

7: O.Berlin P 12630.
Ed.: HOPR pls. 10–11 and DeM-online = KRI V, 594–5. Ramses III (?or IV?). **Bib.**: Wente (1990, 162).

8: O.Berlin P 12654.
Ed.: HOPR pls. 12–15 and DeM-online = KRI VI, 344–5. Year 2 Ramses IV (or V). **Bib.**: Janssen (1982, 133–47); Eyre (1979, 91 n. 57) is hesitant about this attribution.

9: O.BM EA 65938 [= O.Nash 5].
Ed.: HO LIII. 2 = KRI V, 471–2, and Demarée (2002, pls. 187–8). Year 20 Ramses III. **Bib.**: Allam (1973, 221–2); McDowell (1999, 34); Helck (2002, 239–40); Eyre (1979, 91 n. 57) is hesitant about this attribution.

10: O.Bodleian Library Eg. Inscr. 253.
Ed.: HO LXIV. 2 = KRI V, 485. Year 23 Ramses III. **Bib.**: Allam (1973, 40–2); McDowell (1999, 33); Helck (2002, 250).

11: O.DeM 59.
Ed.: Černý (1935, pl. 46–46A). Twentieth Dynasty. **Bib.**: Allam (1973, 84–5).

12: O.DeM 73.
Ed.: Černý (1935, pls. 50–50A) = KRI V, 472–3. Year 20 Ramses III. **Bib.** Allam (1973, 88–9); Helck (2002, 240–1); Janssen (2005, 36).

13: O.DeM 553.
Ed.: Sauneron (1959a, pls. 2–2A) = KRI V, 658–9. Ramses III. **Bib.**: Allam (1973, 127–8).

14: O.DeM 828 + O.Vienna H. 1.
Ed.: Zonhoven (1979, fig. 1) and Grandet (2000, 212).[61] Year 25 Ramses III. **Bib.**: McDowell (1999, 69–72).

15: O.Florence 2620.
Ed. HOPR pls. 34–5 = KRI V, 467. Year 17 Ramses III. **Bib.**: Allam (1973, 147); Helck (2002, 235).

16: O.Florence 2621.
Ed. HOPR pls. 36–9 = KRI V, 478–80. Year 21 Ramses III.

17: O.Florence 2625.
Ed.: HOPR pls. 34–5 = KRI V, 501. Year 25 Ramses III. **Bib.**: Wimmer (1995, 94); Helck (2002, 266).

18: O.Michaelides 1 [= O.Grdseloff 1].
Ed.: Goedicke and Wente (1962, pl. LI) = KRI V, 451–2. Year 10 Ramses III. **Bib.**: Allam (1973, 204–5); Helck (2002, 227); Janssen (2005, 28).

[61] Publication of the missing part of the O.Vienna H. 1 (= Černý, Notebook 114, 47–8).

19: O.Nicholson Museum R. 97.
Ed.: Eyre (1979, 88–9) = KRI VI, 151–2. Ramses III^{end}–Ramses IV.[62]

20: O.Turin N. 57381 [= O.Turin suppl. 9611].
Ed.: HOPR pl. 68–9; López (1978, pls. 119–119a) = KRI VII, 286–7. Year 18 Ramses III.
Bib.: Helck (2002, 238).

21: P.Berlin P 10496.
Ed.: HOPR pls. 80–4 = KRI V, 476–8. Year 21 and 24 Ramses III. **Bib.**: Blackman (1926, 177–81) and DeM-online (see the remarks about the hands of this documents).

This list—with select bibliography[63]—is intended merely as a survey of the documentary texts that have been tentatively attributed to Amennakhte by Egyptologists. With the identification of scribal hands being still highly problematic,[64] the methodological stance adopted here is the following: these documents can serve as a 'test corpus' in order to investigate whether the kinds of variation found within them correlate with the kinds of graphemic and linguistic variations found in the main corpus. However, I explicitly refrain from attributing these texts *en bloc* to Amennakhte.[65]

§4. GRAPHEMIC VARIATION: REGULARITY AND MOTIVATED VARIATIONS IN HIERATIC SPELLINGS

At first glance, the examination of this dimension of variation[66] might appear to be somewhat inadequate: the three documentary texts in the corpus must have been written by Amennakhte himself, but, setting aside any kind of palaeographical consideration, the literary texts might well be copies of Amennakhte's compositions made by other scribes. However, the variations between the witnesses of T1 at the graphemic level are limited, in both quantity and quality, so that we may quite safely infer that the scribes who copied such

[62] The reason why Helck (2002, 514) suggests dating this document to Year 16? of Ramses IX escapes me.

[63] Full bibliographical information may be found in the Deir el-Medina Database (http://www.leidenuniv.nl/nino/dmd/dmd.html).

[64] See, however, the interesting methodological suggestions made in van den Berg and Donker van Heel (2000) regarding the identification of handwritings, which would benefit from considering large palaeographical units.

[65] Issues linked with identification of hands in the material from Deir el-Medina during the Twentieth Dynasty are discussed in Dorn and Polis (2016).

[66] The research on this part of the paper has been facilitated by the use of the *Ramses* database developed at the University of Liège, which allows encoding of the hieroglyphic spellings; see Rosmorduc, Polis, and Winand (2009), Polis, Honnay, and Winand (2013), and Winand, Polis, and Rosmorduc (2015); see ramses.ulg.ac.be.

texts paid a great deal of attention to the formal side of their undertaking.[67] Inductively, it would be surprising if this were not to apply to other literary texts produced by Amennakhte. Hence, I consider all the spellings of the literary corpus to be representative of Amennakhte's own.

In this section, one will observe (1) the high degree of regularity of the spellings in Amennakhte's writings, (2) the importance of the iconic potential of the hieratic script through the analysis of some motivated variations of classifiers,[68] and (3) variations in the spellings that are characteristic of given genres and the result of Amennakhte's deliberate choice.

As a first illustration, one may examine the variation found within substantives.[69] If we exclude some marginal cases, such as the variation between (TA, 3.11) vs / (SG/PL systematic; *passim*), there is only one example of apparently unmotivated variation in the literary texts (143 lexemes; thirty-three occur in two texts or more [23 per cent]) and one example in the documentary texts (172 lexemes; thirty-two occur in two texts or more [18.6 per cent]):

- *ỉmw* 'boat' (T1L, 2; similar in other witnesses of T1) vs (T3, 5);
- *šgr* 'wooden ?box?' (TB, v° 5.15) vs (TB, v° 5.11), certainly due to a lexical borrowing.[70]

[67] Burkard (1977, 68–71 and 142–5) showed that the texts were not written to dictation but copied; see also McDowell (1996, 607) and the comment made by Parkinson (1999, 158).

[68] On the use of the term 'classifier' and its relevance for analysing the Ancient Egyptian writing system, see Goldwasser and Grinevald (2012) and Lincke and Kammerzell (2012).

[69] Proper names have been excluded here.

[70] See Janssen (1975, 200; 2009, 84), who does not acknowledge the spelling with *ḫꜣ*. The alternation between *ꜥl* (Wb. I, 208.11) and *ỉnr* (Wb. I, 97–8) is probably not to be considered as a case of graphemic variation within TB between a syllabic and an older spelling. Indeed, both lexemes are attested in Coptic, respectively ⲗⲗ 'pebble, stone' and ⲱⲛⲉ 'stone' (see Černý 1976, 4 and 228). The difference in the meaning of each word, however, is not self-evident in TB. In the same context, compare: *ḫr ptr, kfꜣ* PN_1 *ḥnꜥ* PN_2 *ꜥl* () *ḥr ṯbn n pꜣ ỉs n Wsỉr* PN_3 'but look, PN_1 and PN_2 removed a stone on the top of the tomb of the Osiris PN_3' (r° 4.4–6); *ḫr ptr=tn tꜣ s.t-ꜥḥꜥ* () *n ṯꜣty* PN *ḥr tꜣ s.t-ỉn ỉnr* () 'but you have seen (i.e. you are aware of) the position of the vizier PN regarding the removing of stones' (r° 4.10); *dỉ ꜥꜣ-n-ỉs.t* PN, *pꜣy=ỉ ỉt, rmṯ r ỉn(.t) ỉnr ỉm=s* 'the chief of the gang PN, my father, appointed someone to remove stones therein' (r° 4.11). Additionally, the phrase *ỉn ꜥl* (parallel to *ỉn ỉnr* in TB) appears in another document related to the violation of a tomb: *ptr n={tw}tn r ỉn ꜥl ỉm=f r-bnr* 'pay attention, you_{pl}, not to remove stones therefrom to the outside' (Block Edinburgh Society of Antiquities 912.3 [DZA 21.900.630]), and, judging from Crum (1939, 3–4), the meaning 'hail stone' is still well attested in Coptic for ⲗⲗ. It is worth noticing here that, besides other occurrences in the Ramesside period (P.Anastasi I, 23.3; 24.2; P.Mag.Harris, 4.7; O.Cairo CG 25651, v° 2.2–2.3; O.DeM 1038, v° 3, probably written by the *ỉdnw* Hay who was a contemporary of Amennakhte, see Dorn (2009, 77; 2011, 190–1)), sometimes related to Tomb Robberies (P.BM EA 10052, v° 14.4–5: *mtw=tw gm.t=ỉ ỉw dgs(=ỉ) pꜣy ꜥl m rd=ỉ, ỉw=f r tp-ḫt* 'if one discovers that I trampled this stone with my foot, I will be impaled'; Block Edinburgh Society of Antiquities 912.7 [DZA 21.900.640]), it occurs in the letter linked to Amennakhte's circle on the verso of P.Turin 1879 (I, 2.4; see Hovestreydt (1997) and here n. 59).

Except for these two cases, the spellings of the substantives are overwhelmingly regular. This phenomenon may be illustrated with three types of motivated variation at the graphemic level:

1. Number

   The singular vs plural number is spelled consistently (even when quite infrequent 'orthographies' are used for the plural). For example, *s.t* 'place' is written (both in literary and documentary texts) and the two occurrences of the plural are written the same way: (TA, rº 4.10 and TB, rº 4.4; another occurrence of this spelling is P.Anastasi IV, 4.9 (= LEM 39.5)).

2. Feminine writings

   The absolute vs suffixal states of the feminine substantives have different but coherent spellings. For example: *sbꜣy.t* 'teaching' (T1A, 1) vs *sbꜣy.t=k* 'your teaching' (T1A, 10; T1L, 5; etc.), here with the second person singular masculine suffix pronoun (2SGM)

3. The influence of the discursive environment

   The opposition between (TB *passim*, TC, b, vº 1) and (TB) is perfectly coherent. One always finds the first spelling in dates and the second when the lexeme is included in the main text; see, e.g., *twn ḥḳr.(wy)n, ỉw hrw 18 ʿḳ m pꜣ ꜣbd* ( ) 'we are hungry, the eighteenth day of the month is there (and no ration arrived)' (TB, rº 1.2).

   The opposition between (e.g. T1B, 2; TB *passim*; TC, b, vº 1, vº 7; etc.) and (e.g. T1N, 5; TB, rº 1.3, vº 2.9, 3.26, 3.29, 4.15; etc.), or (TC, rº 2, b, vº 8) and (TB *passim*), follows the strict distribution <title in headings and 'signatures'> (*sš* PN; when it is written, the classifier A1 appears after the PN) vs <title or function in the main text> (e.g. *pꜣ sš n pꜣ ḫr* 'the scribe of the Tomb', *ỉry=k sš* 'may you be a scribe', etc.).

   In TB, the word *ỉs.t* 'gang' (or) appears without the quad in the title *ꜥꜣ-n-ỉs.t* 'chief of the gang' solely; or are spellings found in the phrase *pꜣ-ꜥꜣ-n-ỉs.t 2*, see vº 2.9, 3.25, 3.28, 4.14; also occurs in *ꜥꜣ-n-ỉs.t* PN, see vº 6.6; rº 3.7, 4.2. When Amennakhte refers to the whole gang as such, in the noun phrase *tꜣ ỉs.t*, the classifiers of the seated man and the plural strokes are always present.[71]

Furthermore, it should be stressed that the writings of the substantives are consistent across genres (310 lexemes; 13 per cent (n = 40) occur both in literary and documentary texts): there is no significant variation of spellings between literary and documentary texts. This means that the degree of carefulness of the handwriting does not directly affect the spellings. Within the documentary texts, however, one observes an influence of cursive handwriting (e.g. *hrw* 'day'

[71] The only exception is to be found in a list of vº 4.16 (*tꜣ ỉs.t*), which deals with the quantity of vegetables that a gardener has to deliver. It should also be noted that is the only spelling attested in TA.

(TA, r° 1.3; also in T5, r° 1) → (e.g. TB, r° 1.1) → (e.g. TB, v° 6.6) → (e.g. TB, v° 8.7)) and processes of abbreviation (*ḥmty* 'copper' (TA, r° 5.7; TB, v° 5.18) → (TB, v° 5.4); *ḥry* 'superior' (TB, r° 4.16) → (e.g. TB, v° 3.5); *smn* 'price' (TB, v° 5.3) → (e.g. TB, v° 5.2); *smw* 'vegetable' (e.g. TB, v° 1.8) → (e.g. TB, v° 4.14)), which are virtually absent from the literary texts. Consequently, it clearly appears that the strong coherence and the high consistency of the spellings, pointing to the existence of—at least 'idiolectal'—writing conventions, would make the graphemic level a worthwhile criterion to investigate when arguing in favour for authorship.

The above-mentioned cases of variation already show that Amennakhte is likely to have had strong scribal habits when producing hieratic texts. It can be further demonstrated, through motivated variations in his use of classifiers, that he also exploited the iconic dimension of the hieratic script, thereby illustrating the fact that—much like the hieroglyphic script[72]—hieratic is not simply a way to write down a string of spoken language,[73] but a complex semiotic system in its own right.[74] The iconic potential of the hieratic writing system broached thereafter is an illustration of the importance of writing 'beyond its function as [a] vehicle of linguistic sequences'.[75]

Variations in classifiers are found in literary and documentary texts alike in order to specify the referent in context: (e.g. T1P, 3) vs (T5, 8); (T4, r° 8) vs (TC, 3) vs (e.g. T5, r° 1; TB, r° 2.4); (e.g. TB, r° 4.15; TC, 6) vs (TA, r° 2.1; TB, 1.x+16). The influence of the referent on the classifier is obvious in the alternation between (*ḫrd.w ꜥḥꜣwty.w* 'the male children', TA, r° 3.10) vs (*bn i͗.i͗n.tw tꜣy.i͗ 3 ḫrd.w ḥr.i͗* 'my three (female) children will not be allowed to go to court against me', TB, v° 6.4–5) vs (when the two genders are concerned; e.g. TA, r° 4.7; TB, r° 4.18); this observation remains true regardless of the genre under consideration. The specification of the referent through the use of a classifier may also reflect the selection of a particular meaning with polysemic lexemes; see, e.g., *ꜥ.wy* 'hands' or (T4, 6; T6, r° 3) vs *ꜥ* 'authority' (T6); *sbꜣy.t* 'teaching' or (e.g. T1A, 1 or T1K, 1) vs *sbꜣy.t* 'punishment' (*i͗.i͗r.tw n=f sbꜣy.t m pꜣ ꜥrḳ=f rn n pr-ꜥꜣ ꜥ.w.s i͗m* 'it is because of my (lit. his) swearing here by the name of Pharaoh l.p.h. that I (lit. he) will receive a punishment', TB, r° 2.10).

With very few exceptions (see the two cases above), we do not encounter cases of free variation at the graphemic level when studying the spellings of the substantives in Amennakhte's corpus. We mostly have to deal with conventionalized spellings or motivated variations.

[72] See especially Loprieno (2001).

[73] Another cogent example for the period is the discrimination in writing between two individuals called *Mꜣꜣ-nḫtw=f* (see Dorn (2006)), which has been discussed by Loprieno (2006, 167).

[74] See already the comments in Broze (1996, 129–56), with previous literature on the topic, regarding the 'manipulations graphiques' and their consistency in the tale of Horus and Seth, which undoubtedly point to a very high degree of elaboration of the written performance.

[75] Loprieno (2006, 167).

As has been stressed, the genres do have a minimal influence on the spellings of the substantives. As far as this distinction is concerned, no conclusion can apparently be drawn from the graphemic level of variation. However, Amennakhte's habit of writing the second person masculine singular suffix pronoun is worth investigating further in this respect. Indeed, the alternation between the spellings , , and (or the like) of this pronoun appears to be overwhelmingly regular and might be symptomatic both of literary registers and of an 'idiolectal' conception of the syntagmatic environments where each of these spellings occurs.

The spelling is the usual spelling of the second person masculine singular suffix pronoun[76] but, in a proportion of approximately 1 to 3, two other types of spellings occur:

1. *ky*

 ky is consistently used after dual inflexions: *ỉr.ty=ky* 'your eyes' (T1A, 4 (= T1B, 7 = T1J, 1 = T1K, 5–6); T3, 7; T4, 5); *ʿ.wy=ky* 'your arms' (T4, 6). This infrequent spelling of the suffix pronoun, which occurs most of the time in monumental contexts (in phrases like *ẖr ṯb.ty=ky* 'under your feet', e.g. in Urk. IV, 1661.5, 1754.7; KRI I, 96.13, etc. or *ẖr rd.wy=ky* 'under your legs', e.g. in KRI II, 249.12), is also attested once in a parallel version to P.Anastasi I, 19.4–5 (O.DeM 1005+1662, 7: *ʿ.wy=ky*), as well as in a parallel version to P.Anastasi IV, 3.4 (O.Gardiner 28, vº 1: *ỉr.ty=ky*), and, strikingly, three times in the P.Chester Beatty IV (vº 4.9: *rd.wy=ky*; vº 4.12 and 5.2: *ʿ.wy=ky*).

2.

 (with its variants and) is a hieratic spelling usually considered[77] to have been influenced by the first person singular ending of the Stative (also known as Pseudo-Participle inflexion in Late Egyptian).[78] This 'long' spelling is characteristic of the literarily elaborated registers that one finds in the wisdom literature *sensu lato*,[79] in the Love Songs and in the Laudes Urbis, as well as in the closely related registers of the didactic literature[80] during the Ramesside period. If we add to this corpus some ten examples coming from other literary compositions (such as P.Raifé-Sallier III, Two Brothers (1 ex.: 14.6), Horus and Seth (2 exx.: 7.7 and 15.2)), the number of occurrences of the long spelling of the suffix pronoun is 147 vs 20 (88 per cent) in favour of the 'literary'

[76] Unfortunately, the 2SG.M suffix pronoun occurs only once in the non-literary corpus, i.e. in TB, rº 2.14.

[77] After Erman (1933, §65–7) who has given the fullest description of the phenomenon to date.

[78] It should be noted that, in the texts where the long spelling of the 2SGM suffix pronoun occurs, the full spelling of the first person pseudo-participle ending represents less than 50 per cent of the attestations.

[79] See, e.g., P.Anastasi I (twenty occurrences), Teaching of Ani (nine occurrences in P.Boulaq 4), P.Chester Beatty IV, Menna's Laments, Prohibitions.

[80] See, e.g., P.Lansing (with O.DeM 1044 and O.Florence 2619); P.Anastasi II; P.Anastasi IV (with O.Gardiner 28); P.Anastasi V; P.Koller; P.Leiden 348; P.Turin A, B, and D; T.Brussels E. 580.

registers. The main syntactic environments in which these spellings appear in the whole Late Egyptian corpus are:

- After plurisyllabic prepositions (like *r-ḥꜣ.t*, *r-ḥr*, *m-bꜣḥ*, *m-ẖmt*, *m-dỉ*, *ḥnʿ*).
- After some substantives (especially with dual inflexions[81]).
- After *sḏm=f* forms (mainly as subject of the Perfective and the Subjunctive[82]).

When occurring in documentary texts,[83] spellings like are mostly found in the introductory formulae of letters and in letters to superiors (probably to be understood in relation to diastratic variation) down to the reign of Ramses III.[84] Consequently, even if some phonological motivations may originally lie behind the use of this spelling,[85] it is safe to assume that the spelling of the 2SG.M suffix pronoun became somehow indexical of the more formal registers. It is therefore not surprising to find it in literary texts by Amennakhte.

Moreover, the syntactic environments in which the long spelling occurs in Amennakhte's corpus display some interesting regularities. Unlike in the other texts of the Late Egyptian corpus, it does not occur after prepositions, but it does occur as:

- the possessive pronoun after three substantives: *Ḥꜣty=k* 'your heart' (T1B, 10,[86] T3, 2)[87]; *sẖr.w=k* 'your course of action' (T1L, 3); *rn=k* 'your name' (T3, 3);
- the subject of the (mostly dependent) Subjunctive (*ʿm=k* (T1A, 5 = T1B, 8 = T1K, 6, similar spelling in P.BM EA 10326, vº 17: *r dỉ.t ʿm=k* 'in order that you know'); *mdw=k* (T1A, 6 = T1B, 11; similar spelling in O.DeM 1108, 4: *ḫft mdw=k* 'when you speak'), *pẖr.k* (T1B, 12), *rwỉ.k* (T1L, 11), *sḥḏ=k* (T6, rº

[81] See, e.g., *ʿ.wy=k*: P.Anastasi I, 19.4; *ʿnḫ.wy=k*: O.DeM 1253, 2.3; *ꜣḫ.ty=k*: O.Turin 6618, 6; *ỉr.ty=k*: O.DeM 1616, 3.8; *rd.wy=k*: P.Harris 500, rº 6–7.12.

[82] Less often as the object of the infinitive (fifteen occurrences); see the examples already quoted in Erman (1933, §65).

[83] Sometimes also in older constructions, such as the negative perfective *bw sḏm=f* in O.DeM 554, 4.

[84] See, e.g., P.Northumberland I, rº 4 and vº 2; O.DeM 581, 3–4; P.Cairo CG 58059, 2; P.Brooklyn 37.903 L, 5. Later occurrences of the long spelling of the 2SGM suffix pronoun are very infrequent. Note that, among the clear cases of long writings in non-literary texts after Ramses III (see P.Mallet, 6.11 and P.Mayer A, vº 9.19), three occurrences come from Dhutmose's letters (P.BM EA 10326, rº 15 and vº 17; P.BN 196 II, vº 3).

[85] See Erman (1933, §67). The long spelling is never used with monosyllabic prepositions like *n* (maybe with the exception of P.Harris 500, rº 6–7.3), *m*, *r*, or *ỉw* (in Amennakhte's literary corpus, see the short spelling in T5, 5: *ỉw=k r nḥḥ* 'you will last forever') and *mtw*.

[86] But in T1A.

[87] For this spelling, see also P.BM EA 10326, 15 (= LRL 18.7): *m dy ḥꜣty=k m-sꜣ=ỉ m md.t nb* 'do not worry about me regarding anything' and P.BN 196 II, vº 3 (= LRL 22.2).

6)) and of *rḫ*[88] in the negative construction *bw rḫ.k*  in a circumstantial clause (T1A, 15; same construction and spelling in P.Turin D, 2.4 = LEM 131.7).

In conclusion, it might be argued that, given the observed regularities, the spelling of the 2SGM suffix pronoun could be used as an interesting criterion with which to corroborate the attribution of a literary text to Amennakhte or, more broadly, to Amennakhte's 'school'. Indeed, if the explanation of the affinity of the long spelling with specific lexemes and restricted syntactic environments remains open to further investigation, the combination in a text of the spelling  after dual inflexions and of the spelling  (or ) after the Subjunctive (and some substantives) could be taken as a worthwhile criterion. Quite interestingly, this happens at least in two didactic compositions: O.Gardiner 28 (= HO CXIII, 1; a copy of P.Anastasi IV, 3.4–4.7) and, strikingly, P.Chester Beatty IV, v°, which, as mentioned earlier (see above §2), has been tentatively attributed to Amennakhte himself by Posener based on internal thematic criteria as well as geographic and diachronic compatibility between the manuscripts. Of course, this criterion is not sufficient in itself, but rather should be taken as an indication that this possibility actually holds.[89]

§5. DIAPHASIC VARIATION: A MULTIDIMENSIONAL APPROACH TO REGISTER ANALYSIS

In order to examine the variation between the registers used by Amennakhte when composing texts belonging to different genres and to show thereby, through the various selections that he deliberately made within the scribal repertoire of his time, his full mastery of the writing conventions, I will first focus on the types and distributions ('register features') of the main predicative constructions attested in each text of the corpus.[90] In a second step, other distinctive linguistic features ('register markers') will be acknowledged so as to

[88] This spelling is to be related to the rather frequent long spellings of the 2SGM suffix pronoun when it is the subject of the dependent subjunctive of *rḫ* in the construction *rdỉ.t rḫ*; see, e.g., O.DeM 289, 1: *dỉ=ỉ rḫ=k pꜣ ktḫ ỉṯꜣy <m> pr ỉ pwy*; O.Petrie 92, r° 5 (= HO 42.1); P.Koller, 5.7 (= LEM 120, 14); O.Gardiner 86, 2; P.Leiden 348, v° 10.1 (= LEM 136.10). See also P.Boulaq 4, 17.7: *nn rḫ=k ḏd sw* 'when it is impossible for you to express them (properly) [i.e. the words]'. This last example is to be added to the examples dealt with in Polis (2011).

[89] The text, usually attributed to the early Twentieth Dynasty in Thebes (see, e.g., Quirke (1996, 382)), should be systematically compared with Amennakhte's production. See also the thematic proximity between P.Chester Beatty IV, v° 4.8 and T3 noted in Vernus (2010, 491).

[90] In the corpus under investigation, I consider that a single register is used in each text, admittedly simplifying things quite a bit.

suggest a more fine-grained picture of variation between registers during the first part of the Twentieth Dynasty.

Given the relatively small size of the corpus, one has to use both qualitative and quantitative criteria in the analysis of linguistic features responsible for register variation.[91] Accordingly, the predicative constructions will be envisioned both in terms of types (i.e. occurrence vs non-occurrence of a construction) and in terms of distribution (i.e. percentage of occurrence of each construction).

As shown in Figure 5.1, the range of predicative constructions[92] attested in Amennakhte's corpus is relatively wide. One finds predicative constructions (verbal morphology included) that are: (a) characteristic of Late Egyptian (left of the chart); (b) common to Late Egyptian and *Égyptien de tradition* (centre of the chart); and (c) inherited from Earlier Egyptian, but no longer productive in Late Egyptian (right of the chart). Consequently, the texts may be arranged according to the types of predicative constructions that occur in their respective registers; this corresponds to different parts of the scale of written formality:

- The registers of T1 and T5–6 filter out the more recent constructions that are strongly indexical of the lower part of the formality scale (periphrastic constructions with *ỉrỉ*, Future III, Sequential, and Conjunctive). Additionally, the selections within the repertoire in the registers of T1 and T5 are oriented towards the higher part of the formality scale, which is illustrated by the occurrences of constructions that are no more productive in the documentary corpus of the time.
- T2 and T3 are literary compositions whose registers are largely open to constructions that entered the written repertoire during the New Kingdom. The small size of these two texts prevents additional conclusions, but they seem not to be entirely closed to constructions belonging to the older, more formal, part of the repertoire.
- The documentary registers of TA and TB are, as expected, fully open to the latest development of the written language of the time and closed to the older constructions and verbal morphology typical of Earlier Egyptian.

The continuum of distinct selections in the available written repertoire is therefore nicely illustrated by the analysis of the types of predicative constructions

[91] It is worth noticing that the present approach relies on linguistic features only in distinguishing registers. This means that one of the more effective criteria for register distinction, namely the lexical similarities between texts belonging to the same genre (which result from the influence of common situational features), has been left out of the present study. For this kind of approach, see Gohy, Martin Leon, and Polis (2013).

[92] For the sake of clarity, the participles and relative forms have been excluded from the chart because of the important number of different morphological units. Their interest for the identification of registers is, however, beyond any doubt. One might think, for example, of the high frequency of the construction [INF. *ỉr.n* NP] in legal and administrative documents.

	i.ir.t=f sḏm	Fut. III	Sequential	Conjunctive	*i.ir=f sḏm* (emph.)	Infinitive (narr.)	Perfective		Imperative		Subjunctive		Present I			Adj. Pred.	Subst. Pred.	Exist. Pred.	(*i.*)*sḏm=f* (emph.)	*bw* (*ir=f*) *sḏm*(*=f*)	2nd Pred.	*iw=f r* NP	*mrr.f*	*sḏm=f* (imperf.)	*sḏm.n.f*
							+	-	+	-	+	-	inf.	psp.	adv.										
T1							2		9	3	16		4	3	5	4	4	2	1	4	3	2	1		1
T5							4				2		3	19	6	1		1			1	1		2	
T6									2		12	1		1	4		2	1							
T2					1				1		1		1	1	3	2		1						1	
T3				2	1				1				4		2	1	1								
TA		10	1		1		5	1			2		2	1	1		1								
TB	1	9	15	10	6	29	24	1	7	2	17	7	17	7	14	1	4	8	3						

Fig. 5.1. Predicative constructions (and verbal morphology) in the main texts of Amennakhte's corpus (only the constructions whose analysis suffers little or no doubt have been included in the chart)

in the corpus. This observation alone shows the inadequacy[93] of Groll's approach to the literary verbal system in Late Egyptian, for she did not properly recognize that the Late Egyptian literary texts never constituted a homogenous linguistic system, but rather a continuum of registers on the formality scale.[94]

The analysis in terms of types of predicative constructions could create the impression that, roughly speaking, the registers of T1 and T5 are similar, as are the ones of T2, T3, TA, and TB. In fact, this may be proven inaccurate by taking into consideration the statistical distribution of the constructions in terms of type-token frequency. In order to make this point clear, I will succinctly limit the discussion to the differences between the registers of T1 and T5, but the same obviously holds, even if to a different extent, for the other texts.

In T1 (see Figure 5.2), one observes a sharp dominance of verbal morphology with manipulative function: together, the Imperative and the Subjunctive represent approximately 45 per cent of the predicative constructions. The high proportion of verbal forms with such function is ultimately linked to the situational features of the register under examination, i.e. that of a teaching, the aim of which is to give advice and instructions to a pupil in an elaborated literary composition.

The variety of other predicative patterns is also to be mentioned, for it reflects both the opening of T1's register to constructions that belong to strata of the repertoire that are common to literary and documentary texts, but also strong intertextual relationships with the linguistic material of the past in related genres.[95] This explains some of the occurrences of linguistics features belonging to the higher part of the formality scale in the register of T1.

Figure 5.3, on the other hand, shows that, even if the registers of T1 and T5 are quite similar with respect to the types of predicative constructions selected, the

[93] See, inter alios, Quack (1994, Introduction).

[94] This does not mean that the literary registers do not display a cohesive behaviour with respect to other linguistic features.

[95] See Dorn (2004, 50–5). For *tr wnn=k* in T1A, 11 (and other witnesses), certainly add Ptahotep P 7.9–10: *šms ib=k tr n wnn=k* 'follow your heart as long as you live'.

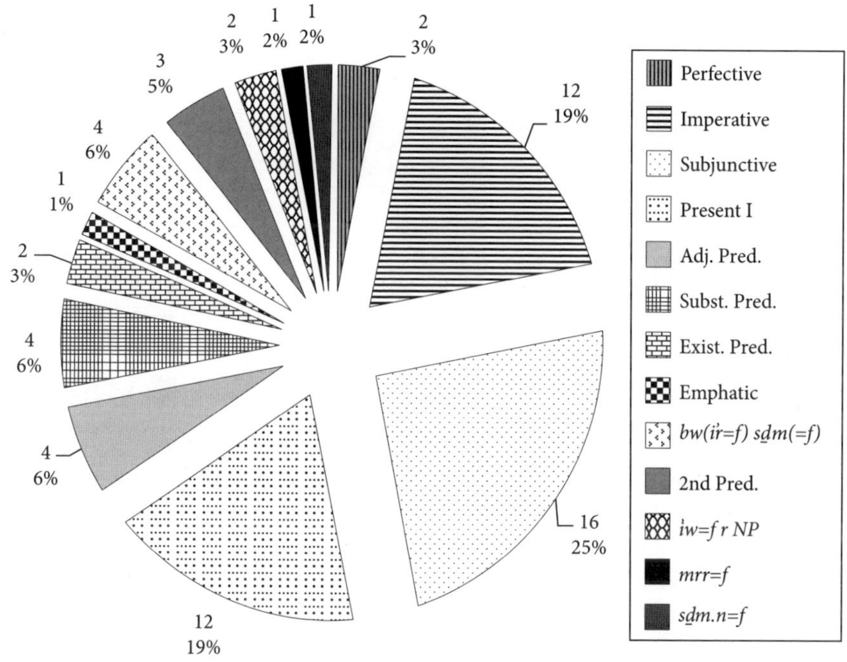

Fig. 5.2. Distribution of the predicative constructions in T1

distribution of this dimension of variation differs substantially between the two registers: the range of predicative constructions is lower and, crucially, the verbal paradigms with solely manipulative function are absent. The description of the recently reinstalled peace and joy in this encomium of Ramses IV leads to a statistically striking over-representation of the Present I with Stative predicates.

This short case study is intended to illustrate the fact that the identification of a register depends not only on the occurrence vs non-occurrence of an individual feature, but also on the relative frequency of features among the various registers. Moreover, the predicative constructions of the registers of T1 and T5 are, to be sure, not representative of this dimension of variation in the registers of the teachings and encomia in general. Only a large-scale and quantitative investigation of these genres would allow refinement of the figure.

Another way to account for the continuum of selections in the written scribal repertoire is to analyse the distribution of the 3PL suffix pronoun. As is well known, the new suffix pronoun =*w* supersedes the suffix pronoun =*sn* during the Ramesside Period. Winand[96] showed that the older pronoun =*sn* is not replaced at the same pace in every syntactic position by the more recent suffix pronoun =*w*. The spread of the new suffix pronoun =*w* was apparently quicker

[96] Winand (1995a, 193–5), with previous literature.

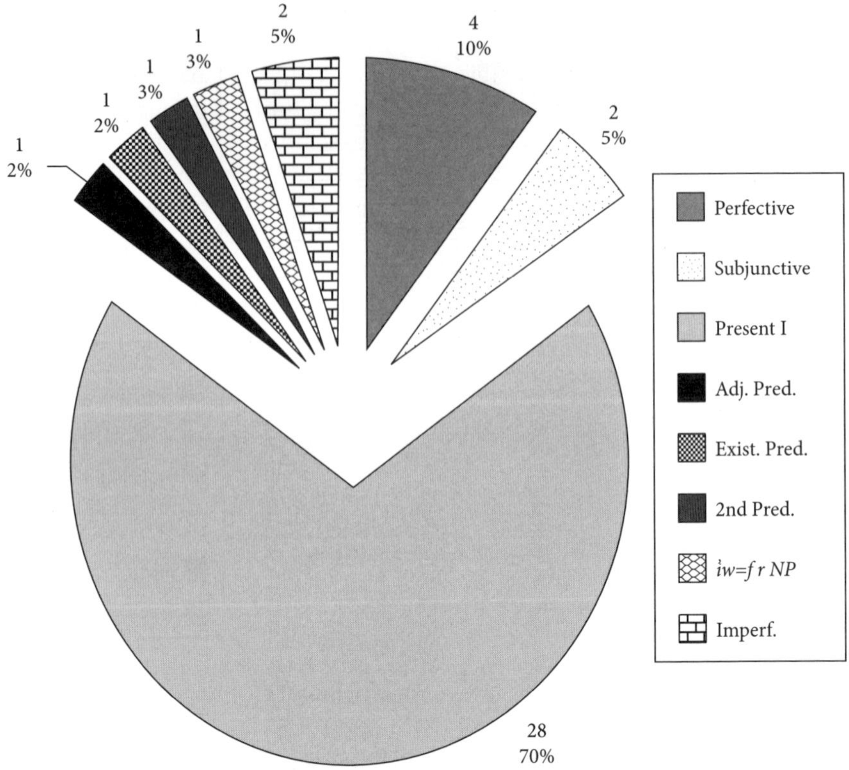

Fig. 5.3. Distribution of the predicative constructions in T5

after *ỉw* and definitely after the infinitive (*status pronominalis*). In the documentary corpus that he investigated, the replacement is almost completed by the beginning of the Twentieth Dynasty: under Ramses III, *=sn* is limited to two environments, namely after prepositions (two occurrences; 18 per cent) and after *ỉw* (two occurrences; 5 per cent).

The distribution of these two pronouns in Amennakhte's corpus is worth looking at in several respects and, even if the figures are very low, some tentative observations may be put forward (see Figure 5.4). Among the literary registers, the ones of T1 and T5 are the more conservative: the occurrences (2) of the 3PL suffix pronoun in T1 are realized with the older form and T5 retains *=sn* as the subject of the *sḏm=f* forms,[97] as well as in the possessive determiner *nꜣy=sn*. This correlates with the above-mentioned distribution of the predicative

[97] One notices that these two cases of *=sn* (r° 5 and 6) occur after the old imperfective *sḏm=f* form. Do we have to posit a relation between the occurrence of older verbal morphology and the appearance of the older suffix pronoun? This hypothesis might be corroborated by the fact that the sole occurrence of *=sn* in TB after a verbal form is with the quotative verb *ỉ.n=sn* 'they said' (r° 2.17).

construction: both texts use registers that are manifestly very high on the formality scale.

In the registers of the other literary texts, the set of acceptable syntactic positions for the suffix pronoun *=w* is larger, since one finds no occurrence of *=sn* in these texts. This is puzzling considering the fact that *=sn* occurs both in TA and TB and calls for two comments. First, as stated above, during the Twentieth Dynasty, some literary registers are amply opened to the latest evolutions of the written repertoire; this case is nothing but a direct illustration of the phenomenon. Second, we might be dealing here with real-time diachrony and the evolution of the habits of one scribe. Indeed, even if we have no idea about the dates of composition of T2 and T7, both T6 and TA[98] were composed and written down several years after TB. This explanation is to be treated with caution, but it should be kept in mind as a working hypothesis.

The two dimensions of register variation broached to this point are sufficient to demonstrate the necessity of conceptualizing registers as a continuous rather than discrete construct by putting the focus of the analysis on the relative distribution of common linguistic features.

Some other linguistic features—while maybe not strong enough to be considered 'register markers' strictly speaking, i.e. distinctive indicators of a register[99]—are definitely characteristic of some registers, as opposed to others in the investigated corpus. As opposed to the other texts, T1 and T6 use the old spelling of one negation: *nn* (strongly indexical of the higher part of the formality

		Inf.	Subst.	*ỉw*	(*ỉ.*)*sḏm=f*	Poss.	Preposition		
							m/r/mỉ-ḳd	*ḥr*	*n*
T1	*=sn*				1				1
	=w								
T5	*=sn*				2	1			
	=w		3	1					
T6	*=sn*								
	=w				1				3
T2	*=sn*								
	=w		1	1	1		1		2
T7	*=sn*								
	=w				1		1		
TB	*=sn*			1	1			1	12
	=w	5	2	7	4	1	1	1	
TA	*=sn*								1
	=w	1		7	2	2	3		1

Fig. 5.4. Distribution of the 3PL suffix pronouns in the corpus

[98] For the sole occurrence of *=sn* in TA as a possible trace of formality and written norm, see bullet number 1, p119.

[99] See Biber (1995, 28–9).

scale, see T1A, 6 (= B, 10) and T1A, 14 (= T1L, 8); T6, rº 5–6), instead of the regular Late Egyptian negation *bn* , which occurs both in other literary (T5, 5) and documentary texts (eighteen occurrences, never *nn*).

The topicalizing particle *ỉr* 'as for' is avoided in literary registers. In T5, one finds: ø *nꜣ ḫꜣr.wt, pr.{t}w wn* 'the widows, their houses are open' (see also T5, 6); in T1A, 6 (= B, 10), ø *smỉ ꜥꜣ, nn sw r s.t=f* 'an arrogant announcement is out of place'. In the documentary registers, on the other hand, the topicalizing particle is systematically present: *ỉr ỉnk, ỉnk nmḥ n pꜣ tꜣ n pr-ꜥꜣ* 'as for me, I am a free woman of the land of Pharaoh' (TA, 2.1); *ỉr pꜣ wꜣḥ nb ḏr.t=f |ḥr ḏr.t=ỉ| ỉm=w, ỉw=ỉ r dỉ.t n=f ꜣḫ.t=ỉ* 'whoever among them has been a helping hand, I will give him my goods' (TA, 2.6); *ỉr pꜣ nty bwpw=f dỉ.t n=ỉ, bn ỉw=ỉ r dỉ.t n=f m ꜣḫ.t=ỉ* 'as for he who did not give me (anything), I will not give him anything of my goods' (TA, 2.7); *ỉr pꜣ[y] 4 ẖrd.w ỉnk <bn> ỉw=w r ꜥḳ r pšs.t m ꜣḫ.t=ỉ nb.t* 'as for these four children of mine, they will not have a part of any of my goods' (4.7; sim. in 3.7, 4.9, rº 5.1 and 5.3); *ỉr pꜣy=tn ḏd* (…) 'concerning your[PL] saying (…)' (TB, rº 3.1–2). This opposition between literary and documentary registers does not seem to suffer any exception.

In the literary registers, the morpheme *ỉw* is avoided for introducing circumstantial clauses of non-existence[100] (see, e.g., the virtual circumstantial clauses in T1A, 15 (= T1L, 9); T5, 6–7: *bn pꜣ nwḥ* 'there is no more hauling';[101] and T6, rº 5–6), as well as before the adjunctal stative that is left unconverted[102] in T1A, 3 (*nḏm zp-2 gm z ỉp m kꜣ.t nb.t* 'it is really pleasant to find a man able in every work') and in the other witnesses, except for T1K, 3–4, which resorts to the converted construction *ỉw=f ỉp m kꜣ.t nb.t* 'who is able in every work'.

Finally, lexical diversity is a dimension of variation that deserves close attention when adopting a multidimensional approach to register analysis. Indeed, the richness of the lexical stock, which is typically captured by the type token ratio V/N,[103] is expected to vary across genres and registers.[104] A simple example that focuses on the adjectival category will be sufficient here in order to illustrate the line of reasoning.

[100] In this respect, the occurrences of the negative relative converter *ỉwty* in T1 (e.g. K, 15: *ỉwty ỉr.t=f* 'the one without discernment [lit. who has no eye]') and T2.4 (*ỉwty ḥbs.w=f* 'the one without clothes') is to be pointed out. However, the vitality of the *ỉwty* morph in demotic and Coptic (especially the host-class expansion of the *ỉwty*-constructions) should warn us against identifying it as a sign of formality (diatopic parameters of variation might possibly be relevant in this case).

[101] On the so-called 'predicative *bn*', see Vernus (1985, especially pp. 155–63 dealing with the construction *bn* + definite subject).

[102] In a similar vein, the definite article *pꜣ* seems to be expressly filtered out in some specific syntactic environments, e.g. before substantival occurrences of the infinitive; see T1A, 3 and 12 (with the other witnesses: *nḏm [zp-2] gm* + OBJ. and *nḏm ḳnḳn*) vs T3, 3 (*nfr.wỉ n=k pꜣ |ꜥš| rn=k*).

[103] Where *V* is the size of the vocabulary of the text and *N* is the number of tokens of the same text; see, e.g., Stamatatos, Fakotakis, and Kokkinakis (2001, 474–5 and 481–2).

[104] A first study of this dimension of register variation in Late Egyptian is proposed in Gohy, Martin Leon, and Polis (2013), where it is used as an effective heuristic device in automatic text categorization.

	Word	Token	Percentage	Type
T1	331	12	3.6%	10
T3	83	3	3.6%	2
T5	195	7	3.5%	5
T6	166	5	3%	4
T7	76	2	2.6%	2
T4	61	1	1.6%	1
T2	81	1	1.2%	1
TB	2074	15	0.72%	6
TA	536	2	0.37%	2

Fig. 5.5. Frequency of occurrence of the adjectival part-of-speech

There are nineteen different 'adjectives' attested in the corpus (among which four occur both in literary and documentary texts: *wr*, *ꜥꜣ*, *nfr*, and *ṯꜣy*): fourteen of them are used in T1–7 and eight in TA–C. As is shown in Figure 5.5 (and even if the shortness of the texts is likely to be responsible for uncontrolled statistical variation), the literary registers are characterized by a higher text frequency of the adjectives than the documentary registers, at least in a proportion of 2 to 1 (but more significantly in most cases). Moreover, there is a clear tendency towards high frequency of adjectives in the registers of the compositions that have been characterized as more formal according to the previous dimensions of register variation (especially T1 and T5), which is probably to be understood as a sign of literary elaboration.[105] Hence, the interest of a multidimensional approach to register variation is again made quite obvious: different linguistic features, when considered together, can help gain a more accurate description of the registers.

The various case studies that have been presented above deal with a restricted number of features, and a proper description of the registers would require taking into consideration both other parameters of variation and as many texts as possible for each register. However, this caveat has no impact on the present argument, for the methodological point to be made is the fundamental usefulness of such a multidimensional approach to Ancient Egyptian registers. Indeed, it shows that an individual scribe, depending on the circumstances of production, was able to play with different parts of the written repertoire that belong to different diachronic strata of the Egyptian language.

[105] We would reach similar conclusions studying the type-token ratio of the prepositions in the corpus. One may notice, for example, that the two poems of the O.Gardiner 25 (T2 and T3) attest eight different prepositions, among which six also occur in the documentary corpus (75 per cent). The Teaching of Amennakhte (T1), on the other hand, has thirteen different prepositions, but only six of them also appear in TA–TC (46 per cent).

§6. WRITTEN CONVENTIONS AND STANDARDIZED REGISTERS

Up to this point, the important issue of standardization, conventionalization, or levelling of the written performance has been left almost untouched, beyond the different types of conventions at the graphemic level that were studied in §4. In this section, I briefly discuss two other kinds of regularities in Amennakhte's writings, pertaining respectively to the graphemo-morphological and constructional levels. These could point to the existence of a somewhat normative conception that Amennakhte—consciously or not—had of written performance.[106]

(a) The imperative plural of *ỉwỉ* 'to come'[107] is systematically written with the grapheme  or  representing the phoneme /n/ in Amennakhte's corpus:[108] *myn*  'come^PL' (T6, r° 2; the referent is likely to be *nṯr.w nb.w* in r° 1; see also *myn*  in r° 6); *myn* () *r-ẖnw* 'come^PL (back) inside' (TB, r° 1.4). This contrasts with the spellings of the imperative singular, where the is not written,[109] see T1L, 14 () and T7, v° 7: *my* () *ỉry.k ḥb* 'come to celebrate'.

The second person plural imperative of *ỉwỉ* does not occur very frequently in the Late Egyptian corpus *sensu lato*, but, when it does, it is usually written with the grapheme  or as in Amennakhte's texts:[110] *myn* () *r-ḥnꜥ=ỉ, dỉ=tn n=ỉ ḏr.t* 'Come^PL next to me in order to help me [lit. to give me a hand]' (P.Anastasi I, 5.7); *mꜣꜥ.ty nb, myn* () *mꜣꜣ=tn* (. . .) 'every righteous man, come^PL so to see (. . .)' (P.Sallier I, 8.9 (= LEM 86.14–15)); *myn* (), *ỉry=n n=f nꜣy=f ḥb.w n.w p.t* 'come^PL, let us celebrate for it its festivals of heaven' (P.Anastasi III, 2.11 (= LEM 22.12–13)); *myn r-dr=w*  'Come^PL you all (so that we give praise to him together)' (Medinet Habu, Great Inscription of

[106] I suggest below that one way of showing the conventionalized nature of some registers is to observe the relaxing of the scribe's attention in the course of writing a text.

[107] For the existence of an isomorphic imperative for *ỉwỉ* 'to come', see the arguments for and against respectively in Schweitzer (2008) and Quack (2004).

[108] See also O.IFAO 1255 A, r° 5 to be published by P. Grandet. This case is to be distinguished from the imperatives plural written with the plural strokes [Z2], like in *hꜣb* (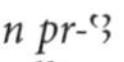) *n pr-ꜥꜣ* 'write^PL to Pharaoh!' (TB, r° 2.4). Indeed, it is difficult to ascertain whether this kind of spelling refers to an underlying phonological reality (compare *ḏd* [] *sw m-mꜣꜥ.t* 'say^PL it truly' (TB, r° 2.17) with *m ỉr snỉ* [] *r mry.t* 'do^PL not cross in direction of the riverbank' (TB, r° 3.11)) or is merely a graphemic device that specifies the plurality of the form. The same kind of problem holds for the distinction between the masculine  (or the like) and the feminine  (see, e.g., LES 48.16: *mỉ n=ỉ mw.t ꜣs.t tꜣy=ỉ mw.t* 'come to me, mother Isis, my mother'; P.BM EA 9997, IV 4: *mỉ r-ḥnꜥ-ỉ* 'come with me') of the singular. Whether such spellings relate to the opposition between ⲁⲙⲟⲩ (masc.) and ⲁⲙⲏ (fem.) in Coptic remains an open question. On this issue, see Erman (1933, §354) and Junge (2001, 81).

[109] In P.Turin CG 54051, compare similarly §4.22 (pl. ) with §11.6 (sg. ).

[110] See Erman (1933, §354 and 362), Caminos (1954, 79), Černý and Groll (1993, 348), and Wb. II, 35.15–17.

Year 8 (= KRI V, 38.7–8)); *myn* () *r tꜣ mry.t* 'come^{PL} to the riverbank' (O.Cairo CG 25264, 4); *myn n=ỉ* ()[111] *ḥm.wt-nswt, sꜣ.t-nswt, sn.wt-nswt* 'come^{PL} to me, royal wives, royal princesses, and royal sisters' (Piankhy, l. 34). Examples of this spelling of the imperative before the reign of Ramses II are highly infrequent (see possible cases such as *my* () *mꜣꜣ=tn mnw nfr wꜥb* 'come^{PL} so as to see the beautiful and pure monument', Urk. IV, 862, 12;[112] however cf. n. 108), but they become more and more usual after the New Kingdom[113] and are beyond any doubt to be related to the Coptic ⲁⲙⲱⲓⲛⲓ (Bohairic), ⲁⲙⲟⲓⲛⲓ (Fayumic), and ⲁⲙⲏ(ⲉ)ⲓⲛⲉ (Akhmimic).[114] During the Ramesside period, 2PL imperatives of *ỉwỉ* (with *n*) do apparently occur almost exclusively in the higher registers (e.g. monumental performance, literary texts, and didactic literature) before spreading down to the lower part of the formality scale. Interestingly, and even if it remains difficult to prove given the low density of the documentation, Amennakhte might have acted as an actual agent in systematizing this spelling in the documentary texts.

(b) Winand notes '[c]omme pour le séquentiel, c'est la disparition progressive de la préposition *ḥr* qui constitue le fait le plus marquant dans le paradigme du présent I.'[115] This general observation is unquestionable, but one of the interests of a small-scale approach to linguistic variation is that one can sometimes refine the picture by focusing on micro-level phenomena of motivated (or at least recurrent) patterns of variation. In Amennakhte's corpus, the preposition *ḥr* is always written in the *independent* occurrences of the analytical construction of the Present I with infinitival predicate (see, e.g., *twk ḥr ỉr.t msꜥy.w n bnw* 'you are doing expeditions worthy of a millstone' (T3, 4–5); *twk ḥr ỉr.t ḳd.w n ỉmw* 'you are doing the round trip of a boat' (T3, 5); *st ḥr sꜥḳ mšꜥy.w, nꜣ ẖnm.wt ḥr nhm ḥr ḏd nꜣy=sn ẖn.w n hnhn* 'they let the travellers enter, the childminders are thrilled while singing their lullabies' (T5, 5); *ptr twỉ ḥr ḏd n=tn tꜣy=ỉ wšb.t* 'behold, I am giving you my stance' (TB, rº 4, 21; see also rº 3.7); *ḫr ptr, bn st ḥr ỉr.t ḫr.t=ỉ gr ỉnk* 'and, see, they are not looking after me in my turn'). It is never written in *dependent* circumstantial syntactic position (namely after *ỉw*; as second predicate *ḥr* is written, see T5.5 quoted above), e.g.: *ỉ.ỉr.w wrš ỉw.w* (*ḥr*) *ssm.t m rn.s* 'they do nothing else but moan all the day long in her name' (T2, 1–2); *ỉ.ỉr.tw swhꜣ pꜣ nty mỉ-ḳd.k, ỉw.f* (*ḥr*) *ỉr.t bỉꜣ.t ꜥꜣ.t* 'one mentions the one like you only because of the extremeness of his character' (T3, 5–6);

[111] See Logan and Westenholz (1972, 112–13). The emendation into *mỉ.<t>n* suggested by Grimal (1981, 63 n. 146) escapes me.

[112] Similar spelling without the *n* occurs in P.Leiden I 343, rº 3.12: *my n=ỉ zp-2*  'come to me, come to me'; see also Kadesh §161 (L2, 42). In Ptolemaic texts, Kurth (2008, 751–3) also mentions, next to a 'Form *mj.n*', the occurrences of a 'Form *mjw*', with spellings such as , , and 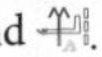.

[113] See Spiegelberg (1925, 98–9 (§216)); Sauneron (1952, 50–1, with previous literature); Lustman (1999, 86 (§14.1.2)), who signals also one occurrence of  after the imperative of *šms* (I owe this reference to J. F. Quack).

[114] See Crum (1939, 7b).

[115] Winand (1992, 413).

ỉw.k (ḥr) ỉr.t pꜣ nty ỉm 'while you act as someone yonder'; *ỉw=w (ḥr) ḥṯ ḥr nḫ̮n ṯꜣy msy.w n hꜣỉ nfr* 'while they are taking care of the full term male children' (T5, 5[116]). A regularity of this kind would deserve checking in a broader corpus in order to specify its spread beyond the idiolectal level,[117] but it has per se the interest of showing how the syntactic environment might have had an influence on the actuation of a construction[118] (here, with or without the preposition *ḥr*). Additionally, the lack of counter-examples points to a possible awareness of a written norm regarding this construction, one that ultimately led to levelled registers in Amennakhte's case.

The importance of levelling processes may be further illustrated by examining the 'respect' of a norm in a single text. In TA, the elegance of the calligraphy seems to be reflected in the spellings and in the language itself that tends to be highly uniform and overwhelmingly regular. At the graphemic level, an illustration of motivated variations may be found in the *status pronominalis* of the substantive *ḫ.t* 'thing' (see above §4.2). The actual phonetic realization of the /t/ is underlined in the spellings by the systematic appearance of the grapheme :  (1.4),  (2.6; 2.7; 3.8),  (4.8), which contrasts clearly with  (2.3),  (4.9),  (5.2).

The prepositions *ḥr* and *r* of the analytic predicative constructions (Present I, Future III, Sequential) are always written, which does not match the general evolution trends of these constructions for the period.[119]

It could be argued that these features are not register-dependent, but are rather a general characteristic of Amennakhte's written production (who could turn out to be a rather conservative scribe). This assumption is, however, contradicted by the data of TB: this text was written years before TA and displays several features that are more advanced from a diachronic viewpoint (formality scale) and less regular (standardization scale) than TA (see, e.g., the frequent, but non-regular and apparently non-motivated, omission of the prepositions in the above-mentioned analytical predicative constructions). This constitutes a noteworthy argument in favour of the existence of a rather vivid language ideology that played a decisive part even in the registers that are not located at the higher end of the formality scale.[120] This formal and conventionalized character

[116] See Meeks (1998, 78.2464).

[117] This is compatible with—but markedly different from—the tendency observed by Winand (1992, 415–16) in the broader corpus of the Twentieth Dynasty. He gives the following figures, depending on the syntactic environment: *ḥr* is present 41 per cent of the time when the Present I occurs in an independent syntactic position while only 22 per cent of the time after the circumstantial *ỉw*.

[118] In the same vein, Winand (1992, 508–10) analysed the possible influence of different syntactic environments on the occurrence vs non-occurrence of the allative preposition *r* within the Future III construction.

[119] See Winand (1992, 414–19, 449–54, and 504–10).

[120] In this respect, see Winand (1992, 418) who commented on the 'particularismes de scribe' regarding the frequent occurrence of the preposition *ḥr* with the Present I in some texts. Given the examples quoted, I would be tempted to postulate here register rather than scribal variation and

of the written register of TA, when compared to other documentary texts, is arguably further demonstrable thanks to minor changes that could point to the decreasing attention of Amennakhte in the course of his writing:[121]

- change from 3PL suffix pronoun *=sn* to *=w* after the preposition *n* (a conservative environment, see §5): *ỉw=ỉ ḥr dỉ.t n=sn* 'and I gave them' (2.3) vs *r rdỉ.t rḫ.tw nꜣ rmṯ-ỉs.t ḥm.wt ỉ.dỉ=s n=w* 'list of the members of the gang and women to whom she gave' (3.1);
- the quantifier *nb* agrees consistently in gender with the antecedent. This is a written hypercorrection, since this type of gender agreement is no longer required during the Twentieth Dynasty, but in column 4.9 we find *ꜣḫ.t nb* (and again in column 5.7);
- change from  to  as the grapheme of the prothetic yod of the perfective relative form, i.e. from the older and infrequent spelling of the Late Egyptian relative form to the newer and usual spelling:  (3.1),  (3.9),  (3.11),  (4.1),  (4.11),  (5.3).

Before concluding this section and in order to summarize the various facets that have been studied above, the dimensions of variation can be tentatively and sketchily presented on a two-dimensional graph[122] (Figure 5.6, which includes only the main texts of the corpus). The horizontal axis represents the continuum of register features (verbal morphology, lexical diversity, etc.) while the vertical axis combines the numbers and types of register markers and the degree of conventionalization.

It should be noted that this graph does not capture the degree of variation within a single register. Expectedly, some registers have a well-defined norm, entailing relatively little variation, while other registers are less specified linguistically, so that there are considerable differences among the texts mobilizing this register.

to link it expressly to a language ideology probably developed through the norm of the didactic literature.

[121] Some mistakes are certainly due to the same phenomenon: (1) omission of the negation: *ỉr pꜣy 3 ẖrd.w ỉnk, <bn> ỉw=w r ꜥḳ r pš.t m ꜣḫ.t=ỉ nb* 'as for these three children of mine, they shall <not> participate in the division of any of my goods' (4.7–8); (2) *pꜣy=ỉ*  written instead of  (5.3). See Winand (this volume, Chapter 6) for similar changes of the scribal practices in the course of writing a document in the Tomb Robberies corpus.

[122] This description of the registers is culturally free, i.e. not based on etic criteria that depend on the preconstructed categories of genres and registers. In this respect, it complements the emic approach explored by Donker van Heel and Haring (2003 (Introduction)): 'A modern attempt at classifying ancient texts inevitably results in a modern classification. It has been tried to minimize this anachronism by taking Egyptian terminology as the main point of departure.'

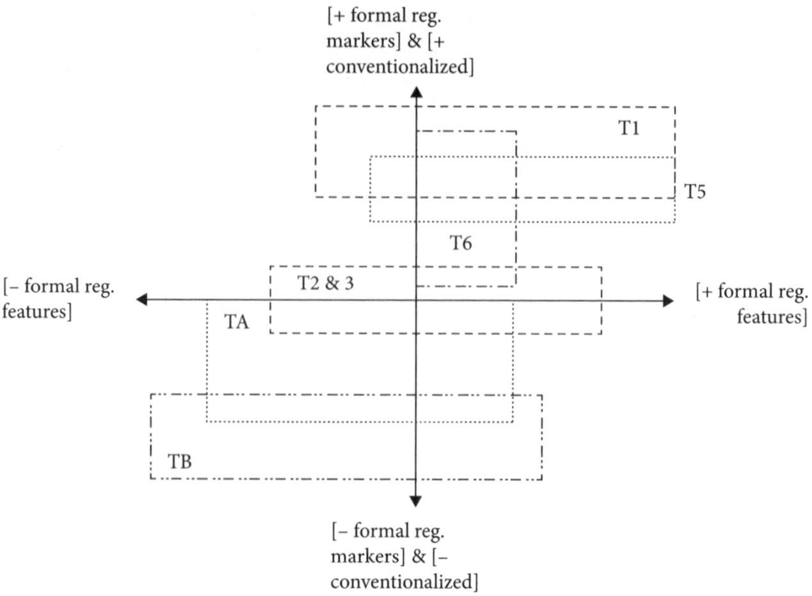

Fig. 5.6. Two-dimensional representation of the register variation in Amennakhte's corpus

§7. IDIOLECTAL FEATURES AND THE IDENTIFICATION OF SCRIBES IN DEIR EL-MEDINA

In this last section, a possible idiolectal feature of Amennakhte will be described before questioning the feasibility of using graphemic and linguistic features as valuable criteria for identifying a scribe or an author in the community of Deir el-Medina, especially during the first part of the Twentieth Dynasty.

The construction of abstract deverbal substantives with the substantive *s.t* 'place' + verbal root is a well-known derivational strategy in Ancient Egyptian.[123] However, if it represents a well-established noun formation pattern in Earlier Egyptian, it has not often been acknowledged for the texts of the New Kingdom. I suggest recognizing two instances of such a construction in TB, r° 4.10: *ẖr ptr=tn tꜣ s.t-ꜥḥꜥ* *n ṯꜣty* PN *ḥr tꜣ s.t-ỉn ỉnr.w* 'but you are aware of the position of the vizier PN regarding the fact of bringing stones'. This 'particularism' is coherent and expected, but in the documentation at our disposal seems to be peculiar to Amennakhte.[124]

[123] See already Firchow (1954, 93–4).

[124] Another rare feature in Amennakhte's writings is the use of suffix pronoun-*ỉmy* in attributive position with possessive function, see TA, 2.2 *ỉry=ỉ sḫpr pꜣy 8 bꜣk=tn-ỉmy* 'I brought up these eight servants belonging to you(r group)'. In the Late Egyptian corpus, I know of a single parallel

Given the high degree of the variation between registers, the discussion of Amennakhte's authorship based on linguistic features is mainly to be achieved by comparing similar registers. In the present case, however, the numerous cases of regularities and motivated variations that have been noticed in the course of the study, both within and across registers, might lead to interesting results.

Before proceeding, it should be emphasized that converging graphemic and linguistic criteria will hardly ever constitute definite proof in favour of attributing a text to an individual scribe. From the outset, these need be supplemented by a close study of the handwriting, by an examination of the other dating criteria, and by taking into consideration thematic similarities[125] in the case of literary compositions. In order to test this methodology, I restrict the following analysis to three texts.

The general principles are first tested on P.Ashmolean 1945.97, cols. 5.9–sq. (§7.1), i.e. the end of TA that directly follows Amennakhte's text and has been written by another hand, perhaps that of his son Horisheri (see n. 55). Given the fact that we deal here with the same genre on the same document, very little variation is expected. As such, the question will be whether some criteria mentioned above are able to account for the distinction between scribes. Second, Dorn suggested that '[e]in möglicher Schluss der Lehre Amunnachts dürfte in O.DeM 1219 vorliegen',[126] whereas Bickel and Mathieu were rather of the opinion that 'l'O.Gardiner 341, s'il n'appartient pas à la fin de cet *Enseignement*, semble lui être apparenté'.[127] Both hypotheses will be reviewed here in order to see whether the texts could possibly be attributed to Amennakhte (§7.2). Finally, a documentary text belonging to the 'test corpus' will be looked at (O.Berlin P 10633), in order to determine whether the regularities and motivated variations of the main corpus corroborate an attribution, suggested on onomastic and palaeographical grounds, to Amennakhte (§7.3).

in KRI VI, 571.7–8: [DATE] *wsf n tꜣ ỉs.t (n) pꜣ ẖr ỉw=sn ḥḳr.w gꜣb.w m ḥtr.w=sn-ỉmy* '[DATE] no work by the gang of the Tomb: they were hungry and lacking their wages'. Another possible characteristic feature of Amennakhte's style is 'l'emploi enclitique de -ʿꜣ, que l'on retrouve cinq fois (*dnj-ʿꜣ* et *smj-ʿꜣ* dans l'*Enseignement* [T1], *bjꜣ.t-ʿꜣ.t* dans le « Poème satirique » [T2] et l'hymne de l'O.CGT 57002 [T5; for the meaning of this expression, see Posener 1964; Guglielmi 1985, 141; and Vernus 2010, 493 n. 9. Note the use of the antonym, *bỉꜣ.t nfr.t*, in P.Chester Beatty IV, v° 5.6], *nb-ʿꜣ* dans l'hymne de l'O.CGT 57001)' (Bickel and Mathieu (1993, 48)).

[125] Here, thematic similarities are to be distinguished from phraseological similarities. One may think, for example, of the use of *ỉ.nw n ỉr.ty=ky* 'look with your eyes' (both in T1B, 7 and in T3, 7; see the numerous parallels quoted in Hintze (1954, 35), Posener (1955, 64 and 67), Guglielmi (1985, 141), and Dorn (2004, 53)). A topos of this kind is manifestly dependent on the register rather than the author, *pace* Bickel and Mathieu (1993, 48).

[126] Dorn (2004, 55), partly based on the remarks made by Fischer-Elfert (1997, 16); see now also Dorn (2013).

[127] Bickel and Mathieu (1993, 32).

§7.1. The End of the Testamentary Deposition of Naunakhte

The variations between TA and the end of the document are striking at several levels and, setting aside the differences of handwritings, they would lead to recognizing two distinct scribes. See, e.g.:

- [DATE] *hrw pn wḥm spr r ḳnb.t in rmṯ-is.t* PN '[date] on this day, the workman PN appeared again in court' (col. 5.9). The phraseology is identical to that of TA (see 1.4), but dissimilarities appear at the graphemic level: *hrw* is written here vs (TA, 1.4) and *rmṯ-is.t* is written vs in TA (eleven occurrences, no variation).
- As regards the spellings, one can also quote: *ʿnḫ-n-niw.t* (5.10) vs in TA (eight occurrences, no variation); *niw.t-nḫt* (5.10) vs in TA (1.5).
- The *status pronominalis* of feminine substantives is written without the grapheme (see 5.9–10: *nꜣ sš i.ir ʿnḫ-n-niwt* PN *ḥr ꜣḫ.t.s* ( ) 'the documents which the citizen PN wrote concerning her goods'), whereas all the occurrences of TA do have the longer spelling.
- The negative Future III (col. 5.11) with substantival subject reads: *bn iw* PN *ø pš im.w* 'PN shall not share in it', with *iw* NP and no preposition *r*. This contrasts clearly with all the other occurrences of the Future III in TA.

§7.2. O.DeM 1219 and O.Gardiner 341

When comparing the respective compatibilities of O.DeM 1219 and O.Gardiner 341 with Amennakhte's scribal habits, the lexemic criteria will be expressly avoided in order not to influence the results with elements of content. I will only discuss the formal graphemic and linguistic features that have been identified in the main corpus.

Several features speak in favour of Dorn's hypothesis[128] regarding O.DeM 1219:

- The spelling of the substantive *sbꜣy.t* 'teaching' *status pronominalis* with the grapheme (r° 3) as in T1A, 10 ( ).
- The long spelling of the 2SGM suffix pronoun in syntagmatic environments similar to T1: after *mdw/md.wt* 'speak/words' (r° 4 identical to T1A, 6) and *ini* 'bring' (v° 16 in the *bw sḏm=f* construction, cf. T1A, 15); see also v° 18 after a lacuna. The short spelling is found after *it* 'father' and *ḏr.t* 'hand' (v° 16 and 17).
- Use of the 3PL suffix pronoun *=sn* (r° 6 and 7 (not *=w*)), which is also systematic in T1.

[128] For the lexemic, phraseological, and thematic similarities, see Fischer-Elfert (1997, 12–16).

- Identical spellings for almost all the lexemes: *nḏm* 'sweet' (, r° 5 = T1A, 11), *ʿḳ* 'to enter' (, r° 6, always the same spelling in the corpus (six occ.; see, e.g., TA, 4.2, TB, r° 1.2)), *ḫpr* 'to become' (,[129] v° 15 and 19 = T1B, 5 and T1K, 4), *ḳỉ n* NP 'form, nature, manner of NP' (, v° 16 = T4.1), *ỉwty* REL.NEG (, v° 17 = T1P, 1), *kꜣ.t* 'work' (, v° 18 = T1A, 3), *ỉb* 'heart' (v° 19 = *passim*), *ṯs.w* 'maxims' (, v° 20 = T1A, 1).

Against the attribution of this text to Amennakhte himself, or more narrowly to the very Teaching of Amennakhte, I am able to mention only one argument: the use of the negation *bn* in the construction *ỉw=ỉ ḫpr bn ỉb=ỉ m ẖ.t=ỉ* 'lit. it happened that my heart was not in my body anymore', instead of the negation *nn* that seems to be the norm in T1. However, the negation *bn* occurs in other literary registers very close to that of T1 (see especially T6, r° 5–6). Moreover, given the fact that we are possibly at the very end of the text, a decrease in the level of indexical formality cannot to be ruled out (see §6). Anyhow, the graphemic and linguistic features of this composition seem to be mostly in agreement with the data collected in the study of Amennakhte's corpus.

The suggestion made by Bickel and Mathieu regarding O.Gardiner 341 receives less support. The attribution to Amennakhte relies principally on the occurrence of two lexemes that are also found in T1:

- *dnỉ* (l. 3 and 3) 'dam, dyke' (in the expression *dnỉ pw Mꜣʿ.t* 'Maat is a dam'; this lemma also occurs in T1A, 3 (and other witnesses) with a similar spelling;
- *bỉꜣ.t* (l. 5) 'character' () that also occurs in T3, 6, with a slightly different spelling: .

Now that T1N has been connected to T1, one could also quote the spelling of *mrỉ* 'to love' on l. 1 (), which seems to be identical to T1N, l. 11. I see no other criteria that would confirm the attribution of this ostracon to our author, but given the very short size and fragmentary nature of this text, as well as the absence of any strong counterargument, it would be risky to deny the possibility of its attribution to Amennakhte. The question must remain open.

§7.3. O.Berlin P 10633

Several features of this text are closely related to the documentary registers of the main corpus:

[129] On this spelling (cf. Coptic ϣⲱⲡⲉ), see Erman (1933, § 49) and Fischer-Elfert (1984a). The spelling occurs in other witnesses of T1 as well as in T5, 4; in T6, v° 3.

- A very good correspondence between the spellings of this text and the ones of the main corpus, see especially *ỉmn-nḫ̮t* 'Amennakhte',[130] *smỉ* 'to make a report', *ỉs.t* 'team', *hrw* 'day', *ꜣbd* 'month', *dỉw* 'rations', *bd.t* 'emmer'.
- Same formulation in l. 2 (*20 n hrw ꜥḳ.w m pꜣ ꜣbd*) and in TB, rº 1.2 (*ỉw hrw 18 ꜥḳ m pꜣ ꜣbd*) with the identical full spelling of *ꜣbd* ()—the different expressions of cardinality are, however, noteworthy.
- The distribution of the 3PL suffix pronouns that is expected for a text from Year 29 of Ramses III written by Amennakhte, i.e. with the 3PL suffix *=w* after the infinitive and *=sn* after the preposition *n* 'to': *ỉw=tw Ḥr dỉ(.t)=w n=sn* 'and one gave them to them'.

Taken separately, none of these criteria would be meaningful, but once considered together,[131] they could militate for an attribution to Amennakhte or a closely related member of the community, who shared his scribal habits. Furthermore, if we consider the rather unusual introduction of the text [DATE] *ỉn sš ỉmn-nḫ̮t* '[DATE] by the scribe Amennakhte' and the mention of the nomination of To as Vizier of Upper and Lower Egypt (see n. 8), there seems to be little room left for doubting Amennakhte's authorship.

The three case studies presented above are definitely not intended to exhaust the subject. Rather, they show that a close look at the scribal habits and, more specifically, at the types of regularities and variations attested for an individual, could be used as a heuristic device when it comes to identifying authors and scribes in the Deir el-Medina community. A large body of convergent evidence (which is not always possible when dealing with small texts on ostraca) will always be needed, and this criterion alone will admittedly never be sufficient. However, as illustrated in this section, it would be worth taking this dimension systematically into consideration.

§8. CONCLUSIONS

This paper is first and foremost a plea for a variationist approach to the Ancient Egyptian linguistic material. Indeed, we are lucky enough to have first-hand access to texts that, unlike, e.g., the writings of most of the classical Greek and

[130] To the well-known occurrences of his name, add Grandet (2003, 351) and O.DeM 10034, rº 1: , Grandet (2006, 225).

[131] Other less decisive criteria could be added. (1) There is the occurrence of the construction *bw sḏm.w* NP in l. 3 (*bw dy n=n dỉw* 'the rations have not been delivered to us') with a quite unusual spelling of the verb *rdỉ*: (a spelling mainly characteristic of the negative verbal complements). This negation is not attested in the main corpus, but the ending of this spelling is not surprising and even quite consonant with what we found in TB, rº 3.2 with the perfective passive participle: *ỉs ỉnk pꜣ ṯꜣty dỉ r nḥm* 'am I by any chance the kind of vizier appointed in order to deprive?' (2) The preposition *ḥr* is always written with the sequential and *=tw* as subject (ll. 5, 6, and 7); in TB, the preposition *ḥr* tends not to be written, but is there when the subject is *=tw;* see rº 2.5.

Latin authors, have not (or have to a very small extent) been standardized by a long homogenizing scribal tradition. This means that, not only writing communities or subgroups of the Egyptian society, but also individual scribes may come to the fore and that significant patterns of variation become discernable at different levels of linguistic analysis.

In order to fully benefit from these (re-)humanized Egyptological linguistic data, one has to accept the texts as they stand, in their diversity, and to resist the normative temptation to emend the data. The description of variation[132] at the micro level of the scribes—that is too often analysed in terms of 'exceptions to' or 'violations' of 'rules'—is one of the keys and a prerequisite for a sound approach of Ancient Egyptian diachrony.

As has been made clear several times, the present study is programmatic. However, the descriptions of Amennakhte's writing habits quite explicitly showed that the variation at the level of an individual scribe is far from being random and is almost entirely free from unmotivated or asystemic idiosyncrasies. On the contrary, a number of intra- and extralinguistic factors have been identified in order to account for the variations within and across registers. As such, if the ancient Egyptians left us with virtually no metacomments on their own linguistic system, this type of investigation shows how a scribe of the Ramesside period was, beyond any doubt, conscious of the registers he used depending on the communicative context. He was able to play with linguistic features and indexical markers intentionally selected[133] in a wide multiglossic scribal repertoire that had been progressively enriched by the history of the language through textual heritage.

Finally, two promising avenues for future research, which have not been directly addressed on empirical grounds here, can be pointed out. (1) The study of individual scribal practices is a necessary first step, but it is to be complemented and expanded by relating it to the linguistic variation within a community a broader region, or at the level of entire bodies of texts. The dynamics of language in a community, such as the identification of innovative scribes and agents of propagation and stabilization of features recently integrated in the written repertoire belongs, to be sure, to the future of our field. (2) The present study was mainly oriented towards a synchronic description of register variation, but one of the ensuing goals will be to refine our approach to the Ancient Egyptian diachrony, starting from an accurate description of register variation for each period. Indeed, as Biber puts it, 'a register perspective is crucial to complete an understanding of the processes of language development and change: [...] linguistic change interacts in complex ways with changing patterns of register

[132] 'Variation is at the very heart of the mechanism responsible for selected, adaptive evolutionary change' (Givón (2002, 17–18)).

[133] On this point, see Stauder's (2013a) results regarding the *Égyptien de tradition* of the Eighteenth Dynasty.

variation.'[134] The Ancient Egyptian corpus is a tantalizing one for analysing how structural changes enter a language in particular registers[135] and subsequently evolve at different rates in different registers, as well as for determining the situational and cultural parameters that make possible and support such evolutions through the permanent mobilization and (re)construction of an evanescent, although pervasive, language ideology.

[134] Biber (1995, 13); see also Romaine (1980 and 1982).

[135] See Goldwasser (1991) about 'dynamic canonicity' and Junge (2001, 21) who stated that 'the norms of registers change for written languages also. The speed with which changes appear in particular types of texts depends upon their relative position in the norm hierarchy: the more developed the norm, the slower it changes.'

6

Words of Thieves

Jean Winand

This study[1] deals with the dossier of juridical documents known collectively as the Late Ramesside Tomb Robbery Papyri. These documents, which date to the end of the Twentieth Dynasty, record the proceedings of the interrogation of those prosecuted for robbing the royal tombs and tombs of high officials in western Thebes. In judicial matters, one might expect a maximal trend towards standardization. When variation occurs, it signals what is exceptional (as opposed to common), personal (as opposed to general), or remarkable (as opposed to banal). To sum up, it marks the unexpected. At first glance, in our corpus, the depositions made by the defendants should be the place of choice for free and multifaceted discourse, while the procedural sentences should favour a formalized and rigid phraseology. This assumption is supported by the evidence only up to a certain point. This paper will show that diversity is found where uniformity is expected, while some kind of uniformity is encountered where variation should be the rule.

§1. INTRODUCTION

The Great Tomb Robbery papyri, as Peet felicitously named them,[2] have been known to Egyptologists for more than eighty years. Very recently, in the 1990s, a new papyrus, P.Rochester, came to light.[3] This papyrus is more loosely related

[1] I would like to thank Gaëlle Chantrain, Eitan Grossman, and Stéphane Polis for their comments and suggestions. I also warmly thank Jennifer Cromwell and Eitan Grossman for improving my English. This study is part of the general Ramses Project ©, an annotated database of Late Egyptian (see Winand, Polis, and Rosmorduc (2015)).

[2] This points to the title of Peet's magistral publication, Peet (1930). To this must be added Peet (1920), as well as Capart, Gardiner, and van de Walle (1936). On P.Ambras, see most recently Salah el-Kholi (2006) and Winand (2011b). In this paper, I shall always refer to the whole dossier under the name Late Ramesside Tomb Robbery Papyri, or by the acronym TR.

[3] Goelet (1996), with comment from Quack (2000).

I	P.Abbott	y. 16 of Ramses IX
	P.Léopold II-Amherst	y. 16 of Ramses IX
II	P.BM EA 10054	y. 16 (of Ramses IX)
III	P.BM EA 10068, r°	y. 17 of Ramses IX
	v° 2–8	y. 12 (*wḥm msw.t*)
	v° 1	same as v° 2–8 (?)
	P.BM EA 10053, r°	y. 17 of Ramses IX
IV	P.BM EA 10053, v°	y. 9 (R. XI or *wḥm-msw.t*)
	P.BM EA 10383	y. 2 (*wḥm-msw.t*)
V	P.Rochester	y. 1 of *wḥm-msw.t*
	Abbott Dockets	y. 1 of *wḥm-msw.t*
	P.BM EA 10052	y. 1 of *wḥm-msw.t*
	P.Mayer A	y. 1 and 2 of *wḥm-msw.t*
	P.BM EA 10403	y. 2 of *wḥm-msw.t*
VI	P.Mayer B	(Ramses IX?)
VII	P.Ambras	y. 6 of *wḥm-msw.t*

Fig. 6.1. List of the papyri in chronological order

to the Late Ramesside Theban juridical papyri, which of course form the main part of my corpus, as it is not concerned with the thefts committed on the Theban west bank. The papyrus consists of a list of some goods stolen from the Amun temple of Karnak by a chief doorkeeper named Djehutyhotep. This person is well known from other sources, namely the Tomb Robbery papyri, and acts as a link to the general corpus.

The arrows to the right of Figure 6.1 suggest possible regroupings according to the scribe's hand.[4] P.Abbott and P.Léopold II-Amherst were reportedly written by the same scribe.[5] The same is generally said for the two long papyri P.BM EA 10052 and P.Mayer A.[6] It has also been suggested that P.BM EA 10053 v° and P. BM 10403 share some characteristic features with P.BM EA 10052 and P.Mayer A; however, a conclusive identification of the scribe's hand in these two papyri is still pending.[7] In the second part of this study, I will discuss the problems raised in identifying the scribes based on palaeography.

[4] The Roman numbers in the first column correspond to the classes made by Peet.

[5] See JEA 22.

[6] See Peet (1920, 135), who already unhesitatingly stated, 'It [i.e. P.BM EA 10052] is written the same way up on both sides by the same hand as Mayer A.'

[7] As Peet wrote (1920, 169), the handwriting of P.BM EA 10403 'is remarkably like that of Pap. 10052 and Mayer A, but differences in the forms of certain crucial signs, and variants in spelling…prevent our ascribing 10403 to the same writer as the other two.'

Table 6.1. Classification of the papyri according to their content

Internal report	P.Abbott
Testimonies of thieves	P.Mayer B
	P.Léopold II-Amherst
	P.BM EA 10053, r° and v°
	P.BM EA 10383
	P.BM EA 10052
	P.BM EA 10403
	P.Mayer A
Intermediary documents	P.BM EA 10054
	P.Rochester
Lists	P.BM EA 10068
	Abbott Dockets
Journal of the Necropolis	KRI VI, 590–8
Recapitulative list of documents	P.Ambras[8]

It has long been recognized that the Tomb Robbery papyri belong to more than one genre. In his presentation of the material, Peet grouped together the documents dealing with the same case, in chronological order. In the list shown in Table 6.1, the documents have been rearranged according to their contents. The bulk of the material consists of the testimonies of thieves. Of course, placing a document in a group is no simple matter, as the content of some papyri may be heterogeneous. The list should thus be considered a rough classification.

Recently, the corpus of the Tomb Robbery papyri has been extensively used in fixing the chronology and the history of the transition from the Twentieth to the Twenty-first Dynasty.[9] The questions I would like to address in this study are directly related to those individuals who wrote the Tomb Robbery papyri, i.e. the scribes. I shall start with a very general question: how did the scribes process the material, starting from the questioning of the accused to the production of the final document? I shall then move on to specific questions related to the process of the writing itself. How did the scribes handle what they heard? This chiefly concerns, of course, the declarations made by the defendants, but also the questions posed by the officials.

§2. PRODUCING AN ADMINISTRATIVE DOCUMENT

Producing the final report was undoubtedly the achievement of a long and, to be sure, tiresome process. One could guess that it usually involved three steps:

[8] On this papyrus, see Winand (2011b).

[9] The bibliography has now become abundant: see Jansen-Winkeln (1992 and 1997) and Thijs (1998–2001, 2007, and 2009).

taking notes during the questioning, making a preliminary draft, and writing down the final document.

In the present state of our documentation, there is no evidence to support the existence of the first step. It is difficult to guess what form it would have taken: more or less loose sentences, names and titles written in full or abbreviated, key words for formulaic parts such as oaths, questions, denials, and so on. One can also only guess what material was used to write it down (e.g. papyrus, tablets, or ostraca).[10]

In most cases, going directly from the notes to the final document was hardly possible. Some sort of intermediary document was probably needed. It has been suggested that P.BM EA 10054 and P.Rochester could be examples of precisely that kind of document.[11] P.BM EA 10052 also clearly shows that spaces, which are sometimes quite large, had been included by the scribe to allow for insertions that were never made. It is difficult to decide whether this is sufficient grounds to view the papyrus as an intermediary document, or if it was from the outset conceived as the definitive output. The final documents that were produced for the record were sometimes magnificent pieces of elegant writing, as shown by P.Léopold II-Amherst.

Ideally, all steps should be performed by a single scribe, and it was most desirable that not too much time should elapse between the different steps. In the particular case of the Tomb Robbery Papyri, one can guess that this was, in fact, what happened, considering the political implications up to the highest level of the Egyptian state.

Thus, in many cases, an intermediary document was probably needed. We are most often presented with depositions, written in an invariably correct and sometimes subtle, if not always elegant, Late Egyptian. It seems clear that the evidence given by the defendants could hardly have been well articulated during the trial between two beatings. The confessions, more often than not, were obtained by force. One must also reckon with the low level of literacy of some defendants, with the inevitable slips of memory, the contradictions that are all too common in such circumstances, and so on.

As already noted, it has been suggested that two papyri, P.BM EA 10054 and P.Rochester, could be intermediary documents. Goelet observed that the names of the officials were not recorded in the latter papyrus. He also pointed to a lack of certain details that are expected in this kind of document, but this may be

[10] The way proceedings were reported in Greek and Latin judicial systems (*oratio obliqua* vs *oratio recta*; *verbatim* or *non-verbatim*) is still debated. As observed by Coles (1966, 16), the scribes did not need to make a complete version during the hearings; they simply could have recorded in note form what was essential: 'in drafting his finished version the scribe would have put his condensed speeches back into colloquial language and arranged the whole in an Oratio Recta quasi-verbatim form.' I thank the anonymous OUP reviewer for pointing out this reference to me.

[11] Thijs (1998, 105 n. 42).

subjective.[12] As noted by Quack, recapitulative sums are lacking at the end of the document, which ends rather abruptly.[13] As regards P.BM EA 10054, Thijs suggested that the arrangements of the different parts of the writing on the papyrus might reveal a work in progress.[14] In his opinion, it is a sign that the scribe was still waiting for some piece of information before completing the final report. The potential use of drafts in scribal work has already been studied, more particularly in connection with the material of Deir el-Medina.[15] The Tomb Robbery papyri probably give us a rare opportunity to see how the scribes rearranged the raw material they collected during the trials in order to produce a document that could eventually be presented to the highest authorities before being stored in the archives.

§3. STANDARDIZING THE DOCUMENTS

In legal documents, some sort of uniformity is only to be expected. This can be observed in every culture where there is an administration. Uniformity can manifest itself in:

- the lexicon
- spellings
- morphosyntax
- phraseology and style
- the general layout of the document

The documents dealing with interrogations of the suspects unmistakably share an air of familiarity. This can be observed in:

- the expository sections
- the questions posed by the officials
- the answers given by the defendants

As regards the last two points (the discourse sections), it is generally assumed that some kind of rephrasing took place. Before going into the details, an important preliminary issue is the identification of the scribes' hands. According to our present knowledge, some papyri are considered to have been written by the same scribe (see Table 6.1). P.Abbott and P.Léopold II constitute the first group; the P.BM EA 10052 and P.Mayer A, a second group to which one should

[12] Goelet (1996, 119) curiously writes that the papyrus 'reads as if it were an abridged edition of a more carefully executed and complete document', which seems very unlikely.

[13] Quack (2000, 229–30). [14] Thijs (1998).

[15] Donker van Heel and Haring (2003, ch. 1–2).

perhaps attach P.BM EA 10053 and 10403. In what follows, I shall examine some issues, taking the whole corpus into consideration. In the second part, I shall focus more thoroughly on two closely related papyri, namely P.BM EA 10052 and P.Mayer A.

As already noted, in documents like the Tomb Robbery papyri, some kind of standardization is unavoidable, at least in the narrative sections. A first case is what can be labelled an adaptation to the administrative style. For instance, at the end of a deposition, it is common to find a list of the stolen items as reported by the accused. It seems very unlikely that what has been recorded corresponds to what was actually said, as, to be sure, nobody ever spoke like that in Egypt.

1. P.Léopold II 2.19–3.1
ỉw 20 n dbn n nbw hꜣy r.n n z nb m pꜣ 8 rmṯ ỉr n nbw dbn 160

‘and twenty *deben* of gold fell to us, for each one, that is the eight people, which makes 160 *deben* of gold.’

2. P.BM EA 10053 v° 3.15
ỉw.n dỉ.t n.f nbw ḳd.t 1 gs, dmḏ ỉ.dy.t n A : *nbw ḳd.t 4 gs*

‘and we gave him one and a half *kite* of gold, the total of what has been given to A: four and a half *kite* of gold.’

3. P.BM EA 10054 r° 1.7
ỉw nbw ḳd.t 4 hꜣy m z nb pꜣ 5 rmṯ wꜥ nb 4 ỉr n nbw dbn 8

‘and four *kite* of gold fell to each of the five men, which means four (*kite*) for each, that is eight *deben* of gold.’

These three examples demonstrate distinctive marks of administrative language: the absence of articles, the word order used, the use of the archaic passive participle, the recapitulative sum at the end, and so on. The following example shows what was probably nearer to the colloquial language, as shown by the syntax of the numerals:

4. P.BM EA 10403 2.1
ỉw ꜣꜥꜥ pꜣy-sr ỉṯꜣy pꜣy.ỉ 10 n dbn n ḥmw ỉw ꜣꜥꜥ ḥr-m-wꜣs.t… ỉṯꜣy pꜣ 10 n dbn n ḥmw n X

‘and the foreigner Payser took my ten *deben* of copper, and the foreigner Horemwaset… took the ten *deben* of copper of X.’

One can also suppose that the scribe sometimes needed to add some information that could hardly have been uttered by the accused when questioned. In the next example (5), Amenpanufer admits that he committed his thefts with a fellow named Hapy-wer:

5. P.Léopold II-Amherst, 1.16–17
ỉw.ỉ ḫpr [ṯꜣ]w.t [m nꜣ mꜥ]ḥꜥ.w m d[wn zp 2 ỉ]rm ẖrty-nṯr ḥꜥpy-wr sꜣ mr-n-ptḥn tꜣ ḥw.t wsr-mꜣꜥ.t-rꜥ mrỉ-ỉmn, ꜥnḫ, wḏꜣ, snb r-ḫt sm ns-ỉmn n pr pnḫr ỉr ḥsb.t 13 [n pr-ꜥꜣ] ꜥnḫ, wḏꜣ, snb pꜣy.n [nb] ꜥnḫ, wḏꜣ, snb ḫpr 4 rnp.t r tꜣy…

'and I began to steal [in the to]mbs ve[ry regularly w]ith the necropolis worker Hapy-wer, son of Merenptah, who belongs to the temple Usermaatre-Meriamun, life, prosperity, health, under the *sem*-priest Nesamon of this estate; and in year 13 [of Pharaoh], life, prosperity, health, our [lord], that is four years from now…'

It is very doubtful that Amunpanufer actually recited the whole curriculum vitae of Hapy-wer. He probably did not say more than his name and patronym. The affiliation of Hapy-wer and the name of his superior were most likely added later by the scribe. It is equally improbable that the epithets *ꜥnḫ, wḏꜣ, snb* (*ꜥ.w.s.*), followed by *pꜣy.n nb ꜥ.w.s.*, were pronounced by the defendant during his trial. It is also possible, albeit very difficult to prove, that the phrase *ḫpr 4 rnp.t r tꜣy*, 'that is four years from now', was actually a gloss added by the scribe. That is, unless one prefers to consider it in the reverse perspective, taking *ḫpr 4 rnp.t r tꜣy* as the original phrase and the opening phrase *ḫr ir ḥsb.t 13*, 'and in year 13' as the gloss added by the scribe. In a way, this would even make better sense, since it is highly disputable that everybody would have been fully aware of the official calendar.

§4. REWRITING THE DEPOSITIONS

Although it is perhaps less palpable, there was also some kind of rewriting of the lengthy depositions made by the accused. It seems that the scribes more or less conformed to what can be called a storyline when faced with certain matters. For instance, a complete declaration on the robbing of a tomb usually follows certain steps presented in a relatively fixed order following a logical and temporal line, and using a fixed phraseology:[16]

- entering the tomb
- finding the coffins
- tearing them to pieces
- setting them on fire
- stripping them of their gold and silver
- stealing the gold and silver
- parcelling out the booty

Now, in some cases, one has the distinctive feeling that the report includes some kind of verbatim quotations.[17] This happens more frequently in some environments such as:

[16] The best example of this is probably P.Léopold II-Amherst II 2.4–3.6, but consider also P.BM EA 10052 r° 3.5–7; r° 6.1–6; P.BM EA 10053 v° 2.11–14; v° 3.7–10; v° 3.12–17; P.BM EA 10054 r° 1.3–11; r° 2.13–16; P.BM EA 10403 1.11–2.3.

[17] Of course, even in these cases, some kind of rewriting could have taken place.

1. exceptional tales that do not conform to the habitual pattern
2. reported speech within a declaration
3. exceptional grammatical constructions
4. the use of slang

The first two points do not require much discussion, so I will focus mainly on the last two.

§5. VERBATIM QUOTATIONS

§5.1. Exceptional Constructions

The Tomb Robbery corpus sometimes shows constructions that are either exceptional with regard to the body of Late Egyptian texts or completely unparalleled. In such cases, one is greatly tempted to admit that the scribe faithfully reproduced what was actually spoken by the defendants. Consider the following example, where *ḫpr* 'to become' is used as an aspectual auxiliary of inchoativity:

6. P.BM EA 10052 8,9
ỉw.w ḫpr ꜥḥꜥ sḏd r-ḏd 'and they began to quarrel(, saying)'

The presence of *ḫpr* in a complex aspectual construction is already attested, albeit rarely and sporadically, in the Nineteenth Dynasty, always co-occurring with an Old Perfective.[18] It can also be used to add an inchoative meaning to an aspectually neutral construction, as in the following example:

7. RAD 77.5
sḫꜣ r pꜣ ḫpr i.ir A *ṯṯṯ ỉrm* B 'report concerning the fact that A began to have a row with B'[19]

In a sequential construction, which naturally gives an inchoative meaning to atelic verbs,[20] using *ḫpr* is a kind of redundant encoding. Compare in this respect how people weep in the Late Egyptian Tales, an exceedingly common behaviour.[21] In the Two Brothers, one finds the simplex *ỉw.f (ḥr) rm* (Two Brothers 13.3),[22] but a complex construction, using one of the posture auxiliaries *ꜥḥꜥ*, *ḥmsỉ* or *sḏr* before an infinitive, is also attested without any notable nuance:

[18] Cf. Battle of Kadesh (KRI II, 88,8), or the instance on an ostracon written in the time of Ramses II (KRI III, 542,12).

[19] One will note the presence of the verb *ṯṯṯ*, whose meaning is very close to that of *sḏd* in the preceding example.

[20] See Winand (2006, 180–2, 325–9).

[21] This, of course, is reminiscent of the Homeric poems where mortal and divine characters alike come to tears very quickly.

[22] LES 10–30.

8. Two Brothers 8.1
ỉw.f ḥr ʿḥʿ ḥr rmy.t n.f kꜣ 'and he began to weep loudly because of him'

This complex pattern surfaces again in Horus and Seth,[23] a tale composed in the Twentieth Dynasty:

9. Horus and Seth 8.11
ʿḥʿ.n ꜣs.t ḥms ḥr rm 'and Isis began to weep'

One must wait until the Tale of Wenamun,[24] well into the Twenty-first Dynasty,[25] to encounter an example of the double complex pattern in a literary piece. However, it remains exceptional even in this tale, as witnessed by the more common pattern *ḫpr* + infinitive:

10. Tale of Wenamun 2.64
ỉw.ỉ ḫpr ḥms.tw rm 'and I began to weep'

11. Tale of Wenamun 2.67
ỉw pꜣ wr ḫpr rm m-dỉ nꜣ md.t ỉ.ḏd.w n.f
'and the prince began to weep because of the words that were told to him'

These examples, taken from the literary corpus, show the gradual introduction of *ḫpr* to express inchoativity in narrative patterns. Of course, one could argue that the literary texts and the documentary texts do not reflect exactly the same level of Late Egyptian. In this case, the construction under discussion does not appear, in the literary corpus, before the Tale of Wenamun, a text which can be considered linguistically closer to the non-literary corpus than the New Kingdom compositions. Thus, the appearance of *ḫpr* as an auxiliary of inchoativity in the Tomb Robbery corpus can be regarded as an innovative trait.

The use of *ḫpr* in contexts where it was usually absent before can again be observed in the contrastive pair appearing in P.Mayer A:[26]

12. P.Mayer A 6.23
ḫr ỉr tw.ỉ m ỉy r-ḫry, ỉw.ỉ gm wʿb ṯꜣṯꜣ-šrỉ
'as I was coming down, I found the wab-priest Tjata-sheri'

13. P.Mayer A 2.7
ỉw.ỉ ḫpr m ỉy.t r-ḫry, ỉw.ỉ sḏm ḫrw <n> nꜣ rmṯ ỉw.w m-ḫnw pꜣy r-ḥḏ
'and I began to come down, and I heard the voice of the men who were inside this treasury'

[23] LES 37–60. [24] LES 61–75. [25] See most recently Winand (2011a).

[26] One can also note the use of *ḫpr* in a deposition found in P.BM EA 10403 (3, 5–6 : *ḫr ḫpr.ỉ ḥms.kwỉ ḥkr.tw ḫr nꜣ nhꜣ, mtw ḫpr nꜣ rmṯ ỉr.t šw.t n ḥmw, ỉw.n ḥms.wyn ḥkr.wyn, ỉ.n.ỉ n.f*) '"and it happened that I was sitting hungry under the sycamores, when people started trading copper as we were sitting hungry," I said to him', with an inchoative force in the narrative conjunctive (on this, see Winand 2001), but with a different sense in the opening line, where it means something like 'it happened that'.

The second example of what I call a remarkable construction is the use of an emphatic *ỉ.ir.f* pattern with an adverbial predicate, i.e in the construction that will be known later as the second tense of the first present.[27] The context is very clear and definitely favours a contrastive–emphatic reading:

14. P.BM EA 10052 5.21–3

ỉr tꜣ s.t ỉ.ḏd.k : ỉn<.n> nꜣ ṯbw n ḥḏ ỉm k.t s.t ꜥꜣ.t tꜣy, rwỉ.tw pꜣy ḥḏ ꜥꜣ ḏd.f ꜥḏꜣ ỉ.ỉr nꜣ ṯbw r pꜣy ḥḏ ꜥꜣ ỉ.ḏd.ỉ n.tn ꜥn wꜥ s.t wꜥty tꜣ wn.n

'as for the place you said that you [lit. we] took the silver vessels from, it is another great place, distinct from this treasure. He said, "False! It is to this big treasure I've already told you about that those vessels belong. It is one single place that we opened." '

As a third example, one can also add an instance of *wn* before an indefinite subject in the negation of the perfective, i.e. the *bwpw.f sḏm* pattern. The use of *wn* (a form of the verb *wnn* 'to be') before an indefinite subject is very far from being systematic in Late Egyptian; it will later become grammaticalized, but only in constructions following the pattern of the Present I. The presence of *wn* here is somewhat unexpected in other grammatical environments. It can possibly be explained as an analogical process at this particular moment of the development of Later Egyptian. Sporadic uses of *wn* in syntactically close grammatical contexts can be observed in the corpus of the late Ramesside times and in the Third Intermediate Period.[28]

15. P.BM EA 10052 3.18–19

ꜥḏꜣ pꜣ ḏd.k 10 n dbn n ḥḏ n z nb nꜣ dy n pꜣ rmṯ ḥnꜥ nꜣy.f ỉry.w bwpw wn zp n.tn ḏd.f wn zp n.n z nb ỉry.n šw.w <r> wnm st

'it is false what you said, that ten *deben* of silver to each man was what was given to this man and his accomplices and that there was nothing left for you. He said, "There was something left for each of us; we traded them <to> eat them." '

§5.2. Slang

All languages have a slang register, and Egyptian was undoubtedly no exception. Further research is still needed in order to provide the data needed to handle this topic properly.[29] Slang can be defined both as variation according

[27] On the autofocal second tense construction in Coptic, see Shisha-Halevy (1986, 75–6).

[28] *wn* + Ø-noun phrase (henceforth NP) is also found in the Future III (LRL 15.8) and in the negative *bw-ỉr.f* pattern (Urk. VI 123.20): see Winand (1989). Müller (2006b, 336 n. 2), followed by Lefevre (2008. II, 15), suggested another explanation for the sequence *bwpw wn ḥtr ỉy* found in a letter from el-Hibeh, analysing *wn-ḥtr* as a proper name, which is not without problems either. This solution also leaves the instances of *wn* in the other, non-Present I-like patterns completely in the dark.

[29] See Vernus (1996, 555–6); Winand (forthcoming b) for a detailed discussion.

to some idea of normativity in linguistic use and as substandard in terms of use of linguistic register. Use of slang is common in some parts of society. Ancient Egypt seems to conform to well-known patterns in its use of slang in matters related to sex and crime. The following examples illustrate some possible uses:

16. P.BM EA 10052 1.8
ỉw.s ḏd n.ỉ gm nhꜣ rmṯ wꜥ šsp n ꜥḳ.w ḥn.n wnm.k sw ỉrm.w – ỉn.s n.ỉ

'and she said to me, "Some men have found a haul of dough. Let's go so that you can wolf it down with them." So said she to me.'[30]

17. P.BM EA 10052 3.5
my r-bnr ḥn.n ỉn.n pꜣy ꜥnḫ-ꜥḳ <r> wnm

'come out! Let's go, we will bring this piece (?) of dough <to> wolf it down'

18a. P.BM EA 10052 8.11
shꜣ.k <wỉ> m pꜣ ḥḏ 'you conned <me> out of the silver'

18b. P.Mayer A 9.20
shꜣ.k wỉ ẖr.f m wꜥ n pꜣy.f ỉry 'you conned me, so they kept saying to one another'

19. P.Mayer A 1.21
sḏm(.ỉ) r-ḏd nꜣ rmṯ ḥn r ỉr.t hꜣw m pꜣy pr-n-sṯꜣ

'(I) heard that the men went to do their business with the portable shrine'

§6. VARIATION WITHIN STANDARDIZATION

Administrative records are, of course, the first candidates where strict standardization can be expected. However, even there, scribes can offer variation in formulae that one could be tempted to see as completely frozen. In what follows, the field of investigation has been restricted to P.BM EA 10052 and P.Mayer A.

a) Curiously enough, the well-known formula 'he was interrogated with the stick' has a different look in the two papyri. In P.BM EA 10052, the formula in the first ten columns is invariably the periphrastic passive *ỉr smtr.f m bḏn*. From col. 11 onwards, the passive construction is sometimes replaced by the Present I *sw smtr m bḏn*. In P.Mayer A, the formula is always *sw smtr m ḳnḳn m bḏn*, which is the second formula found in P.BM EA 10052, with the insertion of *m ḳnḳn* 'by beating'(Table 6.2).[31] This kind of variation between the two documents is not at all exceptional, as will be made clear in the following sections.

[30] See already Peet's comment (1920, 158 n. 4).
[31] One will note here that the practice of P.BM EA 10403 reflects that of P.Mayer A.

Table 6.2. The beating formulae in P.BM EA 10052 and P. Mayer A

	Passive	Present I
P.BM EA 10052	*ỉr smtr m bḏn* (34 times, without exception until 11.15)	*sw smtr m bḏn* (sometimes from 11.16 on)
P.Mayer A		*sw smtr m ḳnḳn m bḏn*

b) Another interesting instance of variation can be observed when the defendant tells the officials to bring a witness to charge him. Such an invitation can happen as part of an oath or as the concluding sentence of a deposition. In the examples below, O stands for oath and D for deposition:

20. P.BM EA 10052 10.16
O: *ỉmy ỉn.tw pꜣy-nḫ... ỉry.f sꜥḥꜥ.s*
'let Payankh be brought so that he may accuse her'

21. P.BM EA 10052 13.8
D: *ỉmy ỉn.tw nfw ns-ỉmn ỉry.f sꜥḥꜥ.ỉ*
'let the sailor Nesamun be brought, so that he may accuse'

22. P.BM EA 10052 12.27; 15.8
D: *ỉmy ỉn.tw pꜣ nty ỉ[w.f s]ꜥḥꜥ.ỉ mtw.f sꜥḥꜥ.ỉ*
'let the one who will accuse me be brought and let him accuse me'

23. P.Mayer A 8.24
O: *ỉmy ỉn.tw rmṯ r sꜥḥꜥ.ỉ*
'let someone be brought to accuse me'

24. P.BM EA 10052 14.5
D: *ỉmy ỉn.tw rmṯ r sꜥḥꜥ.ỉ*
'let someone be brought to accuse me'[32]

The recurrent formula *ỉmy ỉn.tw* X can be followed by a subjunctive, *ỉry.f sꜥḥꜥ.ỉ/f*, by a conjunctive, *mtw.f sꜥḥꜥ.ỉ*, or by a prepositional phrase, *r sꜥḥꜥ.ỉ*. Interestingly enough, P. Mayer A always sticks to the PrepP, which is also known to P.BM EA 10052. In the latter one, however, the subjunctive and the conjunctive are more common.[33]

c) Another striking difference in formulae can be observed in the opening statement of the accused when the question is resumed after a

[32] Cf. P.Mayer A 4.14.

[33] As was pointed out to me by Stéphane Polis, the alternation of the subjunctive (*ỉry.f sꜥḥꜥ.ỉ*) vs *r* + infinitive (*r sꜥḥꜥ.ỉ*) should perhaps be explained by the position of the subject of *ỉn.tw* on the animacy scale: the subjunctive seems to be preferred when the witness is higher on the scale. In exx. 20 and 21, the subject is a proper name, whereas in exx. 23 and 24, it is the generic noun *rmṯ* 'somebody'. In the first case, the subjunctive is used, but in the second one, *r* + infinitive has been preferred. This, of course, requires further investigation.

beating. In P.BM EA 10052, the suspect usually says *i͗.wꜣḥ, ḏd.i͗* 'stop! I'll speak!',[34] an exclamation never found in P.Mayer A. The formula of denial *wꜣ r.i͗, wꜣ r ḥꜥ.t.i͗* 'far from me! far from myself!', which occurs six times in P.BM EA 10052,[35] never appears in P.Mayer A. In four cases, the same defendant appears in both documents: Nesparai (P.BM EA 10052 11.2 and P. Mayer A 8.10), Ankhefenamun (P.BM EA 10052 11.11 and P. Mayer A 8.15), Pa'irsekheru (P.BM EA 10052 11.15 and P. Mayer A 9.24), and Ahautynefer (P.BM EA 10052 15.22 and P. Mayer A 10.9). It is thus difficult to understand why there is such a difference in formulation.

d) The question posed by an official on the modus operandi of the thieves can take different forms, as shown by the four following groups:[36]

1. The *i͗.ḏd (n.i͗)* group

i͗.ḏd n.i͗ rmṯ nb i͗.wn i͗rm.k m nꜣ s.wt ꜥꜣ.t 'Tell me all the people who were with you in the great places' (P. BM EA 10052 1.7, 3.1, 5.11, 7.15)

i͗.ḏd pꜣ sḫr n šm i͗.i͗r.k r pḥ nꜣ sw.t ꜥꜣ.t šps.t 'Tell how you managed to reach the great and venerable places' (P. BM EA 10052 1.14, 3.23, 5.5, 12.14; P. Mayer A 2.11, 2.18, 8.4, 8.17, 8.20)

i͗.ḏd pꜣ i͗.i͗r.k // i͗.ḏd pꜣ sḫr i͗.i͗r.k 'Tell what you did // tell how you did it' (P. BM EA 10052 1.17)

i͗.ḏd my n.i͗ i͗n bwpw.k šm r tꜣ s.t 'Tell me please if you did not go to the place' (P. BM EA 10052, 4,2)

i͗.ḏd n.i͗ rmṯ nb i͗.sḏm.k i͗.ptr.k 'Tell me all the people you heard and saw' (P. BM EA 10052 4.3)

i͗.ḏd n.i͗ rmṯ nb rdy n.w ḥḏ m pꜣy ḥḏ 'Tell me all the people that were given silver from this silver-hoard' (P. BM EA 10052 5.18)

i͗.ḏd pꜣ sḫr n pꜣ ḥḏ i͗.ptr.k m-di͗ A 'Tell how you saw the silver in the possession of A' (P. BM EA 10052 7.5; P. Mayer A 8.11)

i͗.ḏd my + NP 'Tell please + NP' (P. Mayer A 4.2, 4.4, 5.3)

2. The *i͗ḫ pꜣ sḫr n* + infinitive group

i͗ḫ pꜣ sḫr n šm i͗.i͗r.f (*i͗rm* A) 'How did he go (with A)?' (P. BM EA 10052 4.6, 4.16; P. Mayer A 1.9, 2.2, 3.3, 3.20)

i͗ḫ pꜣ sḫr n šm i͗.i͗r.f r nꜣ s.wt 'How did he go the places?' (P. BM EA 10052 8.18)

i͗ḫ pꜣ sḫr n šm i͗.i͗r.f r pḥ nꜣ s.wt 'How did he manage to reach the places?' (P. BM EA 10052 8.3, 11.15, 14.12, 16.18)

i͗ḫ pꜣ sḫr n šm i͗.i͗r.f r VB 'How did he + VB?' (P. Mayer A 1.22)

i͗ḫ pꜣ sḫr n VB *i͗.i͗r.f* 'How did he + VB?' (P. BM 10052 10.14, 11.5, 13.2; P. Mayer A 1.14, 5.10)

i͗ḫ pꜣ sḫr n pꜣy ḥḏ i͗.i͗n X 'What is the matter of the silver that X brought?' (P. BM EA 10052 10.13, 10.17, 11.7v)

[34] P. BM EA 10052 1.13, 1.17, 3.17, 4.1, 4.18, 5.9, 5.13, 5.15, 5.17, 7.16, 8.14, 11.16, 12.16.

[35] P. BM EA 10052 4.8, 8.4, 11.2, 11.11, 11.15, 15.22.

[36] In each group, the formulae are subject to variation as regards their lexical components. They are only intended to give an idea of the different patterns that can be found.

3. The *i͗ḫ ḫr.k* + NP[37]

    i͗ḫ ḫr.k tꜣ md.t n + NP 'What would you say concerning the matter of + NP?' (P. BM 10052 7.10, 10.3, 11.20, 13.11, 14.2, 15.5)

    i͗ḫ ḫr.k pꜣy sḫr n pḥ i͗.ir.k... (P. BM 10052 11.10)

    i͗ḫ ḫr.ṯ pꜣy ḥḏ i͗.in X (P. BM 10052 11.5, 12.25v; P. Mayer A 10.2, 10.18)

    i͗ḫ ḫr.k + NP (P. BM 10052 13.15, 15.1, 15.20; P. Mayer A 4.16, 4.18, 6.14, 7.1, 8.23)

4. The *i͗ḫ ḫr.k* group 'What would you say?'

    (P. BM EA 10052 10.17, 11.2, 11.18, 13.9, 13.23; P. Mayer A 3.23, 3.25, 9.1, 9.6, 9.10, 9.13, 9.15, 9.16, 9.22, 10.10, 10.25).

Tables 6.3 and 6.4 provide the statistics of use for the two papyri. The numbers along the top of the columns indicate the sheets of the papyrus, and the numbers in the columns the number of occurrences of each example. The formulae have been arranged according to decreasing degree of complexity.

As a conclusion, one can see that the distribution is roughly the same in both papyri. As (t)he(y) approach(es) the end of the papyrus, the scribe(s) show(s) a strong tendency to favour shorter formulae, leaving aside the most complex ones. In P.BM EA 10052, the *i͗.ḏd* group is prominent in the first seven columns; it disappears thereafter, with an exception in col. 12. The *i͗ḫ ḫr.k r* NP group and the *i͗ḫ ḫr.k* group, the shortest one, are totally absent before col. 7. P.Mayer A offers the same general profile. In the last five columns of the papyrus, the two *i͗ḫ ḫr.k* groups appear fourteen times, while the *i͗.ḏd* group, which was no longer present since col. 6, occurs four times in col. 8.

This tendency towards abbreviation can also be observed in the spellings. Figure 6.2 shows the different writings of the pervasive word *smtr* 'testimony' in P.BM EA 10052 and the P.Mayer A. In P.BM EA 10052, there are nine different

Table 6.3. Introduction of a question: P.BM EA 10052

P.BM EA 10052	1	2	3	4	5	6	7	8	9	10	11	12	13	14	15	16
i͗.ḏd	3		2	2	4		2					1				
i͗ḫ pꜣ sḫr				2				2	1	3	4		1	1		1
i͗ḫ ḫr.k r NP							1			1	3	1	2	1	3	
i͗ḫ ḫr.k										1	2		2			

Table 6.4. Introduction of a question: P.Mayer A

P.Mayer A	1	2	3	4	5	6	7	8	9	10
i͗.ḏd		2		2	1			4		
i͗ḫ pꜣ sḫr	3	1	2		1					
i͗ḫ ḫr.k r NP				2		1	1	1		2
i͗ḫ ḫr.k			2						7	2

[37] On the meaning of *ḫr.k* in this case, see Winand (forthcoming a).

III	IV	V	VI	VII	VIII	IX	X	XI
2	7	1	21	21	2	2	1	1

Fig. 6.2. Spellings of *smtr* in P.BM EA 10052

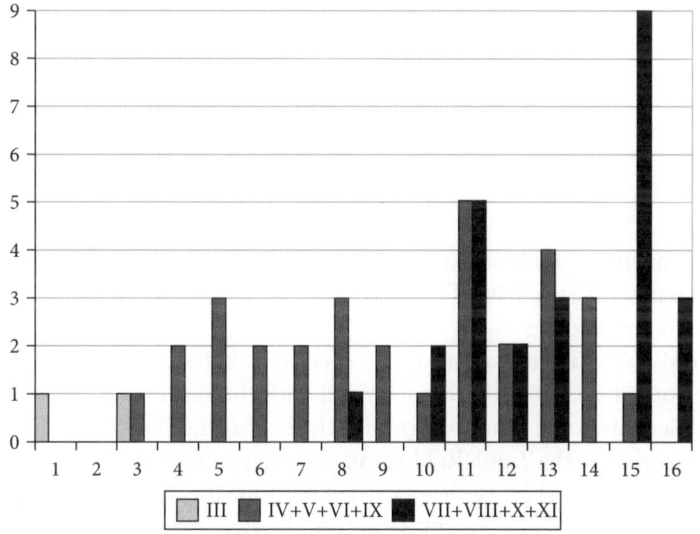

Fig. 6.3. Distribution of the spellings of *smtr* in P.BM EA 10052

spellings, which can be grouped into three sections (as shown by the shadings) according to an increasing degree of simplification.[38]

In the first group, *smtr* has been written in full; in the second group, some abbreviations occur but the group *mt* is still written; in the third and last group, the word is fully abbreviated (with some differences in the choice of classifier). The distribution of the data (Figure 6.3) shows a striking succession of the three groups.

The full written form (III) is present only at the beginning of the papyrus, and the last group (VII+VIII+X+XI) is increasingly used from the second part of the papyrus onwards. In P.Mayer A, the difference is even stronger. The full written form ( ) is present only once, in the very first line of the papyrus. The abbreviated form ( ) is the only one used (forty-five times) in the rest of the document, with one minor exception in col. 8.19 ( ).

Another striking difference between the two papyri is offered by the words *bḏn* 'stick' and *mnn*, another kind of instrument of torture, perhaps a device for

[38] The first group starts with III, and not I. The reason for this is that the first two classes, which represent other spellings, are not attested in this papyrus. The order of the spellings reflects their first occurrence in the text. This explains the position of spelling IX, which belongs to the second group, in the middle of the third group.

Table 6.5. The spellings of *bḏn* in P.BM EA 10052 and P.Mayer A

bḏn				
BM 10052			**36**	
Mayer A	25/1	4	2	2

Table 6.6. The spellings of *mnn* in P.BM EA 10052 and P.Mayer A

mnn			
BM 10052	**11**		
Mayer A		5	3

twisting the limbs. Tables 6.5 and 6.6 show the distribution of the two words in the two papyri. Again, P.BM EA 10052 and P.Mayer A seem to operate according to different choices.

If P.BM EA 10052 and P.Mayer A sometimes behave differently, they also display some features that are not shared with the rest of the Tomb Robbery papyri. Here are some examples, both at the lexical and the graphic level.

In the corpus of the Tomb Robbery papyri, there are two verbs closely related in meaning: *wšwš* and *ḳḳ*. Both are used to describe the stripping off of precious metals from wooden equipment. However, the two verbs consider the process from opposite angles: *ḳḳ* takes the point of view of the metal (*ỉw.w ḳḳ nbw m nꜣ ḥtr.w* 'they stripped off some gold from the doorjambs'),[39] whereas *wšwš* considers the process from the point of view of the equipment (*ỉw.w wšwš nꜣ wt.w* 'they broke the coffins into pieces'). In this case, the metal is not mentioned, but it is clear from the context that the process of *wšwš* is in direct connection with the stripping of the gold and silver that were plated on the furniture, as is clear from the following example:

25. P.Mayer A 3.4
ỉw.f wšwš pꜣ pr-n-sṯꜣ ỉw.f ỉn nꜣ ḥmw ỉm.f

'and he broke the portable shrine into pieces, and he carried the copper parts out of it'

ḳḳ does not seem to be attested outside the Tomb Robbery corpus, but *wšwš* is known elsewhere.[40] Table 6.7 shows the distribution of both words in the corpus of the TR. Some strong tendencies appear: P.BM EA 10052 and P.Mayer A use

[39] *ḳḳ* is still attested in Ptolemaic times with the meaning of 'to peel off'. It is also known in Coptic (ⲕⲱⲕ) with the same meaning; see Crum (1939, 100b–101a). The demotic *ḳwḳe* that appears in P.Magical London–Leiden 3.21 in the expression *ḳwḳe n swḥ.t n msḥ* 'crocodile egg shell' is possibly linked to the same root.

[40] In describing some kind of beating: P.Anastasi III 5.8–9; P.Anastasi IV 9.7; P.Anastasi. V 10.7; P.Sallier I 3.9; P.Chester Beatty IV v° 6.1; in the Necropolis Journal, in a section dealing

Table 6.7. *wšwš* and *ḳḳ* in the TR corpus

	wšwš	*ḳḳ*
P.BM EA 10052	3	
P.BM EA 10053		6
P.BM EA 10054	2	6
P.Mayer A	1	

Table 6.8. The spellings of *iṯ3y* 'thief' in the TR

P.Abbott	16		
P.Ambras			3
P.BM EA 10052	2		18
P.BM EA 10053		11	
P.BM EA 10054		3	
P.BM EA 10068	13		
P.BM EA 10403	1	1	3
P.Léopold II-Amherst	11		
P.Mayer A	1		24
Total	**44**	**15**	**48**

only *wšwš*, whereas P.BM EA 10053 exclusively favours *ḳḳ*. P.BM EA 10054 is the sole document that uses both words.[41]

Significant differences in spellings also appear throughout the corpus. Although the variations may sometimes seem very slight, they gain significance because they bear upon nouns that are used extensively. Two examples will suffice here.

The word for thief, *iṯ3y*, is well attested for obvious reasons. In the Tomb Robbery corpus, it appears 112 times (although only 109 occurrences can be used due to lacunae). The spellings can be sorted into three classes according to what is written just before the two classifiers: Ø, *-y*, or *-w*. The choice of the spelling has nothing to do with the number: each one can be used for singular and plural. As is clear from Table 6.8, each papyrus tends to favour one spelling. One will note here that the scribe of P.BM EA 10053, which is sometimes said to be very close to that of P.BM EA 10052 and P. Mayer A, did not choose the same option for the writing of *iṯ3*.

with a tomb robbery during the reign of Ramses IX (KRI VI, 579,8–9 and 11); and in P.Anastasi I 26.1, for describing a chariot broken to pieces. See also P.Anastasi I 19.9, in a damaged context. The verb is still known in Coptic (ⲟⲩⲟϣⲟⲩⲉϣ), where it means something like 'to trash'; see Crum (1939, 504b).

41 It can be shown that this has something to do with an empiric linguistic tendency I have elsewhere termed the Principle of Thematic Continuity, which makes the prediction that, if one is given the choice between two differently oriented processes, one tends to select the verb that has the thematic entity as its direct object (Winand 2012).

Table 6.9. The spellings of *bwpw*, the negative marker in the TR

 (and var.)	P.Abbott (6)
	P.Léopold II-Amherst (1)
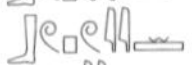	P.BM EA 10053 (1)
	P.BM EA 10403 (1)
	P.BM EA 10052 (48)
	P.BM EA 10403 (6)
	P.Mayer A (24)
	P.Mayer A (1)

Another good example is provided by the spellings of the negative marker *bwpw*, which appears eighty-eight times in the corpus. As shown in Table 6.9, its spellings can easily be sorted into two groups: the *bwp-* group and the *bp-* group,[42] which nicely match the chronological ordering of the manuscripts (see Figure 6.1).

§7. HANDLING A CASE: SOME INTERESTING ISSUES

In the Tomb Robbery corpus, a single case is sometimes dealt with in several documents. This gives us the rare opportunity to get an idea of how the scribes handled the testimonies. A case can be presented twice, in the same document or in two different ones. The testimony can be given by a single defendant, but it can also be presented by two different ones. Parallel wording can also occur with completely distinct cases implying unrelated defendants. In what follows, these possibilities are examined.

§7.1. One Case, Two Witnesses, and One Papyrus

This category can be illustrated by a case reported twice in P.BM EA 10052 by two witnesses:

26. P.BM EA 10052 r° 3.20–21: Deposition of the incense-burner Shedsukhonsu
sḏm.ỉ r-ḏd wꜥ ksks.t ỉw.s mḥ.tỉ m nbw m-dỉ ḥry-ꜥꜣ ḏḥwty-ḥtp ỉw ns-sw pꜣ ḫr

'I heard that one basket full of gold is in the possession of the doorkeeper Djehutyhotep, although it belongs to the Tomb.'

27. P.BM EA 10052 r° 4.4–5: Deposition of the trumpeter Perypatjau
sḏm.ỉ r-ḏd wꜥ ksks.t m-dỉ ḥry-ꜥꜣ ḏḥwty-ḥtp ỉw.s mḥ.tỉ m nbw ỉw ns-sw pꜣ ḫr

[42] On the spellings of the negative *bwpw*, see Winand (1992, 202–8).

'I heard that one basket is in the possession of the doorkeeper Djehutyhotep, being full of gold, although it belongs to the Tomb.'

The two depositions differ in one point only: the position of the phrase *m-dỉ ḥry-ꜥꜣ ḏḥwty-ḥtp* 'is in the possession of Djehutyhotep'. In the second deposition (only a few lines later), the scribe undoubtedly intended to reproduce what he had written in the first one. In doing so, he probably relied too confidently on his memory. As a result, he cut *wꜥ ksks.t* 'one basket' from its expansion *ỉw.s mḥ.tỉ m nbw* 'full of gold'. These two passages strongly suggest that the second deposition is a mere copy-and-paste reproduction of the first one. The odds that the second witness reproduced exactly the same phrasing seem rather weak.

§7.2. One Case, One Witness, and Two Papyri

In the second category, a case is reported by a single witness. In exx. 28 and 29, it seems that the defendant was interrogated about the same case on two different occasions. The two testimonies share a striking air of similarity, but there are differences, too, which can be explained in different ways. It is possible, and actually very probable, that Sekhahatyamun confessed more or less the same facts, but it is debatable, to say the least, that he chose exactly the same words in the same order. In fact, what is truly surprising is the fact that the two depositions are so close. It is difficult to escape the feeling that the latter deposition is an adaptation of the former one:

28. P.BM EA 10052 8.6–11

[a] *dỉ.ỉ nhꜣ-n ỉt n rmṯ-ist pꜣ-nfr* [b] *ỉw.f dỉ.t n.ỉ ḳd.t 2 n ḥḏ* [c] *ỉw.ỉ gm.t.w* [d] *ỉw.w bỉn* [e] *ỉw.ỉ šm r ḫꜣꜥ.w n.f* [f] *ỉw mnỉw ỉhy-mḥ, pꜣy sn n ỉw.f-n-ỉmn, ỉy n-bnr* [g] *ỉw.w ḏd n.ỉ* [h] *ḥn.k r-ḫnw* [i] *ỉw.<w> dỉ.t ꜥḳ.ỉ r tꜣ [s.t-]ḥms n pꜣy.w pr* [j] *ỉw.w ḫpr ꜥḥꜥ sḏd r-ḏd* [k] *shꜣ.k (wỉ) m pꜣ ḥḏ ḫr.f m wꜥ ḏd n pꜣy.f iry im.w* [l] *iw ink ỉ.dỉ ptr.k pꜣ ḫr ỉ.n.f m pꜣ šrỉ n pꜣ-nfr pꜣy rmṯ-ist n mnỉw ỉhy-mḥ*

'[a] I gave some barley to the workman Panefer, [b] and he gave me two *kite* of silver, [c] but I found [d] that they were bad,[43] [e] and I went to give them back to him. [f] The herdsman Ihumeh, the brother of Iuefenamen, then came out, [g] and they said to me [h] 'Come inside!', [i] and <they> let me into the living [room] of their house. [j] Then they began quarrelling:[44] [k] 'you conned (me) out of the silver', so they kept saying to one another,[45] [l] although it is me that showed you the tomb, so said he the son of Panefer, the workman, to the herdsman Ihumeh.'

[43] As already noted by Peet, the intended meaning of *bỉn* cannot be precisely defined: either it has to do with the quality of the silver (some problem with the fineness of the metal?), or it alludes to the illicit provenance thereof.

[44] It is difficult to assess the syntactic status of this phrase: it may be circumstantial (as they were starting to quarrel) or sequential. The presence of the inchoative auxiliary *ḫpr* makes the first option less attractive.

[45] On the meaning of *ḫr* in reported speech, see Winand (forthcoming a).

29. P.Mayer A 9.17

[a] dỉ.ỉ nhꜣ ỉt 3 ẖꜣr n ḥmwty pꜣ-nfr n pꜣ ḫr [b] ỉw.f dỉ.t n.ỉ ḥḏ ḳd.t 2 [c] ỉw.ỉ ỉṯꜣ.w n.f r-ḏd [d] bỉn [e] ỉw.ỉ tm gm.t.f [f] ỉw mnỉw ỉhy-mḥ ỉy r-bnr [g] ỉw.w dỉ.t ꜥḳ.ỉ r wꜥ šnꜥ [h] ỉw.ỉ sḏm m-dỉ.w [i] ỉw.w ꜥḥꜥ ṯtṯt ḥr wꜥ ḥḏ r-ḏd [j] shꜣ.k wỉ ḫr.f m wꜥ n pꜣ n pꜣy.f ỉry

‘[a] I gave some barley (three *khar*) to the coppersmith of the Tomb, Panefer, [b] and he gave me two *kite* of silver. [c] I took them for him (i.e. to return them to him?) thinking [d] (they were) bad, [e] but I did not find him. [f] Then the herdsman Ihumeh came out [g] and they made me enter a storehouse. [h] I then could hear them[46] [i] as they were having a row over a quantity of silver [j] “you conned me,” so they were saying to one another.’

The version in P.Mayer A is obviously an abridged version of that in P.BM EA 10052. Some sentences of P.BM EA 10052 (e, f, g, h, and l) are missing in P.Mayer A. There are also differences that are purely lexical, such as sentence (j) of P.BM EA 10052 and (i) of P. Mayer A, which have *sḏd* and *ṯtṯt*, respectively, two verbs that are semantically very close. In the opening sentence of Mayer A, there is information on the quantity of grain that has been given, which is absent from the version in P.BM EA 10052. This could well be a new piece of evidence given by Sekhahatyamun during the second interrogation.[47] More significantly, however, sentences (c–e) of P.BM EA 10052 have been obviously misunderstood in P. Mayer A, with the last one missing. This is, in my opinion, a strong argument in favour of a dependence of P. Mayer A's redaction on the version offered by the P.BM EA 10052.

§7.3. Two Cases, Two Witnesses, and One Papyrus

The next pair of examples illustrates a parallel wording found in two different cases reported by two distinct witnesses (Sekhahatyamun and Ankhefenamun) in the same papyrus (P.BM EA 10052). The last sentence of both depositions follows a very similar pattern, even if small differences can be identified. It is very close to a modern bureaucratic form, in which one only has to complete what is changing: ‘If you want to kill me for (blank) such or such reason, it is (blank) him or them that did it.’ Once again, there is some suspicion that the scribe reused a formula he had already written for the second deposition. It is, of course, impossible to decide whether this formula was actually produced by the former witness and taken over by the scribe for the second deposition, or if it was part of the phraseological stock of the scribe.

[46] The indirect construction, *sḏm m-dỉ* NP, instead of *sḏm* + SN, suggests that the witness could not hear directly what was said, because not all of the protagonists were in the same room, hence my translation with ‘can’.

[47] The precise stating of the function of Panefer's role—he is said to be a coppersmith—might be an addition by the scribe.

30. P.BM EA 10052 8.4

ḏd n.f ṯꜣty

Q: *ỉḫ pꜣ sḫr <n> šm ỉ.ỉr.k <r> pḥ nꜣ s.wt ꜥꜣy ỉrm nꜣ rmṯ wn {ỉ.wn} ỉrm.k*
ḏd.f

A: *wꜣ r.ỉ, wꜣ r ḥꜥ.t.ỉ nꜣ sw.t ꜥꜣy ỉnn ỉw.tw ẖdb.ỉ ḥr nꜣ mꜥḥꜥ.w n ỉw-mr-ỉtrw mntw nꜣ wn.ỉ ỉm*

'The vizier said to him:

Q: "How did you manage <to> reach great places with the men who were with you?"
He said:

A: "Far be it from me! Far be it from myself, these great places! If I have to be killed on account of the tombs of Iumiteru, then they are the ones I have been in." '[48]

31. P.BM EA 10052 11.12

dỉdỉ.tw n.f ꜥnḫ n nb ꜥnḫ, wḏꜣ, snb ꜥnḫ, wḏꜣ, snb r-ḏd

O: *mtw.ỉ ḏd ꜥḏꜣ ỉw.f ḫšb, dỉdỉ.tw <r> kš*
ḏd.tw n.f

Q: *ỉḫ ḫr.k pꜣy sḫr <n> pḥ ỉ.ỉr.k nꜣ s.wt ꜥꜣy.t ỉrm* X
ḏd.f

A: *wꜣ r.ỉ wꜣ r ḥꜥ.t.ỉ bw rḫ.ỉ nꜣ mꜥḥꜥ (ỉ)n nꜣy.ỉ rmṯ <nꜣ> nty <m> ỉmnt.t ḫr ḥn r pꜣ ḫr ỉnn ỉw.tw ẖdb<.ỉ> ḥr rmṯ mntf tꜣy.ỉ ṯꜣw.t*

'He was given an oath by the Lord, life, prosperity, health life, prosperity, health:

O: "If I say something false, I'll be mutilated and deported <to> Nubia."
It was said to him:

Q: "What's about how you reached the great places with A."
He said:

A: "Far be it from me! Far be it from myself! I do not know the tombs. It is my men who are <in> the West,[49] and also who went to the Tomb. If <I> have to be killed because of someone, my crime is his!" '[50]

§7.4. Two Cases, Two Witnesses, and Two Papyri

In my last example, we have exactly the same wording for two different cases, concerning two different witnesses and recorded on two different papyri.

32. P.BM EA 10052 12.18

bwpwy.ỉ ptr ỉnn ỉw.k ḏd ỉ.gꜣ, gꜣy.ỉ

'I did not see (anything). If you say, "Lie!", I will lie.'[51]

[48] See most recently Collier (2006, 183 ex. 3).

[49] This sentence is usually translated with a past ('who were in the West'), *pace* Peet (1920, 153). In this case, one would rather expect a past converter (cf. *mntw nꜣ ỉ.wn.ỉ ỉm*: P.BM EA 10052 8.5, cf. ex. 30 above). I prefer to understand it as a present; the accused is probably making a general statement here.

[50] Cf. Collier (2006, 192 ex. 18).

[51] Cf. Collier (2006, 192 ex. 19).

33. P.Mayer A 8.8
bwpwy.ỉ ptr ỉnn ỉw.tn ḏd ỉ.gꜣ, gꜣy.ỉ
'I did not see (anything). If you say, "Lie!", I will lie.'

Once again, one must not discount the possibility that the two witnesses wanted to show their good faith, but the odds that they both used the same colourful expression, making the same allusion to a possible obligation of lying, seem very low. The verb *gꜣỉ* 'lie' is found elsewhere, in different phraseological contexts:

34. P.BM EA 10052 11.21
m ỉr gꜣ, bn mꜣꜥ ỉwnꜣ 'Do not lie, it is absolutely not true.'[52]

35. P.BM EA 10052 14.17
m ỉr <dỉ.t> gꜣ.ỉ, bwpw.ỉ ptr 'Do not <make> me lie. I did not see (anything).'

36. P.Mayer A 9.4
ỉry.tw.f <mỉ> ỉḫ, ỉnk m ỉr <dỉ.t> gꜣ.ỉ
'How could it be done? As for me, do not <make> me lie!'

§8. CONCLUSION

The study of the Tomb Robbery material opens an exceptional window into the work of the scribes while dealing with their administrative business. The complexity of the issues, as well as the number of defendants and witnesses, undoubtedly forced the scribes to handle the cases very methodically. To be sure, the Pharaonic administration had the necessary expertise to handle such difficulties. The mysterious ways that preside over the preservation of the documentary evidence in ancient Egypt have brought to light the dossier of an assassination attempt on Ramses III, a major case in judicial history that was not so remote in time (about seventy years) from the Tomb Robbery proceedings.

Immediately following the first edition of the Tomb Robbery corpus, scholars could hardly believe that the written records were verbatim reports of the witnesses' declarations. Gardiner wondered if the depositions were not simply faked.[53] A more nuanced approach was taken by Wainwright. For him, the depositions needed to be partly rewritten to gain the internal coherence they would have otherwise lacked:[54] 'The papyrus is of course not a verbatim report

[52] The spelling of *gꜣỉ* prevents the same reading as in the next two examples. In the two last examples, I inserted the causative *rdỉ* because *gꜣỉ* does not seem to have a factitive meaning (to make someone lie), judging by the evidence provided by the two papyri. Except for a disputable instance in the Wisdom of Amenemope (XII, 4), the word does not appear outside these two papyri.

[53] JEA 22, 187.

[54] See also more recently Thijs' opinion (see above, n. 9).

of the proceedings, but a précis giving the gist of the endless cross questions and crooked answers by which some approximation to some facts got into writing. For instance, no man comes into court and states boldly "I committed this, that, and the other crime". Nor does he call himself a thief; that, of course, is the clerk's designation of the accused.'[55]

The opinion of these distinguished scholars was more an assumption than the result of a clear and neat demonstration. The present study shows that the reality is more subtle.

When reworking the rough data taken during the trials, the scribes undoubtedly proceeded towards some kind of standardization. This process is manifested in the lists, especially in the lists of the stolen items, or the lists of the thieves, where an administrative tone was adopted. They also had the opportunity to add some missing information, such as the father's name, the institutional affiliation, and so on.

Standardization also occurred in phraseology. In the narrative, but also in the questions asked and in the answers that were given, there is an air of familiarity, a feeling of déjà vu. This strongly suggests that a certain degree of rephrasing took place at some point. For lengthier depositions, it is even possible to speak of a restyling, as the scribes tried to follow a storyline in the presentation of the facts. This, of course, implies that drafts were sometimes produced from notes taken between the time of the trial and the final writing of the document. The purpose of this was to bring some coherency to the document. It also made it easier to compare the depositions when looking for factual evidence. This reminds me of a personal experience of mine. Some time ago, I was asked to provide evidence before a court. I made my deposition before a judge, who did not take any notes while I was speaking. He then dictated to his clerk (his scribe) what would eventually become my deposition. He condensed my ten-minute speech into a one-page declaration. He slightly modified the order of the sentences, sometimes keeping my own words, sometimes adding his own. The result was a masterpiece of clarity and logic. I put my signature at the bottom of the page, and it thus instantly became my declaration (I must make it clear that it was written as an oral statement in the first person).

When dealing with a case reported by several witnesses, the scribes somewhat inevitably came across the same formulations. When dealing with the same case twice, they were also tempted to shorten the second version. In some instances, they probably relied too confidently on their memory, which can explain certain oddities in the redaction.

Now, the scribes obviously did not have a modern approach to standardization in the sense that it did not mean for them an exact reproduction *ne varietur*. The evidence shows that a fair degree of variation was acceptable. The scribes did not work with copy and paste. This is, of course, to be expected if the scribes

[55] Wainwright (1938, 59).

were different, but it also happened with a single scribe. The scribes undoubtedly had their idiosyncrasies, and they could even change their habits as they proceeded to the end of their work.

The Tomb Robbery papyri fall into different categories as regards the choice or the spellings of certain words. In some cases (*ỉṯꜣỉ*, *bḏn*, *mnn*, *bwpw*) this neatly supports the conclusion drawn from the palaeographical evidence. Nevertheless, there are also notable differences. The study of two such closely related papyri as P.BM EA 10052 and P. Mayer A reveals some interesting points. The main results are tabulated in Table 6.10.

Comparison of the two documents leads to the following observations:

- Generally speaking, P.Mayer A did not bother with details that are present in P.BM EA 10052.
- Some formulae that are present in P.BM EA 10052 are absent in P. Mayer A.
- The spellings of common words in P.Mayer A are generally abbreviated, much more so than in P.BM EA 10052.
- The scribe who wrote P.Mayer A probably had P.BM EA 10052 relatively close to him, but was sometimes too confident about his memory, which inevitably led to some inaccuracies.
- The tendency in any single document was to abbreviate phraseology (*ỉ.ḏd* > *ỉḫ ḫr.k*) or spellings (*smtr*). This is a very common trend across cultures. The questions asked by the official could take different forms: from a long and articulated sentence to something very brief, such as *ỉḫ ḫr.k*, which corresponds more or less to modern Egyptian Arabic '*eh da?*'. In P.BM EA 10052 and P. Mayer A, a change from the most elaborate to the simplest formulae can be observed throughout the papyrus. The scribe gradually abandoned the longer expressions as he approached the end. The choice of

Table 6.10. Comparison of certain formulae in P.BM EA 10052 and P.Mayer A

		P.BM EA 10052	P.Mayer A
ỉ.wꜣḥ, ḏd.ỉ	'stop! I'll speak!'	x	---
wꜣ r.ỉ, wꜣ r ḥꜥ.t.ỉ	'far from me! far from myself!'	x	---
ỉr smtr.f m bḏn	'he was interrogated with a stick'	x	---
sw smtr m bḏn	'he has been interrogated with a stick'	x	---
sw smtr m ḳnḳn m bḏn	'he has been interrogated with a beating by a stick'	---	x
... ỉ ry.f sꜥḥꜥ.ỉ	'so that he accuses me'	x	---
... mtw.f sꜥḥꜥ.ỉ	'and he will accuse me'	x	---
... r sꜥḥꜥ.f	'to accuses him'	(x)	x
mn	'torturing'	x	---
mnn	'torturing'	---	x
bḏn	'stick'	x	---
bḏr	'stick'	---	x

formula has nothing to do with the official rank of the person asking the question. Anyone involved in the procedure is treated equally, whether vizier, royal butler, priest, or scribe.

- More disturbingly, some differences between P.BM EA 10052 and P.Mayer A have been noted that would be difficult to explain if both documents were written by the same hand. Here, I have essentially in mind the different choices that were made at the lexical level, because this was probably deeply rooted in the scribe's consciousness.

When comparing two documents, similarities are less interesting than differences. Similarity is not sameness, for similarities can be explained variously. As a last example, I would like to briefly discuss a sentence that is found in P.BM EA 10052:

37. P.BM EA 10052 3.16

pꜣ i̓ꜣw šꜣšꜣ, bi̓n tꜣy.f i̓ꜣw.t i̓r i̓w.k ẖdb.tw, i̓w.k ḫꜣꜥ.tw r pꜣ mw i̓w ni̓m wḫꜣ.k

'O doddering old man,[56] how bad is his old age. If you are killed and thrown into the water, who will search after you?'

A nearly exact parallel can be read in the Tale of Wenamun:[57]

38. LES 66, 14–67,1

i̓n i.i̓r.f ḥn.k n pꜣy ḥry-mnš ḏrḏr r di̓.t ẖdb.f tw mtw.w ḫꜣꜥ.k r pꜣ ym, wn i.i̓r.w wḫꜣ pꜣ nṯr m-di̓ ni̓m, mntk m-r-ꜥ i.i̓r.w wḫꜣ.k m-di̓ ni̓m m-r-ꜥ

'If he entrusted you to this barbarian ship's captain, is it not to have him kill you and have them throw you into the sea? From whom would one then seek the god? And also you, from whom would one seek you?'[58]

It would, of course, be very odd to explain the passage in the Tale of Wenamun as a conscious citation of P.BM EA 10052. This would be a very strange case of intertextuality. One is probably on safer ground if one views it as a shared phraseology. The association of killing someone and throwing him into the water is also found in three letters belonging to the Late Ramesside Letters corpus, which are almost contemporary with the Tomb Robbery documents:[59]

39. P.Berlin 10488 r° 6–v° 1

…mtw.k ẖdb(.w) mtw.k ḫꜣꜥ.w <r> pꜣ mw m grḥ i̓w m dy ꜥm rmṯ <n> pꜣ tꜣ i̓m.w

'…and kill (them), and throw them <into> the water at night without letting anyone <on> earth have knowledge of them.'

[56] See Peet (1920, 146 and n. 22) for the translation of *š(ꜣ)š(ꜣ)*.

[57] See Winand (2011a). [58] See Grossman (2007).

[59] Cf. P.Berlin 10487 7; 10489 v° 1–2 (on this, see Winand forthcoming c). Throwing something into the water at night in order to escape someone's notice is also known from the Tale of Horus and Seth (LES 55 1–2). See also O.Caire CG 25761 2, a love poem; however, the text is very badly damaged.

The final sentence is an indirect echo of the last part of the expressions found in P.BM EA 10052 and the Tale of Wenamun: it is made perfectly clear that nobody would be able to search for the poor wretches who were probably involved in some state secrets.[60]

This shows that much caution is needed. A similarity of expression in two documents does not imply common authorship. The natural conclusion of this is that it would be of the utmost interest to have a reappraisal of the palaeography of these two eminently interesting documents.

[60] On this, see Jansen-Winkeln (1995b).

7

Scribal Habits at the Tebtunis Temple Library

On Materiality, Formal Features, and Palaeography

Kim Ryholt

§1. INTRODUCTION

The purpose of this paper[1] is to present the Tebtunis temple library as a case study of scribal habits at an Egyptian temple of the Roman period. I will not go into detail concerning the complicated history of the library's discovery; suffice it to say that it included an estimated four hundred papyrus manuscripts found *in situ* within the temple, where it had apparently been abandoned when the temple ceased to function in the early third century CE.[2] Its scope and the known archaeological context present an ideal situation that allows us to study scribal habits and scribal variation within a narrowly defined geographical, temporal, and social context.

The temple library from Tebtunis, which is located in the southernmost part of the Fayum Oasis, is the only large-scale institutional library preserved from ancient Egypt. It was discovered at the main temple at the site which was dedicated to Soknebtunis, 'Sobek, Lord of Tebtunis', and the frequent mention of this deity in the texts leaves little doubt that they were intended for use within this temple. More specifically, the papyri were found stored or deposited in two small subterranean cellars in a building located next to the temple inside its enclosure wall. The manuscripts as a whole are very poorly preserved; on average less than 10 per cent of the individual papyri survive. While this is highly regrettable, it does not diminish their overall importance. This collection of manuscripts provides a unique insight into a whole range of aspects concerning the operation of an actual Egyptian temple library. What type of material did it include? What was its size? How was material collected, copied, collated,

[1] My thanks are due once more to Cary Martin for checking my English.
[2] See now Gallazzi (forthcoming); Ryholt (forthcoming d).

edited, and distributed? What was the lifespan of a manuscript? Was there systematic maintenance? How many scribes were involved in the operation of the library? Were they specialized? Such insights may, in turn, help to provide a framework for the interpretation of much other extant material lacking a larger context. The focus of the present paper is the materiality of the manuscripts, certain formal features of the texts, and the palaeography of the scribes involved.

Surveys of the texts from the library have been published elsewhere and it is not necessary to go into detail here.[3] As already mentioned, it has tentatively been estimated that the extant remains represent around four hundred manuscripts. The latest-dated papyrus belongs to the early third century CE and it may be assumed that the library was abandoned not too long afterwards. The oldest manuscript so far identified is a legal manual from the first century BCE (repaired in antiquity),[4] while the bulk of the material may be assigned to the second half of the first century and the second century CE. The relatively limited number of papyri prior to the second century BCE indicates that the average lifespan of these manuscripts, most of which seem to have been in active use, did not exceed a century.

About one third of the texts are written in hieratic and two thirds in demotic, while a smaller number were written in hieroglyphic or Greek.[5] The hieratic script was used for texts more directly associated with the cult, such as ritual texts, hymns, and various cultic reference works, while the bulk of the demotic texts preserve lengthy historical and mythological narrative material and handbooks on divination, medicine, and other subjects.

Due to their fragmentary nature, the contents of the temple library have not yet been fully tallied, although there has been enormous progress over the last twenty-five years. A fundamental issue that still remains to be resolved is whether or not the material represents the remains of the whole library in the state it was when it was abandoned, or whether we are merely dealing with part of it. It is not impossible that the manuscripts belonging to the temple were stored in more than one location, and we must also entertain the possibility that manuscripts could have been removed for use or reuse when the library was abandoned. This problem should, however, not have any great impact on the present discussion.

[3] See Ryholt (2005) for a general survey; von Lieven (2005) for the religious texts; Quack (2006c) for the hieratic and hieroglyphic texts. Since these surveys were written, several further volumes of papyri from the library have been published or completed (Ryholt 2006, 2012, forthcoming a; von Lieven 2007; Sérida, 2016; Töpfer, 2015).

[4] P.Carlsberg 301 + PSI inv. D 1: Bresciani (1981) [Florence fragments]; Chauveau (1991, 103–23, pls. 8–9) [Copenhagen fragments].

[5] To the list of Greek papyri mentioned in Ryholt (2005, 143–4) may now be added the 'illustrated herbal from Tebtunis' as well as a fragment of the Iliad, Book 10, preserving the book title at the end (Ryholt 2013).

§2. FRESH VS REUSED PAPYRUS

Examining the physical manuscripts from the library, it is immediately clear that the temple of Soknebtunis—although among the larger temples in Egypt—did not have available enough new and unused papyrus for its needs during the Roman period. Fresh papyrus was evidently not used *ad libitum*, and in many cases the scribes had to resign themselves to reusing older, discarded papyri, or extensively repairing older texts rather than recopying them. This marks a contrast to the Egyptian literary texts of the Ptolemaic period that were found in the rubbish heaps right outside the enclosure wall of the temple and reveal much less evidence of reuse.[6] These texts similarly include rituals, hymns, divination, and narratives, and they are likely to have formed part of the temple library before they were discarded. The cause of this situation is not immediately clear. It is possible that a significant proportion of the papyrus production was appropriated for the vast Roman imperial administrative apparatus after the annexation of Egypt in the late first century BCE and, consequently, the use of papyri became more economic in at least some social contexts.[7]

Proceeding from the list of manuscripts so far catalogued, nearly half of the demotic texts were written on the reverse of previously used papyri, while the same was true for only a sixth of the hieratic texts.[8] Clearly, therefore, priority was given to the hieratic texts. This is hardly surprising, as the hieratic script was mainly used for texts directly associated with the cult. This priority is also reflected in the care with which the hieratic texts were written and the extensive use of different types of formatting lines and rubra in order to create an aesthetically pleasing text and, above all, to facilitate its use. It is also noteworthy that all the demotic medical texts were written on fresh papyrus, whereas many of the divination texts—mainly astrological texts and dream books—were not. In the case of ritual texts and other texts closely related to the cult, the preference for fresh, clean papyrus is likely related to the strict rules governing ritual purity, where papyri previously used for other, profane purposes were likely viewed as a potential source of pollution that might negate the efficacy of the rituals.[9]

[6] Personal observation; none of these papyri has yet been published. An account of the hieratic papyri can be found in Guermeur (2008; 2015) and a description of a few of the demotic literary texts in Di Cerbo (2004, 118).

[7] Around the time of the transition from Ptolemaic to Roman rule, we also witness—as far as Egyptian legal texts are concerned—a disappearance of the characteristic large papyri with lavish margins and texts that often occupy just half or even a third of the papyrus (e.g. Adler et al. 1939; Hughes and Jasnow 1997). Legal documents from the Roman period generally make much more economic use of the papyrus by using shorter lengths or pieces with the texts covering most of the surface (e.g. Lippert and Schentuleit 2010).

[8] As far as the hieroglyphic texts are concerned, all except one of nine inventoried texts (here excluding a few scribal exercises) are written on fresh papyrus.

[9] On ritual purity in Egyptian religion in general, see Quack (2013, 115–58).

The vast majority of previously-used papyri put to secondary use in the temple library are Greek administrative records with blank backs (Figure 7.1), but there are also a number of Egyptian literary papyri in both hieratic and demotic (presumably from the library itself) and, quite exceptionally, two Latin papyri.[10] Very few of the Greek texts have so far been published and a systematic study of the whole has yet to be undertaken. Two documents seem to relate to Karanis, indicating that at least some of the reused papyri were either acquired outside of Tebtunis or brought to the temple.[11] It is too early to speculate whether this might indicate a trade in scrap paper; this must await a proper examination of the material. It is noteworthy that the reuse of papyri from the library itself is relatively infrequent.

The discarded papyri were prepared for reuse by merely rerolling them inside out so that the blank reverse could be inscribed. They would probably have had to be left to settle in for some time after their rolling in order to relax the fibres; otherwise, scribes would have found it difficult to write on them. Another otherwise well-attested method of reusing papyri, that of washing out the original texts, seems to be rather exceptional in the temple library, where there are very few examples of palimpsests. One noteworthy example is P.Carlsberg 14, where the original Greek text on the recto had been washed out, but in the end, the later scribe nonetheless decided to use the blank verso instead, perhaps because he was not satisfied with the cleaning of the recto.[12] The limited number of palimpsests might indicate that the scribes generally found it too arduous a task to thoroughly clean an entire roll.

Some of the reused papyri were substantial and long enough to accommodate their new content; for instance, three Greek administrative records had at least thirteen (two papyri)[13] and fourteen[14] numbered columns respectively and some were probably much longer. Frequently, however, this was not the case. In such cases, the scribes would trim and join together different papyri (Figure 7.1). I have so far found more than twenty examples of joins between different rolls. Given that less than 10 per cent of the individual papyri survive on average, and that most such joins would therefore now be lost, this indicates

[10] For the two Latin papyri, P.Carlsberg 555 (demotic narrative) and P.Carlsberg 671 (hieratic ritual?), see Ryholt (2012, viii, 143–4). The two papyri, with additional fragments in Florence and Berlin, are currently being prepared for publication by Hilla Halla-aho.

[11] P.Carlsberg 159 (demotic narrative): see the brief description and illustration in Ryholt (2012, 1–3, pl. 23). P.Carlsberg 600 (demotic, Myth of the Sun's Eye): unpublished.

[12] The demotic text is published in Volten (1942); see also Quack and Ryholt forthcoming. Another published palimpsest is P.Carlsberg 424 and P.Carlsberg 499 (two pieces cut from the same papyrus) where both sides were washed clean and where the recto has traces of guidelines: Ryholt (2012, 157–70, pls. 20–1). A further example is the unpublished hieroglyphic P.Carlsberg 787.

[13] P.Carlsberg 68+123 (demotic, Inaros Epic): unpublished. P.Carlsberg 100 (demotic, astrological): unpublished.

[14] P.Tebt.Tait 8 (demotic, Myth of the Sun's Eye): see Tait (1977, 35). Personal observation, the column number is not noted in the publication.

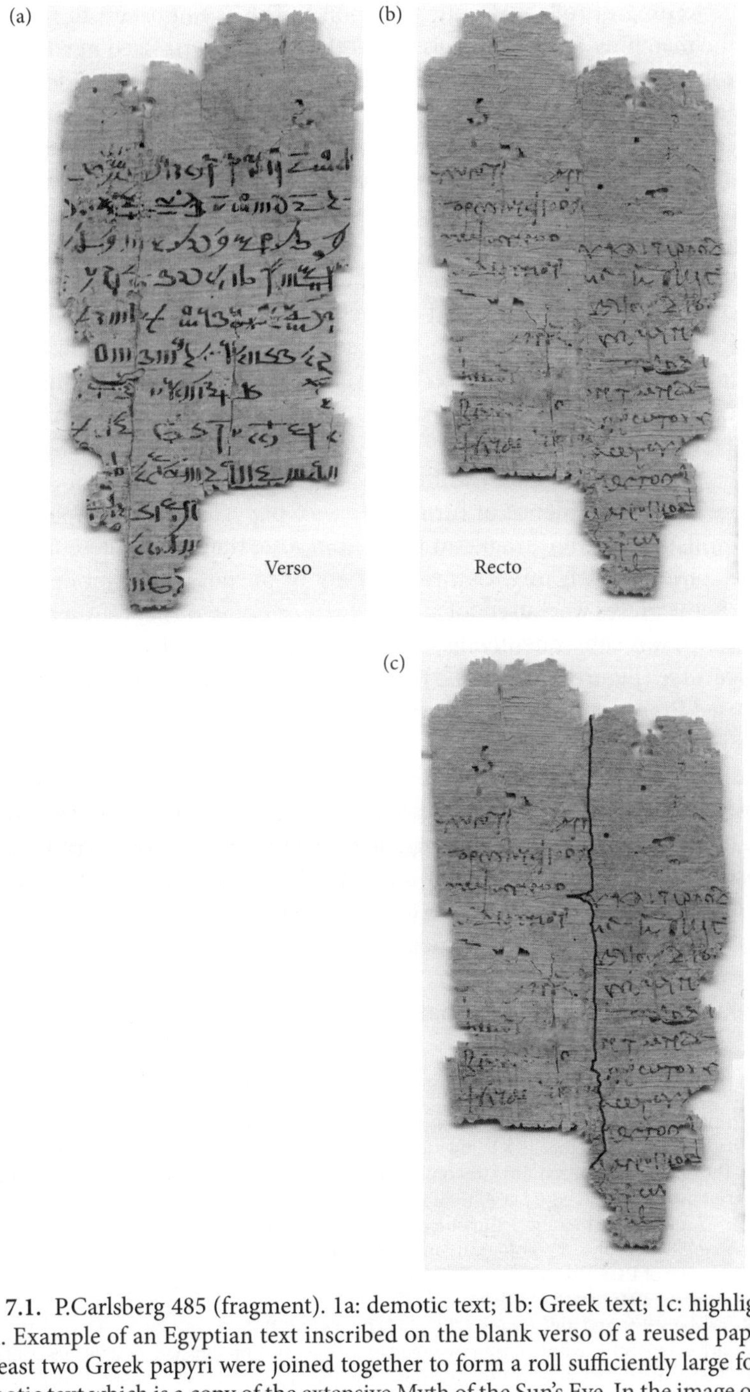

Fig. 7.1. P.Carlsberg 485 (fragment). 1a: demotic text; 1b: Greek text; 1c: highlighted join. Example of an Egyptian text inscribed on the blank verso of a reused papyrus. At least two Greek papyri were joined together to form a roll sufficiently large for the demotic text which is a copy of the extensive Myth of the Sun's Eye. In the image on the lower right, the edge of the join has been drawn up in black to show it more clearly.

that the joining of rolls was quite common.[15] This is important to recognize since the matching of recto texts is one of the main criteria used in sorting the numerous fragments of different reused manuscripts inscribed in identical or very similar hands on the verso.

In addition to the large-scale reuse of older manuscripts, there are other symptoms of the limitations on fresh papyrus. In some cases, scribes had to content themselves with fresh papyrus that was plainly too short for the text in question. Instead of adding sheets to the end of the roll, the text was instead continued on the back.[16] In other cases, the margins and intercolumnia were kept to an absolute minimum and the text itself was written in very long lines and in a much smaller hand than usual so that as much as possible could be fitted into the available space. A scribe responsible for at least two manuscripts, to judge from the hand, offers an extreme example: one single column contains more text than five full columns in the format of a well-known text such as Papyrus Spiegelberg (Figure 7.2).[17]

There is ample evidence of further reuse of papyrus in the temple library. When rolls became too fragile to be used *in toto*, they would be cut up into smaller pieces, which might serve a variety of purposes, like modern scrap paper. Some pieces were used for shorter texts or notes; one cut from a hieratic manuscript was subsequently inscribed in demotic with a list of divine names on its reverse (Figure 7.3),[18] while two others cut from the same ruled papyrus were used for excerpts from the beginning of the Prophecy of Petesis.[19] Other pieces were used to patch damaged manuscripts.

A different kind of secondary use, one that did not entail the discarding of the main text, is the deployment of blank spaces on the reverse for smaller texts, notes, or mere jottings. For instance, two longer demotic narratives, one historical and one mythological, both have shorter hieratic ritual texts concerning Soknebtunis inscribed on the blank backs,[20] and a demotic medical text is similarly inscribed with a hieratic religious or magical text.[21] More curiously, a number of demotic papyri of a different nature—astronomical, astrological, herbal, and narrative—have various types of accounts inscribed on

[15] An example of a demotic literary text with a different origin written on two Greek administrative papyri pasted together is Khamwase and Siosiris now in the British Museum (P.BM EA 10822). The Greek texts pertain to Crocodilopolis in the ninth Upper Egyptian nome, while the manuscript itself was purchased at Aswan; see Griffith (1900, 67–8).

[16] For example, the hieratic P.Carlsberg 1 (hieratic, Book of Nut): see von Lieven (2007). P. Carlsberg 158 (demotic, mythological): unpublished.

[17] The scribe of P.Carlsberg 66 and P.Carlsberg 164; see comments below.

[18] P.Carlsberg 204: Ryholt (forthcoming a).

[19] P.Carlsberg 424 and 499: Ryholt (2012, 157–70, pls. 20–1).

[20] P.Carlsberg 400 (demotic narrative, Nakhthorshena): unpublished, briefly described in Ryholt (2004a, 504–5). P.Carlsberg 460 (demotic mythological narrative): unpublished, described in Kockelmann (2014, 116–23).

[21] P.Carlsberg 172: unpublished. The text on the reverse begins with the words 'I am Horus…', followed by several further first-person nominal sentences expressing identification.

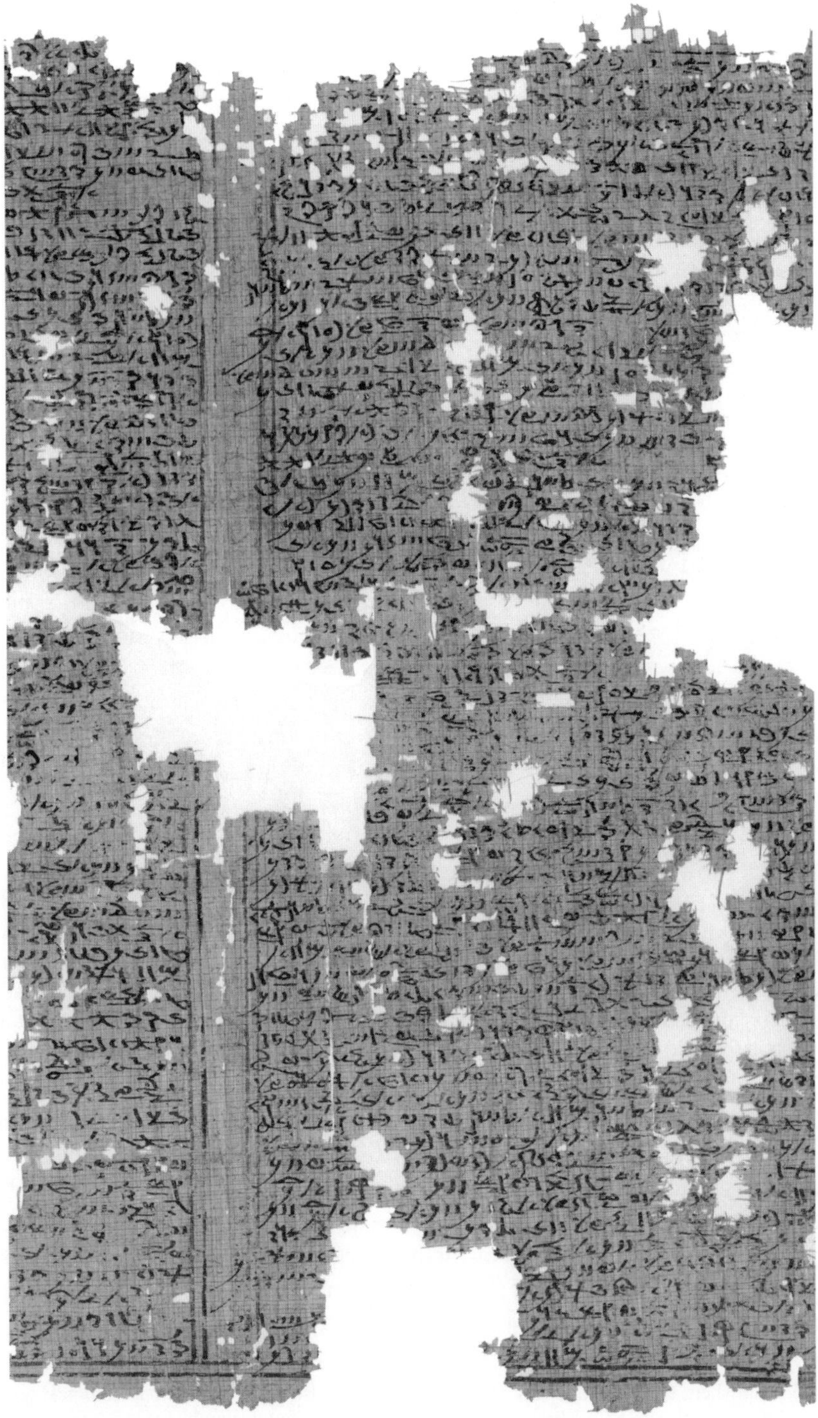

Fig. 7.2. P.Carlsberg 66 (astronomical manual; section). The scribe provided the whole papyrus with neatly drawn frames, but very narrow margins, and he cramped much text in a minute hand into the frames.

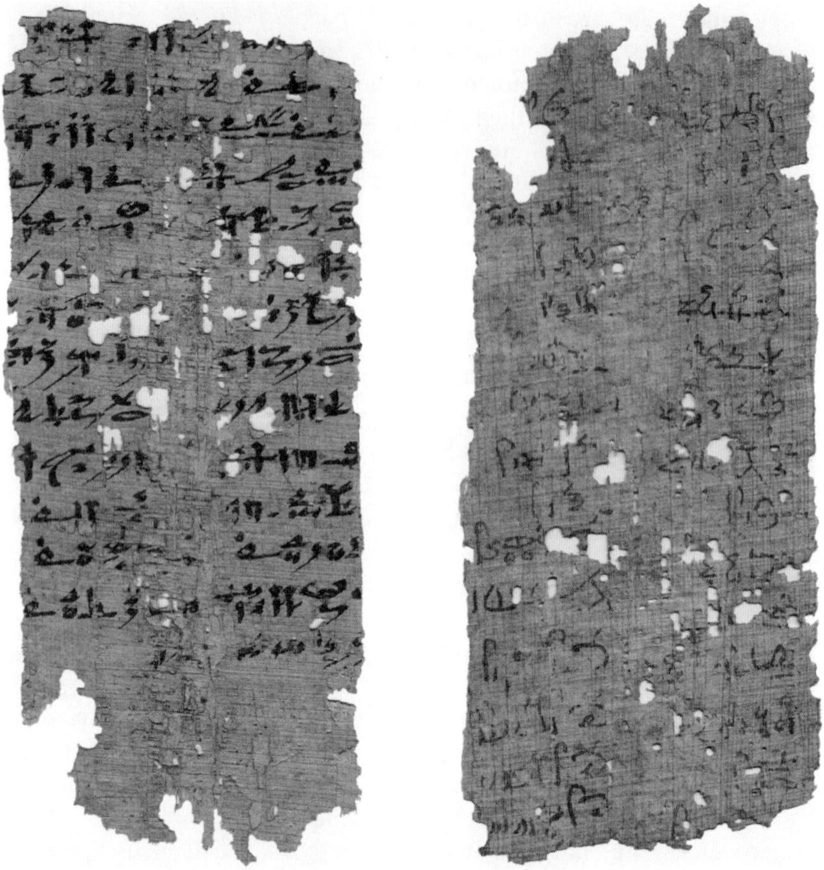

Fig. 7.3. P.Carlsberg 204. A hieratic text (left) was cut up in order to use the blank reverse to write a list of deities in demotic (right). It may be noted that the hieratic text has faint red guidelines laid out with the help of a row of evenly spaced red dots which are visible on the right side of the papyrus.

their backs.[22] It is not obvious under what circumstances this came about. Since the temple library does not otherwise include accounts, the manuscripts would seem to have retained their original use, i.e. that connected with the literary texts. This is also indicated by the fact that the manuscripts were not cut up, although some of them include larger blank sections on the back. The observation is significant since texts secondarily inscribed in this manner would often be considered to be no longer used for their original purpose.

[22] P.Carlsberg 9 (demotic astronomical text) and P.Carlsberg 79 (demotic astrological text): accounts unpublished. P.Carlsberg 230 (demotic herbal): account unpublished; see description and illustration in Tait (1991, 50, pl. 6). P.Carlsberg 324+394 (demotic narrative): account unpublished; see description and illustration in Ryholt (2006, 27–8, pl. 22).

But under what circumstances did this happen? Are we to imagine that the scribes in question simply happened to have these manuscripts at hand and did not have access at that moment to other, more suitable papyrus? Were the papyri at that time kept in the library and had they perhaps been taken out, or borrowed? Do these accounts represent drafts of texts that were later copied onto other papyri before the manuscripts were returned to their original use? And was it considered acceptable to write on material belonging to the library?

§3. LAYOUT OF COLUMNS: FORMATTING LINES

§3.1. Types of Formatting Lines

The different types of formatting lines attested in the Tebtunis manuscripts can be divided into three main groups: horizontal lines separating the text from the upper or lower margin (here called margin lines), vertical lines separating the text columns (here called intercolumnia lines), and horizontal guidelines separating the individual lines of writing.[23]

Within the temple library, the most common layout consists of a combination of guidelines and intercolumnia (Figure 7.4). The scribes sometimes seem to have made use of some kind of a ruler and occasionally provided the manuscript with dots beforehand in order to create a balanced and aesthetic page (Figure 7.5). In other examples, the lines seem to have been drawn up freehand. A less common formatting at Tebtunis is the combination of margin and intercolumnia lines, which may either be drawn up separately or integrated into actual column frames (Figure 7.2).

§3.2. Frequency

In the centuries prior to the Roman period, formatting lines do not seem to have been in general use, at least as far as non-funerary manuscripts are concerned. Formatting lines are not used in any of the published literary fragments from Saqqara dated to the fourth century BCE, and the earliest absolutely-dated example of frame lines is a demotic papyrus from Soknopaiou Nesos from the reign of Augustus.[24] This impression may, however, be skewed by the fact that few larger groups of Egyptian manuscripts have been preserved from the intervening Ptolemaic period.

[23] For a detailed discussion of various types of guidelines in demotic papyri, see Tait (1986).
[24] P.Vienna D 6951: Hoffmann (1999, 219).

Fig. 7.4. P.Carlsberg 180. Example of layout with a combination of guidelines and intercolumnia, typical for hieratic texts in the Tebtunis temple library.

Within the Tebtunis temple library, the use of formatting lines is exceedingly common and some general trends are observable. The majority, about two thirds, of hieratic manuscripts have formatting lines, while they are attested in only about one eighth of the demotic manuscripts. This distribution is evidently directly related to the nature of the texts. As has already been observed, the hieratic texts mostly concern cultic purposes and were therefore generally more carefully prepared than the demotic texts.

Is the use of formatting lines at Tebtunis representative of the period? It was observed about thirty years ago that virtually all papyri with guidelines derive from this site.[25] In the light of material (re)discovered since then, the situation has changed. Above all, it may be observed that the use of guidelines in the unpublished material from Tanis seems no less regular than that from Tebtunis.[26] Moreover, as far as the Book of Thoth is concerned, there are copies from other sites that make use of guidelines, e.g. one demotic manuscript from Soknopaiou Nesos,[27]

[25] Tait (1986, 74).

[26] Personal observation made in 2008, 2009, 2010; see Ryholt (forthcoming e).

[27] P.Vienna D 6343 with further fragments: Jasnow and Zauzich (2005, 87–8, pls. 62–3) [V01+V02+V03]. That V01, V02, and V03 form part of the same manuscript was pointed out by Quack (2007, 263). Note that it was only partially provided with guidelines; they are used in the

(a) (b)

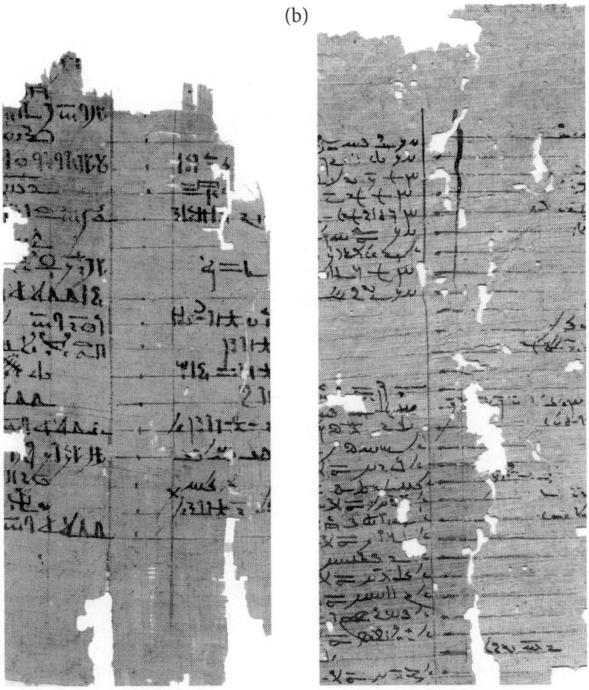

P. Carlsberg 1a P. Carlsberg 13

Fig. 7.5. a) P.Carlsberg 1a; b) P.Carlsberg 13. Examples of guidelines and intercolumnia drawn up by evenly spaced dots.

another probably from the same site,[28] and a hieratic manuscript possibly from Elephantine.[29]

The only substantial, published material available for comparison with Tebtunis is the large collection of literary manuscripts from Soknopaiou Nesos and some further, still unidentified, sites in the Fayum, preserved mainly in Vienna, Berlin, and the Louvre. Here, it will be observed, the predominant types of formatting lines are column frames consisting of either single[30] or double[31] lines, while there are also examples of intercolumnia lines only,

right column of the fragment designated V02, but not in the left column nor in the columns represented by the fragments designated V01.

[28] P.Louvre E 10488 with further fragments: Jasnow and Zauzich (2005, 86–7, pls. 43–59) [L01].

[29] P.Louvre AF 13035 + E 10614: Jasnow and Zauzich (2005, 87, pls. 60–1) [L02].

[30] For example, P.Krall (demotic, Contest for Inaros' Armour): Hoffmann (1996). P.Vienna 6165 and 6165A (demotic, both Petechons and Sarpot): Hoffmann (1995a). P.Vienna D 6257 (demotic medical text): Reymond (1976). P.Vienna D 6319 (demotic, Book of the Temple): Reymond (1977, 45–105).

[31] For example, P.Vienna D 12006 (demotic divination): Stadler (2004). P.Berlin 8027 with further fragments (demotic, Book of Thoth): Jasnow and Zauzich (2005, pls. 17–26, 30, 63) [B04+B05+B06+B13+V04; for the identification of these sigla as belonging to the same papyrus, see Quack (2007, 262)].

Fig. 7.6. P.Carlsberg 468. Hieroglyphic texts with thick double frame lines.

without demarcation of the upper and lower margins.[32] One factor that might play a role in the predominance of this type of layout is the fact that these texts are primarily written in demotic, since we see at Tebtunis that guidelines were mainly used for hieratic texts.

Turning to the hieroglyphic texts from Tebtunis, most of these have a double border, which in some cases is drawn with very thick lines (Figure 7.6).[33] The individual lines of writing, whether vertical or horizontal, are nearly always separated by column lines or guidelines.

Some manuscripts, all inscribed with hieratic texts, have more elaborate intercolumnia. In a few texts we find triple intercolumnia or, perhaps more correctly, intercolumnia drawn with three lines instead of two. In at least two of these texts, the extra space created by the division of the intercolumnia has been used for creative text formatting. In the Book of Nut, it is used for tabulation,[34] while in a ritual in favour of Soknebtunis it is used for a refrain written in a vertical line, 'Awaken, O Soknebtunis!'.[35] Refrains written in vertical lines are also attested in at least two further texts, one a hieratic ritual and

[32] For example, P.Vienna D 6343 (demotic, Book of Thoth): Jasnow and Zauzich (2005, pl. 62) [V01].

[33] For example, P.Carlsberg 56 (hieroglyphic, Book of Fayum): Beinlich (1991; 2013, 123–129, pls. 22–24). P.Carlsberg 305 and 306 (copies of tomb inscriptions from Assiut): Osing and Rosati (1998, 55–100, pls. 6–13).

[34] P.Carlsberg 1 (hieratic, Book of Nut): von Lieven (2007).

[35] P.Carlsberg 667 (hieratic, Daily Ritual and Offering Ritual): unpublished.

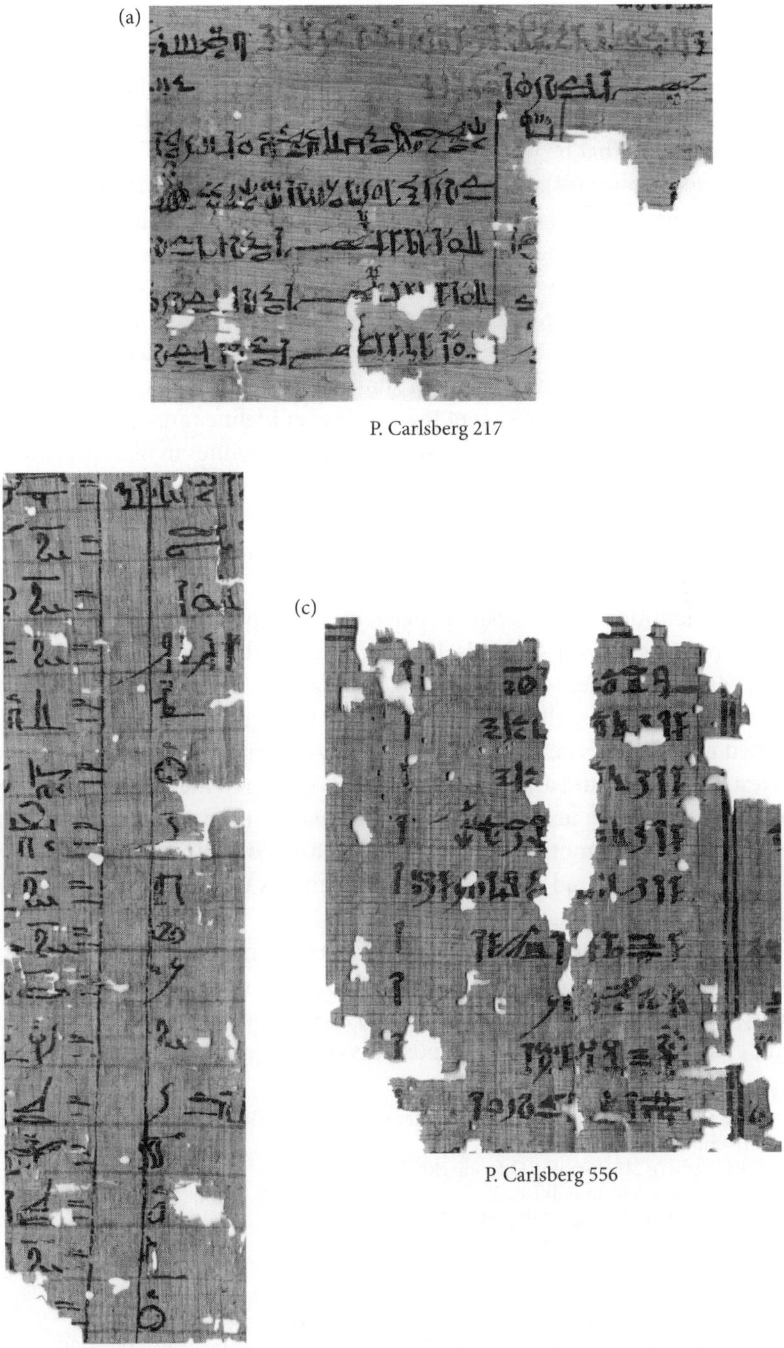

(a)

P. Carlsberg 217

(b)

P. Carlsberg 206

(c)

P. Carlsberg 556

Fig. 7.7. Examples of intercolumnia in papyri from the Tebtunis temple library: a) P.Carlsberg 217; b) P.Carlsberg 206; c) P.Carlsberg 556.

another a demotic hymn to Horus-of-Vine.[36] In both cases, the refrain is written on the outside of the right border of the intercolumnia (Figure 7.7b). In the third example, another hieratic text, the scribe has inserted the vertical lines in the middle of a column, at its bottom, so that it could cover the first five lines of the invocations that he was able to squeeze in (Figure 7.7a).[37]

The most elaborate layout in terms of framing lines from the temple library occurs in the fragment of a hieratic ritual text in favour of Soknebtunis.[38] Here, the columns were framed by thick double lines, and at the same time the manuscript contained finely drawn guidelines together with an additional pair of intercolumnia lines drawn in an equally fine hand (Figure 7.7c). The closest parallel I have come across is the hieratic purification ritual preserved in a papyrus found in cartonnage from Abusir el-Melek.[39] This text is laid out in exactly the same manner, except that the fine guidelines and intercolumnia are both written in red ink in one section and the guidelines in black in another.

§3.3. Red vs Black Lines

Having mentioned the Abusir el-Melek manuscript, we may turn to the use of red formatting lines at Tebtunis. It is employed both for intercolumnia, margin lines, and guidelines, as well as for tables, and it is attested for manuscripts written in all scripts, although it is relatively infrequent.

Red guidelines occur in a few hieratic manuscripts, including a copy of the Priestly Manual[40] and an unidentified text,[41] while red margin lines are attested in a single demotic text.[42] Red intercolumnia are used in at least two hieratic papyri.[43] Three demotic astronomical and astrological manuscripts preserve tables drawn up in red ink, a phenomenon that is well attested for Greek texts of the same nature (Figure 7.8).[44]

Some manuscripts combine black and red formatting lines. One demotic text has black guidelines and red intercolumnia,[45] while two others have black margin lines in combination with the red intercolumnia.[46] Still more elaborate, and evidently for decorative purposes, is the use of black and red formatting

[36] P.Carlsberg 206 (hieratic ritual): Töpfer (2015). P.CtYBR 414 + P.Carlsberg 530 (demotic hymn): unpublished.

[37] P.Carlsberg 217 (hieratic, Offering ritual): unpublished.

[38] P.Carlsberg 556: unpublished. [39] P.Berlin P 13242: Schott (1957).

[40] P.Berlin 14447: Osing (1998, 259–75, pls. 27–8).

[41] P.Carlsberg 204: Ryholt (forthcoming e).

[42] P.Carlsberg 249: unpublished. It is written in a hand very similar to the Sarpot text, just like P.Carlsberg 2.

[43] P.Carlsberg 482 and P.CtYBR 4535: both unpublished.

[44] P.Carlsberg 31 and P.Carlsberg 32: Parker (1962); Neugebauer and Parker (1969, 217–20, 240–3, pl. 79). A third text, of which I have identified several fragments in Berlin, is unpublished.

[45] PSI s.n. + P.Carlsberg 655: unpublished.

[46] P.Carlsberg 2 (demotic, Insinger Wisdom): Volten (1940) [Copenhagen fragments]; Pezin (1986) [Lille fragment]. PSI inv. D 39 (demotic astrological): unpublished.

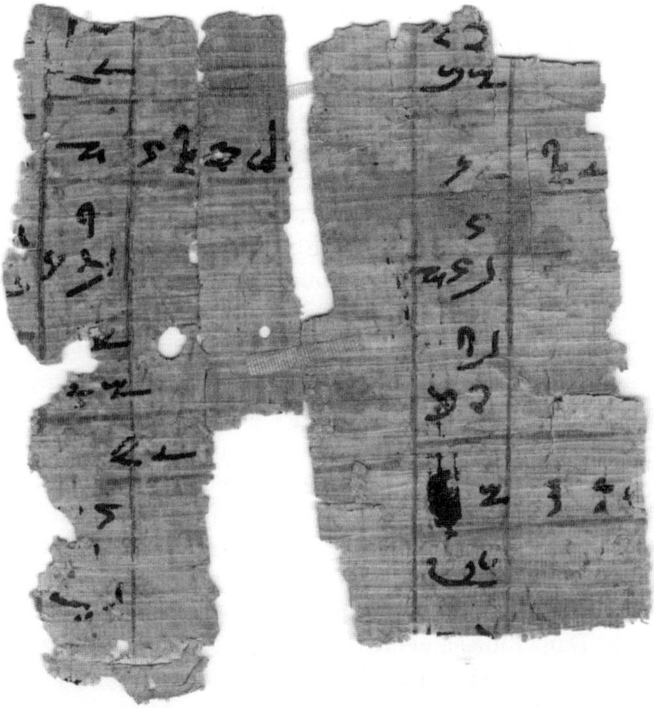

Fig. 7.8. P.Carlsberg 31. Astronomical table laid out with red guidelines.

lines side by side in some manuscripts; a demotic text preserves a red and black intercolumn with horizontal bars similarly in red and black, while a hieroglyphic text is written in columns demarcated by red and black lines.[47]

§3.4. Special Features

The last text formatting I would like to mention is a quite exceptional example of the use of red ink. In an unpublished fragment from the temple library (PSI inv. I 182), preserving part of a hieroglyphic text, red ink was used to paint the background onto which, it seems, the names of a series of demons were subsequently written. Provided that we are in fact dealing with demons, the red background here seems to be functionally equivalent to writing the names of dangerous entities in red ink. Painted backgrounds are also attested for hieroglyphic legends associated with vignettes in the Book of the Dead, but these are consistently painted yellow and we are here dealing with a functionally very different phenomenon.

[47] P.Carlsberg 682: unpublished. PSI inv. I 1: Rosati (1990).

§4. PAGINATION

§4.1. Frequency

Pagination, the numbering of columns, is a relatively rare phenomenon prior to the Graeco-Roman period.[48] From the fourth century onwards, it seems to be used gradually more often, but it never becomes common and pagination in itself was evidently not considered essential. Within the Tebtunis temple library, there are about twenty-five paginated manuscripts representing little more than 6 per cent of the total holdings.

§4.2. Purpose

There seems to be no clear pattern in the use of pagination, although some general observations can be made. Perhaps not surprisingly, it is mainly attested in longer texts. Examples from the temple library include copies of the narratives of the Myth of the Sun's Eye with 124 columns,[49] the Inaros Epic with 46 columns (written in a very minute hand!),[50] the Mythological Manual with 41 columns,[51] the Daily Ritual and the Offering Ritual (alongside one another on the same manuscript) with at least 30 columns,[52] Naneferkasokar and the Babylonians with at least 27 columns,[53] the Priestly Manual with at least 26 columns,[54] and a morning hymn with at least 17 columns.[55] There are, however, exceptions such as the Cairo manuscript of Khamwase and Naneferkaptah (from an uncertain Upper Egyptian provenance), which was only six columns long and which might therefore have been thought not to require pagination.

More importantly, pagination seems mainly to be attested in manuscripts for which some care had been taken in the production. A good illustration is a copy of the Book of the Temple, which was committed to a new papyrus of good quality provided with guidelines and written in a clear and consistent hand.[56]

[48] Černý (1952, 21) could cite only the medical P.Ebers from the New Kingdom and P.Cairo CG 30646 from the third century BCE which is inscribed with Khamwase and Naneferkaptah.

[49] PSI inv. D 104 + P.Carlsberg 790 (demotic): unpublished.

[50] P.Carlsberg 164 (demotic): unpublished. These 46 columns could correspond to *c.*125 columns in the format of the Leiden copy of the Myth of the Sun's Eye or 240 columns in the format of the Papyrus Spiegelberg copy of the Contest for the Benefice of Amun, when measured as an estimated number of signs per column.

[51] PSI inv. I 98: unpublished. Editions of this papyrus and P.Carlsberg 667, cited in the following footnote, are in preparation by Jürgen Osing, who kindly brought both manuscripts to my attention and provided me with details.

[52] P.Carlsberg 667 (hieratic): unpublished.

[53] P.Carlsberg 303 (demotic): unpublished.

[54] P.Carlsberg 182 + PSI inv. I 77 (hieratic): Osing (1998, 219–58, pls. 23–6). The highest preserved column number in the publication is 23. I have since discovered a fragment of the 26th column.

[55] P.Carlsberg 767 (hieratic): unpublished.

[56] P.Carlsberg 313 (hieratic): unpublished.

This could be taken to imply that, at least in some cases, manuscripts with pagination were used as originals for copy purposes, where neatly written manuscripts in a clear hand would naturally be an advantage for the copyist. This impression is further supported by the fact that most of the paginated manuscripts contain copies of texts that can be considered particularly important and which were kept in multiple copies: the Book of the Temple (approximately twenty copies; one has pagination), the Priestly Manual (at least three copies; one has pagination), the Mythological Manual (at least five copies; two have pagination), the Myth of the Sun's Eye (at least seven copies; four have pagination), the initiation ritual known as the Book of Thoth (approximately ten copies; two have pagination), and the historical narrative of the Inaros Epic (at least four copies; one has pagination).[57] The relatively large number of copies of the Myth of the Sun's Eye provided with pagination is noteworthy, as is the fact that two of them have dual pagination, in one case using both demotic and Greek (see below).

There are other substantial and important texts for which pagination is not attested, such as the Book of Fayum, the Daily Ritual, or the very long narrative of the Petese Stories, nor do any of the astrological texts preserve pagination. This may be a mere accident of preservation or identification, given the generally poor preservation of the manuscripts. Moreover, one must consider the possibility that pagination was not added until it was actually decided that a specific text would be copied. Although it is difficult to prove, the pagination in at least some manuscripts seems very likely to be secondary, i.e. not belonging to the original copy process. Thus, for instance, one copy of the Book of Thoth has pagination in much bolder writing,[58] while—as already mentioned—a copy of the Myth of the Sun's Eye has pagination in Greek.[59] In both cases, the pagination is also much fainter than the main text, indicating that the scribe has dipped his pen and written column number after column number while unrolling the papyrus and without redipping the pen very often, thus allowing the ink to get dryer and dryer (Figure 7.9). Moreover, in all but one of the hieratic manuscripts, the pagination is written in demotic.

§4.3. Format, Script, and Position of Pagination

The pagination consistently takes one of three formats: either just the column number (x), the column number preceded by *mḥ* as *mḥ*-x, or the latter preceded by the definitive article as *pꜣ mḥ*-x (Figure 7.9 and Table 7.1). About half

[57] See Ryholt (2005, 148–9, 156). To the list of manuscripts inscribed with the Myth of the Sun's Eye listed there may now be added the unpublished P.Carlsberg 102 + PSI inv. 3024.

[58] P.Carlsberg 616 (demotic): Jasnow and Zauzich (2005, pl. 2) [C02].

[59] P.Carlsberg 600 (demotic): unpublished.

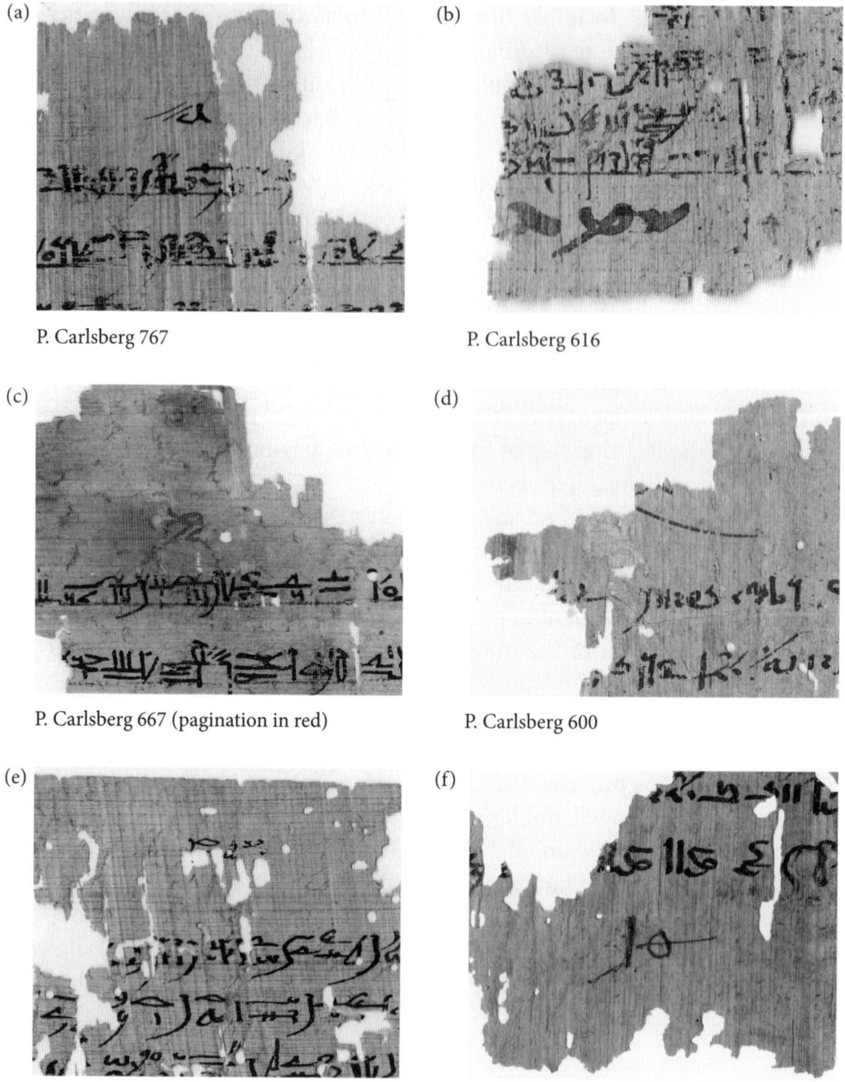

(a) P. Carlsberg 767
(b) P. Carlsberg 616
(c) P. Carlsberg 667 (pagination in red)
(d) P. Carlsberg 600
(e) P. Carlsberg 593
(f) P. Carlsberg 600

Fig. 7.9. Examples of pagination in papyri from the Tebtunis temple library: a) P.Carlsberg 767; b) P.Carlsberg 616; c) P.Carlsberg 667; d) P.Carlsberg 600; e) P.Carlsberg 593 (pagination in red); f) P.Carlsberg 600.

of the manuscripts with pagination use the simple format, while the two formats with *mḥ* are about equally common and make up the other half.

The pagination is written in either the upper or the lower margin. There seems to be no preference for one or the other. It is usually centered in relation to the text column and it is nearly always written in demotic, whether the

Table 7.1. The three types of pagination

x	(Column) x
mḥ-x	(The) xth (column)
pꜣ mḥ-x	The xth (column)

text itself is demotic or hieratic. So far, only a single hieratic text with hieratic pagination has been identified;[60] the other hieratic texts all have demotic pagination.[61] More surprising is the example of dual pagination in Greek and demotic in a demotic text.

For purposes of comparison, it may be noted that two texts among the published demotic literary fragments from Saqqara (fourth century BCE) are provided with pagination.[62] In both cases, it takes the format *mḥ*-x and is written in the lower margin.

§4.4. Special Features (Dual Pagination, Red Ink, and Greek)

A few manuscripts display exceptional features. Most noteworthy is the use of dual pagination in at least six manuscripts, four demotic and two hieratic. These manuscripts preserve, respectively, the Inaros Epic,[63] the Myth of the Sun's Eye (two copies),[64] the Book of Thoth,[65] the Mythological Manual,[66] and a copy of the Daily Ritual and Offering Ritual inscribed together.[67] In two of them, the columns are counted from the beginning—as usual—in one margin, while they are counted from the end in the other, and the same is likely also to apply to the other four more damaged manuscripts. Again it may be assumed that this method of pagination was deployed to facilitate the copying process: with dual pagination, the scribe would not only know which column he was at, but also exactly how many columns were left, without having to unroll the lengthy papyrus. Miscalculations about the length of texts happened all too often, as demonstrated by texts from various periods and locations that were

[60] P.Carlsberg 593 (Mythological Manual): unpublished.

[61] P.Carlsberg 182 + PSI inv. I 77 (Priestly Manual): Osing (1998, 219–58, pls. 23–6). P.Carlsberg 313 (Book of the Temple): unpublished. P.Carlsberg 667 (Daily Ritual and Offering Ritual): unpublished. P.Carlsberg 767 (morning hymn): unpublished.

[62] P.Dem.Saq. 1 and P.Dem.Saq. 2 front (both narratives): Smith and Tait (1983, 1–64, 70–109, pls. 1–3, 4–5).

[63] P.Carlsberg 164: unpublished.

[64] P.Carlsberg 600 and PSI inv. D 104 + P. Carlsberg 790: both unpublished.

[65] P.Carlsberg 616: Jasnow and Zauzich (2005, pl. 2) [C02]. The publication includes only fragments with pagination in the lower margin. I have since discovered further fragments that preserve the pagination in the upper margin.

[66] PSI inv. I 98: unpublished.

[67] P.Carlsberg 667: unpublished.

copied onto papyri too short to contain them in full.[68] Apart from a contemporary hieratic funerary papyrus of unknown provenance in the Cairo Museum,[69] the phenomenon of dual pagination is only known to me from Tebtunis, and the examples thus date to the Roman period.

Somewhat surprising is the fact that the dual pagination in one of the manuscripts inscribed with the Myth of the Sun's Eye is written in demotic in the upper margin, but in Greek in the lower margin. The reason for using Greek rather than demotic is not obvious, but it may reflect nothing other than the ability of many Egyptian priests to communicate and write in both Egyptian and Greek. One might even entertain the possibility that the text was about to be copied by someone particularly well versed in Greek for the purposes of translation, seeing that a translation of the Myth of the Sun's Eye is known from a British Library manuscript (P.British Library inv. 274 = P.Lond.Lit. 192), but this would probably be stretching the evidence too far.

Also worth noting, but less spectacular, is the use of red ink for pagination in two manuscripts. One is the aforementioned hieratic ritual of Sobek with dual pagination, while the content of the other text has yet to be identified.[70]

§5. CORRECTION AND COLLATION

There are numerous evident cases of careful collation, and a very large number of the manuscripts preserve textual corrections and additions. Some mistakes were evidently discovered during the copying process and were immediately corrected, while others were only spotted during later use or collation with other manuscripts. Mistakes were corrected in a variety of ways. Very frequently, we find that missing signs or words have been added, mostly above the line, and that incorrect signs or words have been washed out and rewritten. Less commonly, erroneous signs and words were encircled with dots,[71] deleted with strokes,[72] or blotted out with a thick black square (Figure 7.10).[73]

[68] A good example dating to the Middle Kingdom is afforded by the copy of the Eloquent Peasant (Parkinson 1991: xiv–xviii).

[69] P.Cairo CG 58034: Golénischeff (1927, 209–15, pl. 35). The one preserved column has the number *mḥ-3* in the upper margin and *mḥ-2* in the lower; accordingly, the text would seem to have been only four columns long. The pagination is written in demotic.

[70] PSI s.n.: unpublished.

[71] For example, P.Carlsberg 62 (demotic, Myth of Sun's Eye?), P.Carlsberg 100 (demotic astrological), and P.Carlsberg 163 (demotic narrative): all unpublished. P.Tebt.Tait 4 (demotic narrative): Tait (1977, 24–6, pl. 2).

[72] For example, P.PeteseTebt. A (demotic narrative): Ryholt (1999, 8–9). PSI inv. I 3 + P.Carlsberg 305 + P.Tebt.Tait add 2 (hieroglyphic copy of Assiut tomb inscriptions): Osing and Rosati (1998, 55).

[73] For example, P.Carlsberg 85 (demotic narrative) and P.Carlsberg 652 (hieratic, invocation of Isis): both unpublished.

(a)

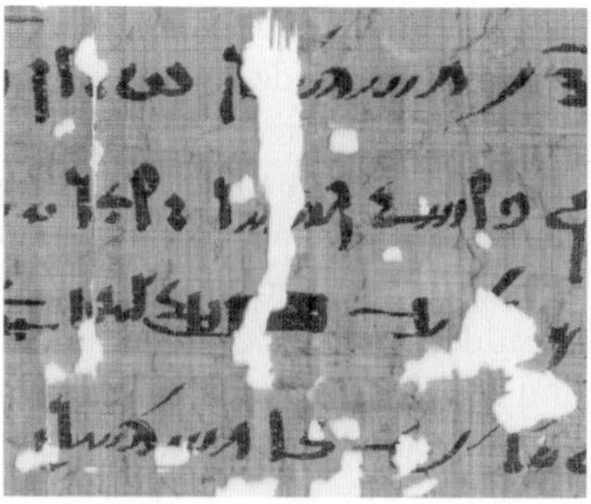

P. Carlsberg 85: erasure with square block in line 3

(b)

P. Carlsberg 652: erasure with square block in line 4

(c)

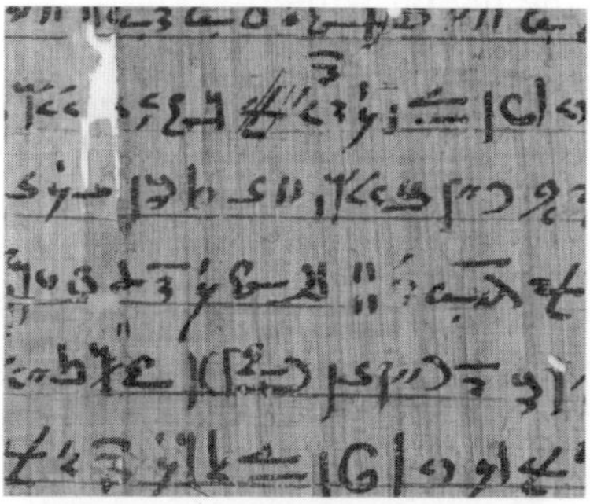

P. Carlsberg 165: erasure by striking out in lines 2 and 5

(d)

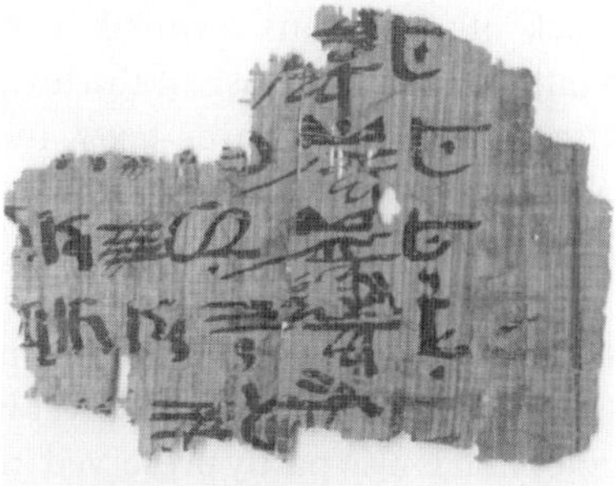

P. Carlsberg s.n.: erasure by striking out in lines 3 and 4

(e)

P. Carlsberg 100: erasure by encircling with dots in last line

(f)

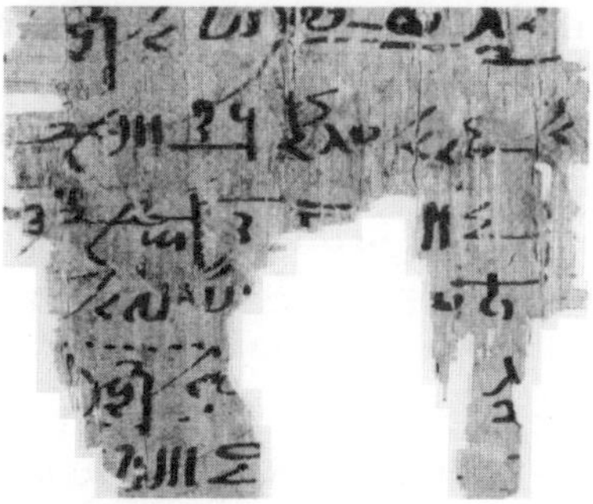

P. Tebt. Tait 4: erasure by encircling with dots in line 5

Fig. 7.10. Examples of corrections in papyri from the Tebtunis temple library: a) P.Carlsberg 85 (erasure with square block in line 3); b) P.Carlsberg 652 (erasure with square block in line 4); c) P.Carlsberg 165 (erasure by striking out in lines 2 and 5); d) P.Carlsberg s.n. (erasure by striking out in lines 3 and 4); e) P.Carlsberg 100 (erasure by encircling with dots in last line); f) P. Tebt. Tait 4 (erasure by encircling with dots in line 5).

A prime example of how details may be added is the Great Tebtunis Onomasticon, which was written in hieratic and provided with glosses in demotic and Old Coptic (Figure 7.4).[74] The secondary recording of textual variants, presumably also based on collation, is not infrequent in texts relating to the cult. Sometimes these are explicitly marked with the words *ky ḏd* 'another (copy) says…'. Some noteworthy examples include a hieroglyphic religious text where many textual variants have been added in hieratic as well as in Old Coptic, some next to the relevant words and some in the margins,[75] while the fragment of a hieratic list of *materia sacra* has a variant recorded on the back of the roll.[76]

A different and more pedestrian type of correction is the secondary addition of rubra. The examples from the temple library consist of reference works where the original scribe for some reason wrote the entire text in black ink and thus omitted to highlight the catchwords with rubra that would facilitate the use of the text. This rewriting of catchwords in red ink is attested in at least three texts, two demotic[77] and one hieratic.[78] The same phenomenon is attested in a recently published hieratic divinatory text from Hermopolis.[79]

In one of the rarely-preserved colophons from the temple library, pertaining to a demotic astrological text, the process of collation is implied.[80] It is incompletely preserved but can be restored with some certainty, since an identical colophon is also partly preserved in P.Krall.[81] This, in turn, indicates that we are dealing with a standard colophon. It reads: *ỉw=f pw nfr* [*ỉw=f*] *sẖ.w ỉw*[*=f nf r-*]*ẖ.t pꜣy-sẖ wb=f* 'This is its very end, it being written (i.e. copied) and it being correct in accordance to that which was written before him (i.e. collated).'[82] The implications of the colophon are not without interest. By using the wording 'being correct in accordance to that which was written before him', the two scribes made no claim that their texts were intrinsically correct, but simply that they were correct insofar as their immediate originals were concerned. In other words, they were reliable copies, but the scribes did not vouch for their contents as such.

[74] P.Carlsberg 180: Osing (1998, 25–218, pls. 1–22).

[75] P.Carlsberg 468: unpublished. With the variants written in Old Coptic, the hieratic group *ky ḏd* is written to the left of the words since the reading direction is left to right.

[76] P.Carlsberg 588: unpublished.

[77] P.Carlsberg 711 + PSI inv. D 42 + P.Cairo CG 50143 (astrological): Cairo fragment published in Spiegelberg (1932a, 105–6, pl. 59). P.Carlsberg 700 (Book of Thoth): Jasnow and Zauzich (2005, pl. 32) [C06].

[78] P.Carlsberg 720 (religious geography): unpublished.

[79] P.Berlin 23057 A–J: Stadler (2004, 234).

[80] P.Carlsberg 420: unpublished.

[81] Hoffmann (1996, 397–9).

[82] The relevant part of P.Krall may be restored as [*ỉw*]*=f sẖ ỉw=f tn*[*f r-ẖ.t pꜣy-sẖ*] *wb=f*. Note that *pꜣy-sẖ* is a common demotic orthography for the participle *pꜣ-ỉ.sẖ*.

§6. REPAIR

Papyrus manuscripts gradually deteriorate, especially when used on a regular basis and over longer periods of time. Evidence of ancient repairs can often help in reconstructing the history of a specific manuscript and thereby shed indirect light on the text or texts it contains. Unfortunately, it happens all too frequently that text editions provide little detail on the actual state and condition of the physical manuscripts beyond what is most obvious. Especially the backs of manuscripts are often entirely ignored, presumably because editors frequently work from photographs or scans and have not inspected the originals. To judge from the Tebtunis temple library, the repair of ancient manuscripts is much more common than might be assumed.

A nice example is afforded by one of the oldest texts from the library, the Tebtunis Legal Manual.[83] This manuscript is about a century older than the bulk of the manuscripts and, in the course of its more than two-centuries-long lifespan, it was evidently consulted often enough that it had to be patched and strengthened on several occasions. The same is true for numerous other manuscripts. I shall give some more examples, but first it might be instructive to look briefly at the different types of patches.

As one might expect, patches would generally be cut to match the size of the area in need of repair. The patches may, broadly speaking, be divided into three groups: small square patches, tall vertical strips running the full height of the papyrus, and larger sheets similarly matching the full height of the papyrus. The small patches are by far the most common (Figure 7.11). The full-height strips and sheets were mainly used as protective sheets attached to the beginning and sometimes also the end of the rolls. The vertical strips were, moreover, used to reinforce weak points where the papyrus was in danger of coming apart, such as the vulnerable area around sheet joins.

An example of extensive repair is attested for a manuscript inscribed with the Petese Stories.[84] Not only was this manuscript repaired and reinforced with patches in several places, with one patch being the size of a whole sheet of papyrus, but there are even indications that an entire section of the papyrus was recopied onto a different roll because of its poor state of preservation.[85]

Another even more noteworthy example is the London–Leiden Magical Papyrus, which is generally assumed to be of Theban provenance.[86] In 2008, I had the chance to study carefully the reverse of the London frames, and it took me entirely by surprise to discover the presence of about forty patches; in some cases with newer patches overlapping older ones. This is the most extensive

[83] P.Carlsberg 301 + PSI inv. D 1 (demotic): Bresciani (1981) [Florence fragments]; Chauveau (1991, pls. 8–9) [Copenhagen fragments].

[84] P.PeteseTebt. A (demotic): Ryholt (1999, 1–3).

[85] Cf. comments in Ryholt (2006, 147–8).

[86] Dieleman (2005).

Fig. 7.11. P.Carlsberg 489 (section of the reverse). Two patches were pasted onto the back of the papyrus to strengthen damaged points. The lower patch was cut from a Greek papyrus.

example of repair that I have come across, and the London frames represent only a portion of a much larger manuscript with an even longer section preserved in Leiden, while both the beginning and the end of the manuscript are lost. If the London frames are representative of the manuscript as a whole, it might easily have been patched more than a hundred times!

Also interesting is a copy of the Book of Thoth, perhaps from Soknopaiou Nesos, where an entire sheet was cut away in antiquity and replaced by a new one.[87] The fact that the entire right intercolumn and half of the left one are preserved rules out the possibility that the scribe had merely forgotten to write that column and that it was later inserted. The repair must have happened some time after the text had originally been written, since the new sheet is inscribed in a different hand and not provided with guidelines. The secondary sheet joins were not smoothened and are clearly visible in the published plates.

Examples such as these illustrate how—if anyone were to doubt it—even texts found in contexts dating close to the end of the Pharaonic civilization (both manuscripts were 'abandoned' in the third century CE) were still very much part of a living tradition, and how they were still being copied, read, and cared for.

§7. THE ANCIENT SCRIBES

The last aspect of the temple library I would like to comment on, on the present occasion, is that of the ancient scribes themselves. To date, no more than three or four scribes responsible for papyri in the temple library are known by name.[88] Three individuals are explicitly recorded as scribes in the colophons of papyri; two names are completely preserved and one only partially. These are Psuphis son of Pakebkis and an individual of whose name only the initial element Pete... survives, both of whom copied demotic narratives,[89] and Pakebkis who made a hieratic copy of the Book of Fayum.[90] The latter text is stated to have been written by the *wab*-priest Pakebkis for the high priest of Soknebtunis and Geb, i.e. the high priest of the temple to which the library belonged. Psuphis

[87] P.Louvre E 10488 with further fragments: Jasnow and Zauzich (2005, pl. 58) [L01, column 2]. The replacement of the sheet is not noted in the publication.

[88] The identity of a further scribe is partially preserved (patronym only) in the demotic colophon of a hieratic ritual papyrus of the second or first century BCE, found in the dump next to the temple; see Guermeur (2008, 119).

[89] Psuphis son of Pakebkis wrote PSI inv. 1730 (Ryholt, forthcoming c), a tall narrow fragment which mentions 'the children of Hareus' and might be related to the Story of Hareus son of Pahat. The latter is edited in Ryholt (2012, 1–21, pls. 1–3). Pete[...] wrote PSI inv. D 6 + P.Carlsberg 423 (unpublished) of which I have identified a large number of fragments. It preserves a new story about Setne Khamwase.

[90] PSI inv. I 71: Botti (1959, 72–3, pl. IX), lines 8–16; Beinlich (2014, 193–9, pls 26–33).

son of Pakebkis was also a *wab*-priest. In principle, the two *wab*-priests Pakebkis and Psuphis son of Pakebkis could be father and son; but although they have the same title and were attached to the same temple around the same date, the name Pakebkis is much too common to render this more than a mere possibility. A fourth scribe who may have been active in the temple library is Phanesis son of Pakebkis. One or two demotic letters of his are written in a hand that is very similar to some of the literary texts from the library, and there are indications that these letters were actually found with the library.[91]

A few more scribes may well be identified, but it seems clear that the majority will remain anonymous to us. There are, however, many instances of texts written in hands that are so similar that one suspects that the same scribe was responsible. It would also be surprising if matters were otherwise, since we are dealing with a temple library where, it must be imagined, some scribes would have operated for years. A number of distinct and sometimes quite dissimilar handwritings are attested at Tebtunis (see Figures 7.12 and 7.13 for the range of demotic and hieratic hands). This is an important observation insofar that it warns us not to be too restrictive in the attribution of 'typical' hands to a specific site; evidently, contemporary or near-contemporary hands could vary considerably. With time, it should be possible to classify the hands attested in the library and thus gain an impression of how many scribes were responsible for the extant texts. A very tentative guess would be in the order of around fifty.

After the Roman annexation, the use of Egyptian scripts soon became very restricted and more or less confined to the native temples. This insularity seems to have intensified a process whereby both the hieratic and demotic scripts developed marked local characteristics with regard to palaeography as well as orthography. Thus, for instance, it is not difficult to distinguish between the typical demotic handwritings of Tebtunis, Soknopaiou Nesos, Narmouthis, and Akhmim.

For the same reason it is tempting to attribute to Soknopaiou Nesos a large historical narrative about the prince Nakhthorshen, which is written in a hand that can only be described as typical of that town.[92] There can, however, be little doubt that this papyrus formed part of the temple library in Tebtunis, since it was found within the cellars with the other papyri. Moreover, the reverse of the papyrus has a hieratic text praising Soknebtunis. Another example is a mythological narrative, which is written in a hand that is not typical of Tebtunis; also, this manuscript was similarly found in the cellars and it, too, has a ritual text praising Soknebtunis inscribed on its back.[93]

What do we make of this? First of all, it is clear that we should be very careful in dismissing a Tebtunis origin for texts that are written in hands that are not

[91] P.Cairo CG 31220 and P.Tebt.Tait 22: Tait (1977, 71–8, pl. 5).
[92] P.Carlsberg 400: unpublished.
[93] P.Carlsberg 460: unpublished; see the description in Kockelmann (2014, 117).

(a) P. Carlsberg 69
(b) P. Carlsberg 304
(c) P. Carlsberg 400
(d) P. Carlsberg 164
(e) P. Carlsberg 460
(f) P. Carlsberg 85

Fig. 7.12. Samples of demotic hands attested in papyri from the Tebtunis temple library: a) P.Carlsberg 69; b) P.Carlsberg 304; c) P.Carlsberg 400; d) P.Carlsberg 164; e) P.Carlsberg 460; f) P.Carlsberg 85.

characteristic for Tebtunis. Second, this may be taken to indicate either that there was a trade or other movement in manuscripts between different temples or that scribes trained in one temple might later find themselves working in another. It is important to note that the two examples presented above are by no means the only ones of this kind. At least two manuscripts are written in a hand

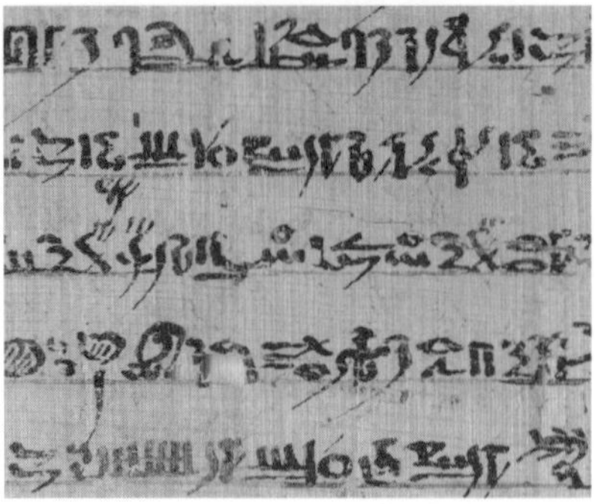

P. Carlsberg 724

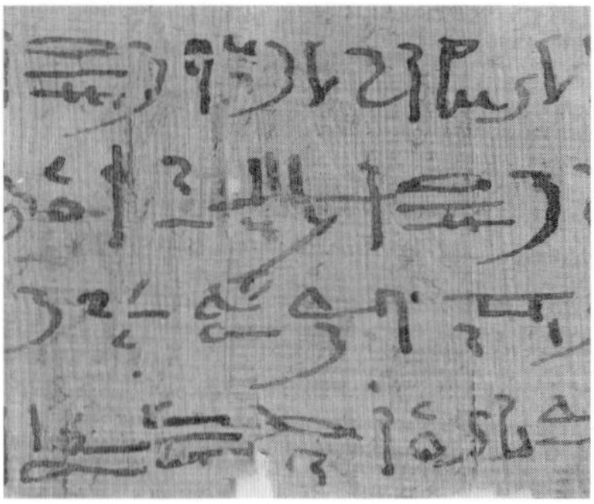

P. Carlsberg 406

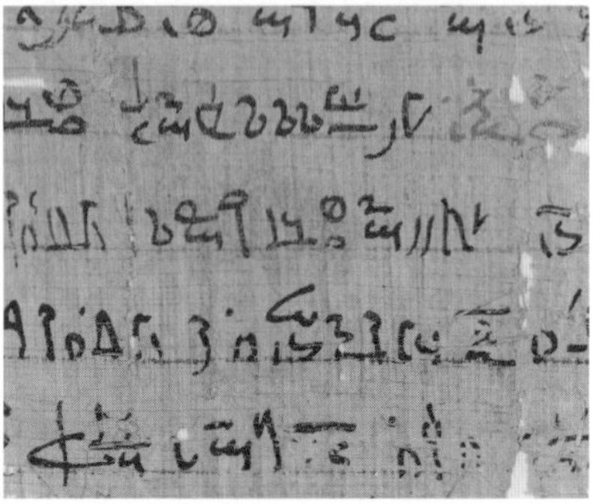

P. Carlsberg 315

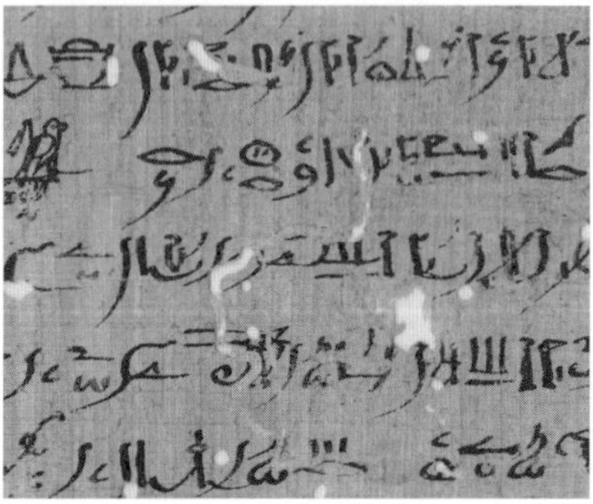

P. Carlsberg 593

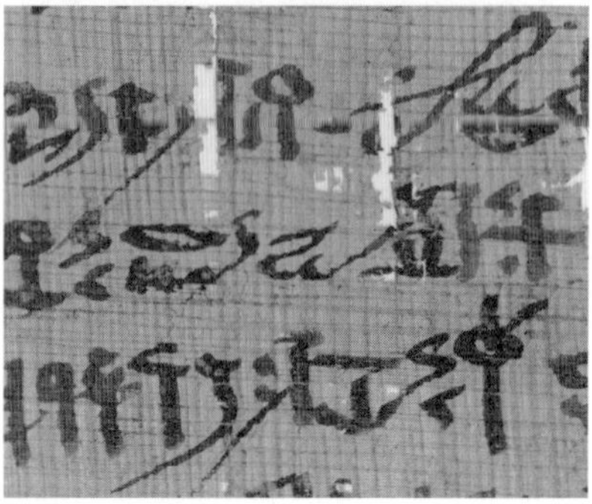

P. Carlsberg 392

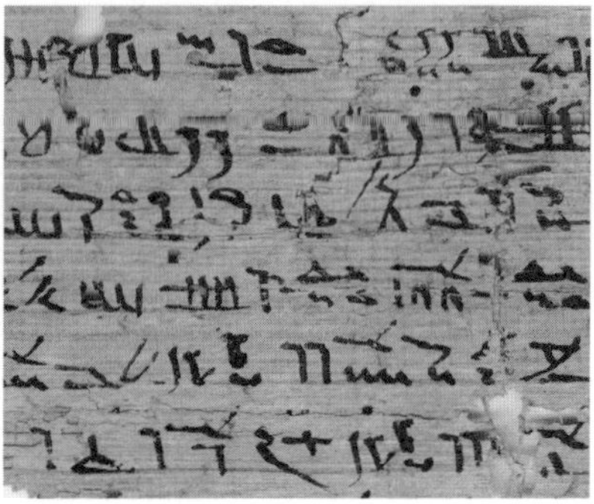

P. Carlsberg 588

Fig. 7.13. Samples of hieratic hands attested in papyri from the Tebtunis temple library: a) P.Carlsberg 724; b) P.Carlsberg 406; c) P.Carlsberg 315; d) P.Carlsberg 593; e) P. Carlsberg 392; f) P.Carlsberg 588.

that is quite similar to that attested in the Narmouthis ostraca,[94] and there are several other hands that one might hesitate to attribute to Tebtunis.

Another important aspect of the individual scribes concerns the nature of their activities within the temple. Were the scribes specialized in the sense that they would work exclusively on specific types of texts? Lacking direct information about the scribes of virtually all the texts, we are confined to the study of palaeography and orthography. I am generally inclined to regard texts in very similar hands to have been written by the same scribe, though this is difficult to prove. There is, however, some degree of consistency in the hands and the formal layout of the papyri with which they are associated. Thus, for instance, both texts written in the Narmouthis hand use fresh papyrus, double frame lines, small margins, very long lines, and a minute script, and they manage to squeeze in between forty-five and sixty lines per column (Figure 7.2). All these shared features seem to indicate personal habits.

Accepting this approach, there would not appear to be any noticeable genre specialization. To give a few examples relating to demotic texts, the aforementioned scribe wrote a historical narrative (the Inaros Epic) and an astrological text; another scribe wrote three historical narratives (including the Inaros Epic) and an astrological text;[95] one wrote a historical narrative, an unidentified divination text, and the Book of Thoth;[96] while yet another scribe (the abovementioned Pete[...]) wrote a wisdom text as well as both a mythological and a historical narrative.[97] It remains uncertain whether the predominant hand at Tebtunis—the so-called Nun hand[98]—represents an individual (as I am inclined to believe) or merely the local handwriting.[99] At any rate, we find in this hand many historical narratives,[100] a mythological narrative,[101] a cult-geographic manual,[102] a cosmology,[103] a religious hymn or manual,[104] an

[94] P.Carlsberg 66 and P.Carlsberg 164: both unpublished, but there is a description of the former in Chauveau (1992), who notes the close similarity with the Narmouthis hand.

[95] P.Carlsberg 80 (narrative, Inaros Epic), P.Carlsberg 411 (narrative about king Sesostris), and PSI inv. D 35 (astrological): all unpublished. P.Carlsberg 433 + P.Tebt.Tait 2 (narrative, Contest for the Benefice of Amun): Tait (2002, pls. 11–12).

[96] P.Carlsberg 129 (narrative, Inaros story) and P.Carlsberg 150 (divination): both unpublished. P.Carlsberg 700 (Book of Thoth): Jasnow and Zauzich (2005, pl. 32) [C06].

[97] P.Carlsberg 423 (narrative about Setne Khamwase), P.Carlsberg 460 (mythological narrative), and P.Berlin 23728 (Insinger Wisdom). The latter is published in Zauzich (1975).

[98] For the Nun hand, see Quack (Chapter 8 in this volume).

[99] The different texts in this hand are also regarded as the work of a single scribe by von Lieven (2007, 17 n. 38).

[100] P.Carlsberg 57+465 (Inaros story): unpublished. P.Carlsberg 68+123 (Inaros Epic): unpublished. P.Carlsberg 125 (Inaros story): Ryholt (2012, 89–102, pls. 11–13). P.Carlsberg 128+434 (Contest for the Benefice of Amun): one fragment published by Tait (2002, 59–61, 75–82, pl. 13). P.Carlsberg 421: (Ryholt (2012, 103–30, pls. 14–17).

[101] P.Tebt.Tait 8 (Myth of the Sun's Eye): Tait (1977, 35–7, pl. 3).

[102] P.Carlsberg 387 (Book of Fayum): Beinlich (2017, 30–92, pls. 42–45).

[103] P.Carlsberg 302: Smith (2002).

[104] P.Carlsberg 69 (hymn to Bastet): unpublished; see Hoffmann and Quack (2007, 305–11).

astrological text,[105] a dream book,[106] and a prophecy,[107] to mention just some of the texts.

A further number of scribes can similarly be identified on the basis of the hieratic hands. To give again a few examples, one scribe wrote two copies of the Book of the Temple, a copy of the Votive Cubit, and priestly regulations.[108] Another wrote a copy of the Book of the Temple and the hieroglyphic dictionary.[109] One wrote a copy of the Book of the Temple, the Book of Nut, and the Mythological Manual,[110] while yet another wrote two copies of the Book of Nut.[111]

Although the scribes were plainly not specialized, it is noteworthy that there are at least a few examples of individuals that wrote more than one copy of the same text. A further question to consider is whether some scribes may have been responsible for writing both hieratic and demotic texts. This is indicated by copies of religious manuals, such as the Book of Nut and the Book of Fayum, where the original text in the hieratic script is accompanied by a running commentary in demotic.[112] The constant shift between two scripts in these papyri makes it unlikely that two different scribes were at work, and we seem to have examples here of scribes who were proficient in both scripts.

§8. CONCLUDING REMARKS

This paper began with the statement that the Tebtunis temple library allows us to study scribal habits and scribal variation within a narrowly defined geographical, temporal, and social context. Within such a context, one might expect to see some degree of uniformity, but it is perhaps not as great as one might anticipate. I have chosen here to focus on a selection of formal features, and, to take an obvious example, the range of distinctive hands is noteworthy. This could be taken to indicate that many of the scribes in question had not been trained together; scribes may have received apprentice training, rather than

[105] P.Carlsberg 668: unpublished.

[106] P.Carlsberg 14: Volten (1942); Quack and Ryholt forthcoming.

[107] P.Carlsberg 399 + PSI inv. D 17 + P.Tebt.Tait 13: Quack (2002b, pls. 9–16).

[108] P.Carlsberg 313 (Book of the Temple), P.Carlsberg 385 (Book of the Temple), P.Carlsberg 386 (temple regulations), and P.Carlsberg 419 (Votive Cubit): unpublished except for the latter, for which see Quack (2006d). See the comments on the scribe ibid., p. 39.

[109] The latter is P.Carlsberg 7: Iversen (1958). Personal communication by J. F. Quack.

[110] P.Carlsberg 393 + PSI inv. I 74 + P.Berlin 14947 (Book of the Temple), P.Carlsberg 308 (Mythological Manual), and P.Carlsberg 228 (Book of Nut): unpublished except for the latter for which see von Lieven (2007). See the comments on the scribe ibid., p. 17.

[111] P.Carlsberg 1 and P.Carlsberg 1a: von Lieven (2007, 16–17). See the comments on the scribe *ad loc.*

[112] P.Carlsberg 1 and P.Carlsberg 1a (Book of Nut): von Lieven (2007, 16–17). P.Carlsberg 387 and 613 (Book of Fayum): Beinlich (2017, 30–92, pls 42–45, and 173–198).

being confined to school training alone, or there may have been a considerable element of physical mobility. There was also no fixed system for making deletions of incorrect text, which may be washed out or cancelled by strokes, blotted out with a thick square, or encircled with dots. This again seems to have been the result of personal preference. There is more uniformity when it comes to the actual layout of texts. Layout, as well as the choice of fresh vs used papyrus, was largely determined by the nature of the texts, and we see that about two thirds of the hieratic texts have guidelines while the same is only true for about one eighth of the demotic texts. In general, and perhaps hardly surprisingly, more care was taken in the case of texts relating to the cult.

How typical is the Tebtunis temple library as regards Egyptian scribal habits? This question cannot be answered in detail without similar studies of material from other sites, which have yet to be undertaken, but a personal examination of the recently rediscovered, contemporary papyri from the temple of Tanis suggests that Tebtunis is not atypical for the Roman period. See Ryholt (forthcoming e). Again we see a range of clearly distinct hands at work and witness a deliberate choice as to layout—with or without guidelines—and the use of fresh vs used papyrus with cultic texts being given priority. It may be noted that the Tanis papyri do not represent a temple library, but an assemblage of discarded papyri found in the basement of a private house that included temple texts comparable to those found at Tebtunis, as well as accounts and private documents. Another *desideratum*, in a broader perspective, would be a comparison between Egyptian scribal practices and those of contemporary Greek scribes in Egypt.[113] This, too, is likely to yield interesting results, but also falls outside the scope of the present paper.

As work on the Tebtunis temple library progresses and more manuscripts are identified, studied, and published, we will undoubtedly learn much more about the scribes, their habits, and the operation of the library as a whole. The present paper has sought to summarize the observations of certain formal features, while others—such as the use of illustrations, different colors and types of ink, abbreviations, or the use of blank spaces between signs or lines to indicate new paragraphs[114]—have been left for a future occasion. Postscript: Since the present paper was written, an analysis of inks from the Tebtunis temple library and other sources has been undertaken by *Ancient Ink as Technology*, a subproject of *CoNeXT* (dir. Prof. Sine Larsen) which is funded by the University of Copenhagen Excellence Programme for Interdisciplinary Research. The first results are published by Christiansen et al. (2017). A survey of illustrated papyri from the Tebtunis temple library is currently in preparation by the present author.

[113] See in particular the seminal study of Greek papyri by Turner (1987) and the more recent study of Oxyrhynchus papyri by Johnson (2004).

[114] Some brief remarks on the use of blank spaces at Tebtunis may be found in Ryholt (2012, 131, 145); see further, Tait (1986, 66–7).

8

On the Regionalization of Roman-Period Egyptian Hands

Joachim Friedrich Quack

§1. INTRODUCTION

In ancient Egypt, for most of its history, hieratic script was the dominant everyday form of writing, a cursive form mainly written with ink on a support of easy mobility such as papyrus, pottery sherds, or limestone flakes. Later, a form of writing called 'demotic' was developed, through a further abbreviation of the hieratic sign forms.[1] While most scholars simply describe demotic as being cursive, a more precise definition of 'cursive', as a writing where the signs are linked to each other, requires a more flexible approach: while on a diachronic level most of the demotic Egyptian signs result from ligatures of several hieroglyphs, on a synchronic level it is quite possible (and especially for the Roman period not infrequent) that the individual demotic signs do not touch each other in writing (i.e. they are not ligatured). While I am aware of this terminological problem, in what follows I simply use 'cursive' as a shorthand expression that does not exclude the possibility that there are specimens where the writing signs do not actually touch each other.

Modern scholars, too impressed by the optically alluring hieroglyphic inscriptions on their more durable stone support, often forget to reckon with the far more important impact the cursive writing had on the life of the people. While there are writings with literary and religious content, by far the greatest amount of cursive writing in Egypt is likely to have taken place in the administrative and economic sphere.[2] This is of some importance for my approach insofar as these activities have a clear relationship with centre and periphery. At the same

[1] While there is no in-depth study of demotic writing from a theoretical point of view, for a short overview see Quack (2010); a more detailed discussion in Quack (2014).

[2] This is typical for ancient cultures in general, regardless of the writing system (Quack 2006a, 79). I would not be surprised if it still holds true for modern times, if we were to include text types such as receipts in our reckoning.

time, the socially dominant side in the process of the writing is likely to have been most influential as far as the development of hand types is concerned. I will return to this point later.

§2. REGIONALIZATION IN THE OLD-NEW KINGDOMS

For the older periods of Egyptian history, it seems quite impossible to define a clear distinction between regional types of hands in cursive writing. Certainly there is nothing in the Old and Middle Kingdom that can be connected in this way. For the New Kingdom, more specifically for the Ramesside period (*c.*1300–1070), some scholars, especially Erman and Möller, have suggested that differences between Upper and Lower Egyptian hands did exist.[3] Their conclusions are based mainly on the Great Harris Papyrus, a manuscript written by several hands and listing donations for different temples.[4] Their main idea was that the geographical setting of the relevant temple would also be an indication as to the origin of the scribe who wrote the section.[5] They tried to bolster their claims by including some Late Egyptian miscellany manuscripts in which there are some indications that shed light on the geographical origin of the scribes in question.[6]

Still, the evidence from subsequent manuscript finds has rather cast doubt upon the supposed distinction, since there were too many cases where papyri had supposedly Upper Egyptian forms for some signs, but supposedly Lower Egyptian ones for others.[7] It seems doubtful, then, that even such a broad distinction can be established, and there is certainly no hope for differentiating individual hand types of different cities. In any case, the divergent forms observed by Erman and Möller were restricted to fairly few signs, fewer than a dozen, and, even for those, there was nothing like an overall trend which would imbue the hands with something which could be described as distinctive global styles. The reason for this global trend of unified development will have to be discussed in more detail below once the later change in trend has been documented.

§3. REGIONALIZATION IN DEMOTIC TEXTS

This change seems to begin in the Ptolemaic period. From then on, there is an increasing tendency towards regionalization in cursive writing, in hieratic as

[3] Erman (1903, 459–63); Möller (1927, 2–3).

[4] For the modern edition, see Grandet (1994).

[5] Of course, this is far from self-evident; the scribe could also be only the secretary of the central administration responsible for the accounting of the expenditure of this particular temple.

[6] This is also a rather risky procedure given that some parts of the contents are model letters whose place of origin does not necessarily have to be identical with the training place of the scribe who copied them in the specific manuscript.

[7] See Quack (1994, 10).

well as demotic texts. The latter is easier to follow, especially for the Ptolemaic period, because it is much more abundantly attested, and, most especially, there are enough different well-attested find-spots for demotic papyri to make comparison meaningful, while almost all major hieratic texts, insofar as they have a documented or deducible provenance, are from Thebes.

The most obvious point is that the training of lawyers was intense and undertaken locally, thus forming strong traditions with their own scribal habits.[8] For example, even though the cities of Thebes and Gebelein are geographically rather close to each other, they have independent notaries, and the hand types look quite different; e.g. for Gebelein it is typical to dissociate the article *pꜣ* into two separate parts. There seems to be a general tendency for local notaries to keep to a specific writing style, and often over a fairly long time. This may be connected to the specific training received for juristic formulations, especially since writing habits are not limited to sign forms: the way stipulations are formulated and their individual sequences have also been proved to be patterned according to geographical origins.[9] For many places, the actual attestation of manuscripts makes it impossible to go beyond such a limited group of textual genres.

However, it should be pointed out that in cases where we have attestations of very different genres of texts from one place, the dominating factor is the local one, not the text genre. A good example is Late Ptolemaic (and perhaps also Early Roman) Akhmim. P.Moscow, Pushkin Museum nº 123, dated to 68 BCE, is a demotic testament from the site.[10] At the same time, there are three major well-preserved literary texts whose provenance from Akhmim is reasonably well established, namely the Teachings of Khasheshonqi in P.BM EA 10507, the narrative of the strife over the benefice of Amun (P.Spiegelberg), and the great demotic wisdom book attested in P.Insinger.[11] A number of demotic funerary texts from this place are also known.[12] The whole group of papyri from Akhmim look quite similar and share characteristic points in their palaeography and orthography, so much so that it is possible to identify smaller fragments[13] as belonging to the same group. Some of the writing habits of this group of texts can even be found in a legal manual, which seems to be quite a bit older but already exhibits some similar preferences for certain sign forms.[14]

[8] Zauzich (1968, 157–228).
[9] Zauzich (1968).
[10] Edited by Malinine (1967); the similarity of that papyrus to the literary material from Akhmim was pointed out by Hoffmann (1995b, 38).
[11] Editions Glanville (1955); Spiegelberg (1910); Suten-Xeft (1905). For the provenance of the texts, see Lexa (1926, part 4, 3); Smith (1994).
[12] Principal editions Smith (1987); Smith (1993).
[13] I know of a number of unpublished fragments probably belonging to a funerary manuscript now preserved at Aberdeen. The mathematical exercises in P.BM EA 10520 published by Parker (1972, 2, 64–72, pls. 19–24) also look quite similar, as well as an unpublished fragmentary model for marriage contracts (P.Heidelberg D 688), which shows a close similarity in the clauses to P.Cairo CG 30601 (Eheverträge 17) and P.Mainz (Eheverträge 21) that actually come from Akhmim.
[14] Lippert (2004, 11–17).

At the same time, parallel copies of the same composition from other places can look completely different. For example, copies of the great demotic wisdom book from Soknopaiou Nesos and Tebtunis (from the Roman period) do not resemble the writing style of P.Insinger (and those from Tebtunis are also different from those of Soknopaiou Nesos).[15] A funerary papyrus (P.Harkness, dating to 61 CE) containing, among other texts, a direct parallel to one of the Akhmim funerary manuscripts[16] is in a somewhat different writing style, even though part of that impression is due to the fact that it is written with a very thin split reed pen (a calamus), not the usual broader writing tool. As far as information on its provenance is available, it comes from a region quite near Akhmim,[17] so a derivation of the hand from the same general school would be reasonable.

§3.1. Tebtunis

A quite similar situation can be documented for Roman-period Tebtunis. Firstly, it should be stated that there are quite a lot of Ptolemaic-period papyri from Tebtunis. However, practically all of the published ones are documentary,[18] and in any case they look quite different from the Roman texts. This in itself is a remarkable point to which I will return later.

Among the Roman-period manuscripts, most are literary or subliterary. Still, a few published documentary papyri are available.[19] They share generally the same type of hand with the literary material; in some cases, I even have suspicions that they might be the product of the very same scribe. For example, the hand of the document P.Carlsberg 431[20] (Figure 8.1) looks very similar to the manuscript of the Ritual for Entering the Chamber of Darkness now distributed between P.Berlin 23854, PSI Inv. D 18a, D 19/2, D19/3, and D 19/12 (Figure 8.2).[21] P.Carlsberg 582, another documentary text (Figure 8.3),[22] is in a writing at least very similar to unpublished literary texts such as P.Carlsberg 640 or 643 (Figure 8.4).

The general impression of the demotic Tebtunis hands is an impressive neatness, with a penchant for rather angular strokes and straight lines. Some sign structures are very characteristic, e.g. the form  of *ỉw=w* with two small lines

[15] For an overview of the fragmentary parallels see Quack (2016, 113 n. 117); there are two small fragments at Heidelberg which might also be parallel manuscripts of that composition (inv. D 52 and 661).

[16] Edition Smith (2005). [17] Smith (2005, 15–16).

[18] A Ptolemaic-period literary papyrus, which perhaps comes from Tebtunis, is the Tale of Naneferkasokar and the Babylonians; see Spiegelberg (1932b) and Quack (2016, 48–50).

[19] Ryholt (2004b). [20] Published by Ryholt (2004b, pl. 41).

[21] Published by Jasnow and Zauzich (2005, pls. 30 and 39–41); for the attribution of those fragments to a single papyrus, see Quack (2007, 263).

[22] Ryholt (2004b, pl. 42).

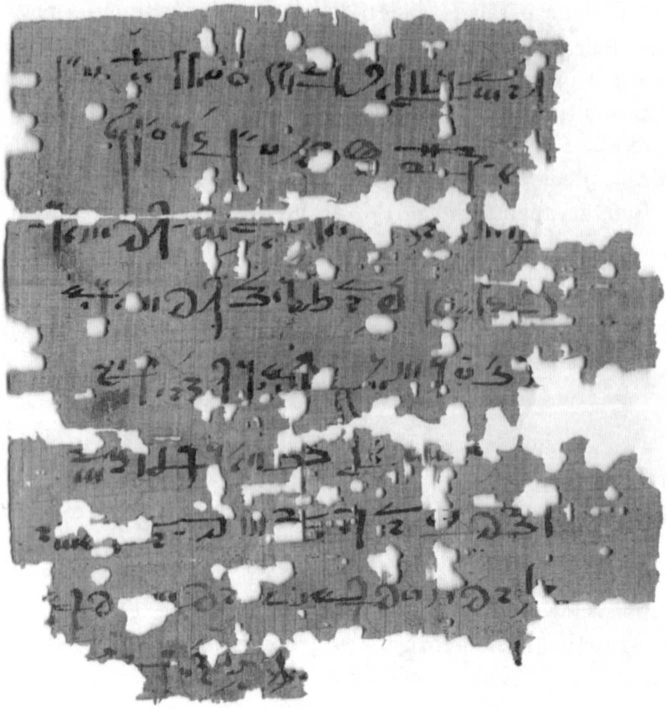

Fig. 8.1. P.Carlsberg 431

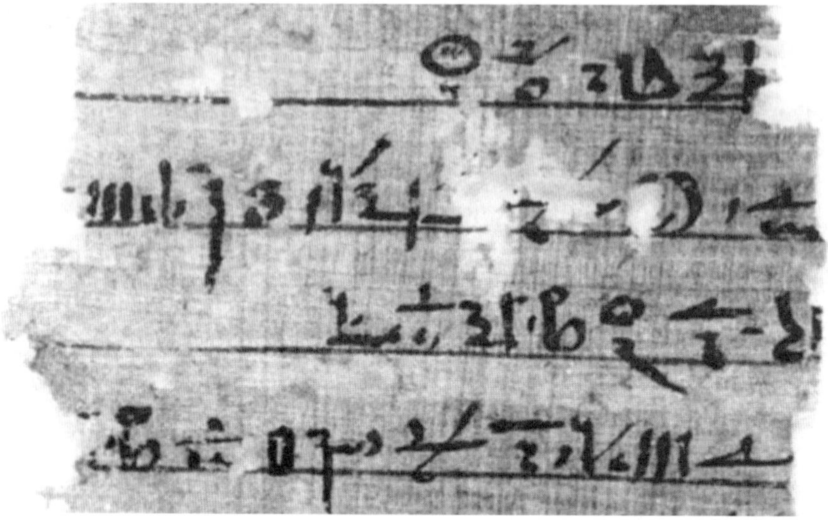

Fig. 8.2. P.Berlin 23854, PSI Inv. D 18a, D 19/2, D19/3, and D 19/12

Fig. 8.3. P.Carlsberg 582 (documentary text)

high up, the second one touching the main vertical stroke. The *l*-sign typically goes down not in a straight diagonal but slanting. The three vertical lines of the *y* are elaborated by giving the third one a marked extension to the left. Filling dots above and below signs are quite frequent. In the details, several subtypes can certainly be established,[23] but I do not intend to go too much into specifics here.

[23] A preliminary assessment of the demotic Tebtunis hands was done by Tait (1977, viii–ix). This is now in need of considerable updating and partial revision, but such a work exceeds the possibilities of this paper.

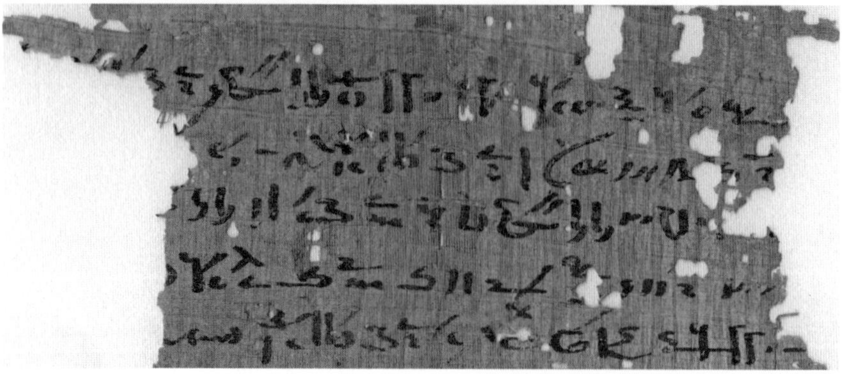

Fig. 8.4. P.Carlsberg 640

There is a very frequent hand at Tebtunis that is nowadays called the 'Nun-scribe' by specialists,[24] because he copied one theological treatise on Nun, the primeval ocean.[25] This is a bit more organized in round curves than is otherwise typical for Tebtunis hands, but is still broadly within the same range. The copyist in question seems to have been the most prolific of his time: about twenty different manuscripts can be attributed to his hand, most of them narrative texts, but there is also a dream book (P.Carlsberg 14),[26] a song for a festival of drunkenness, and an astrological treatise. Even though he was prolific, he was either not the most respected or not the wealthiest scribe around, because almost all of his writing took place only on the verso (i.e. back) of discarded Greek administrative texts. The only recto (i.e. front) manuscripts from him known to me are a copy of the Book of Fayum[27] and the song for the festival of drunkenness for Bastet.[28]

One orthographic speciality of the demotic texts from Tebtunis should be noted. As this is a Fayumic place, the language shows lambdacism, and this is also indicated in the writing. Among the alphabetical signs, the *l* is generalized to the exclusion of *r*. Furthermore, I would like to single out the typical spelling *smwꜣ* for 'to bless', ancient *smꜣꜥ*, which seems to be in accordance with the Coptic form ⲥⲙⲟⲩⲉ, which is supposed to be Middle Egyptian, but might have to be considered southern Fayumic. In any case, the writing which is omnipresent at Tebtunis does not accord with the normal Fayumic form ⲥⲙⲟⲩ.

Page border (i.e. margin) lines and guidelines for the individual lines of writing are fairly frequent among the Tebtunis texts, although not present in all manuscripts; in particular, the Nun-scribe does not normally make use of them.

[24] On the 'Nun-scribe', see also Ryholt's contribution to the current volume (Chapter 7).
[25] Edited by Smith (2002). [26] Published by Volten (1942). [27] Beinlich (2017).
[28] Unpublished; translation of the better-preserved parts in Hoffmann and Quack (2007, 305–11).

Hieratic hands from Tebtunis show the same overall characteristics as the demotic ones, especially the tendency for neatness, rather straight lines, and sharp, well-defined angles. A direct comparison of hieratic and demotic types is possible for the Nun-scribe, as he wrote a hieratic manuscript of the Book of Fayum (P.Carlsberg 387) with demotic translation and commentary (Figure 8.5). In the details, there is some variation, but the overall coherence of the papyri is obvious. Most of them are calligraphically of a high standard, obviously stemming from well-trained scribes who had reached a mature and consistent hand with a good standard of legibility. Often, they appear to the eye as being rather close to hieroglyphic forms. An instructive case is the hieratic copy of the Book of Fayum (Figure 8.6).[29] For that manuscript, it has even been said that its hand was specifically influenced by a hieroglyphic model,[30] but by now we know that this type of hand is well attested at Tebtunis also for compositions for which a hieroglyphic model is unlikely, such as the Book of the Temple (Figure 8.7).

Fig. 8.5. P.Carlsberg 387 (Book of Fayum) with demotic translation and commentary

[29] Edited by Botti (1959). [30] Thus Vernus (1979, 115).

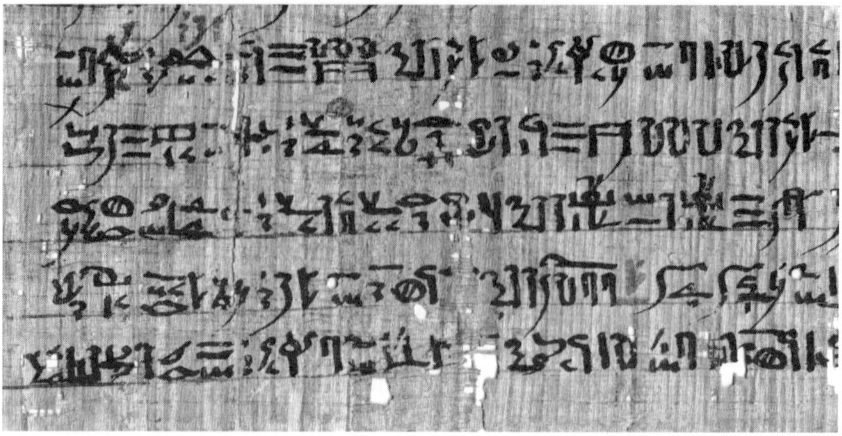

Fig. 8.6. Botti A (Book of Fayum)

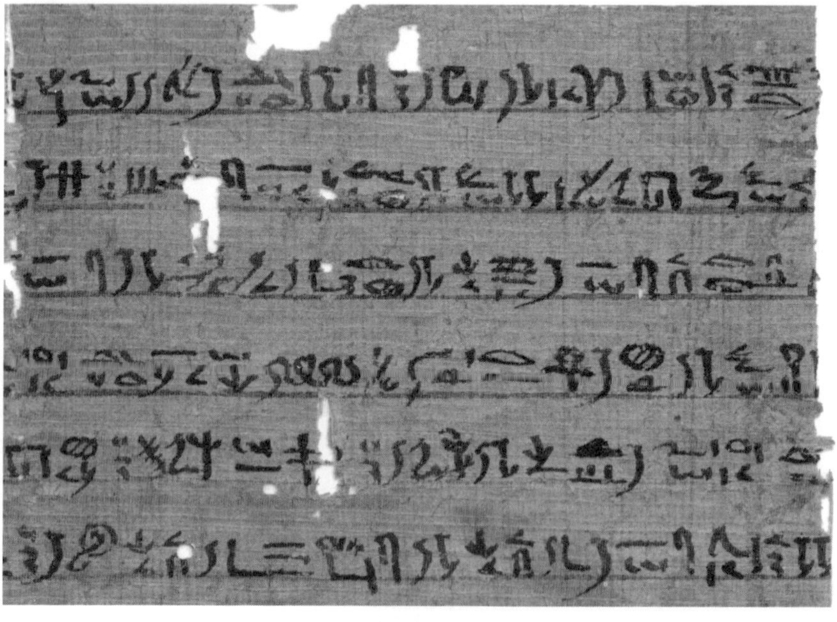

Fig. 8.7. P.Carlsberg 313 (Book of the Temple)

There are only rare cases of hands with an untidy or hasty appearance. One such example is P.Carlsberg 312, a hieratic copy of the Book of the Temple (Figure 8.8), which, while obviously the work of an experienced scribe, was visibly written by somebody who was not a calligraphist and whose main concern was speed. Additionally, this hand stands out due to the relatively large size of the signs, as hieratic hands of the Roman period normally produce individual signs of a relatively small size.

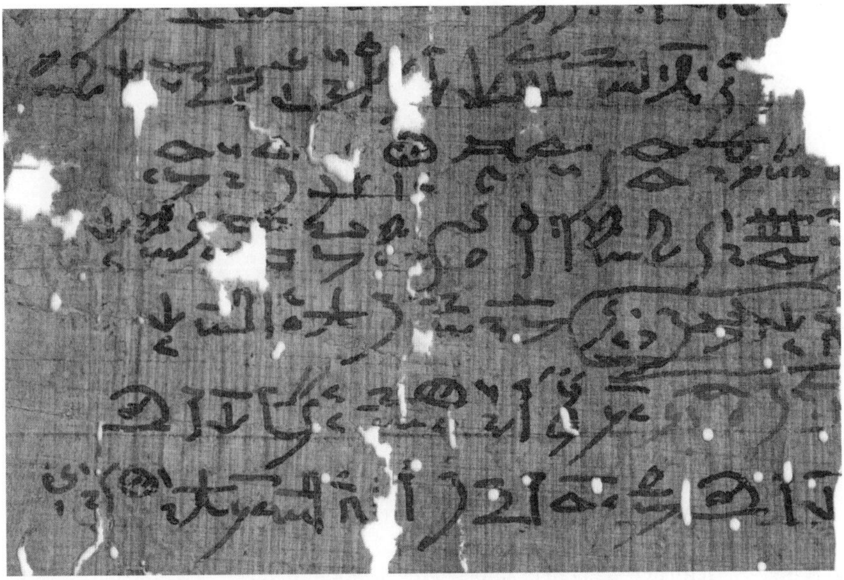

Fig. 8.8. P.Carlsberg 312 (hieratic copy of the Book of the Temple)

§3.2. Soknopaiou Nesos

Soknopaiou Nesos, from the northern border of the Fayum, is directly north of Lake Moeris. Together with Tebtunis, Soknopaiou Nesos is the major find-spot for demotic papyri of the Roman period. The situation here is in some ways more complicated than for Tebtunis, which is perhaps due to the fact that here we have even less documentation for the papyrus finds than we do for Tebtunis. However, we are better served in that administrative documents from Soknopaiou Nesos in demotic Egyptian script are quite numerous, and they can normally be attributed to this place based on internal criteria, such as the gods and place names mentioned. The documentation starts already in the Ptolemaic period,[31] but here, as in Tebtunis, we observe the phenomenon that the Ptolemaic hands look quite different from the Roman ones. In this case, we can even fix the date rather exactly. First attested in a document of 20 BCE, we see a highly characteristic/distinctive hand type that is very different from the Ptolemaic ones and, even more remarkably, highly persistent (Figure 8.9).[32]

Actually, for about two hundred years, until the very end of demotic documentation for administrative papyri from that place, this is the only type of hand ever attested in administrative texts. This has even incited some scholars to suppose that it was the only writing style present at all in Roman-period

[31] Principal editions are Bresciani (1975) and Schentuleit and Vittmann (2009).

[32] Lippert and Schentuleit (2010, 403–10). It should be noted that the hand of Stotoes is much less neat and tidy than that of Satabus.

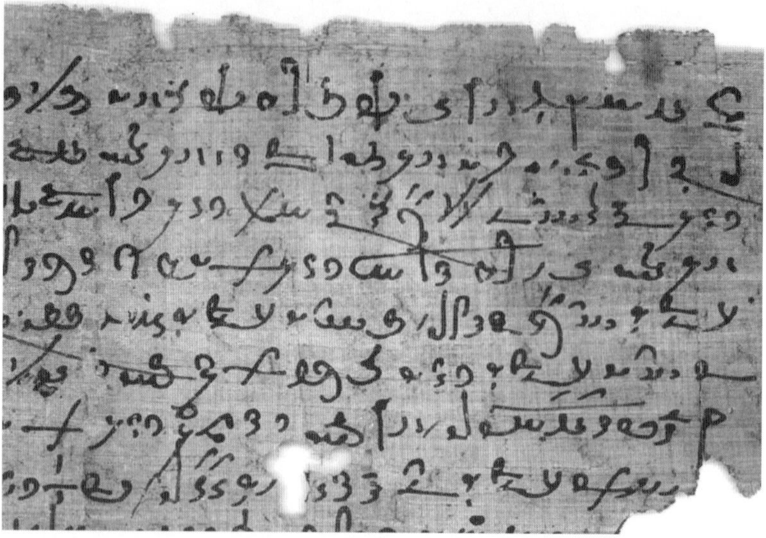

Fig. 8.9. P. Vienna D 4856 (an example of the Satabous hand)

Soknopaiou Nesos—an opinion which I do not share.[33] This hand is absolutely unmistakeable, and at the same time quite idiosyncratic in its appearance. Perhaps the best word to describe it is 'baroque', because it abounds in curves where straight lines would be normal in demotic. The uniformity of its forms through time is so great that specialists can use only very few signs, especially the flesh-determinative, to tell individual hands apart.[34]

One of the earliest scribes for whom this style is attested is Satabus (Egyptian *ḫtbꜣ*) for whom we have fairly ample documentation.[35] He also wrote literary texts; most notably, the only surviving copy of the Prophecy of the Lamb (P.Vienna D 10000) has his name preserved in the colophon.[36] The subliterary divinatory treatise in P.Vienna 12006 is also in this style although no scribal name is preserved,[37] as is a literary manuscript of uncertain content (perhaps the introductory section of the great demotic wisdom book)[38] and a number of liturgical papyri.

Satabus does not seem to be the inventor of this type of hand; it comes about at a time when he is young, and it is started not only by him but also by another man, Stotoes, son of Harpbekis, so their master, whose name is still unknown,

[33] It is formally belied by the evidence of P.Louvre E 10488 and P.Carlsberg 9 (see below), as well as the fact that P.Berlin 8043, the main manuscript for the daily ritual of Sobek of Pay, also shows a hand very different from the Satabus type.

[34] Lippert and Schentuleit (2006b, 7–8).

[35] See Zauzich (1976); Schentuleit (2007).

[36] Zauzich (1983b).

[37] Edition Stadler (2004); for the correct interpretation of the text see the reviews by Quack (2005b), Richter (2008c), and Devauchelle (2008), and especially the interpretation of the number system by Naether (2010, 333–6). I will further deal with the question in the forthcoming edition of a new manuscript of this composition.

[38] Knigge Salis, Müller, and Widmer (2012, 89–91).

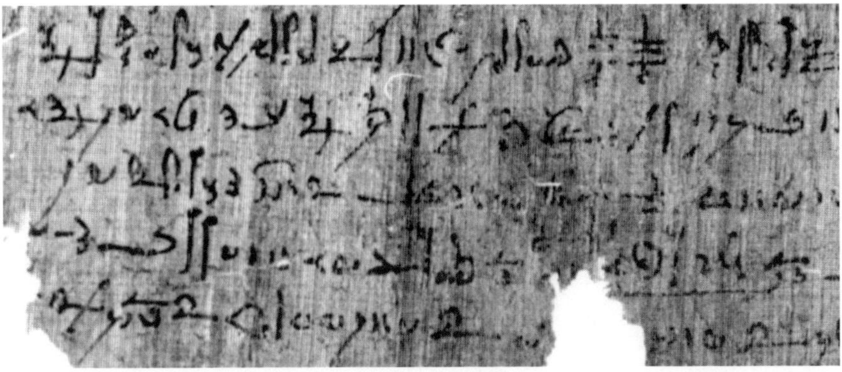

Fig. 8.10. P.Vienna D 10014+10103a+b (unpublished)

was probably the real innovator.[39] Nevertheless, there is one point that might just have contributed to the long-term prevalence of it at Soknopaiou Nesos, namely the standing of Satabus in later memory. There is some evidence that he was deified after his death.[40] Thus, in a cultic inventory, there is a mention of 'Satabus the god',[41] and a Greek-language dedicatory inscription has to be understood in the same way.[42] Furthermore, the name is in a few cases written with the divine determinative.[43] Even if Satabus was not the original instigator of this type of hand, the fact that he used it and that he was a local hero—and even became considered a god—might have greatly contributed to the astonishing longevity of the writing style. Of course, such an approach raises questions about the cultural standing of individual hands or the appreciation of a certain type of calligraphy which, to my knowledge, have never really been posed for ancient Egypt.[44]

But now for different demotic hands at Soknopaiou Nesos. As already hinted, I do not think that the Satabus type is the only demotic type at Roman-period Soknopaiou Nesos, dominant as it might be. Specifically in copies of literary or subliterary texts, I think that different types can be established. I will start with the hand of the theological treatise P.Vienna D 10014+10103a+b (unpublished; Figure 8.10).[45] On the one hand, it could still be considered marginally within the spectrum of the Satabus type, even if it looks rather untidy compared with most of the latter's products. On the other hand, in hindsight, you can see the new directions taking shape here (and that this hand marked a starting point for change). The overall impression of the hand is fairly hectic and without rest.

[39] This is based on a personal communication from Maren Schentuleit; for the actual manuscripts, see Lippert and Schentuleit (2010).

[40] See von Lieven (2008).

[41] Doussa, Gaudard, and Johnson (2004, 148 and 191–3).

[42] Edition Bernand (1975, 157–8, pl. 58, no. 78); see Bingen (1998, 311–13). For the interpretation, I follow von Lieven (2008).

[43] Lippert and Schentuleit (2006a, 53).

[44] If this is not going into a completely mistaken direction, the best comparison would probably come from East Asia with its significant place accorded to calligraphy (made slightly known to the West in movies, e.g. one of the key sequences in 'Hero' (China 2002)).

[45] The Greek text of the front has been edited by Messeri (2001).

The next step is probably reached by hands like that of the medical text P. Vienna D 6257 (Figure 8.11).[46] While still characterized by somewhat flowing lines, the hand has become quite a bit calmer and slightly straighter. The overall effect is quite pleasing to the eye. Rather similar is a manual of textile dyeing (Figure 8.12).[47] Also somewhat in that range, but a bit more at rest in its lines, is

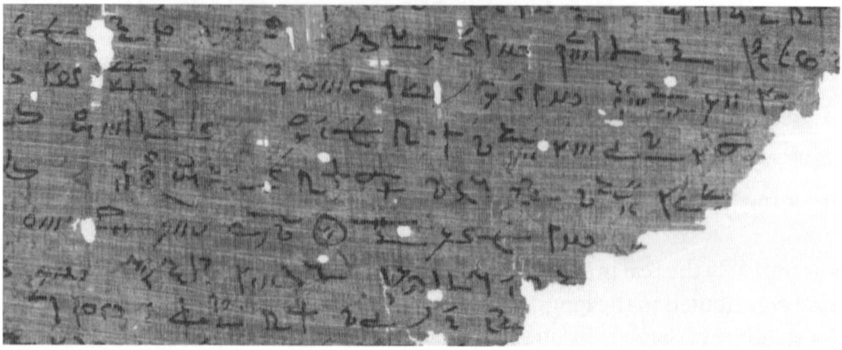

Fig. 8.11. P.Vienna D 6257

Fig. 8.12. P.Vienna D 6321 (manual of textile dyeing)

[46] Published in a quite unsatisfactory way by Reymond (1976); a new edition by Friedhelm Hoffmann will be published soon, where it is also demonstrated why the attribution to Crocodilopolis claimed in the *editio princeps* is incorrect.

[47] Published by Reymond (1977, 111–16, pl. IV) and Reymond (1976, 82–5, pl. 1, columns 1 and 2) who attributed the fragments to two different compositions (without noticing direct joins) and did not understand the purpose of the text.

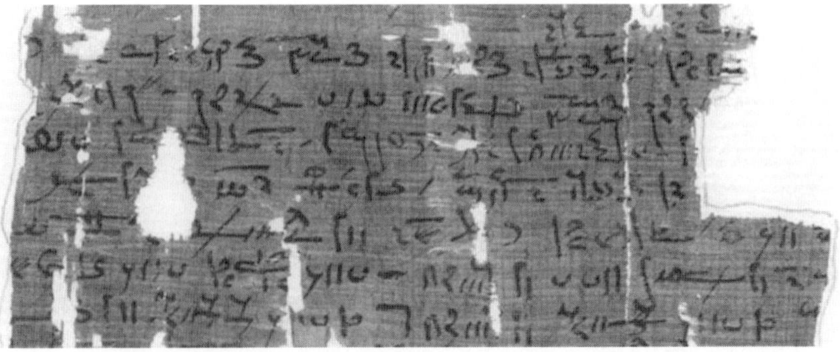

Fig. 8.13. P.Vienna D 6319

the best preserved demotic manuscript of the Book of the Temple (P.Vienna D 6319; Figure 8.13).[48] These manuscripts can be grouped together as forming a second type of demotic hand from Soknopaiou Nesos.

A subgroup of this seems to be constituted by a few texts, especially P. Carlsberg 2 (Figure 8.14; in my opinion, certainly not from Tebtunis and probably from Soknopaiou Nesos).[49] There is also one manuscript of the Ritual for Entering the Chamber of Darkness (P.Louvre E 10488; Figure 8.15),[50] which, while very much a character of its own, shares some typological similarity. This presents one additional complication for the analysis. One of its pages (Figure 8.16) is a later insertion, written in a different hand and without the guidelines so typical for the rest of the manuscript. While quite close in general appearance to the second type, they constitute a bit of a step towards the next group in going further towards the reduction of curved lines.

The next and probably final step is taken by a group of closely related manuscripts, perhaps the work of a single scribe.[51] Good examples are the main manuscript of the Amazon story,[52] the Lille manuscript of the Myth of the Sun's Eye (Figure 8.17), a manuscript with animal omina,[53] and an unpublished wisdom text.[54] I will designate this group as the third demotic type. They have

[48] Originally edited by Reymond (1977, 45–105, pls. 1–3); a new edition by me is in preparation.

[49] Already Volten (1951, 72) doubted the attribution to Tebtunis. It is significant that for this text, contrary to all others published by Volten (1940), no single additional fragment has come to light in places holding Tebtunis papyri, while those really belonging to it (like those published by Zauzich (1975) and Pezin (1986)) are associated with Soknopaiou Nesos material.

[50] Jasnow and Zauzich (2005, pls. 43–59). The provenance of this manuscript from Soknopaiou Nesos is certain because one fragment of it was found by the archaeological excavations of the University of Michigan at that place.

[51] On this type, see Quack (2005a, 112f.).

[52] Newly edited by Hoffmann (1995a) and additionally Hoffmann (1995b, 27–9).

[53] Unpublished; short description in Quack (2006b, 175–9).

[54] Some short indications in Quack (2016, 134).

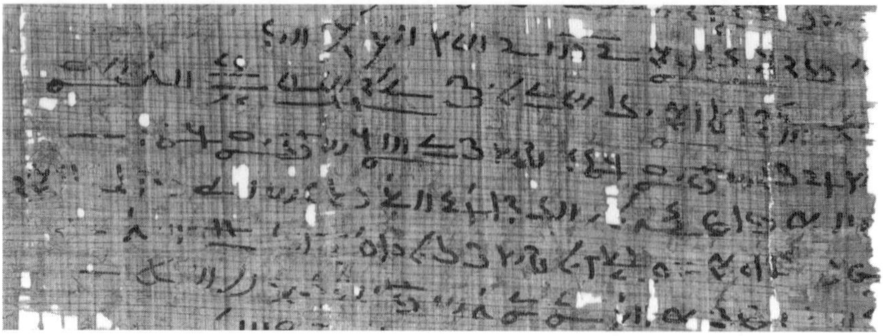

Fig. 8.14. P.Carlsberg 2

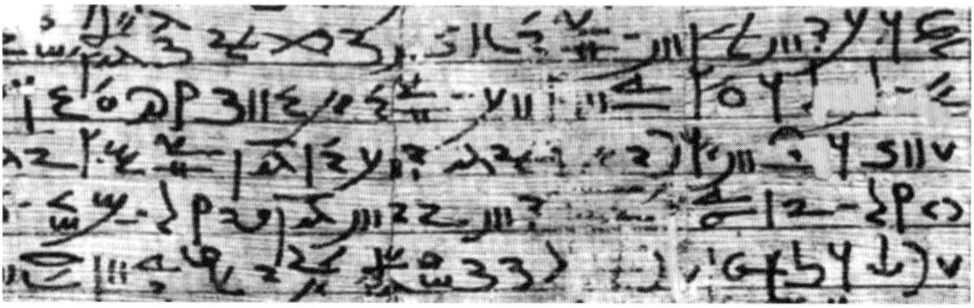

Fig. 8.15. P.Louvre E 10488. © Musée du Louvre / Georges Poncet

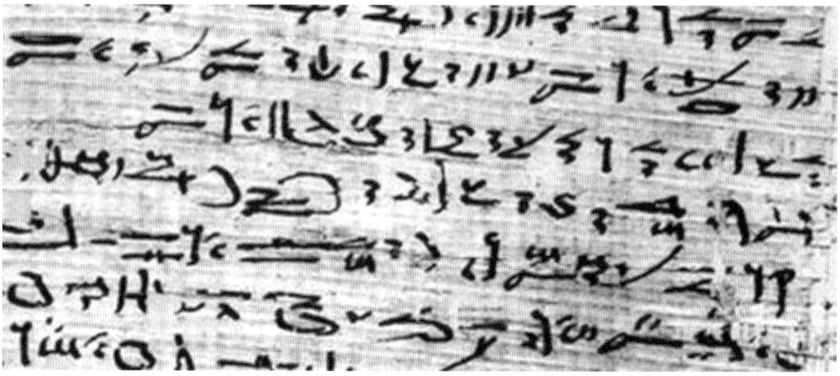

Fig. 8.16. P.Louvre E 10488 (page 2). © Musée du Louvre / Georges Poncet

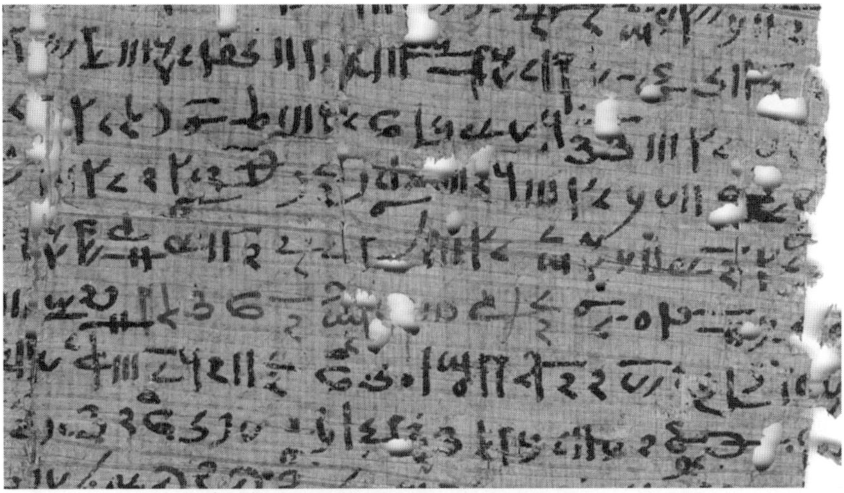

Fig. 8.17. P.Lille (Myth of the Sun's Eye). © Institute Papyrology and Egyptology Lille (HALMA UMR 8164)

almost completely lost the baroque roundedness that was characteristic for Soknopaiou Nesos, using quite straight, restrained, and clear lines. On the fringe of this type is also P. Carlsberg 9, which is certainly not from the same scribe but shows a general similarity.[55]

Types 2 and 3 also exhibit some orthographic peculiarities worth mentioning. First, there is the question of *r* and *l*. In these hands, the clear tendency is to generalize the sign for *r* in all cases, even where all Coptic dialects show *l*. The demotic sign for *l* is used only very sporadically (and then often in a somewhat special form with an extra flourish). Secondly, there is the orthography of 'to bless'. In these hands, the normal writing is *smʿ*, with the ʿ clearly indicated by a one-consonantal sign not otherwise normal in demotic orthography for this word. The verb *ḫꜣʿ* becomes, in type 3, quite dissociated into two elements, of which the first part is placed below the second one, resulting in the form , which can almost be mistaken as *šm* with *ḫr* below it. Finally, in hands of type 3, the group for *mtw* often has a peculiar abbreviated form ,[56] looking almost like alphabetical ʿ, while hands of type 2 have a penchant for the writing *mt* (with the following suffix) in a grouping of the signs not very typical for demotic orthography.

It seems possible to link hieratic hands to Soknopaiou Nesos as well. It is a bit more difficult to demonstrate this, because most of the liturgical manuscripts

[55] Published in Neugebauer and Parker (1969, 220–5, pl. 65). For that papyrus, the provenance from Soknopaiou Nesos can be proven by the fact that on the unpublished verso there are jottings in the typical Satabus type, including even a mention of the god Sobek of Pay.

[56] Example taken from Myth of the Sun's Eye, Lille A 16.

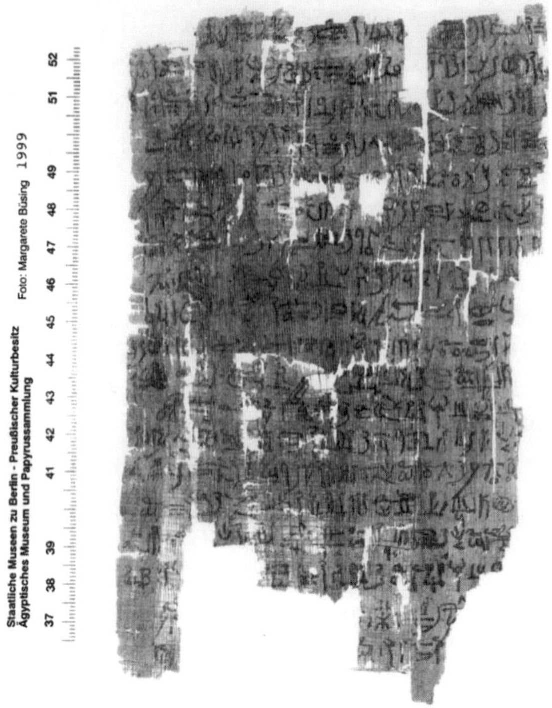

Fig. 8.18. P. Berlin 23071 v°.

from that place are written in demotic script (all of the examples known to me are in the Satabus type), and thus we cannot argue for the hieratic ones from the fact that Sobek lord of Soknopaiou Nesos is a principal figure in them. We have, of course, still the fact that certain types of hieratic hands turn up consistently in collections or specific acquisitions of collections which can be generally attributed to Soknopaiou Nesos, e.g. by the predominance of the Satabus type in documentary demotic texts. Still, a bit more is possible because in some cases of reused papyri, we have cases of different writings on the two sides.

A useful case is P.Berlin 23071. On the (still unpublished) recto, there is a demotic account in a variant of the typical Satabus hand, and it is even ascertained that the fragment comes from the excavations of Zucker in Soknopaiou Nesos. On the verso, we have a version of the Book of the Temple in hieratic script (Figure 8.18).[57] This exhibits what I would like to term the hieratic type 1 at Soknopaiou Nesos. This is a fairly rounded hand with a tendency to avoid sharp angles. A typical sign is also ⊜ with only one slanting stroke in it. I would

[57] Originally published by Burkard (1990); new edition in preparation.

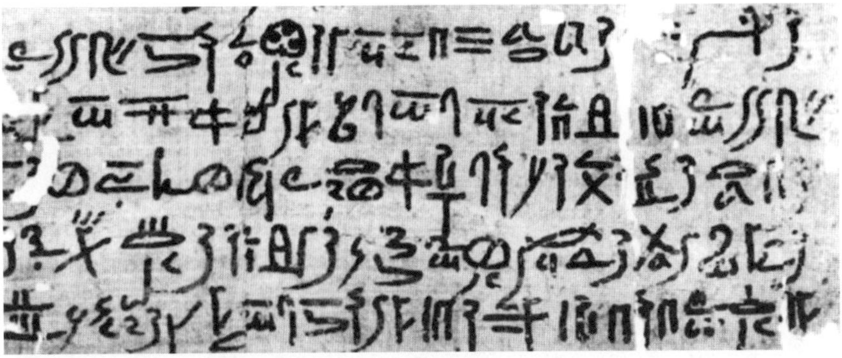

Fig. 8.19. P.Vienna Aeg 6345+

Fig. 8.20. P.Berlin 14399

also single out the form of (the seated man) with a straight base line and a single unbroken curve in its left part. There are similar hands in other manuscripts, although not all necessarily from the same person—they might be just the hieratic pendant to the omnipresent demotic Satabus type. One example of a recto text is another copy of the Book of the Temple, P.Vienna Aeg 6345+ (Figure 8.19, unpublished), as is the hymn on the verso of P.Berlin 23514.[58]

Another case of a similar hand can be demonstrated by P.Berlin 14399 (Figure 8.20), still another copy of the Book of the Temple (unpublished). This makes a very different impression from type 1, at first glance, but if you look

[58] Knigge Salis, Müller, and Widmer (2012, 92–3 and 96).

Fig. 8.21. P.Strasbourg BNU hieratic 19

closely, you can still detect structural similarities. The main difference is that it is forced here into a somewhat too small frame of guidelines, which gives a very crowded appearance to the writing and also favours a more slanting direction of the strokes. Some specific differences are the form of ⊜ with two slanting strokes in it and the form of 𓀭, which has a break in the flow of its base line and also goes slightly below the base line in its left part. This is an example of type 2.

Furthermore, P.Strasbourg BNU hieratic 19 is of interest. The verso contains barely legible remnants of what is probably a list of dates for the rotation of the phylae (temple staff working for one month at a time) by the moon calendar. On the recto, however, we have yet another hieratic copy of the Book of the Temple (Figure 8.21). This shows a hand that exhibits the same general tendency towards a baroque roundedness but has obvious characteristics of its own. The overall appearance has some similarity to the demotic type 2 from Soknopaiou Nesos.

Other types of hieratic hands are a bit less easy to attribute to Soknopaiou Nesos because the only direct evidence provided is that they come from acquisitions or turn up in collections that otherwise contain material clearly from Soknopaiou Nesos. Here, there is always a risk that material became mixed up by antiquities dealers. Still, the fact that the papyri I am talking about show the same consistent associations through several collections gives me some confidence that my attribution is correct. Besides, sometimes it can be bolstered by the fact that several demotic hands of types 2 and 3 include a number of signs of words in hieratic form and thus allow palaeographical comparison.

Some hieratic hands are of baroque appearance. One of them, a hieratic copy of the Book of the Temple, looks quite surprising (Figure 8.22). Even though all of its signs are indeed hieratic, the outward impression, of abstract short lines, is such that about half of the fragments had been inventoried at Vienna as demotic before I undertook close analysis of the material. Perhaps one can say that

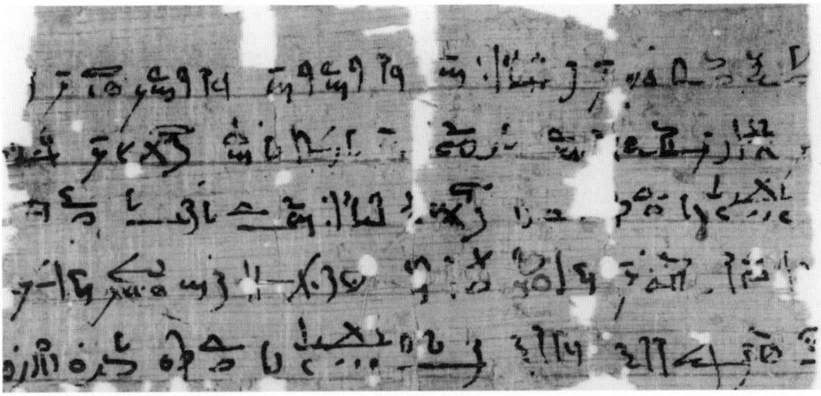

Fig. 8.22. P.Vienna Aeg 6339+8447+8449 (Book of the Temple)

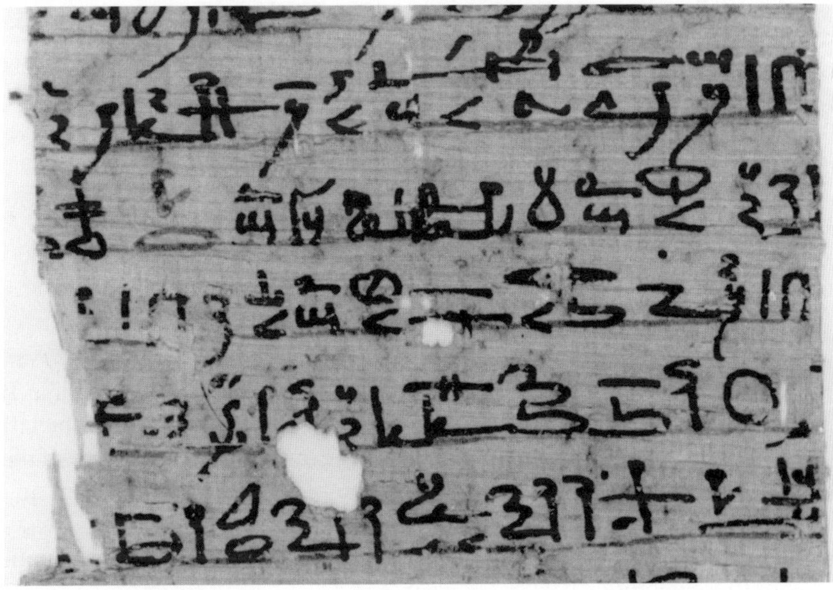

Fig. 8.23. P. Vienna 4851a

the scribe, while consciously writing hieratic, was dreaming in demotic, or at least had his habits formed by training in demotic calligraphy. Another copy of the Book of the Temple, while having fewer round flourishes, still has structural similarities in orthography and a tendency for ligatures (Figure 8.23).

One interesting example is the sole hieratic copy of the Ritual for Entering the Chamber of Darkness (P.Louvre E 10614; Figure 8.24).[59] This still has some movement but is, in general, less extreme in its forms. It has an overall resemblance

[59] Published in Jasnow and Zauzich (2005, pl. 60–1).

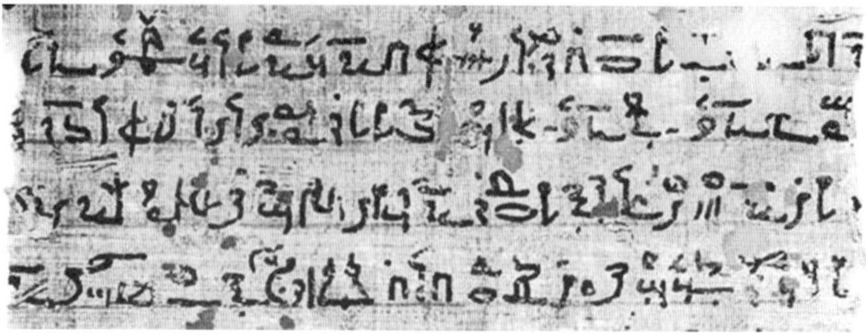

Fig. 8.24. P.Louvre E 10614. © Musée du Louvre / Georges Poncet

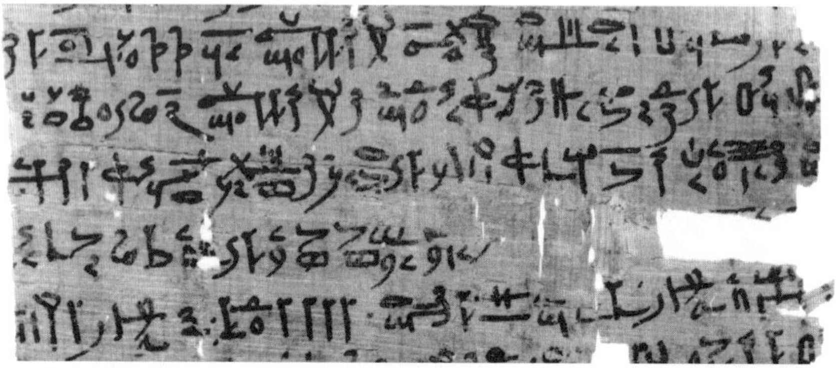

Fig. 8.25. P. Vienna D 4851b

to some examples of type 2 in the demotic hands, especially hands like P. Carlsberg 2 (Figure 8.14). Furthermore, it is already moving towards the last type of hieratic hands from Sokopaiou Nesos, again illustrated by a copy of the Book of the Temple (Figure 8.25), which completely achieves the calm and restrained forms characteristic for the demotic type 3 at Soknopaiou Nesos. I actually suspect that papyrus to have been written by the same scribe responsible for those demotic texts.[60]

One general comment can be offered on the Soknopaiou Nesos hands. In general, I find them quite a bit more difficult to read than the ones from Tebtunis. It is not that they are ugly or less carefully written; on the contrary, they have a considerable style and character of their own. However, while the tendency at Tebtunis aims more for clarity, the tendency at Soknopaiou Nesos is more towards flourishes and extremes in sign forms. While only based on my subjective impression, I would guess that for an ancient Egyptian outsider also the Soknopaiou Nesos style must have been a lot harder to read.

[60] Quack (2005a, 112).

Beyond hands, some questions of manuscript layout also seem bound up with these school traditions. One important aspect is the question of borders and guidelines. In Soknopaiou Nesos, quite often you do not have any. Especially for some of the demotic literary hand types, like the Vienna medical text D 6257, the Myth of the Sun's Eye (Lille manuscript), there are only page borders, with the first line written on top of the upper border. This is also not infrequent for liturgical manuscripts in the Satabus type like P.Berlin 6790, P.BM EA 76638, or P.Vienna D 6950. Hieratic texts can exist also without any guidelines or borders, but altogether they seem more frequent in this material, especially in those cases where we do not have type 1 hands.

§3.3. Narmouthis

Yet another hand type is represented by Roman-period Narmouthis.[61] A detailed comparison is hampered by the fact that we have practically only demotic ostraca, in a few cases also with hieratic writing, and that the material seems to be a bit younger than the bulk of the Egyptian-language Tebtunis and Soknopaiou Nesos texts. I will limit myself to noting that in writing style as well as orthographic habits, they are quite peculiar and different from other Fayumic material (even if they quite consistently indicate lambdacisms).

§3.4. Texts That Do not Fit the Scheme

In general, then, Tebtunis and Soknopaiou Nesos manuscripts look quite distinct. Of course, there are always cases that can destroy an all-too-neat scheme. Some might be due to the mobility of texts or scribes. A case in point is the narrative about Nakhthorshena (P.Carlsberg 400; Figure 8.26). While certainly coming from Tebtunis, as evidenced clearly by the presence of fragments at Florence among the excavated material, the hand is most evidently a Soknopaiou Nesos hand of the Satabus type. There are also at Vienna a very small number of scraps in the Nun hand, and it is unknown whether the manuscripts travelled in antiquity or whether isolated Tebtunis material was mixed up with the Soknopaiou Nesos finds in modern times by some dealer. Finally, there are the mavericks that do not fit in where they appear. One classical case is P.Krall (Figure 8.27).[62] While the distribution of its fragments strongly suggests that it was found in Soknopaiou Nesos, its hand does not really fit there, neither from the perspective of palaeography nor from orthography. The loose, untidy hand

[61] See the publications of Brescani, Pernigotti, and Betrò (1983); Gallo (1997); Bresciani et al. (2002); Menchetti (1999–2000); Menchetti (2003); Menchetti (2005).

[62] New edition by Hoffmann (1996).

does not closely resemble any of the certain Soknopaiou Nesos types. Furthermore, this papyrus has generalized the writing *l* instead of *r*, which is otherwise not usual for Soknopaiou Nesos; and the text has even extended this to words that have *r* even in Fayumic Coptic.[63]

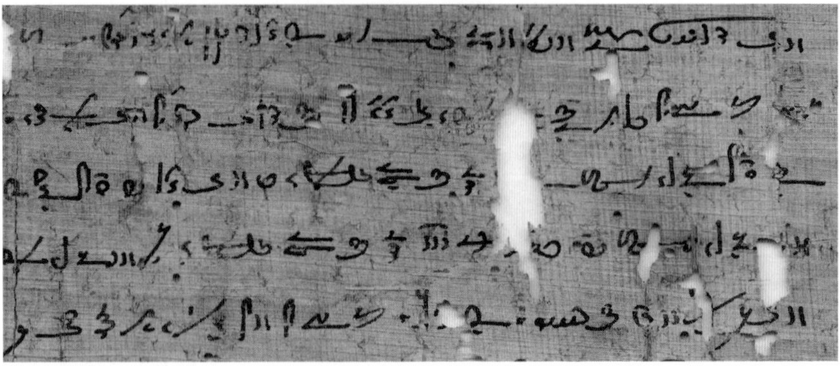

Fig. 8.26. P.Carlsberg 400

Fig. 8.27. P.Krall

[63] See the discussion in Hoffman (1996, 28); since there is no special *l*-form for the sign ⊂⊃, his classification as a historical spelling is not adequate.

§3.5. Thebes

Completely different in appearance from all the Fayum manuscripts are those from Roman-period Thebes. Here, we are in a more difficult situation for research since we have only funerary manuscripts for the hieratic side, and only some very few demotic literary texts. Documentary demotic texts are mainly restricted to tax receipts. Up to now, hardly anything has been worked out for a classification of the hands, although the source material of the hieratic funerary manuscripts is by now sufficiently large to allow for a fruitful analysis.[64] Several types can be recognized, but lack of space prevents me from going into the details. It should be sufficient to say that it would be almost impossible to mistake any of them for a Fayumic hand. Equally, the demotic literary texts such as the Leiden manuscript of the Myth of the Sun's Eye or the London–Leiden Magical Papyrus[65] are very much a world of their own as far as palaeography and orthography are concerned.

§4. CONCLUDING REMARKS

I hope to have shown sufficiently that hieratic as well as demotic hands in the Roman period are quite regionalized, and even regionalized in rather small areas; the Fayum alone has several seriously divergent writing schools. Another point to be noted is that there is a tendency for one important break at some point being followed by rather stable development for subsequent periods. What does that mean, and how can the change, in comparison to the earlier Egyptian periods, which do not exhibit regionalization, be explained?

One technical point should not be forgotten. The period about which I am talking here saw an important change in writing tools—from the traditional Egyptian rush to the Greek-style reed pen. The new tool at the same time required new ways of handling and also permitted a more free-flowing movement of the strokes. This probably contributed to the greater individuality of Roman-period hands compared to earlier material. Still, the technological aspect can be only part of the explanation, at best. More fundamental is the question of school training and the models being emulated.

Unfortunately, we know less about scribal training than we would like to.[66] Already during the Old Kingdom, biographical inscriptions and titles indicate the existence of a court school.[67] For the Middle Kingdom, the Satire of the Trades shows the existence of a school at the residence (of the King), which

[64] See especially the plates in Herbin (2008).

[65] For palaeographical analysis, the plates in Leemans (1839) and Hess (1892) should be used, as the standard edition by Griffith and Thompson (1904–9) does not sufficiently display the original sign shapes and layout of the manuscript.

[66] The basic study is still Brunner (1957).

[67] Brunner (1957, 11f.).

took pupils from all over the country.[68] Such an institution would obviously do much to create a normative writing style and orthography, especially if its alumni were later sent out throughout the country in order to take up administrative jobs. Another factor to be mentioned in connection with the residence is not the direct teaching but the setting of standards. The residence certainly sent many written missives to the provinces, and we can safely assume that their prestige status made them models to be emulated by the local scribes. Thus, in times of a strong central government, the writing style of the residence would probably dominate in the country.

Obviously, besides the central residential school, we should suppose the existence of many local schools throughout Egypt. It would have been impossible to send all children so far away from home to the residence, and thus there must have been decentralized teaching institutions. The Book of the Temple attests to a teaching of the children of the priests, which was organized in the framework of the temple.[69] To what degree there were special institutions for teaching civil administration is difficult to say.

In addition, there was the famulus system where an experienced functionary would take up a younger man (often his son) as an apprentice and teach him the job on the spot. We can suppose this system to have been especially important.

How does this relate to the special situation of the Graeco-Roman period and its regionalized writing styles? We can reasonably doubt that there was still centralized teaching of Egyptian writing systems at the residence of Alexandria. Especially during Roman times, the authorities obviously did not actively encourage the use of indigenous Egyptian writing systems, and for administrative purposes, they fell increasingly out of use, remaining relevant mainly for temple-internal affairs.[70] Furthermore, we can suppose that all missives emanating from the residence would be written in Greek, and thus they could no longer provide high-prestige models for writing in Egyptian scripts.[71]

For the Ptolemaic period, Egyptian-language notaries no doubt played a significant part. Here, instruction passing from father to son is plausible, as the offices themselves tended to be hereditary in actual practice. It would be logical that in this situation, not only the wording and sequence of stipulations, but also the very styles of handwriting, tended to be passed on. However, this diminishes in importance for the Roman period, although it still has some relevance for the texts on which I have focused here. At least I suspect that the fact that at Soknopaiou Nesos we have only the Satabus type for documentary texts, while the other types are restricted to religious and literary texts, is tied

[68] See Jäger (2004, 130f.). [69] Quack (2002a).

[70] Zauzich (1983); Lewis (1993); Lippert and Schentuleit (2010, 4–5).

[71] This opens up the interesting question of whether Greek hands during the Roman period are regionalized in any way or rather uniform across the country. As a reviewer pointed out to me, there seems to be a *communis opinio* that **no** regional features can be pinned down. Turner (1987, 17f.) has some interesting but essentially (and understandably) evasive remarks.

up with the special transmission of competence in administrative techniques and legal intricacies.

For the other points, especially the appearance of several different but related types at one place, I would suppose that they are due to the training received at the temple schools. These would, of course, be locally based at the more important temples, with pupils from there also serving the small outlying chapels.[72] These schools would be relatively autonomous, receiving only limited input from foreign styles of writing, and thus each would tend to cultivate their own locally entrenched style of writing.

This would mean that the regionalization of many different styles of writing was intricately linked with sociopolitical processes of serious magnitude: the loss of relevance of the political elite, and thus the lack of a super-regional, dominant centre, left the remaining niches of use of these writing systems free to adopt their own specific forms.[73] They would become accustomed to their styles and few outsiders would have any need to read their texts, and thus even the development of quite extreme forms would not hamper them, but only modern scholars who need a sufficient amount of texts from a place to understand their specificities.[74]

Another point concerning this should be touched upon, at least briefly. There has been some limited discussion about recognizing different dialects in demotic.[75] As far as I can see, the only really convincing cases concern manuscripts of the Roman period. Why is this so? In principle, it is highly likely that there were regional dialects in Egypt also in earlier times. Is it simply due to the fact that in their diachronic development, it was only during the Roman period that the different dialects came close enough to their Coptic equivalent to allow the modern scholar to recognize them? Or might it be that only now, with the completely regionalized writing conventions, writing in accordance with the local non-standard pronunciation had free rein?

This still leaves one last question, and perhaps here the specific human—or possibly superhuman—factor comes into play. As I noted above, for Tebtunis as well as Soknopaiou Nesos, at one time, probably around the turn from the Ptolemaic to the Roman period, there were serious changes in the writing styles. These led to a new standard, which afterwards commanded long-time adherence. Why was this so? The starting point would probably be specific teachers at the local schools, but why did their hands prove to be so persistent?

[72] See, for example, the Narmouthis ostraca; Gallo (1997, especially xliv–xlvii).

[73] In this line, it is probably also relevant that during the First Intermediate Period, hieroglyphic writing seems to have produced specific regional forms.

[74] In principle, such an approach should be expanded to other areas of the culture, the specific monumental temple orthography (many of the specific 'Ptolemaic' sign values cluster at specific places and are uncommon elsewhere), or even the local traditions of funerary texts, but to do so would go beyond the limits of the present study.

[75] Lexa (1934); Lexa (1947–51, 126–36); Hoffmann (1996, 27–32).

For Satabus at Soknopaiou Nesos, I have raised the question of whether the level of respect that he commanded in his community is the reason why his writing style became a model associated with prestige. Obviously, I am in no position to prove such an idea, and perhaps it seems like idle speculation not worthy of writing down. Still, perhaps raising this issue will help us to remain vigilant for possible evidence that might either bolster or disprove it.

9

κατὰ τὸ δυνατόν

Demotic–Greek Translation in the Archive of the Theban Choachytes

Rachel Mairs

§1. INTRODUCTION

Two parallel legal systems, Greek and Egyptian, operated in Ptolemaic Egypt.[1] If documents originally drawn up in demotic were to be brought as evidence in a case before Greek officials, then translations needed to be made. We have occasional references in the papyri to the production and use of translations of legal documents, such as in UPZ II 162,[2] where an attorney supplied 'copies of Egyptian contracts, translated into Greek' (ἀντίγραφα συγγραφῶν Αἰγυπτίων, διηρμηνευμένων δ' Ἑλληνιστί) in support of his client's case.[3] Instances where we have such translations actually preserved are rather fewer, and cases where both the demotic original and the Greek translation have survived are rare indeed. One example from early Roman Soknopaiou Nesos (in the Fayum), consisting of a demotic sale document and no fewer than five, very slightly different, Greek translations, has been studied by Schentuleit.[4] As well as the

[1] According to a royal decree of 118 BCE (P.Tebt. I 5, 207–20; Pestman (1985c)), the language of the documents, and not the ethnicity of the parties involved, is to determine whether a case is taken before the *chrêmatistai* or the *laokritai*, judges in Greek or Egyptian courts. The documents considered in this paper date to the 140s and 130s BCE, and the jurisdiction of the courts at this point is not entirely clear: see further, Mairs and Martin (2008/2009, 55).

[2] Col. 5, 3–4; = P.Choach.Survey 48, 117 BCE.

[3] References to translated documents, where neither the original nor the translation is preserved: UPZ II 218, col. II 11–14 (131–130 BCE, Thebes); UPZ II 161, 38–9 (119 BCE, Thebes); UPZ II 162, col. V, 3–4 (117 BCE, Thebes); P.Lips. I 9, 14 (233 CE, Hermopolis); P.Oxy. XIX 2231, 26–8 (241 CE, Oxyrhynchus); P.Oxy. I 43 R, 16–18 (195 CE, Oxyrhynchus); P.Oxy. XX 2276, 6–7 (late third–fourth century ce, Oxyrhynchus).

[4] Schentuleit (2001 and 2007).

potential of a translation to clarify readings in the original demotic, the language choices of the translator are of great interest in themselves.[5]

In the archive of the Theban choachytes[6] we have two such sets of translated documents, drawn up for the same family some ten years apart: P.Choach.Survey 12 and 17 (136 BCE).[7] The two sets of papers concern the transfer of rights to perform liturgies and receive income from certain tombs in the Theban necropolis. Some of the same personnel are involved: for example, Horos II son of Horos I, one of the recipients of the transfer of P.Choach.Survey 12, was the husband of Sachperis, the recipient of P.Choach.Survey 17. Martin[8] suggests that both translations were made in *c.*134 BCE for the same court case, a dispute with a group of *necrotaphoi* (buriers of the dead) which was taken before a Greek official, the *epistatês*—hence the need for Greek versions to be used as evidence.[9]

Both sets of documents have an extremely long publication history. Those of P.Choach.Survey 17 were the subject of a study by Berger in 1889.[10] The documents of P.Choach.Survey 12 actually played a role in the decipherment of demotic. In 1822, Thomas Young was entrusted with the Greek papyrus by a collector who had purchased it 'of an Arab in Thebes'. He quickly realized that this was a translation of a demotic text in Paris of which he had received a copy from Champollion.[11] 'A most extraordinary chance', Young writes, 'had brought into my possession a document which was not very likely, in the first place, ever to have existed, still less to have been preserved uninjured, for my information, through a period of near two thousand years: but that this very extraordinary translation should have been brought safely to Europe, to England, and to me, at the very moment when it was most of all desirable to me to possess it, as the illustration of an original which I was then studying, but without any other reasonable hope of being able fully to comprehend it; this combination would, in other times, have been considered as

[5] In what follows, I will not be considering those 'bilingual' texts where a Greek registration statement (compulsory from 146 BCE; see Pestman (1985b)) was appended to a demotic document, or where one of the parties supplied a subscription in Greek. My interest here is in texts where the information in one language is reproduced in the other.

[6] The choachytes were a close-knit priestly community who lived on the west bank at Thebes. They had responsibility for making offerings at tombs in the area, and were paid a fee for this. The 'ownership' of such tombs, and the right to receive the income from them, was frequently passed from one person to another, through sale or inheritance, like any other kind of property. 'Sales' were often fictive, and used to give legal weight to processes such as the consolidation of a family's fragmented holdings into a single 'package'. Both men and women could be choachytes in name, although women did not perform the libations themselves. I use the anglicized 'choachytes' in most of my text, and the transliterated Greek term *choachytês* where the emphasis is on the term itself.

[7] New editions of the texts of P.Choach.Survey 17 are published in Mairs and Martin (2008/2009). For further details on the parties, their family relationships, and the transactions, the original publication should be consulted.

[8] Mairs and Martin (2008/2009, 58–60)

[9] UPZ II 185 = P.Choach.Survey 19.

[10] Berger (1889). This thesis, which Wilcken was unable to locate and of which Spiegelberg appears to have been unaware (see Mairs and Martin (2008/2009, 22–3)), is now available on Google Books (http://books.google.co.uk).

[11] Young (1823, 56–61).

affording ample evidence of my having become an Egyptian sorcerer.' As if the association with Young were not sufficient scholarly pedigree, these documents (and Young's studies on them) were discussed by Edward Hincks in his groundbreaking paper on the 'Enchorial Language of Egypt', which also contained his reflections on the Greek term *choachytês*.[12]

Young's work happens to contain an early expression of an opinion still frequently encountered in classical scholarship, that 'the Greeks and Romans, either from national pride, or from a want of philological talent, were extremely deficient in their knowledge of all such languages as they called barbarous, and they frequently made up for their ignorance by the positiveness of their assertions, with regard to facts which were created by their own imagination.'[13] Young furthermore describes the Greek translation of P.Choach.Survey 12 as being 'in very bad Greek'. Pestman's more recent assessment of the translation of P.Choach.Survey 17 as 'not very good' is only a little kinder.[14] It is beyond the scope of this paper to rehabilitate the Greeks as bad linguists and moreover as linguistic chauvinists—the anglophones of the ancient world—although the growing body of scholarship on bilingualism and language contact in antiquity should make any such 'isolationist' position less and less tenable.[15] But with the question of what makes a good translation we can go a little further, and look in some detail at how these Greek translations were constructed. The existence of two sets of translations from the same archive also allows for cross-comparison, enabling us to assess whether the author of each translation worked in the same way, and considered the same terminology to be equivalent.

§2. THE TEXTS

In what follows, the demotic documents are listed under **A** and the Greek under **B** in each section.

§2.1. P.Choach.Survey 12: 15 December 146 BCE

Sale of liturgies (*mortis causa*) by Onnophris, son of Horos and Senpoeris, to Horos, son of Horos and Senpoeris, and Hasos, son of Horos and Senpoeris.

A: P.Berl.Dem. II 3119
Recto: agreement (dem.); tax payment (Gr.); registration (Gr. – not copied in B).
Verso: 16 witnesses (dem.).

[12] Hincks (1833); see also Ray (1994). [13] Young (1823, 1).
[14] Pestman (1993, 333). [15] Adams, Janse, and Swain (2002); Adams (2003).

B: P.Lond. I 3
Recto: agreement (Gr.); 16 witnesses (Gr.); tax payment (Gr.).
Verso: blank?

For the Greek text of both documents, see UPZ II 175. There is a transcription of the demotic in Erichsen's *Demotische Lesestücke* II.[16]

§2.2. P.Choach.Survey 17: 30 January 136 BCE

Sale of liturgies by Taesis, daughter of Psenamounis and Taesis, to Sachperis, daughter of Amenothes and Thathas.

A: i) P.Berl.Dem. II 5507 (sale)
Recto: agreement (dem.); subscription (dem.).
Verso: 16 witnesses (dem.).

ii) P.Berl.Dem. II 3098 (cession)
Recto: agreement (dem.).
Verso: 16 witnesses (dem.).

B: P.Leid. I 413
Recto: agreement (Gr.).
Verso: blank.

For the demotic and Greek texts of all three documents, see now Mairs and Martin (2008/2009).

For P.Choach.Survey 12 we have only the sale document (*sẖ-n-ḏbꜣ-ḥḏ*) and for P.Choach.Survey 17 both the sale and the accompanying cession document (*sẖ-n-wy*), in which the selling party relinquished their rights to the property in question. Both were necessary for a demotic transaction to have legal force, but typically only the sale document was translated to go as evidence before a Greek law court.

§3. DESCRIBING A TRANSLATION

P.Choach.Survey 12	P.Choach.Survey 17
1. ἀντίγραφ[ον συ]νγραφῆς Αἰγυπτίας μεθηρμηνε[υ]μένης κατὰ δύ[ναμιν].	1. [ἀντίγρ(αφον) συγγραφῆς Αἰγυπτίας με]θηρμηνεθμέν[ης Ἑλληνισ]τὶ κατὰ τὸ δυ[ν]ατόν.
'Copy of an Egyptian document translated as far as possible.'	'Copy of an Egyptian document translated into Greek as far as possible.'

[16] Erichsen (1939, 18–24).

Each Greek document begins with the statement that it is a copy (ἀντίγραφον[17]) in translation of an Egyptian original. This is the standard way of introducing a Greek translation of a demotic legal text. Only a relatively small number of such translations survive, with very similar, but not identical, introductory formulae:

1. P.Giss. I 36 (145–116 BCE, Pathyris)
[ἀντίγρ(αφον) συγχ(ωρήσεως) Αἰγυπτ]ί[ας με]θ̣η[ρ]μ̣η̣ν̣[ευ]μ̣ένης Ἑλληνιστὶ κατὰ τὸ δυνατόν.

2. P.Tebt. I 164 (112 BCE, Kerkeosiris)
ἀντί[γραφον συγγραφῆς Αἰγυπτίας ...] μεθη[ρμηνευμένης ...] ... κατὰ [τὸ δυνα]τὸν.

3. BGU III 1002 (56/55 BCE, Hermopolis Magna)
ἀντίγραφον συνγραφῆς πράσεως Αἰγυπτίας μεθηρμηνευμένης κατὰ τὸ δυνατόν.

4. PSI V 549 (42–41 BCE, Oxyrhynchus)
[ἀντίγραφον συγγραφῆς Αἰγυπτίας με]θηρμηνευμένης κατὰ τὸ δυνατόν.

5. BGU XVI 2594 (8 BCE, Chennis)
ἀντίγραφον ὁμολογίας Αἰγυπτίοις γράμμασι μεθηρμηνευμένη(ς) Ἑλληνικοῖς γράμμασι κατὰ τὸ δυνατόν.

6. CPR XV 1 (3 BCE, Soknopaiou Nesos)
[ἀντίγραφον ἀποστασίου συγγραφῆς Αἰγυπτίας] Ἑ̣λ̣λ̣[ηνιστὶ με]θ̣ηρμην̣[ευμένης] κατὰ τὸ δυ[νατόν].

7. CPR XV 2 (11 CE, Soknopaiou Nesos)
ἀν[τίγ]ραφον Αἰγυπ[τίας] πρ[ά]σεως Ἑλ[ληνι]σ̣τὶ μεθηρμηνευ̣μένης κατὰ τὸ δυνατόν.

8. CPR XV 3 (11 CE, Soknopaiou Nesos)
ἀντίγραφον [συγ]γραφῆς Αἰγυπτίας πράσεως Ἑλληνιστὶ μεθηρμηνευμένης κατὰ τὸ δυνατόν.

9. CPR XV 4 (11 CE, Soknoapaiou Nesos)
[-] κατὰ τὸ δυν[α]τ̣[όν].

10. SB I 5231 (11 CE, Soknopaiou Nesos)
[ἀν]τί[γ]ρ[αφ]ον Αἰγυπτίας π[ρά]σ̣ε̣ως Ἑ[λ]ληνιστὶ μ̣ε̣θ̣ηρμηνε[υ]μένης [κα]τὰ [τὸ δ]υνατόν.

[17] ἀντίγραφον ('transcription', 'copy') in itself bears no connotations of anything other than simple copying of a document. The Greek tax payment of P.Choach.Survey 12, for example, is copied more or less faithfully from the original (where it had already been in Greek), and is still introduced as an ἀντίγραφον. In another document from the same archive, UPZ II 162 = P.Tor. Choach. 12, ἀντίγραφον is used in a similar way, to refer both to 'copies' of Greek documents and to 'copies of Egyptian documents, translated into Greek'. The demotic term used for a copy in the archive of the Theban choachytes is *ḫ pꜣ sẖ* ('wording of the document'), or variants thereof: see Pestman (1993, 333).

11. SB I 5275 (11 CE, Soknopaiou Nesos)
ἀντίγραφον ἀπ᾿ ἀντιγράφου Αἰγυ[πτ]ίας πράσε[ως Ἑλληνιστὶ με]θ[η]ρμ[ηνε]υμ[ένη]ς κατὰ τὸ [δυνατόν].

The latter six examples all come from the archive of Satabus, a priest from early Roman Soknopaiou Nesos, and the latter five are in fact near-identical translations of the same original demotic sale document, P.BM EA 262.[18]

The caveat κατὰ τὸ δυνατόν ('according to what is possible', 'as far as possible', 'to the best of [my] ability') appears universally in such descriptions of a translation. Our document P.Choach.Survey 12 is the only appearance of the variant κατὰ δύναμιν in this sense—if it has been correctly restored, and is not simply to be read κατὰ δυ[νατόν] without the article, which is of course 'bad Greek'—but the meaning is the same. κατὰ τὸ δυνατόν also appears in a number of Roman-period translations from Latin into Greek.[19] The recurrence of the term over such a long time period, and its ubiquity in translations of legal documents, suggests that this is a piece of legalese, not the 'modest words'[20] of a not-very-good translator with poor written Greek. It is a formula, in the same way as the rest of the introduction to a translation, not a statement of personal linguistic competence or confidence. The possible advantages to introducing a translation with such a caveat are evident: the translator is absolved of responsibility for any mistakes, and all concerned are assured that the contents of the translation have been transmitted in good faith.

The use of κατὰ τὸ δυνατόν shows that there was at least some awareness that translation was not an exact science, the simple rendering of information in one language into another, but had the potential to introduce errors or differences in emphasis. But the role of the interpreter or translator as an active agent in proceedings is at best neglected, at worst deliberately obscured. Translators and interpreters throughout the ancient Mediterranean world have a tendency to be 'invisible', as if, despite the key role they played, they are considered to have no form of authorship. The authors of translations (and copies) in Egypt are almost always anonymous, as too are our few examples of oral interpreters (ἑρμηνεῖς) employed in Roman-period court cases (see, e.g., P.Oxy. II 237, 186 CE, the 'Petition of Dionysia'). In the very few cases in which the name of the translator is given, it is always because he fulfils some important role which

[18] Schentuleit (2001).

[19] P.Harr. I 67 (*c*.150 CE): ἑρμηνεία Ῥωμα[ι]κῶν κατὰ τὸ δυνατόν; BGU VII 1662 (182 CE, Philadelphia): Ῥωμ[α]ι[κῇ διαθή]κῃ … μεθηρμηνευμένῃ ἑλληνιστὶ κατὰ τὸ δυνα[τὸν; P.Diog. 9 (186–224 CE, Philadelpheia?): ἀ̣ντί[γρ(αφον)] διαθήκ̣[η]ς Ῥ̣[ω]μ̣αι̣κῆς ἑρμηνευθείσης κα̣τὰ τὸ̣ [δυνατόν; P.Oxy. XIX 2231 (241 CE, Oxyrhynchus): ἀντίγραφο̣ν̣ [ἑ]ρ̣μ̣ηνευθὲν Ἑλλη̣νι̣κο̣ῖς γρ̣άμ̣μασι κατὰ τ[ὸ] δ̣υνατὸν; P.Oxy. LXIV 4435 (early third century CE, Oxyrhynchus): κεφάλαιον ἐκ νόμου Λα̣ι̣[τ]ω̣ρίου ἑρμην[ε]υ̣θέντος κ̣[ατὰ τὸ δυ]ν̣ατὸν̣. κατὰ τὸ δυνατόν should also most probably be restored in the lacuna in BGU I 140 (119 CE): ἀν[τί]γρα(φον) ἐπ̣ισ̣τ[ολ(ῆς) τοῦ κυρίου με]θηρμ[ην]ευμένης [- *c*.9 -]. I do not provide a thorough treatment of translations between Greek and Latin in the papyri here.

[20] Pestman (1993, 333).

goes beyond that of a mere linguistic technician.[21] I am aware of only three named (written) translators. One possible example is from a Ptolemaic document, in which Theon son of Theon, a Persian of the *epigonê*,[22] testifies that he translated the preceding testimonies for a case before the *stratêgos* (P.Heid. VIII 416, before 176 BCE, Herakleopolis). This instance is, to my mind, dubious. Theon may well have translated Egyptian oral testimonies to be transcribed in Greek. The other two named translators are from the Roman period and translated from Latin into Greek. In BGU I 326 (194 CE, Karanis), one Gaios Loukkios Geminianos, an 'expert in Roman law' (νομικὸς Ῥωμαικὸς) certifies that he has translated the preceding document and that it is 'in conformity with the original will' (ἐστιν σύμφωνον τῇ αὐθεντικῇ διαθήκῃ). In SB VI 9298 (249 CE, Oxyrhynchus), an Aurelios Aiguptos describes himself in the same way and also certifies that the document he has translated conforms to that previously registered in Latin. The concern here is evidently accountability, and the reason the translators—who are also legal experts—name themselves is to certify that their translations are accurate representations of the original Latin legal papers and valid in a court of law.

One of our few possible pieces of evidence for the authorship of an earlier translation between demotic and Greek comes from P.Tebt. I 164 (112 BCE). This Greek translation of a demotic contract was written on the back of a report from the office of the well-known Menches, village scribe (κωμογραμματεύς) of Kerkeosiris.[23] One of the parties to the contract is also named Menches, and he is most likely identical with this Menches the village scribe. Verhoogt[24] argues on the basis of the almost literary hand used, and the fact that the translation was made some years after the original contract, that this is a writing exercise. But the two groups of documents discussed here from the archive of the Theban choachytes are ample demonstration that it might be necessary to make a Greek translation of old documents long after they had been drawn up. In P.Tebt. I 164, Menches has an additional Greek name, Asklepiades, as do his father and grandfather, although the women of the family bear only Egyptian names. Both parties are described as Ἕλλην ἐνχώριος (= dem. *Wynn ms n Kmy*), Greeks 'born in Egypt' or 'country-born', and they were clearly operating, to whatever extent, in both Greek and Egyptian cultural and linguistic spheres. The possibility that Menches is the author, as well as the transcriber, of the translation of P.Tebt. I 164 is an intriguing one.

[21] This follows the general pattern throughout the classical world that, where interpreters do become 'visible' in the papyrological or epigraphic record, it is not because of their language abilities per se, but because they use them in a defined and prestigious professional role: see, e.g., the Roman military personnel who commemorate themselves as *interpretes* in several first- and second-century CE tombstones from the Danube region (AE 1988, 938; AE 1951, 103; CIL III, 10505; CIL III 14349; CIL III 14507). On Graeco-Roman Egypt, see Mairs (2012a), and on the Roman provinces of northern and north-western Europe, see Mairs (2012b).

[22] See Clarysse (1994). [23] Verhoogt (1998). [24] Verhoogt (1998, 51–2).

On the identity of the translator(s) of P.Choach.Survey 12 and 17, we really have little or no information, even circumstantial. The fact that the translations were made for the same law case might suggest that they were produced by the same translator—although, as will be discussed below, some crucial differences in their approaches to the translation process cast doubt on this. The hands of the two Greek documents are certainly very similar, although I would not like to state definitively that they are identical. The time gap between the production of demotic originals and Greek translations may indicate that neither of the original scribes (P.Choach.Survey 12: Horos son of Phabis; P.Choach.Survey 17: Paes son of Peteesis) were involved, but this should not be ruled out in other cases. It is best, in the face of the anonymity of most of our translators from demotic to Greek, to suspend judgement on their personal ethnic or linguistic backgrounds. Although it is generally considered to have been more common for Egyptians to 'hellenize' rather than vice versa, the complicated identities of individuals such as Menches-Asklepiades the Ἕλλην ἐνχώριος almost render such bipolar distinctions meaningless. As well as monolingual Egyptian and Greek speakers, there must always have been a sizeable percentage of the population who grew up with exposure to both. The author(s) of our translations cannot, of course, have been just any bilinguals, but people who had had a literate education in both demotic and Greek. Their knowledge of the structure of a demotic contract (see below) also suggests that they had some professional familiarity with demotic legal documents.

§4. STRUCTURE AND PHRASEOLOGY

It is the demotic sale document, not the accompanying cession, which is rendered into Greek. In both cases, the structure and phraseology follow the demotic rather closely: this is a translation of a demotic legal document with all its appropriate clauses, not an attempt to construct a legal document in the Greek mould. Thus, for example, the introductory *d̠d* of the contracts is kept in the Greek as τάδε λέγει ('says these things'), and even the slightly more idiomatic *tw=t mtre ḥꜣt.t̠=y* (P.Choach.Survey 17.3: 'you have caused my heart to be satisfied') or *ḥꜣ.t̠=y mtre.w* (P.Choach.Survey 17.9: 'my heart is satisfied') becomes ἀπηυδόκησάς με ('you have made me content'). There appear to have been no set rules for making a copy or translation: the dating formula could be transmitted in full or in an abbreviated form, names of witnesses could be copied or omitted, the scribe of the original may be named in brief or with his full title.[25] What was clearly most important in the case of both sets of documents was the list of tombs: it was their ownership which was at stake.

[25] See Pestman (1993, 331 and Table 11); Mairs and Martin (2008/2009, 56–7).

In each case, as may be seen from the parallel texts in Mairs and Martin (2008/2009, 47–50), the author of the Greek feels free to condense and paraphrase. The demotic listings of tombs and their occupiers, for example, often follow the format 'the people of N', 'N and his children', or 'N and his children and his people'. The concern of the Greek, in each case, is to record the name of the principal tomb-owner, and additional occupants may be omitted, or signalled by ὁμοίως or ὡσαύτως ('likewise': P.Choach.Survey 12 and P.Choach. Survey 17) or καὶ πάντων ('and everyone/everything': P.Choach.Survey 12). (On the treatment of the demotic titles *ḥsy* and *ḥry* for tomb-owners, see further below.) The Greek of P.Choach.Survey 17 does not even bother to repeat the word for 'tomb', usually preferring to list each new share simply as ἄλλος or ἕτερος ('another one'). The most significant abridgements are in the demotic dating formulae, where the lengthy listing of royal titles and eponymous priests is jettisoned in favour of a simple μετὰ τὰ κοινά ('according to the usual (formulae)'). The Greek of P.Choach.Survey 17 also abbreviates the lengthy, and repetitive, concluding legal clauses of the demotic original to καὶ τὰ ἄλλα τὰ κοινὰ ('plus all the other usual clauses'). The author(s) of the Greek translations, whatever their backgrounds, were at least familiar enough with the structure and clauses of demotic contracts to abridge. The tendency of P.Choach.Survey 12 to transmit the demotic legal undertakings more fully may be ascribed to the fact that they are rather briefer in this document and would have taken little trouble to translate.[26]

§5. TERMINOLOGY: TRANSLATION AND TRANSLITERATION

In general, the texts show a high degree of internal coherence in their choices of equivalent vocabulary, usually fairly literal—an indication that in terminology, if not in structure, there was an established set of translation equivalents, or at least common usage among bilingual speakers. Tables 9.1 and 9.2 do not give a comprehensive listing of equivalent Greek–demotic vocabulary,[27] but a glossary of the more technical terms relating to the choachytes, their duties, and their charges. These are not items of basic vocabulary, but the kind of domain-specific terms for which we have preserved a few Greek–Latin bilingual glossaries from Roman-period Egypt.[28] Whether similar bilingual 'crib sheet' wordlists might be made for the use of scribes translating between demotic and Greek can only be a matter of conjecture.

[26] Mairs and Martin (2008/2009, 57).
[27] For which see the indexes to Pestman (1993).
[28] Kramer (1983 and 2001).

Table 9.1. Terminology in P.Choach.Survey 12

2	*wn n Ỉmn Ỉpy*	3	χ[οα]χύτης
2	*wn n Ỉmn Ỉpy*	6	omitted
3	*wn n Ỉmn Ỉpy*	16	τῶν αὐτῶν χοαχυτῶν
2	*šty.w*	7	λογείας
3	*šty.w*	17–18	καρπειῶν
3	*šty.w*	19–20	καρπειῶν
4	*šty.w*	21	καρπειῶν
3	*šms.w*	9	λειτουργιῶν
3	*tꜣ ḥ.t n Nbwnn*	8	Θυναβουνοὺν
4	*tꜣ s.t n Pꜣ-dj-Nfr-tm*	20	θυπατεστήμει
4	*tꜣ s.t n Pꜣ-dj-Ḫnsw pꜣ f(ꜣ)y mhn*	22	τση Πετεχών[σ]ιος γαλακτοφόρου
4	*pꜣ mꜣꜥ n pꜣ ḥry G-ḏꜣḏꜣ pꜣ ḥsy*	22–3	τόπου ἀσιῆτος καλουμένου Φρεκάγυτο[ς]

Table 9.2. Terminology in P.Choach.Survey 17

5	*wn n Ỉmn*	12	Παστοφόρου Ἄμμωνος
3	*šty.w*	4	[τῶν καρπειῶν]
7	*šte.w*	25	τ]ὰς... καρπε[ία]ς
8	*šte.w*	30	ἀι καρ]πεῖαι
3	*ḥ.t.w*	4	τά]φων
3 ff.	*ḥ.t*	6 ff.	τάφος (but often just ἄλλος or ἑτέρος)
4 ff.	*pꜣ ḥsy*	8 ff.	ὑπο]βρυχ<ί>ου
6	*ỉn-wwe*	20	ἰσιον[όμου
7	*šḳꜣ.w*	24	[<τὰ> κατάγαια]
8	*šḳꜣ.w*	28	<τὰ> κατάγαια
7	*s.t.w*	25	<τὰ>] παστοφόρ[ια
8	*s.t.w*	29	<τὰ> παστοφόρ]ια
7	*ỉḫy.w*	25	<τὰ> προσπίπ[τοντα
8	*ỉḫy.w*	30	τὰ προσπίπ[τον]τα
7	*šms.w*	26	<τὰς> λειτουργίας
9	*šms.w*	30–1	ἀι λειτουργία[ι
8	*ꜥrš.w*	26	[lacuna]
9	*ꜥrš.w*	31	[lacuna]

In P.Choach.Survey 17, *ḥ.t* ('tomb') is translated by the Greek equivalent τάφος—where the Greek bothers to translate it at all, and does not simply say ἄλλος or ἕτερος ('another one'). *šḳꜣ.w* ('grave shafts') are κατάγαια (lit. 'underground').[29] The remuneration and duties which come with the tombs are listed in the same way each time they appear in both the demotic and the Greek. *šte.w* ('revenues') are καρπεῖα, *ỉḫy.w* ('incomes') are προσπίπτοντα, and *šms.w* ('services') are λειτουργίαι; for *ꜥrš.w* ('offerings') we have two unfortunately placed lacunae in the Greek. Both the Greek and the demotic original of P.Choach.

[29] The use of near-identical formulae means that the Greek of line 24 may confidently be restored from line 28.

Survey 12 are rather briefer and more freely phrased, omitting any word for 'tomb', except in four special cases, considered below. As in P.Choach.Survey 17, *šms.w* are λειτουργίαι. Our attempt to find a Greek equivalent for *ʿrš.w* ('offerings') is frustrated by the choice of the scribe to abbreviate here to καὶ τῶν ἄλλων ('and the other things'). Although in P.Choach.Survey 54 the Greek term used is τὰ ἁγνευτικά, Pestman[30] suggests that the lacunae in P.Choach.Survey 12 and 17 contained instead the Greek translation of 'and everything that comes from it' and omitted to translate *ʿrš.w*. Again, *šty.w* are for the most part καρπεῖα, except in line 2 where they are λογεῖα ('collections', 'contributions').

There are a few outright mistakes.[31] The *s.t.w* of P.Choach.Survey 17 should not really be παστοφόρια (buildings within the temple enclosure where priests dwelt), but tombs, interchangeable with *ḥ.t.w*. In two of the 'special' tombs of P.Choach.Survey 12, *s.t* is simply transliterated. In line 6–19 of P.Choach.Survey 17, *bsn̂ṯ* ('smith') becomes πορθμέως ('ferryman'), despite being correctly rendered as σιδηρουργὸς in two other places. Personal names do not always transition successfully from original to translation. A tomb-owner named *Ḥr* in P.Choach.Survey 17, demotic sale line 5 = Greek line 12—and also in the companion cession document—becomes Paurios (*Pa-Ḥr*) in Greek, rather than the expected Horos. Five of the sixteen witnesses in P.Choach.Survey 12 are transposed incorrectly into Greek (see Table 9.3).

These mistakes are curious, since the scribe has earlier rendered the names of the parties and tomb-owners correctly into Greek. One possible explanation for his sloppiness is that the witness list (omitted in the translation of P.Choach. Survey 17) was irrelevant to the lawsuit for which the translations were made, tempting him to dash off the names carelessly.

In other places, differences between original text and translation reveal that these documents were created by individuals with knowledge of the people and transactions involved. In P.Choach.Survey 12, demotic sale line 3 = Greek line 16, the scribe refers to the brother of the addressee as *pꜣy=k sn* 'your brother',

Table 9.3. Demotic and Greek names, adapted from Pestman (1993, 75)

Demotic	Greek	Actual dem. equivalent of the Greek
Ḥr	Πετεῦρις	*Pꜣ-dj-Ḥr*
Ns-pꜣ-mtr	Σναχομνεῦς	*Ns-nꜣ.w-Ḫmn.ỉw*
Pꜣ-dj-Nfr-ḥtp	Πετεῦτῆμις	*Pꜣ-dj-Nfr-tm*
Ỉmn-ỉw	Ἀμονορταῖσις	*Ỉmn-ỉ.ỉr-dj.t-s*
Šlwl	Μίρσις	*Mrš*

[30] Pestman (1993, 460 n. 6).

[31] On scribal errors in the archive of the Theban choachytes as a whole, see Pestman (1985a). It may also be mentioned in passing that demotic copies in the archive occasionally use different writings of a word than the original, a possible result of different traditions of scribal schools, for which see Pestman (1993, 333).

expanded in the translation to τῶι νεωτέρωι σου ἀδελφῶι 'your younger brother', which is correct.[32] We should remain open to the possibility that some of the other 'errors' are in fact corrections.

Where things become interesting is with idiosyncratically Egyptian phenomena, and here there are some important differences between the approaches of the two translations, sufficient to argue that the same translator was not responsible for both. The key decision is the choice of whether to try to find an appropriate Greek equivalent, or simply to transliterate the Egyptian. With priestly titles, this is apparently unproblematic. The crucial term *wn(-pr) n Ỉmn Ỉpy* (παστοφόρος, but freely used instead of *wꜢḥ-mw* to refer to choachytes) is rendered as χοαχύτης in P.Choach.Survey 12 but as 'παστοφόρος of Ammon' in P.Choach.Survey 17. It is perhaps significant that in P.Choach.Survey 12 it is the parties to the transferral of choachyte rights who are being referred to, whereas the (female) parties to P.Choach.Survey 17 are not actually named as choachytes at all: the appearance of *wn* in this document is as the title of a tomb-owner. It would be interesting to know how the author of P.Choach.Survey 12 might have approached the *ỉn-wwe* / ἰσιονόμος of P.Choach.Survey 17.[33]

Two special categories of tomb-owners, *ḥsy.w* ('blessed') and *ḥry.w* ('masters', 'exalted ones') show a difference in approach between the two translations.[34] The Greek of P.Choach.Survey 17 renders *ḥsy* as ὑποβρύχιος ('underwater', 'drowned'). This is the only text which translates *ḥsy* in this way, and, while those who had drowned were counted among the blessed dead, the *ḥsy.w* were a much broader category. In P.Choach.Survey 12, *ḥsy* is simply transliterated as ἀσιης, which is also the policy followed by the translator of UPZ II 180a (from the same archive). As will be argued below, this should not necessarily be regarded as a failing on the part of the translator. *ḥry* is omitted altogether from the translation of P.Choach.Survey 17, while the author of P.Choach.Survey 12 again follows his policy of transliteration: the name-and-title combination *pꜢ ḥrj G-ḏꜢḏꜢ* ('the master G-djadja') becomes the portmanteau name Φρεκαγυτος / Phrekagutos.

The four 'special' tombs in P.Choach.Survey 12 show the strongest tendency to transliterate or partially transliterate rather than translate into Greek, and are also potentially most revealing of the grounds on which this decision was commonly made.[35] A large Ramesside private tomb used extensively by the choachytes during the second century BCE for their mummies, the tomb of Nebwennenef (*tꜢ ḥ.t n Nb-wnn (sic)*),[36] becomes in Greek the Θυναβουνοὺν—as Pestman notes, undeclined. Similarly, *tꜢ s.t n PꜢ-dy-nfr-tm* becomes θυπατεστήμει (this time declined in the dative). *S.t* is again transliterated, this time as a stand-alone

[32] See Pestman (1993, 335), for examples from other copies and translations in the archive.
[33] See Depauw (1998). [34] See Mairs and Martin (2008/2009, 60–7).
[35] I follow here the corrections to the Greek text suggested by Pestman (1993, 76).
[36] Pestman (1993, 451).

word, undeclined, in *tꜣ s.t n Pꜣ-dj-Ḫnsw pꜣ f(ꜣ)y mhn* = τση Πετεχών[σ]ιος γαλακτοφόρου, although the title 'carrier of the milk jar' is translated. The (less technical?) *mꜣꜥ* of *pꜣ ḥrj G-ḏꜣḏꜣ pꜣ ḥsy* ('place of the master G-djadja the blessed') is translated literally as τόπος ('place'), where, as already noted above, both the deceased's titles *ḥsy* and *ḥry* are transliterated, ἁσιης as a stand-alone, Φρε as a prefix to his name.

Schentuleit suggests in her study of a sale document and translations belonging to the priest Satabus of Soknopaiou Nesos[37] that there may be a tendency for more commonly-used priestly titles to be given a Greek translation (*ḥm-nṯr* = προφήτης) whereas the more recherché titles (*nb wꜥb ḥry šy wꜣḏ-wr Nꜣ-nfr-ỉr-šty.t* = νεβουάπει ῥισῆι γέτου Νεφορσάτει) are given a phonetic transcription.[38] This would certainly not be unexpected, for certain words in more common currency to be more amenable to translation. The very fact that it is priestly titles and tomb names in which we see the greatest tendency of our documents to transliterate rather than translate is in itself an illustration of this fact. However, I would also like to suggest that transliteration is something more than a simple failure to cope on the part of the scribe, but may itself exist as a bilingual strategy. Some of the titles of P.BM EA 262, for example, could easily have been translated into Greek, but the scribe appears to have made a deliberate choice to transliterate (e.g. in l. 1 *ḥm-Ny.t* = ἐμνιθης; *ỉry-pꜥ.t* = ὀρπεει or ὀρπαις; and *ḥꜣ.t-pꜥ.t* = τοπεεις or τοπααις).

These documents are not just being translated into Greek, but into Greek-of-Egypt, a language spoken by people resident in the country, familiar with its society and culture, and with frequent exposure to, even if not necessarily competence in, the Egyptian language. Transliteration is a more than acceptable option when the translation is to be used by people perfectly au fait with the titles and institutions being described; here, transliteration may even be a more accurate and appropriate way of communicating the precise identity of the terms under discussion. Code-switching has been recognized as a strategy characteristic not of speakers with a poor command of the language, but of highly competent bilinguals,[39] and it is possible that many of the individuals who created, used, and consulted these documents were functionally bilingual in some way, making the transliteration of culturally Egyptian terminology a kind of literate code-switching.

A parallel can be seen in a Greek inscription from the other end of the Hellenistic world, the edicts of the Indian emperor Aśoka set up at Kandahar, in ancient Arachosia, in the first part of the third century BCE.[40] Arachosia had a population of Greek descent, from the army of Alexander the Great. The region came under the rule of the Indian Mauryan dynasty, and Aśoka, in

[37] Schentuleit (2001): P. BM EA 262, 11 ce. [38] Schentuleit (2001, 135–7; 2007, 108).

[39] See, for example, the discussion in Hamers and Blanc (2000, 258–9).

[40] Schlumberger et al. (1958).

common with his policy elsewhere in his empire, set up copies of a series of decrees promulgating Buddhism. The Kandahar decree is generally considered to be written in excellent literary Greek, in contrast to our Egyptian Greek legal documents. Despite rendering Indian ethical terminology appropriately into Greek, however, the titles of two religious groups, *bramenai* (βραμεναι / Brahmins) and *sramenai* (σραμεναι / Buddhist mendicants) are transliterated. The conclusion to be drawn should not be that the accomplished translator has failed, but that his audience are well aware of what these terms mean.[41] Transliterating foreign religious terms may not make for 'good Greek', but it is a perfectly cromulent, culturally appropriate, local use of the language.

§6. TRANSLATIONESE

Young was one of the first, but by no means the last, to judge that these translations, and other papyrological documents, were written in 'bad Greek'. They are certainly not elegant Attic prose, but then they are not trying to be: they are koine Greek, and they are translations made for practical purposes. Their objective is to transmit accurately certain pieces of information, not to recast Egyptian texts *à la grecque*—hence their preservation of the rhythm and phraseology of the demotic, rather than rewording, and encumbering, the text with all the clauses of a Greek legal document. Recent studies of ancient bilingualism focus less on some ideal state of perfect, native competence in two languages, but more on the question of functionality, the ability to communicate effectively in particular domains.[42] There is a certain amount of evidence of interference from demotic in some Greek documents translated from demotic originals, but this may have as much to do with the fact that these texts are translations, as with their authors' competence in Greek.[43]

Achieving one's purpose in a second language is about more than technical grammatical competence. A 'bad translation' (and the Greek of our texts is really not that bad) may even deliberately be constructed with the intention of allowing a bilingual reader to access the structure and terminology of the original. At an extreme, the use of calques, or 'loan translations', as a translation strategy can go horribly wrong. A much-loved example is Pedro Carolino's *New Guide of the Conversation in Portuguese and English*,[44] a nineteenth-century English phrasebook for Portuguese speakers:

> <u>With a Bookseller</u>
>
> 'What is there in new's litterature?'
> 'Little or almost nothing, it not appears any thing of note.'

[41] Schmitt (1990, 50). [42] Adams (2003, 8); Mairs (2011).
[43] See, e.g., Mussies (1968) on P.Giss. I 36 and BGU III 1002.
[44] Fonseca and Carolino, with an Introduction by Millington (1884); Monteiro (2004).

> 'But why, you and another book seller, you does not to imprint some good works?'
> 'There is a reason for that, it is that you cannot to sell its. The actual-liking of the public is depraved they does not read for to amuse one's self any but to instruct one's.'

The authors—fairly obviously—could not actually speak English, but worked from a Portuguese–French phrasebook and a French–English dictionary. The clumsy pseudo-reflexive 'for to amuse one's self', for example, is clearly a ham-fisted attempt at translating *pour s'amuser*. This literal rendering of one language into another by an incompetent speaker, without regard for idiom or nuances of vocabulary, in Fonseca and Carolino's work produces such other creatures as 'the stone as roll not heap up not foam'—barely comprehensible as an English proverb, but a little clearer if you know that it is badly translated French, which permits the double negative and where the word *mousse* can mean both 'foam' and 'moss'.

Sometimes, unidiomatic translations can have a purpose. To give another, less than serious, example, Miles Kington's *Let's Parler Franglais!*, a spoof guide to French conversation, aims deliberately for the effect the *New Guide* achieves quite by accident.[45] It is predicated upon the idea that an English readership will be functionally fluent in Bad French:

> Lesson Vingt-Sept: Le Hangover
>
> *Mari*: Oh. Ouf. Oah.
> *Femme*: Comment, oh, ouf, et oah? Tu n'aimes pas les cornflakes?
> *Mari*: Non, je n'aime pas les cornflakes. Ils font un bruit comme un division de Panzers.
> *Femme*: Ah! Tu as un hangover!
> *Mari*: Ce n'est pas seulement un hangover. C'est la fin du monde.

This is not really French, but calqued English, and the humour is dependent upon the reader knowing the English words and phrases from which it has been over-literally translated. Yet nor is it nonsense: poor French it may be, but it is still fairly comprehensible.

The Greek translations of P.Choach.Survey 12 and 17 were produced by more accomplished bilinguals. Although they were to go before a Greek court, positing that at least some of their intended audience were also to be bilinguals makes us look at their structure and choices of terminology in a different way—not as imperfect renditions into Greek, but as a skilled preservation of the flavour and sense of the demotic original within a functional Greek framework. There are sound reasons for the translation strategies employed in these documents, and often close reading of the texts can allow us to identify what these strategies were and reveal how and why they were chosen. In the case of religious terminology, where titles and concepts from an Egyptian belief system and religious hierarchy

[45] Kington (1979).

must be rendered into Greek, scribes choose between two strategies: that of finding a Greek translation equivalent, or of simple phonetic transcription. One of these strategies is selected over the other, not because of the scribe's linguistic incompetence, but because it allows better communication of the precise meaning of the term in question. This, in turn, may tell us something about how cultural difference was communicated between ethnolinguistic communities in Hellenistic Egypt: Egyptian words for culturally specific terms such as priesthood titles might become naturalized in the local Greek idiom. The Greek translations of legal documents considered in this paper are first and foremost functional, designed to adequately and accurately replicate information contained in their demotic originals, but their authors are also skilled communicators, sensitive to cultural nuance and accomplished in a range of translation strategies.

10

Scribes in Private Letter Writing

Linguistic Perspectives

Hilla Halla-aho

§1. INTRODUCTION

Many, if not most, private letters from Roman Egypt (and generally in antiquity) were written by a person other than the one who appears as the sender. This article addresses questions concerning the manner of composition of private letters and the scribe's part in this process. Because private letters are important witnesses for language variation and change in text languages, we need to be able to assess the implications of this scribal aspect of letter writing for a linguistic study.

One might quite justly ask why it is important to know who produced the language of a letter. It is possible to argue that, regardless of who produced the language, it still is a reflection of epistolary language of the time and, as such, important for a linguist. To some extent, this of course is true. However, at least on a theoretical level, there are reasons why knowing something about the process of language production is useful, and even necessary. For example, should one wish to establish a connection between the language use and the actual sender, it is essential to know whose linguistic competence is presented in the linguistic form. On a larger scale, and concerning the value of papyri for linguistic research, if the language in many cases was produced by scribes, it is the output of a considerably smaller and more educated group of persons than the profiles of the actual senders of the letters would suggest. Generally, however, scribes do not constitute an insurmountable barrier between the scholar and the author's own words.[1]

[1] Bergs (2005, 79–80), Bagnall and Cribiore (2006, 8), and Verhoogt (2009). Note that Berg's observation concerns the forms of the personal pronouns, a feature that would have been easy for the scribe to change.

Many recent studies have touched upon this question.[2] Bagnall and Cribiore (2006) especially offer much interesting material and several important observations. Outside classical studies, scribal issues have been dealt with, for example, in connection with letters from late medieval England (the Paston Letters), and recently by Dutch linguists concerning the so-called sailing letters.[3]

Before proceeding to the actual linguistic aspects, some general questions on scribal practices need to be addressed.

§2. SCRIBES IN LETTER WRITING IN EGYPT

§2.1. Who Used Scribes and Why?

Letters from Roman Egypt usually do not mention that a scribe was used.[4] In the typical case, a scribe can be identified as the writer when another hand has written something on the papyrus sheet. This is often the closing salutation.[5] Sometimes the author of the letter even added a longer postscript in his own hand. In other cases, the sender proofread the letter and introduced corrections in the text.[6] On the other hand, if we have more than one letter from the same person, and they have been written by different hands, it seems clear that a scribe was used for at least some of them.

One possibility is that the same hand has written letters that have been sent by different people.[7] This does not happen often in the papyrus material, but there are occasional cases.[8]

Motivations for using scribes probably differed somewhat according to social class and level of education.[9] The members of the upper levels of the society (at least the men) were usually literate, but also had the opportunity to use private secretaries. Their motivations for using scribes were at least partly

[2] Bagnall and Cribiore (2006), Verhoogt (2009), and Evans (2010a and 2012).

[3] Bergs (2005 and Chapter 3 of the current volume) on the Paston Letters; Nobels and van der Wal (2009) on the sailing letters (I owe this reference to Marja Vierros).

[4] See Bagnall and Cribiore (2006, 6–8). One letter where the scribe identifies himself is P.Oxy. LVI 3860; see Bagnall and Cribiore (2006, 45). On the other hand, sometimes there is a reference in the letter itself to the writing process that indirectly points to an autograph, cf. νυκτ[ό]ς σοι ἔγραψα [τ]ὴν ἐπισστολὴν ταύτην εὑρὼν εὐκαιρίαν 'I wrote you this letter at night, having found an opportunity' (P.Mich. VIII 476, 20); see Nobels and van der Wal (2009, section 4.1).

[5] See Luiselli (2008, 689–92). Bagnall and Cribiore (2006, 46–8) point out that what at first sight looks like a second hand might actually be the same hand writing in a smaller and more cursive script, as if more hastily.

[6] See Bagnall and Cribiore (2006, 60).

[7] See Nobels and van der Wal (2009, section 4.2).

[8] For example, O.Claud. I 126 and 127 (on which see below).

[9] These have been discussed in Cribiore (2001, 229–30) and Bagnall and Cribiore (2006, 6–7 and 59–63).

comfort and ease. Even for a fully literate person, employing a scribe would have made the process easier, faster, and in many cases rendered a better result, in terms of handwriting and orthographic standards. Letters had to be written in large and clear letters, and the work was therefore slow and troublesome. In addition, using a scribe would enable the sender to attend to other duties while dictating.[10] Furthermore, there undoubtedly was a custom of using scribes in antiquity, so that people who had the opportunity would rather use a scribe than write themselves simply because it was the normal thing to do. Thus, those who were most likely to write themselves did not do so.[11]

While upper-class households may have employed scribes among their servants (or, in any case, persons who had received adequate schooling to be used as scribes), we have to presume that the average member of the population, of lower social standing and more limited financial means, could buy scribal services from professional scribes that were available in the markets or in the streets. Among these groups, illiteracy must have been common. Sometimes the scribes would have been literate family members, and, at least for women, whose literacy was at a lower level than that of men, the easiest way would often have been to ask a male relative to write the letter on their behalf.[12] Thus, a scribe in a private letter is not necessarily a professional scribe. The term 'social scribe' has been used for these writers.[13]

The same person might on one occasion use a scribe, and on another write himself. The letters P.Mich. VIII 483 and 484 are both written by Iulius Clemens, a legionary centurion. All of 484 is written by the same hand that wrote the farewell wish in 483, and this can thus be identified as that of Iulius Clemens himself. It is characterized by the editors Youtie and Winter as a 'large, upright, elegant hand with little linking of letters'. Both letters are written in a good orthographical standard. Iulius Clemens employed a scribe even though he demonstrably was a good writer himself. It is possible that the use of a scribe in only one of these letters derives from a difference in the status of the receivers. We know that in elite circles it was regarded as polite to write in one's own hand, undoubtedly because it took more time, thus showing the writer's commitment and warm feelings towards the recipient.[14] It is difficult to tell whether the fact that Iulius Clemens wrote the letter P.Mich. VIII 484 to Arrianus in his own hand is indicative of the same feeling or not. Arrianus is addressed as a brother (ἀδελφός, which at least indicates a familiar relationship even if not actual brotherhood). The other letter (P.Mich. VIII 483), for which he used a scribe,

[10] Cribiore (2001, 229); Small (1997, 171–5).
[11] Bagnall and Cribiore (2006, 6 and 47).
[12] Verhoogt 2009; Bagnall and Cribiore (2006, 7).
[13] By Nobels and van der Wal (2009).
[14] See Cic. Q fr. 2.2.1 and 2.16.1. It is not a coincidence that the remarks on the use of a secretary in the letters of Cicero are all in letters to Quintus or Atticus, the two persons who would recognize Cicero's handwriting (and those two to whom he usually wrote in his own hand); see Richards (1991, 69).

was written to a person called Socration in a respectful tone. But there may have been various reasons why a scribe on one occasion was used and on another was not. Sometimes scribes may have been unavailable or unaffordable. One factor that probably played a role every now and then was privacy: the author perhaps preferred to write a letter without the help of a scribe if the conveyance of personal information or feelings was needed.[15]

§2.2. Passing on the Message: Dictating

What do we know about the ways by which information was passed from the author to the scribe? This question is closely intertwined with the question of how the scribe contributed to the composition of the letter text and linguistic expression. Naturally, there is no one answer to these questions, as the situation will have varied from case to case.[16]

The most common way of passing information to the scribe was by dictation, at least in private letters. Normally, this would have happened at a relatively low speed, syllable by syllable (*syllabatim*), without (almost) any alterations to what the author said.[17] In some cases, the scribe would have modified the language of the author to varying degrees (for example, by producing a standard form instead of non-standard, or adding a particle). At the other end on the scale of scribal intervention are those cases where the scribe composed the letter text according to instructions given by the author.[18] In private letters on papyri, composing a draft that the scribe then rewrote as an actual letter must have been relatively rare, and done only in special cases.[19]

An essential aspect related to dictation, and one that is often wrongly interpreted, is the relationship of dictating to speaking. Dictating should not be equated with speaking (speaking in the sense of 'producing unplanned spoken language').[20] A person dictating a letter knows that (s)he is composing a written text. What is relevant for language production is whether the speaker or writer plans beforehand what he is going to say or write. Moreover, written language and spoken language often show diverging conventions (e.g. in expressing salutations, but

[15] Cribiore (2001, 230).

[16] See Richards (1991, 23–53 and 97–111) and Bagnall and Cribiore (2006, 59–65) on different ways to compose a letter.

[17] See Sen. Ep. 40.9 for evidence that the pace of dictation was substantially slower than that of speaking. See Small (1997, 173–5) for further references on dictation in ancient sources. The ability of Cicero's private secretary Tiro to take down whole periods at a time, using shorthand, naturally was an exception; see Cic. Att. 13.25.3 and Richards (1991, 99). For evidence of dictation taking place in a Vindolanda letter, see Adams (1995, 90; on tab.Vindol. II 234).

[18] See Bagnall and Cribiore (2006, 7–8) and below on P.Amh. II 131 (=P.Sarap. 80).

[19] A draft letter of Flavius Cerialis is known from Vindolanda (tab.Vindol. II 225).

[20] Despite what is implied in Bagnall and Cribiore (2006, 31).

also in other areas). Dictating is thus equivalent to producing written language in spoken form.[21]

Part of this confusion is caused by the notion of 'orality'. Language produced by dictation is 'oral' only as much as this refers to the physical action of using one's mouth. This does not necessarily imply immediacy, informality, emotive language, or lack of control (note that among Cicero's letters, the more formal ones are those that he dictated, and the more informal ones are those that he wrote in his own hand!).

Dictated letters and autograph letters by less literate persons share many essential characteristics: the lack of connecting and ordering devices that are normally used in written language (particles and other connectives, hypotactic structures). This collection of features is labelled as an 'oral style' by Bagnall and Cribiore, in keeping with their conception of dictation as an oral process.[22] However, it would perhaps be best to call it 'simple written language'. The fact that a letter is not written in a fluent and elegant epistolary style, or that it is even clumsy by some standards, does not mean that it is a transcript of spoken language. The essential point is that we are dealing with variation within written language.

§3. THE LINGUISTIC APPROACH: SCRIBES AS PARTICIPANTS IN THE LANGUAGE PRODUCTION PROCESS

Because the relationship between scribe and language is different with respect to different levels of language, they are best dealt with separately. A distinction can be made between the orthographical/phonological/morphological and syntactic levels.

§3.1. Orthography/Phonology/Morphology

Because the scribe was the person who actually wrote the words down, a reasonable assumption is that orthography was always produced by the scribe. After all, it is a rather simple process of encoding the phonetic/phonological shape of a word into writing according to certain rules. Most of the common non-standard orthographical forms, including but not restricted to iotacisms in Greek, reflect sound changes that by the Roman period would have penetrated the whole Greek-speaking community, and even when there was variation in pronunciation, it would have been up to the scribe to decide what to write. The orthographic appearance of a letter is thus indicative, first and foremost, of the

[21] Cf. Small (1997, 182): 'dictating what one has composed in one's head'.

[22] Bagnall and Cribiore (2006, 61–4).

educational level of the scribe, and only in very rare cases is directly motivated by the pronunciation of the author.

A professional scribe could (and would) produce standard orthography regardless of who was dictating, and how.[23] Similarly, a social scribe would stick to his idiosyncrasies when writing a letter for another person. An example is presented by a set of ostraca from Mons Claudianus. The three ostraca O.Claud. I 137–9 have all been written by the same hand. O.Claud. I 137 is a letter from Valerius Palmas to Valerius Longus, and O.Claud. I 138 is a letter from Maximus to his sister Sarapias. In 139, the sender's name has not been preserved. The editor, Bülow-Jacobsen, suspects that Maximus, who sends his greetings at the end of O.Claud. I 137, is the writer of all three letters.[24] Maximus' orthography shows certain substandard features that occur in all three letters: a double <c> written where a single one is expected (137.13 and 21; 138.18; 139.12, 14, and probably 4), and omitting the <α> in the name Οὐαλέριος (137.1 and 2; 138.5; 139.15).[25]

The Mons Claudianus ostraca provide even more evidence for a social scribe producing his own idiosyncratic forms in a letter. A man named Dioskoros apparently grew vegetables somewhere near the main fort. We have many letters from him, nearly all of which deal with the delivery of vegetables (O.Claud. II 224–42). The editor notes the discrepancy between Dioskoros' trained handwriting and his difficulties with Greek syntax, especially cases. This is visible most clearly in the opening address, where Dioskoros does not inflect the names of the addressees, not even when they are Greek and not Egyptian:

1. O.Claud. II 225.1–3

Διόσκορος Δράκων καὶ Ερημησις καὶ Ἀμμωνιανὸς κουράτωρ ἀμφοτέροις τοῖς φιλτάτοις πολλὰ χα(ίρειν)

'Dioscorus to Dracon and Eremesis and Ammonianus curator, all his best friends, many greetings.'

If the editor is right in identifying the handwriting (very likely in view of the plates of O.Claud. II), Dioskoros also wrote one letter for another person, the *curator* Antonius Nepotianus (O. Claud. II 381, addressed to Iulius Ammonianus, the *curator* of Claudianus). The same inability to choose the correct morphological form can be detected in this letter:

2. O.Claud. II 381.1–5

Ἀντωνίῳ Νεπωτιανὸς κουράτωρ{ος} πρεσιδί[ου ...] ⟦χαί(ρειν)⟧ Ἰούλις Ἀμμων[ιανῷ] κουράτωρ Κλ̣[αυδιανοῦ] (5) χαίρ(ειν)

'Antonius Nepotianus, curator of the fort...to Iulius Ammonianus, curator of Claudianus, greetings.'

[23] Adams (1995, 87–90); Evans (2010a, 66).

[24] This agrees well with the idea of Verhoogt (2009) that the name of the social scribe would normally appear at the end of the letter, sending greetings to the recipient.

[25] These are just two examples among a larger body of deviant spellings.

The conception of literacy and writing skills was subject to varying standards, especially, no doubt, in such remote places as Mons Claudianus and its surroundings, but still it is difficult to imagine the context in which a person with such a poor command of Greek ended up acting as a scribe for a superior.

But even professional scribes with experienced hands sometimes produced non-standard forms. A case where confusion is due to language contact is presented by a set of Greek-influenced spellings in one of the Latin letters of Claudius Terentianus (P.Mich. VIII 468). These are the accusative plural *nostrous* with <ou> (P.Mich. VIII 468.62), the accusative singular *illan* (P.Mich. VIII 468.28) with <n>, and the form *uetranus* corrected from *utranus* (P.Mich. VIII 468.6, *utranus* from the common Greek spelling οὐτρανός). As pointed out by Adams, these forms should be attributed to the scribe, who was accustomed to writing Greek, or was a Greek speaker himself. This conclusion is supported by the fact that by orthographical standards, letter 468 plainly stands out as the poorest of the Terentianus letters, abounding in phonetic spellings.[26] The case serves as a reminder that Greek-influenced forms in the letter of a bilingual person are not necessarily produced by the author.[27] This conclusion is important for the evaluation of Terentianus' Latin skills. The Greek influence can be seen in the orthography (morphology) and was produced by the scribe, not by Terentianus, although he was bilingual.[28]

§3.2. Syntax and Composition

In the sphere of syntax, things become more complicated, and there is a range of options available, according to the production process. If the letter was dictated to the scribe, he probably was not able to make alterations, at least other than inserting a particle or a conjunction here and there. However, there are also instances where the scribe was probably responsible for most of the wording and phrasing in a letter, and the author merely indicated the contents of his message.

[26] Adams (2003, 542). On the difference in orthographical standards in the Latin letters of Terentianus, see Halla-aho (2003).

[27] For similar points raised in connection with Graeco-Egyptian bilingualism, see Clarysse (2010, 47–8).

[28] P.Mich. VIII 468 is, in all probability, not an autograph. Strassi (2008, 27) suggests that the letter P.Mich. VIII 469 is an autograph of Terentianus. It is written in a less careful and practised hand than the other letters, and it has different orthographic variants of the same word. Noteworthy is also the fact that the handwriting clearly becomes more careless towards the end of the letter (see the photograph in ChLA 42, 1216), another fact that points to a non-professional writer; see Bagnall and Cribiore (2006, 45). Of the Greek letters, only 479 has the closing salutation by a different hand, of the Latin letters only 472 (the letter by Tiberianus). Concerning possible autographs in the Latin letters of Terentianus, one should, however, note that the letters P.Mich. VIII 470 and 471 have been written by the same hand.

In the usual state of affairs, when only one letter survives from one person, it is not possible to compare the language and writing practices in a series of letters. This is why those cases where we happen to have more than one letter from the same person are especially important for research into scribal practices. Nevertheless, even in those cases where more than one letter is preserved from one person, it is often difficult to say what elements in the language derive from the author and what from the scribe.

For example, P.Mich. VIII 490 and 491 are both letters from an Egyptian recruit in the Roman fleet in Misenum to his mother. They are written by different hands (by different scribes), and 490 has a postscript by a second hand, presumably that of Apollinarius himself. Letter 490 is written in a somewhat less elegant style: there is repetition of the verb δηλῶ and there are sentence beginnings introduced with καί. Furthermore, there apparently is an error in the opening salutation, where πρὸ παντὸς ἔρρωσό μοι ὑγιαίνουσα τὸ προσκύνημά σου ποιῶν παρὰ πᾶσι τοῖς θεοῖς 'Before all else I wish you good health and make obeisance on your behalf to all the gods', has ἔρρωσό combined with ποιῶν, instead of the normal, and correct, εὔχομαί σε ὑγιαίνειν, continued with the participle ποιῶν.

In the other letter (P.Mich. VIII 491), there seems to be more of an attempt at typical letter phraseology with γεινώσκειν σε θέλω 'I wish you to know' (lines 4–5), ἐρωτῶ σε οὖν 'I ask you to' (line 9), καλῶς δε ποιήσ<εις> γράψασ{σ}ά μοι ἐπιστολὴν 'Please write me a letter' (lines 11–12), and the vocative μήτηρ 'mother' (lines 5 and 9). Note also τῇ μητρεὶ καὶ κυρίᾳ πολλὰ χαίρειν 'to his mother and lady' in the opening salutation (490 has only τῇ μητρί).

The use of connectives is in line with this conclusion, although no dramatic difference is evident. The range of particles in both letters is normal with δέ, γάρ, and in 491 also οὖν. Once in 491 καί opens a new construction (line 13), but in 490 this happens three times (lines 5, 7, and 9).

Thus, letter 491 shows a more elegant form of epistolary Greek in all respects, even if the difference is not striking. Accordingly, even with a couple of scribal mistakes, this letter shows a form of language closer to what must have been perceived as an epistolary standard. It is, however, impossible to say whether this variation derives from the two scribes' different linguistic standards and styles, or whether one of the letters in fact reflects the linguistic competence of Apollinarius himself that the scribe reproduced on the papyrus.[29] It is possible that the other scribe was better educated and more independent in composing the letter text. Furthermore, at the end of 490, we find the salutation of Asclepiades to the recipient, thus rendering Asclepiades a candidate for being a social scribe.[30]

[29] In support of the latter interpretation one can note the idiom ὀκνέω γράφειν 'to hesitate to write' that appears in both letters: καὶ σὺ δὲ μὴ ὤκνι γράφιν περὶ τῆς σωτηρίας σου 'do not delay to write about your health' (P.Mich. VIII 490.12–13) and οὐ μὴ ὀκνήσω σοι γράφιν 'I will not delay to write to you' (P.Mich. VIII 491.14).

[30] See above (n. 24).

The opening salutations are those parts in a letter that most easily could reflect the practices of the scribe instead of those of the author. In the letters of Apolloniarius, for example, one may note the additional address κυρίᾳ in the 'better' letter. In Claudius Terentianus' Latin letters, the opening salutation varies from letter to letter, the one in P.Mich. VIII 467 being the longest and most elaborate. Three of his Greek letters (P.Mich. VIII 476, 477, and 478), on the other hand, show the same long opening salutation, but these are all possible or probable autographs.[31] In the Zenon archive, there is some evidence that letters written by scribes more often have longer salutation formulae than autograph letters.[32]

The authorship and language use of women writers has been treated extensively in Bagnall and Cribiore (2006). The questions about scribes and authorship concern men, too, even if in the case of women authors they are more prominent because the literacy of men was, on average, both more common and at a higher level of competence. The results of Bagnall and Cribiore show that in many cases, the language use of women authors is still visible even in dictated letters.[33] In these cases, practised handwriting and good orthography are combined with relatively simple syntax. The main characteristics of this simple style are the use of few connecting particles, little subordination, and mostly main clauses combined in a sequence by the means of καί.[34] On the other hand, in the rare instances when dictated and autograph letters of the same person can be compared, differences (of varying degrees) can be observed between autographs and dictated letters. It is thus possible to distinguish between two types of scribal behaviour: transcribing (more or less directly) from dictation and composing the letter text more or less independently. It appears that these two types can be found in letters authored by men as well.

Lucius Bellienus Gemellus is the author of several letters, of which a number are published as P.Fay. 110–20.[35] Of these, P.Fay. 110 is written in a 'well-formed, uncial hand of a literary type' (according to the editors Grenfell and Hunt). This one is the earliest of the extant letters of Gemellus, and the later letters show his own handwriting.[36] His letters consist, for the most part, of a sequence of imperatives linked to each other with the simple καί.[37] The interesting thing

[31] Letter 476 was written by Terentianus at night (see n. 4 above) and is thus in all probability an autograph. The hand in 476 is similar to that in 477 and 478; see the descriptions of the editors Youtie and Winter in P.Mich. VIII (pp. 54, 58, and 63). See also White (1986, 173).

[32] Evans (2012). [33] Bagnall and Cribiore (2006, 59–63).

[34] On connective particles, see Clarysse (2010, 36–43) and Evans (2010b).

[35] White (1986, nos. 95–8). See now Ast and Azzarello (2012) for the archive and new texts belonging to it.

[36] Among the new (unpublished) texts of the Gemellus archive there is another letter authored by Gemellus but written in another hand; see Ast and Azzarello (2012, 70).

[37] See Clarysse (this volume, Chapter 11): A short and somewhat abrupt style with plain imperatives is typical in letters from high to low. However, the extensive use of καί is not in itself an inherent feature of such letters.

here is that P.Fay. 110 also shows this same style, despite the good quality of the handwriting as well as the orthography. Furthermore, the following parallel expressions can be found when comparing P.Fay. 110 and 112 (one of Gemellus' autograph letters):

3.
a) P.Fay. 110.3–5: εὖ ποιήσεις[38] κομισάμενός μου τὴν [ἐ]πιστ[ο]λὴν ἀναγκάσας ἐκχωσθῆναι τὸ ἐν αὐτῶι κόπριον 'When you receive my letter, please have the manure heaped up.'[39]
b) P.Fay 112.1–2: εὖ πυήσις διῶξαι τοὺς σκαφήτρους τῶν ἐλαιώνον 'Please urge on the hoeing of the olive groves.'

4.
a) P.Fay. 110.34: μὴ οὖν [ἄ]λλως ποιήσῃς 'Therefore, do not act otherwise.'
b) P.Fay. 112.21: μὴ οὖν ἄλλως πυήσῃς 'Make sure that you do not act otherwise.'

5.
a) P.Fay. 110.16–17: καὶ γνῶθι εἰ πεπότισται ὁ [ἐ]λαιὼν δυσὶ ὕδασι 'And find out whether the oliveyard has been watered twice.'
b) P.Fay. 112.15–16: ἐπίγνοθι εἰ ἐσκάφη ὡ τῆς Διονυσιάδος ἐλαιών 'Find out whether the olive grove at Dionysias was hoed.'

The obvious conclusion is that the scribe who wrote P.Fay. 110 closely followed Gemellus' dictation and produced what he heard without almost any alterations.

Similar cases in which there is an apparent mismatch between professional handwriting combined with standard orthography and less polished language have been presented by Bagnall and Cribiore. Such letters are, for example, P.Oxy. VI 932,[40] a letter written by a woman called Thais, and a letter from the Tiberianus archive (P.Mich. VIII 473) sent to Tiberianus by a woman called Tabetheus.[41] The specific substandard characteristics of each letter are different (the letter of Thais shows omission of linguistic elements whereas Tabetheus' letter presents a disorganized narrative), but both seem to be the products of a professional scribe faithfully taking down the dictation of a less literate person. In this, they are clearly parallel to the letter of Gemellus, P.Fay. 110. The latter, however, is a particularly important witness because of the series of autograph letters that confirm that what we see in P.Fay. 110 is the product of Gemellus himself, and not a scribe who controlled orthography well but syntax less so.

[38] This phrase appears in two further letters of Gemellus: εὖ οὖν πυήσας ἐξαυτῆς πέμσις αὐτὸν ἐξαυτῆς 'Therefore, please send him immediately' (P.Fay. 113.10–12) and εὖ οὖν πυήσας κομισάμενός μου τὴν ἐπιστολὴν πέμσις μυ Πίνδαρον εἰς τὴν πόλιν 'Upon receipt of my letter, please send Pindaros to me at the city' (P.Fay. 114.3–5).

[39] The translations of P.Fay. 110–13 are from White (1986, nos. 95–7).

[40] Discussed in Bagnall and Cribiore (2006, 297–8).

[41] Discussed in Bagnall and Cribiore (2006, 136–7).

Sometimes, however, when we have many letters from the same author, the letters written by a scribe are more elegant in their turn of phrase and composition. An example is provided by two letters from Sarapion (P.Amh. II 131 and 132 = P.Sarap. 80 and 81).[42] The first of these, written by a scribe, is addressed to Sarapion's wife Selene. It is twice as long as the other letter that Sarapion himself wrote to his son Eutychides. In this case, the conclusion seems to be that whereas letter 132 presents Sarapion's own language use, the other letter was in fact formulated by a competent scribe.

I cite here the first half of P.Amh. II 131 (representative of the style and tone of the letter as a whole) together with the full text of 132. Both letters are concerned with practical matters, so difference in topics does not explain the notable difference in style:

6. P.Amh. II 131.1–13 (=P.Sarap. 80)
Σαραπίων Σελήνηι τῆι ἀδελφῆι χαίρειν. ἕως ἂν ἐπιγνῶ τὸ ἀσφαλὲς τοῦ πράγματος περὶ οὗ κατέπλευσα ἐπιμενῶ, (5) ἐλπίζω δὲ θεῶν θελόντων ἐκ τῶν λαλουμένων διαφεύχεσθαι καὶ μετὰ τὴν πεντεκαδεκάτην ἀναπλεύσειν. μελησάτω σοι ὅπως ἀγορασθῇ τὰ κενώματα καὶ ὅπως τὰ παιδία (10) περὶ τὴν ἰδιοσπορίαν ἡμῶν καὶ τοὺς γεωργοὺς ἐπιμελῶς ἀναστραφῶσιν, μάλιστα δὲ περὶ τοὺς τọὺ̣ς ἐν Ὑφαντῶṿι[43] ὅπως μὴ δίκας λέγωμεν.

'Sarapion to his sister, Selene, greeting. Until I learn that the matter about which I sailed down is settled, I will remain, but I hope, the gods willing, to get away from talking and, after the fifteenth, to sail up. Make sure that the empty jars are bought and that the servants occupy themselves with the sowing of our private land and with the cultivators, and especially that they be concerned about the woven things, lest we have to speak about restitution.'[44]

7. P.Amh. II 132 (=P.Sarap. 81)
Σ̣αραπίων Εὐτυχ(ίδῃ) τῶι υἱῶι χαίρειν. περισ<σ>ῶς μοι ἔγραψας περὶ τοῦ μισθοῦ τῶν ἐργατῶν, σὺ γὰρ διὰ σαυ- (5) τοῦ ἶ. ἐπίγνωθι οὖν τὸ ἀσφαλὲς τί Πολεῖς διδοῖ τοῖς αὐτοῦ καὶ σὺ δός. δότω σοι δὲ Ὡρίων ὁ ἱερεὺς ἀργύριον χάριν τον ἐργατῶν. αὔριον δὲ σοι (10) Ἀχιλλᾶν πέμψο ἵνα καὶ σὺ εἰς Ἑρμούπολ(ιν) ἔλθῃς

'Sarapion to his son, Eutychides, greeting. You wrote to me unnecessarily about the wages of the labourers, for you yourself are in charge. Therefore, find out—to be safe—how much Polis pays his workers and you pay the same. Let Horion the priest give you the money for the labourers. Tomorrow I will send Achillas to you in order that you too may come to Hermopolis.'

In the first excerpt, one notes the elegant beginning with ἕως ἄν, the genitive absolute θεῶν θελόντων (although it admittedly was a stock phrase), the use of ὅπως

[42] White (1986, no. 106).
[43] Interpreted by Grenfell and Hunt in P.Amh. II as περὶ τῶν ἐνυφαντῶν.
[44] Translations of P.Amh. II 131–2 are from White (1986, no. 106).

(twice),[45] and the use of the emphasizing expression μάλιστα δὲ in the sequence of orders. After the initial part cited here, the letter continues with careful sentence connection (οὕτως δὲ...ἐχρησάμεθα οὖν...ἐκ γὰρ ὧν...ἐπέμψαμεν δ'ὑμῖν). The second letter, on the other hand, begins bluntly with a reproach περισ<σ>ῶς μοι ἔγραψας, and has a parenthetical expression τὸ ἀσφαλὲς 'the safe thing to do' (lines 4–5) , as well as καὶ σὺ δός 'and you pay (the same)' (line 7) without an explicit object. It is worth pointing out that the first letter (131) also contains a reproach, οὕτως δὲ ἠμελήσατε ἡμῶν ὡς ἀνειρημένων τὸ ἀναβολικὸν καὶ ἐχόντων ἐκ τούτου εἰς ἡμᾶς δαπανῆσαι 'You were negligent towards me, assuming as though I had received the deferred payment and could pay my expenses out of that' (lines 13–16). It is interesting that the correspondence related to Sarapion and that related to Gemellus are contemporary (early second century CE) and similar in their topics, both concerning the management of a large family property. The linguistic competence of Gemellus and Sarapion was well suited for handling practical matters, even if lacking in epistolary elegance. The letter P. Amh. II 131 shows what a competent scribe could do with this kind of 'raw material'.

A similar case to that of Sarapion, by a woman writer, is presented by the two letters of Klematia (P.Oxy. XLVIII 3406 and 3407).[46] The one that she wrote herself (3406) is, according to Bagnall and Cribiore, characterized by an oral, paratactic style. They refer to the frequent use of καί introducing new requests, to the use of two consecutive imperatives in καὶ π̣ε̣ίρα καὶ ἔρεον ἀνένικον (lines 6–7), and to the variation in the use of plural and singular imperative forms (παραμέτρησον line 3, βοήθησον line 5, and ἀπέτησον line 9 are in the singular, but μὴ ἀμελήσεται line 8 is in the plural). By contrast, letter 3407 is written in a more polished style. Bagnall and Cribiore point out the range of connectives used (ἀλλὰ line 13, οὖν line 18, δέ lines 21 and 23), together with the fact that the occasional instances of καί never open new instructions.[47]

§4. CONCLUDING REMARKS

The main points of this paper may be summarized as follows:

- On the levels of orthography and phonology, as well as (perhaps to a lesser degree) morphology, we see predominantly the output of the scribe, and

[45] For ὅπως as the more formal or learned conjunction (when compared with ἵνα), see Clarysse (2010, 43–5).

[46] Bagnall and Cribiore (2006, 213–16).

[47] One does note the form ἐμέναν (line 21), but it really is not surprising given the late date of this text. The active role of the scribe in this letter is probably also shown by the fact that the sender is referred to as 'the landlady' in the opening address, without her proper name (the identification with the Klematia of 3406 is based on other factors, such as the name of the recipient, Papnouthis); see Bagnall and Cribiore (2006, 215).

only in special cases should we suspect that the author's idiolectal forms have been reproduced on the papyrus.

- The syntax and composition of a letter often represent the author's dictation, which the scribe reproduced on the papyrus.
- Dictated language produced by less educated authors can be called 'simple written language'. Being planned beforehand, it does not necessarily bear any close resemblance to actual spoken language.
- Although following the author's dictation word-by-word was a normal and perhaps even prevalent practice, letters on papyri show clear instances of letters not only penned but also composed on the behalf of their senders by a competent scribe, and being stylistically far removed from the language and style that the authors themselves were able (or wanted) to produce.
- The analysis of the letters by Lucius Bellienus Gemellus and Sarapion supplements some of the results of Bagnall and Cribiore by pointing out that similar processes were at work also in letters authored by men.

11

Letters from High to Low in the Graeco-Roman Period

Willy Clarysse

§1. INTRODUCTION

Polite formulae in letters from low to high have often been studied because their phrases can be catalogued rather easily.[1] Letters from superiors to subordinates also contain particular topics, which remain largely unchanged over time, though the formulae through which they are expressed may change. In the present contribution, I examine how landowners and other superiors in the private sphere addressed their stewards (often called *phrontistai* in the Roman period) and other agents, including sons as junior business partners.

I have concentrated on a few archival groups of texts between the third century BCE and the third century CE: the archive of Zenon, with letters of the *dioiketes* (the minister of finance) Apollonios to his stewards Panakestor and Zenon, belongs to the third century BCE; for the late first and second century CE, the focus is on the letters which L. Bellienus Gemellus, a Roman veteran and landowner, wrote to his manager-slave Epagathos and his manager-son Sabinus, and on the correspondence of the sons of Patron, owners of a large estate in the district of Polemon, with their *phrontistai*; in the archive of Heroninus, the Alexandrian grandee Appianus and his representative Alypios, a high-ranking metropolite, give orders to Heroninus and a few other estate managers in Theadelpheia and its surroundings *c.*250 CE.

These test cases provide a set of topics and a set of formulae that I checked with the Duke Databank of Documentary Papyri[2] in order to find similar texts elsewhere. In doing so, I came across a few (fewer than I expected) individual letters that belong to a similar setting.[3] Additionally, I have also undertaken a comparison with the archive of the gymnasiarch Chairemon (from Bakchias,

[1] Steen (1938); Koskenniemi (1956, 54–154); Papathomas (2007).

[2] The Duke Databank (DDbDP) can be accessed at http://papyri.info/ddbdp/.

[3] For example, BGU II 624 (the addressee is φίλτατος 'dear'); P.Oxy. LXVII 4624 (letter by a gymnasiarch to his *phrontistes*); P.Tebt. II 419 (letter to a *phrontistes*); P.Hamb. IV 256.

*c.*100 CE),[4] where the relationship between the landowner and his collaborator(s) is remarkably different. It would be interesting to compare how government officials addressed their subordinates, but that must await a different study.

In a few cases where we do have both the letter of a superior to his inferior and the answer of the subordinate, we can see how the same topic is formulated from the two sides.

§2. THE DOCUMENTATION

§2.1. The Zenon Archive

For the Zenon archive (261–228 BCE),[5] I have concentrated on letters by the *dioiketes* Apollonios to his managers Panakestor (five letters) and Zenon (forty-four letters), ranging between 266 and 254 BCE.

P.CairZen. II 59179 is a letter addressed by Apollonios to Zenon, including a copy of two letters to Krataimenes and Paramonos in Memphis. Zenon receives these copies ὅπως παρακολουθῇς 'in order that you may follow up the case'. The letters to Krataimenes and Paramonos are almost identical, but Krataimenes is addressed with the polite formula [κα]λ̣ῶς ποιήσεις συντάξας τὰ γενήματα [δια]τηρῆσαι, 'please give order to guard the crops', whereas for Paramonos the scribe uses ἐπιμελές σοι γενέσθω ὅπως τὰ γενήματα διατηρηθῇι, 'it is your duty that the crops should be guarded'. Krataimenes is the judge who has to settle a dispute about vineyards and, as such, is an independent person of some weight; Paramonos (his name suggests that he was a slave or a freedman) is the manager of Apollonios' Memphite estate. The former is addressed with a polite 'please' formula, while the latter receives an order with the typical third person imperative. Clearly, such details mattered in the hierarchy of officials and managers surrounding the minister.

PSI V 502 is a letter of rebuke from Apollonios to Panakestor, Zenon's predecessor as estate manager of the estate (*dorea*) in Philadelpheia. Criticism is a recurrent theme in letters from superiors to inferiors. In the present case, we also have the answer, a long letter in which Panakestor defends himself against the curt rebuke of the *dioiketes*, who wrote 'I am astounded by your negligence because you have written nothing, neither about the valuation (of the crop) nor about the gathering in (of the harvest). Even now, write to us in what state everything is.' In Panakestor's answer, the sharp verb κατεπλησσόμην ('I am astounded') is

[4] For this archive, see the description provided on the Trismegistos website, http://www.trismegistos.org/arch/detail.php?tm=16. For the archives under discussion, see Vandorpe, Clarysse, and Verreth (2015, 70–73 [Chairemon-Apollonios], 132–136 [Epagathos-Gemellus], 170–175 [Heroninus], 271–279 [descendants of Patron], and 447–455 [Zenon]).

[5] For the archive, see Clarysse and Vandorpe (1995).

weakened into a more neutral θαυμάζω (line 12; 'I am surprised') and καταγινώσκων (line 29; 'condemning'). Panakestor adds that 'it is not possible for somebody in your service to be negligent.'

§2.2. The Archive of L. Bellienus Gemellus (Epagathos)

The archive of L. Bellienus Gemellus (hereafter Gemellus), a Roman veteran whose estate was spread over several Fayum villages, was found by Grenfell and Hunt in 1899 in a house in Euhemeria. The house was no doubt that of Epagathos, the manager-slave of Gemellus, who should thus be considered the real owner of the archive. Of about a hundred documents, ranging from 94 until 122 CE, only twenty-five are fully published; twenty-eight receive a short description in P.Fay. and thirty-three are still unpublished.[6] I have included twelve letters in my database (these are the only ones written from high to low). Seven of these are written by Gemellus and his son Sabinus to their manager Epagathos (six plus one); three are addressed by Gemellus to his son Sabinus, who in the earlier period functions as a manager for his father's farms and is treated as a subordinate in the letters.

Most of the letters by Gemellus and his son as estate holders consist of orders in the aorist imperative and in the second person of the future tense, but the first order is typically introduced by the polite formula εὖ ποιήσεις, 'please' (Olsson (1925), nos. 52, 54, 55 after a πάντη πάντως, 'by all means', beginning, 56, 58, 62, 63, 64; not 53, which starts with μέμφομαι, 'I blame you'; the beginning is missing in 57 and 60). In seven of the twelve letters, the formula μὴ οὖν ἄλλως ποιήσῃς, 'make sure to do it properly', usually at the end, insists that orders should be carried out.

The son Sabinus is treated similarly to Epagathos (so in Olsson (1925), nos. 55–6), though we note the use of ἐάν σοι δόξῃ 'please' in no. 59, and also a longer beginning formula (χαίρειν καὶ διὰ πάντος εὐτυχεῖν, 'greetings and success for ever') and end formula (ἐρρῶσθαι σὲ εὔχομαι εἰς τὸν ἀεὶ χρόνον, 'I pray that you may be healthy for ever'). In no. 61, Gemellus uses the philophronetic formula ἐπιμέλου σαυτοῦ, 'take care of yourself', again in a letter to his son. ἀσπάζου greetings (as opposed to χαίρειν greetings) occur not only for Sabinus (no. 61), but twice also for Epagathos (nos. 54, 57). Gemellus himself addresses his son with υἱός, 'son', but Epagathos he calls either φίλτατος, 'dear', the most general laudatory epithet,[7] or τῶι ἰδίωι, 'my own', which sounds friendly and familiar (like Latin *suus*), but at the same time stresses the relationship of master and slave.[8]

[6] Several of these are in the papyrus collection of the Egypt Exploration Society, housed in the Sackler Library, Oxford. For this archive, see now Ast and Azzarello (2012 and 2013).

[7] Koskenniemi (1956, 97–100).

[8] The expression occurs seven times in the archive of L. Bellienus Gemellus but rarely elsewhere (O.Leid. 330; P.Oxy. VI 932; P.Oxy. XLIX 3505; SB XVI 12322; O.Krokod. 81). All examples date from the first and second centuries CE. Influence of Latin *suus* is possible; see the note with P.Oxy. XLIX 3505 and Koskenniemi (1956, 104).

One single letter is written by Sabinus to his father Gemellus, whom he addresses with his praenomen Lucius and as τιμιώτατος, 'honourable' (P.Fay. 261, unpublished). In another letter, P.Fay. 123 (= Olsson (1925), no. 65), a certain Harpokration, otherwise unknown, addresses Sabinus as ἀδελφός, 'brother'. Here we find twice the polite formula ἐάν σοι δόξηι, 'please', followed by the ἀσπάζου greetings for Gemellus' brothers Lykos and NN. This is a private rather than a business letter, containing messages rather than orders. The tone is clearly different from the other letters.

§2.3. The Descendants of Patron

The sons of Patron belonged to a far higher social level than the veteran Bellienus Gemellus. They occupied important functions in the metropolis, but were also landowners in Tebtunis, where their papyri were found in the famous *cantina dei papiri*, a storeroom near the processional avenue leading to the temple.[9] Kronion, who is the addressee of eight letters, is explicitly called φροντιστής, 'estate manager'. Laches and Turbo no doubt occupied a similar function. Turbo may have been the last manager, who kept the papyri until they were put aside in the *cantina*,[10] but as the texts bear no year dates (with one exception: P.Mil. Vogl. IV 217 of 125 CE), the chronological order of the *phrontistai* cannot be established. I have taken into account twenty-two letters, of which eight are addressed to Kronion and three each to Laches and Turbo.

Again, most letters consist of multiple orders in short sentences, mostly in the aorist imperative ('go to this person or that place'; 'send me some goods'; 'receive things from a messenger'; 'take care of some things'). In most cases, the addressee is only addressed by his name; φίλτατος is used only once for Kronion and twice for Laches, who is also called πατήρ, 'father',[11] and was therefore considered by Vogliano as the paterfamilias of this aristocratic family. But the tone of the letter clearly excludes this, as was shown some time ago.[12] Exceptionally, in P.Mil.Vogl. VI 281, Kronion is addressed as τιμιώτατος, 'honourable'. In this group of texts, the first order in the series is sometimes introduced by καλῶς ποιήσεις, 'please', but far less frequently than with Bellienus Gemellus (only four instances out of twenty-two).[13]

In one single instance, Patron (the reading is ascertained by the verso, see BL X, p. 202) seems to pay a visit to the family of Laches in Alexandria and brings

[9] For the *cantina*, see Gallazzi (1990).

[10] See the article by R. Smolders available online at: http://www.trismegistos.org/arch/detail.php?tm= 66&i=1.

[11] P.Mil.Vogl. II 50 and in an unpublished fragment in Milan; see Clarysse and Gallazzi (1993, 64 n. 3).

[12] Clarysse and Gallazzi (1993, 63–8).

[13] P.Mil.Vogl. II 51; 62; VI 281; 282 (writers and addressees are each time different).

with him greetings (SB VIII 9643; but perhaps he just sends greetings to Laches' sister and family; [καὶ εἶδο]ν, 'I have seen your sister' in line 20 is a supplement). Maybe he even asks for information about the health of his correspondent (εὐθέως μοι δήλωσον - - τῷ ἀμερίμνωι, 'show me immediately - - not worried'). This writer uniquely addresses Laches as κύριε, 'sir', in the last sentence. A κύριος Patron, no doubt the landlord himself, is mentioned in line 7. In my opinion, the author of the letter may well be a colleague of Laches rather than a member of the landlord's family. A palaeographic investigation of the handwritings may provide a solution here, but the publication does not contain a photograph.

Again, as an interesting contrast, two letters are addressed to the estate owners. In one of these Ptollarion is addressed as κύριος both in the prescript (where his name precedes that of the writer Serapyllos) and in the address (P.Mil.Vogl. I 61). Serapyllos starts with a report of his activities in the indicative, then continues with imperatives, adding εἰ δοκεῖ σοι κύριε, 'if this pleases you, sir' (line 12). The other letter, dated 117 CE, is addressed to Paulus, probably identical with Paulinos, one of the three sons of Ptollarion, in a very different semi-literary style.[14]

§2.4. The Heroninus Archive

The archive of Heroninus contains a similar correspondence, but is more than a century later, *c.*250 CE. Heroninus and his colleague Eirenaios were *phrontistai* in the area of Theadelpheia and Euhemeria, in the north-west Fayum. They looked after part of the estate (a *phrontis*) of Appianus, a rich Alexandrian landowner. The tightly organized estate, with land spread over many villages in the Fayum, is directed by Alypios, clearly a member of the metropolite gentry, like the sons of Ptollarion in the previous archive. The Alexandrian grandee Appianus stands even higher on the social scale. Excluding the twenty-seven orders for payment, which are too short and stereotyped to be of any use for our subject, we are left with seventy-two 'real' letters, of which sixty-five are addressed to Heroninus.

A conspicuous difference with the second-century letters is the heading, which starts with an abbreviated παρά, 'from NN', followed by the name of the sender (Appianus, his brother Ophellius, Alypios, and Ischyrion, who was probably Alypios' right-hand man).[15] The name of the addressee is found only on the back, in the address. Letters between equals (e.g. letters addressed to Heroninus by his colleagues Eirenaios, Herapion, Syros, or Horion) and letters from low to

[14] It was studied by Foraboschi (1968) and need not occupy us here, except for the striking contrast in style and vocabulary.

[15] The only exceptions are P.Flor. II 180, where Appianus addresses Heroninus with τῶι φιλτάτωι χαίρειν, 'dear' and P.Flor. II 204, where the two formulas are mixed up: παρὰ Ἰσχυρίωνος Ἡρωνίνωι χαίρειν, 'from Ischyrion to Heroninos, greetings'.

high preserve the traditional form with χαίρειν. The παρά introduction is a sign that the sender is a hierarchical superior of the addressee.[16] The only sender who seems to use both forms is Herakleides, but perhaps we should distinguish two different persons with this common name.[17]

Again, the typical verbal form is the imperative aorist. The polite εὖ or καλῶς ποιήσεις formula has completely disappeared. Though it is still very much alive in letters between equals or to superiors, it is not used from high to low in the hierarchy of the Appianus estate. More often than before, orders are now expressed by subordinate sentences of the type 'I have ordered you that..., I have sent (ἀπέστειλα) NN so that', followed by ἵνα, ὅπως, and ὥστε, 'in order that'.

It is interesting to compare the forty-nine letters by the chief steward Alypios with the twelve letters by the landowner Appianus himself. The tone and style are similar, except that Appianus usually omits the greeting formula ἐρρῶσθαι σὲ εὔχομαι, 'I wish you good health', at the end.[18]

There are, therefore, at least four different ways of starting and ending a letter:

- παρὰ NN, addressee not named, no χαίρειν, no ἐρρῶσθαι: used by Appianus when addressing the local *phrontistai*.
- παρὰ NN, addressee not named, no χαίρειν, ending with ἐρρῶσθαι: used by Alypios, Ischyrion, and Ophellius when addressing the local *phrontistai*.
- ὁ δεῖνα τῶι δεῖνι (ἀδελφῶι, φιλτάτωι) χαίρειν, 'NN to NN (brother, dear) greetings', ending with ἐρρῶσθαι σὲ εὔχομαι: used by *phrontistai* when writing to one another.
- χαίροις κύριέ μου, 'be greeted, sir' (P.Flor. II 10 verso) and τῶι κυρίωι μου Ἀλυπίωι παρὰ Ἡρωνίνου, 'to Mr. Alypios from Heroninus' (P.Prag. II 200): used by *phrontistai* when addressing their hierarchical superiors (only a few examples are preserved).

There are a few exceptions to the rule, like P.Flor. II 180 above, but by and large it is possible to distinguish between higher and lower managers using this method.

Appianus' letters are even curter than those of Alypios and often contain rebukes and threats, which are rare and less specific with Alypios.[19] Perhaps

[16] Rathbone (1991, 67) mentions in passing that 'all Ischyrion's letters, like all Alypios' and all but one of Appianus', begin bluntly "from Ischyrion" instead of the more usual and comradely "X to Heroninos greetings"'. The different headings, together with polite phrases, deserve a more systematic study.

[17] παρὰ Ἡρακλείδου is found in P.Flor. II 185*, where the correspondent is addressed as πατρί, 'father', and in 185**; Ἡρακλείδης Ἡρωνίνωι χαίρειν is found in P.Flor. II 185 with τῷ φιλτάτῳ, 'dear'; 186, with τῷ ἀδελφῷ; 187, with τῶι πατρί; SB XVI 12577 (a letter of rebuke!).

[18] Only three of Appianus' twelve letters have the formula, including P.Flor. II 180, which also uses χαίρειν (see above); the other two are P.Flor. II 171 and 177. Alypios omits the formula only in his payment orders, which are signed with σεσημείωμαι, 'I have signed', and which I have left out of the picture.

[19] P.Flor. II 148; 150; 162; SB VI 9468; 9469.

Appianus wanted to affirm that he was the master or he became involved personally only when things had gone seriously wrong. In any case, he does not seem to have been an easy person, as can be seen from the following quotes:

1. P.Flor. II 170.3–8
κἂν νῦν οὖν διάπεμψαι ἵνα [μ]ὴ ὡς τοιούτῳ σοι χρησώμε[θα]. εἰ περὶ τῶν οὐθαμίνων ἀμελεῖτε πόσῳ μᾶλλον τῶν ἀναγκαιοτέρων

'Even now, send them, so that we do not treat you as such. If you are careless about things of no importance, how much more will you be about things that do matter?'

2. P.Flor. II 171.12–13
πρὸ γὰρ τοσούτων ἡμερῶν ἀκούσας τοῦτο, ἐνθάδε ἠμέλησας

'Having heard this so many days ago, you have remained here without caring.'

3. P.Flor. II 175.15–17
εἰδὼς ὅτι ἐὰν [ἐν τ]ούτῳ καταγνωσθῇς, σὺ αὐτοῦ αἴτιος γείνῃ

'knowing that you will be responsible, if you are condemned for this'

4. P.Flor. II 176.2–13
κἂν τὸ βραχύτατόν τις ἀναπέμπῃ ὀφείλει <μ>ετὰ γραμμάτων ἀναπέμπειν καὶ δηλοῦν τί ἀνεπέμφθη διὰ τίνος - - - ἐνεφαίνετο δὲ ἐκ τῆς τῶν σύκων κακίας καὶ ξηρότητος καὶ δίψης ἡ τοῦ χωρίου ἀμέλια.

'If anyone sends up even the most trifling item, he should send it with a note and make clear what has been sent and through whom - - - From the bad quality and the dryness and the thirst of the figs the careless handling of the field became clear.'

5. P.Flor. II 177.2–6
καὶ πρὸ ἡμερῶν ἐπέστειλα ἵνα ἀρτίδια καλὰ ποιήσηται καὶ ἀναπέμψηται ἡμεῖν καὶ οὐκ ἐπ<οι>ήσατε

'And some days ago I ordered that you should make good loaves and send them[20] up to us, and you did not do it.'

6. SB VI 9056
Concluding: οὕτω οὖν γενέσθω καὶ ἤδη

'That is how it should happen and quickly.'

§3. A TYPE OF LETTER?

Our documentation allows us to follow one particular type of correspondence, from high to low, over a period of about five hundred years, instances of which share some characteristic features.

[20] ποιήσηται καὶ ἀναπέμψηται here stands for ποιήσητε καὶ ἀναπέμψητε. These cannot be passive forms, as interpreted by the editor; cf. χρήζεται and ὀφείλεται in lines 11 and 16, which have been corrected in the Papyrological Navigator (http://www.papyri.info).

1) The letters are usually short. The format follows that of other letters of the same periods, i.e. broad letters written against the fibres covering lengthwise the height of the roll in the early Ptolemaic period; narrow letters written along the fibres covering the height of the roll from top to bottom in the Roman period.[21]
2) The brevity of the letters is partly due to the absence of the usual introductory and concluding philophronetic formulae (the main subject, in fact, of most studies on papyrus letters): the letters contain no *formula valetudinis* of the type *si vales bene est, ego quoque valeo*, 'if you are well, then it is all right, I myself am well', and no interest in the health of the addressee, no *proskynemata*, no thanks, no allusions to the 'ideology of friendship',[22] and rarely greetings to third persons. In fact, most of the subjects discussed by Koskenniemi are missing in our letters. In the Heroninus archive, the typical *chairein* (χαίρειν) formula, used throughout the Ptolemaic and Roman periods, is replaced by παρά + name of the sender, without the name of the addressee, who appears only in the address on the back.
3) In the Roman period, the addressee is often addressed as φίλτατος; just once, unexpectedly, he is τιμιώτατος, 'most honoured'. ἴδιος is only used by Gemellus for his manager-slave Epagathos, while πατήρ is possible for older persons like Laches. The reverential κύριος is nowhere used, but it appears as soon as *phrontistai* write to their landlords.
4) Most letters contain orders in the aorist imperative, more rarely the present imperative or the future indicative (especially πέμψεις), as shown in Table 11.1. Circumscriptions by means of δεῖ, 'it is necessary', βούλομαι, 'I want', ἀπέστειλα or ἔπεμψα ἵνα or ὥστε, 'I have sent in order that', come to the fore in the Heroninus archive. The third person imperative is commonly used, also outside such stereotypical expressions as φροντίς σοι ἔστω, 'it should be in your care'. One wonders if this was still a living verbal form in the Roman period, or if it sounded like officialese. In private letters, for instance, it is hardly ever found.[23]
5) A recurrent theme is that of urgency. In 73 out of 163 cases, orders are accompanied by ταχέως, ταχύ, τάχος, 'quickly'; τὴν ταχίστην, 'as fast as possible'; ἤδη, αὔθωρον, ἐξαυτῆς, 'immediately'; κατὰ σπουδήν, 'in a hurry'; or more colourful circumscriptions like νύκτα ἡμέραν ποιούμενος, 'making the night a day'; νυκτὸς μετ' αὔριον, 'in the night, at dawn';

[21] For the change in format, see now Fournet (2009).

[22] I take the term from Parsons (1981, 9).

[23] Mandilaras (1973, 302) counts 500 instances of the second person vs 70 of the third person, i.e. 14 per cent (including typical Byzantine circumlocutions such as μανθανέτω ἡ σὴ διάθεσις, 'may your disposition learn' i.e. 'hear'); in our documentation, there are 217 second person imperatives vs 40 third person, i.e. 18 per cent. In the Heroninus archive, however, when the style is fully developed, one imperative in three is third person.

Table 11.1 Modes and tenses

	Zenon	Bellienus	Ptollarion	Heroninus
Number of texts	49	12	18	61
Imperative: aorist/present	58/11	28/4	39/4	71/6
Imperative: third person	4	5	6	25
Future indicative	1	17	1	1
Subordinate sentence	5	0	0	41
Polite formulae	2	8	6	0
Warnings[24]	3	1	6?	3

ὀρθρίσας, 'early in the morning'; πάντα ὑπερθέμενος, 'putting everything off'; or σπουδή σοι γενέσθω, 'hurry up'.

6) Closely linked to the theme of urgency are the many superlatives, in which I include the use of words like πᾶς ('all of them') and οὐδείς ('none of them'), which are used in 50 texts out of 163. Steen uses the term 'expression d'intensité'.[25] In this he also includes the formulae (ὅρα) μὴ ἀμελήσῃς or μὴ ἄλλως ποιήσῃς, 'mind that you do not neglect', often used at (or towards) the end of the letter.
7) Superiors have the right (and even a duty) to rebuke inferiors (40 cases of 163). The most commonly-used verb in this respect is μέμφομαι, 'I blame you'. Sometimes criticism is strengthened by a threat of punishment, as in P.Lond. II 356 (ἐὰν ἄλλως ποιήσῃις γίνωσκε ἕξοντα πρὸς ἐμέ, 'if you do otherwise, know that you will have (a problem) with me'), P.Flor. II 162 (ἐὰν ἀμελές τι ποιῇις - - καὶ τὰ παλαιὰ ἁμαρτήματα ἐπεξελεύσεως τεύξεται, 'if you do anything careless - - your old mistakes will receive punishment'), P.Flor. II 148 (εἴ τις ἐμβάλοι παρὰ τὴν ἐμὴν ἐγκέλευσιν - - ζημιώθη ζημίαν ἣν μὴ προσδοκᾷ, 'if anybody puts in anything contrary to my orders - - he will be punished with a punishment which he does not expect'[26]). The impatience of the writer can also be expressed by θαυμάζω πῶς, 'I am surprised that you (dare)' (this expresses not surprise, but rather anger at the behaviour of the correspondent) and ἔτι καὶ νῦν (you are not behaving correctly, and now you get a last chance). Congratulations for a job well done are found only in a few letters from Apollonios to Zenon (ὀρθῶς ἐποίησας, 'you did well' in P.CairoZen. II 59142, 59180, 59202; P.Ryl. III 560).

None of these characteristics is unique for our type of text. The common formula (ὅρα) μὴ ἀμελήσῃις, 'take care that you do not neglect', for instance, is also found in family letters and in letters among equals. The genre is perhaps best defined by what is not there: there are no wishes for good health and no questions about

[24] The formula ὅρα μὴ ἀμελήσῃις, 'take care that you do not neglect', has not been included.
[25] Steen (1938, 153–68). [26] The translation is that of Rathbone (1991, 249).

the health of the addressee; compliments are absent except for four Zenon texts (P.CairoZen. II 59142, 59180, 59202, and P.Ryl. III 560[27]); there are hardly any wishes for friendly exchange of letters, which are so common in family correspondence (no *philanthropon*[28] here and no *kolakeia*[29]); and we find no excuses by the writer for something he did not do (as, for instance, not writing earlier), hardly any greetings to third persons, and no proposals to send goods to the addressee. This kind of letter seems to consist mainly of orders and (a few) interdictions, sometimes with a short motivation. Even the use of polite phrases like εὖ / καλῶς ποιήσεις, 'please' is limited and completely disappears in the Heroninus archive, whereas expressions for 'please' like ἐὰν θέλῃς or ἐάν σοι δόξῃι are hardly ever used.[30]

Even the 'raumliche Entfernung'[31] between writer and addressee is absent: the landlord is always nearby and ready to come for inspection (even for Appianus, who clearly spent part of his time in the Fayum). Some of the letters are in fact written confirmation of oral orders, and the *phrontistai* also have to report by letter (cf. P.Flor. II 176, quoted above in example 4: καὶ ἂν τὸ βραχύτατόν τις ἀναπέμπῃ ὀφείλει μετὰ γραμμάτων ἀναπέμπειν καὶ δηλοῦν τί ἀνεπέμφθη διὰ τίνος).

In the preceding sections, I have already pointed out the very different tone in the few cases where the employee addresses his superior. When managers of Appianus write among each other the curt tone is only slightly adapted, though they do use the more polite *chairein* formula. Many of these letters, however, consist of a few stereotyped formulae: deliver the goods, make the payment, etc.

On the whole, this type of letter can be fairly well distinguished from letters between business correspondents or family members. In one archive, however, the relationship between landlord and manager was more personal (Olsson (1925), nos. 41–7). The landlord Chairemon is a gymnasiarch; the manager is a certain Apollonios.[32] We have letters in both directions, but Chairemon clearly treats his manager as an equal, rejoicing when he has received a letter, thanking him, using 'please' expressions, sending greetings to his children, etc. The relationship between Appianus and Alypios may well have been of a similar kind, two aristocrats of whom one acts as a representative of the other, being on equal terms. For this reason, the nine letters between Chairemon and Apollonios have been left out from the present discussion.

[27] These four letters are from the *dioiketes* to Zenon between 256 and 254 BCE, each using the expression ὀρθῶς ἐποιήσας.

[28] As in PSI IV 429, where Zenon reminds himself to write a friendly letter (φιλάνθρωπον) to Theophilos.

[29] As in O.Narm. (OGN) 1–19 with commentary by Bingen (1995, 307).

[30] Kruse (2010, 38) offers a very similar description for official letters from superiors to inferiors: 'Stand der Adressat in sozialem Rang bzw administrativer Dienststellung deutlich unter dem Briefschreiber, so verzichtete man in der Regel auf jedes schmückende Beiwerk.'

[31] The phrase used by Koskenniemi (1956, 169).

[32] For this archive, see Smolders (2005).

Letters from superiors to inferiors (usually landowners to their estate managers) have a curt and urgent tone, and are often critical, but they do not have formulae of their own. They belong to the subtype of 'orders', in which the appellative function of the language predominates over the descriptive and expressive, and the writers tend to dissociate themselves from the addressees rather than to accommodate to them.[33] They can rather be identified by what is not there: their usual brevity is largely due to the lack of philophronetic formulae and polite phrases found in other types of letters.

[33] See Bergs (2004).

12

Greek or Coptic? Scribal Decisions in Eighth-Century Egypt (Thebes)

Jennifer Cromwell

§1. INTRODUCTION

The corpus of Coptic documentary material from western Thebes, dated to the seventh and eighth centuries CE, including the village of Djeme and its surrounding monasteries,[1] comprises a variety of text types written on ostraca (i.e. potsherds and limestone flakes), papyrus, and, in much smaller numbers, animal skin. These differ in their length and complexity: papyrus and skin were used predominantly for long legal documents composed of extended clauses of formulary and rhetoric; receipts, lists, and letters were written on ostraca, but this simple distinction is not always adhered to. Approximately a hundred and fifty legal documents (by the above definition) survive, and they predominantly fall into the following categories: sales, settlements of dispute (including inheritance, and financial and business arrangements), testaments, and donations to religious institutions.[2] Many of these legal documents are signed by the scribe

[1] The village of Djeme was built in and around the ancient mortuary temple of Ramses III, Medinet Habu, on the Theban west bank; as general introductions, see Hölscher (1954) and Wilfong (2002, 1–22). The most concise overview of the region—of the surviving archaeological and textual evidence—remains Wilfong (1989), although this, of course, does not include important work undertaken in the area over the past couple of decades, notably, for example, the hermitage at MMA 1152 (Górecki (2007)) and the monastery at Deir el-Bachit (Burkard and Eicher (2007) and Beckh, Eichner, and Hodak (2011)). As a brief overview of recent work undertaken in the area, see Choat and Cromwell (2016).

[2] These have been published primarily in P.KRU and P.CLT, with texts also in P.Mon.Epiph., O.Crum, O.CrumST, and O.CrumVC (although the O.Crum/ST/VC volumes do not exclusively contain Theban material). The publication of the correspondence of the monk Frange, O.Frange, in 2010 (see also the contribution of Boud'hors in Chapter 13 of the current volume) represents a significant contribution to the body of written material from Thebes, but he did not write legal documents. The recent publication of texts from other monastic settlements in Thebes, notably the *topos* of St Mark, O.Saint-Marc (see Boud'hors in current volume) and the monastery at Deir el-Bachit (available online at http://www.koptolys.gwi.uni-muenchen.de/splash.php) have also expanded the available body of Coptic non-literary material from Thebes.

who wrote them, meaning that dossiers of individual scribes can be compiled.[3] In turn, the professional careers of several individuals can be followed, providing information about what types of documents they wrote, for whom they wrote, when they wrote, and so on.[4] The Theban region therefore provides a bounty of written evidence, from a well-defined community, for analysis.

One question concerning these scribes is how they were trained to construct such technical texts. This is not so easily traced, and the training of Coptic documentary scribes is a poorly understood area of study.[5] Examination of the original manuscripts shows that they differ in several ways. The most immediate, i.e. visual, difference is their palaeography, which in turn is reflected in the range of formularies and orthographies found across the corpus. This indicates that scribes at Djeme were trained in different ways, but can this training be identified, and, if so, how? I propose that similarities between scribes, based on the three factors of palaeography, formulary, and orthography, will indicate shared training. While this provides no information about where such education took place, whether in the village, in one of the surrounding monasteries, or outside Thebes,[6] and no information about teachers, it will help to identify how many different schools of practice existed and how they differed, and will provide material for comparison with other corpora. Connections between individual Theban texts will help identify the milieu within which different individuals operated and may indicate possible education environments, whether in town or monastery, or somewhere in between.

In order to determine the level of similarity between scribes, a systematic analysis of the manuscripts is required. In the following discussion, however, I focus upon a single element of the documents: the religious invocation at the beginning of the documents. Through close examination of this formula, the analysis of this case study will show the importance and potential for further

[3] I use here 'scribe' as a convenient term to refer to the individuals who wrote these legal documents. I do not use it as a professional label or title, although I will refer to this issue again later in my discussion (§6).

[4] The documents written by Aristophanes son of Johannes, the most prolific scribe from Djeme, is the subject of Cromwell (2017). See Richter (1998) for a linguistic analysis of the work of David son of Psate. For the work of a single scribe, albeit not a writer of legal documents, see the introduction to the texts in O.Frange.

[5] The most important work undertaken on education in Egypt has focused on Greek evidence from the Ptolemaic and early Roman periods, especially Cribiore (1996 and 2001). For Coptic school exercises, which are often difficult to differentiate from their Greek counterparts, see P.Rain. UnterrichtKopt., although this does not contain detailed analysis of the texts involved. There is now Bucking (2011), which focusses on a seventh century manuscript used for elementary instruction in Coptic (probably from a monastery). Specifically for documentary scribes in late antique (i.e. Byzantine and early Islamic) Egypt, there is only Bucking (2007a), although Coptic epistolary training is briefly discussed by Cribiore (2007). For the earlier, Greek, evidence, see Cribiore (1996).

[6] Djeme's archaeological record (see n. 1) is such that school facilities in the village cannot be identified. For the monasteries of Apa Epiphanius and Apa Paul, see respectively Bucking (2007b) and Eicher and Fauerbach (2005).

such studies of close analysis of variation for the identification of scribal networks and training.

§2. INVOCATION FORMULAE

A religious invocation at the beginning of legal documents had been a requirement since the end of the sixth century.[7] In the documents from Djeme, this forms part of a protocol that also includes the date and, in some instances, mention of the current local official(s). There were multiple forms of the invocation—the typology established by Bagnall and Worp lists over twenty different versions.[8] Within this typology, the formulae are divided into four categories, dedicated respectively to (i) Christ; (ii) the Holy Trinity; (iii) the Holy Trinity, Mary (and the Saints); and (iv) Christ, Mary, and the Saints. With the exception of the first of these, variations are found with each type, creating twenty-six different forms.[9]

All invocations from Djeme are dedicated to the Holy Trinity. Two types predominate, 2E and 2J, which have a Greek and a Coptic version. Additionally, 2L and 2R are also found.

> 2E: ἐν ὀνόματι τῆς ἁγίας καὶ ζωοποιοῦ καὶ ὁμοουσίου τριάδος πατρὸς καὶ υἱοῦ καὶ ἁγίου πνεύματος
>
> 'In the name of the holy, life-giving, and consubstantial Trinity, the Father, the Son, and the Holy Spirit.'
>
> 2J (Greek): ἐν ὀνόματι τοῦ πατρὸς καὶ υἱοῦ καὶ ἁγίου πνεύματος
>
> 2J (Coptic): ϩⲙⲡⲣⲁⲛ ⲙ̅ⲡⲉⲓⲱⲧ ⲙⲛⲡϣⲏⲣⲉ ⲙⲛⲡ̅ⲛ̅ⲁ̅ ⲉⲧⲟⲩⲁⲁⲃ
>
> 'In the name of the Father, the Son, and the Holy Spirit.'
>
> 2L: ϩⲙⲡⲣⲁⲛ ⲙ̅ⲡⲉⲓⲱⲧ ⲙⲛⲡϣⲏⲣⲉ ⲙⲡ̅ⲛ̅ⲁ̅ ⲉⲧⲟⲩⲁⲁⲃ ⲧⲉⲧⲣⲓⲁⲥ ⲛϩⲟⲙⲟⲟⲩⲥⲓⲟⲛ
>
> 'In the name of the Father and the holy consubstantial Trinity.'
>
> 2R: ἐν ὀνόματι τοῦ θεοῦ τοῦ παντοκράτορος
>
> 'In the name of God Almighty.'

As a result of the vagaries of preservation, the invocation has not always survived and so the available corpus does not comprise all known legal documents from

[7] For the introduction of the invocation and its legal necessity, see Bagnall and Worp (2004, 99–109).

[8] Bagnall and Worp (2004, 100–1).

[9] The typology established by Bagnall and Worp lists twenty-five types, separated by 'what are in some cases relatively minor variants like the presence and absence of particular epithets'. They specifically note a variant of type 2I, but do not include it as a separate form. In Cromwell (2010b), I argue that this should instead be labelled 2R and it is as such that I refer to it throughout this paper. Other variations exist that could similarly expand this typology (note especially P.KRU 9 and 35 in the Appendix).

western Thebes. The Appendix includes the seventy-seven examples that are available for analysis.[10] However, in order to better understand who used what formula and why, the following discussion is based only on documents attributable to known individuals, i.e. signed documents and those that can be attributed to particular scribes with a high degree of certainty. This results in a smaller corpus of forty-four documents, written by twenty-six men. These are collated in alphabetical order in section II of the Appendix. If texts that are currently anonymous—or even unpublished—are at some point assigned to specific scribes, they can be inserted into the established framework at that time. One problem with the analysis of these texts, however, is that there is very limited information for the scribes who wrote them, beyond their name. It cannot even be determined absolutely, in all cases, that the scribe comes from or was trained in the Theban region (as discussed in §6). Differences that do occur may therefore be attributable to dialectical variations, but in most cases this cannot be proven (see §4). Nevertheless, it seems to be the case that the majority of documents from this region were written by local scribes.

Across all seventy-seven examples, there is a distinct preference for type 2E (34/77: 44.2 per cent). The Coptic version of 2J is the second most common form, occurring twenty-one times (27.3 per cent). These are not equally represented in the restricted corpus under analysis here, in which 2E predominates to an even greater degree (30/44: 68.2 per cent). The restricted corpus is not, then, representative of the wider picture at Djeme. However, this is a problem of preservation, and, for the purposes of making connections between known scribes, this is an issue to be borne in mind, but not one that prohibits the use of such a methodology.

§3. GREEK OR COPTIC?

There is a distinct difference when it comes to the language of these formulae: 2E and 2R are written exclusively in Greek, 2L only in Coptic, while 2J has both a Greek and Coptic version.[11] The Greek in the Greek variants conforms to Greek syntax and consists entirely of Greek lexemes, mostly in full and with correct

[10] Note that this includes only legal documents, not letters. The latter can be prefixed by a short invocation of God, either in Greek or Coptic, e.g. P.KRU 122 ⲉⲛ ⲟⲛⲟⲙⲁⲧⲓ ⲧⲟⲩ ⲕ̅ⲩ̅ ⲉ ⲁⲅⲓ ⲧⲣⲓⲁⲥ 'In the name of the Lord and the Holy Trinity' (I have retained here the original editor's transcription, rather than convert it to Greek; I discuss the issue of the Greekness of these invocations later), and P.KRU 123 ϩⲙ ⲡⲣⲁⲛ ⲡⲛⲟⲩⲧⲉ ⲛϣⲟⲣⲡ ⲛϩⲱⲃ ⲛⲓⲙ 'In the name of God, above everything' (more common is the shorter ϩⲙ ⲡⲣⲁⲛ ⲙⲡⲛⲟⲩⲧⲉ 'In the name of God'). This heavily abridged version is only found with letters and shows little, if any variation, and is thus not incorporated into the taxonomy of invocation formulae.

[11] Again, one could argue that these should be listed as different forms, at least 2J(i) and 2J(ii) respectively for the Greek and Coptic.

declination, although orthographic variations are found (see §4). This is a special use of Greek in Coptic documents. In general terms, the use of Greek in Coptic documents falls into two broad categories (although, by the end of §5, I will argue for three categories). In the first category are loanwords, in which Greek lexical items are integrated into the matrix of the dominant language (Coptic) and conform to Coptic syntax.[12] The second category comprises whole phrases in which there is a switch from Coptic to Greek. Such clauses are brief—at the longest they amount to only a dozen words or so—and are both intersentential, in that the switch happens at the end of a clause, and intrasentential, when the switch happens within a clause.[13] One notable feature of these phrases is that, except in rare examples, it is only here that the Greek conjunction ⲕⲁⲓ (καὶ) is found, either written in full or represented by the sinusoid symbol (ϛ).[14] The same phrase can be written with either, although the use of the symbol is less common, e.g. ⲕⲁⲧⲁ ⲡⲁⲥⲁⲛ ⲛⲟⲙⲏⲛ ⲕⲁⲓ ⲇⲉⲥⲡⲟⲧⲉⲓⲁⲛ (P.KRU 10.50, 12.44, 14.68–9, 27.51, 39.52, 43.60–1, 47.49, 58.19) vs ⲕⲁⲧⲁ ⲡⲁⲥⲁⲛ ⲛⲟⲙⲏⲛ ϛ ⲇⲉⲥⲡⲟⲧⲉⲓⲁⲛ (P.KRU 28.31, 50.57) 'according to all regulations and rights of ownership'.

The conjunction καὶ is also written in the invocation formula.[15] Here the sinusoid symbol appears only twice, in P.KRU 59, by Komes son of Abraham, and P.KRU 71, by Swai son of Philotheos (see Appendix, section II).[16] It appears more rarely elsewhere in the protocol: P.KRU 70.3–4 and 5 (first linking toponyms and then two dating systems, the latter by the sinusoid), and 106.6 and 8 (linking two officials and again two dating systems). The Greek invocations, as with the other Greek insertions, are highly formulaic, set phrases that the scribe learned and inserted at the appropriate position within the document. While I do not want to digress into a discussion on the competency of these scribes in Greek,

[12] Richter (2008a, 72–4) discusses the percentage of Greek word types in different documents.

[13] The definitions employed here are James Adams' (2003, 23 and 24). Sometimes, the same phrase can be used as both an inter- and an intrasentential insertion. For example, ⲛⲧⲁⲣⲧⲁⲁⲩ ⲛⲁⲓ ⲇⲓⲁ ⲭⲉⲓⲣⲟⲥ ⲉⲓⲥ ⲭⲉⲓⲣⲁ 'which you gave to me, from hand to hand' (P.KRU 25.25; see also P.KRU 36.44 and 37.104) vs ⲧⲉⲧⲓⲙⲏ ⲛⲧⲓⲙⲓⲛⲉ ⲁⲥⲉⲓ ⲉⲧⲟⲟⲧⲛ ϩⲓⲧⲟⲟⲧⲧⲏⲩⲧⲛ ⲛⲧⲱⲧⲛ ⲛⲉⲛⲧⲁⲓⲟⲩⲁⲛϩⲟⲩ ⲉⲃⲟⲗ ⲛⲧⲡⲉ ⲇⲓⲁ ⲭⲉⲓⲣⲟⲥ ⲉⲥ ⲭⲉⲓⲣⲁ ⲟⲓⲕⲟⲑⲉⲛ ⲛⲛⲟⲩⲃ ⲛⲇⲟⲕⲓⲙⲟⲛ ⲁⲩⲱ ⲛⲕⲉⲫⲁⲗⲁⲓⲟⲛ 'The price, thusly, has come to me from you, those whom I've mentioned above, from hand to hand, from one's own resources, of tested and headed gold' (P.KRU 11.41–2; see also P.KRU 4.45–8, 5.34–5, 10.41–2, 14.48–52, 15.48–51, 22.11–15).

[14] The sinusoid symbol appears, albeit rarely, in name strings: ⲓⲱ^{ⲁ} ⲩⲓ^{o} ⲙⲁⲕ/ ⲡⲁⲡⲛⲟⲩ^{θ} ϛ ⲭⲁⲏⲗ ⲩⲓ^{o} ⲥⲉⲩⲏⲣⲟⲩ ϛ ⲡⲉⲏⲩ ⲩⲓ^{o} ⲙⲁⲕ/ ⲑⲱⲙⲁⲥ 'Johannes son of the late Papnouthios, and Chael son of Severos, and Peu son of the late Thomas' (P.KRU 5.64). This particular example, however, could be treated as written entirely in Greek. Of more significance is the following example, which is the only Theban example in which the symbol is used in what is certainly a Coptic sentence, ⲡⲣⲟⲥ ⲧⲁⲓⲧⲏⲥⲓⲥ ⲛϥⲓⲗⲟ^{θ} ⲥⲉⲛⲟⲩ^{θ} ϛ ⲙⲁⲣⲓⲁ ⲧⲉϥⲥϩⲓⲙⲉ 'at the request of Philotheos (son of) Senoute and his wife Maria' (P.KRU 90.23).

[15] The Greek versions of the invocation also set themselves apart by the use of the Greek definite article, τοῦ, τῆς (rather than Coptic ⲡ-, ⲧ-). As with καὶ, the Greek definite article is never found, in standard Coptic, before Coptic or Greek lexemes. I mention this here simply to emphasize further how the invocation differs linguistically from the main body of the documents.

[16] Note that, in his collection of Greek words in Coptic documents, Förster (2002, 363) does not include attestations of the sinusoid, only variants of καὶ.

it should be stressed that these short clauses cannot be used as evidence for Coptic–Greek bilingualism, just as botanists' use of Latin names does not mean all botanists know Latin.[17]

In terms of language use, therefore, two broad schools of practice existed. Scribes either wrote their invocation in Coptic or in Greek.[18] If the latter, this Greek is similar to other loan-phrases found in Coptic documents. Yet, the invocation does differ from these in one key way, namely the use of script, which is the topic of §5.

§4. ORTHOGRAPHY

Two scribes who wrote the Greek invocation 2E, Abraham son of David and Job son of Alexander, employ orthographic variants[19] that are not replicated—in their entirety—elsewhere, although certain features do occur in other texts in isolation.[20]

Abraham son of David (P.KRU 68)
[ⲉⲛ ⲟⲛⲟⲙⲁⲧⲓ] ⲧⲏⲥ ⲁⲅⲓⲁⲥ ⲕⲁⲓ ⲍⲱⲡⲉⲓⲟ (ζωοποιοῦ) ⲱⲙⲟⲓⲱⲥⲓⲟⲩ (ὁμοουσίου) ⲧⲣⲓⲁⲇ̣[ⲟⲥ ⲡⲁⲧⲣ]ⲟⲥ ⲕⲁⲓ ⲁⲓⲟⲥ (υἱοῦ) ⲕⲁⲓ ⲁⲅⲓⲱ (ἁγίου) ⲡ̅ⲛ̅ⲁⲙⲁⲧⲟⲥ (πνεύματος)

Job son of Alexander (P.KRU 88)
ⲉⲛ ⲟⲛⲟⲙⲁⲧⲓ ⲇ̣ⲏⲥ (τῆς) ⲁⲅⲓⲁⲥ ⲍⲱ^{ⲡⲟ}ⲩ (ζωοποιοῦ) ⲱⲙⲱⲥⲓⲟⲩ (ὁμοουσίου) ⲇ̣ⲣⲓⲁⲧⲟⲥ (τριάδος) ⲡⲁ^{ⲧ}ⲣⲟⲥ ⲅⲁⲓ (καὶ) ⲧⲱ^{ⲩ} ⲱ [=ⲧⲱ ⲩⲱ[21]] (τοῦ υἱοῦ) ⲅⲁⲓ (καὶ) ⲇ̣ⲟⲩ (τοῦ) ⲁⲅⲓⲟⲛ (ἁγίου) ⲡ̅ⲛ̅ⲁ̅ (πνεύματος)

[17] The issue of Coptic–Greek bilingualism has yet to receive thorough treatment and is generally neglected in studies of bilingualism in the ancient world. For Egypt, studies focus on Latin–Greek and Demotic–Greek: for example, Adams (2003); Adams, Janse, and Swain (2002); and Mairs in Chapter 9 of the current volume.

[18] Another formulaic element that exhibits the same division in language use is the scribal notation at the end of the document. Like the invocation, this is written either in Coptic or Greek, the choice of which normally follows the language of the invocation (with the exception of Christopher son of Demetrios, P.KRU 57 (invocation in Coptic, notation in Greek), and Shmentsnêy son of Shenoute, P.KRU 12, 13, and 106 (invocation in Greek, notation in Coptic)). When in Greek, it again conforms to Greek syntax and can be classified as a set phrase.

[19] I use 'variant', not 'error', in discussing the orthography of these texts in order not to impose a standard upon the texts to which the actual writer may not have adhered. Further, 'variant' keeps open the possibility of dialectical features, which I will turn to later. However, in this respect, note Walter Crum's comment that precedes his discussion of the dialect of Theban texts: 'It should be premised that certain common phenomena, rather errors in orthography than facts of phonetic significance, will be here left out of account' (Crum and Winlock 1926, 236). Determining where 'errors in orthography' become regional (if not dialectical) features is a more difficult matter.

[20] Bucking (2007a) raises the issue of what standard should be used for Greek orthography in late Byzantine documents (and the same applies to Greek in Coptic documents), as Attic standard can hardly be employed. However, until such a standard is determined, competency in Greek orthography can only be measured against this.

[21] ⲧⲱ^{ⲩ} ⲱ, in which the superlinear writing is clear by the scribe, is apparently a miswriting of ⲧⲱ ⲩⲱ: ⲱ in each instance is for οῦ.

Job is the only scribe in this corpus to show variant spellings of both the definite article (τοῦ and τῆς) and conjunction (καὶ). P.KRU 86, which is unsigned, exhibits the same variation between ⲧ and ⲇ (see the Appendix), among other variants, none of which are shared with Job. These features of Job's Greek (i.e. Graeco-Coptic) spellings persist throughout the rest of his document. Many of these involve the alternation of ⲇ and ⲧ, which are interchanged in repeated writings of the same word:

- δωρίζω (to give, present) = ⲇⲱⲣⲓⲍⲉ (line 5), ⲇⲱⲍⲉ (line 10), ⲧⲱⲣⲓⲍⲉ (line 4)
- εὐλαβέστατος (most pious, humble) = ⲉⲩⲗⲁⲃⲉⲥⲧⲁⲇⲟⲥ (line 18)
- πραιτώριον (governor's residence) = ⲡⲣⲁⲓⲇⲱⲣⲓⲟⲛ (line 14)
- τόπος (topos, place, shrine) = ⲧⲱⲡⲟⲥ (line 6), ⲇⲱⲡⲟⲥ (lines 9, 11, 13)

Other variants primarily involve vowels and do not occur on a consistent basis (in the following examples, 'standard' orthography is given second in each instance): ⲇⲓⲏⲕⲩⲧⲏⲥ (line 3) > διοικητής (magistrate);[22] ⲏⲛⲉⲅⲉ (line 13) > ἐνάγω (to bring to court, accuse);[23] ϩⲟⲗⲟⲥ and ϩⲱⲗⲟⲥ (lines 13 and 17) > ὅλως (altogether);[24] ⲡⲣⲱⲉⲓⲥⲧⲟⲥ (lines 3 and 18) > προεστώς (superior);[25] ⲥⲉⲛⲏⲇⲱⲥⲓⲥ (line 10) > συνείδησις (conscience, guilt).[26] Variations in his Coptic are less common but do occur, including ⲧⲩⲣⲟⲩ (lines 6 and 7) > ⲧⲏⲣⲟⲩ (all), ϣⲱⲛⲏ (line 8) > ϣⲱⲛⲉ (to become sick; illness), and ⲟⲩⲉⲓϣ (line 11) > ⲟⲩⲟⲉⲓϣ (time). Job was sufficiently competent as a scribe to draw up a legal document, here the donation of a child to the monastery of Apa Phoibammon, and he wrote in a competent ligatured hand.[27] Yet, either he was a poor speller, perhaps writing some words based on phonetic estimations, or another factor is at play here. It is possible that Job's writing reflects, at least in part, regional or dialectical variations. Unfortunately, the most consistent changes that occur in

[22] This is the only example of this spelling in Förster (2002, 201–2), but other unique Theban variants include: ⲇⲓⲉⲓⲕⲉⲧⲏⲥ (P.KRU 86.11), ⲇⲓⲏⲕⲉⲧⲏⲥ (P.KRU 4.4), and ⲧⲓⲏⲕⲓⲧⲏⲥ (P.KRU 20.12). Note, 'magistrate' serves here only as a convenient translation for the title *dioiketes*.

[23] The same variant spelling is employed by Abraham in P.KRU 68, while a number of other variants also start with eta; see Förster (2002, 256).

[24] The first spelling is common in Coptic texts, but the second less so; see Förster (2002, 575), although it should be noted that Förster has not included this example.

[25] Variants with initial ⲡⲣⲱ are less common than those with ⲡⲣⲟ, but a number are attested; see Förster (2002, 679–80).

[26] There are four Coptic texts in Förster (2002, 776) that contain this word, with four variants, three of which are Theban.

[27] Consultation of this document, British Library Papyrus LXXXVII, shows that Job was certainly a competent writer. Yet, analysis of his writing seems only to raise further questions. While the hand is advanced enough to be that of a professional scribe, there is a distinct unevenness to it and certain letters are written in a Greek style (such as that discussed below). Of particular note are ⲇ and ⲡ, but more so ⲃ: in the name ⲫⲟⲩⲃⲁⲙⲱⲛ (Phoibammon) in line 6, Job uses a standard majuscule form, but in the same word in line 9, he reverts to the minuscule form. This is quite unusual in Coptic words.

P.KRU 88, namely ⲏ for ⲉ, ⲱ for ⲟ, and the interchange of ⲇ and ⲧ, are found in texts throughout central and southern Egypt, and the consonantal change is especially common in Greek words.[28] Without any information about Job himself (see §6), it is difficult to state it definitively, but it is possible that Job was not from Thebes and his orthography reflects other regional influences and therefore a different scribal practice. It is certainly the case that not all the scribes that wrote the legal documents in this corpus actually came from Thebes, as I note below.

Abraham's work also includes non-standard Graeco-Coptic spellings, but these are not as prevalent as Job's, and his document, P.KRU 68, the testament of Elizabeth, is longer and more complex than P.KRU 88. One particularly noteworthy writing is ϩⲱⲙⲟⲓⲟⲥⲓⲟⲥ > ὁμοούσιος (consubstantial), which appears in the main body of his document (line 21). However, in the invocation it is written ⲱⲙⲟⲓⲱⲥⲓⲟⲩ. The writing in line 21 reflects standard features of Graeco-Coptic orthography: rough breathing (ὁ) is replicated by use of ϩ before the vowel,[29] and Greek adjectives occur in Coptic as genderless common nouns without case agreements (hence the nominative ending -ⲟⲥ). The other vocalic variant that occurs, ⲟ for ⲱ in the centre of the word (ϩⲱⲙⲟⲓⲟⲥⲓⲟⲥ for ⲱⲙⲟⲓⲱⲥⲓⲟⲩ), cannot be accounted for so easily, but there is still some consistency in Abraham's use of the vowel sequence -ⲟⲓⲟ-/-ⲟⲓⲱ- for -οου-. However, the most ready explanation for these differences is that Abraham learned the invocation with a set spelling (as no other legal documents written by him are known, this fact cannot be checked) that conformed to Greek grammar, but when writing the rest of the document he employed standard Graeco-Coptic writings. This, again, serves to isolate the invocation as a separate element from the rest of the document.

Abraham and Job may have learned the Greek invocation 2E from a bad model (the use of models will be mentioned again in §7), may have misremembered it if working from memory, or may have written it from dictation, with attempted spellings of unfamiliar words, although there is no evidence to support dictation in the production of legal documents. Beyond these two examples, which exhibit the greatest level of variation, the variation found in the rest of the corpus is predominantly confined to the writings of τριάδος (father) and υἱοῦ (son). Variation with the former occurs with ⲇ and ⲧ, as seen above with Job: ⲇⲣⲓⲇⲧⲟⲥ (P.KRU 1, 2, 4, and 70) and ⲧⲣⲓⲇⲧⲟⲥ (P.KRU 100). Writings of the latter are more varied: ⲩⲓⲟⲩ (P.KRU 12, 13, 24, 30, 36, 59, 106, P.CLT 1), ⲩⲟⲩ (P.KRU 100), ⲩⲓ° (P.KRU 1, 4, 54), and ⲩ° (P.KRU 2, 6, 71). All these variants occur in invocations transcribed by the original editor in Coptic script; all those transcribed as Greek employ the standard writing, with rare exceptions.

[28] See Kahle (1954, 70–1, 90, 95, and 130–1) for attestations of these features in texts throughout Egypt. Kahle divides his texts into broad regions, of which these features are found in C (Oxyrhynchus to Bawit), D (from Assiut to Abydos), and E (from Coptos to Hermonthis).

[29] This feature is also found in the invocation in the writing of ἅγιος, which is correctly declined in the invocation (ⲁⲅⲓⲱ), but occurs throughout the rest of the document as ϩⲁⲅⲓⲟⲥ, as is standard in Coptic texts.

The originals of each need to be checked before definitive statements can be made concerning the choice of script (see §5) and its connection with orthographic standards, or even the scribe's confidence and competency in writing Greek.

It might be significant that the child donation documents (P.KRU 78–103), as a group, show the most varied orthography. In addition to the use of ⲧⲟⲩ and ⲗ̣ⲟⲩ in the above-mentioned P.KRU 86, this document is also notable for its other spellings: ⲍⲱⲱⲡⲓ/ > ζωοποιοῦ, ⲟⲙⲟⲥⲓⲟ^{ⲩ} > ὁμοουσίου, ⲉⲓⲟ^{ⲩ} > υἱοῦ, ⲁⲅⲟ^{ⲩ} > ἁγίου. Other deeds include unusual abbreviations: ⲡ̄ⲣ̄ⲥ̄ for πατρὸς is found in both P.KRU 81 and 84.[30] This abbreviation is found once outside the donation text corpus, in P.KRU 59 by Komes son of Abraham, which concerns a loan. In addition, *πνεύματος* is abbreviated to ⲡⲛⲁⲟⲥ in P.KRU 81. While these are documents of the same type, the scribes who wrote them are not a homogenous group. For example, the scribe of P.KRU 96 is a priest from Hermonthis (see Table 12.1), while Aristophanes son of Johannes, a scribe certainly based in Djeme, wrote P.KRU 87, 95, 101, and 103, as well as a large number of documents concerning the administration of taxes in the village. I return to this point in §6.

Orthographic consistency has so far only been discussed in connection with Greek lexemes. All examples of Coptic 2J and 2L conform to standard spellings. This greater degree of conformity in the Coptic versions may be the result of scribes writing in their first language, and the level of proficiency that they achieved in it. The only variant found is with ⲉⲓⲱⲧ, 'father', which sometimes appears without ⲉ: ⲓⲱⲧ, by Johannes son of Lazarus (P.KRU 21, 35, and 38) and Christopher son of Demetrios (P.KRU 57). Concerning Christopher, there is only one occurrence of (ⲉ)ⲓⲱⲧ in P.KRU 57 and this is the only document that he is known to have written. Whether this spelling is standard for him cannot be determined. It is the standard orthography for Johannes (P.KRU 21.51,75 and P.KRU 38.19,40), except when written after ⲩ: ⲡⲉⲩⲉⲓⲱⲧ, 'their father' (P.KRU 38.13). However, ⲓⲱⲧ for ⲉⲓⲱⲧ is so common at Thebes that it can hardly be considered a non-standard variant.

§5. PALAEOGRAPHY

A cursory glance at the texts in the Appendix reveals that the Greek invocations (2E and 2R) are sometimes transcribed as Coptic, while other times as Greek. The decision as to how to transcribe them was not made arbitrarily by the original editor of the texts (for the most part), but rather represents a change in palaeographic style by some scribes for the writing of the protocol.[31] Palaeographic

[30] Förster (2002, 629) lists only one example of this abbreviation and it is not from either of these texts (but from P.CLT 4.1).

[31] Examination of the original documents reveals that the original editor, Walter Crum, was not, however, always consistent in his transcription method. Aristophanes son of Johannes always

changes occur in the overall appearance of the script and individual letter formation. Aristophanes son of Johannes, Cyriacus son of Petros, David son of Psate, and Swai son of Philotheos all made use of this practice. For Aristophanes, I have discussed this in detail elsewhere,[32] and so what follows will focus, briefly, on Cyriacus son of Petros.

Cyriacus' Greek script (Figure 12.1) is notably different from his Coptic one (Figure 12.2). It is more compact, even though spaces between lines are greater, with distinctively long ascending and descending strokes that are not replicated in the Coptic, which is, with exceptions, written as if between two lines.[33] Individual letters are also written in a different way. This is most readily apparent with ʙ, ʌ, ⲡ, and ⲩ, and to a lesser extent ⲙ, as shown in Figure 12.3. This is exactly the same practice as exhibited by Aristophanes.[34]

Not only is the language of the invocation different from the body of the document, it is also visually different. Not all scribes who wrote a Greek

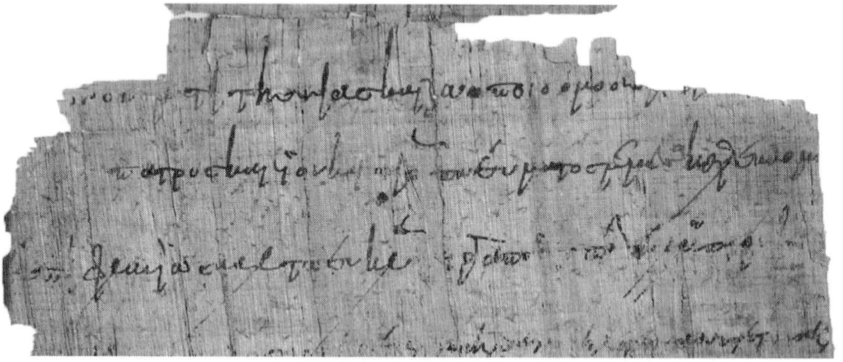

Fig. 12.1. P.KRU 50.1–3. © The British Library Board, Or. 6721/10

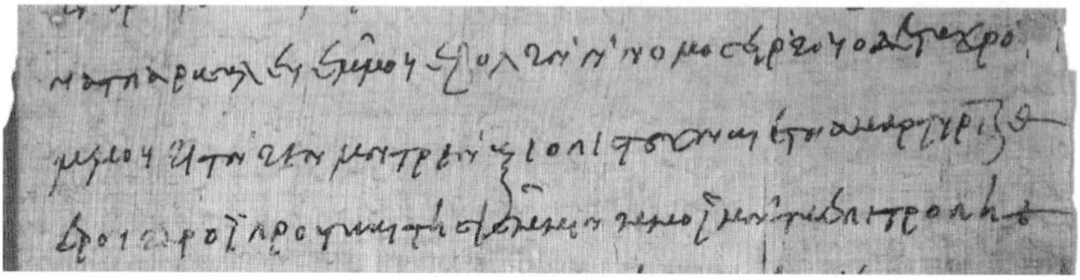

Fig. 12.2. P.KRU 50.8–10. © The British Library Board, Or. 6721/10

wrote his protocol in the same Greek style, yet, for P.KRU 41, Crum transcribes the invocation and reference to the current officials in Coptic but the date in Greek (and similarly for the damaged P.KRU 47). This error has been amended in the current paper.

[32] Cromwell (2010a).

[33] In the terminology proposed by Delattre (2007, 127), text between two lines is 'bilineaire', while that with ascenders and descenders is written as if between four lines, thus 'quadrilineaire'.

[34] These are displayed graphically in Cromwell (2010a, 227).

	Coptic	Greek
ⲃ/β		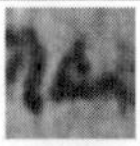
ⲗ/λ		
ⲙ/μ		
ⲡ/π		
ⲩ/υ		

Fig. 12.3. Greek and Coptic letter formations (Cyriacus son of Petros)

invocation changed their script to do so. Into this category fall Psate son of Pisrael and the above-mentioned Abraham son of David. In P.CLT 1, Psate wrote every section of the document in the same style, with unchanging letter formation throughout.[35] The protocol is instead made distinct from the main body by the internal spacing of the text: there is a clear and intentional gap between the two sections, which is approximately three times the standard line spacing throughout the rest of the papyrus. In fact, the text is laid out such that the invocation and date are one unit, and reference to the current official is a second but closely connected unit. This is achieved visually through the use of text indentation: the first unit comprises two lines, the second of which is indented; the second unit is written on a single line that begins at the left margin.

Figure 12.4 shows the first twelve lines of P.KRU 68, by Abraham, including the invocation and the introductory clauses of the document proper. As can be seen in the image, there is no change in script from one to the other (the cross approximately one third along line 3 marks the end of the Greek protocol). Abraham's letter formation is also different from that of Cyriacus. He writes in an unligatured bilinear hand, not the cursive, heavily ligatured hand found in Figures 12.1 and 12.2.

This practice shows that there are three types of Greek in Coptic documentary texts: (1) loanwords (Graeco-Coptic); (2) Greek clauses in Coptic script; and (3) Greek clauses in a second script. The above observations show that

[35] This is one of the rare Djeme documents for which there is a published image: P.CLT pl. I–III, which is also available online through the Metropolitan Museum of Art's online catalogue, by its inventory number 24.2.3 (http://www.metmuseum.org/collections/search-the-collections).

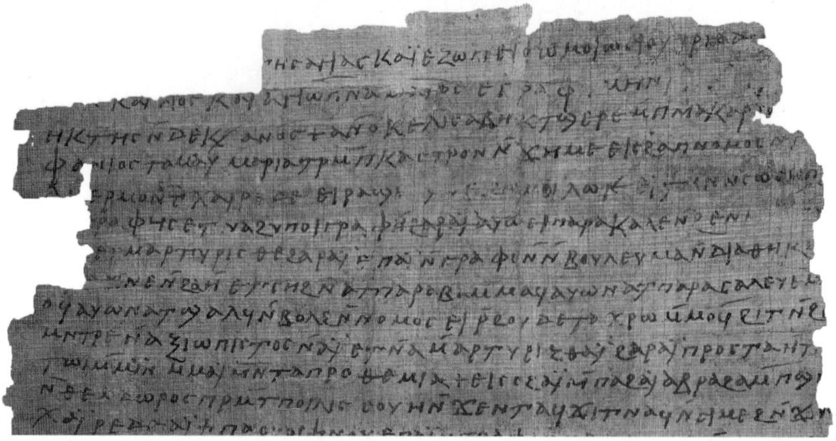

Fig. 12.4. P.KRU 68. 1–12. © The British Library Board, Or. 1062

the invocation, when written in Greek, can fall into either category (2) or (3). Clauses that comply with the third pattern exhibit bigraphism, the use of two different scripts in the same text by a single scribe.[36] This practice extends beyond the invocation formula. For Aristophanes son of Johannes, this includes the notation at the end of the document, the repetition of the property price in sale documents, the amount of tax paid and the date in tax receipts, as well as a small number of other passages.[37]

Transition to Greek in a different script served a particular purpose: to write administrative components. The shift indicates a diglossic relationship. This is not to say that one language (and here script) was of a higher status than the other; James Adams has shown that diglossia is not restricted to such a black and white two-tiered system.[38] There is a conscious bipartite relationship between Coptic and Greek in the work of certain scribes, whereby the function of the two is clearly delineated. As a brief side note, this practice is not confined to Djeme but is also found elsewhere, including the monastery of Apa Apollo at Bawit, Hermopolis (el-Ashmunein), and Aphrodito, to give examples only of well-known sites from which large bodies of written material have survived.[39] Bigraphism therefore distinguishes between schools of training,

[36] Adams (2003) and Price and Naeh (2009) use the term 'biliteralism'. As this could be misinterpreted as connected to 'literal' or even 'literacy', I reject the term in favour of bigraphism, which focuses entirely on the graphic nature of the writing.

[37] I have discussed this aspect of his work at length in Cromwell (2010a).

[38] Adams (2003, 539–40).

[39] For texts from Bawit, see the plates provided in P.BawitClackson, P.Brux.Bawit, P.LouvreBawit, and P.Mon.Apollo. This practice is not always evident in texts from Hermopolis

and three basic divisions exist: (1) Coptic invocation with no script change (e.g. Johannes son of Lazarus); (2) Greek invocation with no script change (e.g. Abraham son of David and Psate son of Pisrael); and (3) Greek invocation in a different script (e.g. Aristophanes son of Johannes, Cyriacus son of Petros, David son of Psate, and Swai son of Philotheos).

§6. THE SCRIBES THEMSELVES

Individual scribes have been mentioned throughout this study, but only in reference to the documents that they wrote and not what information we have about them that might help indicate how they were trained. The majority of scribes did not include a title or any other information about themselves when they wrote their notation at the end of the document. The most common writings are variations of 'written by me, X', whether in Greek (e.g. P.KRU 14.103: δι' ἐμοῦ Ἀριστοφάνου υἱὸ(ς) Ἰωάννου ἐγένετο, by Aristophanes son of Johannes) or in Coptic (e.g. P.KRU 21.113: ⲓⲱⲁⲛⲛⲏⲥ ⲛⲗⲁⲍⲁⲣⲟⲥ ⲁⲓⲥⲙⲛⲧⲥ, by Johannes son of Lazarus). It is mostly impossible to identify a scribe as belonging to a particular milieu, or to say anything at all about their background. Of the twenty-two known scribes in the restricted corpus used here, only six bear titles (Table 12.1). For other titles held by scribes not included in this corpus, see below.

Of these, only one states the name of the ecclesiastical institution to which he belongs: Shmentsnêy son of Shenoute held a position within the holy church of Djeme.[40] One of these six was not from Djeme. Elisaios clearly states that he is

Table 12.1. Scribes bearing titles

Scribe	Text	Title
Abba Apater	P.KRU 100.76	μοναχός, monk
Elisaios	P.KRU 96.99–100	πρεσβύτερος, priest (from Hermonthis)
Moses son of Shenoute	P.KRU 7.65	ἀρχιπρεσβύτερος, archpriest
Shenoute son of Shmentsnêy	P.KRU 2.60, 4.94, 54.24	πρεσβύτερος, priest (from *castrum* Memnonion)
Shmentsnêy son of Shenoute	P.KRU 12.67–9, 13.84–5, 106.242–3	πρεσβύτερος + ἡγούμενος, priest and governor (of the holy church of Djeme)
Zacharias	P.CLT 10.30–1	ἀρχιπρεσβύτερος, archpriest

(Ashmunein) published, for example, in P.Ryl.Copt., or from Aphrodito, published in P.Lond. IV, but is clear upon consultation of the papyri themselves.

[40] This was the main church in Djeme, built within the second courtyard of the ancient temple; see Hölscher (1954, 51–4).

from Hermonthis (Armant), approximately 20 km south of Thebes. This is significant as it provides important evidence for the use of the invocation formula 2R: there is no evidence that scribes at Djeme used it.[41] The level of variation at Thebes is therefore reduced to three invocation formulae, not four: 2E, 2J, and 2L.

Although most scribes do not provide specific details about themselves, some are particularly well known in the village. Most scribes, as already stressed, do not refer to themselves as scribes; designations such as γραμμάτευς or Coptic ⲥⲁϩ are rare,[42] and there is certainly no equivalent of κωμογραμματεὺς, 'village scribe'. Yet, these are certainly professional scribes working in the village, for villagers and officials. Their dossiers, including texts written on ostraca, show the type of documents that they were most involved in writing and highlight more general connections between individuals. Three scribes in the village were heavily involved not only in the production of legal documents, but also in the writing of tax receipts: Aristophanes son of Johannes, Johannes son of Lazarus, and Psate son of Pisrael (each of whom have been mentioned several times already). These three scribes, bearing no titles, are located within the same functional domain.

Analysis of their documents shows that, despite these connections in their professional activities, they were not trained in the same way. The scribal repertoires of Aristophanes, Psate, and Johannes vary significantly and to different extents. The first two write Greek 2E, but Johannes writes the Coptic invocation 2L, and is the only person to whom this variant can securely be attributed (the scribes responsible for the writing of P.KRU 9 and 20 are unknown[43]). As noted above, however, Aristophanes and Psate used different palaeographic styles to write the same formula. Indeed, the three broad schools of practice identified in §5 are represented here: (1) Coptic with no change of script by Johannes; (2) Greek with no change of script by Psate; and (3) Greek with a change of script by Aristophanes.

Other repertorial differences exist in the work of these men, as is evident from the protocol alone, without having to look further through the documents.

[41] I have discussed this in detail elsewhere: Cromwell (2010b).

[42] The title ⲛⲟⲙⲓⲕⲟⲥ (νομικός) appears in seven documents, in connection with the execution of the document: 'It was read out to me before the *nomikos*' (P.KRU 89.48; 92.55; 96.90; 100.66) and 'It was executed before the *nomikos*' (P.KRU 23.65; 36.65; 37.96). The second formula is only used by Psate, who makes one further reference to this official: ⲁⲛⲥⲙⲛ ⲇⲓⲁⲗⲩⲥⲓⲥ ⲛⲁⲛⲉⲛⲉⲣⲏⲩ ϩⲓⲡⲛⲟⲙⲓⲕⲟⲥ ⲙⲡⲕⲁⲥⲧⲣⲟⲛ 'We drew up the settlement together, before the *nomikos* of the *castrum*' (P.KRU 36.27). This title is never used by any scribe to refer to themselves, and Psate is not referring to himself as such here. The title γραμματεύς is less common still (there are four examples from Djeme, which refer to three men: Athanasios in O.Lips.Copt. 43.14 and P.Mon.Epiph. 163.15, Damianos in P.KRU 105.45, and Theodore in P.KRU 65.98), and is not used by any of the scribes under discussion here. The Coptic term ⲥⲁϩ is problematic. Not only does it mean scribe, it can also mean teacher and master of a craft (see Crum 1939, 383b–4a).

[43] For P.KRU 9, see the accompanying note in the Appendix.

One set of examples illustrates this point. Continuing the linguistic cohesion of the protocol, Aristophanes and Psate write the date in Greek, but their use of formula differs:

Aristophanes (P.KRU 10.2, 11.2, 14.2, 15.2, 41.3)
εγρ/ μ [month/X] [day/Y] ι/δ [year/Z] = ἐγρ(άφη) μ(ηνὶ) X Y ἰ(ν)δ(ικτίωνος) Z
'Written in month X, day Y, indiction year Z.'

Psate (P.KRU 36.2–3, P.CLT 1.2)
ⲉⲛ ⲙⲏⲛⲓ [month/X] [day/Y] ⲓⲛⲇⲓⲕⲧⲓⲟⲛⲟⲥ [year/Z] = ἐν μηνὶ X Y ἰνδικτίονος [=ἰνδικτίωνος] Z
'In month X, day Y, indiction year Z.'

Johannes (P.KRU 35.6–7, 38.5–6)
ϩⲙ ⲡⲟⲟⲩ ⲛϩⲟⲟⲩ ⲉⲧⲉⲥⲟⲩ[day/Y] ⲙⲡⲉⲃⲟⲧ [month/X] ⲛⲧⲓⲣⲟⲙⲡⲉ [year/Z][44]
'Today, the Y day of X, year Z.'

Johannes' use of Coptic—and Coptic free from any Greek loans—immediately sets him apart from Aristophanes and Psate. Only Aristophanes introduces the date by a verbal construction. Psate uses the preposition ⲉⲛ (ἐν), Johannes the adverb 'today', ϩⲙ ⲡⲟⲟⲩ ⲛϩⲟⲟⲩ. The level of variation matches that catalogued by Bagnall and Worp for invocations (creating typologies for all the formulae found in these documents would be the most comprehensive way of comparing scribes and their work). As with palaeographic styles, the formulae employed represent three different groups.

Functional domain is therefore not a unifying factor in terms of the training received. Chronological connections are more significant. Aristophanes, the only one of these three to exhibit bigraphism in his legal documents, is attested from 724 to 756.[45] His contemporaries include the three other bigraphic scribes mentioned at the beginning of §5: Cyriacus son of Petros (726–41), David son of Psate (738–48/9, although possibly as late as 763), and Swai son of Philothesos (749–65).[46] Those scribes using only one script worked during the earlier part of the century: Psate son of Pisrael (698–728), Johannes son of Lazarus (698–739), and Abraham son of David (723–4). Unfortunately, not only are most documents not securely dated, some of the dates provided in the prosopographic reference work for Thebes (Till 1962) need to be revised. Till, as was the general consensus at the time, used the civil year as starting on Thoth 1 (=29/30 August), but it has since been demonstrated that the civil year started earlier, on

[44] Slight variation is found in P.KRU 21.6–7: ϩⲙ ⲡⲟⲟⲩ ⲛϩⲟⲟⲩ ⲉⲧⲉⲡⲁⲓⲡⲉ ⲥⲟⲩ [as above] ⲓⲛⲇ/°.

[45] These dates for Aristophanes are certain, as three of his documents are among the few from Djeme that bear an absolute date: P.Bal. 130 Appendix A (=724), P.KRU 14 (=756), and P.KRU 15 (=756). See Cromwell (2017, chapter 2) for further discussion of Aristophanes' dates.

[46] These dates are all taken from Till (1962).

Pachon 6 (=1 May).[47] This means that many of his dates have to be altered and backdated by one year. Until such a revision is accomplished, establishing an accurate timeline for Theban scribes is not possible.[48]

§7. CONCLUSIONS AND FURTHER STUDY

Djeme scribes showed a distinct preference for writing the Greek invocation 2E, followed by Coptic 2J. Greek 2J is less common, 2L less common still, and 2R was not in fact used by scribes from the village. This does not indicate that there were two main schools of practice. Palaeographic differences between the scribes who wrote 2E indicate that at least three main schools existed, with other groups using the less common varieties. A rough division of the schools of practice, purely on the basis of variation found within this single formula, produces six groups:

(1) 2E (Greek) in Greek script
(2) 2E (Greek) in Coptic script
(3) 2J (Coptic)
(4) 2J (Greek) in Greek script
(5) 2J (Greek) in Coptic script
(6) 2L (Coptic)

Within these groups, a range of orthographic capabilities is found, although it is difficult to reach conclusions as to what this signifies: the scribe learned from a bad model, the scribe wrote imperfectly from memory, the scribe wrote unknown or unfamiliar words from dictation, or the scribe simply was not a good speller.

Information about the scribes themselves is too sparing to determine where or from whom they learned to write legal documents. As Bergs in the current volume points out, even scribal identification does not necessarily mean we have sufficient sociolinguistic data with which to work. However, close attention to the variation found can be used to group individual scribes together. What data we have can help locate people in different environments.

The case study presented here collects several scribes into one group, based on the three criteria used throughout: formulae, palaeography, and orthography. These scribes fall into the proposed category (1) above and are Aristophanes

[47] See Gonis (2004, 157) and further references therein.

[48] Other factors also need to be considered when revising the dates of these texts, especially in relation to each other. Detailed analysis of the palaeography of a single scribe over several manuscripts can be used to establish a relative chronology of those texts, often with greater certainty than other prosopographic information; see, for example, the specific case study of Isaac son of Constantine in Cromwell (2010c).

son of Johannes, Cyriacus son of Petros, David son of Psate, and Swai son of Philotheos. Their style is different from that exhibited by Psate son of Pisrael and Johannes son of Lazarus, their predecessors, who can be located within categories (2) and (6) respectively. Similar treatment of all formulae found across the documentary corpus at Djeme can confirm this and should be the next step in the process of identifying scribal groups in Thebes. It is vital in such future studies that the linguistic and visual aspects of the documents be combined, as working from published editions alone (without images) obscures important differences between the scribes. Without analysis of the palaeography, the differences between types 2E and 2J are lost, and the use of bigraphism by the scribes in category (1) goes unseen. The notion of diglossic bigraphism, in which different scripts were used for different purposes, has consequently not been analysed for Coptic manuscripts.[49] However, understanding the development of this practice is essential if we are then to understand how it was introduced into Coptic legal documents and why. This, in turn, has a major bearing on the question of from whom these scribes received their training.

On this issue, there are several routes of enquiry. As all of the scribes discussed in detail in sections §5–7 are from Djeme, the first point of contact for them are the scribes who produced the large volume of texts from the monasteries of the Theban west bank.[50] Moving beyond Thebes, Coptic texts from other sites provide other points of comparison, which are vital for determining how widespread schools of practice were. From the beginning of the eighth century, a large corpus of Coptic and Coptic-Greek documents from Aphrodito (250 km north of Thebes) exhibit features similar in style to the Theban scribes in category (1).[51] The third route is contemporary Greek documents. Very few Greek documents derive from Thebes, other than tax receipts, and the best-known late-seventh-/eighth-century Greek document found at Thebes, SB III 7240, was not written at Thebes but was issued from the office of a Hermopolite official, Flavius Atias. Such Greek texts may have provided models for Coptic documentary practice. Comparisons with textual production from elsewhere in Egypt will contextualize the Djeme texts, revealing how they fit into trends

[49] This phenomenon has been noted for other languages and scripts found in Egypt, although no detailed treatments have yet been undertaken. Dieleman (2005, 47–8) has discussed the use of hieratic and Greek in demotic magical texts, noting that use of multiple scripts served 'as a vehicle to convey a message in a language' and that to understand the use of such scripts and the underlying scribal practice involved 'it is necessary to determine which scripts the ancient compilers deemed most suitable for conveying which message, this is to say, to discover the functional specialisation of each script'. Adams (2003, 531 and 536) has discussed a number of case studies for bigraphism in Demotic–Latin receipts and Greek–Latin documents in Egypt. The convention found in the latter, in which Latin is used in a formal bureaucratic way to endorse petitions, is similar to that found at Djeme. Diglossic bigraphism was therefore a practice familiar to, and used by, scribes across language and chronological barriers.

[50] See n. 1 and 6.

[51] Consultation of these texts suggests that the texts of Theodore (for whom see Richter 2010a, 214) will be especially illuminative for comparative analysis.

in non-literary text production throughout the country. However, in order to undertake a comparison with contemporary texts, whether in Coptic or Greek, and to draw significant conclusions, it is necessary to have well-dated and securely provenanced documents, as well as access to the original manuscripts or images in order to compare palaeographic features.[52]

The variation found in the invocation formulae—in the formula used, its language, and its script—is not arbitrary, but connected to the different backgrounds of the scribes themselves. Identifying the networks within which scribes operated, their influences, and their level of training will provide the underlying reasons for the level of variation found in these texts. This case study provides one way to tackle scribal repertoires, and anticipates a complete analysis of the rich dataset provided by Coptic papyri of the eighth century.

APPENDIX: INVOCATIONS IN DJEME DOCUMENTS

I. All Djeme Invocations

Type	Known Scribes	Subtotal	Anonymous	Subtotal	Total
2E	P.KRU 1, 2, 4, 5, 6, 10, 11, 12, 13, 14, 15, 19, 24, 27, 30, 36, 41, 45, 47, 50, 54, 58, 68, 70, 71, 88, 100, 106; P.CLT 1; O.CrumST 97	30	P.KRU 22, 86, 99; O. Medin.HabuCopt. 61	4	34
2J (Coptic)	P.KRU 7, 57, 62, 64, 69, P.CLT 2, 10, O.CrumST 429; O.CrumVC 6	9	P.KRU 16, 56, 61, 73; P.Mon.Epiph. 92; O. Crum 140; O.CrumST 45, 60, 107, 412; O.Medin. HabuCopt. 57, 74	12	21
2J (Greek)	P.KRU 59	1	P.KRU 64, 81, 84; P.CLT 4, 6; O.CrumST 59	6	7
2L	P.KRU 21, 35, 38	3	P.KRU 9, 20; O.Crum 393	3	6
2R	P.KRU 96	1	P.KRU 80, 118	2	3
Unclear			P.KRU 74, 82, 102, 109; P.CLT 7	5	5
Outside the typology			O.CrumVC 8	1	1
		44		33	77

[52] The online papyrological tool http://www.pappal.info aims to facilitate the study of ancient writing by collecting images of dated papyri. At present (May 2015), only twenty-three texts are available for 690 to 800, which actually represents only a small percentage of the available dated manuscripts. This, however, is because PapPal relies upon access to original images and the permission to reproduce them on its site, which is dependent upon the policy of the institutions that hold the material. Furthermore, the website is currently restricted to texts written in Greek or Latin.

II. Invocations Attributable to Known Scribes (Alphabetical Order)

1. Apa Apater (2E)
- P.KRU 100: ⲉⲛ ⲟⲛⲟⲙⲁⲧⲓ ⲧⲏⲥ ⲁⲅⲓⲁ/ ⲍⲱⲟⲡⲟⲓⲟⲩ ⲟⲙⲟⲟⲩⲥⲓⲟⲩ ⲧⲣⲓⲁⲧⲟⲥ ⲡⲁⲧⲣⲟⲥ ⲕⲁⲓ ⲧⲟⲩ ⲩⲟⲩ ⲕⲁⲓ ⲧⲟⲩ ⲁⲅⲓⲟⲩ ⲡ̅ⲛ̅ⲁⲧⲟⲥ

2. Abraham son of David (2E)
- P.KRU 68: [ⲉⲛ ⲟⲛⲟⲙⲁⲧⲓ] ⲧⲏⲥ ⲁⲅⲓⲁⲥ ⲕⲁⲓ ⲍⲱⲡⲉⲓⲟ ⲱⲙⲟⲓⲱⲥⲓⲟⲩ ⲧⲣⲓⲁⲇ̣[ⲟⲥ ⲡⲁⲧⲣ]ⲟⲥ ⲕⲁⲓ ⲁⲓⲟⲥ ⲕⲁⲓ ⲁⲅⲓⲱ ⲡ̅ⲛ̅ⲁⲙⲁⲧⲁⲟⲥ

3. Ammonios son of Chael (2E?[53])
- O.CrumST 97: [ⲉⲛ ⲟⲛⲟⲙⲁⲧⲓ ⲧⲏ]ⲥ ⲁⲅⲓⲁⲥ ⲕⲁⲓ ⲍⲱⲟⲡⲓⲟ^{ⲩ}ⲙⲟⲩⲥⲓⲟⲩ ⲧⲣⲓⲁ[ⲇ̣ⲟⲥ]

4. Andreas the priest (2J: Coptic)
- O.CrumST 429: ϩⲙ ⲡⲣⲁⲛ ⲙ̅ⲡⲉⲓⲱ^{ⲧ} ⲙ̅ⲛ̅ ⲡϣⲏⲣⲉ ⲙ̅ⲛ̅ ⲡⲉⲡⲛⲁ ⲉⲧⲟⲩⲁⲁⲃ

5. Aristophanes son of Johannes (2E)
- P.KRU 10: ἐν ὀνόματι τῆς ἁγίας καὶ ζωοποιοῦ ὁμοουσίου τριάδος πατρὸς καὶ υἱοῦ καὶ ἁγίου πνεύματος
- P.KRU 11: [ἐ]ν ὀνόματι τῆς ἁγίου καὶ ζωποιοῦ ὁμοουσίου τριάδος πατρὸς καὶ [υἱοῦ] καὶ ἁγίου πνεύματος
- P.KRU 14: ἐν ὀνόματι τῆς ἁγίας καὶ ζωοποιοῦ ὁμοουσίου τριάδος πατρὸς καὶ υἱοῦ καὶ ἁγίου πνεύματος
- P.KRU 15: ἐν ὀνόματι τῆς ἁγί[ας κα]ὶ ζωοποιοῦ ὁμοουσίου τριάδος πατρὸς καὶ υἱοῦ καὶ ἁγίου πνεύματος[54]
- P.KRU 27: ἐν ὀνόματι τῆς ἁγίας καὶ ζωοποι[οῦ ὁμο]ουσίου τριάδος πατρὸς καὶ υἱοῦ καὶ ἁγίου πνεύματος
- P.KRU 41: ἐν ὀνόματι τῆς ἁγίας καὶ ζωοποιοῦ ὁμοουσίου τριάδος πατρὸς καὶ υἱοῦ καὶ ἁγίου πνεύματος
- P.KRU 47: [ἐν ὀνόματι τῆς ἁγίας καὶ ζωοποιοῦ ὁμοουσίου τριάδος πα]τρὸς καὶ υἱοῦ καὶ ἁγίου πνεύματος[55]
- P.KRU 58: [ἐν ὀνόματι τῆς ἁ]γίας καὶ ζωοποιοῦ ὁμοουσίου τριάδος πα[τρος]

6. Christopher son of Demetrios (2J: Coptic)
- P.KRU 57: ϩⲙ ⲡⲣⲁⲛ ⲙⲡⲓⲱⲧ ⲙⲛ ⲡϣⲏⲣⲉ ⲙⲛ ⲡⲉⲡ[ⲛⲁ ⲉⲧⲟⲩⲁⲁⲃ]

7. Cyriacus son of Petros (2E)
- P.KRU 50: [ἐν] ὀνόματι τῆς ἁγίας καὶ ζωοπιοῦ ὁμοουσί[ου] τρ[ιάδος] πατρὸς καὶ υἱοῦ καὶ ἁγίου πνεύματος

8. David son of Psate (2E)
- P.KRU 5: [ἐν ὀνόματι τῆς ἁγία]ς καὶ ζωοποιοῦ ὁμοουσίου τριάδος πατρὸς καὶ υἱοῦ καὶ ἁγίου πνεύμ(ατος)

[53] The beginning of the formula conforms to 2E, but the original editor reconstructs after ⲧⲣⲓⲁ[ⲇ̣ⲟⲥ the name of the first party. If there are no lost lines, this cannot be 2E, but such a truncated variant is not found in Bagnall and Worp's typology.

[54] The orthography of this passage is corrected from the original publication.

[55] In the original publication, Crum does not transcribe the invocation in full and also fails to transcribe it as Greek: [ⲉⲛ ⲟⲛⲟⲙⲁⲧⲓ ⲡⲁ]ⲧⲣⲟⲥ ⲕⲁⲓ ⲩⲓⲟⲩ ⲕⲁⲓ ⲁⲅⲓⲟⲩ ⲡⲛⲉⲩⲙⲁⲧⲟⲥ.

- P.KRU 19: ἐν ὀνόματι τῆς ἁγίας καὶ ζωοπιοῦ ὁμοουσίου τριάδος πατρὸς καὶ υἱοῦ καὶ ἁγίου πν(εύμ)α(τος)
- P.KRU 24: ἐν ὀνόματι τῆς ἁγίας καὶ ζωοποιοῦ ὁμοουσίου τριάδος πατρὸς καὶ υἱοῦ καὶ ἁγίου πνεύμ(ατος)[56]

9. Demetrios (2E)
- P.KRU 30: [ⲉⲛ ⲟⲛⲟ]ⲙⲁⲧⲓ ⲧⲏⲥ ⲁⲅⲓⲁⲥ ⲕⲁⲓ ⲍⲱⲟⲡⲟⲓⲟⲩ ⲟⲙⲟⲟ[ⲩⲥⲓⲟⲩ ⲧⲣⲓⲁⲇ̣ⲟⲥ ⲡⲁⲧⲣⲟⲥ ⲕⲁⲓ ⲩⲓⲟⲩ ⲕⲁⲓ ⲁⲓⲟⲩ ⲡⲛⲉⲩ]ⲙⲁⲧⲟⲥ

10. Elisaios the priest (2R)
- P.KRU 96: ἐν ὀνόματι τοῦ θεοῦ το(ῦ) παντοκράτωρ

11. Isaac son of Zacharias (2E)
- P.KRU 70: ⲉⲛ ⲟⲛⲟⲙⲁⲧⲓ ⲧⲏⲥ ⲁⲅⲓⲁⲥ ⲕⲁⲓ ⲍⲱⲟⲡⲟⲓⲟⲩ ⲟⲙⲟⲟⲩⲥⲓⲟⲩ ⲧⲣⲓⲁⲇ̣ⲟⲥ ⲡⲁⲧⲣⲟⲥ ⲕⲁⲓ [ⲩⲓⲟ] ⲕⲁⲓ ⲁⲅⲓⲟⲩ ⲡⲛⲉⲩⲙⲁⲧⲟⲥ

12. Job son of Alexander (2E)
- P.KRU 88: ⲉⲛ ⲟⲛⲟⲙⲁⲧⲓ ⲇ̣ⲏⲥ ⲁⲅⲓⲁⲥ ⲍⲱⲡⲓⲟⲩ ⲙⲱⲥⲓⲟⲩ ⲇ̣ⲣⲓⲁⲧⲟⲥ ⲡⲁⲧⲣⲟⲥ ⲅⲁⲓ ⲧⲱ ⲩⲱ[57] ⲅⲁⲓ ⲇ̣ⲟⲩ ⲁⲅⲓⲟⲛ ⲡ̅ⲛ̅ⲁ̅

13. Johannake son of Johannes[58] (2E)
- P.KRU 45: ἐν ὀνόματι τῆς ἁγίας καὶ ζωοποιοῦ ὁμοουσίου τριάδος πατρὸς καὶ υιοῦ καὶ ἁγίου πνεύματος

14. Johannes (2J)
- O.CrumVC 6: ϩⲙ̅ ⲡⲣⲁⲛ ⲙ̅ⲡⲓⲱⲧ ⲙ̅ⲛ̅ ⲡϣⲏⲣⲉ ⲙ̅ⲛ̅ ⲡⲉⲡⲛⲁ ⲉⲧⲟⲩⲁⲁⲃ

15. Johannes son of Lazarus (2L)
- P.KRU 21: ϩⲙ ⲡⲣⲁⲛ ⲙⲡⲓⲱⲧ ⲙⲛ ⲡϣⲏⲣⲉ ⲙⲛ ⲡⲉⲡⲛⲁ ⲉⲧⲟⲩⲁⲁⲃ ⲧⲣⲓⲁⲥ ⲛϩⲟⲙⲟⲟⲩⲥⲓⲟⲛ
- P.KRU 35: ϩⲙ ⲡⲣⲁⲛ ⲙⲡⲓⲱⲧ ⲙⲛ ⲡϣⲏⲣⲉ ⲙⲛ ⲡⲉⲡ̅ⲛ̅ⲁ̅ ⲉⲧⲟⲩⲁⲁⲃ ⲧⲣⲓⲁⲥ ⲛϩⲟⲙⲟⲟⲩⲥⲓⲟⲩ ⲉⲧϫⲏⲕ ⲉⲃⲟⲗ ⲁⲩⲱ ⲛⲣⲉϥⲧⲁⲛϩⲟ[59]
- P.KRU 38: ϩⲙ ⲡⲣⲁⲛ ⲙⲡⲓⲱⲧ ⲙⲛ ⲡϣⲏⲣⲉ ⲙⲛ ⲡⲉⲡ̅ⲛ̅ⲁ̅ ⲉⲧⲟⲩⲁⲁⲃ ⲧⲣⲓⲁⲥ ⲛϩⲟⲙⲟⲟⲩⲥⲓⲟⲛ

16. Komes son of Abraham (2J: Greek)
- P.KRU 59: ⲉⲛ ⲟⲛⲟⲙⲁⲧⲓ ⲧⲟⲩ ⲡ̅ⲣ̅ⲥ̅ ϛ ⲧⲟⲩ ⲩⲓⲟⲩ ϛ ⲧⲟⲩ ⲁⲅⲓⲟⲩ ⲡ̅ⲛ̅ⲥ̅

17. Moses son of Shenoute (2J: Coptic)
- P.KRU 7: [ϩⲙ ⲡⲣⲁⲛ] ⲙⲡⲓⲱⲧ ⲙⲛ ⲡϣⲏⲣⲉ [ⲙⲛ ⲡ]ⲉⲡⲛⲁ ⲉⲧⲟⲩ[ⲁⲁⲃ]

18. Paulos son of Johannes (2J: Coptic)
- P.KRU 62: ϩⲙ ⲡⲣⲁⲛ ⲙⲡⲉⲱⲧ ⲙⲛ ⲡϣ[ⲏⲣⲉ] ⲙⲛ ⲡⲛⲁ ⲉ[ⲧⲟⲩⲁⲁⲃ]

[56] The entire protocol is erroneously transcribed in Coptic script in the original publication.

[57] For this correction to the original, see the discussion on Job above.

[58] The notation at the end of P.KRU 45 is lost, but a palaeographic and linguistic comparison with P.KRU 46 attributes this document to Johannake.

[59] While Bagnall and Worp (2004, 295) classify this extended form as 2L, it should be understood as a separate form.

19. Petros son of Theophilos (2J: Greek)

- P.KRU 64: [ⲉⲛ ⲟ]ⲛⲟⲙⲁⲧⲓ ⲧⲟⲩ ⲡⲁⲧⲣⲟⲥ ⲕⲁⲓ ⲧⲟⲩ [ⲩⲓⲟⲩ] ⲕⲁⲓ ⲧⲟⲩ ⲁⲅⲓⲟⲩ ⲡⲛⲁⲩⲙⲁⲧⲟⲥ

20. Psate son of Pisrael (2E)

- P.CLT 1: ⲉⲛ ⲟⲛⲟⲙⲁⲧⲓ ⲧⲏⲥ ⲁⲅⲓⲁⲥ ⲕⲁⲓ ⲍⲱⲟⲡⲟⲓⲟⲩ ⲟⲙⲟⲟⲩⲥⲓⲟⲩ ⲧⲣⲓⲁⲇⲟⲥ ⲡⲁⲧⲣⲟⲥ ⲕⲁⲓ ⲩⲓⲟⲩ ⲕⲁⲓ ⲁⲅⲓⲟⲩ ⲡ̅ⲛ̅ⲉ̅ⲩ̅ⲙ̅ⲁⲧⲟⲥ
- P.KRU 36: ⲉⲛ ⲟⲛⲟⲙⲁⲧⲓ ⲧⲏⲥ ⲁⲅⲓⲁⲥ ⲕⲁⲓ ⲍⲱⲟⲡⲟⲓⲟⲩ ⲟⲙⲟⲟⲩⲥⲓⲟⲩ ⲧⲣⲓⲁⲇⲟⲥ ⲡⲁⲧⲣⲟⲥ ⲕⲁⲓ ⲩⲓⲟⲩ ⲕⲁⲓ ⲁⲅⲓⲟⲩ ⲡ̅ⲛ̅ⲉ̅ⲩ̅ⲙ̅ⲁⲧⲟⲥ

21. Severos son of Samuel (2J: Coptic)

- P.KRU 69: ϩⲙ ⲡⲣⲁⲛ ⲙⲡⲉⲓⲱⲧ ⲙⲛ ⲡϣⲏⲣⲉ ⲙⲛ ⲡⲉⲡ̅ⲛ̅ⲁ̅ ⲉⲧⲟⲩⲁⲁⲃ

22. Shenoute son of Shmentsnêy (2E)

- P.KRU 1:[60] ⲉⲛ ⲟⲛⲟⲙⲁⲧⲓ ⲧⲏⲥ ⲁⲅⲓⲁ ⲕⲁⲓ ⲍⲟⲟⲡⲓⲟⲩ ⲟⲙⲟⲟⲩⲥⲓⲟⲩ ⲇⲣⲓⲁⲧⲟⲥ ⲡⲁⲧⲣⲟⲥ ⲕⲁⲓ ⲧⲟⲩ ⲩⲓ^{ⲟ} ⲕⲁⲓ ⲧⲟⲩ ⲁⲅⲓⲟⲩ ⲡ̅ⲛ̅ⲁ̅
- P.KRU 2: ⲉⲛ ⲟⲛⲟⲙⲁⲧⲓ ⲧⲏⲥ ⲁⲅⲓⲁ ⲕⲁⲓ ⲍⲟⲟⲡⲓⲟⲩ ⲟⲙⲟⲟⲩⲥⲓⲟⲩ ⲇⲣⲓⲁⲧⲟⲇ ⲡⲁⲧⲣⲟⲥ ⲕⲁⲓ ⲧⲟⲩ ⲩ^{ⲟ} ⲕⲁⲓ ⲧⲟⲩ ⲁⲅⲓⲟⲩ ⲡ̅ⲛ̅ⲁ̅
- P.KRU 4: ⲉⲛ ⲟⲛⲟⲙⲁⲧⲓ ⲧⲏⲥ ⲁⲅⲓⲁ ⲕⲁⲓ ⲍⲟⲟⲡⲓⲟⲩ ⲟⲙⲟⲟⲩⲥⲓⲟⲩ ⲇⲣⲓⲁⲧⲟⲥ ⲡ̅ⲁ̅ⲧ̅ⲣ̅ⲟ̅ⲥ̅ ⲕⲁⲓ ⲧⲟⲩ ⲩⲓ^{ⲟ} ⲕⲁⲓ ⲧⲟⲩ ⲁⲅⲓⲟⲩ ⲡ̅ⲛ̅ⲁ̅
- P.KRU 54: ⲉⲛ ⲟⲛⲟⲙⲁⲧⲓ ⲧⲏⲥ ⲁⲅⲓⲁⲥ ⲕⲁⲓ ⲍⲟⲟⲡⲓⲟⲩ ⲟⲙⲟⲟⲩⲥⲓⲟⲩ ⲧⲣⲓⲁⲧⲟⲥ ⲡⲁⲧⲣⲟⲥ ⲕⲁⲓ ⲧⲟⲩ ⲩⲓ^{ⲟ} ⲕⲁⲓ ⲧⲟⲩ ⲁⲅⲓⲟⲩ ⲡ̅ⲛ̅ⲁ̅

23. Shmentsnêy son of Shenoute (2E)

- P.KRU 12:[61] ⲉⲛ ⲟⲛⲟ[ⲙⲁⲧⲓ ⲧⲏⲥ ⲁⲅⲓⲁⲥ ⲕⲁⲓ ⲍⲱⲟⲡⲟⲓⲟⲩ ⲟⲙⲙⲟⲩⲥⲓⲟⲩ ⲧⲣⲓⲁⲇⲟⲥ] ⲡⲁⲧⲣⲟⲥ ⲕⲁⲓ ⲩⲓⲟⲩ ⲕⲁⲓ ⲁⲅⲓⲁ ⲡⲛⲉⲩⲙⲁⲧⲟⲥ
- P.KRU 13: ⲉⲛ ⲟⲛⲟⲙⲁⲧⲓ ⲧⲏⲥ ⲁⲅⲓⲁⲥ ⲕⲁⲓ ⲍⲱⲟⲡⲟⲩⲙⲟⲟⲩⲥⲓⲟⲩ[62] ⲧⲣⲓⲇⲟⲥ ⲡⲁⲧⲣⲟⲥ ⲕⲁⲓ ⲩⲓⲟ^{ⲩ} ⲕⲁⲓ ⲁⲅⲓⲁⲥ ⲡⲛⲉⲩⲙⲁⲧⲟⲥ
- P.KRU 106: ⲉⲛ ⲟⲛⲟⲙⲁⲧⲓ ⲧⲏⲥ ⲁⲅⲓⲁⲥ ⲕⲁⲓ ⲍⲱⲟⲡⲓⲟⲩ ⲟⲙⲟⲟⲩⲥⲓⲟⲩ ⲧⲣⲓⲁⲇ^{ⲟ}/ ⲡⲁⲧⲣⲟⲥ ⲕⲁⲓ ⲧⲟⲩ ⲩⲓⲟⲩ ⲕⲁⲓ ⲧⲟⲩ ⲁⲅⲓⲱ ⲡⲛⲉⲩⲙⲁⲧⲟⲥ

24. Swai son of Philotheos (2E)

- P.KRU 6: ἐν ὀνόματι τῆς ἁγίας καὶ ζωοποιο^{ῦ} ὁμοουσίο^{υ} τριάδος πατρὸς καὶ υ(ἱ)ο$^{(ῦ)}$ καὶ ἁγίο^{υ} πνεύματος
- P.KRU 71: ἐν ὀνόματι τῆς ἁγίας ζωοποιο^{ῦ} ὁμοουσίο^{υ} τριάδο(ς) πατρὸς καὶ υ(ἱ)ο(ῦ) ϛ ἁγίο(υ) πνεύματος

25. Theodoros son of Moses (2J: Coptic)

- P.CLT 2: ϩⲙ ⲡⲣⲁⲛ ⲙ̅ⲡⲉⲓⲱⲧ ⲙⲛ ⲡϣⲏⲣⲉ ⲙ̅ⲛ̅ ⲡ̅ⲡ̅ⲛ̅ⲁ̅ ⲉⲧⲟⲩⲁⲁⲃ

26. Zacharias the priest (2J: Coptic)

- P.CLT 10: ϩⲙ ⲡⲣⲁⲛ ⲉⲙⲡⲉⲓⲱⲧ ⲙⲛ ⲡϣⲏⲣⲉ ⲙⲛ ⲡ̅ⲛ̅ⲁ̅ ⲉⲧⲟⲩⲁⲁⲃ

[60] P.KRU 1 is not signed but can certainly be attributed to Shenoute on formulaic, orthographic, and palaeographic grounds.

[61] Only the beginning and end of the formula are preserved in P.KRU 12. This reconstruction may not be accurate and other orthographic variations (of which there are a number in the preserved sections of this and his other documents) may have occurred.

[62] Shmentsnêy makes a curious orthographic error here, in which the -ⲟⲩ ending of the first word doubles as the beginning of the second.

III. Invocations Not Attributable to Known Scribes

2E

- P.KRU 22: ⲉⲛ ⲟⲛⲟⲙⲁⲧⲓ ⲧⲏⲥ ⲁⲅⲓⲁⲥ ⲕⲁⲓ ⲍⲱⲟⲡⲟⲓⲟⲩ ⲟⲙⲟⲟⲩⲥⲟⲓⲩ ⲧⲣⲓⲁⲇⲟⲥ ⲡⲁⲧⲣⲟⲥ ⲕ[ⲁⲓ] ⲩⲓⲟⲩ ⲕⲁⲓ ⲁⲅⲓⲟⲩ [ⲡⲛⲉⲩⲙⲁⲧⲟⲥ]
- P.KRU 86: ⲉⲛ ⲟⲛⲟⲙⲁⲧⲓ ⲧⲟⲩ ⲧⲏⲥ ⲁⲅⲓⲁⲥ ⲕⲁⲓ ⲍⲱⲱⲡⲓ/ ⲟⲙⲟⲥⲓⲟ^ⲩ ⲧⲣⲓⲁⲇⲟⲥ ⲡⲁⲧⲣⲟⲥ ϗ ⲇⲟⲩ ⲉⲓⲟ^ⲩ ϗ ⲇⲟⲩ ⲁⲅⲟ^ⲩ ⲡⲛⲉⲩⲙⲁⲧⲟⲥ
- P.KRU 99: ⲉⲛ ⲟⲛⲟⲙⲁⲧⲓ ⲧⲏⲥ ⲁⲅⲓⲟ^ⲩ ⲕⲁⲓ ⲍⲱⲟⲡⲟⲓⲟ^ⲩ ⲟⲙⲟⲟⲩⲥⲓⲟ^ⲩ ⲧⲣⲓⲁⲇⲟⲥ ⲡⲁⲧⲣⲟⲥ ⲕⲁⲓ ⲩⲓ^ⲟ ⲕⲁⲓ ⲁⲅⲓⲟ^ⲩ ⲡ̅ⲛ̅ⲁ̅
- O.Medin.HabuCopt. 61:[63] ⲉⲛ ⲟⲛⲟⲙⲁⲧⲓ ⲧⲏⲥ ⲁⲅⲓⲁⲥ ⲕⲁⲓ ⲍⲟⲡⲓ^ⲩ ϩⲟⲙ^ⲩ ⲧⲣⲓⲁⲧⲟⲥ ⲡⲁⲧⲣⲟⲥ ⲕⲁⲓ ⲓ^ⲩ ⲕⲁⲓ ⲁ^ⲅ ⲡ̅ⲛ̅ⲁ̅ⲧⲟⲥ

2J (Coptic)

- P.KRU 16: ϩⲙ ⲡⲣⲁⲛ ⲙⲡⲉⲓⲱⲧ ⲙⲛ ⲡϣⲏⲣⲉ ⲙⲛ ⲡⲉⲡⲛⲁ ⲉⲧⲟⲩⲁⲁⲃ
- P.KRU 56: ϩⲙ ⲡⲣⲁⲛ ⲙⲡⲉⲓⲱⲧ ⲙ[ⲛ ⲡϣⲏⲣⲉ ⲙⲛ ⲡ]ⲉⲡⲛⲁ ⲉⲧⲟⲩⲁⲁⲃ
- P.KRU 61: ϩⲙ ⲡⲣⲁⲛ ⲙⲡⲓⲱⲧ ⲙⲛ ⲡϣⲏⲣⲉ ⲙⲛ ⲡⲉⲡ[ⲛⲁ] ⲉⲧⲟⲩⲁⲁⲃ
- P.KRU 73: ϩⲛ ⲡⲣⲁⲛ ⲙⲡⲉⲓⲱⲧ ⲙⲛ ⲡϣⲏⲣⲉ ⲙⲛ ⲡⲉ[ⲡ̅ⲛ̅ⲁ̅ ⲉⲧⲟⲩⲁⲁⲃ]
- P.Mon.Epiph. 92: ϩⲙ ⲡⲣⲁⲛ ⲙⲡⲉⲓⲱⲧ ⲙ̅ⲛ̅ ⲡϣⲏⲣⲉ ⲙⲛ̅ ⲡⲉⲡ̅ⲛ̅ⲁ̅ ⲉⲧⲟⲩⲁⲁⲃ
- O.Crum 140: ϩⲙ ⲡⲣⲁⲛ ⲙⲡⲉⲓⲱⲧ ⲙⲛ ϣⲏⲣⲉ [ⲙⲛ ⲡⲉⲡⲛⲁ] ⲉⲧⲟⲩⲁⲁⲃ
- O.CrumST 45: ϩⲙ ⲡⲣⲁⲛ ⲙⲡⲉⲓⲱⲧ ⲙ̅ⲛ̅ ⲡϣⲏⲣⲉ ⲙ̅ⲛ̅ ⲡⲛⲁ ⲉⲧⲟ^ⲩ[ⲁⲁⲃ]
- O.CrumST 60: [ϩⲙ ⲡⲣ]ⲁⲛ ⲙⲡⲓ̈ⲱⲧ[64] ⲙ̅ⲛ̅ ⲡⲉⲡ̅ⲛ̅ⲁ̅ [ⲉ]ⲧⲟⲩⲁⲁⲃ
- O.CrumST 107: ϩⲙ ⲡⲣⲁⲛ ⲙⲡⲉⲓⲱⲧ ⲙⲛ ⲡϣⲏ[ⲡ]ϣⲏⲣⲉ ⲙⲛ ⲡⲉⲡ̅ⲛ̅ⲁ̅ ⲉⲧⲟⲩⲁⲁⲃ
- O.CrumST 412: ϩⲙ ⲡⲣⲁⲛ[65] ⲙ̅ⲛ̅ ⲡϣⲏⲣⲉ ⲙⲛ ⲡⲉⲡⲛⲁ ⲉⲧⲟⲩⲁⲁⲃ
- O.Medin.HabuCopt. 57: ϩⲙ̅ ⲡⲣⲁⲛ ⲙⲡⲉⲓ̈ⲱⲧ ⲙⲛ̅ ⲡϣⲏⲣⲉ ⲙⲛ̅ ⲡⲉⲡ̅ⲛ̅ⲁ̅ ⲉⲧⲟⲩⲁⲃ
- O.Medin.HabuCopt. 74: ϩⲙ ⲡⲣⲁⲛ ⲙⲡⲉⲓⲱⲧ ⲙⲛ ⲡϣⲏⲣⲉ ⲙⲛ̅ ⲡⲉⲡ̅ⲛ̅ⲁ̅ ⲉ[ⲧⲟⲩⲁⲁⲃ]

2J (Greek)

- P.KRU 64: [ⲉⲛ ⲟⲛ]ⲟⲙⲁⲧⲓ ⲧⲟⲩ ⲡⲁⲧⲣⲟⲥ ⲕⲁⲓ ⲧⲟⲩ [ⲩⲓⲟⲩ] ⲕⲁⲓ ⲧⲟⲩ ⲁⲅⲓⲟⲩ ⲡⲛⲁⲩⲙⲁⲧⲟⲥ
- P.KRU 81: ⲉⲛ ⲟⲛⲟⲙⲁⲧⲓ ⲧⲟⲩ ⲡ̅ⲣ̅ⲥ̅ ⲕⲁⲓ ⲧⲟⲩ ⲓ̅ⲟ̅ⲩ̅ ⲕⲁⲓ ⲧⲟⲩ ⲁⲅⲓⲟⲩ ⲡⲛⲁⲟⲥ
- P.KRU 84: ⲉⲛ ⲟⲛⲟⲙⲁⲧⲓ ⲧ^ⲩ ⲡⲁⲧⲣⲟⲥ ⲕⲁⲓ ⲧⲟⲩ ⲓⲟⲩ ⲕⲁⲓ ⲧⲟⲩ ⲁⲅⲓ^ⲩ ⲡⲛⲉⲩⲙⲁⲧⲟⲥ
- P.CLT 4: ⲉⲛ ⲟⲛⲟⲙⲁⲧⲓ ⲧⲟⲩ ⲡ̅ⲣ̅ⲥ̅ ϗ ⲧⲟⲩ ⲩⲓⲟⲩ ϗ ⲧⲟⲩ ⲁⲅⲓⲟⲩ ⲡ̅ⲛ̅ⲥ̅
- P.CLT 6: ⲉⲛ ⲟⲛⲟⲙⲁⲧⲓ ⲧⲟⲩ ⲡⲁⲧⲣⲟⲥ ⲕⲁⲓ ⲧⲟⲩ ⲩⲓⲟⲩ ⲕⲁⲓ ⲧⲟⲩ ⲁ[ⲅⲓⲟⲩ...]
- O.CrumST 59: ⲉⲛ ⲟⲛⲟⲙⲁⲧⲓ ⲧⲟⲩ ⲡⲁⲧⲣⲟⲥ ⲕ/ ⲧⲟⲩ ⲩ̈ⲓⲟⲩ ⲕ/ ⲧⲟⲩ [ⲁⲅ]ⲓⲟ ⲡ̅ⲛ̅ⲁ̅

2L

- P.KRU 9: [...] ⲧⲉⲧⲣⲓⲁ[ⲥ] ⲛϩⲟⲙⲟⲟⲩⲥⲓⲟⲥ ⲁⲩⲱ ⲛⲣⲉϥⲧⲁⲛϩⲟ[66]
- P.KRU 20: ϩⲙ ⲡⲣⲁⲛ ⲙⲡⲉⲓⲱⲧ ⲙⲛ ⲡϣⲏⲣⲉ ⲙⲛ ⲡⲉⲡⲛⲁ ⲉⲧⲟⲩⲁⲁⲃ ⲧⲣ[ⲓ]ⲁⲥ ⲛϩⲟⲙⲟⲟⲩⲥⲓⲟⲛ

[63] This is possibly written by one Joseph, ⲁⲛⲟⲕ ⲓⲱⲥⲏⲫ ⲉⲅⲣ/, but the location of the notation, before the witness statements, is unusual. On this basis it is not included in the restricted corpus of notations attributable to named scribes (it could be a witness statement).

[64] ⲙⲛ ϣⲏⲣⲉ has been omitted by the scribe.

[65] ⲙⲡⲉⲓⲱⲧ has been omitted by the scribe.

[66] As with P.KRU 35, although the invocation is mostly lost, this could be considered a separate form, not only an extended version of 2L (perhaps 2S?). Alternatively, although the reference to the Trinity is at the end, this could be the Coptic version of 2E. This typological problem remains for another day.

- O.Crum 393:[67] [ϩ]ⲙ ⲡⲣⲁⲛ ⲙⲡⲉⲓⲱⲧ ⲙⲛ ⲡϣⲏ[ⲣⲉ ⲙⲛ] ⲡⲉⲡ̅ⲛ̅ⲁ̅ ⲉⲧⲟⲩⲁⲁⲃ ⲧⲉⲓⲁ̣ⲣⲓⲁⲥ ⲉⲧⲟⲩⲁⲁⲃ ⲛϩⲟⲙⲟⲟⲩⲥⲓⲟⲥ

2R

- P.KRU 80: ⲉⲛ ⲟⲛⲟⲙⲁⲧⲓ ⲧⲟⲩ ⲑⲉⲟ^{ⲩ} ⲡ̅ⲣ̅ⲥ̅ ⲟ ⲡⲁⲛⲧⲟⲕⲣⲁⲧⲱⲣ
- P.KRU 118: ⲉⲛ ⲟⲛⲟⲙⲁⲧⲓ ⲧⲟⲩ^{ⲑ} ⲧⲱ ⲡⲁⲛⲧⲟⲕⲣⲁⲧⲱⲣ

Unclear

- P.KRU 74: [ⲉⲛ ⲟⲛⲟⲙⲁⲧⲓ . . . ⲡⲛ]ⲉⲩⲙⲁⲧⲟⲥ
- P.KRU 82: ⲉⲛ ⲟⲛⲟⲙⲁⲧⲓ ⲧⲟⲩ ⲡⲁⲧⲣⲟⲥ ⲕ[ⲁⲓ . . .]
- P.KRU 102: [. . .] ϛ ⲩⲓⲟⲩ ⲕⲁⲓ ⲁⲅⲓⲟⲩ ⲡ[ⲛⲉⲩⲙⲁⲧⲟⲥ]
- P.KRU 109: [. . .] ⲕⲁⲓ ⲁⲅⲓⲟⲩ ⲡ̅ⲛ̅ⲁ̅
- P.CLT 7: ⲉⲛ ⲟⲛⲟⲙⲁⲧⲓ [. . . ⲡⲁⲧⲣⲟ]ⲥ ⲕⲁⲓ ⲧⲟⲩ ⲩⲓⲟ[ⲩ . . .]

Outside the typology

- O.CrumVC 8: ϩⲙ ⲡⲣⲁⲛ̅ ⲙⲡⲉⲓⲱ^{ⲧ} ⲙⲛ̅ ⲡϣⲏⲣⲉ ⲙⲛ̅ ⲡⲉⲡⲛⲉⲩⲙⲁ ⲉⲧⲟⲩⲁⲁⲃ ⲧⲉⲧⲣⲓⲁⲥ ⲉⲧϩⲛ̅ ⲟⲩⲙⲛ̅ⲧⲟⲩⲁ ⲛⲁⲧⲡⲱϣ ⲁⲩⲱ ⲛⲁⲧϣⲁϫⲉ ⲉⲣⲟⲥ

[67] O.Crum 393 is a variant of 2L: [ϩ]ⲙ ⲡⲣⲁⲛ ⲙⲡⲉⲓⲱⲧ ⲙⲛⲡϣⲏ[ⲣⲉ ⲙⲛ]ⲡⲉⲡ̅ⲛ̅ⲁ̅ ⲉⲧⲟⲩⲁⲁⲃ ⲧⲉⲓⲁ̣ⲣⲓⲁⲥ ⲉⲧⲟⲩⲁⲁⲃ ⲛϩⲟⲙⲟⲟⲩⲥⲓⲟⲥ, but does not strictly conform to that type.

13

Copyist and Scribe: Two Professions for a Single Man?

Palaeographical and Linguistic Observations on Some Practices of the Theban Region According to Coptic Texts from the Seventh and Eighth Centuries

Anne Boud'hors

§1. INTRODUCTION

During the last forty years, two archaeological sites on the Theban west bank have provided a large amount of Coptic ostraca (more than one thousand in each case) that make it possible to study in detail the writing activity of two individuals. One of these sites is called the '*topos* of St Mark' and is located on the hill of Gournet Mourray (above the ancient workers' village, Deir el-Medina). It was excavated by the French (Institut Français d'Archéologie Orientale (IFAO)) in 1970–3.[1] The remains include a church and some annexes, which did not necessarily constitute a monastery, but may have been used for accommodating the people in charge of the church, as well as for hosting visitors. Almost all the ostraca found there are fragmentary and of limited significance. However, among the 450 useful pieces, about 200 belong to the dossier of a certain Mark, who was first deacon, then priest and hegemon of the *topos* at the beginning of the seventh century, and who is also known from texts from other places in the same area.[2] The other site is Theban tomb (TT) 29, which once belonged to Amenemope, vizier of the pharaoh Amenhotep II, located on

[1] See Sauneron (1971, 1972, 1973). The results of the excavation are still almost completely unpublished.

[2] See Heurtel (2007 and 2010). The ostraca of Gournet Mourray have been published in Boud'hors and Heurtel (2015). In this article, they will be quoted according to their catalogue number preceded by O.Saint-Marc.

the southern part of the hill of Sheikh abd el-Qurna, that is to say, some hundreds of metres from the *topos* of St Mark. The excavation of the tomb by the Université Libre of Brussels between 1999 and 2006[3] brought out remains of Coptic occupation: brick walls inside the tomb, remains of a pit that could have contained a loom in the yard, a large quantity of ceramics, and more than 1,200 ostraca.[4] The place may have been a kind of hermitage occupied by one or two ascetics at the same time. As it is located among many pharaonic tombs similarly reused, it is likely that the whole complex was a type of ascetic community with a central church. Among the 800 published ostraca, more than 600 are connected with the activity and correspondence of Frange, the monk who inhabited the place in the first half of the eighth century. To be more precise, the ostraca of this dossier are in the great majority of letters written by Frange. This fact is surprising; however, it is less exceptional than it appears at first sight.[5] In any case, it provides a very useful set of materials for palaeographic and linguistic study. In addition, about fifty of the ostraca from TT29 are to be dated to the beginning of the seventh century, a time when a certain Moses had lived there, and several of these ostraca were written by the hand of the very Mark mentioned above.[6]

To sum up: it should be emphasized that both textual documentations are in quite a privileged situation in contrast with many other Coptic documents. Here are texts with clear archaeological provenance, dated by a set of reliable criteria, written (or 'produced') by people whose personalities are at least partially known, and numerous enough to establish some consistent facts. To compare the two dossiers is very tempting, all the more because both Mark and Frange not only wrote letters, but also were copying literary manuscripts. That is what I will try to do in this article, taking into account various points of view intertwining with each other, namely palaeography, language, social history, and chronology. There are differences between the two men with regard to the last two points, since their position in society, as well as their level of education and skills, were not the same, and at least one century elapsed between their respective lives, during which time the Arab conquest took place. How these differences are visible in the written production and how, in turn, they influence it will be central questions of my successive examination of the two dossiers.

[3] Mission archéologique dans la nécropole thébaine (Mant), under the direction of Roland Tefnin and, after his death, of his successor Laurent Bavay.

[4] On the archaeological discovery, see Tefnin (2002); for a first overview of the documentation, see Boud'hors and Heurtel (2002); a full bibliography concerning the ostraca is to be found in their comprehensive catalogue (Boud'hors and Heurtel 2010), which are now referred to by the papyrological standard O.Frange.

[5] Explanations for this are proposed in Boud'hors and Heurtel (2010, 9). To a lesser extent, the situation is the same for the dossier of Mark.

[6] See Heurtel (2008a).

§2. WRITING ACTIVITIES OF MARK, PRIEST OF THE *TOPOS* OF ST MARK

§2.1. Handwriting

Mark's hand is typical of his time, as a majuscule one, sloping to the right, with consistent size and spacing and few ligatures. This is the kind called 'semi-professional' by Crum and in use in many documents of the seventh century. Mark's hand contains, however, some individual features,[7] which make it possible to identify it even if his name is not mentioned or despite variations due to the material, either limestone (Figure 13.1) or pottery (Figure 13.2). Variations can also be connected to the content, as can be seen in the verso of the limestone ostracon just mentioned, where the signature is quick and somewhat flowery (Figure 13.3). It can be useful to compare this writing with the hand of Moses, Mark's contemporary and correspondent (Figure 13.4), where the spacing is bigger and separating signs are used (see more on this writing below, §3.4).

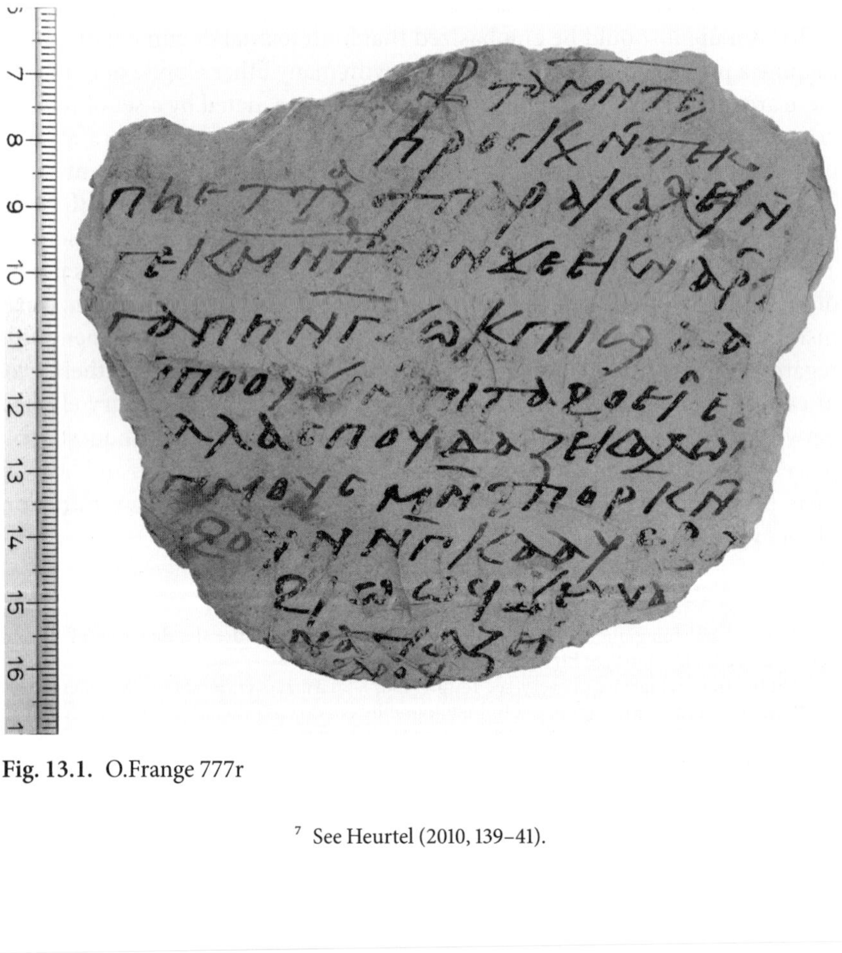

Fig. 13.1. O.Frange 777r

[7] See Heurtel (2010, 139–41).

Fig. 13.2. O.Frange 781

Crum had already identified Mark's hand in several documents of the Theban region, particularly in some ostraca from the so called 'Deir Epiphanius', another ascetic settlement located on the hill of Sheikh abd el-Qurna, and possibly in the wall inscriptions of the same place (copies of literary texts attributed to Damian of Alexandria and Severus of Antioch).[8] If this identification is correct, it witnesses well the diversity of Mark's activities, his mobility, and the close relations between the different sites of the area called the 'mountain of

[8] See Crum's commentary on P.Mon.Epiph. 84.

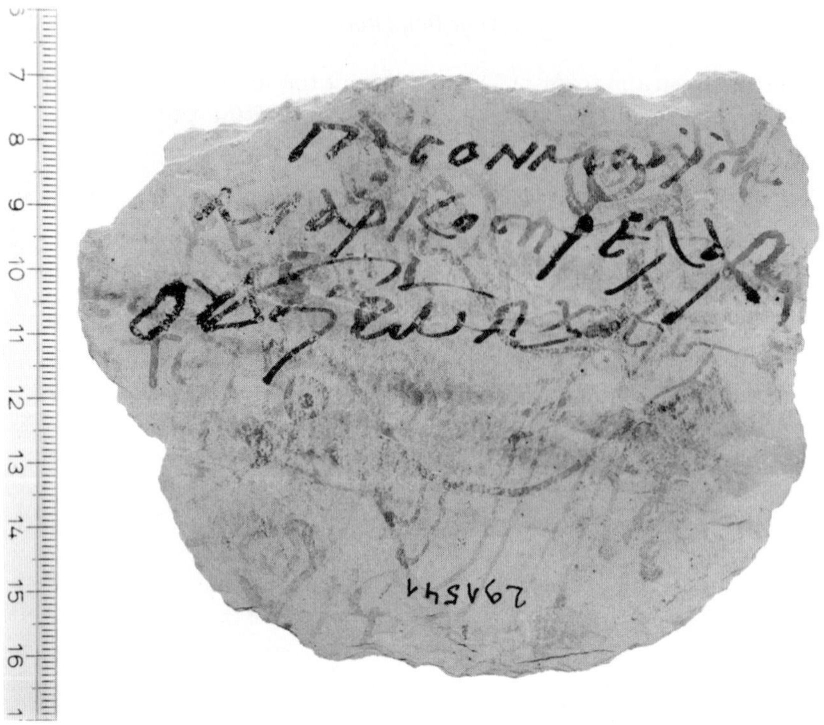

Fig. 13.3. O.Frange 777v

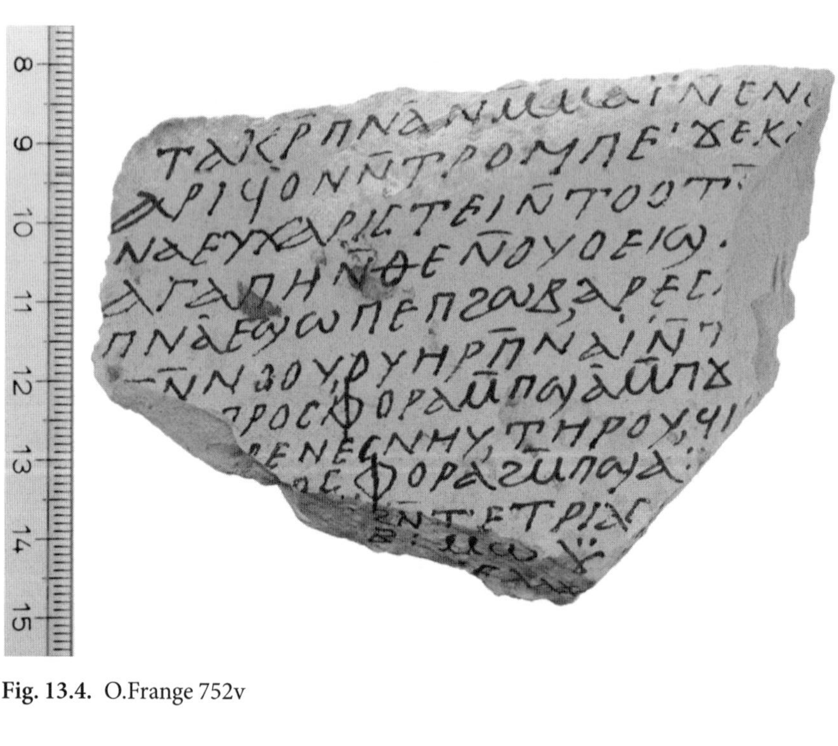

Fig. 13.4. O.Frange 752v

Djeme', between the town of Djeme (around the temple of Ramses III in Medinet Habu) and the monastery of Phoibammon (on the upper part of Hatshepsut's temple in Deir el-Bahari).

§2.2. Mark as a Copyist

It should not be a surprise if Mark's abilities led him to copy manuscripts as well as wall inscriptions. In the correspondence between Mark and Moses (see §2.1) several letters concern books and their copying—for instance, one where Mark mentions that he has received an order for a *sticheron*, that is to say a liturgical work in verse (O.Frange 779). It is tempting to connect this ostracon with the manuscript P.Mon.Epiph. 592 (Figure 13.5), a work in verse that could be by Mark's hand,[9] as well as with a Greek *trisagion* written on another ostracon from TT29 (O.Frange 791; Figure 13.6). Palaeographic similarities are also to be observed with P.Bodmer 58, a papyrus codex from the Theban region containing various theological texts.[10] It must be noted that the sloping majuscule of both manuscripts (P.Mon.Epiph. 592 and P.Bodmer 58) is quite exceptional, since at this time such script is used for documents, while literary manuscripts are most often written with a 'Biblical majuscule'.[11] Nevertheless, a sloping hand is often used in liturgical manuscripts, so that here its use can be connected either with the copyist (Mark) or with the kind of text (liturgical).[12] Finally, another trace of Mark's literary activity is provided by an ostracon written by him and dated 601, on which the drawing of a rosette is likely to be a practice sketch of this common decorative motif in Coptic manuscripts (Figure 13.7).[13]

§2.3. Letters and Documents by Mark

Mark's letters are generally of practical content, concerning requests about daily life. Such requests are more or less developed according to the circumstances and the addressees. For instance, by contrast with the long letter on limestone written to Moses about the *sticheron* (see above), the following message is quite brief: '+ Be so good and forgive me that I neglected (ἀμελεῖν) to send the firewood, because Peter was not able to come. Now, then, I have sent it. Do not take issue about it, for it is perfectly (καλῶς) good. Above all, pray for

[9] For this hypothesis, see Boud'hors (2008, 153–5; 2010a, 183–4).

[10] The texts are edited in Crum (1915). I have studied again the features of this manuscript in a typological sketch of the Theban codex: Boud'hors (forthcoming).

[11] See Boud'hors (2008, 151). [12] See Boud'hors (2010a, 184).

[13] Ostracon C 7134 of the Egyptian Museum in Turin (=SBKopt. II 1238), mentioning a solar eclipse; the most recent study of it is in Gilmore and Ray (2006).

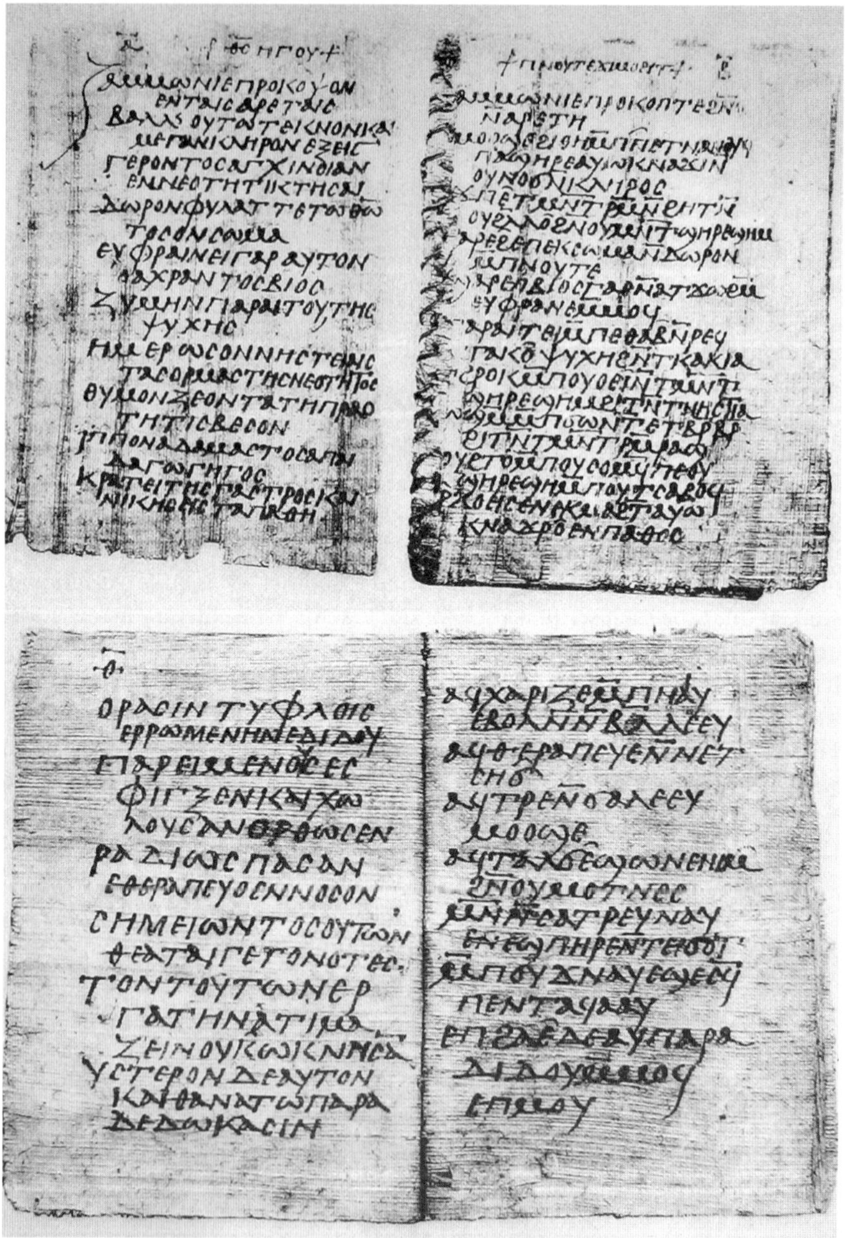

Fig. 13.5. P.Mon.Epiph. 592 (Crum and Evelyn White 1926)

Fig. 13.6. O.Frange 791r

Fig. 13.7. O.Turin C7134v

me by charity, until I come to the north! To be given to my brother Ezekiel from the humblest Mark' (O.Frange 787). Some letters are connected to Mark's office, for, as a priest and hegemon of the *topos* of St Mark, he had administrative and economic duties, as is attested by many documents found at Gournet Mourray, namely lists, accounts, and receipts. He also wrote private legal texts, among others a work contract for a camel driver[14] and a request for arbitration.[15] His ecclesiastical authority must have been quite significant, judging by the addressees of his letters, particularly Abraham, bishop of Hermonthis at the beginning of the seventh century, who resided at the monastery of Phoibammon.[16] It remains, of course, difficult to establish a chronology of all these activities, which may have been simultaneous, successive, or, most probably, alternating.

§2.4. The Role of Greek

Mark must have received scribal training in both Coptic and Greek.[17] It is not that he makes clear distinctions between them, but he cannot help writing the Greek words and formulae with a slightly different, somewhat more cursive hand, as, for instance, in an ostracon from Gournet Mourray (O.Saint-Marc 68), where the expression ἅγι(α) τρί(ας) in the final greetings is written in that way, while the preceding ⲏ (= Greek article ἡ) is written in the Coptic manner, in the flow of what precedes it (Figure 13.8). Also noteworthy in Mark's writing is the habit of abbreviating Greek words (ⲡⲣⲟⲥⲕ(ⲩⲛⲉⲓ), ⲭⲁⲣⲧ(ⲏⲥ), etc.) and the very standardized spelling of the Greek words. To what extent this scribal training has to do with a 'Greek education' in terms of literature and culture is a different matter that would need further investigation and will not be dealt with here.

§2.5. Linguistic Features

The language of the documents written by Mark is a standard, almost 'classic' Sahidic.[18] This is clear from both the orthographic and syntactic points of view. Noticeable for the former point are the lack of dialectal or 'southern' spellings to be found, although they are generally frequent in Theban texts,[19] and the

[14] Ostracon edited by Heurtel (2003).

[15] Ostracon kept in the Museum of Antiquities in Basel: see Heurtel (2013, 81–3).

[16] On Abraham's activity and correspondence, see Krause (1956). A fragmentary letter on papyrus found at Gournet Mourray and addressed to Abraham is by Mark's hand.

[17] As it was the case for the scribes of Djeme a century later: see the writing of Aristophanes son of Johannes studied by Cromwell (2010a).

[18] Nevertheless, this adjective should be treated with caution. For instance, in Mark's writings, the absolute forms of the infinitive are constructed directly with the object, without ⲛ-, which is not 'classical', but is almost the rule in the Theban texts.

[19] See Crum and Winlock (1926, 232–56); Kahle (1954, 48–192).

Fig. 13.8. O.Saint-Marc 68. © IFAO

'correctness' of the spelling of Greek words. This may be the result of the training he had received (see above), as well as a required feature for the somewhat official texts he had to write, without personal involvement. Even in the private letters written by him, a kind of formality or self-discipline is perceptible. As for syntax, none of the typically Theban constructions, such as the 'protatic' or 'apodotic' *efsotm*,[20] are to be found: the conditional ⲉϥϣⲁⲛⲥⲱⲧⲙ is always used by Mark in non-negative contexts; moreover, for final clauses, the most frequent construction is with ϫⲉⲕⲁⲥ + Future II (see §3.5.1 for the use of other constructions by other writers). In order to judge the extent and the reasons for this standardization, it is useful to compare Mark's letters with the ones written to him:

- O.Saint-Marc 50, from Antony to Mark the priest; the writing is skilful and the language quite standardized on the whole, only ϭⲛⲁⲩⲛⲉⲩⲉ instead of ⲕⲓⲛⲁⲩⲛⲉⲩⲉ (Greek κινδυνεύειν) being remarkable;
- O.Saint-Marc 51, from Pesunthios to Mark the priest; this writing is not so elegant as Mark's hand, but quite fluent; there are some Theban spellings:

[20] See Shisha-Halevy (1973, 1974, 1976); Grossman (2009b).

ϭⲥⲁⲩⲛ (line 8) = ⲕⲥⲟⲟⲩⲛ (S), 'you know'; ⲛϥⲧⲛⲛⲁⲩⲧ (line 9) = ⲛϥⲧⲛ̄ⲛⲟⲟⲩⲧ (S), 'so that he sends me';

- O.Saint-Marc 60, addressed to Mark the deacon; the hand is clumsy;[21] the text displays many Theban features: ⲛϣⲱⲣⲡ ⲙⲏⲛ (line 1/2) = ⲛϣⲟⲣⲡ ⲙⲉⲛ (S); ⲛⲏⲕ ⲛⲣⲏⲥⲧⲉ (line 8) = ⲛⲁⲕ ⲛⲣⲁⲥⲧⲉ (S); and the following constructions: ⲉⲡⲛⲟⲩⲧⲉ ⲧⲁϣ ⲉⲓ[ⲧⲁⲁϥ ⲛ]ⲥⲟⲩⲟ ⲛⲁⲕ, 'if God orders, I will give you the corn', where both protatic and apodotic *efsotm* are to be found, in contrast to other forms with the same function used by Mark (conditional in the protasis and future in the apodosis): ⲉⲣϣⲁⲛⲡϫⲟⲉⲓⲥ ⲣ̄ϩⲛⲁϥ ϯⲛⲁⲛ̄ⲭⲁⲣⲧ(ⲏⲥ), 'if God wills, I will bring papyrus' (O.Frange 778).

These examples show how many nuances there are between Mark's 'classicism' and a language more or less marked by local features. Such features are all the more numerous as the writing is less skilful, which indicates a lesser level of education. On the other hand, the spreading of local trends in the language of Theban texts seems to have grown as time went on. The whole matter has to be investigated further by taking into account all the texts from this period (the beginning of the seventh century), including a detailed study of the correspondence of Abraham of Hermonthis and Pisenthios of Koptos, both archives being likely to provide information about different standards of language according to the senders.

§3. FRANGE'S EPISTOLARY ACTIVITY

In several of the points mentioned above, Frange's dossier is very different from Mark's. His social position is more difficult to determine and the great number of texts gives him an importance that does not perhaps correspond to the role he really played. Actually, the contents of the documentation are more private. Furthermore, several steps in his monastic career are perceptible, which seems also to be paralleled by an evolution of his writing.

§3.1. Frange's Hand

Frange's usual writing does not belong to a set type. It is quite bilinear, with some letters clearly descending below the writing line (for instance, the ϩ); it sometimes slopes a little, at other times not at all. It varies according to the

[21] Same hand in O.Saint-Marc 61. It remains uncertain whether or not this Mark is the same as the priest. If he is not, there is no longer certainty about the date of these two ostraca.

Fig. 13.9. O.Frange 213

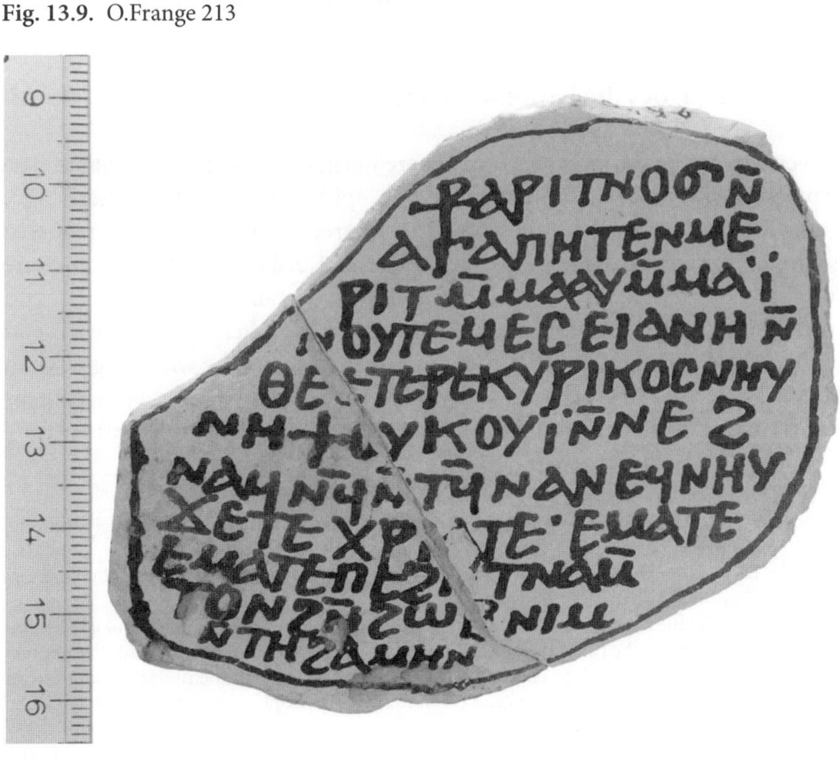

Fig. 13.10. O.Frange 83v

material (limestone/pottery, more or less ribbed pottery, etc.: see Figures 13.9 and 13.10) and can have very different sizes. However, one letter allows the reader to identify Frange's hand quite surely, which is the ⲉ, as it is open at the upper part. This usual writing is the one used by Frange to write dozens of letters to various people, from a simple greeting to an urgent request of a needed thing, including some ascetic advice. All these texts contribute to display a kind of manifold landscape of places and people, ascetics, and laymen of various ranks living on both banks of the Nile.[22] Frange himself was born in Petemout, today al-Madamoud, where his 'sister' Tsie was still living and was in charge of supplying him with food and working material.[23] However, there is no administrative or legal text among them, nor is there any account or list. Frange's correspondence is entirely private, one could even say egocentric.[24] He was not a professional scribe as was, at the same time, Aristophanes son of Johannes,[25] or as Mark probably was. On the other hand he was copying manuscripts, according to his own statements and to some palaeographic peculiarities of his daily messages (see below §3.4). He also taught some people around him how to write, as is shown by the great number of exercises and models written by him or by others.[26] He may not have had any difficulty in disguising his hand. Therefore, it is not always easy to identify his hand when his name is not mentioned or to justify the mention of his name as sender when the hand does not look like his. What follows is a brief survey of specific questions about this writing.[27]

§3.2. What Does the Expression 'Frange Writes by His Hand' Mean?

Eleven ostraca bear this expression, where his hand is clearly identifiable. The expression is borrowed from the Pauline epistles (Col. 4:18, 2 Thess. 3:17, Philem. 19) and seems sometimes to replace the greeting in case of urgent requests: '+ This is Frange who writes by his hand to David. Kurikos had taken the measure (artaba) of corn and put it at your place so that you can bring it to me; but you were careless and did not bring it. Now then, I have taken the trouble to send you my father Victor. Give him the measure of corn and he will bring it when he comes, for I am in great need of it' (O.Frange 62). In two cases, Frange introduces himself in detail so that the precision may have helped to authenticate

[22] To get an idea of this, see Heurtel (2008b).

[23] Tsie's letters to Frange are numerous. He seems to have kept them more willingly than the ones of other people: see Heurtel (2008c).

[24] The psychological side of this dossier is interesting, although quite tricky to deal with.

[25] See Cromwell (2010a).

[26] This may be the reason why he calls himself several times ⲥⲁϫⲱ, which is not a common term here, but refers to the function of teacher (like ⲥⲁϩ). On the other hand, I have the impression (which, however, should be checked) that copyists scarcely call themselves ⲅⲣⲁⲫⲉⲩⲥ or ⲕⲁⲗⲗⲓⲅⲣⲁⲫⲉⲩⲥ, these titles being instead given to them by people writing to them or speaking of them: is it because of modesty?

[27] More details about these questions can be found in Boud'hors and Heurtel (2010, Introduction, §1.2).

the ostracon he gave to this messenger: '+ This is Frange, originating from Petemout and living on the mountain of Djeme, who writes by his hand. Be so good as to act according to God and to show to this man (the way) of the house of Iona, the servant originating from Petemout, because it is absolutely needed' (O.Frange 201). In a last occurrence, the mention 'Frange writes by his hand' has been added above a message from him where his name was at first not specified.

§3.3. Traces of Progress in Frange's Writing?

About twenty ostraca addressed by Frange are written with upright and less skilful writing, which does not look like Frange's hand (see Figure 13.11). Specific

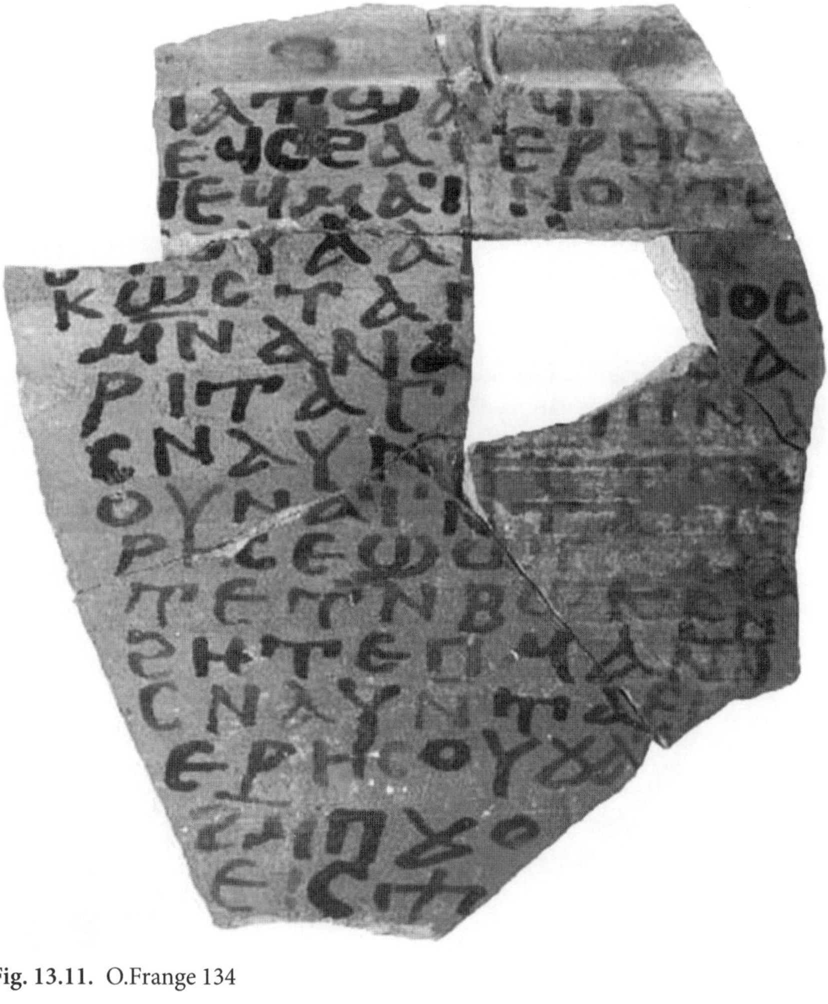

Fig. 13.11. O.Frange 134

to this writing are the two points of the dieresis on either side of the letter ⲓ, the typical ⲙ, and the ⲧ with small vertical strokes at both ends of the horizontal part; ⲉ does not have the special shape mentioned above. Moreover, Frange's name is spelled ϥⲣⲁⲅⲅⲉ instead of the usual form ϥⲣⲁⲛⲅⲉ. An explanation for such features could be that these ostraca were not written by him. However, another hypothesis is that this is Frange's novice hand, from a time when he was not yet sure of the spelling of his (strange) name and had not yet attained the authority and self-confidence he would have later. This hypothesis is supported by the occurrence of another form of his name in the same group of ostraca, namely ⲫⲣⲁⲅⲅⲁⲥ (O.Frange 5), while ⲫⲣⲁⲛⲅⲁⲥ is also found several times in letters carefully written and addressed to important people with many respectful expressions.

§3.4. Variation and Imitation in Frange's Writing

It has been mentioned above that some variations in Frange's writing were due to the influence of his professional hand, as a copyist of literary manuscripts (see Figure 13.12, where the two kinds of writing are mixed up). Given that he was able to disguise his hand, it is not unlikely that he imitated the writing of Moses, his predecessor in the tomb (see §1 above), either on some occasions or more systematically in order to create his own style. A good example of this

Fig. 13.12. O.Frange 486

possibility is provided by O.Frange 190 (Figures 13.13 and 13.14): in this letter from Frange to Azarias, Frange's usual hand is clearly recognizable on the recto, while the writing of the address on the verso is different and quite similar to Moses' hand, considering the shapes of ⲉ, ⲙ, ⲧ, and the many separating signs (see Figure 13.4). In some cases, particularly when there is no proper name, it is difficult to decide by whose hand the ostracon is written—for instance, in O.Frange 80 (Figure 13.15), where the subject of the letter (black ink) could concern both Frange and Moses, and the writing does not solve the question. In the latter case, the ostracon was eventually attributed to Frange because of linguistic features (see below). As we will see now, the relation between palaeography and language in this dossier is often important.

Fig. 13.13. O.Frange 190r

Fig. 13.14. O.Frange 190v

Fig. 13.15. O.Frange 80

§3.5. Frange's Language, between Imitation and Idiolectal Traits

Frange's language has many Theban phonological features, which do not appear systematically but vary from one text to another and even inside a single text. There is nothing different here from what can be observed in Theban texts of this period. More revealing for our purpose are the morphosyntactic features, especially when they show oppositions between Frange's and Mark's phrasing.[28]

[28] It is not the purpose of this paper to list all the specific features of Frange's language. See Boud'hors and Heurtel (2010, Introduction, §4).

§3.5.1. *Construction of the verbs of demand*

The use of ϫⲉⲕⲁⲥ followed by Future II, while frequent in Mark's ostraca (see above §2.5), particularly as the almost exclusive construction of ⲡⲁⲣⲁⲕⲁⲗⲉⲓ, 'to ask for',[29] is scarcely used by Frange and seems to be reserved for rather solemn demands:

1. O.Frange 211

ϯⲧⲁⲙⲟ ⲙ̄ⲙⲱⲧⲛ̄ ϫⲉⲕⲁⲥ ⲉⲧⲉⲧⲛⲁⲥⲱⲧⲙ̄ ⲛ̄ⲥⲁⲡⲁⲥⲟⲛ ⲡⲁϩⲁⲙ

'I exhort you[30] to obey my brother Paham.'

2. O.Frange 120

ⲉⲓ̈ⲡⲁⲣⲁⲕⲁⲗⲓ ⲙ̄ⲙⲟⲕ ϫⲉⲕⲁⲥ ⲉⲕⲛⲁⲁⲁⲥ ⲉⲧⲃⲉⲡⲛⲟⲩⲧⲉ

'I ask you to act in the name of God...'

The so-called Future III is also used, in letters possibly written at the beginning of Frange's monastic life:

3. P.Mon.Epiph. 376

ϯⲡⲁⲣⲁⲕⲁⲗⲓ ⲛⲧⲉⲕⲙⲛⲧϫⲟⲉⲓⲥ ⲛⲥⲟⲛ ϫⲉⲕⲁⲥ ⲉⲕⲉⲣⲧⲛⲟϭ ⲛⲁⲅⲁⲡⲏ

'I ask Your brotherly Lordship to have the great goodness...'

4. O.Crum 396 (letter signed by 'Phrangas')

ϫⲉⲕⲁⲥ ⲉⲓϣⲁⲛⲣⲡⲉⲕⲙⲉⲉⲩⲉ ⲉⲓⲉⲙⲱϩ ⲛⲣⲁϣⲉ

'...so that,[31] when I think of you, I will be full of joy.'

In the following example, the breaking of the construction after ϫⲉⲕⲁⲥ is noteworthy:

5. O.Frange 48

ⲉⲓ̈ⲡⲁⲣⲁⲕⲁⲗⲉⲓ ⲛ̄ⲧⲉⲕⲙⲛ̄ⲧϫⲟⲉⲓⲥ ⲛ̄ⲥⲟⲛ ⲉⲧⲛⲁⲛⲟⲩⲥ ϫⲉⲕⲁⲥ ⲉⲕϣⲁⲛⲥⲱⲧⲙ̄ ⲛⲉⲥϩⲁⲓ̈ ⲛ̄ⲧⲁⲙⲛ̄ⲧⲉⲗⲁⲭ(ⲓⲥⲧⲟⲥ) ⲙ̄ⲡⲣ̄ⲁⲙⲉⲗⲓ

'I ask Your good brotherly Lordship, when you hear the letter of my humility, do not be careless...'

As a more general trend, Frange resorts to a construction with the causative Infinitive (ⲉⲧⲣⲉϥ-) or with the Conjunctive. Moreover, for final clauses, ϫⲉ is much more frequent than ϫⲉⲕⲁⲥ and is constructed with the following forms of Future: ϫⲉⲓⲛⲁ-/ϫⲉ ⲉⲓⲛⲁ- (1SG); ϫⲉ ⲉⲕⲛⲁ- (2MSG); ϫⲉⲣⲁ- (2FSG); ϫⲉϥⲁ-/ϫⲉϥⲛⲁ- (3MSG); ϫⲉⲛⲁ- (1PL).

[29] However, there is at least one occurrence of ϫⲉ + Future II (O.Frange 777).

[30] Note the unusual meaning of ⲧⲁⲙⲟ here, while the meaning 'to inform' is common.

[31] ϫⲉⲕⲁⲥ introduces here a final clause, not a completive one.

§3.5.2. *Theban forms of the Conditional*

The standard form of Conditional ⲉϥϣⲁⲛ- is relatively rare in Frange's letters, while it is very common in Mark's (see above §2.5). In example 5, the use of ⲉⲕϣⲁⲛⲥⲱⲧⲙ and of ϫⲉⲕⲁⲥ is probably to be connected with a certain rhetorical emphasis, as it is in the following example:

6. O.Frange **139**

ⲁⲣⲓⲧⲁⲅⲁⲡⲏ <u>ⲉⲕϣⲁⲛ</u>ⲉ̈ⲓ ⲉⲃⲟⲗ ⲁⲙⲟⲩ ⲛ̄ⲧⲁϭⲛ̄ⲡⲉⲕϩⲙ̄ϩⲁⲗ

'Have the goodness, when you go out, to come so that I can meet your servant.'

However, the most frequent conditional form is the 'protatic *efsotm*', very common in Theban texts and already found in an ostracon addressed to Mark:[32]

7. O.Frange 106

<u>ⲉⲕ</u>ⲉⲓ ⲛⲁ̈ⲓ ⲙ̄ⲡⲉⲥⲟⲡ ⲙⲛ̄ⲧⲉⲕⲣ̄ⲧⲁⲡⲱⲕⲣⲓⲥⲓⲥ ⲡⲁϩⲏⲧ ⲛⲁϩⲓⲥⲉ [for ⲙⲛ̄ⲧⲉⲕ-, see below]

'If you come to me this time and you do not give the answer, my heart will suffer.'

8. O.Frange 22

<u>ⲉ</u>ⲡⲛⲟϭ ⲛ̄ⲣⲱⲙⲉ ⲉⲓ ⲛϥ̄ⲣⲁⲉⲓⲥ ⲉⲡⲉϥⲙⲁ ϯⲛⲏⲩ ⲉⲣⲏⲥ

'If/when the great man comes and watches his house, I will go south…'

9. O.Frange 585

<u>ⲁ</u>ⲣⲱⲙⲉ ϯ ϫⲟⲟⲩ ⲙ̄ⲙⲟⲟⲩ ⲛⲁⲓ 'If people resist, send them to me!'

Remarkable in the last example is the 'southern' coloration of the conjugation basis (ⲁ- and not ⲉ-[33]).

To express a negative condition Frange does not use the form ⲉϥ-ⲧⲙ̄-ⲥⲱⲧⲙ̄, although it is very common in Theban texts,[34] but rather the form ⲙⲛⲧⲉ-:[35]

[32] See above §2.5 and note 20.

[33] This form seems, however, to be unattested until now. The Akhmimic dialect has an occurrence of conditional ⲁⲧⲉⲧⲛ-, but no form ⲁ- for the prenominal; Bohairic and Fayyumic have ⲁⲣⲉ- for the prenominal form, and there is another occurrence of ⲁⲣⲉ- as the prenominal in early Sahidic (see Shisha-Halevy 1974, 370 n. 10 and 372 exx. 2 and 26–9).

[34] On the other hand, ⲉϥϣⲁⲛⲧⲙ̄ⲥⲱⲧⲙ̄ seems to be completely absent in these texts: see Grossman (2009b, 52 n. 14). As for Frange's dossier, it contains three occurrences of ⲉϥⲧⲙ̄ⲥⲱⲧⲙ̄: one is in a letter addressed to him (O.Frange 320), another one is in a letter addressed by his name but written by a hand different from his (O.Frange 177: see the comment on ex. 17 below), and the third one is indeed in a letter written by him to the nun Tsie (O.Frange 215), but it does not really have a conditional sense, instead having a meaning akin to 'even if': ⲉⲣⲧⲙⲟⲩⲱϫⲉ ϩⲟⲉⲓⲧⲉ ⲛⲁ̈ⲓ ⲉⲛⲉϩ ⲛ̄ⲧⲓⲛⲁⲃⲱϣ '(even) if you do not ever weave clothes for me, I will not be nude.'

[35] Which is in accordance with Grossman (2009b, 52): '…in the grammatical system of the Theban documents, it is rather ⲙⲛⲧ(ⲉ)ϥⲥⲱⲧⲙ and the ⲉϥⲧⲙ̄ⲥⲱⲧⲙ that constitute the negative protatic subsystem, while the affirmative is constituted by the opposition between ⲉϥⲥⲱⲧⲙ and ⲉϥϣⲁⲛⲥⲱⲧⲙ.'

10. O.Frange 51

<u>ⲙⲛ̄ⲧⲉⲕ</u>ϫⲟⲟⲩⲥⲟⲩ ⲛⲁ̈ⲓ ϩⲛ̄ⲟⲩϭⲉⲡⲏ ⲡⲉⲕϩⲏⲧ ⲛⲁϩⲓⲥⲉ

'If you do not send them to me quickly, your heart will suffer.'

The latter form is also typically Theban and occurs overwhelmingly in Frange's letters, not only with a conditional value, but also in negative final clauses ('lest…')[36]:

11. O.Frange 68

ⲙⲡⲣϭⲱ ⲛϣⲟⲩϫⲟⲟⲩⲥ <u>ⲙⲛⲧⲉ</u>ⲡⲉⲕϩⲏⲧ ϩⲓⲥⲉ

'Do not stay without sending it, lest your heart should suffer.'

§3.5.3. *Two specific constructions by Frange*

§3.5.3.1. Grammaticalized use of ϭⲛⲧⲥ̄

This form is to be analysed as the pronominal form ϭⲛⲧ- of the Infinitive ϭⲓⲛⲉ, 'to find', with an Imperative value, followed by the suffix -ⲥ, here neutral and cataphoric. It had already been found by Crum in some Theban texts[37]:

12. P.Mon.Epiph. 173

ⲕⲁⲓ ⲅⲁⲣ ⲙⲡⲉⲓϭⲙ̄ⲧⲩⲡⲟⲥ ⲛ̄ⲉⲓ ⲙ̄ⲙⲟⲛ <u>ϭⲛⲧⲥ̄</u> ⲁⲓⲉⲓ ⲛⲙ̄ⲙⲁϥ

'Indeed I did not find the way of coming; otherwise, <u>depend upon it</u>, I would have come with him.'

This value of ϭⲛⲧⲥ̄, reinforcing the 'apodotic perfect', is confirmed by two clear examples in Frange's letters and by another letter not written by him. Therefore, Frange's dossier now provides the widest attestation of this construction[38]:

13. O.Frange 160

ⲉⲛⲉⲟⲩⲛϩⲟⲧⲉ ⲛ̄ⲧⲉⲡⲛⲟⲩⲧⲉ ϩⲙ̄ⲡϩⲏⲧ ⲙ̄ⲡⲁϩⲁⲧⲣⲏ ⲛ̄ⲑⲉ ⲛ̄ⲧⲁϥⲛⲁⲩ ⲉⲣⲟ̈ⲓ ⲉⲓⲟ ⲛ̄ϫⲟⲗⲏ <u>ϭⲛ̄ⲧⲥ̄</u> ⲁϥⲉⲓ ⲉⲡⲉⲧⲉⲙⲟⲩⲧ

'If there were fear of God in Pahatre's heart, when he saw I was angry, <u>depend upon it</u>, he would have come to Petemout.'

[36] Where it can be opposed to uses of the Conjunctive. For a detailed description of ⲙⲛⲧⲉ-, see Boud'hors (2010b).

[37] Crum (1939, 820b).

[38] For more details, see Boud'hors and Heurtel (2010, Introduction, § 4.3.2). The translation 'to be sure' (= 'depend upon it') had already been proposed by the editors of O.Medin.HabuCopt. 139, which is written by Frange. As for the ostracon not written by him (O.Frange 358), it is addressed by a woman called Susan to Moses the priest and it is puzzling to observe that, while the hand is very skilful, almost professional, the phrasing is amazingly close to Frange's syntax (it contains particularly an occurrence of the form ⲙⲉϥ-ⲥⲱⲧⲙ described below, §3.5.3.2): could Frange have dictated or even written this letter?

§3.5.3.2. The ⲙⲉϥⲥⲱⲧⲙ form

Although there are probably occurrences of this form to be found outside Frange's dossier, they are still rare and uncertain. Obviously, the form is distinct from the negative 'aorist', the latter having almost always a vowel 'a' (ⲙⲁϥⲥⲱⲧⲙ) in Theban texts, as well as a modal value (future or impossibility). The paradigm is attested as follows: ⲙⲉⲓ- (ex. 3), ⲙⲉⲕ- (ex. 12), ⲙⲉⲣ- (ex. 2), ⲙⲉϥ- (ex. 1), ⲙⲉⲥ- (ex. 1).[39] The examples quoted below show that these forms are equivalent to the negative Perfect (ⲙⲡⲉϥⲥⲱⲧⲙ).

14. O.Frange 164

ⲉⲡⲓⲇⲏ ⲁϊϫⲟⲟⲩ ⲕⲩⲣⲓⲕⲟⲥ ⲛⲁⲕ ⲡⲉⲗⲟⲩⲥⲧⲣⲉ <u>ⲙⲉⲕ</u>ⲥⲱⲧⲙ̄ ⲛ̄ⲥⲱϊ

'Although I sent you Kurikos, Peloustre, you did not obey me…'

In the same context, the negative Perfect is used in an ostracon perhaps written by Frange's hand, but addressed by Patermoute to Heleseos:

15. O.Frange 155

ⲉⲡⲓⲇⲏ ⲁϊϫⲟⲟⲩ ⲛⲁⲕ ⲉⲧⲃⲉⲡϩⲱⲃ ⲙ̄<u>ⲡⲕ</u>ⲣⲁⲡⲟⲕⲣⲓⲥⲓⲥ ⲛⲁϊ ϣⲁⲧⲉⲛⲟⲩ

'Although I sent you a message about the matter, you did not give an answer to me till now.'

Having been only the scribe of the letter, Frange may have followed the syntax of the sender.

Another kind of opposition appears in the two following examples, which are both from letters addressed by Frange, the first one written by his hand, the second one with a sloping professional script that does not correspond to any of his known hands:

16. O.Frange 127

†ⲣ̄ϣⲡⲏⲣⲉ ⲙⲙⲟⲕ ϫⲉ ⲁⲕⲣⲡⲉⲟⲩⲟⲉⲓϣ ⲧⲏⲣϥ <u>ⲙⲉⲕ</u>ⲉⲓ ⲛⲁⲓ

'I am amazed at your spending all this time without coming to me.'

17. O.Frange 176

†ⲣ̄ϣⲡⲏⲣⲉ ⲙⲙⲟⲕ ϫⲉ ⲁⲕⲃⲱⲕ ⲉⲡⲉⲧⲉⲙⲟⲩⲧ <u>ⲙ̄ⲡⲕ̄</u>ⲛ̄ⲧⲟⲩ

'I am amazed at your going to Petemout without bringing them to me.'

The addressee of O.Frange 176, namely a man called Mahenknout, is taken to task once more in O.Frange 177. There again the negative Perfect is used in reproaching him for his bad behaviour and there again the hand, although different from the one in O.Frange 176, does not look like any of Frange's ways of

[39] ⲙⲉⲓ- and ⲙⲉϥ- are also likely to be identified in O.Vind.Copt. 154. See the presentation of all the occurrences in Boud'hors and Heurtel (2010, Introduction, §4.3.3).

writing.[40] Therefore, it seems that in Frange's dossier the negative Perfect is found in opposition with the form ⲙⲉⲕ- in specific palaeographic contexts.

On the other hand, the prevailing number of occurrences with the second person singular suggests that it could be a kind of specialized use associated with contexts of reproach or anger. In fact, the expected form of the negative Perfect is also found outside such a context:

18. O.Frange 186

ⲁⲣⲓⲧⲁⲅⲁⲡⲏ ⲛ̄ⲅ̄ⲕⲱ ⲛⲁⲛ ⲉⲃⲟⲗ ϫⲉ ⲙ̄ⲡⲉⲕϭⲛ̄ⲧⲛ̄ ϩⲙ̄ⲡⲙⲁ

'Have the goodness to forgive us for not having found us here.'

Examples with the first and third persons are more difficult to explain. Moreover, the former are very few when compared with the frequent use of ⲙⲡ(ⲉ)ⲓ-.[41]

§4. CONCLUSION

If one adds to the syntactic features just described some lexical peculiarities, particularly the use of the Stative ⲁⲛⲓⲧ in the relative construction ⲉⲧⲁⲛⲓⲧ, 'that is good', as an alternating form for the more common ⲉⲧⲛⲁⲛⲟⲩϥ, Frange's language can be characterized as strongly marked both by Theban traits and personal habits. This does not mean that he was ignorant of the rules of the epistolary rhetoric, since, on the contrary, some of his letters demonstrate how skilfully he resorted to it, but his functions and concerns led him to use various registers of language. By contrast, in Mark's case, we are facing a well-standardized form of language where neither local trends nor personal marks appear. This is, for a great part, the result of a higher level of education and a different social position, which can also be noticed in the unequal graphic skills. Moreover, the chronological gap may have played a role. To judge the impact of this chronological factor, one should consider the written production of the professional scribes in the eighth century. Obviously, their skills in writing remain excellent, with growing cursivity, as can be observed in the long legal texts of Djeme. Nevertheless, the language of these documents shows a kind of 'destandardization', both from the phonological and morphosyntactic points of view, with the emergence (or the resurgence) of constructions perhaps stemming from the local spoken language. Such a development could be connected with a general change in life after the Arab conquest.

[40] It should be recalled that in this very letter (O.Frange 177) the negative conditional form ⲉϥⲧⲙ̄ⲥⲱⲧⲙ, unusual in Frange's syntax, occurs (see above, n. 34).

[41] It may be useful to make clear that the form ⲙⲡⲁⲧⲉ-, 'not yet', also occurs with all persons, even if less frequently, which is the case for every kind of text. Therefore, ⲙⲉϥⲥⲱⲧⲙ cannot be interpreted as an alternating form for ⲙⲡⲁⲧⲉϥⲥⲱⲧⲙ, although the meaning sometimes fits this interpretation.

14

A Scribe, His Bag of Tricks, What It Was For, and Where He Got It

Scribal Registers and Techniques in Bodl.Mss.Copt.(P) a.2 & 3

Tonio Sebastian Richter

§1. TWO ALCHEMICAL MANUSCRIPTS AND ONE ANONYMOUS SCRIBE

The scribe that will be observed at work in the following lines left us two specimens of his skills, both kept today in the Bodleian Library, Oxford.[1] The two manuscripts, Bodl.Ms.Copt.(P) a.2 and Bodl.Ms.Copt.(P) a.3 (Figures 14.1 and 14.2), are written in vertical format (*transversa charta*) on the horizontal fibres (verso) of the papyrus strips, which measure 70 cm by 25 cm and 80 cm by 25 cm, respectively. This format is one of the more conspicuous features of the manuscripts.[2] Private letters in Arabic are written on the vertical fibres (recto) of both manuscripts, which are earlier than the Coptic texts.[3] There is no overt or even

[1] I am grateful to the Sarah J. Clackson Fund and the Alexander von Humboldt Foundation who endowed my research visit at Oxford in Autumn 2017. I am also grateful to the authorities and staff of the Oriental Reading Room of the New Bodleian Library who kindly assisted me in autumn 2004, 2006, and 2007, and my Leipzig colleague Susanne Beck in autumn 2009, when we had to handle the bulky frames containing Bodl.Mss.Copt.(P) a.1, a.2, and a.3. Last but not least, I am indebted to my colleagues at the Oxford Oriental Institute, Prof. John Baines and Prof. Mark Smith, who kindly granted logistical support on these occasions.

[2] Some contemporary medical and magical texts, such as P.Louvre AF 12530 (90 cm by 9 cm) edited by Richter (2014), the magical P.Heid.inv.Kopt. 500+501 (121 cm by 21.5 cm) edited by Bilabel and Grohman (1934), and the famous Papyrus Médical Copte (248 cm by 27 cm) of the Institut Français d'Archéologie Orientale (IFAO) edited by Chassinat (1921), display similar vertical formats, which were otherwise typical for seventh- and eighth-century Coptic legal documents from Upper Egypt.

[3] P.Bodl.Arab. 1 (on the recto of Bodl.Ms.Copt.(P) a.3) and P.Bodl.Arab. 2 (on the recto of Bodl.Ms.Copt.(P) a.2) were edited by Margoliouth (1893), as Prof. Petra Sijpesteijn (Leiden) kindly informed me.

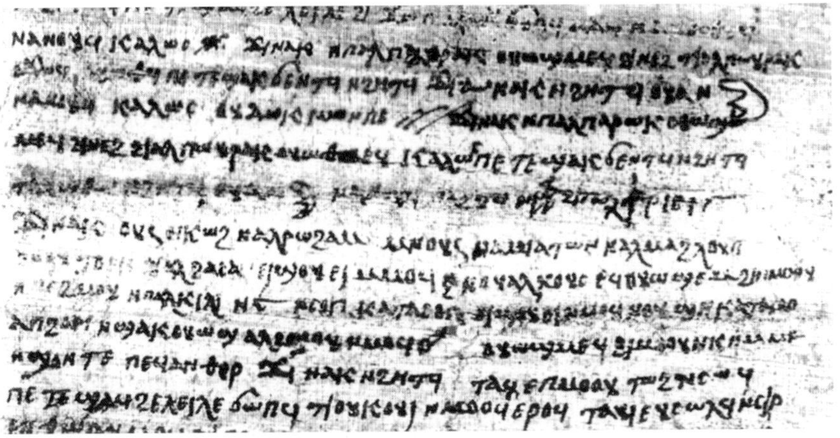

Fig. 14.1. Bodl.Ms.Copt.(P) a.2, 20–30: 'Informal' bimodular uncial (descending ⲗ, ⲣ, ϣ, ϥ, ϩ; ascending ⲃ, ϫ and ϭ). © University of Oxford, Bodleian Library

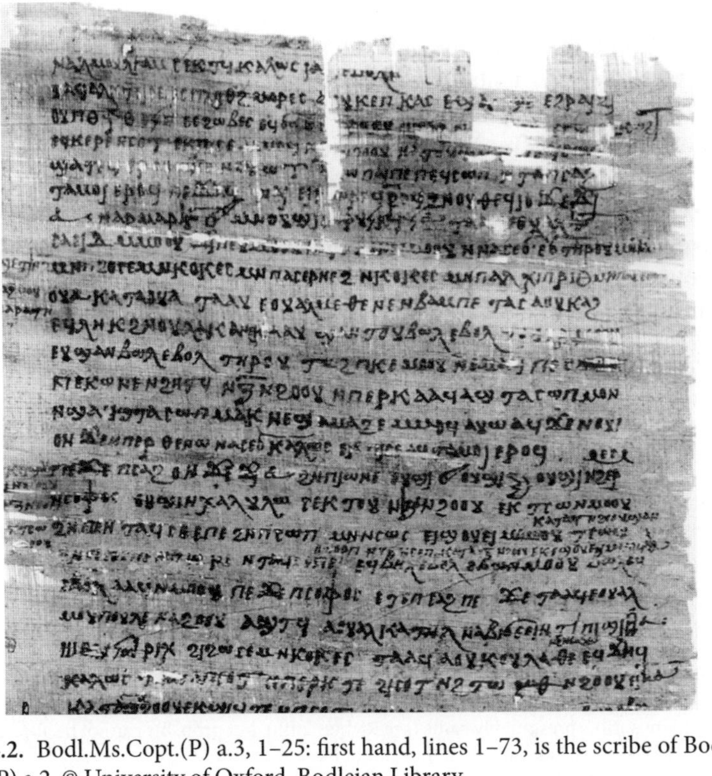

Fig. 14.2. Bodl.Ms.Copt.(P) a.3, 1–25: first hand, lines 1–73, is the scribe of Bodl.Ms. Copt.(P) a.2. © University of Oxford, Bodleian Library

traceable connection between the Arabic recto and the Coptic verso of both manuscripts, although there may once have been one.[4] The Coptic writing can be dated, on palaeographic grounds, to the tenth or eleventh century CE; however, the use of papyrus makes a tenth-century date more likely than a later one.

Bodl.Mss.Copt.(P) a.2 and a.3, as well as a third item, Bodl.Ms.Copt.(P) a.1, were brought to Oxford in 1890 by the Reverend John Greville Chester.[5] All three papyri bear texts on the same uncommon subject—alchemy—and together might have formed part of the 'reference library' of a tenth-century Coptic-reading alchemist.[6] Together with a fourth item, the tenth-century parchment quire British Library (BL) Or. 3669(1),[7] these manuscripts constitute a small but significant corpus of Coptic alchemical texts[8] that provides evidence for the reception and appropriation of contemporary scientific knowledge from Arabic sources in medieval Egypt. This process is similar to (and roughly contemporary with) the much better investigated transmission of knowledge via translation from Arabic into Latin in medieval Spain.[9]

The content of these manuscripts, more or less elaborate compilations of alchemical recipes, shall not be dealt with here. Instead, I will focus on the means of presentation used by their anonymous scribe. Viewed from this angle, Bodl.Mss.Copt.(P) a.2 and a.3 show a striking diversity of distinct graphic codes. Although the great bulk of textual substance is encoded in one writing system and style—the 'matrix system', as we shall call it—there are also several alternative codes, one applied in a more regular way, the others sporadically embedded in the matrix. Also striking is the fact that the alternative graphic codes are not functionally necessary: whatever is written in them could well have been written by means of the standard code of the matrix system. In terms of conveying the essential semantic content of the text, their use is apparently gratuitous or sportive. Like a bag of tricks, these codes seem as though they were meant to surprise the audience.

[4] Texts found on the same writing support can have different degrees of relatedness; in some cases, it is almost certain that no relationship existed. The reuse of commercially sold and bought second-hand writing material might account for such cases, a scenario that has been mentioned explicitly regarding the Cairo Genizah material by Goitein (1967–93.II, 233).

[5] This information is taken from the Oriental Reading Room's card catalogue of 'Manuscripts: Donors and Vendors'. For the Reverend Chester, an antiquity hunter and trader who had business with a number of British collections, see Dawson and Uphill (2012, 119–20).

[6] This is additionally indicated by the fact that P.Bodl.Ms.Copt.(P) a.1 and one of our scribe's manuscripts, P.Bodl.Ms.Copt.(P) a.3, provide two versions of the same text.

[7] This manuscript was acquired by the German Egyptologist Eisenlohr slightly earlier than the Bodleian manuscripts and purchased by the British Museum roughly at the same time; see the *editio princeps* (Stern 1885) and the information provided by Crum (1905, 175) concerning P.Lond. Copt. I 374. It was discovered in the same region of Upper Egypt, around Sohag, from where the Bodleian manuscripts presumably came (see Richter 2015), but probably cannot be allotted to the same alchemist's 'bookshelf' in which they might have been stored.

[8] The edition of the Coptic alchemical corpus is under preparation; see the preliminary working reports by Richter (2009, 2010b, and 2015).

[9] See Burnett (2009) and, for alchemy in particular, Vinciguerra (2009).

However, just as sports and tricks have their rules, so might our scribe's choices also have been governed by rules, whether intentional or not. As such, we should ask what purposes these tricks served for the master of the bag—what functions, beyond semantic ones, they had. Eventually it might be worthwhile to look for the origin of the codes brought together in the two alchemical manuscripts by our scribe, and for what purposes and for whom they originally served. It is also interesting to speculate on the social milieus, forms of education, and paths of manuscript transmission that they may reveal. Although their contexts differ in some respects—for instance, in age—they still may have something in common: an intersection within which our scribe's own origins as a writing individual, including his scribal education and his aims, must be somehow located.

§2. THE 'MATRIX SYSTEM'

Before dealing with the kind of writing system and style used to encode the vast majority of the textual substance of Bodl.Mss.Copt.(P) a.2 and a.3, I will briefly discuss the formal types and functions of later Coptic bookhands.[10]

§2.1. Unimodular and Bimodular Uncial

Later (ninth- to eleventh-century) Coptic literary manuscripts are usually written in one of two types of bookhand that have been termed by Viktor Stegemann, the author of the most important treatise on Coptic palaeography available to

[10] In this discussion, I shall adhere to the terminological conventions established in the field of Coptic studies, although some of them might look unusual or outdated through the eyes of Greek palaeographers. There has been little research on Coptic palaeography so far, which may well account for certain shortcomings. It is, however, important to note that Coptic writing styles, once derived from Greek prototypes, did not only undergo formal developments of their own, but were working in a functional framework different from that of the (Greek) donor system. Therefore, it might not be wise simply to transfer the achievements of Greek palaeography to the classification of Coptic scripts, and a terminological standardization of Coptic terms along the lines of the current standard Greek terminology would be misleading. The term 'uncial', which remains common in palaeographical descriptions of Coptic (and so is used in the present study), might seem an inappropriate choice due to unwanted Latin implications. However 'majuscule' would not be an obvious choice either in a palaeographic framework were no such thing as a 'minuscule' exists, i.e. due to likewise unwanted Greek implications. While 'sloping dotted majuscule' in terms of Greek palaeography means a fourth-/fifth-century Greek bookhand (Crisci 1985), what Coptologists call 'sloping uncial' is a display typeface mainly of the ninth- to twelfth-century display typeface (see below §2.2), thus something functionally and chronologically quite remote from its Greek counterpart and original model. Further, the formal distinction into 'unimodular' and 'bimodular' of the two main Coptic bookhands of tenth- to twelfth-century literary manuscripts, used side by side in one scriptorium in Upper Egypt (see below), seems more adequate than attributing the name of the town of Alexandria and that of a seventh- to eighth-century Greek majuscule style to one of the two (i.e. 'Alexandrian majuscule').

date,[11] 'thick style' (*Dicker Stil*) and 'narrow style' (*Schmaler Stil*), referring to their overall appearance. Both of these are principally based on the formal canon of uncial, i.e. generally speaking, the idea of keeping every alphabetic sign, regardless of its individual shape, within a certain space unit or module. These two types of uncial are also called unimodular uncial (corresponding to Stegemann's thick style) and bimodular uncial (corresponding to Stegemann's narrow style).[12] While the thick style is based on a single module being the square unit, the narrow style alternates between two modules, the square unit and the half-square unit. The latter of these was used for otherwise broad, round letters, such as epsilon (ϵ as opposed to ⲉ), sigma (ϲ as opposed to ⲥ), and omicron (ο as opposed to ⲟ), resulting in their conspicuously narrow forms.

§2.2. Sloping Uncial

The contemporary scribal repertoire of the scriptorium includes yet another bookhand, which is sometimes called 'sloping uncial'.[13] This style, however, was not in competition with the aforementioned uncials, but served instead as a functional complement to the two. It was regularly used for paratextual units, such as page numbers, titles, and scribal colophons, within a literary text. Its formal traits, such as a slight inclination of the letters to the right (i.e. their sloping stance) rather than the strongly upright stance of letters in the uni- and bimodular uncial, and often also its significantly smaller size, allowed readers to take in the textual segmentation of a book page almost automatically. Some distinctly shaped signs include the asymmetric upsilon (ⲩ), the split kappa (ⲕ), and the reduced mu (ⲙ), hardly distinguishable from eta (ⲏ).

Reserved for paratextual units—second-degree texts, so to speak[14]—this writing style can be classified functionally as an *Auszeichnungsschrift* ('writing style used for markups'), to adopt a palaeographical term used by the Byzantinist Herbert Hunger,[15] or *Subscriptionsstil*, as Stegemann put it,[16] in reference to the typical usage of sloping uncial in subscribed book titles and colophons.

§2.3. Coptic *Kleinliteratur*

As was first noticed by Till,[17] sloping uncial could occasionally be used as the only style throughout an entire manuscript. This is striking, since sloping uncial usually occurs only in functional opposition to a uni- or bimodular uncial, with

[11] Stegemann (1936). [12] I owe this terminology to Emmel (2004.I, 107).
[13] Corresponding to what is called '9th class' by Zoëga (1810), the earliest approach to Coptic palaeography. For a study of the early development of this style, see Boud'hors (1997).
[14] In the terms used by Genette (1982). [15] See Hunger (1977), as well as Crisci (1985).
[16] Stegemann (1936, 19–20). [17] Till (1942).

the former representing or marking the auxiliary or secondary status of a textual unit vis-à-vis the main body of the text. However, even when used outside of this opposition, its function of indicating a hierarchically lower textual level is still maintained. The use of sloping uncial as a matrix system was apparently restricted to texts of supposedly lower 'literary value', thereby revealing attitudes about 'literariness' as held by the Coptic scribes themselves. Till covered the spectrum of late Sahidic texts which were 'allowed' to be entirely written in sloping uncial under the label *Kleinliteratur*, 'minor literature'. Coptic *Kleinliteratur* included, for example, the tenth-century compositions of what has been called 'Coptic folk literature',[18] liturgical manuscripts,[19] Coptic magical texts,[20] and medical[21] or, more broadly speaking, scientific writing.[22] It comes as no surprise that this very type of 'low' or 'minor' literature, if compared to the contemporary production and transmission of Coptic literary (in a narrow sense) manuscripts, usually exhibits also a lower degree of linguistic standardization.[23]

§2.4. The Scribal Matrix of BL Or. 3669(1) and Bodl.Ms.Copt.(P) a.1

The use of sloping uncial in Coptic scientific texts is found in parts of the Coptic alchemical corpus. The hand of the parchment quire BL Or. 3669(1) (Figure 14.3), a palimpsest written on top of the incompletely erased lines of a literary text, looks like a very practised specimen of this type, closely resembling the fluent hand of P.Berlin 9287,[24] a late Coptic poetry manuscript.[25] In terms of proficiency, we may imagine that this hand belonged to a professional scribe. The papyrus quire Bodl.Ms.Copt.(P) a.1 (Figure 14.4), despite having the same sort

[18] Erman (1897); Junker (1908/1911).

[19] Such as Pierpont Morgan M 574, edited by Quecke (1970).

[20] The typical Coptic magical writing style is basically an informal sloping uncial (for example, the Heidelberg Magical Book of Mary and the Angels, P.Heid.inv.Kopt. 685 (Meyer 1996)), but there are also more formal, scriptorium-like specimens, e.g. the Magical Book of Cyprianus (P.Heid.inv. Kopt. 684 (Bilabel and Grohmann 1934)) or P.Heid.inv. 518 (Bilabel and Grohmann 1934, plate 10).

[21] These include the aforementioned Papyrus Médical Copte (see n. 2) and a number of manuscripts from the small corpus of Coptic medical texts, such as the pages of a parchment codex formerly kept in the Borgia collection (Bouriant 1888; Zoëga 1810, 629–39 (no. 278)), the parchment bifolium P.Leuven University Library fragment 114 (Till 1952, 159–63; SB Kopt. I 1), BKU I 26, SB Kopt. I 2 and 5, and P.Ryl.Copt. 104, 106, 107, 108.

[22] Examples include the arithmetic problems of BL Or. 5707 (Drescher 1948/9; P.Rain. UnterrichtKopt. 331 and plates 138–43).

[23] It is also notable that many late Coptic documentary texts, such as the eleventh-century legal documents from the Teshlot archive (Green 1985, Richter 2000, Schenke 2007), are written in sloping uncial, indicating their scribes' education in a scriptorium context, and thereby the non-existence of dedicated documentary scribal training at that time.

[24] Junker (1908/1911, pl. I).

[25] Edited by Junker (1908/1911). For further comparative examples, cf. those in the catalogue of Coptic manuscripts in the British Library (P.Lond.Copt. II 71 (pl. 1) and 176 (pl. 8)).

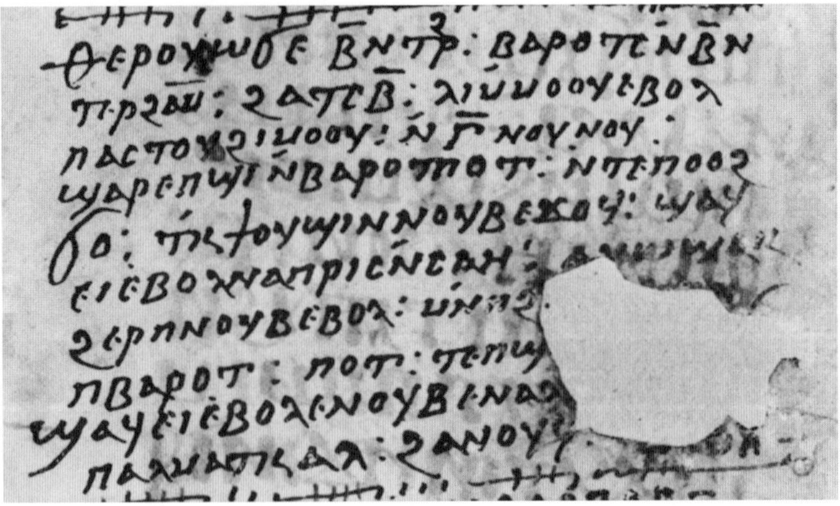

Fig. 14.3. BL Or. 3669(1), fol. 7r°, 6–15: Formal sloping uncial (*Stegemann's 'Subskriptionsstil'*). © The British Library Board

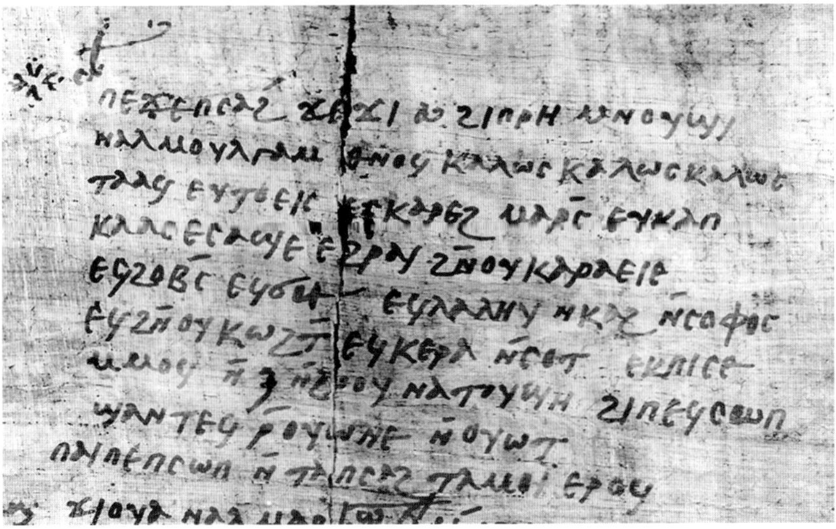

Fig. 14.4. Bodl.Ms.Copt.(P) a.1, fol. 1v°, 1–10: Informal sloping uncial. © University of Oxford, Bodleian Library

of style, bears a less elegant appearance and is presumably the work of a non-professional scribe.[26] Viewed from a functional perspective, the choice of sloping uncial for alchemical texts conforms well with Till's concept of *Kleinliteratur*, and seems to be a perfectly appropriate choice in such terms.

§2.5. The Scribal Matrix of Bodl.Mss.Copt.(P) a.2 and a.3

In contrast, the scribe of Bodl.Mss.Copt.(P) a.2 and a.3 (Figures 14.1 and 14.2) chose another basic style for his work. What he aimed to produce was a bimodular uncial, albeit a rather less formal, somewhat unstylized variety, using vertically shaped letters such as lambda (ⲗ), rho (ⲣ), and fai (ϥ) with descenders. Tall letters such as beta (ⲃ), djandja (ϫ), and kyima (ϭ) ascend above the average line,[27] and, generally speaking, letters do not always stand in a perfectly upright position.

The use of a bimodular uncial, a supposedly 'high variety' of bookhand, for writing alchemical texts is only at first glance a surprising choice. It points to a significant difference between the two aforementioned Coptic formal bookhands, the unimodular and the bimodular uncial. In fact, the more archaic of the two,[28] the unimodular style, was more narrowly restricted to high-prestige literature, while the bimodular uncial was not exclusively bound to the function of a bookhand proper. Often enough, it is actually used as an *Auszeichnungsschrift*. In cases where the basic text was written in unimodular uncial,[29] the distinction between first and second degree textual units was managed through the difference in formal type, i.e. producing the same effect as if sloping uncial had been used. In cases where bimodular uncial was chosen also for the main text,[30] the only (albeit sufficiently) distinguishing difference between the main textual and paratextual units as two functional varieties of one formal type was their different size. The extended functionality of the bimodular uncial as a functional equivalent to sloping uncial seems to be the rationale behind its choice for Bodl.Mss.Copt.(P) a.2 and a.3. The conspicuously small size of the bimodular uncial in these manuscripts eventually leads to the same conclusion: our scribe, had he adopted Hunger's and Till's terminology, would have intended to use an *Auszeichnungsschrift* in order to copy a piece of *Kleinliteratur*.

[26] We owe parts of the medical recipes of P.Louvre AF 12530 to the same scribe; see Richter (2014, 167).

[27] A good comparison is the Gospel of Matthew (Balestri and Ciasca, 1898, no. 37).

[28] More directly descending from the ancient biblical uncial, this fine Greek writing style is known from such famous manuscripts as the Codex Sinaiticus, the Codex Vaticanus, and the Codex Alexandrinus, the earliest extant copies of the entire Bible (fourth to fifth century CE).

[29] As in, for example, the Gospel of Luke (Balestri and Ciasca, 1898, no. 93).

[30] As in, for example, the Shenoute (and Athanasius) Codex, Paris, Bibliothèque nationale F130.5 fol.128v°, or Zoëga (1810) pl. v, specimen XXIIX (= Ms. CCXLIX).

§3. A 'BAG OF TRICKS'

As mentioned before, our scribe used a remarkable number of alternative graphical codes. These include minuscule (3.1), a cryptographic code (3.2), Arabic letters (3.3), and a set of alchemical symbols (3.4), in addition to his basic choice of bimodular uncial as the matrix style.

§3.1. Minuscule Forms

In certain contexts, the canon of letter shaping according to bimodular uncial is regularly abandoned by our scribe for the use of minuscule forms. One might even call these Greek minuscule forms, were there not a body of evidence from earlier (seventh- to eighth-century) Coptic documentary papyri in which quite similar formal types of letters were used.[31] Our scribe's choice of minuscule forms is triggered essentially by two contexts: abbreviations (3.1.1) and numbers (3.1.2 and 3.1.3).

§3.1.1. Abbreviations

Abbreviations of the *apokopê* (ἀποκοπή, 'cut-off') type generally trigger a switch from uncial to minuscule forms. The most frequent case is that of the word *miliaresion* (μιλιαρήσιον),[32] always abbreviated μι$^{\lambda}$, thus fully spelled in minuscule-type letters (exx. 1–6):

1. Bodl.Ms.Copt.(P) a.2,2
ϫⲓ μιλ αϛ ⲛϩⲏⲧϥ ⲙⲛμι$^{\lambda}$ α ⲛϩⲁⲧ 'take 1½ Mil. of it and 1 Mil. of silver.'

2. Bodl.Ms.Copt.(P) a.2,7
ⲧ̣ⲁ̣ⲗ̣ⲟ̣ μ̣ι̣$^{\lambda}$ [.] 'add [. . .] Mil.'

[31] For this writing style in documentary Coptic, see Cromwell (2010a) and Chapter 12 in the current volume. While minuscule was standardized in Greek palaeography and elevated to the rank of a book style by the ninth century, minuscule forms of several characters in Coptic remained limited to the scribal register of non-literary writing. Although documentary writing styles had ceased to be used at the time when the alchemical manuscripts were written, documentary scribal strategies were obviously still known and transmitted. A cursive style that strikingly resembles the eighth-century documentary hands occurs, e.g. in tenth-century Coptic ink inscriptions and graffiti.

[32] Originally designating an early Byzantine silver coin (Latin: *milliarense*), which did not survive the fourth century; a flat and broad silver coin under the name *miliaresion* was reintroduced in the seventh century, possibly as an equivalent to the Sassanid and Arabic silver currencies. In later Byzantine medical and alchemical writing, the word is used to designate a weight (Olympiodor, Aëtos; see LSJ 1134a; Sophocles, *Greek Lexicon*, 760f.; Du Cange, *Glossarium ad Scriptores Mediae et Infimae Graecitatis*, 933–4). The Coptic–Arabic glossary Scale copte 44 of the Bibliothèque nationale de Paris (ed. Munier 1930) has ⲙⲓⲗⲓⲁⲣⲏⲥⲓⲟⲛ as the equivalent of *dirham* (fol. LVIII*v*° 56: ⲙⲙⲓⲗⲓⲁⲣⲉⲥⲓⲛ = *darâhim*).

3. Bodl.Ms.Copt.(P) a.2,53–4
ϫⲓ ⲛⲁⲕ ⲛⲏⲧϥ δ ⲛⲓⲱⲧ ϩⲓμι^{λ} α ⲛⲁⲃⲓϭⲉⲉⲓⲛ 'take 4 (corns of) barley on 1 Mil. of glass.'

4. Bodl.Ms.Copt.(P) a.2,54
ⲥⲉⲧ μι^{λ} α ϩⲓϫⲱ μι^{λ} ι 'throw 1 Mil. on 10 Mil.'

5. Bodl.Ms.Copt.(P) a.3, r° 22–23
ⲧⲓⲡⲓϣⲓ μι^{λ} α: *ⲛⲁϣⲓϣ*ⲣⲓⲭ 'give the very quantity (of) 1 Mil. of Ashirikh.'

6. Bodl.Ms.Copt.(P) a.3, r° 74
ⲡϣⲓ μι^{λ} ϛ 'the quantity of 6 Mil.'

In other cases, the switch from uncial to minuscule forms occurs word-internally. The word to be abbreviated begins in uncial, while the final, superscript letter (and sometimes the preceding one) is in the minuscule form (exx. 7–8):

7. Bodl.Ms.Copt.(P) a.3, r° 7–8
ϫⲓ α ⲛⲁⲣⲙⲁⲣⲕⲁ^{σ}/ 'take 1 (portion) of *Al-Markas(ita)*.'

8. Bodl.Ms.Copt.(P) a.3, r° 56
ⲟⲩϣⲓ…ⲛⲁⲗ^{ϖ} ☉ ⲟⲩϣⲓ ⲛⲁⲗ^{ϖ} ☽ 'a portion…of gold filings (*al-p[urate]*), a portion of silver filings (*al-p[urate]*).'

Text-internal switches seem, even more than the full minuscule spelling of the word *mil*(*iaresion*), to explain that choice. The rationale seems to be a correspondence between abbreviating strategies, text types, and writing styles respectively. In Coptic literary texts (i.e. the type of text usually written in uni- or bimodular uncial), the commonest way of abbreviating is the so-called compendium, the omission of the middle part of the abbreviated word. A supralinear stroke overlining the remaining initial and final letters of the word serves as the abbreviation marker, as in ⲓ̅ⲥ̅ (Jesus), ⲇ̅ⲁ̅ⲇ̅ (David), and ⲡ̅ⲛ̅ⲁ̅ (*pneuma* 'spirit'). The number and range of abbreviations of this type is narrowly limited, by convention, to a closed repertoire mainly including the names of holy places and persons.[33] This is why compendium-like abbreviation was not a possible choice for our scribe. For his purpose, he instead drew on a convention of Coptic non-literary usage: abbreviating words by cutting off their final part (*apokopê*) and marking the abbreviation with a superscript letter and/or a dash, a strategy that had been conventionalized in the Coptic notary practice centuries earlier. Although the repertoire of words to be abbreviated this way is virtually unlimited, local standards associated with particular types of documents and contexts assured the unambiguous comprehensibility of even heavily abridged words.

In order to understand the occasional choice of minuscules by our scribe, the crucial point is that, as often as he made use of the 'documentary strategy' of abbreviating, he also sporadically adopted the prevalent writing style of earlier Coptic documentary text production, the minuscule.

[33] Therefore called *nomina sacra*; see Layton (2004, 34).

§3.1.2. *Numbers*

Alphabetic signs functioning as numbers (ⲁ = 1, ⲃ = 2, ⲅ = 3, etc.) generally occur in Bodl.Mss.Copt.(P) a.2 and a.3 in minuscule form.

Coptic literary manuscripts exhibit a well-known variation in the spelling of numerals according to dialects: while lower Egyptian dialectal varieties tend to use alphabetic signs as numbers (ⲁ = 1, ⲃ = 2, ⲅ = 3, etc.), southern standards of Coptic, such as Sahidic, tend to show a preference for numerals to be written out as full words (ⲟⲩⲁ 'one', ⲥⲛⲁⲩ 'two', ϣⲟⲙⲛⲧ 'three', etc.). In some texts, such as the Gospel of Judas, both practices coexist. In Coptic bookhand environments, numbers represented by letters are usually marked by a supralinear stroke (cf. fig. 14.3, line 3: ⲅ̄ ⲛⲟⲩⲛⲟⲩ 'three hours', with gamma marked by a stroke) or instead (or additionally) framed by colons, and thereby sufficiently distinguished from neighbouring 'common' letters representing phonemes, although their shapes are virtually the same.[34]

The scribe of Bodl.Mss.Copt.(P) a.2 and a.3 generally avoided supralinear marking. Instead, he contrasted alphabetic signs functioning as numbers by using minuscule forms. This contrast worked well enough, since there was no other environment allowing minuscule signs except for the aforementioned abbreviations (and quite a handful of sporadic occurrences of single minuscule-shaped signs).[35] Evidence for the development of a particular minuscule-like Greek alphabet to represent numbers is mainly found in late Greek and Coptic documentary texts.[36] As in his aforementioned abbreviations, our scribe may have drawn on documentary habits in his spelling of numerals. He clearly does so in using the sign 𐅵, which Coptic documents conventionally employed to express '$^1/_2$'.[37]

§3.1.3. *Hybrid spelling of numerals*

Another, even more striking manner of writing numerals in Bodl.Mss.Copt.(P) a.2 and a.3 is a hybrid composition of reduced or adapted numeral words and their alphabetic equivalents, as in exx. 9–11:[38]

[34] The same strategy is applied to pagination, for which Upper Egyptian manuscripts also regularly used alphabetic signs. Pagination belongs to the paratextual parts of manuscripts, where sloping uncial is often found.

[35] Quite frequently in the case of eta, the choice is apparently subject to free variation, as in Bodl. Ms.Copt.(P) a.2,15 ⲛⲟⲩⲟⲩϣ**h** 'one night', Bodl.Ms.Copt.(P) a.2,50 ϣⲁⲛⲧⲉϥⲉⲣⲙⲟⲟⲩ ⲧhⲣ[ⲉ]ϥ 'until it entirely becomes liquid', and Bodl.Ms.Copt.(P) a.2,61 ϥⲧⲟ̣ⲟⲩ ⲛⲧhⲃⲉ 'four fingers'.

[36] Resulting in the set of so-called 'epact' (often wrongly called 'Coptic') numbers, cf. P.Rain. UnterrichtKopt. 294–303, 306a–12, 315, 317–20, 322, 326, 329, 332, and their accompanying plates.

[37] Cf. ex. 1 above and Bodl.Ms.Copt.(P) a.2,44: ⲟⲩϣⲓ ⲛⲓϣ ⲉϥⲡⲟⲥⲉ ϣⲁⲛⲧⲉϥⲡⲱⲧ ⲉⲧⲉϥ𐅵 'a unit of urine being cooked until it was reduced to its half'.

[38] A description of this strategy is given by Kasser (2007, 66–7): *Notation des nombres*: 'Une particularité frappante des textes du Codex Tchacos est leur manière, qu'on pourrait qualifier de désinvolte, de noter les nombres, non seulement par leur nom complet ou par le chiffre correspondant,

9. Bodl.Ms.Copt.(P) a.2,43
ⲧⲁⲗⲱ δ ϩⲓⲙⲉⲧⲓⲁ ⲛⲃⲁⲣⲱⲧ 'add 4 (units) to elleven (units) of copper'

10. Bodl.Ms.Copt.(P) a.2,54
ⲧⲁⲗⲟ α ⲗⲟⲩα 'add 1 (unit) to ole (unit)'

11. Bodl.Ms.Copt.(P) a.3, r° 11
ⲟⲩα ⲕⲁⲧⲁ ⲟⲩⲁ 'ole after the other'

This strategy is shared by the scribe of the alchemical parchment quire BL Or. 3669(1) (see Table 14.1).[39]

Evidence from the Coptic-Gnostic Codex Tchacos (Table 14.2) has recently been dealt with by Rodolphe Kasser,[40] who quoted a number of examples from elsewhere (Table 14.3).

Table 14.1. Hybrid numerals in BL Or. 3669(1)

Attestation	Form	Composed of	Rendering
BL Or. 3669(1) *passim*	ⲟⲩα	ⲟⲩⲁ 'one' + ⲁ '1'	'ole'
BL Or. 3669(1) *passim*	ⲥⲃ	ⲥⲛⲁⲩ 'two' + ⲃ '2'	'2wo'
BL Or. 3669(1) VII^r 6	ⲥⲛⲃ	ⲥⲛⲁⲩ 'two' + ⲃ '2'	'T2wo'
BL Or. 3669(1) VIv 1	ⲥⲍ	ⲥⲁϣϥ 'seven' + ⲍ '7'	'Se7en'

Table 14.2. Hybrid numerals in Codex Tchacos

Attestation	Form	Composed of	Rendering
Codex Tchacos 11,10; 21,21	ϣⲅ̄	ϣⲟⲙⲛⲧ 'three' + ⲅ '3'	'Th3ee'
Codex Tchacos 25,19	ⲥⲍ̄ϥⲉ	ⲥⲁϣϥⲉ 'seven' + ⲍ '7'	'Se7en'
Codex Tchacos 12,15	ⲙⲛⲧ[ⲓⲃ̄]	ⲙⲛⲧⲥⲛⲟⲟⲩⲥ 'twelve' + ⲓⲃ '12'	'Twel2e'
Codex Tchacos 44,21; 46,20	ⲙⲛⲧⲓⲅ̄	ⲙⲛⲧϣⲟⲙⲛⲧ 'thirteen' + ⲓⲅ '13'	'Thirl3en'
Codex Tchacos 24,26	ⲙⲛⲧⲓⲍ̄	ⲙⲛⲧⲥⲁϣϥ 'seventeen' + ⲓⲍ '17'	'Sevenl7en'
Codex Tchacos 13,5; 23,2	ϣⲟⲃ̄	ϣϥⲉⲥⲛⲟⲟⲩⲥ 'seventy-two' + ⲟⲃ '72'	'Se7enty-2wo'

Table 14.3. Hybrid numerals in other corpora

Attestation	Form	Composed of	Rendering
P.Bodmer III, Joh 4,35; 11,39; 19,23	ϥⲇ̄	ϥⲧⲟⲟⲩ 'four' + ⲇ '4'	'fou4'
P.Bodmer III, Joh 6,67	ⲙⲉⲧⲓ̄ⲃ̄	ⲙⲉⲧⲥⲛⲟⲟⲩⲥ 'twelve' + ⲓⲃ '12'	'Twel2e'
Kellia, MSAC 1999, p. 116	ϫⲟⲩⲕⲇ̄	ϫⲟⲩⲧⲁϥⲧ 'twenty-four' + ⲕⲇ '24'	'T2enty-fou4'
P.Lond.Copt. I 524, Kropp I, C12	ϥⲇ̄	ϥⲧⲟⲟⲩ 'four' + ⲇ '4'	'fou4'

"à la grecque", mais aussi, assez souvent, par une formule hybride, surtout si tel graphème du *chiffre* se trouve, par hasard, être identique ou similaire à tel graphème du *nom* du nombre. Example "quatre", chiffre ⲇ̄, nome ϥⲧⲟⲟⲩⲉ, graphie hybride ϥⲇ̄.'

[39] 'Two' is spelled here in three different ways: ⲃ '2', ⲥⲃ '2wo', ⲥⲛⲃ 'T2wo'.

[40] Kasser (2007, 66–8).

In terms of text genre, the distribution of this strategy for spelling numerals is striking. We find very early specimens of Coptic literature such as gnostic and biblical writing, in addition to epigraphic evidence, magic, and late Coptic alchemy. This range of texts closely resembles the distribution of the following phenomenon, the application of cryptographic spellings.

§3.2. Cryptography

Coptic cryptography[41] is based on relatively plain mechanisms of changing letters, all of them depending on Greek cryptographic techniques.[42] The only specifically Coptic aspect of them is the different ways of hiding the six or seven (depending on dialect) specifically Coptic letters not found in Greek. In Bodl. Mss.Copt.(P) a.2 and a.3, this has mostly been managed by writing them upside down. The cryptographic system applied therein works with three rows of letters, inverting the letters of each row and replacing the normal row with the inverted one, such as α, β, γ, δ, ε, ς, ζ, η, θ, ι becoming ι, θ, η, ζ, ς, ε, δ, γ, β, α, etc.[43]

In such a system, the fifth letter of each row, particularly epsilon and nu, would have to change places with itself. In order to avoid this, these letters were replaced by two non-alphabetic signs: three horizontal strokes (standing for E) and three vertical strokes (representing N). Consequently, since epsilon and nu are particularly common letters, virtually every cryptographically spelled word or passage bears the stigma of cryptography on its face; the system was thus hiding and at the same time revealing itself. Coptic cryptography is a phenomenon of limited frequency,[44] and it is clearly restricted in terms of text genres. The spectrum of texts that make occasional use of cryptography turns out to be identical with that of texts that make occasional use of hybrid numeral spellings. It includes scribal colophons from the Gnostic library of Nag Hammadi and from tenth- to twelfth-century Coptic literary manuscripts,[45] epigraphic texts,[46] magical texts,[47] and late Coptic scientific manuscripts including the alchemical Bodl.Mss.Copt.(P) a.1, a.2, and a.3.[48] These scribal strategies are not a purely random, idiosyncratic *Glasperlenspiel*, but rather a highly marked kind of practice. Their occurrence thus strikes me as a shibboleth, a group code indicating not just individual skills, but a specific milieu, a shared intellectual

41 Cf. Wisse (1979) and Doresse (1991).

42 Cf. Menci (2008).

43 Doresse (1991, 65–6).

44 Doresse (1991, 65a) estimated that 'about thirty examples [of textual units] . . . have been recorded'. Their number has increased in the meantime, but not tremendously.

45 This is just one of the numerous features shared by Coptic scribal colophons and Coptic epigraphy.

46 This observation strongly contradicts the implicit assumption that hiding information could have been a concern, or even the main concern, in a scribe's choice to employ cryptography.

47 Erman (1895), Kropp (1930–1), Wisse (1979).

48 As well as the Papyrus Médical Copte (see n. 2).

socialization, a text community, or a scribal network where such skills, as well as the underlying attitudes towards language and writing, were cultivated and transmitted over centuries.[49]

§3.3. Arabic Letters

A rare case of graphic code switching from Coptic to Arabic signs[50] is attested in Bodl.Ms.Copt.(P) a.2, line 69, where, in the middle of a list of different kinds of honey,[51] a string of nine Arabic letters is inserted, possibly to be read (from right to left): *ʾ – q – n – kh – ʾ – n – k – s – h* (ex. 12):

12. Bodl.Ms.Copt.(P) a.2,68–9
ⲙⲛⲟⲩⲱⲓ ⲛⲁⲗⲟⲩⲥⲱⲗ ⲛⲁⲣⲁⲧⲡⲉ ⲙⲛⲟⲩⲥⲱⲗ اقنخانكسه  ⲟⲩⲥⲱⲗ ⲣⲱⲙⲁⲛ ⲛϩⲁⲙⲏⲗ̅ ⲙⲛⲟⲩⲥⲱⲗ ⲣⲱⲙⲁⲛ ϩⲱⲗⲱ

'and a unit of clover honey and… -honey and honey of pomegranate and of figs and honey of sweet pomegranate.'

Their meaning is still not understood, although the context suggests that the reference is to another specification of honey. Although it seems likely that all Coptic alchemical texts were (more or less literally) rendered from Arabic,[52] I do not think we are faced here with a source-language island left behind as a result of incomplete translation, but rather with a code in its own right. However, it is not even certain that the language is Arabic. If not, the direction in which the string should be read is also questionable.

§3.4. 'Scientific Signs': *Sêmeîa Tês Epistêmês*

A further graphical code applied in Bodl.Mss.Copt.(P) a.2 and a.3 involves symbolic signs taken from the repertoire of the so-called *sêmeîa tês epistêmês* (exx. 13–19).[53]

a) ☉ Sun = χρυσός, ⲣⲏ 'gold', e.g.
13. Bodl.Ms.Copt.(P) a.2,14
ϣⲁⲃⲉⲣ☉ ⲉ̣ⲛ̣ⲁ̣ⲛ̣ⲟ̣ⲩ̣ϥ̣ 'it will become fine "gold"'.

[49] One may speculate that a text like the treatise about the mysteries of the letters of the Greek alphabet, recently re-edited by Brandt (2007), may not have been alien to these people.

[50] A rare case of sentence-internal linguistic code switching from Arabic to Coptic and back again is found in tenth-century personal letters; see Delattre et al. (2012). For text-internal switches, see, e.g., the magical text P.Heid.inv.Kopt. 500+501 ed. Bilabel and Grohmann (1934) (see n. 2).

[51] The Coptic word ⲟⲩⲥⲱⲗ is the Arabic *ʿusûl*, plural of *ʿasal*.

[52] See Richter (2009 and 2015). [53] See Zuretti (1932).

b) ☽ Moon = ἄργυρος, ϩⲁⲧ 'silver', e.g.

14. Bodl.Ms.Copt.(P) a.2,21
ϩⲓϫⲱ μιλ α ☽ ⲉⲛⲁⲛⲟⲩϥ 'on 1 Mil. (of) fine "silver" '.

15. Bodl.Ms.Copt.(P) a.2,21
ϫⲓ α ⲛⲁⲕ ⲛϩⲏⲧϥ ⲟⲩⲁ ⲛ☽ 'take 1 (quantity) of it (and) one (quantity) of "silver" '.

c) □ Rectangle = πέταλον, ⲡⲟⲕϥ 'sheet of metal', e.g.

16. Bodl.Ms.Copt.(P) a.2,1
ϫⲓ ⲛⲁⲕ □ ⲛⲃⲁⲣⲱⲑ 'take a "sheet" of copper.'

17. Bodl.Ms.Copt.(P) a.2,3
ⲁ̣ⲁ̣ϥ̣ □ 'make it "a sheet" '

18. Bodl.Ms.Copt.(P) a.2,4–5
ϣⲁⲛⲧⲉⲕⲁⲁϥ ⲛ□ 'until you (have) made it (into) a "sheet" '.

19. Bodl.Ms.Copt.(P) a.3 r° 38–9
ⲉⲕⲓⲣⲉ ⲛⲙⲟϥ ⲛ□ 'while you make it (into) a "sheet".

More closely than any code used by our scribe, this remarkable type of sign is related to one particular kind of text, namely to alchemical literature *strictu sensu*. The connection of planets with metals[54] underlying its pairs of astrological *signifiants* and alchemical *signifiés* (such as sun = gold, moon = silver) evokes the late Egyptian, as well as Stoic and middle Platonic, concept of universal sympathy.[55] The same repertoire of astrological signs symbolizing metals and metallic compounds is attested also in Greek and Arabic alchemical manuscripts, as well as in medieval and early modern Western alchemy, chemistry, and pharmacy. The designation *sêmeîa tês epistêmês* occurs in the most ancient (and most important) witness of the Corpus Chymicum Graecum, the Codex Venice San Marco 299,[56] where a list of signs and their meanings is titled: 'Scientific signs (*sêmeîa tês epistêmês*) of the philosophers as contained in the technical writings, especially in those of the so-called mystical philosophy among them' (Figure 14.5).[57]

[54] In Egypt, this is attested as early as in the second/third century CE in a demotic ostraca from Narmouthis, OMM 1229; see Menchetti and Pintaudi (2007, 230–2, no. 1).

[55] See Richter (2010b).

[56] Ed. Berthelot and Ruelle (1888). Codex Macianus 299 is dated by Greek palaeographers to the late tenth or early eleventh century. Strikingly enough, it is partially written in a bimodular uncial. While the alchemical texts transmitted in this manuscript are written in the Greek minuscule bookhand of the time, the catalogue of *sêmeîa tês epistêmês*, as well as some subtitles to alchemical drawings, are written in this typically Egyptian (sometimes so-called Alexandrian, or Coptic) uncial. This fact seems to provide evidence for an Egyptian stage in the manuscript transmission behind this copy.

[57] Codex Macianus 299 (Berthelot and Ruelle 1888), fol. 6: σημεῖα τῆς ἐπιστήμης τῶν ἐγκειμένων ἐν τοῖς τεχνικοῖς συγγράμμασι τῶν φιλοσόφων καὶ μάλιστα τῆς μυστικῆς παρ᾽ αὐτοῖς λεγομένης φιλοσοφίας. Extant lists of *sêmeîa tês epistêmês* have been edited by Zuretti (1932).

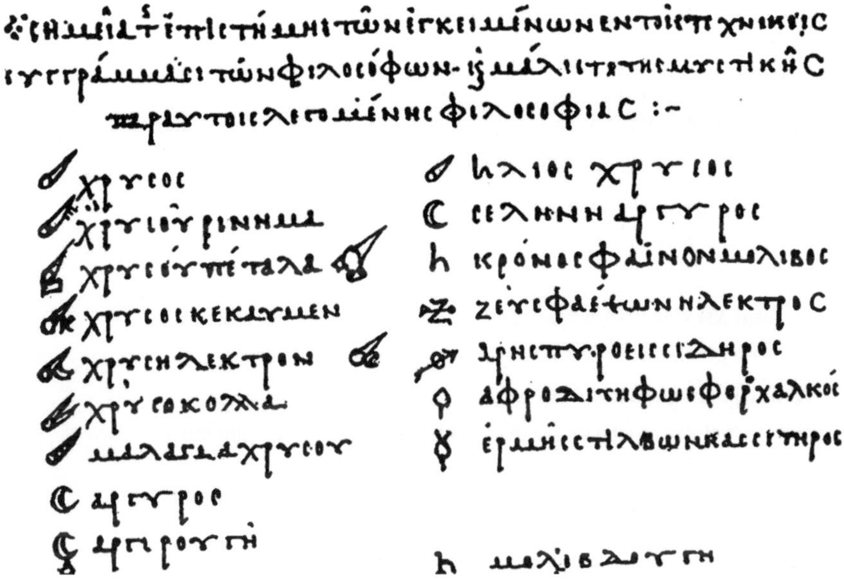

Fig. 14.5. *Sêmeîa tês epistêmês* according to Codex Marcianus 299, fol. 6 (Berthelot 1909, pl. II)

§3.4.1. *Grammatical insertion and syntactic reach of the* sêmeîa tês epistêmês

It is interesting to look at how such different signs as phonetic and symbolic ones interact when combined in a text. Once incorporated into Coptic syntax, the meaning of the symbols ☉ 'gold', ☽ 'silver', and □ 'sheet metal' is not narrowly restricted to pure semantics but can also be integrated into the grammatical framework. There are cases such as the Coptic construct state formation requiring a bare noun, where the pure content of the symbol—the bare sememe ('gold', 'silver')—is sufficient to be used in the Coptic syntactic environment (ex. 20):

20. Bodl.Ms.Copt.(P) a.3, r° 63
ϣⲁⲃⲉⲣ☉ ⲕⲁⲗⲱⲥ 'it will rightly become gold.'

In cases of a marked choice, such as the definite article occurring with an essentially indefinite referent such as the mass noun 'gold', the embedding construction has to be made overt by the explicitly spelled-out article (ex. 21):

21. Bodl.Ms.Copt.(P) a.2,37
ϣⲁⲕⲧⲁⲗⲱϥ ⲉⲡ☉ 'you shall add it to (ⲉ-) the (ⲡ-) gold (☉).'

However, if an unmarked determination (indefinite article) or a construction mediated by morphematic (object-marking or attributive) ⲛ- are required syntactically, these grammatical elements can be implied using the symbol (exx. 22–30):

22. Bodl.Ms.Copt.(P) a.2,17
ⲛⲁⲛⲟⲩϥ ⲉ̣σ̸ ⲙⲛ☽ 'it is better than (preposition ⲉ + indefinite article ⲟⲩ-) gold and (preposition ⲙⲛ + indefinite article ⲟⲩ-) silver.'

23. Bodl.Ms.Copt.(P) a.2,1
ϫ̣ⲓ ⲛⲁⲕ □ ⲛⲃⲁⲣⲱⲑ 'take a (object marker ⲛ- + indefinite article ⲟⲩ-?) sheet of copper.'

24. Bodl.Ms.Copt.(P) a.3, r° 7–8
ϫ̣ⲓ α ⲛⲁⲣⲙⲁⲣⲕⲁ°/ σ̸ 'take 1 (unit) Markas(ita-stone) of (attributive ⲛ-) gold.'

25. Bodl.Ms.Copt.(P) a.2,32
ⲕⲟⲩⲱϣ σ̸ ⲉⲓϭⲣⲓ ⲙⲙⲟϥ 'if you want (object marker ⲛ- + indefinite article ⲟⲩ-) gold, let it melt.'

26. Bodl.Ms.Copt.(P) a.2,39.72
ⲧⲁⲗⲟ ⲟⲩα ⲗⲟⲩα σ̸ 'add one (unit) to one (unit) of (attributive ⲛ-) gold.'

27. Bodl.Ms.Copt.(P) a.2,39–40
ⲉⲕϣⲁⲛⲧⲓ □ ⲛⲗⲁⲗⲩ 'if you add a (indefinite article ⲟⲩ-) white sheet of metal.'

28. Bodl.Ms.Copt.(P) a.2,42
δ □ ⲛⲗⲁⲗⲩ ⲙⲛα ⲛⲧⲁϩⲧ '4 (quantities) of (attributive ⲛ-) white sheet and 1 of lead.'

29. Bodl.Ms.Copt.(P) a.2,66a
ϣⲁⲣⲉⲡⲉϥⲗⲉⲓⲛ ⲉⲓⲛⲉ σ̸ 'its colour will become like (ⲉⲓⲛⲉ ⲛ-ⲟⲩ-[58]) gold.'

30. Bodl.Ms.Copt.(P) a.3, r° 41–2
ⲗⲁⲡⲟⲩⲣⲁⲧⲉ σ̸ ... ⲗⲁⲡⲟⲩⲣⲁⲧⲉ ☽ ... 'filings of (attributive ⲛ-) gold ... filings of (attributive ⲛ-) silver.'

While this implicit junction, as it were, frequently involves 'left-side' implications (this is to say, grammatical affixes which, if spelled out, would stand in front of the symbol), it is only sporadically attested when 'right-side' implications (i.e. functional language following the symbol), such as the relative marker ⲉ-, are concerned (exx. 31–2):

31. Bodl.Ms.Copt.(P) a.2,3
ⲟ̣ⲩϣ̣ⲓ σ̸ ⲟ̣ⲩⲁ̣ⲑ 'one unit of melted (relative construction ⲉ⸗ϥ-ⲟ̣ⲩⲁ̣ⲑ) gold.'

32. Bodl.Ms.Copt.(P) a.2,24
ⲟⲩⲁ ⲛ☽ ⲛⲁⲛ̣ⲟⲩϥ 'one (unit) of fine (relative construction ⲉ-ⲛⲁⲛ̣ⲟⲩϥ) silver'

[58] Crum (1939, 80b).

§4. WHAT WAS THE PURPOSE OF AND WHERE ARE THE ORIGINS OF THE MULTIPLICITY OF CODES?

I would like to conclude by asking what insights this inspection of a tenth-century Coptic scribe's bag of tricks provides, in terms of assumed functions and traceable origins of the tools and practices found therein. Although to some extent we can only speculate about the reasons for our scribe's extra efforts, it seems that explanations can actually be proposed for most of them, such as:

- A general form of professionalism, exposed by specifically scientific scribal registers.
- A particular form of scribal self-consciousness, expressed by a graphemic repertoire of scribal 'group codes' such as cryptography and playful numeral spelling.
- Deliberate incomprehensibility by means of obfuscating strategies applied to texts dealing with secret sciences such as alchemy, in order to keep specific parts of knowledge from unworthy readers.

In terms of the origin of the diverse practices employed by our scribe, we have already mentioned a number of possible places of origin and means of transmission that point to some different directions:

- The Coptic scriptorium tradition, its technical habits and aesthetic standards, its institutional support, and its forms of education.
- The Coptic documentary tradition, i.e. the sphere of (semi-)institutional and (semi-)professional, yet more or less formal production of Coptic day-to-day writings[59]—a tradition which, as far as we know, was no longer productive in the tenth century, but obviously was still known and available to some extent.
- Specific scientific traditions, including not only formalized terminologies but also formalized ways of presenting and symbolizing them.
- Last, but not least, manuscript interference with Arabic, indicating a bilingual milieu of intellectual exchange between Arabs and Copts.[60]

[59] See Bucking (2007a), Cromwell (2010a), Richter (2008a, 1–4).

[60] Another feature of Bodl.Mss.Copt.(P) a.1, 2, and 3 pointing to manuscript interference with Arabic is their use of word division, as opposed to the *scriptio continua* of earlier Coptic manuscripts.

15

'These Two Lines...'

Hebrew and Judaeo-Arabic Letter Writing in the Classical Genizah Period

Esther-Miriam Wagner and Ben Outhwaite

§1. INTRODUCTION

> 'I, whose signature follows at the end of these two lines, am obliged to inform our honourable lord that I have indeed arrived... and am now in Benhā'.
>
> (T-S 10J9.14, a Hebrew letter written in Egypt, *c.*1150 CE)[1]

With 193,000 fragments in the Taylor-Schechter Collection alone, the manuscripts of the Cairo Genizah are a source without parallel for the literary history of the Jews of North Africa and the Middle East. While there is no aspect of Jewish letters (in the broadest sense of the word) that has not been profoundly affected by the nineteenth-century discovery of these manuscripts, the documentary texts of the Genizah, in particular, have opened up new vistas for the study of Jewish life in the Middle East of the Middle Ages, freeing scholars from relying on the scarce contemporary 'historical' accounts, with their attendant problems and unreliabilities.[2]

As primary historical sources, the thousands of letters written by Jews between the end of the tenth century and the middle of the thirteenth century, the 'classical Genizah period' (equating to the periods of Fatimid and Ayyubid

[1] The T-S (Taylor-Schechter), Or. (Oriental), and Mosseri (Jacques Mosseri) manuscripts quoted in this paper are from the Cairo Genizah Collection at Cambridge University Library; the Lewis-Gibson manuscripts are from the Lewis-Gibson Collection at the Bodleian Libraries, Oxford, and Cambridge University Library; ENA is the Elkan Nathan Adler Collection of the Jewish Theological Seminary, New York; Halper is the Halper Collection at the University of Pennsylvania; AIU is the collection at the Alliance Israélites Universelle, Paris; Freer refers to the Freer Collection of Genizah manuscripts at the Smithsonian Institution, Washington DC.

[2] For a general introduction to the Cairo Genizah manuscripts, see Reif (2000).

rule in Egypt), have enabled researchers to meticulously record the social, economic, and political history of the Jewish communities of Iraq, Syria-Palestine, Egypt, and North Africa for a period of several hundred years.[3]

The Jews of Cairo and other leading Jewish communities around the Mediterranean not only frequently wrote letters, but, either through piety—to avoid defacing the name of God or consigning something written in the 'Holy Language' (which perhaps extended to anything in Hebrew characters, rather than just the Hebrew language itself) to the rubbish heap—or through thrift—paper and vellum were expensive and could be (and frequently were) reused—letters from every major period of Jewish life in the medieval East were deposited in the Genizah chamber of the Ben Ezra Synagogue in Fusṭāṭ (Old Cairo). Most importantly for posterity, they deliberately preserved them. The Collection is richest in material from the early eleventh through to the mid thirteenth century, when the Jewish community in Egypt was at its peak of prosperity and culture, before its decline under the more oppressive rule of the Mamluks.

Letters were an essential means of communication for the Jews living under Islam in the Middle Ages. The traditional seats of Jewish learning and halakhic (religio-legal) governance were in Baghdad (the rabbinical academies, the *yeshivot*, of Sura and Pumbeditha) and, to a lesser extent, in Jerusalem (the Palestinian Yeshiva). Their constituencies, though, were scattered across the Jewish world, with the *geʾonim* (the heads of rabbinic academies) of both Babylon (Iraq) and Palestine seeking to maintain a particular hold over their followers in Egypt, the principal source of charitable funds for the academies. Letters frequently passed between Egypt and Palestine and Egypt and Iraq, as Jews in the bustling and prosperous cities sought halakhic knowledge, legal rulings, influence, and political advantage from the *geʾonim*; and the *geʾonim*, the *nesiʾim* (members of the Jewish aristocracy, who could trace their lineage back to the biblical King David), and other dignitaries sought to govern their distant communities, dispense judgement, and ensure the continued flow of funding. At a lower level, letters passed between communal officials and leading citizens, between petitioners and public servants, and across all walks of life, as the deeply literate Jewish community recorded its everyday activities in epistolary form.

Beyond communal governance, however, Jews were also heavily involved in international trade. Whether it was the import of wheat from Libya or copper goods from India, a network of Jewish traders relied upon the written letter to organize their cargoes, settle their debts, or just discuss the latest political rumours. Hundreds of letters exchanged between traders in Cairo, Alexandria, Qayrawān, ʿAyḏāb, and Aden, among other major trading centres, were consigned to the Genizah chamber, preserving an authentic first-hand account of trading life on the Mediterranean Sea and Indian Ocean in the High Middle Ages.

[3] An excellent recent study of the Jews of the Fatimid Empire, based almost entirely on the documentary sources unearthed in the Genizah, is Rustow (2008).

Hebrew, *lešon ha-qodeš*, the sacred Jewish tongue, had not been a spoken vernacular for centuries in the Jewish Near East, yet as a written vernacular—in the form of letters—it flourished in the late tenth and the first half of the eleventh centuries, returning with a revival of interest in the Hebrew language in Egypt in the thirteenth century and, once more, in the sixteenth century with the arrival in the eastern Mediterranean of non-Arabic-speaking Jews from Spain. Previously, Aramaic had been the vernacular of the Jews of Iraq, Palestine, and Egypt, and had been employed in international correspondence, as the *responsa* literature (answers to halakhic queries issued by rabbinical authorities) shows. But with the Arab conquest came a new vernacular, and an initial reluctance to use the written language of the conquerors appears to have led to a revival of Hebrew for correspondence, as widespread knowledge of Aramaic evaporated. Hebrew served most effectively as the language of international Jewry, linking Jews in every country despite their differences in spoken language. Moreover, it was liturgically acceptable and a fitting language for Jewish communication, unlike Arabic; letters in Hebrew could be read out to the assembled congregation in the synagogue, the principal means of spreading news. For this reason, Hebrew was advanced by the *geʾonim* as the language of communication in the Jewish world, until the decline and uprooting of the gaonate in Iraq and Palestine led to a move towards a more local system of Jewish government, and the emphasis shifted to local rather than international communication.

While Hebrew fitted the needs and aims of Geonic communication, and was often emulated at a more local level, for other Jewish letter writers, the vernacular—at least in its Judaized form—was sufficient. Written in Hebrew characters and replete with Hebraisms, dialectal features, and pseudo-classical corrections, Judaeo-Arabic served different Jewish constituencies as a primary means of written communication. For business and trade purposes, for low-level communal activities, and for the exchange of letters between close family members, Judaeo-Arabic was the favoured means of written communication, a more prosaic alternative to the sacred language. From the earliest period of Genizah documents, the late tenth century, Judaeo-Arabic letters are attested alongside Hebrew letters. As time went on, the proportion of Judaeo-Arabic correspondence being written—and, importantly, being deposited in the Genizah—increased, until the late eleventh century, when little Hebrew correspondence can be detected. Subsequent revivals of Hebrew in the late twelfth to early thirteenth centuries, and in the Ottoman period, appear to arise from a combination of a renewed interest in Jewish learning in Egypt and immigration into the area by Jews from non-Arabic-speaking countries.

In the earliest Genizah period, Hebrew and Judaeo-Arabic served side by side as Jewish epistolary languages. It is too simplistic to divide Jewish letter writing purely by function, into Hebrew for Geonic, communal, and international communication, and Judaeo-Arabic for personal, familial, and business communication, or, as has been suggested, between the predominantly aesthetic and the predominantly communicative.[4] The *geʾonim* of both Iraq and Palestine were champions of Hebrew letters, but, from Saʿadya Gaʾon onwards, they increasingly employed Judaeo-Arabic in their literary works. Moreover, on occasion, they resorted to Judaeo-Arabic in their correspondence, too, particularly when dealing with private political matters, when writing to family members, or when they were unsure as to whether their correspondent was sufficiently accustomed to the Holy Tongue to be presented with a whole letter's worth.[5] In these cases, the correspondence often tends to be framed as a Hebrew letter, with the effusively polite opening and closing blessings in Hebrew, but with the main body in Judaeo-Arabic.

The *geʾonim* were the epitome of Jewish culture: the Palestinian Academy was the medieval descendant of the Talmudic Sanhedrin, the seat of Jewish government in the Holy Land. It is no wonder that successive heads of the Palestinian Yeshiva preferred to communicate with their followers in Egypt in the Holy Tongue, the language of the Bible and of the Rabbis. The Jewish mercantile class, however, was immersed in the culture of the ruling empire; Jewish merchants carried out their business in Arabic, they went into partnership with Muslims, and the most influential of them had access to the very highest levels of the Islamic rulership. Eschewing the language of the Bible for their correspondence, their letters reflect the contemporary Arabic-speaking world around them, albeit written in Hebrew characters. Viewed this way, it seems that we are dealing with two very different kinds of letter writing—that of the Geonic tradition, steeped in Jewish history, and that of the integrated Jew, a trader or businessman, who affected a more contemporary communicative mode.

Other than the clear linguistic separation between Hebrew and Judaeo-Arabic letters, stylistically, at a quite superficial level, they can display different traits: for instance, Hebrew letters tend to be more florid than the more concise Judaeo-Arabic letters, and, on the whole, Hebrew letters show a higher degree of penmanship. But this may reflect the general difference in content between the two (diplomatic missives versus business communications, for instance, or a letter to a distinguished scholar versus a letter to a spouse), or it may reflect the educational background of the writer, rather than be derived from a format imposed by the epistolary tradition involved. To what extent can we see these two Jewish worlds—traditional versus contemporary, Hebrew versus Arabic, (more) religious versus (more) secular—codified in the two principal modes of letter writing? Are Hebrew letter writers consciously adopting a more

[4] For instance, Drory (1992, 60–1) sees a division of function between Hebrew and Judaeo-Arabic, the former as opaque and aesthetic, the latter as transparent and communicative. Blau (1999, 232–8) rightly points to this as an oversimplification, but suggests that nevertheless 'the literary-aesthetic facet of Hebrew is more pronounced'.

[5] For an examination of this subject in reference to the Hebrew and Judaeo-Arabic letters of the Palestinian Gaʾon Solomon b. Judah, see Outhwaite (2004).

traditional template when writing? Do Judaeo-Arabic letters strive to emulate Arabic epistolographic traditions? To suggest an answer to these questions, and to assess whether the differences between Hebrew and Judaeo-Arabic correspondence are anything more than the most obvious ones of language or content, we shall examine three major features common to letter writing in the documentary Genizah of the High Middle Ages (known as the 'classical Genizah period', the eleventh to the thirteenth centuries): the manner in which the letter is addressed; the invocation of the deity, if any; and the way in which the letter is dated. Through an examination of these three issues, we hope to establish the extent to which the flowering of the epistolary art in the classical Genizah period owes much to a Jewish tradition of letters or draws greatly upon the wider influence of the surrounding Islamic world.

§2. ADDRESSING A LETTER

> 'To the dear, glorious, honourable, great, and holy, our master and teacher Sahlān, Head of the Row—may God be his aid and his shadow's shade—son of the honourable, great, and holy, our master and teacher Abraham, Member of the Academy—may his soul be bound up in the bundle of life! A great salvation!'
>
> (T-S 13J26.1, address of a Hebrew letter sent from Jerusalem to Egypt, *c.*1029)

In letters from Egypt in the eleventh and early twelfth centuries, the address of the intended recipient is found on the reverse of the leaf, in several lines across the width of the page, often, but not always, upside down in relation to the text on the recto. Once a writer had finished composing his letter, he would fold it up upon itself, starting from the bottom of recto and making small folds at approximately two-inch intervals. Once finished, the address would be written on one or, sometimes, both sides of the resulting folded package in the blank space that had been left for this purpose on the verso of the letter (see Figure 15.1). Letters recovered from the Genizah retain very clear marks of this regular folding, even after nearly a millennium of neglectful storage (see Figure 15.2).

While all letters have this basic shape in the eleventh and twelfth centuries across the Jewish communities of North Africa and the Middle East, the manner in which the address is written noticeably differs across linguistic and geographical boundaries.

In Judaeo-Arabic letters from Egypt and North Africa, the address is written across the width of the leaf, but divided into two sections. On the right-hand side the name of the addressee, with his attendant titles and location, appears, sometimes with the additional embellishment of blessings for his good health

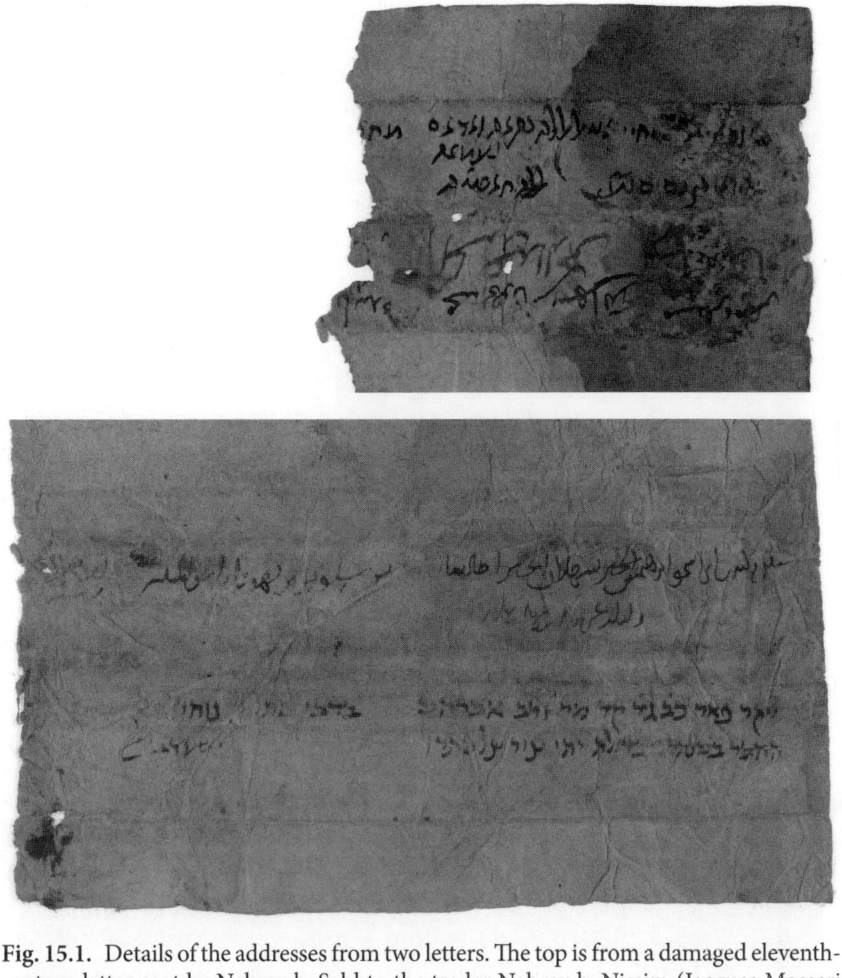

Fig. 15.1. Details of the addresses from two letters. The top is from a damaged eleventh-century letter sent by Nahray b. Sahl to the trader Nahray b. Nissim (Jacques Mosseri Collection at Cambridge University Library, Mosseri Ia.12.2). The sender wrote the address on both sides of the letter, once it was folded up. One side is addressed in Judaeo-Arabic and the other in Arabic (upside down in relation to the other address). The image at the bottom is a detail of the address from the verso of a letter by the Palestinian Gaʾon Solomon b. Judah (Mosseri Ia.27). Again, he wrote the address on both sides of the folded-up letter, but this time in Arabic and Hebrew versions (both oriented the same way up). As is his custom, he writes only the name of the recipient and not the sender. Reproduced by kind permission of the Syndics of Cambridge University Library.

or on his departed father. The left-hand side bears the name of the sender, sometimes accompanied by the sender's motto (in Arabic, his *ʿalāma*) or a general wish for the speedy delivery of the letter or some statement of the relationship between sender and addressee. There is a distinct gap between the two parts of the address. Examples of this format are numerous; T-S 13J17.1, to a leading Jewish trader of the mid eleventh century, is typical:

Fig. 15.2. The verso of a complete letter by Solomon b. Judah, addressed in Arabic (Jacques Mosseri Collection at Cambridge University Library, Mosseri Ia.4). We have added lines in order to highlight the original folds. Reproduced by kind permission of the Syndics of Cambridge University Library.

1. T-S 13J17.1

מן מרדוך בן מוסי נ'נ'	1. לסידי ומולאי אבי יחיי נהראי בן נסים נ'נ'
יצל אל פסטאט אן שא אללה	2. אטאל אללה בקאה ואדאם סלאמה וסעאדתה
1. From Mardūk b. Mūsā,	To my lord and master Abī Yaḥyā Nahray b. Nissim,
2. may it reach Fusṭāṭ, God willing.	may God prolong his life and make his well-being and good fortune lasting.

Although structurally similar, correspondence in Hebrew from the earliest Genizah period does not usually address letters in this way. Geonic letters from Palestine generally note only the name of the addressee on the reverse of the letter, attaching some kind of blessing as politeness dictates; for example, when Josiah Ga'on (d. 1025) writes to his followers in Damietta (Dumyāṭ, in the Nile Delta), the address, in a single line across the width of the page, reads: אל אחינו קהל דמיאט הי כפתור ובית דין הזקינים שמרם צור, 'To our brothers the community of Damietta—'the Isle of Caphtor'—and to the Court of the Elders, the Rock (=God) preserve them' (T-S 13J26.16).[6] The same writer sends a Judaeo-Arabic letter to Gaza (T-S 12.16, with an address in Hebrew), addressed similarly, but over two lines: 'To our master Solomon the judge, son of Saʿadya the judge—his rest be in Eden—and the elders, and the rest of the holy community who dwell in Rafaḥ—may the Rock (=God) preserve them. A good deliverance!'.[7]

A divided address like that of Egyptian Judaeo-Arabic correspondence can be found in letters from Palestine; nevertheless, it usually features only the addressee's name (and that of his father) and titles. For instance, the prolific letter writer Solomon b. Judah addresses two letters, one Hebrew and one Judaeo-Arabic (towards the end of his career, 1045–50) in a virtually identical manner: 'To our precious, honourable, and holy master and teacher Abraham, the precious elder—may the Rock preserve him and bless him', followed by a gap and then 'son of the master and teacher Solomon—his rest be in Eden. A great deliverance!' (T-S 18J4.15, a letter in Hebrew); 'To our great, honourable, holy master and teacher Nathaniel ha-Levi, the honoured elder—may the Rock bless him and protect him', a gap and then 'son of [our] master and teacher Ḥalfon the elder—his rest be in Eden. A great deliverance!' (T-S 18J4.25, a letter in Judaeo-Arabic, but addressed in Hebrew). The sender's name is not noted in the address of the letter because it was the practice of the *ge'onim* to either head

[6] 'The Isle of Caphtor' is a toponym found in the Hebrew Bible (Jeremiah 47:4), which may originally have referred to Crete. It is a feature of Geonic Hebrew letters from Palestine that they often refer to contemporary places using place names taken from the Bible, presumably in order to avoid writing Arabic words in an otherwise Hebrew document. Solomon b. Judah (d. 1051), for instance, writes a letter (T-S 16.261) to a Jewish doctor in 'the fortress of Sinim' (Isaiah 49:12), which is Tripoli, avoiding using the Arabic name Ṭarābulus or Ṭarābulus al-Šām ('Syrian Tripoli', to distinguish it from Tripoli in Libya).

[7] 'A good deliverance', ישע טוב (*yeša ṭov*), was the Ga'on's *ʿalāma* (motto). Appending it to letters was a habit almost certainly derived from the epistolary practices of the Islamic rulers.

their letter with their name and titles (mainly the Babylonian *ge'onim*) or to sign their letter at the end (Solomon b. Judah and some of the other Palestinian *ge'onim*).

One finds Hebrew letters from Palestine that are addressed in an identical manner to that of the Egyptian and North African Judaeo-Arabic correspondence, but they are a distinct rarity in the first quarter of the eleventh century. A letter sent from Ashqelon to Egypt around 1025 (T-S 13J19.15) shows the Egyptian style of address, noting both the addressee ('the two holy communities', which is to say those Jews in Egypt with allegiance to the Palestinian Academy and those with allegiance to the Babylonian Academies) and the sender, the Jewish community in Ashqelon.

2. T-S 13J19.15

Sender	Recipient
1. Seekers of your welfare and inquirers	To the precious, glorious two
2. after your well-being, the community of Ashqelon.	holy communities who dwell in
3. 'May deliverance be hastened in their days!'	Egypt. May they be blessed and supported by kindness.

Because of its good port and connection by sea to Egypt, and because of the difficulties and dangers of overland travel in Palestine, Ashqelon was in many respects closer to the Egyptian and other Mediterranean communities than to the gaonate in Jerusalem.[8]

The origins of the Geonic address format are not clear. Only a few examples of Hebrew correspondence from the preceding pre-Islamic period are preserved (among the Oxyrhynchi papyri, for example) and they are too fragmentary to draw much in the way of conclusions. Bodleian MS. Heb. c. 57, the beginning of an official letter, probably from Fusṭāṭ, Egypt, can be dated to *c.*400 CE.[9] The remains of an address on the verso are illegible, but the letter opens with 'From the heads of the synagogue [and from your brothers] the members of the synagogue which is in [Egypt/Fusṭāṭ]', which is similar to the style used by the earliest letters found in the Genizah, those of the Babylonian *ge'onim*, but which gives no solid evidence as to how the letter might have been addressed on the verso.

While the origins of the Geonic address might be found in the poorly attested Hebrew and Aramaic correspondence of pre-conquest Jewish communities, remarkable parallels to the Egyptian Judaeo-Arabic style can be seen quite clearly in the pre-Islamic epistolary tradition of Egypt. Coptic papyri from Kellis of the fourth century CE, which themselves have borrowed from Greek stylistic traditions, show an identical layout and separation of addressee and

[8] See, for instance, Gil (1992, 757–8), where he notes that in the eleventh century it was argued by a leading Jewish figure, David b. Daniel, that Ashqelon was not actually part of Palestine (Eretz-Israel) at all.

[9] Edited in Cowley (1915, 210–11).

sender on the back of the letter, only reversed (addressee on the left; sender on the right—reflecting the different text direction of Coptic).[10] Clearly, this method of addressing correspondence, necessitated by the narrow folding of finished letters, was in use already in Egypt, before we find so many examples of it in the Genizah.

In Coptic letters, addressee and sender are typically separated by a large X (or cross) or occasionally by more elaborate patterns.[11] Such embellishment is never found in Egyptian Jewish letters, whose epistolary tradition—like that of the Muslims around them—eschewed adornment or religious symbols. The similarity of the layout, however, both in the positioning of the address in relation to the rest of the letter and the grouping of the two elements, is remarkable, and strongly indicates an epistolary tradition that extends over many centuries and crosses cultural boundaries.

By the thirteenth century, Genizah letters as a whole have mostly abandoned these early epistolary traditions. The name of the sender now appears on the front of the letter, in the top left-hand corner, separate from the main body of the text:

3. T-S 13J34.9

מן אם דאוד עמתך

'from Umm Daʾūd, your paternal aunt'

In Judaeo-Arabic correspondence, it is often prefaced with *al-mamlūk*, 'the slave', a formula of obeisance that appears in Arabic petitions from the later Fatimid period:[12]

4. Or. 1080 J28

אלממלוך שלמה ברבי אליה הדיין

'the slave Solomon, son of Elijah the judge'

On the reverse, the intended recipient and sender may still be noted, but typically in an address that reads 'this letter should reach so-and-so, from so-and-so' and lacking the bisection typical of the earlier correspondence. For example, the address of T-S 10J7.2 shows:

5. T-S 10J7.2

1. יצל אלכתאב אלי כב׳ גד׳ קד׳ רבי איליה הדיאן ש״צ
2. מן ממלוכה יוסף אבן יעקב אלכהן

1. 'May this letter reach the honourable, great, and holy Rabbi Elijah the judge
2. From his servant Joseph b. Jacob al-Kohen.'

This is repeated with slight variations in the beginning of the letter on the recto.

[10] See, for instance P.KellisCopt. 11 (P.Kellis V, pp. 128–31 and pl. 4): 'To my master son Psenamoun. X Tsemnouthes your mother.'

[11] See Choat (2006, 114–18).

[12] See the discussion of the petitionary formula, and the examples, in Khan (1993, 306). It first appears in petitions to the Fatimid Caliph al-Āmir (1101–30) and subsequently spread into letter writing.

Often, only the addressee is listed, for example:

6. T-S 13J34.9

1. יצל אלי מחרוסה מצר יסלם לאבן ר׳
2. אליה אלשיך אבו זכרי ושלום

1. 'This letter should arrive to the fortress of Fusṭāṭ to be given to the son of our master
2. Elijah, the *šayḵ* Abū Zikrī. And greetings.'

Or address and sender are written in completely different parts of the page, for example:

7. T-S 13J24.6

i) address:

1. מושב הדרת יקרת צפירת תפארת מרינו ורבינו
2. אליהו הדין החכם והנבון המעוז המגדול ברבי זכריה

1. 'The seat of the glorious, precious, the diadem, the crown, our master and our teacher
2. Elijah the wise and discerning judge, the towering refuge, son of the scholar Zechariah.'

ii) above the address, upside down:

1. מן כאדמה [ושאכר]
2. תפצ׳לה מנצור

1. 'From his servant [and thankful]
2. of his grace, Manṣūr.'

Hebrew letters from Egypt are few in this later period, but those that the Genizah has preserved show a very similar style of address. The writer of T-S 6J2.9, a circa twelfth century Hebrew note asking for assistance in dealing with tax demands, pens his name in a diagonal line above the start of the text, 'His servant Solomon, [who] seeks his well-being.' A letter dated 1212 and addressed to the scholar Anaṭoli b. Joseph (T-S 13J9.9) has an isolated עבדו מנחם, 'his servant Menaḥem' in the top left-hand corner. Although the address is partially lost, it appears to be written in one continuous line, beginning 'Our master and teacher Anaṭoli.'[13]

In the later period, the late twelfth to the thirteenth century, Jewish letters from Egypt and North Africa grow to more closely resemble the style of address

[13] The address of T-S 13J20.18, a Hebrew letter written in Egypt between 1170 and 1189, should not be taken as typical. The letter is finished on the verso, but in place of a simple address we find an extended PS beforehand: 'And no, do not blame me for the handwriting and the paper, because the handwriting is not good and neither is the paper. [I swear that] as our Ga'on lives, I could find no paper better than this. And furthermore, the writing is not good because I am ill and I wrote it [myself]. And I say again: I am ailing in my belly and my eyes, and I cannot stand up. And were it not for the fact that I am ill, I would [have come myself] in place of my letter. And greetings. And may it reach our honourable Ga'on [...].'

used in petitions to the Fatimid and Ayyubid government. The name of the sender—of the petitioner—already appears at the top of Arabic petitions to the Fatimid authorities in the eleventh century, but Jewish letter writers do not absorb and adopt this style until one hundred years later.[14] By that time, however, they are susceptible to further influence, and it is common to find the formula of petitionary obeisance, *al-mamlūk (yuqabbil al-ʾarḍ)* 'the slave (kisses the ground)', used in short or in full, in polite Judaeo-Arabic correspondence.

In the first half of the eleventh century, a distinction can be discerned in the way that Hebrew letter writers, principally the *geʾonim* of Palestine, and Judaeo-Arabic letter writers address their letters. In the twelfth and thirteenth centuries, however, that distinction breaks down, as Hebrew letter writing becomes a waning art, and both Judaeo-Arabic and Hebrew letters come to resemble the formal correspondence of the Islamic state.

§3. INVOKING THE DEITY (*BASMALA* AND ITS EQUIVALENTS)

'In [Your name], O M[erciful] and G[racious One]'.

(T-S 13J20.18, an abbreviated Hebrew invocation on a twelfth-century letter)

The common practice today among orthodox Jews of invoking God's name at the head of a letter can be found in the majority of early modern (i.e. sixteenth century onwards) correspondence from the Genizah, where the abbreviation ב״ה (which stands for בעזרת האל, 'with God's help') is commonplace. This abbreviation is usually written high in the upper margin of the page, separate from the main text, and in some cases in such a highly stylized manner that it is barely intelligible.

The Hebrew invocation 'with God's help' is not used in the earlier period of Genizah letters, the late tenth to late eleventh centuries, at least not as an overarching blessing on the act of writing. It can be found, however, in the address formula used by the Geonic pretender Nathan b. Abraham, in the second quarter of the eleventh century.[15] Here its use is particularly interesting, since it is clearly not intended as a blessing in general—this can be discerned from its

[14] For examples of the different Arabic petitionary forms of the eleventh to thirteenth centuries, see Khan (1993, nos 92–3, 95–6, 99, 101).

[15] Nathan b. Abraham set himself up as a rival to the incumbent Gaʾon of the Palestinian Yeshiva, Solomon b. Judah, in the years 1038–42, a period of great crisis in the Jewish political affairs of Syria-Palestine and Egypt; see Gil (1992, 691–719). During that time, Nathan attempted to appropriate many of the Gaʾon's rights and duties and adopted a more traditional, 'Geonic' style in his letters.

position at the conclusion of the address—but as a Godspeed for the delivery of the letter: 'To the precious, lofty prince, brother of wisdom and discernment, our master and lord Mevorak̠ the wise and discerning, b. [...] David the saint (his rest [be in Eden]). [To] Qayrawān, with God's help (בעזרת אל)' (T-S 8.3, datable to 1037). A variation, 'with God's will' (ברצון אל), is more frequent and occurs in several other letters by the same writer: אלפסטאט ברצון אל, '[To] Fusṭāṭ, God willing' (T-S 8J20.1, datable to 1038) or, with the definite article, פסטאט ברצון האל (Mosseri V.341.1, datable to 1039).

The Arabic–Islamic origins of this blessing on the delivery of the letter become clear when we look at a contemporary Judaeo-Arabic letter, such as that of Abraham b. David, who writes the following address on the verso: לסידי ומולאי אבי אלחסן עלי בן יחזקאל אלחז[א]ן אטאל אללה בקאה ואדאם סלאמתה וסעאדתה אלקדס אן שא אללה 'To our lord and master Abū-l Ḥasan Eli b. Ezekiel the cantor, God preserve him and protect his well-being and his happiness. [To] al-Quds (Jerusalem), God willing' (T-S 12.365, datable to 1039).[16] Clearly the Hebrew phrase *bi-rṣon ha-ʾel* is standing in for the general-purpose Arabic blessing *in šāʾa allāh*, 'God willing', which is found throughout the eleventh century in Judaeo-Arabic and Arabic letters.

The use of *in šāʾa allāh* on the reverse of letters appears towards the end of the second quarter of the eleventh century in Palestinian Jewish correspondence, and may generally be symptomatic of the increasing adoption of the Egyptian Arabic address formula generally, with its clear division between sender and recipient. Prior to the 1030s, the Jerusalem Gaʾon Solomon b. Judah's letters (and indeed those of his predecessors) do not include any blessing on the delivery—only on the recipient as politeness dictates—but by the 1040s we can see that he has adopted a more arabicized version of the address, often actually written in Arabic script, with *in šāʾa allāh* following the addressee's home town: *al-Fusṭāṭ in šāʾa allāh* (Mosseri Ia.4, datable to 1040; T-S 13J23.19, datable to 1042; T-S 13J31.8, datable to 1048).

While *be-ʿezrat ha-ʾel* and its variants appear in the address of Hebrew letters, the more general invocation of God's name, the equivalent of the Arabic–Islamic *basmala*, is notably absent from the earliest extant Hebrew correspondence, which apparently feels no need to call upon the Almighty at the head of the page. This is in clear contrast to Islamic letters of this period, and earlier, which, as a rule, write the *basmala* on a separate line at the head of the text.[17]

[16] Note that in a Judaeo-Arabic letter, the writer is happy to write the Arabic name of the Holy City, Jerusalem, something that would not happen in a Hebrew letter, with its unwillingness to have recourse to the vernacular.

[17] See, for instance, Khan (1990, 8) and the further references given there, and the many examples of Arabic letters opening with the *basmala* in Khan (1992).

Letters written in Judaeo-Arabic also attest a *basmala*, or an equivalent invocation, from an early stage, at least as early as the beginning of the eleventh century; for instance, there is an isolated בשמך, 'in Your name', at the head of a Judaeo-Arabic letter by Yefet b. David of Aleppo, dated to *c.*1010 (T-S 13J35.2). The Arabic *basmala* itself (even in Hebrew characters) is rare, and letter writers use similar expressions, such as על שמך, 'by Your name', which became the most common invocation in the eleventh century—for example, T-S 13J16.23 (datable to 1015), T-S 12.325 (*c.*1030), and T-S Ar. 18(1).101 (1036).

Prefacing the letter with the Arabic *basmala*, *bism illāh al-raḥmān al-raḥīm* 'In the name of God, the merciful and compassionate', either in Arabic script or in Judaeo-Arabic (בסם אללה אלעטים or אללה אלרחמן אלרחים), appears to be a step favoured by only a few Jewish letter writers, most prominent among them Ibrahim b. Farrāḥ, in letters such as T-S 8J18.13 (1050), T-S 8J18.10 (1055), and T-S 13J26.8 (1066). He writes a *basmala* even when he acts as a scribe for others who, in their own correspondence, normally use the 'native' Hebrew or Aramaic form of the invocation—for example, in letters written for Mardūk b. Mūsā, such as T-S 8J20.17 and ENA 2805.21 (both 1046); and contrast Mardūk's letters in his own hand with the invocation בשמך רח' (Halper 385) and בשמ' (AIU VI E 5; both 1046). The *basmala* proper may even be written in Arabic script in a letter otherwise composed completely in Judaeo-Arabic—for example, Mosseri IIIa.11 (1050) and Halper 396 (1030).

Hebrew letter writers do not appear to have adopted the custom of prefacing their text with a concise invocation until some decades after its first use in Judaeo-Arabic correspondence. An equivalent of the Arabic *basmala*—in both form and function—does begin to be used later in the eleventh century, however, with the Aramaic phrase בשמך רחמנא, 'in Your name, O Merciful', and its abbreviated variants (בשמ' רחמ', etc.) prominently heading a number of letters.[18]

That it takes longer to make its way into the stylistic canon of the Hebrew letter writer strongly suggests that the practice had its origins in the Arabic-writing Islamic world, and that it entered Jewish epistolography through Judaeo-Arabic emulation of Islamic stylistics.[19]

[18] It should be noted that in some cases its appearance is anachronistic, since medieval copies were made of the correspondence of prominent personalities, sometimes many decades after their original composition. Sherira Ga'on, for instance, head of the Pumbeditha Yeshiva at the end of the tenth century, opens his letters with his own name and titles, following the style of earlier Babylonian *ge'onim*. Mosseri IV.6, a letter by Sherira in Hebrew and Judaeo-Arabic, prefaces this standard opening with the abbreviation רחמ' בשמ'. The handwriting, however, is not contemporary with the Ga'on, and evidently represents a later period when it had become standard practice among the Jews of the Islamic lands to write a *basmala* or its equivalent at the head of practically any written text.

[19] Supporting this argument is the fact that there is no evidence of a *basmala* or Hebrew/Aramaic equivalent in any of the Genizah letters produced by Jews in Byzantium or by Byzantine Jews living in Egypt. See, for instance, the twelfth- to thirteenth-century Hebrew letter writer Yeḥi'el b. Elyaqim (T-S 13J20.3) or any of the other Byzantine letters edited in Outhwaite (2009).

The Babylonian *geʾonim*, whose formal correspondence is some of the earliest and most carefully executed of the documents represented in the Genizah, do not attest an invocation equivalent to the Islamic *basmala* in their Hebrew letters. Their style was influential and widely emulated, and the conservative nature of their Hebrew ensured that a generally conservative style flourished further west, where their letters were read, recited, and copied. The rare early use of על שמ׳ רח׳, 'by Your name, O Merciful', to open a Hebrew (but not Geonic) letter of *c.*1035 (ENA 4020.24) is interesting and unusual: the fact that the writer is a Maghrebi, but dwelling in Damascus, is probably significant and suggests that far from the main centres of Hebrew letters, a less conservative style may have taken root. One waits a further twenty years for the Hebrew/Aramaic invocation to appear with any kind of regularity in Hebrew letters. Daniel b. ʿAzarya, the Gaʾon of the Jerusalem Yeshiva at the beginning of the second half of the eleventh century, is the first Palestinian Gaʾon to inscribe a Jewish *basmala* (בשמך רח׳ in CUL Or. 1080 J4 and בשמך רחמ׳ in Bodleian Libraries, Oxford, and Cambridge University Library Lewis-Gibson Misc. 103) at the head of his Hebrew correspondence; or perhaps the scribe who wrote these letters for him is responsible.[20] In any case, this stylistic addition is short-lived, as Daniel is at the tail end of the golden age of Hebrew letter writing in the eleventh century; the Jewish leaders who follow him in Palestine and Egypt adopt Judaeo-Arabic as the language of their official correspondence.

The eleventh century shows the greatest use of the Judaeo-Arabic *basmala* invocation, but by *c.*1070, even these letter writers are turning their backs on it, with very few examples cropping up in the Genizah. The abandonment of this practice may be related to the social changes happening in the Islamic world at the time. The disruption of the period 1060–80, with plague, a worsening of economic and social conditions, and the considerable violence of the Seljuk invasions, led to a more inward-looking Jewish community, which sought security within its social borders and in its own cultural identity.[21] Consciously or not, this may have led to a lessening of the influence of Arabic style—of which the *basmala* is surely the most overt—and a return to more 'native' Jewish traditions. On a purely stylistic level, this change appears quite marked, and clear evidence can be seen in the letters of writers such as Benaya b. Moses who uses the Judaeo-Arabic *basmala*, בסם אללה (T-S 12.368), in the year 1060, but, twenty years later, has turned to the Aramaic invocation, בשמך רחמ׳ (T-S 13J23.3).

[20] A number of scholars have examined the origins of this Aramaic invocation, as to whether the phrase itself (rather than its usage) is modelled on, or forms the model for, the Islamic *basmala*. The pioneering Genizah scholar Goitein (1953, 48 n. 26) rejected the idea that *bišmaḵ raḥmana* was drawn from the Arabic and pointed to pre-Islamic attestations of the formula, followed by Friedman (1980.I, 93).

[21] On this unusually harsh and difficult time and its effect on the Jewish communities of Egypt and Palestine, see Goitein (1967–93.V, 114–15) and Cohen (1980, 54–60).

Much later, by the thirteenth century, the process is apparently complete, and Judaeo-Arabic letters employ only the Hebrew–Aramaic invocations and never the *basmala*. Moreover, the position and role of the invocation has changed, so that it bears little resemblance to the Islamic blessing that inspired it. Generally it appears in combination with the introduction of addressee and writer (for instance, Or. 1080 J222; T-S 10J9.10; T-S 13J8.28), and sometimes in combination with biblical citations (rarer, but found, for example, in T-S 13J13.26).

For a comparatively brief period, therefore, mainly under the Fatimid rule of the eleventh century, Jewish letter writing adopted the Islamic custom of *basmala*, even in its Hebrew correspondence, but the social and political pressures at the end of the eleventh century probably put an end to such close emulation of Islamic letters, and a return to a more Jewish invocation followed, cementing a style that lasted for the remainder of the classical Genizah period.

§4. WRITING THE DATE

Letters in Hebrew are rarely dated, the date and time of composition appearing not to be an essential part of the communication. Not one of the letters by the prolific writer Solomon b. Judah is dated, nor are the replies sent to him from Egypt, and nor are the majority of letters from Syria-Palestine generally in the eleventh century.

One body of correspondence that does regularly append a date, however, is that of the *geʾonim* of Babylonia, whose letters address their followers and allies far away in Egypt and North Africa. It is common practice in the letters of Hai, Sherira, and the other heads of the Babylonian *yeshivot* to write a date at the conclusion of the letter, beneath the very last line of the text on the left-hand side of the page, alongside or beneath the writer's *ʿalāma*. The date is always given according to the Seleucid calendar (although this is not made explicit), a system of dating popular in the eastern Jewish communities of the tenth and eleventh centuries.

The practice appears to be regular in some of the earliest attested correspondence of the Babylonian *geʾonim*. Nehemiah ha-Kohen Gaʾon, head of the Pumbeditha Academy, concludes a letter to the community of Safāquṣ (T-S 16.6) with כסלו שנת ע'ד', 'Kislev, the year 74', which is an abbreviated Seleucid date 1274 (א'ש'ע'ד'), which equates to November 962 CE. Although some of the letters have a quasi-legal function (for instance, *responsa*, written replies on matters of Jewish law), the addition of a date appears not to fulfil any kind of legal requirement, since in deeds and other formal court documents, dates are always given in full, with the system of dating usually made explicit.

Hai b. Sherira Gaʾon, head of the Pumbeditha Academy in the early eleventh century, continued in the style of his predecessors and dated his correspondence.

Most of Hai's extant correspondence is in Judaeo-Arabic, yet his overall style is identical to the Hebrew correspondence of the *ge'onim* before him and to his own Hebrew letters. Dates appear at the end of the letter, alongside the *ʿalāma*: י׳ט׳ באדר שנת ש׳י׳ח׳, 'Adar 19, 318' = 9 February 1007 CE (T-S 12.829). Similar dates are found in the letters of Samuel b. Ḥofni, the last Ga'on of Sura, and Hezekiah b. David, the Babylonian exilarch (Mosseri IV.15; T-S 13J9.1, respectively).

Letters from the *yeshivot* in Iraq were presumably dated since they had to travel such great distances to reach the Babylonian Jewish communities of Egypt and the Maghreb, when travel in general was unreliable and journey times were considerably elastic, according to the vagaries of caravans, shipping winds, and the constant difficulties of the road. Although the route between Palestine and Egypt was also prone to disruption and there was no shortage of dangers, the time required for a letter to reach Egypt was much less, and perhaps therefore the Palestinian *ge'onim* never felt a great need to note the time of their letters' execution.[22]

With the renewed interest in writing the Holy Language at the end of the twelfth century, Hebrew letters reappear in the Genizah archive, though not in great numbers, and a number are dated in a similar manner to the earlier Babylonian fashion. A letter by a certain Menaḥem to the Alexandrian Anaṭoli b. Joseph concludes with כ׳ב כסליו א׳ת׳ק׳כ׳ד׳, 'Kislev 22, 1524', a Seleucid date in unabbreviated form, which equates to 1212 CE. Too few Hebrew letters are attested for this period to determine whether the dating of correspondence had become the rule or not, but what little evidence there is suggests that the practice of dating the end of a letter was adopted more generally in Egyptian circles.

There are hundreds of dated letters in Judaeo-Arabic from Egyptian and Maghrebi traders of the eleventh century. They date their letters differently from the Babylonian style, with the date usually occurring in the first few lines of the letter and written in the Classical Arabic style, which introduces the numerals with *li-* combined with the verbs *baqiya* 'remain' and *ḫalā* 'pass',[23]—for example, לה׳ בקין מן אלול (T-S 20.180), 'seven (days) have passed from Ševaṭ' (eleventh-century Maghreb); לה׳ ויקב ומן לולא (T-S 10J9.3), 'five (days) have remained from Elul (= 25th Elul)'. Unlike in the dating used by the Iraqi Jews, the year is rarely given.

In Judaeo-Arabic letters from the early thirteenth century, mostly from the family of the prominent Genizah figure judge Elijah, there seems to be a return to the dating system found in the Geonic letters from Babylonia. The dating

[22] There are exceptions. The pretender Nathan b. Abraham begins to date his correspondence when he proclaims himself rightful Ga'on of Palestine. But, with his conscious adopting of other clearly Babylonian Geonic features in his letters (such as placing his name and titles in two short lines right at the head of the letter), it seems that he is deliberately seeking to emulate the preeminent *ge'onim* of his day.

[23] See Wright (1967.II, 248–9).

formulae are less sophisticated and the date stands at the end of the letter (as in the Geonic letters), instead of the beginning. Moreover, some of the dates are formed with ordinal numbers: כתב עסאב מן שהר ניסן (T-S 12.69), 'it was written on the seventh of Nissan'; כתב יום אלארבעא ו' מן אדר שני (T-S 13J20.24), 'it was written on Wednesday, sixth of the Second Adar'. If the year is given, it is most often in Seleucid dating: לתאמן יום אלאתנין אל תאמן מן שהר מרחשון א'ת'ק'מ'ג' לשטרות (Freer 8), 'on the eighth, Monday, the eighth of Marḥešvan 1543 of the Seleucid era (= 1232 CE)'. Dating according to the Jewish calendar of Creation also occurs: כתב כ'ג' שבט קעה (T-S 10J31.10), 'written on the 23rd of Ševaṭ (4800 +) 175 (= 4975 Era of Creation = 1215 CE)'. The dating does not follow earlier Egyptian epistolary tradition but is similar to the dating in legal documents and in the earlier Geonic letters from Babylonia.

While there is a clear difference between the Palestinian and Babylonian Geonic letters as regards dating, the former rarely writing any kind of date, there are also sufficient differences between the style of dating Hebrew letters and Judaeo-Arabic letters generally to see that they are operating from different traditions. The commercial correspondent of the eleventh century rarely bothers to note the year in the date and mimics standard Arabic syntax exactly in the formula. But for the script (Hebrew) and the system of dating (Seleucid rather than Hijra), the result is identical to what can be found in an Arabic letter. It is most interesting, however, that towards the thirteenth century this is supplanted by a formula that more closely resembles the traditional style of the (Babylonian) *ge'onim*, suggesting that, yet again, there was a gradual shift away from a simple reliance upon the Islamic model.

§5. CONCLUSION

In analysing these three major elements of the Hebrew and Judaeo-Arabic letter, we can see that far from being a unified and stable tradition that extended across the two languages and over the whole classical Genizah period, there was considerable divergence and movement in epistolary fashions. Hebrew letters from Palestine and Babylonia in the first half of the eleventh century do not resemble their Judaeo-Arabic counterparts in Egypt and the Maghreb: they are addressed differently, they tend not to employ an invocation, and they are dated differently (if at all). This self-confident independence, however, more or less comes to an end with the eclipse of the gaonate, first in Iraq and subsequently in Palestine, a process complete by the end of the century, as power shifts from the *yeshivot* to the local centres. That this coincides with a decline in the use of Hebrew is to be expected, since the *ge'onim* and their correspondents were champions of the Hebrew language in the face of Islamic domination. Subsequently, when Hebrew came back into fashion, the resulting letters resemble in form more those of contemporary Judaeo-Arabic writers, rather than the Geonic tradition of old.

At the same time, the writers of Judaeo-Arabic letters show a similar independence, drawing on a native and antique Egyptian tradition, but also feeling secure enough to borrow from the more ostentatious features of Arabic–Islamic correspondence, even to the point of inscribing an Arabic *basmala* at the top of a Jewish letter. However, a major shift, mirroring that which occurred in the Hebrew-language tradition, occurs towards the end of the eleventh century, as turmoil engulfs the region and the self-confidence of the Jewish community secure in their position in the early Fatimid state is replaced by a more introspective and withdrawn approach as political uncertainty increases. This has an interesting twofold consequence: Judaeo-Arabic letters lose some of their more defining features and come more and more to resemble the correspondence around them, yet at the same time, the most overt sign of the Jewish assimilation to the dominant culture of the Islamic state, the adoption of the *basmala*, is deliberately replaced by a native version.

A century later these changes are solidified, so that Jewish letters from the Genizah retain a number of defining features that distinguish them, but overall, stylistically, they resemble more closely the correspondence of the state around them, having made a break with their previous, independent traditions of epistolography.

Bibliography

Adams, J. N. 1995. 'The Language of the Vindolanda Writing-Tablets: An Interim Report', in *Journal of Roman Studies* 85: 86–134.

Adams, J. N. 2003. *Bilingualism and the Latin Language* (Cambridge).

Adams, J. N., Janse, M., and Swain, S. (eds). 2002. *Bilingualism in Ancient Society: Language Contact and the Written Text* (Oxford).

Adler, E. N., Tait, J. G., Heichelheim, F. M., and Griffith, F. L. 1939. *The Adler Papyri* (London).

Allam, S. 1973. *Hieratische Ostraka und Papyri aus der Ramessidenzeit (= Urkunden zum Rechtleben im Alten Ägypten)* (Tübingen).

Allen, J. 1994. 'Colloquial Middle Egyptian. Some Observations on the Language of Heqa-nakht', in *Lingua Aegyptia* 4: 1–12.

Allen, J. 2004. 'Traits dialectaux dans les Textes des Pyramides du Moyen Empire', in S. Bickel and B. Mathieu (eds) *D'un Monde à l'autre. Textes des Pyramides & Textes des Sarcophages (Actes de la Table Ronde Internationale « Textes des Pyramides versus Textes des Sarcophages », IFAO, 24–26 Septembre 2001* (Cairo): 1–14.

Allen, J. 2013. *The Ancient Egyptian Language. A Historical Study* (Cambridge).

Ammon, U., Dittmar, N., Mattheier, K. J., and Trugdill, P. (eds). 2004. *Sociolinguistics/ Soziolinguistik: An International Handbook of the Science of Language and Society.* Volume 1 (Berlin–New York).

Andrássy, P., Budka, J., and Kammerzell, F. (eds). 2009. *Non-Textual Marking Systems. Writing and Pseudo Script from Prehistory to Present Times* (Göttingen).

Andreu, G. (ed.) 2002. *Les artistes de Pharaon. Deir el-Médineh et la Vallée des Rois* (Paris).

Andreu, G. (ed.) 2003. *Deir el-Médineh et la Vallée des Rois. La vie en Égypte au temps des pharaons du Nouvel Empire. Actes du colloque organisé par le musée du Louvre les 3 et 4 mai 2002* (Paris).

Assmann, J. 1975. *Ägyptische Hymnen und Gebete* (Zurich–Munich).

Assmann, J. 1991. 'Die Entdeckung der Vergangenheit. Innovation und Restoration in der ägyptischen Literaturgeschichte', in J. Assmann (ed.) *Stein und Zeit. Mensch und Gesellschaft im alten Ägypten* (Munich): 303–13.

Assmann, J. 1997. 'Gottesbeherzigung: „Persönliche Frömmigkeit" als religiöse Strömung der Ramessidenzeit', in *L'imperio ramesside. Convegno internazionale in onore di Sergio Donadoni* (Rome): 17–43.

Ast, R. and Azzarello, G. 2012. 'A Roman Veteran and his Skilful Administrator: Gemellus and Epagathus in Light of Unpublished Papyri', in P. Schubert (ed.) *Actes du 26e Congrès international de papyrologie (Genève 2010)* (Geneva): 67–71.

Ast, R. and Azzarello, G. 2013. 'New Perspectives on the Gemellus Archive', in C. Arlt and M. Stadler (eds) *Das Fayyûm in Hellenismus und Kaiserzeit* (Wiesbaden): 19–28.

Auer, P., and Schmidt, J. E. (eds). 2010. *Language and Space. An International Handbook of Linguistic Variation. Volume 1: Theories and Methods* (Berlin–New York).

Ausbüttel, E. 1904. *Das persönliche Geschlecht unpersönlicher Substantiva einschließlich Tiernamen im Mittelenglischen* (Halle).

Bagnall, R. S. 2011. *Everyday Writing in the Graeco-Roman East* (Berkeley–Los Angeles).

Bagnall, R. S. and Cribiore, R. 2006. *Womens' Letters from Ancient Egypt 300 BC – AD 800* (Ann Arbor).

Bagnall, R. S. and Worp, K. 2004. *Chronological Systems of Byzantine Egypt*. 2nd edition (Leiden).

Bailey, G. and Tillery, G. 2004. 'Some Sources of Divergent Data in Sociolinguistics', in C. Fought (ed.) *Sociolinguistic Variation: Critical Reflection* (Oxford): 11–30.

Baines, J. 1983. 'Literacy and Ancient Egyptian Society', in *Man NS* 18: 572–99.

Baines, J. 1985. *Fecundity Figures: Egyptian Personification and the Iconology of a Genre* (Chicago).

Baines, J. 1990. 'Restricted Knowledge, Hierarchy, and Decorum: Modern Perceptions and Ancient Institutions', in *Journal of the American Research Center in Egypt* 27: 1–23.

Baines, J. 1996. 'Classicism and Modernism in the Literature of the New Kingdom', in A. Loprieno (ed.) *Ancient Egyptian Literature. History & Forms* (Leiden): 157–74.

Baines, J. 2003. 'Research on Egyptian Literature: Background, Definitions, Prospects', in Z. Hawass (ed.) *Egyptology at the Dawn of the Twenty-first Century. Proceedings of the Eighth International Congress of Egyptologists*. Volume 3 (Cairo): 1–26.

Baines, J. 2007. *Visual and Written Culture in Ancient Egypt* (Oxford).

Baines, J. and Eyre, C. J. 1983. 'Four Notes on Literacy', in *Göttinger Miszellen* 61: 65–96.

Baines, J. and Eyre, C. J. 1989. 'Interaction between Orality and Literacy in Ancient Egypt', in K. Schousboe and M. T. Larsen (eds) *Literacy and Society* (Copenhagen): 91–118.

Balestri, G. and Ciasca, A. 1898. *Sacrorum Bibliorum fragmenta copto-sahidica Musei Borgiani*. Volume 3 (Rome–Naples).

Barnes, J. 1969. 'Graph Theory and Social Networks', in *Sociology* 3: 215–32.

Barton, D. 2007. *Literacy. An Introduction to the Ecology of Written Language* (Oxford).

Barton, D. and Hamilton, M. 1998. *Local Literacies. Reading and Writing in one Community* (London–New York).

Beal, J. C. 2008. 'Variation in Late Modern English: Making the Best Use of "Bad Data"', in S. M. Fitzmaurice and D. Minkova (eds) *Studies in the History of the English Language IV. Empirical and Analytical Advances in the Study of English Language Change* (Berlin): 327–36.

Beckh, T., Eichner, I., and Hodak, S. 2011. 'Briefe aus der koptischen Vergangenheit. Zur Identifikation der Klosteranlage Deir el-Bachît in Theben-West', in *Mitteilungen des deutschen Archäologischen Instituts. Abteilung Kairo* 67: 15–30.

von Beckerath, J. 1983. 'Ostrakon München ÄS 396', in *Studien zur Altägyptischen Kultur* 10: 63–9.

von Beckerath, J. 2000. 'Bemerkungen zu Papyrus Turin 1885 Verso II–III', in R. J. Demarée and A. Egberts (eds) *Deir el-Medina in the Third Millennium AD. A Tribute to Jac J. Janssen* (Leiden): 1–7.

Beinlich, H. 1991. *Das Buch vom Fayum* (Wiesbaden).

Beinlich, H. 2013. *Der Mythos in seiner Landschaft: Das ägyptische „Buch vom Fayum". Band 1: Die hieroglyphischen Texte* (Dettelbach).

Beinlich, H. 2014. *Der Mythos in seiner Landschaft: Das ägyptische „Buch vom Fayum". Band 2: Die hieratischen Texte* (Dettelbach).

Beinlich, H. 2017. *Der Mythos in seiner Landschaft: Das ägyptische „Buch vom Fayum". Band 3: Die hieratisch-demotischen Texte* (Dettelbach).

Bennett, H. S. 1995. *The Pastons and their England: Studies in an Age of Transition* (Cambridge).

Bennett, J. A. W. and Smithers, G. V. (eds). 1974. *Early Middle English Verse and Prose* (Oxford).

Benskin, M. 1991. 'The Fit-technique Explained', in F. Riddy (ed.) *Regionalism in Late Medieval Manuscripts and Texts* (Cambridge): 9–26.

van den Berg, H. and Donker van Heel, K. 2000. 'A Scribe's Cache from the Valley of Queens? The Palaeography of Documents from Deir el-Medina: Some Remarks', in R. J. Demarée and A. Egberts (eds) *Deir el-Medina in the Third Millennium AD. A Tribute to Jac J. Janssen* (Leiden): 9–49.

Berger, J. 1889. *Un nouveau contrat bilingue démotique-grec: thèse présentée à l'École du Louvre et soutenue le 21 janvier 1889* (Paris).

Bergs, A. 2004. 'A New Approach to Text Typology', in *Journal of Historical Pragmatics* 5: 207–27.

Bergs, A. 2005. *Social Networks and Historical Sociolinguistics. Studies in Morphosyntactic Variation in the Paston Letters (1421–1503)* (Berlin–New York).

Bergs, A. 2009. 'The Linguistics of Text Messaging', in C. Rowe and E. L. Wyss (eds) *New Media and Linguistic Change* (Creskill, NJ): 55–74.

Bergs, A. 2015. 'The Linguistic Fingerprint of Authors and Scribes: A Historical Whodunit', in A. Auer, D. Schreier, and R. Watts (eds) *Letters as Evidence* (Cambridge): 156–81.

Bernand, E. 1975. *Recueil des inscriptions grecques du Fayum I. La «méris» d'Hérakleidès* (Leiden).

Berruto, G. 2010. 'Identifying Dimensions of Linguistic Variation in a Language Space', in P. Auer and J. E. Schmidt (eds) *Language and Space. An International Handbook of Linguistic Variation. Volume 1: Theories and Methods* (Berlin–New York): 226–41.

Berthelot, M. 1909. *Die Chemie im Altertum und im Mittelalter* (Leipzig and Vienna).

Berthelot, M. and Ruelle, C.-É. 1888. *Collection des anciens alchimistes grecs* (Paris; reprinted: Osnabrück 1967).

Bex, T. 1996. *Variety in Written English: Texts in Society: Societies in Text* (London–New York).

Biber, D. 1995. *Dimensions of Register Variation. A Cross-Linguistic Comparison* (Cambridge).

Biber, D. and Conrad, S. 2009. *Register, Genre, Style* (Cambridge).

Biber, D., Conrad, S., and Reppen, R. 1998. *Corpus Linguistics: Investigating Language Structure and Use* (Cambridge).

Biber, D. and Finegan, E. (eds). 1994. *Socio-Linguistic Perspectives on Register* (Oxford).

Bickel, S. and Loprieno, A. (eds). 2003. *Basel Egyptology Prize; 1. Junior Research in Egyptian History, Archaeology, and Philology* (Basel).

Bickel, S. and Mathieu, B. 1993. 'L'écrivain Amennakht et son *Enseignement*', in *Bulletin de l'Institut français d'archéologie orientale* 93: 31–51 and pls. i–viii.

Bierbrier, M. L. 1975. *The Late New Kingdom Egypt (c. 1300–664 B.C.) – A Genealogical and Chronological Investigation* (Warminster).

Bierbrier, M. L. 1980. 'Terms of Relationship at Deir el-Medîna', in *The Journal of Egyptian Archaeology* 66: 100–7.

Bilabel, F. and Grohmann, A. 1934. *Griechische, koptische und arabische Texte zur Religion und religiösen Literatur in Ägyptens Spätzeit* (Heidelberg).

Bingen, J. 1995. 'Review of P. J. Sijpesteijn, *Ostraka greci da Narmuthis (OGN 1)*', in *Chronique d'Égypte* 70: 306–8.

Bingen, J. 1998. 'Statuaire égyptienne et épigraphie grecque: le cas de I. Fay. I 78', in W. Clarysse, A. Schoors, and H. Willems (eds) *Egyptian Religion. The Last Thousand Years, Part I. Studies Dedicated to the Memory of Jan Quaegebeur* (Leuven): 311–19.

Black, M. 1997. 'Studies in the Dialect Materials of Medieval Herefordshire'. Unpublished doctoral dissertation (University of Glasgow).

Black, M. 1999. 'AB or Simply A? Reconsidering the Case for a Standard', in *Neuphilologische Mitteilungen* 100: 155–74.

Blackman, A. M. 1926. 'Oracles in Ancient Egypt', in *The Journal of Egyptian Archaeology* 12: 176–85.

Blau, J. 1999. *The Emergence and Linguistic Background of Judaeo-Arabic: A Study of the Orgins of Neo-Arabic and Middle Arabic.* 3rd revised edition (Jerusalem).

Bloomfield, L. 1933. *Language* (New York).

Bolinger, D. 1977. *Meaning and Form* (London).

Botti, G. 1959. *La glorificazione di Sobk e del Fayyum in un papiro ieratico da Tebtunis* (Copenhagen).

Boud'hors, A. 1997. 'L'onciale penchée en copte et sa survie jusqu'au XVe siècle en Haute-Égypte', in F. Déroche and F. Richards (eds) *Scribes et manuscrits du Moyen-Orient* (Paris): 117–33.

Boud'hors, A. 2008. 'Copie et circulation des livres dans la région thébaine (VIIe-VIIIe siècles)', in A. Delattre and P. Heilporn (eds) *« Et maintenant ce ne sont plus que des villages… ». Thèbes et sa région aux époques hellénistique, romaine et byzantine* (Brussels): 149–61, pls. XIV–XV.

Boud'hors, A. 2010a. 'Toujours honneur au grec? À propos d'un papyrus gréco-copte de la région thébaine', in A. Papaconstantinou (ed.) *The Multilingual Experience in Egypt from the Ptolemies to the Abbasids* (Aldershot): 179–88.

Boud'hors, A. 2010b. 'La forme ⲙⲛⲧⲉ- en emploi non autonome dans les textes documentaires thébains', in *Journal of Coptic Studies* 12: 67–80.

Boud'hors, A. Forthcoming. 'À la recherche des manuscrits coptes de la région thébaine', in D. Brakke, S. Davis, and S. Emmel (eds) *Scripta Coptice* (Leuven).

Boud'hors, A. and Heurtel, C. 2002. 'The Coptic Ostraca from the Tomb of Amenemope', in *Egyptian Archaeology* 20: 7–9.

Boud'hors, A. and Heurtel, C. 2010. *Les ostraca coptes de la TT 29. Autour du moine Frangé* (Brussels).

Boud'hors, A. and Heurtel, C. 2015. *Ostraca et papyrus coptes du* topos *de Saint-Marc à Thèbes* (Cairo).

Bouriant, U. 1888. 'Fragment d'un livre de médecin en copte thébain', in *Académie des inscriptions et belles-lettres, comptes rendus 1887*, sér. 4/15: 319–20 and 374–9.

Bouvier, G. and Bouvier, K. 2006. 'L'activité des gens de la Nécropole à la fin de la XXe et à la XXIe dynastie, d'après les graffiti de la Montagne thébaine: le transfert des momies royales', in A. Dorn and T. Hofmann (eds) *Living and Writing in Deir el-Medine. Socio-historical Embodiment of Deir el-Medine Texts* (Basel): 21–9.

Brandt, C. 2007. *Der Traktat „Vom Mysterium der Buchstaben." Kritischer Text mit Einführung, Übersetzung und Kommentar* (Berlin).

Bresciani, E. 1975. *L'archivio demotico dei tempio di Soknopaiou Nesos nel Griffith Institute di Oxford. Volume 1: P. Ox. Griffith nn. 1–75* (Milan).

Bresciani, E. 1981. 'Frammenti da un "prontuario legale" demotico da Tebtuni nell'Istituto Papirologico G. Vitelli di Firenze', in *Egitto e Vicino Oriente: Rivista della sezione oreintalistica dell'Instituto di Storia Antica, Università degli studi di Pisa* 4: 201–15.

Bresciani, E., Menchetti, A., Messeri, G., and Pintaudi, R. 2002. 'The Publication Project of the Ostraka from Medinet Madi (Cairo Museum J.E. 8/4/48/1)', in M. Eldamaty and M. Trad (eds) *Egyptian Museum Collections around the World*. Volume 1 (Cairo): 163–74.

Brescani, E., Pernigotti, S., and Betrò, M. C. 1983. *Ostraka demotici da Narmuti I (nn. 1–33)* (Pisa).

Breyer, F. 2008. 'Das Napatanische. Eine ägyptomeroitische Kreolsprache und ihre Verhältnis zum Altnubischen', in *Lingua Aegyptia* 16: 323–30.

Brunner, H. 1957. *Altägyptische Erziehung* (Wiesbaden).

Broze, M. 1996. *Mythe et roman en Égypte ancienne. Les aventures d'Horus et Seth dans le Papyrus Chester Beatty I* (Leuven).

Bryan, B. 1996. 'The Disjunction of Text and Image in Egyptian Art', in P. Der Manuelian (ed.) *Studies in Honor of William Kelly Simpson*. Volume 1 (Boston): 161–8.

Bucking, S. 2007a. 'On the Training of Documentary Scribes in Roman, Byzantine, and Early Islamic Egypt: A Contextualized Assessment of the Greek Evidence', in *Zeitschrift für Papyrologie und Epigraphik* 159: 229–47.

Bucking, S. 2007b. 'Scribes and Schoolmasters? On Contextualizing Coptic and Greek Ostraca Excavated at the Monastery of Epiphanius', in *Journal of Coptic Studies* 9: 21–47.

Bucking, S. 2011. *Practice Makes Perfect P. Cotsen-Princeton 1 and the Training of Scribes in Byzantine Egypt* (Los Angeles).

Burkard, G. 1977. *Textkritische Untersuchungen zu altägyptischen Weisheitslehren des Alten und Mittleren Reiches* (Wiesbaden).

Burkard, G. 1990. 'Frühgeschichte und Römerzeit', in *Studien zur Altägyptische Kultur* 17: 107–133.

Burkard, G. 2013. 'Amunnacht, Scribe and Poet of Deir el Medina: A Study of Ostrakon O Berlin P 14262', in R. Enmarch and V. M. Lepper (eds) *Ancient Egyptian Literature. Theory and Practice* (Oxford): 65–82.

Burkard, G. and Eicher, I. 2007. 'Zwischen pharaonischen Gräbern und Ruinen: Das Kloster Deir el-Bachit in Theben-West', in G. Dreyer and D. Polz (eds) *Begegnung mit der Vergangenheit. 100 Jahre in Ägypten. Deutsches Archäologisches Institut Kairo 1907–2007* (Mainz): 270–4.

Burnett, C. 2009. *Arabic into Latin in the Middle Ages: The Translators and their Intellectual and Social Context* (Farnham).

Caminos, R. A. 1954. *Late Egyptian Miscellanies* (London–Oxford).

Capart, J., Gardiner, A. H., and van de Walle, B. 1936. 'New Light on the Ramesside Tomb-robberies', in *The Journal of Egyptian Archaeology* 22: 169–93.

Carter, H. and Gardiner, A. H. 1917. 'The Tomb of Ramesses IV and the Turin Plan of a Royal Tomb', in *The Journal of Egyptian Archaeology* 4: 130–58.

Černý, J. 1935. *Catalogue des ostraca hiératiques non littéraires de Deir el Médineh (Nos 1 à 113)* (Cairo).

Černý, J. 1936. 'Une famille de scribes de la nécropole royale de Thèbes', in *Chronique d'Égypte* 11: 247–50.
Černý, J. 1945. 'The Will of Naunakhte and the Related Documents', in *The Journal of Egyptian Archaeology* 31: 29–53 and pls. viii–xii.
Černý, J. 1952. *Paper and Books in Ancient Egypt* (London).
Černý, J. 1956. *Graffiti hiéroglyphiques et hiératiques de la nécropole thébaine* (Cairo).
Černý, J. 1976. *Coptic Etymological Dictionary* (Cambridge).
Černý, J. 2004. *A Community of Workmen at Thebes in the Ramesside Period.* 3rd edition (Cairo).
Černý, J. and Gardiner, A. H. 1957. *Hieratic Ostraca.* Volume 1 (Oxford).
Černý, J. and Groll, S. I. 1993. *A Late Egyptian Grammar.* 4th edition (Rome).
Cerquiglini, B. 1989. *Éloge de la variante: histoire critique de la philologie* (Paris).
Chafe, W. and Tannen, D. 1987. 'The Relation between Written and Spoken Language', in *Annual Review of Anthropology* 16: 383–407.
Chassinat, É. 1921. *Un papyrus médical copte* (Cairo).
Chauveau, M. 1991. 'P. Carlsberg 301: Le manuel juridique de Tebtynis', in P. J. Frandsen (ed.) *The Carlsberg Papyri 1: Demotic Texts from the Collection* (Copenhagen): 103–23.
Chauveau, M. 1992. 'Un traité astrologie en écriture démotique', in *Cahier de recherches de l'Institut de papyrologie et égyptologie de Lille* 14: 101–5.
Choat, M. 2006. *Belief and Cult in Fourth-Century Papyri* (Turnhout).
Choat, M. and Cromwell, J. 2016. 'Thebes in Late Antiquity', in P. Buzi, A. Camplani, and F. Contardi (eds) *Coptic Society, Literature and Religion from Late Antiquity to Modern Times. Proceedings of the Tenth International Congress of Coptic Studies, Rome, September 17th–22nd, 2012, and Plenary Reports of the Ninth International Congress of Coptic Studies, Cairo, September 15th–19th, 2008* (Leuven): 695–8.
Christiansen, T., Buti, D., Dalby, K. N., Lindelof, P. E., Ryholt, K., and Vila, A. 2017. 'Chemical Characterization of Black and Red Inks on Ancient Egyptian Papyri: The Tebtunis Temple Library', in *Journal of Archaeological Science: Reports* (JASREP) 14: 208.
Christophe, L. A. 1957. 'Sur le Graffito 1247 de la Nécropole Thébaine', in *Bulletin de l'Institut français d'archéologie orientale* 56: 173–88.
Clark, C. 1992. 'The Myth of the Anglo-Norman Scribe', in M. Rissanen, O. Ihalainen, T. Nevalainen, and I. Taavitsainen (eds) *History of Englishes. New Methods and Interpretations in Historical Linguistics* (Berlin–New York): 117–29.
Clarysse, W. 1994. 'Greeks and Persians in a Bilingual Census List', in E. Bresciani (ed.) *Acta Demotica: Acts of the Fifth International Conference for Demotists, Pisa, 4th–8th September 1993* (Pisa): 69–77.
Clarysse, W. 2010. 'Linguistic Diversity in the Archive of the Engineers Kleon and Theodoros', in T. V. Evans and D. D. Obbink (eds) *The Language of the Papyri* (Oxford): 35–50.
Clarysse, W. and Gallazzi, C. 1993. 'Archivio dei discendenti di Laches o dei discendenti di Patron?' in *Ancient Society* 24: 63–8.
Clarysse, W. and Vandorpe, K. 1995. *Zénon, un homme d'affaires grec à l'ombre des Pyramides* (Leuven).
Cohen, M. R. 1980. *Jewish Self-Government in Medieval Egypt* (Princeton).
Coles. R. A. 1966. *Reports of Proceedings in Papyri* (Brussels).

Collier. M. 2006. 'The Lure of Alterity: *ỉnn* Conditionals in Late Egyptian', in V. M. Lepper (ed.) *"After Polotsky": New Research and Trends in Egyptian and Coptic Linguistics*; *Lingua Aegyptia* 14: 181–98.

Collier. M. 2009. 'Pragmatics and Meaning Construction in Late Egyptian: Of Implicatures, Pragmatic Scales, and Scope', in M. Müller and S. Uljas (eds) *Proceedings of the Fourth International Conference on Egyptian Grammar (Crossroads IV), Basel, March 19–22, 2009*; *Lingua Aegyptia* 14: 9–26.

Collombert, P. 2008. 'Par-delà Bien et Mal. L'inscription de la reine Katimala à Semna', in *Kush* 19: 285–318.

Compagnon, A. 1998. *Le démon de la théorie. Littérature et sens commun* (Paris).

Cooney, K. M. 2006. 'An Informal Workshop: Textual Evidence for Private Funerary Art Production in the Ramesside Period', in A. Dorn and T. Hofmann (eds) *Living and Writing in Deir el-Medine. Socio-historical Embodiment of Deir el-Medine Texts* (Basel): 43–55.

Coseriu, E. 1980. '„Historische Sprache" und „Dialekt"', in J. Göschel, P. Ivić, and K. Kehr (eds). *Dialekt und Dialektologie. Ergebnisse des internationalen Symposions „Zur Theorie des Dialekts', Marburg/Lahn, 5.–10. September 1977* (Wiesbaden): 106–22.

Coulon, L. 1999. 'La rhétorique et ses fictions. Pouvoir et duplicité du discours à travers la littérature égyptienne du Moyen Empire', in *Bulletin de l'Institut français d'archéologie orientale* 99: 103–32.

Cowley, A. 1915. 'Notes on Hebrew Papyrus Fragments from Oxyrhyncus', in *The Journal of Egyptian Archaeology* 2/4: 209–13.

Cribiore, R. 1996. *Writing, Teachers and Students in Graeco-Roman Egypt* (Atlanta).

Cribiore, R. 2001. 'Windows on a Woman's World. Some Letters from Roman Egypt', in A. Lardinois and L. McClure (eds) *Making Silence Speak. Women's Voices in Greek Literature and Society* (Princeton–Oxford): 223–39.

Cribiore, R. 2007. 'The Coptic School Exercises in the Collection of Columbia University', in B. Palme (ed.) *Akten des 23. Internationalen Papyrologen-Kongresses, Wien 22–28 Juli 2001* (Vienna): 127–30.

Crisci, E. 1985. 'La maiuscola ogivale diritta. Origini, tipologie, dislocazioni', in *Scrittura e civiltà* 9: 103–45.

Croft, W. 2000. *Explaining Language Change. An Evolutionary Approach* (Harlow).

Croft, W., Denning, K., and Kemmer, S. 1990. 'Typology and Diachrony in the Work of Joseph H. Greenberg', in W. Croft, K. Denning, and S. Kemmer (eds) *Studies in Typology* (Amsterdam–Philadelphia): ix–xviii.

Cromwell, J. 2010a. 'Aristophanes son of Johannes: An 8th Century Bilingual Scribe? A Study of Graphic Bilingualism', in A. Papaconstantinou (ed.) *The Multilingual Experience in Egypt from the Ptolemies to the Abassids* (Aldershot): 221–32.

Cromwell, J. 2010b. 'ΕΝ ΟΝΟΜΑΤΙ ΤΟΥ ΘΕΟΥ ΤΟΥ ΠΑΝΤΟΚΡΑΤΟΡΟΣ: Variation and Specificity in Christian Invocation Formulae from Thebes', in *Zeitschrift für Papyrologie und Epigraphik* 174: 151–5.

Cromwell, J. 2010c. 'Palaeography, Scribal Practice and Chronological Issues in Coptic Documentary Texts', in *Journal of the American Research Center in Egypt* 46: 1–16.

Cromwell, J. 2017. *Recording Village Life: A Coptic Scribe in Early Islamic Egypt* (Ann Arbor).

Crum, W. E. 1905. *Catalogue of the Coptic Manuscript in the British Museum* (London).

Crum, W. E. 1915. *Der Papyruscodex saec. VI–VII der Phillipsbibliothek in Cheltenham* (Strasbourg).

Crum, W. E. 1939. *A Coptic Dictionary* (Oxford).

Crum, W. and Evelyn White, H.G. 1926. *The Monastery of Epiphanius at Thebes, Part II: Coptic Ostraca and Papyri* (New York).

Crum, W. E. and Winlock, H. E. 1926. *The Monastery of Epiphanius at Thebes. Part I: The Archaeological Material; The Literary Material* (New York).

Curzan, A. 2003. *Gender Shifts in the History of English* (Cambridge).

Darnell, J. C. 2006. *The Inscription of Queen Katimala at Semna: Textual Evidence for the Origins of the Napatan State* (New Haven).

David, A. 2006. *Syntactic and Lexico-Semantic Aspects of the Legal Register in Ramesside Royal Decrees* (Wiesbaden).

David, A. 2010. *The Legal Register of Ramesside Private Law Instruments* (Wiesbaden).

Davies, B. G. 1999. *Who's Who at Deir el-Medina. A Prosopographic Study of the Royal Workmen's Community* (Leiden).

Davis, N. 1971. *The Paston Letters and Papers of the Fifteenth Century.* Volume 1 (Oxford).

Davis, V. L. 1973. *Syntax of the Negative Particles bw and bn in Late Egyptian* (Munich).

Dawson, W. R. and Uphill, E. P. 2012. *Who Was Who in Egyptology.* 4th edition edited by M. L. Bierbrier (London).

Delattre, A. 2007. *Papyrus coptes et grecs du monastère d'Apa Apollô de Baouit* (Brussels).

Delattre, A., Liebrenz, B., Richter, T. S., and Vanthiegem, N. 2012. 'Écrire an arabe et en copte. Le cas de deux lettres bilingues', in *Chronique d'égypte* 87: 170–88.

Demarée, R. J. 2002. *Ramesside Ostraca* (London).

Demarée, R. J. 2008. 'Letters and Archives from the Necropolis at Thebes', in L. Pantalacci (ed.) *La lettre d'archive. Communication administrative et personnelle dans l'Antiquité proche-orientale et égyptienne. Actes du colloque de l'université de Lyon 2, 9–10 juillet 2004* (Cairo): 43–52.

Demarée, R. J. and Egberts, A. (eds). 1992. *Village Voices. Proceedings of the Symposium 'Texts from Deir el-Medîna and their Interpretation', Leiden, May 31 – June 1, 1991* (Leiden).

Demarée, R. J. and Egberts, A. (eds). 2000. *Deir el-Medina in the Third Millennium AD. A Tribute to Jac. J. Janssen* (Leiden).

Demarée, R. J. and Janssen, J. J. (eds). 1982. *Gleanings from Deir el-Medîna* (Leiden).

Denison, D. 2003. 'Log(ist)ic and Simplistic S-curves', in R. Hickey (ed.). *Motives for Language Change* (Cambridge): 54–70.

Depauw, M. 1998. 'The isionomos or *ỉn-wwy*', in W. Clarysse, A. Schoors, and H. Willems (eds) *Egyptian Religion: The Last Thousand Years* (Leuven): 1131–53.

Der Manuelian, P. 1999. 'Semi-Literacy in Egypt: Some Erasures from the Amarna Period', in E. Teeter and J. A. Larson (eds) *Gold of Praise. Studies in Ancient Egypt in Honor of Edward F. Wente* (Chicago): 285–98.

Derchain, P. 1996. 'Auteur et société', in A. Loprieno (ed.) *Ancient Egyptian Literature. History & Forms* (Leiden): 83–94.

Devauchelle, D. 2008. 'Review of Stadler 2004', in *Die Welt des Orients: Wissenschaftliche Beiträge zur Kunde des Morgenlandes* 38: 242–5.

Di Cerbo, C. 2004. 'Neue demotische Texte aus Tebtynis. Überblick zu den demotischen Papyri der italienisch/französischen Ausgrabung in Tebtynis aus den Jahren 1997–2000', in F. Hoffmann and H. J. Thissen (eds) *Res severa verum gaudium. Festschrift für Karl-Theodor Zauzich zum 65. Geburtstag am 8. Juni 2004* (Leuven): 109–19.

Dieleman, J. 2005 *Priests, Tongues, and Rites: The London-Leiden Magical Manuscripts and Translations in Egyptian Ritual (100–300 CE)* (Leiden).

Dieleman, J. 2010. 'Cryptography at the Monastery of Deir el-Bachit', in H. Knuf, C. Leitz, and D. von Recklinghausen (eds) *Honi soit qui mal y pense. Studien zum pharaonischen, griechisch-römischen und spätantiken Ägypten zu Ehren von Heinz-Josef Thissen* (Leuven–Paris–Walpole, MA): 511–17.

Donker van Heel, K. and Haring B. J. J. 2003. *Writing in a Workmen's Village. Scribal Practice in Ramesside Deir el-Medina* (Leiden).

Doresse, J. 1991. 'Cryptography', in A. S. Atiya (ed.) *The Coptic Encyclopedia*. Volume 8 (New York–Toronto): 65–9.

Doret, É. 1986. *The Narrative Verbal System of Old and Middle Egyptian* (Geneva).

Dorn, A. 2004. 'Die Lehre Amunnachts', in *Zeitschrift für ägyptische Sprache und Altertumskunde* 131: 38–55 + pls. ii–vii.

Dorn, A. 2006. '*mȝȝ-nḫt.w=f*, ein (?) einfacher Arbeiter, schreibt Briefe', in A. Dorn and T. Hofmann (eds) *Living and Writing in Deir el-Medine. Socio-historical Embodiment of Deir el-Medine Texts* (Basel): 67–85.

Dorn, A. 2009. 'Ein Literatenwettstreit und das Ende der Diglossie als Sprachgeschichtliche Schwelle. Essayistische Gedanken zur Literatur des Neuen Reiches', in D. Kessler, R. Schulz, M. Ullmann, A. Verbovsek, and S. J. Wimmer (eds) *Texte – Theben – Tonfragmente. Festschrift für Günter Burkard* (Wiesbaden): 70–82.

Dorn, A. 2011. *Arbeiterhütten im Tal der Könige. Ein Beitrag zur altägyptischen Sozialgeschichte aufgrund von neuem Quellenmaterial aus der Mitte der 20. Dynastie (ca. 1150 v. Chr.)*. 3 volumes (Basel).

Dorn, A. 2013. 'Zur Lehre Amunnachts: Ein Join und Missing Links', in *Zeitschrift für ägyptische Sprache und Altertumskunde* 140: 112–25.

Dorn, A. 2017. 'The *ỉrỉ.n Personal-Name*-formula in Non-Royal Texts of the New Kingdom. A Simple Donation Mark or a Means of Self-Presentation?' in T. J. Gillen (ed.) *(Re)productive Traditions in Ancient Egypt* (Liège): 593–621.

Dorn, A. and Hofmann, T. (eds). 2006. *Living and Writing in Deir el-Medine. Socio-historical Embodiment of Deir el-Medine Texts* (Basel).

Dorn, A. and Polis, S. 2016. 'Nouveaux textes littéraires du scribe Amennakhte (et autres ostraca relatifs au scribe de la Tombe)', in *Bulletin de l'Institut Français d'Archéologie Orientale* 116.

Doussa, T., Gaudard, F., and Johnson, J. H. 2004. 'P. Berlin 6848, a Roman Period Temple Inventory', in F. Hoffmann and H. J. Thissen (eds) *Res severa verum gaudium. Festschrift für Karl-Theodor Zauzich zum 65. Geburtstag am 8. Juni 2005* (Leuven): 139–222.

Drescher, J. 1948/9. 'A Coptic Calculation Manual', in *Bulletin de la Société d'archéologie Copte* 13: 137–60.

Drory, R. 1992. '"Words beautifully put": Hebrew versus Arabic in Tenth-Century Jewish Literature', in J. Blau and S. C. Reif (eds) *Genizah Research After Ninety Years: The Case of Judaeo-Arabic* (Cambridge): 53–66.

Dziobek, E. 1998. Denkmäler des Vezirs User-Amun (Heidelberg).

Eckert, P. 2004. 'Variation and a Sense of Place', in C. Fought (ed.) *Sociolinguistic Variation: Critical Reflection* (Oxford): 107–18.

Edgerton, W. F. 1951a. 'The Strikes in Ramses III's Twenty-Ninth Year', in *Journal of Near Eastern Studies* 10: 137–45.

Edgerton, W. F. 1951b. 'Early Egyptian Dialect Interrelationships', in *Bulletin of the American Schools of Oriental Research* 122: 9–12.

Eicher, I. and Fauerbach, U. 2005. 'Die spätantike/koptische Klosteranlage Deir el-Bachit in Dra' Abu el-Naga (Oberägypten) Zweiter Vorbericht', in *Mitteilungen des Deutschen Archäologischen Instituts, Abteilung Kairo* 61: 139–52, tafeln 21–6.

Emmel, S. 2004. *Shenoute's Literary Corpus*. 2 volumes (Leuven).

Erichsen, W. 1939. *Demotische Lesestücke II. Urkunden der Ptolemäerzeit* (Leipzig).

Erman, A. 1895. 'Zauberspruch für einen Hund', in *Zeitschrift für ägyptische Sprache und Altertumskunde* 33: 132–5.

Erman, A. 1897. *Bruchstücke koptischer Volkslitteratur* (Berlin).

Erman, A. 1903. 'Zur Erklärung des Papyrus Harris', in *Sitzungsberichte der Preußischen Akademie der Wissenschaften* 21: 456–74.

Erman, A. 1933. *Neuägyptische Grammatik*. 2nd edition (Leipzig).

Evans, T. V. 2010a. 'Identifying the Language of the Individual in the Zenon Archive', in T. V. Evans and D. D. Obbink (eds) *The Language of the Papyri* (Oxford): 53–70.

Evans, T. V. 2010b. 'Standard Koine Greek in Third Century BC Papyri', in T. Gagos (ed.) *Proceedings of the Twenty-Fifth International Congress of Papyrology, Ann Arbor, July 29–August 4, 2007* (Ann Arbor): 197–205.

Evans, T. V. 2012. 'Linguistic and Stylistic Variation in the Zenon Archive', in M. Leiwo, H. Halla-aho, and M. Vierros (eds) *Variation and Change in Greek and Latin* (Helsinki): 25–42.

Evans, T. V. and Obbink, D. D. (eds). 2010. *The Language of the Papyri* (Oxford).

Eyre, C. J. 1979. 'A "Strike" Text from the Theban Necropolis', in J. Ruffle, G. A. Gaballa, and K. A. Kitchen (eds) *Glimpses of Ancient Egypt: Studies in Honour of H. W. Fairman* (Warminster): 80–91.

Ferguson, C. A. 1983. 'Sport Announcer Talk: Syntactic Aspects of Register Variation', in *Language and Society* 12: 153–72.

Ferguson, C. A. 1994. 'Dialect, Register, and Genre: Working Assumptions about Conventionalization', in D. Biber and E. Finegan (eds) *Socio-Linguistic Perspectives on Register* (Oxford): 15–30.

Firchow, O. 1954. 'Zu den Wortverbindungen mit ś.t', in *Zeitschrift für ägyptische Sprache und Alterstumkunde* 79: 91–4.

Fischer, O., van Kemenade, A., and Koopman, W. 2000. *The Syntax of Early English* (Cambridge).

Fischer-Elfert, H.-W. 1983. 'Eine literarische „Miszelle": À propos ODeM 1040, 1218 und UC 31 905', in *Studien zur Altägyptischen Kultur* 10: 151–6.

Fischer-Elfert, H.-W. 1984a. 'Textkritische Kleinigkeiten zur „Lehre des Amenemhete" ', in *Göttinger Miszellen* 70: 89–90.

Fischer-Elfert, H.-W. 1984b. 'Ich bin das Schiff – du bist das Ruder. Eine Danksagung an den Lehrer', in *Studien zur Altägypischen Kultur* 11: 335–45.

Fischer-Elfert, H.-W. 1997. *Lesefunde im literarischen Steinbruch von Deir el-Medineh* (Wiesbaden).

Fischer-Elfert, H.-W. 1999. *Die Lehre eines Mannes für seinen Sohn. Eine Etappe auf dem „Gottesweg" des loyalen und solidarischen Beamten des Mittleren Reiches. Textband (i) & Tafelband (ii)* (Wiesbaden).

Fischer-Elfert, H.-W. 2006. 'Literature as a Mirror of Private Affairs: The Case of Menna and his Son Mery-Sekhmet', in A. Dorn and T. Hoffman (eds) *Living and Writing in Deir el-Medine. Socio-historical Embodiment of Deir el-Medine Texts* (Basel): 87–92.

Fleischman, S. 2000. 'Methodologies and Ideologies in Historical Linguistics: On Working with Older Languages', in S. C. Herring, P. van Reenen, and L. Schøsler (eds) *Textual Parameters in Older Languages* (Amsterdam): 33–58.

Fonseca, J. da, and Carolino, P., with an Introduction by J. Millington. 1884. *English As She Is Spoke, or A Jest in Sober Earnest* (London).

Foraboschi, D. 1968. 'Commento a P.Mil. Vogliano 24 (117 d.C.)' in *Studi Classici e Orientali* 17: 43–55.

Förster, H. 2002. *Wörterbuch der griechischen Wörter in den koptischen dokumentarischen Texten* (Berlin).

Fought, C. (ed.). 2004. *Sociolinguistic Variation: Critical Reflection* (Oxford).

Fournet, J.-L. 2009. 'Anatomie de la lettre antique', in R. Delmaire, J. Desmulliez, and P.-L. Gatier (eds) *Correspondances. Documents pour l'histoire de l'Antiquité tardive* (Paris): 23–66.

Frandsen, P. J. 1990. 'Editing Reality: The Turin Strike Papyrus', in S. I. Groll (ed.) *Studies in Egyptology Presented to Miriam Lichtheim.* Volume 1 (Jerusalem): 166–99.

Friedman, M. 1980. *Jewish Marriage in Palestine. A Cairo Genizah Study.* 2 volumes (Tel Aviv).

Fronczak, M. and Rzepka, S. 2009. '"Funny Signs" in Theban rock graffiti', in P. Andrássy, J. Budka, and F. Kammerzell (eds), Non-textual Marking Systems, Writing and Pseudo Script from Prehistory to Modern Times (Göttingen): 159–78.

Funk, W.-P. 1988. 'Dialects Wanting Homes: A Numerical Approach to the Early Varieties of Coptic', in J. Fisiak (ed.) *Historical Dialectology: Regional and Social* (Berlin–New York): 149–92.

Gallazzi, C. 1990. 'La 'Cantina dei Papiri' di Tebtynis e ciò che essa conteneva', in *Zeitschrift für Papyrologie und Epigraphik* 80: 282–8.

Gallazzi, C. Forthcoming. 'I papiri del tempio di Soknebtynis chi li ha trovati, dove li hanno trovati', in C. Gallazzi (ed.) *Tebtynis VI.*

Gallo, P. 1997. *Ostraca demotici e ieratici dall'archivio bilingue di Narmouthis II (nn. 34–99)* (Pisa).

Gardiner, A. H. 1935. *Facsimiles of the Egyptian Hieratic Papyri in the British Museum.* 2 volumes (London).

Gardiner, A. H. 1948. *Ramesside Administrative Documents* (London).

Gasse, A. 1992. 'Les ostraca hiératiques littéraires de Deir el-Medina: Nouvelles orientations de la publication', in R. J. Demarée and A. Egberts (eds) *Village Voices. Proceedings of the Symposium 'Texts from Deir el-Medîna and their Interpretation', Leiden, May 31 – June 1, 1991* (Leiden): 51–70.

Genette, G. 1982. *Palimpsestes. Litterature au second degré* (Paris).

Gies, F. and Gies, J. 1999. *A Medieval Family. The Pastons of Fifteenth Century England* (London).

Gil, M. 1992. *A History of Palestine, 634–1099* (Cambridge).

Gillen, T. J. 2014. 'Ramesside Registers of Égyptien de Tradition: The Medinet Habu Inscriptions', in E. Grossman, S. Polis, A. Stauder, and J. Winand (eds) *On Forms and Functions: Studies in Ancient Egyptian Grammar* (Hamburg): 41–86.

Gilmore, G. and Ray, J. 2006. 'A Fixed Point in Coptic Chronology: The Solar Eclipse of 10 March 601', in *Zeitschrift für Papyrologie und Epigraphik* 158: 190–2.

Gilula, M. 1991. 'The King's Egyptian', in *Lingua Aegyptia* 1: 125–7.

Givón, T. 2002. *Bio-Linguistics. The Santa Barbara Lectures* (Amsterdam–Philadelphia).

Glanville, S. R. K. 1955. *Catalogue of Demotic Papyri in the British Museum. Volume II. The Instructions of Onkhsheshonqi* (London).

Gneuss, H. 1972. 'The Origin of Standard Old English and Aethelwold's School of Winchester', in *Anglo-Saxon England* 1: 63–83.

Goedicke, H. and Wente, E. F. 1962. *Ostraka Michaelides* (Wiesbaden).

Goelet, O. 1996. 'A New "Robbery" Papyrus: Rochester MAG 51.346.1', in *The Journal of Egyptian Archaeology* 82: 107–27.

Goelet, O. 2008. 'Writing Ramesside Hieratic: What the *Late Egyptian Miscellanies* Tell us about Scribal Education', in S. H. D'Auria (ed.) *Servant of Mut. Studies in Honor of Richard A. Fazzini* (Leiden): 102–10.

Gohy, S., Martin Leon, B., and Polis, S. 2013. 'Automatic Text Categorization in Late Egyptian', in S. Polis and J. Winand (eds) *Texts, Languages & Information Technology in Egyptology* (Liège): 61–74.

Goitein, S. D. 1953. 'A Jewish Addict to Sufism: In the Time of the Nagid David II Maimonides', *Jewish Quarterly Review* 44: 37–49.

Goitein, S. D. 1967–93. *A Mediterranean Society: The Jewish Communities of the Arab World as Portrayed in the Documents of the Cairo Geniza*. 5 volumes (Berkeley).

Goldwasser, O. 1990. 'On the Choice of Registers. Studies in the Grammar of Papyrus Anastasi I', in S. I. Groll (ed.) *Studies in Egyptology Presented to Miriam Lichtheim* (Jerusalem): 200–40.

Goldwasser, O. 1991. 'On Dynamic Canonicity in Late-Egyptian: The Literary Letter and the Personal Prayer', in *Lingua Aegyptia* 1: 129–41.

Goldwasser, O. 1992. 'Literary Late Egyptian as a Polysystem', in *Poetics Today* 13: 447–62.

Goldwasser, O. 1995. 'On the Conception of the Poetic Form – A Love Letter to a Departed Wife: Ostracon Louvre 698', in S. Izre'el and R. Drory (eds) *Language and Culture in the Near East* (Leiden–New York): 191-205

Goldwasser, O. 1999. '"Low" and "High" Dialects in Ramesside Egyptian', in S. Grunert and I. Hafemann (eds) *Textcorpus und Wörterbuch. Aspekte zur ägyptischen Lexicographie* (Leiden): 311–28.

Goldwasser, O. 2001. 'Poetic License in Nineteenth Dynasty Non-Literary Late-Egyptian?', in *Lingua Aegyptia* 9: 123–38.

Goldwasser, O. and Grinevald, C. 2012. 'What are "Determinatives" good for?', in E. Grossman, S. Polis, and J. Winand (eds) *Lexical Semantics in Ancient Egyptian* (Hamburg): 17–53.

Golénischeff, W. 1927. *Papyrus hiératiques* (Cairo).

Gonis, N. 2004. 'Tax Receipts on Coptic and Greek Ostraca Re-Read', in *Zeitschrift für Papyrologie und Epigraphik* 147: 157–63.

Górecki, T. 2007. 'Sheikh Abd el-Gurna. Archaeological Activities in the Hermitage in Tomb 1152', in *Polish Archaeology in the Mediterranean* 18: 305–10.

Görlach, M. 1999. 'Social and Regional Variation', in R. Lass (ed.) *The Cambridge History of the English Language. Volume III: 1476–1776* (Cambridge): 459–538.

Goyon, G. 1949. 'Le papyrus de Turin dit 'des mines d'or' et le Wadi Hammamat', in *Annales du Service des Antiquités de l'Égypte* 49: 337–92.

Grandet, P. 1994. *Le papyrus Harris I* (Cairo).

Grandet, P. 2000. *Catalogue des ostraca hiératiques non littéraires de Deîr el-Médînéh. Tome VIII, Nos 706–830* (Cairo).

Grandet, P. 2003. *Catalogue des ostraca hiératiques non littéraires de Deîr el-Médînéh. Tome IX, Nos 831–1000* (Cairo).

Grandet, P. 2006. *Catalogue des ostraca hiératiques non littéraires de Deîr el-Médînéh. Tome X, Nos 10001–10123* (Cairo).

Grandet, P. 2010. *Catalogue des ostraca hiératiques non littéraires de Deîr el-Médînéh. Tome XI, Nos 10124–10275* (Cairo).

Green, M. 1985. 'A Private Archive of Coptic Letters and Documents from Teshlot', in *Oudheidkundige Mededelingen uit het Rijksmuseum van Oudheden te Leiden* 64: 61–122.

Greenberg, J. H. 1990. 'Were there Egyptian Koines?' in Keith Denning and Suzanne Kemmer (eds.) *On Language. Selected Writings of Joseph H. Greenberg* (Stanford): 502–19.

Griffith, F. L. 1900. *Stories of the High Priests of Memphis* (Oxford).

Griffith, F. L. and Thompson, H. 1904–9. *The Demotic Magical Papyrus of London and Leiden*. 3 volumes (London).

Grimal, N.-C. 1981. *Études sur la propagande royale égyptienne I. La stèle triomphale de Pi('ankh)y au musée du Caire (JE 48862 et 47086–47089)* (Cairo).

Grob, E. M. 2010. *Documentary Arabic Private and Business Letters on Papyrus. Form and Function, Content and Context* (Berlin–New York).

Groll, S. I. 1975. 'The Literary and Non-literary Verbal Systems in Late Egyptian', in *Orientalia Lovaniensia Periodica* 6–7: 237–46.

Groll, S. I. 1984. 'A Short Grammar of the Spermeru Dialect', in F. Junge (ed.) *Studien zu Sprache und Religion Ägyptens. Zu Ehren von Wolfhart Westendorf überreicht von seinen Freunden and Schülern* (Göttingen): 41–64.

Groll, S. I. 1987. 'The Negative *sḏm.n.f* System in the Kūbban Dialect', in J. Osing and G. Dreyer (eds) *Form und Mass, Beiträge zur Literatur, Sprache und Kunst des alten Ägypten. Festschrift für Gerhard Fecht zum 65. Geburtstag am 6. Februar 1987* (Wiesbaden): 154–66.

Grossman, E. 2007. 'Protatic *jjr=f sḏm* in the Report of Wenamun: A "Proto-Demotic" Feature?' in *Göttinger Miszellen* 215: 49–55.

Grossman, E. 2009a. 'Periphrastic Perfects in the Coptic Dialects. A Case Study in Grammaticalization', in *Lingua Aegyptia* 17: 81–118.

Grossman, E. 2009b. 'Protatic ⲉϥⲥⲱⲧⲙ̄ revisited', in A. Giewekemeyer, G. Moers, and K. Widmaier (eds) *Liber Amicorum Jürgen Horn zum Dank* (Göttingen): 47–56.

Grossman, E. 2011. 'Destandardization'. Paper presented at *Scribes as Agents of Language Change*, Cambridge 10–12 April 2011.

Grossman, E. Forthcoming. 'Typology, Dialectology, and Diachrony: The Grammaticalization of Prohibitive Constructions in Coptic'.

Grossman, E. and Polis, S. Forthcoming. 'Prohibitive Markers, Constructions, and Cycles in Ancient Egyptian–Coptic', in E. Oréal and J. Winand (eds) *Negation in Ancient Egyptian* (Berlin).

Grossman, E., Polis, S., and Winand, J. (eds). 2012. *Lexical Semantics in Ancient Egyptian* (Hamburg).

Guermeur, I. 2008. 'Les nouveaux papyrus hiératiques exhumés sur le site de Tebtynis: un aperçu', in S. Lippert and M. Schentuleit (eds) *Graeco-Roman Fayum – Texts and Archaeology* (Wiesbaden): 113–22.

Guermeur, I. 2015. 'Les papyrus hiératiques de Tebtynis. Un aperçu du matériel issu des fouilles 2008–2010', in N. Quenouille (ed.) *Von der Pharaonenzeit bis zur Spätantike* (Wiesbaden): 17–37.

Guglielmi, W. 1983. 'Eine „Lehre" für einen reiselustigen Sohn (Ostrakon Oriental Institute 12074)', in *Die Welt des Orients: Wissenschaftliche Beiträge zur Kunde des Morganlandes* 14: 147–66.

Guglielmi, W. 1985. 'Das Ostrakon Gardiner 25 Verso und seine hyperbolischen Vergleiche', in *Zeitschrift für ägyptische Sprache und Alterstumkunde* 112: 139–43.

Gundacker, R. 2010. 'Ein besondere Form des Substantivalsatzes. Mit besonderer Rücksicht auf ihre dialektale und diachrone Bedeutung', in *Lingua Aegyptia* 18: 41–117.

Hagen, F. 2006. 'Literature, Transmission, and the Late Egyptian Miscellanies', in R. J. Dann (ed.) *Current Research in Egyptology 5. Proceedings of the Fifth Annual Symposium, January 2004, Durham* (Oxford): 84–99.

Hagen, F. 2007. 'Ostraca, Literature and Teaching at Deir el-Medina', in R. Mairs and A. Stevenson (eds) *Current Research in Egyptology 6. Proceedings of the Sixth Annual Symposium, January 2005, University of Cambridge* (Oxford): 38–51.

Häggman, S. 2002. *Directing Deir el-Medina. The External Administration of the Necropolis* (Uppsala).

Hale, M. 2007. *Historical Linguistics: Theory and Method* (Malden, MA–Oxford).

Halla-aho, H. 2003. 'Scribes and the Letters of Claudius Terentianus', in H. Solin, M. Leiwo, and H. Halla-aho (eds) *Latin vulgaire — latin tardif VI. Actes du VIe Colloque international sur le latin vulgaire et tardif, Helsinki 29 août — 2 septembre 2000* (Hildesheim): 245–52.

Halle, M. 1962. 'Phonology in Generative Grammar', in *Word* 18: 58–72.

Halleux, R. 1979. *Les textes alchimiques* (Turnhout).

Halliday, M. A. K. 1978. *Language as Social Semiotic. The Social Interpretation of Language and Meaning* (London).

Halliday, M. A. K. 1988. 'On the Language of Physical Science', in M. Ghadessy (ed.) *Registers of Written English: Situational Factors and Linguistic Features* (London): 162–78.

Hamers, J. F. and Blanc, M. H. A. 2000. *Bilinguality and Bilingualism* (Cambridge).

Haring, B. J. J. 2000. 'The Scribe of the Mat, from Agrarian Administration to Local Justice', in R. J. Demarée and A. Egberts (eds) *Deir el-Medina in the Third Millennium AD. A Tribute to Jac. J. Janssen* (Leiden): 129–58.

Haring, B. J. J. 2003a. 'From Oral Practice to Written Record in Ramesside Deir el-Medina', in *Journal of the Economic and Social History of the Orient* 46: 249–72.

Haring, B. J. J. 2003b. 'Pratique écrite et pratique orale à Deir el-Médineh', in G. Andreu (ed.) *Deir el-Médineh et la Vallée des Rois. La vie en Égypte au temps des pharaons du Nouvel Empire. Actes du colloque organisé par le musée du Louvre les 3 et 4 mai 2002* (Paris): 139–56.

Haring, B. J. J. 2006. 'Scribes and Scribal Activity at Deir el-Medina', in A. Dorn and T. Hofmann (eds) *Living and Writing in Deir el-Medine. Socio-historical Embodiment of Deir el-Medine Texts* (Basel): 107–12.

Haring, B. J. J. 2009. "In Life, Prosperity, Health!" Introductory Formulae in Letters from the Theban Necropolis', in D. Kessler, R. Schulz, M. Ullmann, A. Verbovsek, and S. J. Wimmer (eds) *Texte – Theben – Tonfragmente. Festschrift für Günter Burkard* (Wiesbaden): 180–91.

Haring, B. J. J. 2009. 'On the Nature of Workmen's Marks of the Royal Necropolis Administration in the New Kingdom', in P. Andrássy, J. Budka, and F. Kammerzell (eds) *Non-textual Marking Systems, Writing and Pseudo Script from Prehistory to Modern Times* (Göttingen), 123–35.

Haring, B. J. J. and Kaper, O. E. E. (eds). 2009. *Pictograms or Pseudo Script? Non-Textual Identity Marks in Practical Use in Ancient Egypt and Elsewhere. Proceedings of a Conference in Leiden, 19–20 December 2006* (Leiden).

Harrel, J. A. and Brown, V. M. 1989. 'Oldest Geologic Map is Turin Papyrus', in *Geotimes* 34/3: 10–11.

Harrel, J. A. and Brown, V. M. 1992. 'The Oldest Surviving Topographical Map from Ancient Egypt (Turin Papyri 1879, 1899, and 1969)', in *Journal of the American Research Center in Egypt* 29: 81–105.

Harris, W. V. 1989. *Ancient Literacy* (Cambridge, MA).

Haussmann, T. 1991. *Erklären und Verstehen: Zur Theorie und Pragmatik der Geschichtswissenschaft* (Frankfurt).

Helck, W. 1960. *Materialen zur Wirtschaftsgeschichte des Neuen Reiches (Teil II)* (Wiesbaden).

Helck, W. 2002. *Die datierten und datierbaren Ostraka, Papyri und Graffiti von Deir el-Medineh* (Wiesbaden).

Herbin, F.-R. 2008. *Catalogue of the Books of the Dead and Other Religious Texts in the British Museum. Volume IV. Books of Breathing and Related Texts* (London).

Herring, S. C., van Reenen, P., and Schøsler, L. 2000. 'On Textual Parameters and Older Languages', in S. C. Herring, P. van Reenen, and L. Schøsler (eds) *Textual Parameters in Older Languages* (Amsterdam): 1–31.

Hess, J. J. 1892. *Der gnostische Papyrus von London* (Freiburg).

Heurtel, C. 2003. 'Le serment d'un chamelier. O.Gournet Mourraï 242', in *Bulletin de l'Institut français d'archéologie orientale* 103: 297–306.

Heurtel, C. 2007. 'Marc, le prêtre de Saint-Marc', in N. Bosson and A. Boud'hors (eds) *Actes du huitième congrès international d'études coptes (Paris, 28 juin–3 juillet 2004)*. Volume 2 (Leuven): 727–50.

Heurtel, C. 2008a. 'Les prédécesseurs de Frangé: l'occupation de TT29 au VIIe siècle', in A. Boud'hors and C. Louis (eds) *Études coptes X. Douzième journée d'études (Lyon, 19–21 mai 2005)* (Paris): 167–78.

Heurtel, C. 2008b. 'Le petit monde de Frangé : une micro-société dans la région thébaine au début du 8e siècle', in A. Delattre and P. Heilporn (eds) *« Et maintenant ce ne sont plus que des villages... ». Thèbes et sa région aux époques hellénistique, romaine et byzantine* (Brussels): 163–74.

Heurtel, C. 2008c. 'Une correspondance copte entre Djémé et Pétémout', in L. Pantalacci (ed.) *La lettre d'archive. Communication administrative et personnelle dans l'Antiquité proche-orientale et égyptienne (Actes du colloque de l'université de Lyon 2, 9–10 juillet 2004)* (Cairo): 87–108.

Heurtel, C. 2010. 'Écrits et écriture de Marc', in A. Boud'hors and C. Louis (eds) *Études coptes XI. Treizième journée d'études (Marseille, 7–9 juin 2007)* (Paris): 139–50.

Heurtel, C. 2013. 'Trois ostraca de Marc redécouverts', in A. Boud'hors and C. Louis (eds) *Études coptes XII. Quatorzième journée d'études (Rome, 11–13 juin 2009)* (Paris): 77–84.

Hincks, E. 1833. 'The Enchorial Language of Egypt', in *Dublin University Review* 3.

Hintze, F. 1954. 'Ein Bruchstück einer unbekannten Weisheitslehre', in *Zeitschrift für ägyptische Sprache und Alterstumkunde* 79: 33–6.

Hockett, Charles F. 1959. 'The Stressed Syllables of Old English', in *Language* 35: 575–97.

Hoffmann, F. 1995a. *Ägypter und Amazonen. Neubearbeitung zweier demotischer Papyri. P. Vindob. D 6165 und P. Vindob. D 6165 A* (Vienna).

Hoffmann, F. 1995b. 'Neue Fragmente zu den drei großen Inaros-Petubastis-Texten', in *Enchoria: Zeitschrift für Demotistik und Koptologie* 22: 27–39.

Hoffmann, F. 1996. *Der Kampfum den Panzer des Inaros. Studien zum P. Krall und seiner Stellung innerhalb des Inaros-Petubastis-Zyklus* (Vienna).

Hoffmann, F. 1999. 'Die Hymnensammlung des P. Wien D6951', in K. Ryholt (ed.) *Acts of the Seventh International Conference of Demotic Studies* (Copenhagen): 219–28.

Hoffmann, F. and Quack, J. F. 2007. *Anthologie der demotischen Literatur* (Berlin).

Hölscher, U. 1954. *The Excavation of Medinet Habu, V: Post-Ramessid Remains* (Chicago).

Horak, U. 1992. *Illuminierte Papyri, Pergamente und Papiere*. Volume 1 (Vienna).

Hovestreydt, W. 1997. 'A Letter to the King Relating to the Foundation of a Statue (P. Turin 1879 vso.)', in *Lingua Aegyptia* 5: 107–21.

Hudson, A. 1994. 'Diglossia as a Special Case of Register Variation', in D. Biber and E. Finegan (eds) *Socio-Linguistic Perspectives on Register* (Oxford): 294–314.

Hudson, A. 1996. *Sociolinguistics*. 2nd edition (Cambridge).

Hughes, G. R. and Jasnow, R. 1997. *Demotic and Greek Texts from an Egyptian Family Archive in the Fayum* (Chicago).

Hulbert, J. R. 1946. 'A Thirteenth-Century English Literary Standard', in *Journal of English and Germanic Philology* 45: 411–14.

Hunger, H. 1977. 'Minuskel- und Auszeichnungsschriften im 10.–12. Jahrhundert', in G. Cavallo (ed.) *La paléographie grecque et byzantine* (Paris): 201–20.

Hüttner, R. A. M. 2000. 'Die Votivstele des Vorarbeiters Chons (KHM Wien, ÄS Inv.Nr. 8212)', in *Göttinger Miszellen* 178: 59–63.

Iversen, E. 1958. *Papyrus Carlsberg No. VII: Fragments of a Hieroglyphic Dictionary* (Copenhagen).

Jäger, S. 2004. *Altägyptische Berufstypologien* (Göttingen).

Jansen-Winkeln. K. 1992. 'Das Ende des Neuen Reiches', in *Zeitschrift für ägyptische Sprache und Alterstumkunde* 119: 22–37.

Jansen-Winkeln. K. 1995a. 'Diglossie und Zweisprachigkeit im alten Ägypten', in *Wiener Zeitschrift für die Kunde des Morgenlandes* 85: 85–115.

Jansen-Winkeln. K. 1995b. 'Die Plünderung der Königsgräber des Neuen Reiches', in *Zeitschrift für ägyptische Sprache und Alterstumkunde* 122: 62–78.

Jansen-Winkeln. K. 1997. 'Die thebanischen Gründer der 21. Dynastie', in *Göttinger Miszellen*, 157: 49–74.

Janssen, J. J. 1975. *Commodity Prices from the Ramessid Period: An Economic Study of the Village of Necropolis Workmen at Thebes* (Leiden).

Janssen, J. J. 1979. 'Background Information on the Strikes of Year 29 of Ramesses III', in *Oriens antiquus: revista del Centro per la Antichità e la Storia dell'Arte de Vicino Oriente* 18: 301–8.

Janssen, J. J. 1982. 'A Draughtsman who became Scribe of the Tomb: Horshire, Son of Amennakhte', in R. J. Demarée and J. J. Janssen (eds) *Gleanings from Deir el-Medîna* (Leiden): 149–53.

Janssen, J. J. 1984. 'A Curious Error (O. IFAO. 1254)', in *Bulletin de l'Institut français d'archéologie orientale* 84: 303–6.

Janssen, J. J. 1987. 'On Style in Egyptian Handwriting', in *The Journal of Egyptian Archaeology* 73: 161–7.

Janssen, J. J. 1992. 'Literacy and Letters at Deir el-Medîna', in R. J. Demarée and A. Egberts (eds) *Village Voices. Proceedings of the Symposium 'Texts from Deir el-Medîna and their Interpretation', Leiden, May 31 – June 1, 1991* (Leiden): 81–94.

Janssen, J. J. 1994. 'An Exceptional Event at Deir El-Medina (P. Turin 1879, verso II)', in *Journal of the American Research Center in Egypt* 31: 91–7.

Janssen, J. J. 2005. 'Accountancy at Deir el-Medîna: How Accurate are the Administrative Ostraca?' in *Studien zur Altägyptischen Kultur* 33: 147–57.

Janssen, J. J. 2009. *Furniture at Deir el-Medîna, Including Wooden Containers of the New Kingdom and Ostracon Varille 19* (London).

Jasnow R. and Zauzich, K. T. 2005. *The Ancient Egyptian Book of Thoth. A Demotic Discourse on Knowledge and Pendant to the Classical Hermetica* (Wiesbaden).

Johnson, J. 1977. 'The Dialect of the Demotic Magical Papyrus of London and Leiden', in Oriental Institute (ed.) *Studies in Honor of George R. Hughes* (Chicago): 105–32.

Johnson, W. A. 2004. *Bookrolls and Scribes in Oxyrhynchus* (Toronto).

Johnstone, B. 2004. 'Place, Globalization, and Linguistic Variation', in C. Fought (ed.) *Sociolinguistic Variation: Critical Reflection* (Oxford): 65–83.

Jones, C. 2004. 'Discourse Communities and Medical Texts', in I. Taavitsainen and P. Pahta (eds) *Medical and Scientific Writing in Late Medieval English* (Cambridge): 23–36.

Junge, F. 1985. 'Sprachstufen und Sprachgeschichten', in *Zeitschrift der Deutschen Morgenländischen Gesellschaft: Supplement* 6: 17–34.

Junge, F. 2001. *Late Egyptian Grammar: An Introduction*, translation of F. Junge, *Neuägyptisch. Einfürhung in die Grammatik*, Wiesbaden, 1996, by D. Warburton (Oxford).

Junker, H. 1908/1911. *Koptische Poesie des 10. Jahrhunderts* (Berlin).

Kahle, P. E. 1954. *Bala'izah. Coptic Texts from Deir el-Bala'izah in Upper Egypt* (Oxford).

Kammerzell, F. 1998. 'The Sounds of a Dead Language. Reconstructing Egyptian Phonology', in *Göttinger Beiträge zur Sprachwissenschaft* 1: 21–41.

Kammerzell, F. 2005. 'Old Egyptian and Pre-Old Egyptian. Tracing linguistic Diversity in Archaic Egypt and the Creation of the Egyptian Language', in S. Seidelmayer (ed.) *Texte und Denkmäler des ägyptischen Alten Reiches* (Berlin): 165–247.

Kasser, R. 1991. 'Geography, Dialectal', in A. S. Atiya (ed.) *The Coptic Encyclopedia*. Volume 8 (New York–Toronto): 133–41.

Kasser, R. 2007. *The Gospel of Judas. Critical Edition* (Washington DC).

Keller, C. A. 1984. 'How Many Draughtsmen Named Amenhotep? A Study of some Deir el Medina Painters', in *Journal of the American Research Center in Egypt* 21: 119–29.

Keller, C. A. 2003. 'Un artiste égyptien à l'oeuvre: le dessinateur en chef Amenhotep', in G. Andreu (ed.) *Deir el-Médineh et la Vallée des Rois. La vie en Égypte au temps des pharaons du Nouvel Empire. Actes du colloque organisé par le musée du Louvre les 3 et 4 mai 2002* (Paris): 83–114.

Kemp, B. 2006. *Ancient Egypt. Anatomy of a Civilization.* 2nd edition (London–New York).

Kessler, D., Schulz, R., Ullmann, M., Verbovsek, A., and Wimmer, S. J. (eds). 2009. *Texte – Theben – Tonfragmente. Festschrift für Günter Burkard* (Wiesbaden).

Killen, G. and Weiss, L. 2009. 'Markings on Objects of Daily Use from Deir el-Medina: Ownership Marks or Administrative Aids?' in P. Andrássy, J. Budka, and F. Kammerzell (eds) *Non-textual Marking Systems, Writing and Pseudo Script from Prehistory to Modern Times* (Göttingen): 137–58.

King, R. D. 1969. *Historical Linguistics and Generative Grammar* (Engelwood Cliffs, NJ).

Kington, M. 1979. *Let's Parlez Franglais!* (London).

Khan, G. 1990. 'The Historical Development of the Structure of Medieval Arabic Petitions', in *Bulletin of the School of Oriental and African Studies* 53: 8–30.

Khan, G. 1992. *Arabic Papyri: Selected Material from the Khalili Collection* (Oxford).

Khan, G. 1993. *Arabic Legal and Administrative Documents in the Cambridge Genizah Collections* (Cambridge).

Khan, G. 2008. 'Remarks on the Historical Background of Arabic Documentary Formulae', in *Asiatische Studien* 62: 885–906.

Klotz, D. 2006. 'Between Heaven and Earth in Deir el-Medina: Stela MMA 21.2.6', in *Studien zur Altägyptischen Kultur* 34: 269–83.

Knigge Salis, C., Müller, M., and Widmer, G. 2012. 'Spätzeitliche Fragmente religiöser Papyri', in V. Lepper (ed.) *Forschungen in der Papyrussammlung. Eine Festgabe für das Neue Museum* (Berlin): 75–96

Kockelmann, H. 2014. 'Gods at War. Two Demotic Mythological Narratives in the Carlsberg Papyrus Collection, Copenhagen (PC 460 and PC 284)', in M. Depauw and Y. Broux (eds) *Acts of the Tenth International Congress of Demotic Studies, Leuven 26–30 August 2008* (Leuven): 115–25.

Koenig, Y. 1981. 'Notes sur la découverte des Papyrus Chester Beatty', in *Bulletin de l'Institut français d'archéologie orientale* 81: 41–3.

Koenig, Y. 1991. 'Les ostracas hiératiques du musée du Louvre', in *Revue d'égyptologie* 42: 95–116.

Kortman, B. (ed.). 2004. *Dialectology meets Typology. Dialect Grammar from a Cross-Linguistic Perspective* (Berlin).

Koskenniemi, H. 1956. *Studien zur Idee und Phraseologie des griechischen Briefes bis 400 n. Chr.* (Helsinki).

Kramer, J. 1983. *Glossaria Bilinguia in Papyris et Membranis Reperta* (Bonn).

Kramer, J. 2001. *Glossaria bilinguia altera (C. Gloss Biling. II)* (Munich).

Krause, M. 1956. 'Apa Abraham von Hermonthis. Ein oberägyptischer Bischof um 600'. Unpublished doctoral dissertation (Humboldt-Universität, Berlin).

Kretzschmar, W. 2009. *The Linguistics of Speech* (Cambridge).

Kropp, A. M. 1930–1. *Ausgewählte koptische Zaubertexte. Volume I: Textpublikation; Volume II: Übersetzungen und Anmerkungen; Volume III: Einleitung in die koptischen Zaubertexte* (Brussels).

Kruse, T. 2010. 'Briefe und ihre Funktion in der Verwaltung des griechischen und römischen Aegypten', in C. Kreuzsaler, B. Palme, and A. Zdiarsky (eds) *Stimmen aus dem Wüstensand. Briefkultur im griechisch-römischen Aegypten* (Vienna): 35–44.

Kurth, D. 2007 and 2008. *Einführung ins Ptolemäische: eine Grammatik mit Zeichenliste und Übungsstücken*. Volumes 1 and 2 (Hützel).

Labov, W. 1994. *Principles of Linguistic Change. Volume 1: Internal Factors* (Oxford).

Laing, M. 1993. *Catalogue of Sources for a Linguistic Atlas of Early Medieval English* (Cambridge).

Laing, M. 2004. 'Multidimensionality: Time, Space and Stratigraphy in Historical Dialectology', in M. Dossena and R. Lass (eds) *Methods and Data in English Historical Dialectology* (Bern): 49–96.

Laing, M. and Lass, R. 2008–13 and 2013–. *A Linguistic Atlas of Early Middle English, Version 2.1 and 3.2.* Electronic text corpora with accompanying software by K. Williamson, and theoretical introduction and manual (The University of Edinburgh). http://www.lel.ed.ac.uk/ihd/laeme2/laeme2.html.

Laing, M. and Lass, R. 2009. 'Shape-Shifting, Sound-Change and the Genesis of Prodigal Writing Systems', in *English Language and Linguistics* 13: 1–31.

Lass, R. 1980. *On Explaining Language Change* (Cambridge).

Lass, R. 1997. *Historical Linguistics and Language Change* (Cambridge).

Lass, R. 2004. '*Ut custodiant litteras*: Editions, Corpora and Witnesshood', in M. Dossena and R. Lass (eds) *Methods and Data in English Historical Dialectology* (Bern–Oxford): 21–48.

Lass, R. and Laing, M. 2008–. 'Introduction, Chapter 2: Interpreting Middle English', in R. Laing and M. Lass, *A Linguistic Atlas of Early Middle English, Version 2.1 and 3.2.* Electronic text corpora with accompanying software by K. Williamson, and theoretical introduction and manual (The University of Edinburgh). http://www.lel.ed.ac.uk/ihd/laeme2/laeme2.html.

Layton, B. 2004. *A Coptic Grammar*. 2nd edition (Wiesbaden).

Leahy, A. 1981. '*smn* and *di mn*', in *Göttinger Miszellen* 48: 35–9.

Leemans, C. 1839. *Papyrus égyptien démotique à transcriptions grecques du Musée d'antiquités des Pays-Bas à Leide* (Leiden).

Lefevre. D. 2008. 'Les papyrus « d'èl-Hibeh » à la 21ème Dynastie. Étude philologique et prosopographique'. Unpublished doctoral dissertation. 2 volumes (EPHE IVe section, Paris).

Lenker, U. 2000. 'The Monasteries of the Benedictine Reform and the "Winchester School": Model Cases of Social Networks in Anglo-Saxon England?' in *European Journal of English Studies*, 4.2: 225–38.

Lenzo Marchese, G. 2004. 'Les colophons dans la literature égyptienne', in *Bulletin de l'Institut français d'archéologie orientale* 104: 359–76.

Lesko, L. 1990. 'Some Comments on Ancient Egyptian Literacy and Literati', in S. I. Groll (ed.) *Studies in Egyptology Presented to Miriam Lichtheim*. Volume 2 (Jerusalem): 656–67.

Lesko, L. 1994. 'Literature, Literacy and Literati', in L. Lesko (ed.) *Pharaoh's Workers. The Villagers of Deir el-Medina* (London): 131–44.

Lewis, N. 1993. 'The Demise of the Demotic Document: When and Why', in *The Journal of Egyptian Archaeology* 79: 276–81.

Lewis, R. E. and McIntosh, A. 1982. *A Descriptive Guide to the Manuscripts of the Prick of Conscience* (Oxford).

Lexa, F. 1926. *Le Papyrus Insinger. Les enseignements moraux d'un scribe égyptien du premier siècle après J.-C. Texte démotique avec transcription, traduction française, commentaire, vocabulaire et introduction grammaticale et littéraire* (Paris).

Lexa, F. 1934. 'Les dialectes dans la langue démotique', in *Archiv Orientální* 6: 161–72.

Lexa, F. 1947–51. *Grammaire démotique* (Prague).

Lichtheim, M. 1973. *Ancient Egyptian Literature. Volume 1: The Old and Middle Kingdoms* (Berkeley–Los Angeles–London).

Lichtheim, M. 1980. 'The Praise of Cities in the Literature of the Egyptian New Kingdom', in S. M. Burstein and L. A. Okin (eds) *Panhellenica. Essays in Ancient History and Historiography in Honour of Truesdell S. Brown* (Lawrence, KS): 15–23.

von Lieven, A. 2005. 'Religiöse Texte aus der Tempelbibliothek von Tebtunis – Gattungen und Funktionen', in S. Lippert and M. Schentuleit (eds) *Tebtynis und Soknopaiu Nesos. Leben im römerzeitlichen Fajum. Akten des Internationalen Symposions vom 11. bis 13. Dezember 2003 im Sommerhausen bei Würzburg* (Wiesbaden): 57–70.

von Lieven, A. 2007. *The Carlsberg Papyri 8: Grundriss des Laufes der Sterne. Das sogenannte Nutbuch* (Copenhagen).

von Lieven, A. 2008. 'Heiligenkult und Vergöttlichung im Alten Ägypten'. Habilitation thesis (Free University, Berlin).

Lightfoot, D. 1979. *Principles of Diachronic Syntax* (Cambridge).

Lightfoot, D. 1998. *The Development of Language: Acquisition, Change, and Evolution* (Oxford).

Lincke, E.-S. and Kammerzell, F. 2012. 'Egyptian Classifiers at the Interface of Lexical Semantics and Pragmatics', in E. Grossman, S. Polis, and J. Winand (eds) *Lexical Semantics in Ancient Egyptian* (Hamburg): 55–112.

Lippert, S. L. 2004. *Ein demotisches juristisches Lehrbuch. Untersuchungen zu Papyrus Berlin P 23757 rto* (Wiesbaden).

Lippert, S. L. and Schentuleit, M. 2006a. *Demotische Dokumente aus Dime I: Ostraka* (Wiesbaden).

Lippert, S. L. and Schentuleit, M. 2006b. *Demotische Dokumente aus Dime II: Quittungen* (Wiesbaden).

Lippert, S. L. and Schentuleit, M. 2010. *Demotische Dokumente aus Dime III: Urkunden* (Wiesbaden).

Logan, T. J. and Westenholz, J. G. 1972. '*sḏm.f* and *sḏm.n.f* Forms in the Pey (Piankhy) Inscription', in *Journal of the American Research Center in Egypt* 9: 111–19.

López, J. 1978. *Ostraca ieratici N. 57001–57092*. Volume 3/1 (Milan).

López, J. 1982. *Ostraca ieratici N. 57320–57449*. Volume 3/3 (Milan).

Loprieno, A. 1982. 'Methodologische Anmerkungen zur Rolle der Dialekte in der ägyptischen Sprachentwicklung', in *Göttinger Miszellen* 53: 75–95.

Loprieno, A. 1994. 'As a Summary: New Tendencies in Egyptological Linguistics', in *Lingua Aegyptia* 4: 369–82.

Loprieno, A. 1995. *Ancient Egyptian. A Linguistic Introduction* (Cambridge).

Loprieno, A. (ed.) 1996a. *Ancient Egyptian Literature. History & Forms* (Leiden).

Loprieno, A. 1996b. 'Defining Egyptian Literature: Ancient Texts and Modern Theories', in A. Loprieno (ed.) *Ancient Egyptian Literature. History & Forms* (Leiden): 39–58.

Loprieno, A. 1996c. 'Linguistic Variety and Egyptian Literature', in A. Loprieno (ed.) *Ancient Egyptian Literature. History & Forms* (Leiden): 515–29.

Loprieno, A. 2001. *La pensée et l'écriture: pour une analyse sémiotique de la culture égyptienne. Quatre séminaires à l'École pratique des hautes études, Section des sciences religieuses, 15–27 mai 2000* (Paris).

Loprieno, A. 2006. 'As a Conclusion: Towards a Detailed Perspective on Deir el-Medina', in A. Dorn and T. Hofmann (eds) *Living and Writing in Deir el-Medine. Socio-historical Embodiment of Deir el-Medine Texts* (Basel): 165–70.

Lucas, A. and Rowe, A. 1938. 'The Ancient Egyptian Bekhen-Stone', in *Annales du Service des Antiquités de l'Égypte* 38: 127–56.

Luiselli, M. 2003. 'The Colophons as an Indication of the Attitudes towards the Literary Tradition in Egypt and Mesopotamia', in S. Bickel and A. Loprieno (eds) *Basel Egyptology Prize; 1. Junior Research in Egyptian History, Archaeology, and Philology* (Basel): 343–60.

Luiselli, M. 2011. *Die Suche nach Gottesnähe. Die altägyptische „persönlich Frömmigkeit" von der Ersten Zwischenzeit bis zum Ende des Neuen Riches* (Wiesbaden).

Luiselli, R. 2008. 'Greek Letters on Papyrus, First to Eighth Centuries: A Survey', in *Asiatische Studien/Études Asiatiques* 62 (2008): 677–737.

Lustman, J. 1999. *Étude grammticale du Papyrus Bremner-Rhind* (Paris).

MacCoull, L. S. B. 1988. 'Coptic Alchemy and Craft Technology in Early Islamic Egypt: The Papyrological Evidence', in M. J. S. Chiat (ed.) *The Medieval Mediterranean. Cross Cultural Contacts. Medieval Studies at Minnesota* 3 (Minnesota): 101–4.

McDowell, A. G. 1992. 'Awareness of the Past in Deir el-Medîna', in R. J. Demarée and A. Egberts (eds) *Village Voices. Proceedings of the Symposium 'Texts from Deir el-Medîna and their Interpretation', Leiden, May 31 – June 1, 1991* (Leiden): 95–109.

McDowell, A. G. 1994. 'Contact with the Outside World', in L. Lesko (ed.) *Pharaoh's Workers. The Villagers of Deir el-Medina* (London): 41–59.

McDowell, A. G. 1996. 'Student Exercises from Deir el-Medina: The Dates', in P. Der Manuelian (ed.) *Studies in Honor of William Kelly Simpson.* Volume 2 (Boston): 601–8.

McDowell, A. G. 1999. *Village Life in Ancient Egypt. Laundry Lists and Love Songs* (Oxford).

McDowell, A. G. 2000. 'Teachers and Students at Deir el-Medina', in R. J. Demarée and A. Egberts (eds) *Deir el-Medina in the Third Millennium AD. A Tribute to Jac J. Janssen* (Leiden): 217–33.

McEnery, T. and Wilson, A. 1996. *Corpus Linguistics* (Edinburgh).

McIntosh, A. 1956. 'The Analysis of Written Middle English', in *Transactions of the Philological Society* 55: 26–55.

McIntosh, A. 1963. 'A New Approach to Middle English Dialectology', in *English Studies* 44: 1–11.

McIntosh, A. 1974. 'Towards an Inventory of Middle English Scribes', as reprinted (by A. McIntosh, M. Laing, and M. L. Samuels) in M. Laing (ed.) *Middle English Dialectology. Essays on Some Principles and Problems* (Aberdeen): 46–61.

McIntosh, A., Samuels, M. L., and Benskin, M. 1986. *A Linguistic Atlas of Late Medieval English.* 4 volumes (Aberdeen).

Mairs, R. 2011. 'Bilingualism', in R. S. Bagnall, K. Brodersen, C. B. Champion, A. Erskine, and S. R. Huebner (ed.) *The Encyclopedia of Ancient History* (Oxford).

Mairs, R. 2012a. 'Interpreters and Translators in Hellenistic and Roman Egypt', in P. Schubert (ed.) *Actes du 26ᵉ Congrès international de papyrologie (Genève 2010)* (Geneva): 457–62.

Mairs, R. 2012b. '"Interpreting" at Vindolanda', in *Britannia* 43: 1–12.
Mairs, R. and Martin, C. J. 2008/2009. 'A Bilingual "Sale" of Liturgies from the Archive of the Theban Choachytes: P. Berlin 5507, P. Berlin 3098 and P. Leiden 413', in *Enchoria, Zeitschrift für Demotistik und Koptologie* 31: 22–67.
Malinine. M. 1967. 'Partage testamentaire d'une propriété familiale', in *Revue d'égyptologie* 19: 67–85.
Mandilaras, V. G. 1973. *The Verb in the Greek Non-Literary Papyri* (Athens).
Manicas, P. 2006. *A Realist Philosophy of Social Science. Explanation and Understanding* (Cambridge).
Margoliouth, D. S. 1893. *Arabic Papyri of the Bodleian Library* (London).
Markus, M. 1988. 'Reasons for the Loss of Gender in English', in D. Kastovsky and G. Bauer (eds) *Luick Revisited. Papers Read at the Luick Symposium at Schloss Liechtenstein, 15–18.9.1985* (Tübingen): 241–58.
Mäkinen, M. 2006. 'Between Herbals et alia: Intertextuality in Medieval English Herbals'. Unpublished doctoral dissertation (University of Helsinki).
Mathieu, B. 1993. 'Sur quelques ostraca hiératiques littéraires récemment publiés', in *Bulletin de l'Institut français d'archéologie orientale* 93: 335–47 + figs 1–9.
Mathieu, B. 1996. *La poésie amoureuse de l'Égypte ancienne: recherches sur un genre littéraire au Nouvel Empire* (Cairo).
Mathieu, B. 2002. 'Lire et écrire à Deir el-Médineh : combien de lettrés', 'La littérature égyptienne à travers les documents de Deir el-Médineh', and 'Ostracon: *Enseignement d'Amennakhte, fils d'Ipouy*', in G. Andreu (ed.) *Les artistes de Pharaon. Deir el-Médineh et la Vallée des Rois* (Paris): 219, 220, and 221.
Mathieu, B. 2003. 'La littérature égyptienne sous les Ramsès d'après les ostraca littéraires de Deir el-Médineh', in G. Andreu (ed.) *Deir el-Médineh et la Vallée des Rois. La vie en Égypte au temps des pharaons du Nouvel Empire. Actes du colloque organisé par le musée du Louvre les 3 et 4 mai 2002* (Paris): 117–37.
Mathieu, B. 2008. *La poésie amoureuse de l'Égypte ancienne. Recherche sur un genre littéraire au Nouvel Empire*. 2nd edition (Cairo).
Matras, Y. 2008. *Language Contact* (Cambridge).
Matthiew, M. 1930. 'The Ostracon No. 1125 in the Hermitage Museum', in *Publications de la Société Égyptologique à l'Université d'État de Leningrad* 5: 25–7 + pl. 1.
Meeks, D. 1998. *Année lexicographique. Égypte ancienne*. 2nd edition (Paris).
Meltzer, E. S. 1980. 'Dialect Features in Middle Kingdom Inscriptions', in *Newsletter of the American Research Center in Egypt* 112: 34–6.
Meltzer, E. S. 1990. 'The "Prehistory" of Late Egyptian *i*(*w*)*n*(ꜣ): A Hypothesis', in *Göttinger Miszellen* 114: 71–9.
Menchetti, A. 1999–2000. 'Esercizi scolastici in demotico da Medinet Madi', in *Egitto e Vicino Oriente: Rivista della sezione oreintalistica dell'Instituto di Storia Antica, Università degli Studi di Pisa* 22–3: 137–53.
Menchetti, A. 2003. 'Esercizi scolastici in demotico da Medinet Madi (II)', in *Egitto e Vicino Oriente: Rivista della sezione oreintalistica dell'Instituto di Storia Antica, Università degli Studi di Pisa* 26: 23–31.
Menchetti, A. 2005. *Ostraka demotici e bilingui da Narmuthis (ODN 100–188)* (Pisa).
Menchetti, A. and Pintaudi, R. 2007. 'Ostraka greci e bilingui da Narmuthis', in *Chronique d'Égypte* 82: 227–80.

Menci, G. 2008. 'Scritture segrete nell'Egitto romano e byzantine', in *Atene e Roma* n.s. 2: 260–70.

Messeri, G. 2001. 'Registro di pagamenti del Syntaximon (in un quartiere Ebraico?)', in B. Palme (ed.) *Wiener Papyri als Festgabe zum 60. Geburtstag von Hermann Harrauer (P. Harrauer)* (Vienna): 81–92.

Meurman-Solin, A. 2014. 'Historical Dialectology: Space as a Variable in the Reconstruction of Regional Dialects', in J. M. Hernandez-Campoy and J. C. Conde-Silvestre (eds) *The Handbook of Historical Sociolinguistics* (Chichester): 465–79.

Meyer, M. 1996. *The Magical Book of Mary and the Angels (P. Heid. Inv. Kopt. 685)* (Heidelberg).

Milroy, J. 1992a. *Linguistic Variation and Change: On the Historical Sociolinguistics of English* (Oxford).

Milroy, J. 1992b. 'Social Network and Social Class: Toward an Integrated Sociolinguistic Model', in *Language in Society* 21.1: 1–26.

Milroy, J. and Milroy, L. 1985. 'Linguistic Change, Social Network and Speaker Innovation', in *Journal of Linguistics* 21: 339–84.

Milroy, J. and Milroy, L. 1987. *Observing and Analysing Natural Language* (Oxford).

Milroy, L. 1987. *Language and Social Networks* (Oxford).

Milroy, L. 2004. 'Language Ideologies and Linguistic Change', in C. Fought (ed.) *Sociolinguistic Variation: Critical Reflection* (Oxford): 161–77.

Milroy, L. and Gordon, M. 2003. *Sociolinguistics: Method and Interpretation* (Oxford).

Mitchell, J. C. (ed.) 1969. *Social Networks in Urban Situations* (Manchester).

Moers, G. 2001. 'Der Papyrus Lansing: Das Lob des Schreiberberufes in einer ägyptischen „Schülerhandschrift" aus dem ausgehenden Neuen Reich', in O. Kaiser and M. Dietrich (eds) *Texte aus der Umwelt des Alten Testaments: Ergänzungslieferung* (Gütersloh): 109–42.

Moers, G. 2002. 'The Interplay of Reenactment and Memory in the *Complaints of Khakheperreseneb*', in *Lingua Aegyptia* 10: 293–308.

Moers, G. 2008. 'Zur Relevanz der Namenliste des pChester Beatty IV für Versuche einer funktionalen Binnendifferenzierung des gemeinhin als „literarisch" bezeichneten Gattungssystem des Mittleren Reiches', in C. Peust (ed.) *Miscellanea in honorem Wolfhart Westendorf* (Göttingen): 45–52.

Moers, G. 2009. 'Der „Autor' und sein „Werk". Der Beginn der Lehre des Ptahhotep in der Tradition des Neuen Reiches', in D. Kessler, R. Schulz, M. Ullmann, A. Verbovsek, and S. J. Wimmer (eds) *Texte – Theben – Tonfragmente. Festschrift für Günter Burkard* (Wiesbaden): 319–32.

Moers, G. 2010. 'New Kingdom Literature', in A. B. Lloyd (ed.) *A Companion to Ancient Egypt*. Volume 2 (Oxford): 685–708.

Moers, G., Widmaier, K., Giewekemeyer, A., Lümers, A., and Ernst, R. (eds). 2013. *Dating Egyptian Literary Texts. "Dating Egyptian Literary Texts" Göttingen, 9–12 June 2010*. Volume 1 (Hamburg).

Möller, G. 1927. *Hieratische Paläographie. Die aegyptische Buchschrift in ihrer Entwicklung von der fünften Dynastie bis zur römischen Kaiserzeit, Zweiter Band. Von der Zeit Thutmosis' III bis zum Ende der einundzwanzigsten Dynastie* (Leipzig).

Monteiro, G. 2004. 'English as She Is Spoke: 150 Years of a Classic', in *Luso-Brazilian Review* 41: 191–8.

Müller, M. 2004. 'Der Turiner Streikpapyrus (pTurin 1880)', in B. Janowsky and G. Wilhelm (eds) *Texte aus der Umwelt des Alten Testaments, N.F. 1: Texte zum Rechts- & Wirtschaftsleben* (Gütersloh): 165–84.

Müller, M. 2006a. 'Magie in der Schule? Die magischen Sprüche der Schülerhandschrift pBM 10.085 + 10.105', in G. Moers, H. Behlmer, K. Demuß, and K. Widmaier (eds) *jn.t d̠r.w. Festschrift für Friedrich Junge*. Volume 2 (Göttingen): 449–55.

Müller, M. 2006b. 'Ägyptische Briefe', in *Texte aus der Umwelt des Alten Testaments*. Neue Folge Band 3: *Briefe* (Gütersloh): 330–9.

Munier, Henri 1930. *La Scala copte 44 de la Bibliothèque Nationale. Bibliothèque d'études coptes*. Volume 2 (Cairo).

Mussies, G. 1968. 'Egyptianisms in a Late Ptolemaic Document', in E. Boswinkel, B. A. van Groningen, and P. W. Pestman (eds) *Antidoron Martino David Oblatum: Miscellanea Papyrologica (P.L. Bat. XVII)* (Leiden): 70–6.

Naether, F. 2010. *Die Sortes Astrampsychi. Problemlösungsstrategien durch Orakel im römischen Ägypten* (Tübingen).

Naether, F. and Renberg, G. H. 2010. '"I Celebrated a Fine Day". An Overlooked Egyptian Phrase in a Bilingual Letter Preserving a Dream Account', in *Zeitschrift für Papyrologie und Epigraphik* 175: 49–71.

Nelson, M. and Hassanein, F. 1995. '« Sortie au jour » d'un membre oublié de la famille d'Ipouy', in *Mnemonia* 6: 229–36 + pls. xlii–xliii.

Neugebauer, O. and Parker, R. A. 1969. *Egyptian Astronomical Texts. Volume 3: Decans, Planets, Constellations and Zodiacs* (Providence, RI–London).

Nevalainen, T. 1999. 'Making the Best Use of "Bad" Data. Evidence for Sociolinguistic Variation in Early Modern English', in *Neuphilologische Mitteilungen* 100/4: 499–533.

Nevalainen, T., Klemola, J., and Laitinen, M. 2006. '"Triangulation" of Diachrony, Dialectology, and Typology: An Overview', in T. Nevalainen, J. Klemola, and M. Laitinen (eds) *Types of Variation. Diachronic, Dialectal and Typological Interfaces* (Amsterdam–Philadelphia): 3–19.

Nevalainen, T. and Raumolin-Brunberg, H. 2003. *Historical Sociolinguistics* (London).

Nobels, J. and van der Wal, M. 2009. 'Tackling the Writer-Sender Problem: The Newly Developed Leiden Identification Procedure (LIP)', online journal *Historical Sociolinguistics and Sociohistorical Linguistics* 9 (http://www.let.leidenuniv.nl/hsl_shl/Nobels-Wal.html).

Ogura, M. and Wang, W. S.-Y. 1998. 'Evolution Theory and Lexical Diffusion', in J. Fisiak and M. Krygier (eds) *Advances in English Historical Linguistics (1996)* (Berlin): 315–44.

Olsson, B. 1925. 'Papyrusbriefe aus der frühesten Römerzeit'. Unpublished doctoral dissertation (Uppsala University).

Osing, J. 1975. 'Dialekte', in *Lexicon der Ägyptologie*. Volume 1 (Wiesbaden): 1074–5.

Osing, J. 1998. *The Carlsberg Papyri 2: Hieratische Papyri aus Tebtunis 1* (Copenhagen).

Osing, J. and Rosati, G. 1998. *Papiri geroglifici e ieratici da Tebtynis* (Firenze).

Outhwaite, B. M. 2004. '"In the language of the Hagri": The Judaeo-Arabic Letters of Solomon ben Judah', in S. Reif (ed.) *The Written Word Remains: The Archive and the Achievement. Articles in honour of Professor Stefan C. Reif* (Cambridge): 52–69.

Outhwaite, B. M. 2009. 'Byzantium and Byzantines in the Cairo Genizah: New and Old Sources', in N. de Lange, J. G. Krivoruchko, and C. Boyd-Taylor (eds) *Jewish Reception of Greek Bible Versions: Studies in their Use in Late Antiquity and the Middle Ages* (Tübingen): 182–220.

Pantalacci, L. 1996. 'Fonctionnaires et analphabètes: sur quelques pratiques administratives observées à Balat', in *Bulletin de l'Institut français d'archéologie orientale* 96: 359–67.

Papathomas, A. 2007. 'Höflichkeit und Servilität in den Papyrusbriefen der ausgehenden Antike', in B. Palme (ed.) *Akten des 23. Papyrologenkongresses* (Wien): 497–512.

Parker, R. A. 1962. 'Two Demotic Astronomical Papyri in the Carlsberg Collection', in *Acta Orientalia* 26: 143–7.

Parker, R. A. 1972. *Demotic Mathematical Papyri* (Providence, RI).

Parkinson, R. B. 1991. *The Tale of the Eloquent Peasant* (Oxford).

Parkinson, R. B. 1999. *Cracking Codes. The Rosetta Stone and Decipherment* (Cambridge).

Parkinson, R. B. 2002. *Poetry and Culture in Middle Kingdom Egypt. A Dark Side to Perfection* (London).

Parkinson, R. B. 2009. *Reading Ancient Egyptian Poetry among other Histories* (Oxford).

Parsons, P. 1981. 'Background: The Papyrus Letter', in *Didactica Classica Gandensia* 20–1: 3–19.

Peden, A. 2001. *The Graffiti of Pharaonic Egypt. Scope and Roles of Informal Writings (c. 3100–332 B.C.)* (Leiden).

Peet. T. E. 1920. *The Mayer Papyri A & B: nos. M. 11162 and M. 11186 of the Free Public Museums* (Liverpool–London).

Peet. T. E. 1930. *The Great Tomb-robberies of the Twentieth Egyptian Dynasty: Being a Critical Study, with Translations and Commentaries, of the Papyri in which these are Recorded* (Oxford).

Pestman, P. W. 1982. 'Who were the Owners, in the "Community of Workmen", of the Chester Beatty Papyri', in R. J. Demarée and J. J. Janssen (eds) *Gleanings from Deir el-Medîna*: 155–72.

Pestman, P. W. 1985a. 'A Comforting Thought for Demotists? Errors of Scribes in the Archive of the Theban Choachytes', in S. F. Bondi (ed.) *Studi in onore di Edda Bresciani* (Pisa): 413–22.

Pestman, P. W. 1985b. 'Registration of Demotic Contracts in Egypt: P. Par. 65; 2nd cent. B.C.', in J. Ankum, J. Spruit, and F. Wubbe (ed) *Satura Roberto Feenstra sexagesimum quintum annum aetatis complenti ab alumnis collegis amicis oblata* (Fribourg): 17–25.

Pestman, P. W. 1985c. 'The Competence of Greek and Egyptian Tribunals According to the Decree of 118 B.C.', in *Bulletin of the American Society of Papyrologists* 22: 265–9.

Pestman, P. W. 1993. *The Archive of the Theban Choachytes (Second Century B.C.): A Survey of the Demotic and Greek Papyri Contained in the Archive* (Leuven).

Peust, C. 1999a. *Egyptian Phonology. An Introduction to the Phonology of a Dead Language* (Göttingen).

Peust, C. 1999b. *Das Napatanische. Ein ägyptischer Dialekt aus dem Nubien des späten ersten vorchristlichen Jahrtausends. Texte, Glossar, Grammatik* (Göttingen).

Peust, C. 2007. 'Die Konjugation für „gehen" im Neuägyptischen', in *Göttinger Miszellen* 212: 67–80.

Pezin, M. 1986. 'Premiers raccords effectués sur les documents démotiques de Lille', in *Cahier de recherches de l'Institut de papyrologie et égyptologie de Lille* 8: 89–98.

Philips, B. 1995. 'Lexical Diffusion as a Guide to Scribal Intent: A Comparison of ME <eo> vs. <e> Spellings in the Peterborough Chronicle and the Ormulum', in

H. Andersen (ed.) *Historical Linguistics 1993: Selected Papers from the 11th International Conference on Historical Linguistics* (Amsterdam): 379–86.

Pinker, S. and Prince, A. 2001. 'On Language and Connectionism: Analysis of a Parallel Distributed Processing Model of Language Acquisition' (University of Southampton). http://www.users.ecs.soton.ac.uk/harnad/Papers/Py104/pinker.conn.html.

Pleyte, W. and Rossi, F. 1869–76. *Papyrus de Turin* (Wiesbaden, 1981 reprint).

Polis, S. 2011. 'Le serment du P. Turin 1880, v° 2, 8–19. Une relecture de la construction *ỉw bn sḏm.f* à portée historique', in M. Collier and S. Snape (eds) *Ramesside Studies in Honour of K. A. Kitchen* (Bolton): 387–402.

Polis, S. Forthcoming. 'Language and Reality in Ancient Egypt. Norms and Ideologies in the Social Practices of the Ramesside Period', in A. Dorn (ed.) *Filtering Decorum – Facing Reality* (Liège).

Polis, S., Honnay, A.-C., and Winand, J. 2013. 'Building an Annotated Corpus of Late Egyptian. The Ramses Project: Review and Perspectives', in S. Polis and J. Winand (eds) *Texts, Languages & Information Technology in Egyptology* (Liège): 25–44.

Polis, S. and Stauder, A. 2014. 'The verb ib and the construction *ỉb=f r sDm*', in E. Grossman, S. Polis, A. Stauder, and J. Winand (eds) *On Forms and Function in Ancient Egyptian Grammar* (Hamburg): 201–31.

Polis, S. and Winand, J. (eds). 2013. *Texts, Languages & Information Technology in Egyptology* (Liège).

Polotsky, H. J. 1960. 'The Coptic Conjugation System', in *Orientalia* 29: 392–422.

Posener, G. 1938. *Catalogue des ostraca hiératiques littéraires de Deir el-Médineh. Tome i (nos 1001 à 1108)* (Cairo).

Posener, G. 1951a. 'Les richesses inconnues de la littérature égyptienne (recherches littéraires, i)', in *Revue d'égyptologie* 6: 27–48 + pl. i.

Posener, G. 1951b. 'Ostraca inédits du musée de Turin (recherches littéraires, iii)', in *Revue d'égyptologie* 8: 171–89 + pls. 12–13.

Posener, G. 1952. 'Le début de l'enseignement de Hardjedef (recherches littéraires, iv)', in *Revue d'égyptologie* 9: 109–20 + pl. i.

Posener, G. 1955. 'L'exorde de l'instruction éducative d'Amennakhte (recherches littéraires, v)', in *Revue d'égyptologie* 10: 61–72 + pl. iv.

Posener, G. 1964. 'L'expression *bỉꜢ.t ꜥꜢ.t* « mauvais caractère »', in *Revue d'égyptologie* 16: 37–43.

Posener, G. 1972. *Catalogue des Ostraca hiératiques littéraires de Deir el-Médineh. Tome ii/fasc. 3 (nos 1227–66)* (Cairo).

Posener, G. 1977. *Catalogue des Ostraca hiératiques littéraires de Deir el-Médineh. Tome iii/fasc. 1 (nos 1267–1409)* (Cairo).

Posener, G. 1978. *Catalogue des Ostraca hiératiques littéraires de Deir el-Médineh. Tome iii/fasc. 2 (nos 1410–1606)* (Cairo).

Posener, G. 1980a. *Catalogue des ostraca hiératiques littéraires de Deir el Médineh. Tome iii/fasc. 3, (nos 1267–1675)* (Cairo).

Posener, G. 1980b. 'L'auteur de la Satire des métiers', in J. Vercoutter (ed.) *Livre du centenaire 1880–1980* (Cairo): 55–9.

Prada, L. 2013. 'Orthographic Differentiations in Verbal Forms and Converters: An Early Demotic Case Study (P.Ryl. 5)', in S. P. Vleeming (ed.) *Aspects of Demotic Orthography: Acts of an International Colloquium Held in Trier, 8 November 2010* (Leuven–Paris): 69–97.

Price, J. J. and Naeh, S. 2009. 'On the Margins of Culture: The Practice of Transcription in the Ancient World', in H. M. Cotton et al. (eds) *From Hellenism to Islam: Cultural and Linguistic Change in the Roman Near East* (Cambridge): 157–88.

Quack, J. F. 1994. *Die Lehren des Ani. Ein neuägyptischer Weisheitstext in seinem kulturellen Umfeld* (Freibourg–Göttingen).

Quack, J. F. 2000. 'Eine Revision im Tempel von Karnak: Neuanalyse von Papyrus Rochester MAG 51.346.1', in *Studien zur Altägyptische Kultur* 28: 219–32.

Quack, J. F. 2001. 'Ein neuer Versuch zum Moskauer literarischen Brief', in *Zeitschrift für ägyptische Sprache und Alterstumkunde* 128: 167–81.

Quack, J. F. 2002a. 'Die Dienstanweisung des Oberlehrers im Buch vom Tempel', in H. Beinlich, J. Hallof, H. Hussy, and C. von Pfeil (eds) *5. Ägyptologische Tempeltagung Würzburg, 23.–26. September 1999* (Wiesbaden): 159–71.

Quack, J. F. 2002b. 'Ein neuer prophetischer Text aus Tebtynis (Papyrus Carlsberg 399 + Papyrus PSI inv. D. 17 + Papyrus Tebtunis 13 vs.)', in A. Blassius and B. U. Schipper (eds) *Apokalyptik und Ägypten* (Leuven): 253–74.

Quack, J. F. 2002c. 'Beiträge zum Peripherdemotischen', in T. A. Bács (ed.) *A Tribute to Excellence: Studies Offered in Honor of Ernő Gaál, Ulrich Luft, László Török* (Budapest): 393–403.

Quack, J. F. 2004. 'Gibt es einen stammhaften Imperativ *ỉyỉ* „komm?"', in *Lingua Aegyptia* 12: 133–6.

Quack, J. F. 2005a. 'Die Überlieferungsstruktur des Buches vom Tempel', in S. Lippert and M. Schentuleit (eds) *Tebtunis und Soknopaiou Nesos. Leben im römerzeitlichen Fajum* (Wiesbaden): 105–15.

Quack, J. F. 2005b. 'Review of Stadler *Isis, das göttliche Kind und die Weltordnung*', in *Archiv für Papyrusforschung* 51: 174–9.

Quack, J. F. 2006a. 'Die Rolle der Hieroglyphenschrift in der Theorie vom griechischen Vokalalphabet', in W. Ernst and F. Kittler (eds) *Die Geburt des Vokalalphabets aus dem Geist der Piesie. Schrift, Zahl und Ton im Medienverbund* (Munich): 75–98.

Quack, J. F. 2006b. 'A Black Cat from the Right, and a Scarab on your Head. New Sources for Ancient Egyptian Divination', in K. Szpakowska (ed.) *Through a Glass Darkly: Magic, Dreams, and Prophecy in Ancient Egypt* (Swansea): 175–87.

Quack, J. F. 2006c. 'Die hieratischen und hieroglyphischen Papyri aus Tebtynis – Ein Überblick', in K. Ryholt (ed.) *The Carlsberg Papyri 7: Hieratic Texts from the Collection* (Copenhagen): 1–7.

Quack, J. F. 2006d. 'Eine Papyruskopie des Textes der Votivellen (P. Carlsberg 419)', in K. Ryholt (ed.) *The Carlsberg Papyri 7: Hieratic Texts from the Collection* (Copenhagen): 39–52, pl. 5.

Quack, J. F. 2007. 'Die Initiation zum Schreiberberuf im Alten Ägypten', in *Studien für Altägyptische Kultur* 36: 249–95.

Quack, J. F. 2010. 'Difficult Hieroglyphs and Unreadable Demotic? How the Ancient Egyptians Dealt with the Complexity of their Script', in A. de Voogt and I. Finkel (eds) *The Idea of Writing. Play and Complexity* (Leiden): 235–51.

Quack, J. F. 2013. 'Conceptions of Purity in Egyptian Religion', in C. Frevel and C. Nihan (eds), *Purity and the Forming of Religious Traditions in the Ancient Mediterranean World and Ancient Judaism* (Leiden): 115–58.

Quack, J. F. 2014. 'Bemerkungen zur Struktur der demotischen Schrift und zur Umschrift des Demotischen', in M. Depauw and Y. Broux (eds) *Acts of the Tenth International Congress of Demotic Studies. Leuven, 26–30 August 2008* (Leuven–Paris–Walpole, MA): 207–42.

Quack, J. F. 2016. *Einführung in die altägyptische Literaturgeschichte III. Die demotische und gräko-ägyptische Literatur, Einführungen und Quellentexte zur Ägyptologie 3. Zweite, veränderte Auflage* (Berlin).

Quack, J. F. and Ryholt, K. Forthcoming. 'Manuals on Dream Interpretation', in K. Ryholt (ed.) *The Carlsberg Papyri 11: Demotic Literary Texts* (Copenhagen).

Quecke, H. 1970. *Untersuchungen zum koptischen Stundengebet* (Leuven).

Quirke, S. 1996. 'Archive', in A. Loprieno (ed.) *Ancient Egyptian Literature. History & Forms* (Leiden): 379–401.

Quirke, S. 2004. *Egyptian Literature about 1800 BC: Questions and Readings* (London).

Ragazzoli, C. 2008. *Éloges de la ville en Égypte ancienne. Histoire et littérature* (Paris).

Ragazzoli, C. 2010. 'Weak Hands and Soft Mouths. Elements of Scribal Identity in the New Kingdom', in *Zeitschrift für ägyptische Sprache und Alterstumkunde* 137: 157–70.

Rathbone, D. 1991. *Economic Rationalism and Rural Society in Third-Century A.D. Egypt* (Cambridge).

Ray, J. D. 1994. 'Edwards Hincks and the Progress of Egyptology', in K. J. Cathcart (ed.) *The Edward Hincks Bicentenary Lectures* (Dublin): 58–74.

Reiche, C. 2004. 'Zur Anwendung von Netzwerkkonzept, Strukturtheorie und Semiotik bei der Erforschung von Gesellschaft und Kultur Ägyptens im inner- und interkulturellen Kontaktraum', in R. Gundlach and A. Klug (eds) *Das ägyptische Königtum im Spannungsfeld zwischen Innen- und Aussenpolitik im 2. Jahrtausend v. Chr.* (Wiesbaden): 35–69.

Reif, S. C. 2000. *A Jewish Archive from Old Cairo: The History of Cambridge University Library's Genizah Collection* (Abingdon–New York).

Reymond, E. A. E. 1976. *From the Contents of the Libraries of the Suchos Temples in the Fayyum, Part I. A Medical Book from Crocodilopolis. P. Vindob. D 6257* (Vienna).

Reymond, E. A. E. 1977. *From the Contents of the Libraries of the Suchos Temples in the Fayyum, Part II. From Ancient Egyptian Hermetic Writings* (Vienna).

Richards, R. E. 1991. *The Secretary in the Letters of Paul* (Tübingen).

Richter, T. S. 1998. 'Zwei Urkunden des koptischen Notars David, des Sohnes des Psate', in *Archiv für Papyrusforschung und Verwandte gebiete* 44: 69–85.

Richter, T. S. 2000. 'Spätkoptische Rechtsurkunden neu bearbeitet (II): Die Rechtsurkunden des Teschlot-Archivs', in *The Journal of Juristic Papyrology* 30: 95–148.

Richter, T. S. 2004a. 'Zur Sprache thebanischer Rechtsurkunden: Auffällige Konstruktionen im Bereich der Zweiten Tempora', in M. Immerzeel and J. van der Vliet (eds) *Coptic Studies on the Threshold of a New Millennium. Proceedings of the Seventh International Congress of Coptic Studies. Leiden, August 27–2 September 2000* (Leiden): 145–54.

Richter, T. S. 2004b. 'O.Crum Ad. 15 and the Emergence of Arabic Words in Coptic Legal Documents', in L. Sundelin and P. M. Sijpesteijn (eds) *Papyrology and the History of Early Islamic Egypt* (Leiden): 97–114.

Richter, T. S. 2005. 'What's in a Story? Cultural Narratology and Coptic Child Donation Documents', in *Journal of Juristic Papyrology* 35: 237–64.

Richter, T. S. 2006. '"Spoken" Sahidic? Gleanings from Non-Literary Texts', in *Lingua Aegyptia* 14: 311–23.

Richter, T. S. 2008a. *Rechtssemantik und forensische Rhetorik: Untersuchungen zu Wortschatz, Stil und Grammatik der Sprache koptischer Rechtsurkunden*. 2nd revised edition (Weisbaden).

Richter, T. S. 2008b. 'Greek, Coptic, and the "Language of the Hijra". Rise and Decline of the Coptic Language in Late Antique and Medieval Egypt', in H. Cotton, R. Hoyland, and D. J. Wasserstein (eds) *From Hellenism to Islam: Cultural and Linguistic Change in the Roman Near East* (Cambridge): 401–46.

Richter, T. S. 2008c. 'Review of Stadler, *Isis, das göttliche Kind und die Weltordnung*', in *Wiener Zeitschrift für die Kunde des Morgenlandes* 98: 380–6.

Richter, T. S. 2009. 'What Kind of Alchemy is the Alchemy Attested by 10th-Century Coptic Manuscripts?' in *Ambix. Journal of the Society for the History of Alchemy and Chemistry* 56: 23–35.

Richter, T. S. 2010a. 'Language Choice in the Qurra Dossier', in A. Papaconstantinou (ed.) *The Multilingual Experience in Egypt from the Ptolemies to the Abassids* (Aldershot): 189–220.

Richter, T. S. 2010b. 'Naturoffenbarung und Erkenntnisritual. Diskurs und Praxis spätantiker Naturwissenschaft am Beispiel der Alchemie', in H. Knuf, C. Leitz, and D. von Recklinghausen (eds) *Honi soit qui mal y pense. Studien zum pharaonischen, griechisch-römischen und spätantiken Ägypten zu Ehren von Heinz-Josef Thissen* (Leuven–Paris–Walpole, MA): 585–605.

Richter, T. S. 2014. 'Neue koptische medizinische Rezepte', in *Zeitschrift für Ägyptische Sprache und Altertumskunde* 141: 155–95.

Richter, T. S. 2015. 'The Master Spoke: «Take one of *the sun* and one unit of *almulgam*». Hitherto Unnoticed Coptic Papyrological Evidence for Early Arabic Alchemy', in A. T. Schubert and P. Sijpesteijn (eds) *Documents and the History of the Early Islamic World. 3rd Conference of the International Society for Arabic Papyrology, Alexandria, 23–26 March 2006* (Leiden): 158–94.

Ritter, V. 2008. 'Ostraca hiératiques et ostraca figurés. Quelques nouveaux raccords', in *Göttinger Miszellen* 217: 81–7.

Rizzo, J. 2005. '*Bjn*: de mal en pis', in *Bulletin de l'Institut français d'archéologie orientale* 105: 295–320.

Romaine, S. 1980. 'The Relative Clause Marker in Scots English: Diffusion, Complexity, and Style as Dimensions of Syntactic Change', in *Language in Society* 9: 221–47.

Romaine, S. 1982. *Socio-historical Linguistics. Its Status and Methodology* (Cambridge).

Romer, J. 1984. *Ancient Lives* (New York).

Rosati, G. 1990. 'Un modello di cubito "votivo"? (PSI inv. 1 I)', in *Oriens Antiquus* 39: 125–34.

Rosmorduc, S., Polis, S., and Winand, J. 2009. 'Ramses. A New Research Tool in Philology and Linguistics', in N. Strudwick (ed.) *Information Technology and Egyptology (= Proceedings of the XXIst Table Ronde 'Égyptologie et Informatique')* (Piscataway, NJ): 155–64.

Rumelhart, D. E., McClelland, J. L, and The PDP Research Group. 1986. *Parallel Distributed Processing: Explorations in the Microstructure of Cognition* (Cambridge, MA).

Rustow, M. 2008. *Heresy and the Politics of Community: The Jews of the Fatimid Caliphate* (Ithaca, NY).

Ryholt, K. 1999. *The Carlsberg Papyri 4: The Story of Petese Son of Petetum and Seventy Other Good and Bad Stories* (Copenhagen).

Ryholt, K. 2004a. 'The Assyrian Invasion of Egypt in Egyptian Literary Tradition', in J. G. Dercksen (ed.) *Assyria and Beyond: Studies Presented to Mogens Trolle Larsen* (Leiden): 484–511.

Ryholt, K. 2004b. 'Demotic Receipts for Temple-Tax on Property-Transfer at Tebtunis in the Roman Period (P. Carlsberg 268, 431, 432, 469, 582; P. Mich. inv. 664; P. Botti II)', in F. Hoffmann and H. J. Thissen (eds) *Res severa verum gaudium. Festschrift für Karl-Theodor Zauzich zum 65. Geburtstag am 8. Juni 2005* (Leuven): 509–33 + pls. 41–3.

Ryholt, K. 2005. 'On the Contents and Nature of the Tebtunis Temple Library. A Status Report', in S. Lippert and M. Schentuleit (eds) *Tebtynis und Soknopaiu Nesos. Leben im römerzeitlichen Fajum. Akten des Internationalen Symposions vom 11. bis 13. Dezember 2003 im Sommerhausen bei Würzburg* (Wiesbaden): 141–70.

Ryholt, K. 2006. *The Carlsberg Papyri 6: Petese Stories II* (Copenhagen).

Ryholt, K. 2012. *The Carlsberg Papyri 10: Narrative Literature from the Tebtunis Temple Library* (Copenhagen).

Ryholt, K. 2013. 'The Illustrated Herbal from Tebtunis: New Fragments and Archaeological Context', in *Zeitschrift für Papyrologie und Epigraphik* 187: 233–8.

Ryholt, K. (ed.). Forthcoming a. *The Carlsberg Papyri 11* (Copenhagen).

Ryholt, K. Forthcoming b. 'A List of Deities', in K. Ryholt (ed.) *The Carlsberg Papyri 11: Demotic Literary Texts* (Copenhagen).

Ryholt, K. Forthcoming c. 'The End of a Narrative with a Colophon', in K. Ryholt (ed.) *The Carlsberg Papyri 11* (Copenhagen).

Ryholt, K. Forthcoming d. 'Libraries from Late Period and Greco-Roman Egypt', in K. Ryholt and G. Barjamovic (eds) *Libraries before Alexandria* (Oxford).

Ryholt, K. Forthcoming e. *The Carbonised Papyri from Tanis and Thmuis.*

Salah el-Kholi, M. 2006. *Papyri und Ostraka aus der Ramessidenzeit* (Syracuse, NY).

Sapir, E. 1921. *Language* (New York).

Sauneron, J. 1971. 'Les travaux de l'IFAO en 1970–1971', in *Bulletin de l'Institut français d'archéologie orientale* 70: 235–74.

Sauneron, J. 1972. 'Les travaux de l'IFAO en 1971–1972', in *Bulletin de l'Institut français d'archéologie orientale* 71: 189–230.

Sauneron, J. 1973. 'Les travaux de l'IFAO en 1972–1973', in *Bulletin de l'Institut français d'archéologie orientale* 73: 217–63.

Sauneron, S. 1951. 'La tradition officielle relative à la XVIIIe dynastie d'après un ostracon de la Vallée des Rois', in *Chronique d'Égypte* 26: 46–9.

Sauneron, S. 1952. 'Plutarque : Isis et Osiris (chap. IX)', in *Bulletin de l'Institut français d'archéologie orientale* 51: 49–51.

Sauneron, S. 1959a. *Catalogue des ostraca hiératiques non littéraires de Deir el-Médineh (n°s 550 à 623)* (Cairo).

Sauneron, S. 1959b. 'Les songes et leur interprétation dans l'Égypte ancienne', in *Sources orientales* 2 (= *Les songes et leur interprétation*) (Paris): 17–61.

Saussure, F. de. 1986. *Course in General Linguistics*. Edited by C. Bally and A. Sechehaye with the cooperation of A. Riedlinger. Translated and annotated by R. Harris (Chicago).

Schenke, G. 2007. 'P.Köln 466: Übereignung eines Bäckerei-Anteils. Ein neuer Text aus dem Teschlot Archiv', in *Kölner Papyri (P.Köln)* Band 11 (Paderborn): 288–300.

Schenkel, W. 1983. *Aus der Arbeit an einer Konkordanz zu den altägyptischen Sargtexten. Teil I: Zur Transkription des Hieroglyphisch-Ägyptischen (unter Mitarbeit von Rainer Hannig). Teil II: Zur Pluralbildung des Ägyptischen* (Wiesbaden).

Schenkel, W. 1993. 'Zu den Verschluß- und Reibelauten im Ägyptischen und (Hamito) Semitischen. Ein Versuch zur Synthese der Lehrmeinungen', in *Lingua Aegyptia* 3: 137–49.

Schentuleit, M. 2001. 'Die spätdemotische Hausverkaufsurkunde P. BM. 262: Ein bilingues Dokument aus Soknopaiu Nesos mit griechischen Übersetzungen', *Enchoria, Zeitschrift für Demotistik und Koptologie* 27: 127–54.

Schentuleit, M. 2007. 'Satabus aus Soknopaiou Nesos: Aus dem Leben eines Priesters am Beginn der römischen Kaiserzeit', in *Chronique d'Égypte* 82: 101–25.

Schentuleit, M. and Vittmann, G. 2009. *„Du hast mein Herz zufriedengestellt…". Ptolemäerzeitliche demotische Urkunden aus Soknopaiu Nesos* (Berlin–New York).

Schlumberger, D., Robert, L., Dupont-Sommer, A., and Benveniste, E. 1958. 'Une bilingue gréco-araméenne d'Asoka', in *Journal Asiatique* 246: 36–48.

Schmitt, R. 1990. 'Ex Occidente Lux: Griechen und griechische Sprache im hellenistischen Fernen Osten', in P. Steinmetz (ed.) *Beiträge zur Hellenistischen Literatur und ihrer Rezeption in Rom* (Stuttgart): 41–58.

Schott, S. 1957. *Die Reinigung Pharaos in einem memphitischen Tempel (Berlin P 13242)* (Göttingen).

Schweitzer, S. D. 2008. 'Nochmals zum stammhaften Imperativ von *jyi̯/jwi̯*', in *Lingua Aegyptia* 16: 319–21.

Scragg, D. 1974. *A History of English Spelling* (Aberdeen).

Sérida, R. 2016. *The Carlsberg Papyri 14: A Castration Story* (Copenhagen).

Shisha-Halevy, A. 1973. 'Apodotic *efsôtm*: A Hitherto Unnoticed Late Coptic, Tripartite Pattern Conjugation-Form and Its Diachronic Perspective', in *Le Muséon* 86: 455–66.

Shisha-Halevy, A. 1974. 'Protatic ⲉϥⲥⲱⲧⲙ̄: A Hitherto Unnoticed Coptic Tripartite Conjugation-Form and Its Diachronic Connections', in *Orientalia* 43: 369–81.

Shisha-Halevy, A. 1976. 'Protatic ⲉϥⲥⲱⲧⲙ̄: Some Additional Material', in *Orientalia* 46: 127–8.

Shisha-Halevy, A. 1981. 'Bohairic-Late Egyptian Diaglosses: A Contribution to the Typology of Egyptian', in D. W. Young (ed.) *Studies Presented to H. J. Polotsky* (East Gloucester, MA): 314–38.

Shisha-Halevy, A. 1986. *Coptic Grammatical Categories. Structural Studies in the Syntax of Shenoutean Sahidic* (Rome).

Shisha-Halevy, A. 2007a. 'Determination-Signalling Environment in Old and Middle Egyptian: Work-Notes and Reflections', in T. Bar and E. Cohen (eds) *Studies in Semitic and General Linguistics in Honor of Gideon Goldenberg* (Münster): 223–54.

Shisha-Halevy, A. 2007b. *Topics in Coptic Syntax: Structural Studies in the Bohairic Dialect* (Leuven).

Silverstein, M. 1979. 'Language Structure and Linguistic Ideology', in P. R. Clyne, W. F. Hanks, and C. L. Hofbauer (eds) *The Elements: A Para Session on Linguistic Units and Levels* (Chicago): 193–247.

Silverstein, M. 1992. 'The Uses and Utility of Ideology: Some Reflections', in *Pragmatics* 2(3): 311–23.

Small, J. P. 1997. *Wax Tablets of the Mind. Cognitive Studies of Memory and Literacy in Classical Antiquity* (London).

Smith, H. S. and Tait, W. J. 1983. *Saqqâra Demotic Papyri I* (London).

Smith, J. J. 1991. 'Tradition and Innovation in South-West Midland Middle English', in F. Riddy (ed.) *Regionalism in Late Medieval Manuscripts and Texts* (Cambridge): 53–65.

Smith, J. J. 1996. *An Historical Study of English: Function, Form and Change* (London).

Smith, M. 1987. *Catalogue of Demotic Papyri in the British Museum. Volume III. The Mortuary Texts of Papyrus BM 10507* (London).

Smith, M. 1993. *The Liturgy of Opening the Mouth for Breathing* (Oxford).

Smith, M. 1994. 'Budge at Akhmim, January 1896', in C. J. Eyre, A. Leahy, and L. Montagno Leahy (eds) *The Unbroken Reed. Studies in the Culture and Heritage of Ancient Egypt in Honour of A. F. Shore* (London): 293–303.

Smith, M. 2002. *The Carlsberg Papyri 5. On the Primaeval Ocean* (Copenhagen).

Smith, M. 2005. *Papyrus Harkness (MMA 31.9.7)* (Oxford).

Smith, S. T. 2001. 'The Practice of Sealing in the Administration of the First Intermediate Period and the Middle Kingdom', in *Cahier de recherches de l'Institut de papyrologie et égyptologie de Lille* 22: 161–94.

Smolders, R. 2005. 'Chairemon: Alexandrian Citizen, Royal Scribe, Gymnasiarch, Landholder at Bacchias, and Loving Father', in *Bulletin of the American Society of Papyrologists* 42: 93–100.

Spiegelberg, W. 1910. *Der Sagenkreis des Königs Petubastis nach dem Straßburger demotischen Papyrus sowie den Wiener und Pariser Bruchstücken* (Leipzig).

Spiegelberg, W. 1921. *Ägyptische und andere Graffiti (Inschriften und Zeichnungen) aus der thebanischen Nekropolis* (Heidelberg).

Spiegelberg, W. 1925. *Demotische Grammatik* (Heidelberg).

Spiegelberg, W. 1932a. *Die demotischen Denkmäler III. Demotische Inschriften und Papyri* (Berlin).

Spiegelberg, W. 1932b. 'Aus der Geschichte vom Zauberer Ne-nefer-ke-Sokar, Demotischer Papyrus Berlin 13640', in S. R. K. Glanville (ed.) *Studies Presented to F. Ll. Griffith* (London): 171–80 + pl. 21.

Stadler, M. 2004. *Isis, das göttliche Kind und die Weltordnung. Neue religiöse Texte aus dem Fayum nach dem Papyrus Wien D. 12006 Rekto* (Vienna).

Stamatatos, E., Fakotakis, N., and Kokkinakis, G. 2001. 'Automatic Text Categorization in Terms of Genre and Author', in *Computational Linguistics* 26/4: 471–95.

Stauder, A. 2013a. 'L'émulation du passé à l'ère thoutmoside: la dimension linguistique', in S. Bickel (ed.) *Vergangenheit und Zukunft. Die Konstruktion historischer Zeit in der 18. Dynastie* (Basel): 77–125.

Stauder, A. 2013b. *Linguistic Dating of Middle Egyptian Literary Texts. 'Dating Egyptian Literary Texts' Göttingen, 9–12 June 2010*. Volume 2 (Hamburg).

Steen, H. 1938. 'Les clichés épistolaires dans les lettres sur papyrus grecques', in *Classica et Mediaevalia* 1: 119–76.

Stegemann, V. 1936. *Koptische Paläographie* (Heidelberg).

Stenroos, M. 2007. 'Sampling and Annotation in the Middle English Grammar Project', in A. Meurman-Solin and A. Nurmi (eds) *Annotating Variation and Change* (Helsinki). http://www.helsinki.fi/varieng/series/volumes/01/stenroos/.

Stenroos, M. 2009. 'Order Out of Chaos? The English Gender Change in the Southwest Midlands as a Process of Semantically Based Reorganization', in *English Language and Linguistics* 12.3: 445–73.

Stenroos, M. and Mäkinen, M. 2011. 'Manual, Version 2011.1', in M. Stenroos, M. Mäkinen, S. Horobin, and J. J. Smith (compilers), *The Middle English Grammar Corpus*, version 2011.1 (Stavanger). http://www.uis.no/research/history-languages-and-literature/the-mest-programme/the-middle-english-grammar-corpus-meg-c/meg-c-manual/.

Stenroos, M., Mäkinen, M., Horobin, S., and Smith. J.J. (compilers). 2011. *The Middle English Grammar Corpus*, version 2011.1 (Stavanger). http://www.uis.no/research/history-languages-and-literature/the-mest-programme/the-middle-english-grammar-corpus-meg-c/.

Stern, L. 1880. *Koptische Grammatik* (Leipzig).

Stern, L. 1885. 'Fragment eines koptischen Tractates über Alchimie', in *Zeitschrift für Ägyptische Sprache und Altertumskunde* 23: 102–19.

Stockwell, R. P. and Barritt, C. W. 1961. 'Scribal Practice: Some Assumptions', in *Language* 37: 75–82.

Strassi, S. 2008. *L'archivio di Claudius Tiberianus da Karanis* (Berlin–New York).

Strudwick, N. 1995. 'The Population at Thebes in the New Kingdom. Some Preliminary Thoughts', in J. Assmann, E. Dziobek, H. Gucksch, and F. Kampp (eds) *Thebanische Beamtennekropole. Neue Perspektiven archäologischer Forschung* (Heidelberg): 97–105.

Suten-Xeft. 1905. *Suten-Xeft, le livre royal. Édition en phototypie* (Leiden).

Swales, J. M. 1990. *Genre Analysis: English in Academic and Research Settings* (Cambridge).

Swales, J. M. 1993. 'Genre and engagement', in *Revue Belge de Philologie et d'Histoire* 71: 687–98.

Sweeney, D. 1994. 'Idiolects in the Late Ramesside Letters', in *Lingua Aegyptia* 4: 275–324.

Sweeney, D. 1995. 'Women and Language in the Ramesside Period, or, Why Women Don't Say Please', in C. J. Eyre (ed.) *Proceedings of the Seventh International Congress of Egyptologists. Cambridge 3–9 September 1995* (Leuven): 1109–18.

Sweeney, D. 1998. 'Friendship and Frustration: A Study in Papyri Deir el-Medina IV–VI', in *The Journal of Egyptian Archaeology* 84: 101–22.

Sweeney, D. 2003 'Gender and Request Formulation in Late Egyptian Literary Narratives', in M. Hasitzka, J. Diethart, and G. Dembski (eds) *«Das alte Ägypten und seine Nachbarn» – Festschrift zum 65. Geburstag von Helmut Satzinger mit Beiträgen zur Ägyptologie, Koptologie, Nubiologie und Afrikanistik* (Vienna): 132–59.

Tait, W. J. 1977. *Papyri from Tebtunis in Egyptian and in Greek* (London).

Tait, W. J. 1986. 'Guidelines and Borders in Demotic Papyri', in M. L. Bierbrier (ed.) *Papyrus: Structure and Usage* (London): 63–89.

Tait, W. J. 1991. 'P.Carlsberg 230: Eleven Fragments from a Demotic Herbal', in P. J. Frandsen (ed.) *The Carlsberg Papyri 1: Demotic Texts from the Collection* (Copenhagen): 47–92.

Tait, W. J. 2002. 'P. Carlsberg 433 and 434: Two Versions of the Text of P. Spiegelberg', in P. J. Frandsen and K. Ryholt (eds) *The Carlsberg Papyri 3: A Miscellany of Demotic Texts and Studies* (Copenhagen): 59–82.

Tefnin, R. 2002. 'A Coptic Workshop in a Pharaonic Tomb', in *Egyptian Archaeology* 20: 6.

Thijs, A. 1998. 'Reconsidering the End of the Twentieth Dynasty/1: The Fisherman Pnekhtemope and the Date of BM 10054', in *Göttinger Miszellen* 167: 95–108.

Thijs, A. 1998–2001. 'Reconsidering the End of the Twentieth Dynasty', in *Göttinger Miszellen* 167: 95–108; 170: 83–99; 173: 175–91; 175: 99–103; 177: 63–70; 179: 69–83; 181: 95–103; 184: 65–73.

Thijs, A. 2007. 'The Scenes of the High Priest Pinuzem in the Temple of Khonsu', in *Zeitschrift für ägyptische Sprache und Alterstumkunde* 134: 50–63.

Thijs, A. 2009. 'The Second Prophet Nesamun and his claim to the High-Priesthood', in *Studien zur Altägyptische Kultur* 38: 343–53.

Thomason, S. G. and Kaufman, T. 1991. *Language Contact, Creolization, and Genetic Linguistics* (Berkeley).

Tieken-Boon van Ostade, I., Nevalainen, T., and Caon, L. (eds). 2000. *Social Network Analysis and the History of English* (=*European Journal of English Studies* 4.3: 211–16).

Till, W. C. 1942. 'Koptische Kleinliteratur', in *Zeitschrift für ägyptische Sprache und Altertumskunde* 77: 101–11.

Till, W. C. 1952 'Weitere koptische Rezepte', in *Le Muséon* 65 (1952), 159–68.

Till, W. C. 1962. *Datierung und Prosopographie der koptischen Urkunden aus Theben* (Vienna).

Tobin, Y. 1988. *From Sign to Text: A Semiotic View of Communication* (Amsterdam).

Toivari-Viitala, J. 2001. *Women at Deir el-Medina. A Study of the Status and Role of the Female Inhabitants in the Workmen's Community during the Ramesside Period* (Leiden).

Tolkien, J. R. R. 1929. '*Ancrene Wisse* and *Hali Meiðhad*', in *Essays and Studies* 14: 104–26.

Töpfer, S. 2015. *The Carlsberg Papyri 12: Fragmente eines Sothisrituals von Oxyrhynchos aus Tebtunis* (Copenhagen).

Turner, E. G. 1987. *Greek Manuscripts of the Ancient World* (London).

Uljas, S. 2010. 'Archaeology of Language. A Case Study from Middle Kingdom/Second Intermediate Period Egypt and Nubia', in *Studien zur Altägyptischen Kultur* 39: 373–82.

Vachek, J. 1945–9. 'Some Remarks on Writing and Phonetic Transcription', in *Acta Linguistica* 5: 86–93.

Vågslid, E. 1989. *Norske skrivarar i millomalderen* (Oslo).

Valbelle, D. 1985. *« Les ouvriers de la tombe ». Deir el-Médineh à l'époque ramesside* (Cairo).

Vandorpe, K., Clarysse, W. and Verreth, H. 2015. *Graeco-Roman Archives from the Fayum* (Leuven).

Venturini, I. 2007. 'Le statut des exercices scolaires au Nouvel Empire: Balbutiement d'écoliers ou entraînements d'étudiants', in J.-C. Goyon and C. Cardin (eds) *Proceedings of the International Congress of Egyptologists. Actes du neuvième congrès international des égyptologues. Grenoble, 6–12 septembre 2004*. Volume 2 (Leuven): 1885–96.

Verhoogt, A. M. F. W. 1998. *Menches, Komogrammateus of Kerkeosiris: The Doings and Dealings of a Village Scribe in the Late Ptolemaic Period (120–110 B.C.)* (Leiden).

Verhoogt, A. M. F. W. 2009. 'Dictating Letters in Greek and Roman Egypt from a Comparative Perspective' (working paper: http://sites.lsa.umich.edu/wp-content/uploads/sites/235/2015/02/dictating1.pdf).

Vernus, P. 1978. 'Littérature et autobiographie. Les inscriptions de *sꜣ-mwt* surnommé Kyky', in *Revue d'égyptologie* 30: 115–46.

Vernus, P. 1979. 'Un hymne à Amon, protecteur de Tanis, sur une tablette hiératique (Caire J.E. 87889)', in *Revue d'égyptologie* 31: 101–19.

Vernus, P. 1982. 'Deux particularités de l'égyptien de tradition: *nty iw* + présent I; *wnn·f ḥr sḏm* narrative', in *L'égyptologie en 1979*. Volume 1 (Paris): 81–9.

Vernus, P. 1985. 'Études de philologie et de linguistique (IV). XIII. Non-existence et définition du sujet: *bn* prédicatif en Néo-égyptien', in *Revue d'égyptologie* 36: 153–68.

Vernus, P. 1987. 'Études de philologie et de linguistique (VI)', in *Revue d'égyptologie* 38: 163–81.

Vernus, P. 1990. 'Les espaces de l'écrit dans l'Égypte pharaonique', in *Bulletin de la Société française d'égyptologie* 119: 35–56.

Vernus, P. 1992. *Chants d'amour de l'Égypte antique* (Paris).

Vernus, P. 1993. *Affaires et scandales sous les Ramsès. La crise des valeurs dans l'Égypte du Nouvel Empire* (Paris).

Vernus, P. 1994. 'Observations sur la prédication de classe ("Nominal Predicate")', in *Lingua Aegyptia* 4: 325–48.

Vernus, P. 1995. *Essai sur la conscience de l'histoire dans l'Égypte pharaonique* (Paris).

Vernus, P. 1996. 'Langue littéraire et diglossie', in A. Loprieno (ed.) *Ancient Egyptian Literature. History & Forms* (Leiden): 555–64.

Vernus, P. 2002. 'Les vies édifiantes de deux personnages illustres de Deir el-Medineh', in G. Andreu (ed.) *Les artistes de Pharaon. Deir el-Médineh et la Vallée des Rois* (Paris): 57–69.

Vernus, P. 2003. 'La piété personnelle à Deir el-Medineh. La construction de l'idée de pardon', in G. Andreu (ed.) *Deir el-Médineh et la Vallée des Rois. La vie en Égypte au temps des pharaons du Nouvel Empire. Actes du colloque organisé par le musée du Louvre les 3 et 4 mai 2002* (Paris): 281–308.

Vernus, P. 2009. *Dictionnaire amoureux de l'Égypte pharaonique* (Paris).

Vernus, P. 2010. *Sagesses de l'Égypte pharaonique*. 2nd edition (Paris).

Vernus, P. 2012. 'Le verbe *gm(j)*: essai de sémantique lexicale', in E. Grossman, S. Polis, and J. Winand (eds) *Lexical Semantics in Ancient Egyptian* (Hamburg): 387–438.

Vernus, P. 2013. 'La datation de l'*Enseignement d'Aménemopé*. Le littéraire et le linguistique', in G. Moers, K. Widmaier, A. Giewekemeyer, A. Lümers, and R. Ernst (eds) *Dating Egyptian Literary Texts. "Dating Egyptian Literary Texts" Göttingen, 9–12 June 2010*. Volume 1 (Hamburg): 191–236.

Verreth, H. 2009. *The Provenance of Egyptian Documents from the 8th Century BC till the 8th Century AD*. Trismegistos Online Publications (TOP) 3: http://www.trismegistos.org/top.php.

Vierros, M. 2007. 'The Language of Hermias, an Egyptian Notary from Pathyris (c. 100 BC)', in B. Palme (ed.) *Akten des 23. Internationalen Papyrologenkongresses. Wien, 22.–28. Juli 2001* (Vienna): 719–23.

Vierros, M. 2008. 'Greek or Egyptian? The Language Choice in Ptolemaic Documents from Pathyris', in A. Delattre and P. Heilporn (eds) *'Et maintenant ce ne sont plus que des villages…' Thèbes et sa region aux époques hellénistique, romaine et byzantine. Actes du colloque tenu à Bruxelles les 2 et 3 Decembre 2005* (Brussels): 73–86.

Vierros, M. 2012. *Bilingual Notaries in Hellenistic Egypt. A Study of Greek as a Second Language* (Brussels).

Vinciguerra, A. 2009. 'The *Ars Alchemie*: The First Latin Text on Practical Alchemy', in *Ambix. Journal of the Society for the History of Alchemy and Chemistry* 56: 57–67.

Volten, A. 1940. *Kopenhagener Texte zum demotischen Weisheitsbuch (Pap. Carlsberg II, III Verso, IV Verso und V)* (Copenhagen).

Volten, A. 1942. *Demotische Traumdeutung (Pap. Carlsberg XIII und XIV verso)* (Copenhagen).

Volten, A. 1951. 'The Papyrus-Collection of the Egyptological Institute of Copenhagen', in *Archiv Orientální* 19: 70–4.

Vycichl, W. 1958. 'A Late Egyptian Dialect of Elephantine', in *Kush* 6: 176–8.

Wagner, E.-M. 2010. *A Linguistic Analysis of Judaeo-Arabic Letters from the Cairo Genizah* (Leiden).

Wainwright, G. 1938. 'Thoughts on Three Recent Articles', in *The Journal of Egyptian Archaeology* 24: 59–64.

Wente, E. F. 1990. *Letters from Ancient Egypt* (Atlanta).

Werning, D. 2013. 'Linguistic Dating of the Netherworld Books Attested in the New Kingdom. A Critical Review', in G. Moers, K. Widmaier, A. Giewekemeyer, A. Lümers, and R. Ernst (eds) *Dating Egyptian Literary Texts. "Dating Egyptian Literary Texts" Göttingen, 9–12 June 2010.* Volume 1 (Hamburg): 237–81.

White, J. L. 1986. *Light from Ancient Letters* (Philadelphia).

Wickelgren, W. A. 1969. 'Context-Sensitive Coding, Associative Memory, and Serial Order in (Speech) Behavior', in *Psychological Review* 76.1: 1–15.

Wilcken, U. 1935. *Urkunden der Ptolemäerzeit II* (Berlin).

Wilfong, T. G. 1989. 'Western Thebes in the Seventh and Eighth Centuries: A Bibliographic Survey of Jeme and Its Surroundings', in *Bulletin of the American Society of Papyrologists* 27: 169–81.

Wilfong, T. G. 2002. *Women of Jeme: Lives in a Coptic Town in Late Antique Egypt* (Ann Arbor).

Williamson, K. 2004. 'On Chronicity and Space(s) in Historical Dialectology', in M. Dossena and R. Lass (eds) *Methods and Data in English Historical Dialectology* (Bern–Oxford): 97–136.

Williamson, K. 2008–13 and 2013–. *A Linguistic Atlas of Older Scots, Phase 1: 1380–1500, Version 1.1 and 1.2* (The University of Edinburgh). http://www.lel.ed.ac.uk/ihd/laos1/laos1.html.

Wimmer, S. 1995. *Hieratische Paläographie der nicht-literarischen Ostraka der 19. und 20. Dynastie.* 2 Volumes (Wiesbaden).

Winand, J. 1989. 'L'expression du sujet nominal au Présent I en néo-égyptien', in *Chronique d'Égypte* 64: 159–71.

Winand, J. 1992. *Études de néo-égyptien. 1. La morphologie verbale* (Liège).

Winand, J. 1995a. 'La grammaire au secours de la datation des textes', in *Revue d'égyptologie* 46: 187–202.

Winand, J. 1995b. 'Review of W. Schenkel (1990), *Einführung in die altägyptische Sprachwissenschaft*, Darmstad', in *Bibliotheca Orientalis* 52: 307–16.

Winand, J. 2001. 'À la croisée du temps, de l'aspect et du mode. Le conjonctif en néo-égyptien', in O. Goldwasser and D. Sweeney (eds) *Structuring Syntax. A Tribute to Sarah Israelit-Groll* (Göttingen): 293–329.

Winand, J. 2006. *Temps et aspect en ancien égyptien. Une approche sémantique* (Leiden).

Winand, J. 2007. 'Encore *Ounamon* 2,27–28', in *Lingua Aegyptia* 15: 299–306.

Winand, J. 2011a. 'The Report of Wenanum: A Journey in Ancient Egyptian Literature', in M. Collier and S. Snape (eds) *Ramesside Studies in Honour of K.A. Kitchen* (Bolton): 541–59.

Winand, J. 2011b. 'À propos du P. Ambras', in *Chronique d'Égypte* 86: 22–30.

Winand, J. 2012. 'Le verbe et les variations d'actance. Les constructions réversibles (Études valentielles, 2)', in E. Grossman, S. Polis, and J. Winand (eds) *Lexical Semantics in Ancient Egyptian. Proceedings of the Workshop on Lexical Semantics December 2009 (Liège)*. Lingua Aegyptia Studia Monographica 9 (Hamburg): 459–86.

Winand, J. Forthcoming a. 'Des on-dit aux oracles. La clôture de discours *ḫr.f* en néo-égyptien', in S. Aufrère, N. Bosson, A. Boud'hors, and E. Grossman (eds) *Festschrift. A. Shisha-Halevy*.

Winand, J. Forthcoming b. 'As If Spoken: What Do We Really Know About Late Egyptian as a Vernacular Language?' in A. Dorn (ed.) *Proceedings of the International Conference Filtering Decorum – Facing Reality, November 2013* (Liège).

Winand. J. Forthcoming c. 'Un peu d'analyse valentielle, quelques collocations lexicales et un soupçon de classificateurs sémantiques: une note sur le pBerlin 10487', in F. Doyen et al. (eds) *Sur le chemin du Mouseion d'Alexandrie: Études offertes à Marie-Cécile Bruwier*.

Winand. J., Polis. S., and Rosmorduc, S. 2015. 'Ramses. An Annotated Corpus of Late Egyptian', in P. Kousoulis (ed.) *Proceedings of the Tenth International Congress of Egyptologists, University of the Aegean, Rhodes, 22–29 May 2008* (Leuven): 1513–21.

Winter, E. 1963. 'Altorientalische Alterümer in London und Oxford', in *Archiv für Orientforschung* 20: 201–2 + fig. 18.

Wisse, F. 1979. 'Language Mysticism in the Nag Hammadi Texts and in Early Coptic Monasticism', in *Enchoria: Zeitschrift für Paprologie und Epigraphik* 9: 101–20.

von Wright, G. H. 1971. *Explanation and Understanding* (New York).

Wright, R. 2002, *A Sociophilological Study of Late Latin* (Turnhout).

Wright, W. 1967. *A Grammar of the Arabic Language*. 2 volumes. 3rd edition (Cambridge).

Young, T. 1823. *An Account of Some Recent Discoveries in Hieroglyphical Literature, and Egyptian Antiquities. Including the Author's Original Alphabet, as Extended by Mr. Champollion, with a Translation of Five Unpublished Greek and Egyptian Manuscripts* (London).

Zauzich, K.-T. 1968. *Die ägyptische Schreibertradition in Aufbau, Sprache und Schrift der demotischen Kaufverträge aus ptolemäischer Zeit* (Wiesbaden).

Zauzich, K.-T. 1975. 'Berliner Fragmente zum Texte des Pap. Insinger', in *Enchoria: Zeitschrift für Demotistik und Koptologie* 5: 119–22 + pl. 38.

Zauzich, K.-T. 1976. 'Der Schreiber der Weissagung des Lammes', in *Enchoria: Zeitschrift für Demotistik und Koptologie* 6: 127–8.

Zauzich, K.-T. 1983a. 'Demotische Texte römischer Zeit', in *Das römisch-byzantinische Ägypten, Akten des internationalen Symposions 26.–30. September 1978 in Trier* (Mainz): 77–80.

Zauzich, K.-T. 1983b. 'Das Lamm des Bokchoris', in *Festschrift zum 100-jährigen Bestehen der Papyrussammlung der Österreichischen Nationalbibliothek Papyrus Erzherzog Rainer* (Vienna): 165–74 + pl. 2.

Zibelius-Chen, K. 2007. 'Critical Review of Darnell 2006', in *Bibliotheca Orientalis* 64: 377–87.

Zoëga, G. 1810. *Catalogus codicum Copticorum manu scriptorum* (Rome; Hildesheim–New York, 1973, reprint).

Zonhoven, L. M. J. 1979. 'The Inspection of a Tomb at Deir el-Medîna (O. Wien Aeg. 1)', in *The Journal of Egyptian Archaeology* 65: 89–98 + pl. xi.

Zuretti, C.O. 1932. *Catalogue des manuscrits alchimiques grecs. Volume 8: Alchemistica signa* (Brussels).

Index